Managing Your Company Cars:
Expert Opinion

Colin Tourick, editor

Eyelevel Books

Managing Your Company Cars

Expert Opinion

Colin Tourick

editor

Managing Your Company Cars: Expert Opinion
Editor: Colin Tourick
© 2009
Copyright remains with the individual authors as listed on the contents page.

Logos, company names, corporate motifs and identities
remain © or ™ of their respective companies.

Published by:

Eyelevel Books
Worcester

www.eyelevelbooks.co.uk

Printed by the:
MPG Books Group in the UK.

ISBN 9781902528267

To Vera Tourick

For her never-ending encouragement

Expert Opinions

Best practice amongst fleet managers
- Reducing business mileage
- Selecting a leasing company
- Reducing fuel costs and emissions
- Running a green fleet
- Managing a large corporate fleet
- Tackling the grey fleet
- Running a police fleet
- Managing a large fleet

Other topics
- Fleet policy
- A manufacturer's view of the fleet market
- Short-term leasing
- Tyres
- Glass
- Daily hire
- Fast fit
- Brokers
- Telematics
- Roadside assistance
- Remarketing
- Driver risk management
- ECOS, cash for car, salary sacrifice, tax and NI
- Fuel and fuel cards
- Fleet systems
- Credit hire and accident management

- Fleet analytics - a view From Australia
- Setting residuals and maintenance budgets
- International leasing and fleet management
- Reducing business mileage
- Legal aspects of running a car fleet
- Workplace Travel Plans
- Purchasing cars
- Business car information for SMEs
- Meeting the needs of disabled business drivers
- The different ways fleet managers can dispose of vehicles
- Work-related road safety
- Recruiting fleet staff
- Car sharing
- Environmental issues - a manufacturer's view
- The training of fleet professionals
- Saving money, saving CO2
- The sub-prime market
- Fleet management during economic downturn and recession
- Specialist insurances

CONTENTS

FOREWORD

I had been mulling over a question for some time: What do we mean by the term *best practice*?

When I wrote *Managing Your Company Cars* I had a very clear objective in mind; I wanted to write a textbook for people who run car fleets. A textbook is something quite specific; a source of reference that someone can go to when they want to understand something, or perhaps to look up the definition of an expression they have just heard for the first time. A reference book needs to be comprehensive, leave no stone unturned, and explain things very thoroughly.

Managing Your Company Cars was published in 2003 and the feedback was so positive that I wrote the 2nd edition in 2005.

In early 2008 I began thinking about writing the 3rd edition but held back because it was clear that the company car tax rules were about to change and I didn't want to produce something that would be out-of-date as soon as it hit the bookshelves.

In the event I took a different approach and produced a much shorter book, *Managing Your Company Cars in Nine Easy Steps*, a basic primer in fleet management. This was published in May 2008.

Come the autumn of 2008 the new tax rules had been clarified and I started to think again about writing the 3rd edition. But my mind kept wandering back to that expression, *best practice*.

Managing Your Company Cars sets out to explain things but it doesn't describe what the best people in the fleet world are doing right now, and what they are planning for the future. If I was a fleet manager I would want to know these things. Ideally, I would love the opportunity to meet real experts from every corner of the fleet world, get them all into one room and quiz them about their specialist topic: What exactly is such-and-such? How does it work? What benefits does it give? How can I cut my costs when buying such-and-such? How can I reduce my risks? What recent developments have there been in your part of the fleet market? What are the best fleets doing? How are things changing?

I wondered if I could write a book that answered all those questions. I have been in this market for almost 30 years but there is an awful lot I don't know about. No-one knows everything about the fleet market. To write this book I wouldn't be able to sit at a keyboard and just start typing, I'd have to get out there and talk to experts across the fleet world to find out what they were doing. Best Practice is certainly out there but I would have to go out and look for it.

I began to make a list of the people I wanted to talk to. The list was remarkably long. There are many specialist areas in this sector.

I certainly needed to talk to fleet suppliers – contract hire companies, manufacturers, daily hire companies and so on. I also wanted to talk to fleet managers. There are some great things going on out there in Fleet Manager Land but too often these stories don't get heard. And the government is increasingly active in encouraging fleets to go green, reduce accidents and so on, so I would need to talk to those people too. I soon realised that if I was going to do this project justice I would have to talk to an awful lot of people before I could feel sufficiently confident to start on the book.

There are aspects of the recession that are nebulous but one thing is very clear; everybody seems to be incredibly busy. It seems we are all having to work harder to achieve things that – in retrospect – were a little bit easier to achieve a couple of years ago.

This most definitely applies to me so, whilst I was really keen to research best practice, I had to concede that I just didn't have the time to do the project justice. I didn't think my consultancy clients would be happy if I told them I was about to take a couple of months off to write a book.

And, at that point, the penny dropped. Rather than writing this new book from scratch, would it be possible to persuade a group of experts to write a chapter each on their area of expertise? My role would be to recruit them, ask them questions, edit their responses and arrange publication. I had enough time to do that but surely these people wouldn't have enough time in the run-up to Christmas to devote to this exercise?

I tentatively started approaching fleet experts and, to my amazement and delight, they were all enthusiastic and they all said yes.

I set out the ground rules from the start:

> This is going to be a serious book, giving best practice advice to fleet managers. I want it to contain real insights that fleet managers will find valuable. I am going to ask you a series of questions – the sort of questions I think fleet managers would want to ask. You will provide the answers. These questions and answers will form an interview and the interview will form the chapter. Don't think this is a collection of advertorial pieces; it isn't.

And when setting the ground-rules for organisations that provide services for fleets, I added:

> Please remember that you are the representative of your sector of the fleet market; so don't focus exclusively on your company, tell us about your sector.

I approached highly-experienced professionals and organisations – the sort of people I would approach if I wanted expert advice on a fleet issue.

The contributors and I have aimed to produce a book that encapsulates the very best of contemporary fleet management. Have we succeeded? That's for you to decide. I would be very interested to hear your views so please email me via www.tourick.com with your thoughts and observations.

My thanks to everyone who has been involved in this project. There have been a number of nights – when I was still working away at my PC at 4am, thinking of good questions to ask a contributor; providing someone else with the specification of the images to go in their chapter; reading and editing and re-reading and re-editing the chapters (250,000 words in all) – when I might have decided to give up on this gargantuan task. But everyone's enthusiasm for this project has kept me going.

Thank you to Jon Moore of Eyelevel Books, the publisher. This is the fourth book we have produced together and I always find his help, experience and insights to be utterly invaluable. Thank you too to Rachel Mills for her organisational skills and to Hilary Davis for her encouragement.

I must say a special thanks to Paul Harrop of Daimler Fleet Management, Ashley Martin of Ashley Martin Communications and James Langley of the Institute of Car Fleet Management, who kindly threw open their address books and made some important introductions.

And finally I must warmly thank all of the people who have written chapters, many of whom were no doubt bashing away at their PCs at the same time of night as I was, wondering how on earth they had committed themselves to such a major undertaking.

Colin Tourick

About the editor

Professor Colin Tourick MSc FCA FCCA MICFM is a management consultant specialising in vehicle management.

Colin's fleet career started in 1980 as the first accountant at LeasePlan UK, followed by five years in big ticket leasing in the City of London financing aircraft, ships and property. He was general manager of Fleet Motor Management, director of Commercial Union Vehicle Finance and corporate finance director of UFB Humberclyde. For six years he was managing director of CitiCapital Fleet.

For six years he has been a fleet management consultant working for some of the largest banks, motor manufacturers and vehicle leasing companies, in the UK and abroad.

Colin has served as chairman of the BVRLA Training Committee, a member of the BVRLA Leasing and Fleet Management Committee and a member of the Finance & Leasing Association's Motor Finance Division management committee. He is a chartered accountant, a certified accountant and a member of the Institute of Car Fleet Management. He has a Master of Science degree in Accounting and Finance from London School of Economics, is a Visiting Professor at the Centre for Automotive Management at University of Buckingham Business School and a Visiting Fellow at the Centre for Automotive Industries Management at Nottingham Business School.

He is a frequent commentator, writer and speaker on fleet industry issues. His particular interests are reducing fleet management costs and building successful vehicle management businesses.

HOW TO USE THIS BOOK

This book is written for fleet managers. 'Fleet Manager' may not be your job title. You may be an accountant, company secretary, purchasing manager, human resource manager or transport manager, or you may work in a department run by one of these people. You may be a managing director, finance director, commercial director, HR director or operations director or indeed hold any one of a wide range of board positions.

If you are responsible for some aspect of running your company's vehicle fleet – purchasing cars, approving and paying maintenance invoices, selling cars, arranging finance, dealing with a contract hire company, obtaining finance quotes, corporate social responsibility or, indeed, anything whatsoever to do with company vehicles – this book is for you.

Whilst this book is aimed at fleet managers, I am hoping it will be read by people in the many sub-sectors of the fleet industry. If you work in a leasing company, a fuel card company, a car manufacturer, a lease brokerage or an environmental consultancy and want to know what's happening elsewhere in the fleet market, I hope you will find a great deal to interest you in these pages. The contributors have included a great deal of wisdom in their chapters.

As the book is a compilation of chapters written by dozens of contributors you can read it in any order. Different readers will have different interests. Here is a guide to help you find the chapters you might wish to read first:

Are you a newly-appointed fleet manager?

- Reducing business mileage
- Selecting a leasing company
- Reducing fuel costs and emissions
- Running a green fleet
- Managing a large corporate fleet
- Tackling the grey fleet
- Running a police fleet
- Managing a large fleet
- Fleet policy
- Driver risk management

- Legal aspects of running a car fleet
- Work-related road safety
- The training of fleet professionals
- Saving money, saving CO_2

Are you interested in cutting your fleet costs?

- Reducing business mileage
- Reducing fuel costs and emissions
- Managing a large corporate fleet
- Tackling the grey fleet
- Managing a large fleet
- Fleet policy
- Short-term leasing
- ECOS, cash for car, salary sacrifice, tax and NI
- Fleet analytics – a view From Australia
- Purchasing cars
- Car sharing
- Saving money, saving CO_2

Do you wish to operate a green fleet?

- Reducing business mileage
- Reducing fuel costs and emissions
- Running a green fleet
- Tackling the grey fleet
- Tyres
- Telematics
- Fleet analytics – a view From Australia
- Reducing business mileage
- Business Travel Plans
- Car sharing
- Environmental issues – a manufacturer's view
- Saving money, saving CO_2

Would you like to reduce the risks inherent in your fleet?

- Driver risk management
- Setting residuals and maintenance budgets
- Legal aspects of running a car fleet
- Work-related road safety
- Fleet management during economic downturn and recession
- Specialist insurances

Do you want to see what some of the best fleet managers are doing?

- Reducing business mileage
- Selecting a leasing company
- Reducing fuel costs and emissions
- Running a green fleet
- Managing a large corporate fleet
- Tackling the grey fleet
- Running a police fleet
- Managing a large fleet

Do you want to learn about best practice from suppliers to fleets?

- A manufacturer's view of the fleet market
- Short-term leasing
- Tyres
- Glass
- Daily hire
- Fast fit
- Brokers
- Telematics
- Roadside assistance
- Remarketing
- Driver risk management
- ECOS, cash for car, salary sacrifice, tax and NI
- Fuel and fuel cards
- Fleet systems
- Credit hire and accident management
- International leasing and fleet management
- Legal aspects of running a car fleet
- Business car information for the small business
- Meeting the needs of disabled business drivers
- The different ways fleet managers can dispose of vehicles
- Work-related road safety
- Recruiting fleet staff
- Car sharing
- The sub-prime market
- Fleet management during economic downturn and recession
- Specialist insurances

Do you want to consider different approaches to acquiring, funding and disposing of your fleet?

- Short-term leasing
- Daily hire
- Brokers
- Remarketing
- ECOS, cash for car, salary sacrifice, tax and NI
- Credit hire and accident management
- Setting residuals and maintenance budgets
- International leasing and fleet management
- Purchasing cars
- The different ways fleet managers can dispose of vehicles
- Saving money, saving CO_2
- The sub-prime market

Do you want to see how modern technology is being applied in the field of fleet management?

- Reducing business mileage
- A manufacturer's view of the fleet market
- Telematics
- Fleet systems
- Fleet analytics – a view From Australia
- Business car information for the small business

INTRODUCTION

I am writing this in January 2009. It has just become official, Britain is in recession, having experienced two consecutive quarters of negative growth. (Now there's a piece of governmental marketing-speak if ever there was one. *Negative growth*. Why don't they say economic decline?)

Many fleet managers will have experienced the effects of the economic slowdown long before mid-2008, and by now will have plenty of experience of cost-cutting and returning vehicles to leasing companies earlier than planned because of staff redundancy.

As someone who does a lot of work within the fleet industry, it's difficult for me to look back at 2008 without sighing, because it was a shocking year. I won't repeat here the horror stories in full ugly detail. It has, truthfully, been a nightmare, and there's no particular reason to see why this will not continue for some time. Junior government ministers may find themselves being pilloried for suggesting there may be a few green shoots of recovery, but a 'good news' week for the fleet industry at present is one when a client does not go bust, turnover does not decline, a factory doesn't shut down or the used vehicle market does not take another sudden downward turn.

As far as I can tell, there is no part of the fleet industry that has been unaffected. Manufacturers have reduced production in line with falling demand. Contract hire companies have found their funding lines bring squeezed, residual values plummeting, demand for new vehicles reducing and clients extending their payment periods or simply going bust.

I was chatting to a fleet industry insider who said something that stunned me. "You know Colin", he said, "a few contract hire companies are now technically insolvent, they just haven't recognised it yet".

Can that be true?

I have seen evidence of declining margins as contract hire companies have struggled to keep up their market shares, and many players are experiencing reduced order levels. The downturn for them has lasted more than 18 months so it is having an effect on current reported profitability - but surely not by enough to make any business insolvent?

After an 11% decline in the last year (though I have seen conflicting figures) used vehicle prices may be stabilising. These price reductions have had a direct impact on contract hire companies' bottom lines. Assuming an average contract hire company is geared 10:1 (though in many cases they are geared up much more than this by their bank parent companies,) an 11% decline in used vehicle values will certainly dent a company's share capital and reserves but will not of itself make the company insolvent. Then of course there is the effect of bad debts and write-offs, which will be affecting different players differently.

So whilst I don't know of any contract hire companies that are insolvent or are likely to become so in the foreseeable future, I do know that the situation is uncomfortable for many players and that things could get a whole lot worse if used vehicle prices decline sharply.

Turning to other parts of the fleet world, one might think that the companies that supply tyres and glass, or the garages that maintain vehicles, would be insulated from the downturn: After all, surely there will have been no fall-off in the number of tyres and windscreens that need to be replaced or the frequency with which cars will need to re serviced? Sadly not. I am told that consumers are putting off the decision to replace tyres and cracked windscreens, and are trying to find cheaper ways get their cars serviced, which in some cases means not getting them serviced at all. One can only hope that fleet managers won't adopt this approach, because the consequent impact on health and safety will be significant.

My hope is that the downturn will make fleet managers look for value rather than just cutting costs. So, for example, there is a great deal to be said about the advantages of using telematics, driver risk management services and modern fleet systems. Whilst these cost money now they can also generate substantial reductions in costs and risks. Will fleet managers be prepared to invest in these at present? I do hope so.

For those fleet managers who wish to reduce costs, a chat with the finance director might be in order. There are a number of effective ways to reduce the tax cost of operating a business car fleet. The obvious one is to encourage employees to drive low-CO_2 cars. And for many organisations, employee car ownership, cash for car and salary sacrifice schemes can all produce significant savings in tax and national insurance.

Fleet managers are in the front line when it comes to cost-reduction and this book contains plenty of good ideas. The cost of fuel has both soared and plummeted in the last year. What can the fleet manager do to reduce fuel costs? The introduction of business travel plans and car sharing can help, as can getting the fleet policy right in the first place. And fleet managers need tools to measure and control fuel use, which is where fuel cards can be invaluable.

Perhaps the best source of advice and inspiration is to hear from other fleet managers, so this book contains chapters written by some leading fleet managers. They explain how they have faced specific fleet challenges – reducing fuel costs and emissions, running a green fleet, managing a large corporate fleet, changing their leasing company, tackling the grey fleet and even running a police fleet – and how they rose to meet those challenges.

Some fleet topics are perennial; for example, the options when setting up a roadside assistance arrangement, using a credit hire service, deciding how best to manage the immediate aftermath of an accident and deciding how best to buy new cars, so this book contains chapters on these topics too.

If you own your own vehicles, or buy them using one of the purchase-based form of finance (hire purchase, lease purchase, conditional sale, credit sale or contract purchase) you are probably taking the residual value risk in those vehicles. And unless you have an arrangement with a leasing or fleet management maintenance company, perhaps through contract management or maintenance-inclusive contract hire, you will be responsible for the maintenance costs of your vehicles; ie you will be taking the maintenance cost risk. To manage this risk you need information, which is why this book includes a chapter written by a highly experienced data provider.

A vast amount has been said in the last 15 years about pan-European and global fleet deals. It stands to reason that a multinational will want to reduce its costs by leveraging its buying power. Many a global procurement manager will have done global deals for the supply of their photocopiers and IT equipment, then hoped to be able to do the same sort of deals for their fleets, only to discover that fleet vehicles and services are not as straight-forward as some other types of supply. There are too many variables; different currencies, interest rates, tax rules, customs, practices and so on. Yet these deals are being done, in no small measure through the tenacity of some of the international leasing groups who have worked through the issues, determined what is possible and then set out to try to do a good job in delivering what the client wants. One such expert has written a chapter in this book.

In recent years a lot has been done to give people with disabilities the same access to services that able-bodied people take for granted. Disability discrimination legislation provides broad protection for disabled people, yet many fleet managers will be unsure what to do the first time they come across a disabled employee who needs a hire or lease car. So this book contains a chapter on this topic.

One of the most satisfying aspects about making a career in this sector is that fleet management is incredibly multi-faceted; there is always a new angle, always something new to learn. I have been in this industry for nearly 30 years yet I am constantly learning new things, and have certainly learned a lot from the contributions to this book. I hope that in these pages you will learn, as I have, new things across topics as diverse as work-related road safety, the legal aspects of running a car fleet, environmental issues, the sub-prime fleet finance market, recruiting and training fleet staff and upcoming developments in new vehicles.

Thankfully the downturn has not yet affected my own business. We help fleet managers reduce costs and risks. We also help lessors improve their aspects of their businesses - pricing, strategic planning, sales staff performance, etc. These services are still in demand, though like all other small businesses we do worry about the economy.

We're working currently for companies that want to get out of the market and others that want to buy in. One person's downturn is another's golden opportunity.

As the economic clouds grow darker, fleet managers will be wondering how to respond. Is now the time to move from outright purchase to contract hire? Or in the other direction? Or is there some better and cheaper product out there? If redundancies are being discussed, what can be done to avoid large early termination charges from contract hire companies? In fact, what can be done generally to reduce fleet costs?

And what should fleet managers be doing now about the risks inherent in running a fleet of vehicles; residual values, maintenance costs, health and safety, road risk?

Here is a check-list fleet managers may find useful when trying to reduce fleet costs and risks:

- Avoid early terminating leased vehicles: Redeploy them within the business.
- Ensure the early termination clause in your contract hire agreement is as good as you can negotiate.
- Ensure your lease contains a pooled mileage clause.
- Renegotiate contract hire agreements mid-term rather than building up big excess mileage charges.
- Choose the right financial product for your fleet, making sure you include tax costs and benefits in your evaluation.
- Stop providing free private fuel.
- Review your fleet list. Is it delivering the right mix of cars in terms of costs and emissions?
- Move to a fixed list not a user-chooser policy.
- Use whole-life costs to select vehicles for your fleet list. These include fuel, maintenance, depreciation and tax.
- Make sure your cars are serviced regularly, to ensure fuel efficiency and to identify vehicle problems before they become expensive to repair.
- Use demonstrator cars where available.
- Consider taking cars on daily hire rather than allowing employees to use their own.
- Investigate whether it makes sense to have one manufacturer's cars across your whole fleet.
- Consider having pool cars available for occasional journeys.
- If you have a large fleet, consider taking third party motor insurance and self-insuring the comprehensive risk.
- Consider introducing a cash-for-car, salary sacrifice or Employee Car Ownership scheme.
- Encourage the take-up of low CO_2 cars.
- Make sure your driver safety procedures are robust and well-documented.

- Consider introducing an Internal Driving Licence scheme. These operate like conventional driving licences in that the driver has to do certain things (in this case comply with the rules you set) before being granted the Internal Driving Licence (an internally-issued permit to drive on business) for a period of time (perhaps 12 months). A 'totting-up' scheme is set by the company and points are given for various transgressions (motoring offences, failure to return the car in good condition, abuse of vehicle, not having the car serviced, allowing it to be used by unauthorised drivers, etc). The driver's permission to drive is removed if they run up more than 12 points. This system will be accepted by employees if the points are fair and the reasons for the scheme are fully explained.

- If you don't want to take maintenance risk, use a fleet management service or take your vehicles on a maintenance-inclusive lease from a contract hire company. They will remind you when services are due. Their qualified maintenance controllers will carry out pre- and post-event control; they know how long jobs should take, will minimise the hassle of maintaining your vehicles, will negotiate supplier pricing in advance and will pass back the savings to you via a competitive rental or a recharge that reflects their buying power rather than yours.

- If you don't outsource your maintenance control, keep a maintenance history for each car. If you accept a quote, issue an order number and record this on the vehicle maintenance record. This may be a simple file used to log each event - date, cost and work done. Bigger fleets will wish to use fleet software.

- When suppliers' invoices arrive, check these against the maintenance history to ensure the work has been authorised and correctly billed. If so, pass for payment. If not, reject.

- You can reduce fuel costs by using journey-planning tools, satnav, telematics and fleet systems, but remember that a key determinant of mpg is the driver's right foot: If it is too heavy the cost goes straight to your company's bottom line.

- Rather than using employees' cars and paying a mileage allowance, consider using daily hire cars instead.

- Ensure your drivers are prompted to have their cars serviced when due, but don't let them authorise the work or pay the bill. Use an expert to do this; the driver may forget to get their car serviced, may pay too much for the work and may pay for unnecessary work.

- If you allow your drivers to buy their company cars when de-fleeted, beware of 'preconditioning' – drivers asking for additional work to be done at the company's expense just before they buy the car.

- Someone driving 25,000 miles pa is as likely to die on the road as a coal miner working down a coal mine, and more likely than a builder on a building site. As an employer you are responsible for your employees' safety. Implement a health and safety review of workplace driving. Collect data (accident list: 5 years), analyse the data (look for trends, determine the true cost of road accidents), benchmark your accident data with other companies (your insurer will provide info, compare your accident record with other firms), review your accident history, find problem areas, determine steps you can take to reduce accidents, present recommendations to senior management, agree action plan, allocate responsibilities, implement road safety plan, evaluate the effects of the changes regularly.

This is a brief checklist that will hopefully be helpful.

Cars cost so much to run and involve so many risks there will always be things you can do to improve the way you manage your fleet.

Colin Tourick

CT&A

Services for fleet managers

- Fleet cost reduction
- Risk reduction
- Advice on selection of suppliers
- Support when going out to tender

Services for contract hire companies

- Pricing support – Margin Management
- Strategic planning
- Sales team and account manager training
- Benchmarking services
- Merger and acquisition support

Colin Tourick & Associates Limited
London
www.tourick.com

1

REDUCING BUSINESS MILEAGE

Lee Wickens
CSR & Quality Manager
Addison Lee

Some readers, particularly those outside London will be unaware of Addison Lee. What does it do, how big is its vehicle fleet and what is your role in the group?

Addison Lee is London's leading minicab company with the fleet of approximately 2,500 premium minicabs operating around the clock, 365 days a year. Established in 1975, the company has transformed the private hire industry and today enjoys an unsurpassed reputation for moving people and parcels in London. Our vehicles are spacious people carriers fitted with air-conditioning and satellite navigation as standard, and our fleet is more than five times the size of our nearest private hire competitor. Our prices are fixed regardless of the time of day, and with no meters in the cars, the passenger will never pay more than quoted. Addison Lee is, on average, 30% cheaper than black taxis and with the sheer volume of vehicles we own, we have become a genuine rival to the long-established black cab trade. A groundbreaking automatic allocation system allows us to offer a within-15-minute on demand pick-up time within central London, a service unparalleled within the capital.

We are also the founding member of the PHCA (Private Hire Car Association), which represents the private hire operators and drivers of London. As well as our private hire cars we also offer extensive transport services including motorcycle and van couriers, international and overnight deliveries and a large fleet of chauffeur-driven Mercedes Benz. In 2006, Addison Lee purchased Redwing, London's largest coach company, and now also offers coach travel for parties of twenty or more. As part of an ongoing commitment to the environment, Addison Lee has cut its emissions per journey by 17.6% since 2002 (this figure was externally verified by Beardsley Consultants in November 2007) and we are working on a further 6% year-on-year reduction.

Addison Lee is the first minicab company to be certified ISO 9001, ISO 14001 and to obtain the Investors in People accreditation. We also are the first to have combined the three quality standards most applicable to our industry, (ISO 9001, 14001,

18001) into a complete and concise quality, environment and health & safety management system.

I am responsible for overseeing the company's green initiatives and the training provided to staff and drivers.

What is the EST/Department for Transport 'Fleet Heroes' award and how did you get involved in it?

Energy Savings Trust (EST) is an independent, UK organisation focused on promoting action leading to the reduction of carbon dioxide emissions - a key contributor to man-made climate change. EST is impartial, and not tied to any particular commercial organisation or driven by political or corporate motivations. The organisation offers free advice and information for people across the UK looking to save energy. They also help people choose greener ways of travel at home and at work. They have a range of advice services - delivered at a local level - which provide practical solutions to environmental issues with enthusiasm and passion.

When I first started working for Addison Lee PLC I started researching various ways of reducing mileage and cutting emissions. I found EST on the internet and asked them to review our fleet's fuel efficiency. The EST team was extremely helpful and professional. In the course of several meetings they created a 'Green Fleet Review' and provided heaps of advice and tips on how to make the fleet more efficient and help it run smoothly.

Sounds like you were impressed!

They were very professional and passionate about their jobs. These guys really know what they are talking about and they are very eager to help. I found that EST will ask you questions to get to the bottom of your operating system, and this made for a very successful relationship as they had a very detailed insight into our business so they could tailor a plan that suited our organisation. The 'Green Fleet Review' is a brilliant report that did not leave out any part of our fleet operations. Any previous initiatives will be acknowledged, but the report's main focus is looking forward to what you can do to further reduce emissions. There obviously were a few recommendations which came out of the Green Fleet Review which were not practicable as they conflicted with our main business objectives. For example, they suggested we should reduce our six-seater vehicles to four seats in order to save CO_2, which was not possible. Most of the recommendations were extremely enlightening and very business-focused whilst still concentrating directly on the reduction of green house gas emissions.

What did you do to win the award?

Addison Lee won the Best Large Fleet Category in the Green Fleet awards primarily for its technology-focused carbon reduction initiatives, but there were a host of other areas we covered to ensure the whole company was involved and that every process in the business was covered.

The following gives an overview of our main submission data:

- Recyclable fleet sourcing
- Improved staff, supplier and client environmental awareness
- Expansion of home worker network
- Investment in local and socio-economic CSR

OUR FLEET

After extensive research into the market place, we chose the Volkswagen Sharan, Ford Galaxy and Mercedes Benz E and S class for our fleet, as tests showed that these are over 75% recyclable, considerably greener than any other vehicle in their class, and overall far less damaging to the environment than any hybrid vehicle available.

Addison Lee has given serious consideration to incorporating battery-powered vehicles into its fleet. We feel that in time these will prove to the be future of greener vehicles but they are not for us at present because they mainly involve moving CO_2 production away from the car and into power stations that still burn fossil fuels.

After working closely with all of our major clients, we have managed to reduce drivers' 'dead' mileage by 17.6% over the last 5 years, thanks to investment in developing our own scheduling applications and fleet management. I will refer to this further when I talk about IT. Put simply, because our vehicles rarely have to travel more than half a mile to arrive at their next collection point, the emissions are substantially lower than those of our competitors who, owing to their vastly smaller fleet sizes, often need to travel several miles between jobs. This has led to reduction of greenhouse emissions by 17.6% which is around 22,000 tonnes over 5 years. (Addison Lee's baseline is 2002 which is when we started implementing all the new environmental policies and practices).

- Our S class Mercedes exceeds even the 2014 Euro 6 emissions standards
- Our Mercedes E and S-class also exceed the government's 2012 recyclability standards which will require all cars built after the date to be at least 98% recyclable
- Our Mercedes S-class was the world's first car to be awarded an environmental certificate, which recognises the car's compliance with ISO standard 14062.

EMISSIONS

Turning now to emissions, as already mentioned we have reduced each of our drivers' dead mileage by 17.6% over the last 5 years. This has cut greenhouse gas emissions by the same amount, which is a great step towards combating climate change. The choice of our fleet alone has also allowed us to make substantial savings in CO_2 emissions (from 220g/km to 164g/km).

Addison Lee has recently made some further cuts in vehicle emissions. Our allocation and scheduling technology has enabled us to reduce our average distance to pick-up by 50%. This has saved us 16,000 miles per day and is probably one of the biggest breakthroughs for Addison Lee's Environmental Management System so far this year.

We have also saved an impressive 2000 plus miles per day by upgrading our allocation software to allow drivers conducting their last job of the day to be allocated a journey in the direction of their home. This saves 18,000 miles every day of the year which, without a doubt, makes us the most efficient private hire fleet in London.

Over the period of 2002-2008 we are looking at a total carbon reduction of 20-26%. This information will be verified in our 2008 environmental statement and the results will be made available for public viewing.

Addison Lee aims to reduce its CO_2 emissions by 60% by 2025 (the government's new deadline). We therefore have 17 years during which we need to average a 2.5% per year CO_2 reduction to meet the targets, which we believe we can achieve.

Turning now to the future, Addison Lee is working in partnership with The London Climate Change Agency on the first hydrogen powered taxi in London.

Additionally, we are currently working closely with Volkswagen, Ford and Mercedes looking at the new ranges of energy efficient diesels such as Volkswagen's common-rail turbo diesel technology in an effort to improve efficiency and emissions.

We are also consulting Volkswagen about the diesel-based engine technology known as CCS (Combined Combustion System), which, as well as delivering better fuel efficiency will also be able to run on biofuels. Addison Lee tracks biofuel sustainability and advancements through membership of the All-Party Parliamentary Group for Renewable Transport Fuels.

The Energy Savings Trust fleet review looked, amongst other subjects, at our carbon footprint, vehicle allocation policy, fuel economy and driver training. We are now starting to work on the issues highlighted in the report to further reduce our carbon emissions.

Additionally we have just joined Motorvate, a membership scheme for innovative fleet managers implementing measures to reduce carbon emissions. Motorvate is the next logical step after a fleet review for any company that is serious about improving its environmental performance and efficiency. The project, funded by the Department for Transport, measures the progress by certification and Addison Lee is ultimately aiming to achieve the gold level award.

DRIVER TRAINING

We train all our drivers to a NVQ level in Road Passenger Vehicle Driving, free of charge. Among other subjects, we cover defensive driving, the environmental impact of using a car on a daily basis and how to reduce emissions by driving more efficiently. Also, in our monthly internal newsletter BriefLee we regularly include tips on how to save fuel and consequently reduce emissions.

RECYCLING

Addison Lee PLC commits to procure goods from sustainable sources and specifically to increase the proportion of timber and paper products obtained from certified, well-managed forests and through recycling.

Additionally, all of Addison Lee's prospective suppliers are expected to provide an environmental overview of their business operations before being considered, and we send each of them an annual verification report and a supplier assessment survey.

OFFICES

Addison Lee recycles over 98% of all office and garage waste and is looking to improve these figures with the help of Bywaters, a London-based waste management and recycling company.

Our waste carriers include Brent Oil, Bywaters, McGrath and the vehicle manufacturers themselves. A range of waste streams were identified, 515.4 tons in total.

These included:

Vehicle batteries	60 tons
Oil	11 tons
Tyres	156 tons
Discs	207 tons
General waste	52 tons
Dry recyclables	10.4 tons
Brake pads	12.9 tons
Gear boxes	5 tons
Water pumps	0.3 tons
Alternators	0.3 tons
Starter motors	0.04 tons
IT equipment	0.8 tons

RECYCLING

Our furniture is fully recycled, but the volumes have yet to be determined.

Currently, 20 tons of waste goes to landfill, thus 98% of Addison Lee's company waste is recycled.

HOME WORKERS

Addison Lee currently has 80 full time home-based employees and this figure is growing by, on average, 5 per month. This represents a significant reduction in vehicle emissions and office waste. The exact amount of CO_2 they generate through work has yet to be quantified as we simply have not had the time due to the sheer number of other projects and initiatives we are focusing on.

CLIENT REPORTING

All Addison Lee clients can receive comprehensive reports, detailing precise greenhouse gas emissions and particulates generated by their journeys. The report forms part of our bespoke management information and can be produced in a number of ways, as required by the client.

In addition to our account management reports we are working closely with our major clients to reduce the number of unnecessary journeys taken by their staff. This has a dual effect, generating significant cost savings while impacting positively on our environmental objectives.

Addison Lee can provide in-depth analysis of waiting time statistics. The information can highlight trends and regular offenders. The data can often be used to significantly reduce the amount of waiting time. Our drivers will always turn off their engines whilst waiting for prolonged periods for the client.

CERTIFICATION AND INITIATIVES

Addison Lee is acutely aware of its environmental responsibilities. In 2002, we recruited a full time Environmental Awareness Manager and subsequently we have implemented multiple policies to ensure that we continually monitor and improve our commitment to reducing harmful impacts on our planet. Our CSR & Environmental Policy states that we influence the suppliers of services and resources to adopt best environmental practices as part of our vision of a cleaner London.

We have recently been certified ISO 14001 (which recognises our commitment to integrating high standards of environmental responsibility into all of our operations) and all of our employees are involved in an environmental awareness programme.

We are working with the EST to compile a green handbook, containing facts and statistics about environmental issues and climate change. This will be available free of charge to all our staff, clients and suppliers.

We are a member and active participant of the London Green 500. The primary focus of this organisation is to bring together the 500 largest businesses in the capital, with the greatest potential for carbon reduction, to focus on carbon-reduction initiatives.

We are also a member and active participant of the May Day Network, the UK's largest group of businesses and organisations that are committed to collectively tackling climate change by mobilising their companies, employees, suppliers and customers. By sharing best practice, these businesses promise to play a powerful role in reducing the UK's carbon emissions.

W have been talking with the London Climate Change Agency about how we could be involved in any way in furthering their work. The agency was established as the primary delivery vehicle for reducing London's carbon dioxide emissions.

CORPORATE SOCIAL RESPONSIBILITY

This year, we have invested heavily in our internal energy reduction systems, one element of our environmental management system. We have funded a 4KW Solar Photo Voltaic System for Netley School, our local primary school, and we are beginning the installation in December. This will reducing the school's CO_2 output and, more importantly, will prove to be invaluable for the future by educating children from the local community about sustainable energy and other current and emerging environmental technologies.

We donate all superfluous computer equipment to local schools and nurseries. Addison Lee also works with local schools, in conjunction with a local children's charity, to provide fun, educational lessons and workshops relating to environmental issues.

Addison Lee built a computer, media and music facility for the members of the Samuel Lithgow Youth Centre, a not-for-profit local charity.

Addison Lee PLC is a corporate partner of Computer Aid, an organisation which provides high quality, professionally-refurbished computers for reuse in education, health and not-for-profit organisations in developing countries. This has itself cut an amount of CO_2 however this has yet to be quantified due to the complexity of calculating the environmental benefits with any real certainty.

What changes did you have to make in order to reduce your mileage?

We have invested in more efficient management of our fleet as part of our Environmental Commitments Statement. We also made IT changes, and this is the subject of the case study below. Not all of our changes were environmentally-directed but they have been implemented due to the expansion of the company. As a company we are very well organised and look towards the future and to adopting ideas that will help reduce mileage and CO_2 output.

How effective was the introduction of your new IT system?

ADDISON LEE IT CASE STUDY

Summary

Addison Lee's overhaul of its legacy IT systems was the single biggest factor in creating a greener fleet. By integrating a new £1.5m custom-built scheduling and allocation application to provide dynamic, real time scheduling across the entire fleet, this project enabled Addison Lee to grow its fleet by 200% (1000 vehicles) whilst increasing backroom staff by just 100. The company has now reduced its dead mileage by over 17%; booking times have been reduced from 2.5 to 1.5 minutes, while customer response times have been cut by seven minutes.

Addison Lee's use of IT to cut dead mileage and increase fleet efficiency provides an emphatic demonstration that creating a lean business can provide huge environmental benefits.

The Situation

By 2003 Addison Lee's fleet had grown to around 500 cars and it was experiencing customer demand for more minicabs, but even the best human cab controllers were unable to effectively allocate jobs to more than 500 drivers.

Addison Lee's management decided that in order to meet customer demand for a larger fleet, a technological solution was required that could handle higher volumes of passengers and allocate many more jobs at a faster rate. Most minicab companies work to a 'nearest cab takes job' structure, but with such a large fleet servicing anything up to 2,000 jobs an hour within a relatively small area, Addison Lee required a solution that could assess the fleet in its entirety and allocate jobs according to a holistic view of what was most efficient for the fleet as a whole, rather than assessing on a job-by-job basis. Although the primary motivation for implementing this system was to increase capacity and profitability for the fleet, the improved efficiency that would be delivered would provide a significant reduction in journey times, dead mileage and consequently, emissions.

Business Objectives

Addison Lee's objectives for the new technology were as follows:

1 Accelerate the booking and job allocation process to allow faster response and handle greater numbers of jobs

2 Reduce dependency on human input, to cut down on human error and accelerate business processes

3 Improve fleet scheduling, to make the most efficient use of all resources

4 Implement a scalable, flexible, highly-available, future-proof infrastructure to integrate with other, third-party applications as required

5 Reduce emissions for the fleet as a whole by efficient allocation and scheduling

Managing the project in-house, Addison Lee selected a Sybase database and placed it within a multi-tiered architecture that enabled provision of redundancy systems and scalability for future growth. The team also custom-built applications to meet the challenge of allocating thousands of jobs to the fleet of premium minicabs efficiently, to minimize waiting times and reduce 'dead mileage' (miles travelled without customers – at a loss to the company).

The challenge of handling exponentially-increasing volumes of bookings was addressed with a custom-engineered allocation solution. By utilising complex mathematical algorithms and a real time event-based optimisation engine, the allocation system was brought online with a capacity to process 10,000 jobs per hour.

The allocator was the key application in enabling Addison Lee to rapidly expand its operations and grow the fleet from 500 cars up to the current 2,500, whilst ensuring maximum fleet efficiency and a drastic reduction in dead mileage and thus emissions. Individual drivers are profiled so the allocation system can match the best drivers to the highest priority clients and routes are automatically planned using actual road distances instead of 'as the crow flies' to reduce both passenger journeys and wait times – the allocator can even plan jobs for drivers to take them closer to home at the end of the night.

Benefits

By integrating drivers' mobile devices, GPS, Addison Lee's IT systems and the custom-built automated booking and dispatch system, jobs can now be swiftly allocated to drivers whether online, by text or by telephone. 98% of these jobs are now allocated automatically, with no need for human involvement, while the average time for a booking has been reduced from 150 to 90 seconds.

Peter Ingram, IT Director at Addison Lee explains: *'When a customer books one of our drivers, we can tell them exactly where their appointed vehicle is and give them an approximate time when the driver will arrive. If the driver is delayed for any reason, we can then give the customer an updated arrival time based on the drivers' progress. The allocation engine can also optimise the vehicle's efficiency to prioritise pick-up speed, driver earnings, or general efficiency, as required. The benefits in time alone are clear – our booking times have been reduced from 2.5 to 1.5 minutes, while customer response times have been cut by a whole 7 minutes.'*

Naturally, the system has also seen a great increase in efficiency. 'Dead mileage' where drivers are travelling without earning, has been reduced by 17.6%. Drivers can now take 'Going Home' or 'First Thing' jobs, allocating pre-booked jobs according to the driver's route home and location and allowing them to keep working all day without wasting non-work mileage at the start and end of a shift. Just this 'Going Home' function saves the company around 3,000 miles of travelling per day, whilst in a year the fleet itself does three million fewer miles than would have been expected under the previous systems.

The environmental benefits of this cannot be overstated. 20-26% carbon emission reduction from 2002 to the end of 2008 – this will be checked and externally verified in early 2009.

This efficiency has also stretched to training, where training times for call centre staff have been reduced from one month to one week.

The system has also provided great benefits for Addison Lee's drivers themselves. As well as making their job a great deal easier, the system has helped increase their earning potential. Average jobs per driver have increased by two per week, while average driver earnings are up by 5%.

Peter Ingram concludes: *'The project to overhaul our IT systems stemmed from a desire to improve our efficiency, grow our business and increase profits. The fact that this project had such significant benefits in terms of reducing our environmental impact was a very welcome side effect. We're extremely proud of our capability to dynamically schedule our fleet so efficiently in real time and in one of the most complex urban environments in the world.'*

Evaluation: Facts and Figures

· Cost of implementation; £1.5m

· 30% growth in turnover with 65% profit growth per year

· 2004 Profit £3 million

· 2007 Profit £15.2 million

· Growth in fleet; up by 1000 cars (200%) in three years

· Growth in back office employees during same period; under 100

· Dead mileage reduced by 17.6%

· Complaints / pick up errors; down to 0.9%

What vehicles are you currently adding to your fleet?

Our latest fleet addition has been the Ford Galaxy. It produces 165g/km of CO_2 which is 32g/km lower than the VW Sharan it is replacing. We are eagerly anticipating the release of the new VW Sharan which is due early 2010 and we hope both these vehicles will soon be under the 160g/km mark, further reducing our total fleet emissions.

You have personally been involved in an initiative to reduce emissions by driving smarter. Please explain this initiative.

My involvement has been in setting up a college for Addison Lee. This was born out of the lack of suitable training for the industry and made possible by the forward-thinking of Addison Lee as a company and the help of Go Skills, LSC (Learning Skills Council) and Edexcel.

The qualification we are delivering is the RPVD (Road Passenger Vehicle Driving) NVQ at level 2. This is a very well thought out qualification and it has 'fitted' the needs of the transport industry extremely well as shown by the very positive response of employers within the Private Hire industry. The environmental element has been embedded in the qualification from the start as it combines with one of the Health and Safety units. As with all environmental benefits, this includes elements of health and safety and customer satisfaction so that it is not just focused on the environment, and this makes it attractive to all drivers. We have developed our training to exceed the qualification framework.

We are also training the drivers on environmental issues which not only affect them on the road but at home and in their family lives as well.

Quote from our EST Green Fleet Review:

> Addison Lee take an active role in offering their drivers as much training and information as possible, all of which should help the drivers get as much from a gallon of diesel as possible. AL's delivery of NVQ in Road Passenger Driving in connection with LSC and Go Skills is noteworthy and a fine example of positive engagement with employees in a sector where turnover is so high that employers are frequently disinclined to spend time or money on staff.

Do you have any plans to change your current arrangements to further reduce your business mileage?

The company aims to reduce its CO_2 emissions by 60% by 2050, so on average a 2.5% CO_2 reduction is required each year to meet the target.

Would you recommend that other fleet managers follow the same course you have?

I would definitely recommend others follow the same course Addison Lee took. The key thing to take away from our experience is that 'green washing' – green for green's sake - is not an option for fleet managers. By investing in technology to expand our operations and run our fleet more efficiently we have delivered real benefits to the business, improved customer service, eliminated waste (dead mileage) and generally created a leaner organisation.

To a large extent, our experience shows that managing a fleet in the most efficient manner is the key to reducing environmental impact. I cannot stress enough how fundamental a role our new IT systems have played in cutting dead mileage and thus emissions. Since we have developed this technology we have demonstrated our systems to a number of (non-competing) fleet managers and I would welcome enquiries from anyone looking to implement similar systems to contact us and see what we have done here.

If our system can handle the scale of our operations, the challenge of meeting ever-changing customer demands, real-time changes to pick up and drop off points and the complexity of managing our fleet in London's constantly fluctuating traffic system, I see no reason why fleet managers in any other sector should not be able to implement systems as we have and see a similar impact, not only creating a greener fleet, but just as importantly, delivering a faster, leaner and more profitable business.

Lee Wickens
CSR & Quality Manager
Addison Lee

Addison Lee
Environmental
Commitments

V 4.0 8/10/08

35-37 William Road, London NW1 3ER
t 020 7387 8888 e info@addisonlee.com w www.addisonlee.com

2 SELECTING A LEASING COMPANY

> **Keith B Cook,** Chartered MCIPD
> Deputy Financial Controller
> Computacenter UK Limited

Please introduce yourself and your fleet

I've worked in the hi-tech sector for over 25 years, the last 19 of which have been with Computacenter, and I've had stewardship of the Fleet function for a little over 6 years. My background is quite eclectic, with a blend of Financial, Systems and Commercial skills focused on maximising sustainable profitability; especially in terms of cost management. So, when the chance came to take on the overall management of the Computacenter Fleet, it was an opportunity that I just couldn't refuse. The challenge to take on the function and enhance the positive contribution to the bottom line, whilst retaining employee satisfaction, was irresistible.

The Computacenter fleet comprises 2,000 vehicle-eligible employees with around 50% opting to take a vehicle and 50% opting to take cash. Of the vehicles, there are approximately 750 cars and 250 light commercials (LCVs). Around 80% of the fleet is a working fleet, for engineers and sales people visiting client sites, with the balance being 'perk' vehicles. We also have some re-imbursement drivers, often referred to as the 'grey fleet', which covers those employees who do not receive any vehicle benefit so have to make business related journeys in their privately owned vehicle.

Please explain, in outline, how you fund and manage your fleet

We've split our fleet up into a number of contractual elements. The actual day to day management of the fleet is currently outsourced to two fleet management companies (one for cars and one for the LCVs), who also handle our accident management. We decided on the outsource model, as it means we can deliver a scalable and repeatable service to our employees, that couldn't be achieved, cost effectively, through internal resource.

We have a Fleet Contract Manager who oversees the performance of the various contracts, and contractual elements, to ensure that each contract, and supplier, is delivering measurable value and performing to agreed Service Levels. They also act as a point of internal escalation, and proactively seek stakeholder feedback; so we have a holistic view of supplier performance against employee needs, which can often change. We aim to use 'best of breed' providers for each service, so we also have a fuel card provider and daily rental provider that also supplies pre-contract vehicles; invariably on a mini lease.

The Fleet Contract Manager is supported by two administrators who are responsible for validating the scheduled and especially unscheduled charges from our suppliers; ensuring all avoidable costs (eg. parking fines, speeding fines, insurance excess charges, unfair wear and tear charges etc.) are re-charged to employees. The team also manages all aspects of occupational road risk, which is not an inconsiderable task. This includes annual driver license checks, via DVLA, for all drivers; insurance checks, to ensure that cash takers are adequately insured for business travel; and reviewing accident data to identify loss trends and implement loss control measures such as driver training and policy changes.

With regards to funding, we've recently moved to a blend of traditional contract hire and Employee Car Ownership (ECO). The cost to the employee, regardless of the funded product they end up being provided with, is identical.

With a traditional contract hire vehicle, the employee will pay company car tax, related to the scale charge for their vehicle and marginal rate of tax, via a change of tax code. If they go into an ECO vehicle, then they make a 'contribution' to the vehicle that is identical to the company car tax that they would have paid if it were a contract hire vehicle. This has the added advantage of ensuring that employees have a financial incentive to select CO_2 friendly vehicles, regardless of how the vehicle is funded. For the company, there is a 'calculator' that sits behind the selection process and determines which funded product is right for which employee, based on a number of variables (business mileage, vehicle selection, marginal tax rate et al), to ensure that the most cost effective/tax efficient funding option is selected for the company.

Fundamental to this is the fact that, as stated above, the employee remains in a neutral position, regardless of whether they have an ECO or contract hire vehicle. So, the employee experience, from quote, through order to in-life management, remains the same, other than a difference in the paperwork that needs to be signed; as ECO relies on a credit sale agreement (CSA).

Whatever funding option is selected, the employee receives the vehicle fully inclusive of service, maintenance and repair (SMR), insurance, accident management, breakdown assistance & recovery and a relief vehicle if their car is off the road for any reason. Where employees opt for cash, then they have to provide these additional services from the cash they are given. The competitive rates that we can source these services for, by using our 'bulk' purchasing power, means that the vehicle option is compelling. Consequently, it's important that drivers understand, when making any comparisons, that it's not just the 'metal' that they are getting, but a complete package (on that point, they also need to ensure that they are comparing like-for-like mileage profiles and any contract penalties; such as excess mileage charges).

With regards to fuel, fuel reimbursement rates are one of the prime factors in determining the choice between ECO and contract hire. It's also a major item of expenditure in its own right. To set our reimbursement rates we use exactly the same methodology as HMRC use to set their Advisory Fuel Rates. The big advantage that this has is that it's completely transparent for our employees, and there can be no arguments about the integrity of the calculation. However, rather than stick,to the HMRC rates, which remain static for a 6 month period, we review the cost of fuel each month, pass them through the calculation, and, if fuel prices change materially, we review our internal reimbursement rates up or down accordingly. This ensures that we strike the right balance between cost control and employee satisfaction; all the more important when the price of fuel is so volatile.

It's important to note that employees are made aware that, when they are making their car choice, they should select a fuel-efficient vehicle, as this is a core element of the fuel reimbursement calculation. So, if they choose a less fuel-efficient vehicle than the reimbursement model suggests they should choose, the reimbursement they receive will not necessarily cover the cost of the actual fuel used. This is deliberate, and another way in which we encourage drivers to select more environmentally friendly vehicles.

How does your allocation policy work?

We used to allocate car grades on the basis of On Target Earning (OTE), but this created some inequity between roles. So, around 3 years ago we moved to allocating vehicles by Job Family (each job role is a member of one of eight Job Families). There are effectively four vehicle grades, plus two role specific engineering grades, and each Job Family maps across to a grade (a car grade may comprise more than one job family grade). There are also a few director grades. It's a system that works well.

Within each grade we ensure that there is a core selection of 'grade appropriate', and fit for purpose, vehicles available. We achieve this by using external benchmark data to ensure that we offer market competitive vehicles at each grade level. Moving to job families has made this benchmarking process a lot more robust.

We operate a user/chooser scheme – providing drivers with a rate book from which to select a vehicle – with drivers able to upgrade to a maximum of 35% above their entitlement (the total sum they can spend on a vehicle, including company car tax). The user/chooser scheme was driven off the back of employee consultation, and meets the desire of our employees to have the flexibility to choose a vehicle that is appropriate to their lifestyle, so long as it remains fit for purpose. Each month, and especially after manufacturer/suppliers pricing reviews, we validate the rate book, at each grade level, to ensure that the core vehicles remain available within the relevant price band or, if not, that a suitable alternative vehicle is available. Eg. If one of the core vehicles was a Ford, it may be replaced by a similar specification vehicle from a different manufacturer, such as Vauxhall or VW.

Whilst we benchmark against core vehicles, the employee entitlement is to a typical specification of vehicles for the grade, not to a specific make/model. This is because individual makes/models of vehicle can change price materially, but overall an equivalent make/model may remain competitively priced for the grade. This can happen particularly when a make/model comes to the end of its life, or have a major facelift. In providing this level of choice, it's important that employees understand that, at the end of their current contract, they may not necessarily be able to renew their vehicle, on a specific like-for-like basis. However, this can also be positive as, if their renewal coincides with a manufacture promotion on a vehicle that would generally only be available in a higher grade, employees are able to capitalise on this.

For note, almost certainly, where there are like-for-like vehicle comparisons, they can be unreliable, as the actual specification of the make/model will have changed. Typically these will be changes to body styling, or items that were options becoming standard equipment. The key to managing any potential employee dissatisfaction is to ensure that employees' expectations are set at the point of purchase, and that recruiting managers set expectations clearly at interview.

When it comes to daily rental vehicles, and pre contract cars, we provide a single solution of a large-bodied saloon vehicle, unless there are specific circumstances that dictate otherwise (such as an LCV or MPV), or the employee wishes to downgrade. Because we have a lot of high business mileage drivers, this type of vehicle appropriately covers our duty of care under occupational road risk legislation. In reality, this was the grade of vehicle that our employees were justifying upgrades to.

So, by focusing our purchasing power on this one grade of rental vehicle, rather than splitting it across two, we've been able to reduce costs and supply a higher specification of vehicle; a classic win-win.

Are there any vehicles that you would not allow on your fleet?

We try our best to be as flexible as possible, because our employees value the choice to select a vehicle that matches their lifestyle. It also helps when attracting new employees to work for Computacenter. The only real restrictions we impose, are that the vehicle must be fit for purpose for the job role (eg. load space, number of doors), and must be below a CO_2 cap of 230 g/km. This cap has been reduced, and will continue to be reduced, over time. The only manufacturer excluded from the choice list is Alpha Romeo. This was nothing to do with the quality of the cars, but because we had too many replacement engines due to drivers neglecting to top up oil levels regularly.

You use a mixture of contract hire and employee car ownership (ECO) to fund your fleet. Why did you choose this mix of financial products?

Employee Car Ownership delivers significant operational savings to the business, typically for higher business mileage drivers, allowing us to reduce our cost base without diluting employee benefit in any way. However, when we used to run a 'one size fits all' ECO scheme, for all of our drivers, we had a group of low business mileage – typically perk – drivers, on whom we had to pay tax and national insurance (NI) gross-up costs, as a result of this method of funding. By being able to channel these drivers into contract hire the business further optimised the cost of delivering company cars, again without diluting employee benefit in any way.

All employees choose their vehicle on the basis of a 15,000 mile per annum/three year contract term. This ensures that all drivers make their car choice equally, regardless of the actual miles they will drive.

Once the choice has been made, we purchase their contract based on their actual mileage profile, using historic or job role data, as the more accurately we can predict the contract mileage, the more we can ensure that we tailor the contract to the employee. Consequently, whilst it's not an absolute science, there will be fewer under/over mileage contracts at the end of their term, leading to greater certainty over cost. Whilst we have mileage pooling within our supply contract, another benefit of flexing the mileage contracts, for ECO, is that we ensure that the tax and NI gross-up costs, that we incur, are more accurate; as we don't end up 'over paying', where a driver drives substantially fewer miles than if they had had a 'standard' contract.

By utilising a blend of two funding products, we are now able to provide our employees with a vehicle at the most completive cost to the business, without impacting employee entitlement or choice in any way whatsoever. We have also taken the opportunity to extend this to the cash option that we offer. Where we used to offer a 'cash equivalent' to a car, we now offer a 'cash alternative'. This means that we offer a sum of cash that is equivalent to the cost to the business of providing a car for the individual employee. So, the employee receives a baseline monthly cash payment, plus a slightly enhanced fuel reimbursement rate for each business mile driven. This helps emphasise our vehicle purchasing power to employees, and encourages them to take the car choice which, in turn, makes it easier to manage occupational road risk. However, it's essential, when recruiting, to ensure that recruiting managers understand that the benefit/value that they are 'selling' is the car choice available.

You have recently gone through a large tender process and have changed vehicle management suppliers. Please talk us through the process and explain how you chose your new supplier.

We believe in long term relationships with our suppliers, but governance standards mean that, from time to time, we have to put all material items of expenditure out to competitive tender. It was no small exercise.

We began by defining what we were looking for, commercially and functionally, from a new contract. We already had a good idea of how we wanted our scheme to evolve (from a one size fits all classic ECO scheme, to a blended new generation ECO and

Contract Hire scheme, with tailored mileage contracts), and that we needed to lock down as many of the financial elements of supply that we could, leaving the least number of variable elements. With regards to the fixed financial elements, the obvious things to ensure were fixed and competitive, were interest rate margins, management fees, mileage pooling, profit sharing (on tyres, exhausts, windscreens, disposals etc.), and contract end charges such as fair wear and tear. For the variable elements, it was also important that the supplier committed to a price benchmarking mechanism as, given the complexity and tax clearance required within the ECO element of the scheme, we were awarding a sole supply contract, and we needed to ensure that the pricing remained competitive over the full life of the contract. The prime financial variable elements being service, maintenance and repair budgets and residual values.

We also took the opportunity, at this early stage, to seek input from key stakeholders from the across the business. Their early involvement was critical to securing their buy in to the new scheme, as they had an active role in its evolution and architecture. At the end of this process we compiled a Request for Information (RFI) to send to a range of Vehicle Management companies, selected on the basis of their perceived capability and their previously demonstrated desire to work with us.

The RFI went out to around 10 vendors, of various sizes, as we wanted to ensure we understood what we could expect from both large and medium sized suppliers. We kept a very open mind. The RFI was split into three sections;

- Vehicle Management,
- Accident Management, and
- Daily Rental.

Within each section, the supplier was requested to provide specific information, and evidence of capability and price. They could bid for any, or all, of the contractual components, but the stated preference was for a 'one stop shop'. We set out with the intention of appointing the new supplier within 3 months, which helped keep the process focused and moving.

I've been asked, a number of times, why our preference was for a 'one stop shop' approach, and our view was that any efficiency gains that could be made from disaggregating the services, would be at risk of being lost between the gaps created between different suppliers at the handoff points. One supplier means that if anything went wrong, one supplier was responsible, and accountable, for putting it right. More importantly, by owning the end-to-end process they were also in full control of being able to put it right. The tender process ensured that we knew the most competitive price, and levels of innovation, for each contractual component, and this could be embedded in the final contract with the eventual provider. At the end of the day, any gains from disaggregating the service would have been marginal, and one error, that took too long to fix, would have evaporated them.

Once the RFI results were back, we used a pre defined selection matrix to score the responses, to see who we would take through to the final stages. There was a mix of mandatory and desirable criteria. Clearly, the capability to deliver a scalable and repeatable ECO scheme, alongside contract hire, was one of the mandatory criteria. The matrix was completed, separately, by three people, and the consistency of scoring made it easy to narrow the selection down to four potential suppliers. They were each sent a more detailed tender document, drawing on what had been learned from all the responses to our RFI, and factoring in informal input from other Subject Matter Experts within the industry (once you put your fleet out to tender, it's such an incestuous industry, that soon everyone gets to know, and your phone gets pretty hot). The responses to this process were followed by formal presentations.

All of the responses and presentations were of a high quality, but this exercise enabled us to eliminate two further suppliers from the process; primarily because their ECO capability was less well established. This allowed us to take two suppliers to the final stage, which involved a more forensic examination of capability, extensive demonstrations of their database and quoting tools and, very importantly, reference site visits. The site visits were critical, as it was imperative to see how other companies, in similar industries with similar sized fleets, were interacting with these suppliers and to see, first hand, the tools that they were using, how they were being used, and the levels of satisfaction achieved. Both of the final two suppliers were open and flexible with regards to the site visits.

After receiving Best and Final Offers (BAFO) from each supplier, from a commercial perspective, there was very little, if anything, to separate them. It was encouraging to have two commercially favorable proposals, but we clearly needed to find something to differentiate between the two bids and select a winner. As ECO was, and remains, a core product for us, we decided to select the supplier which, in our opinion, had the most established, and demonstrable, pedigree in ECO provision. Both had strong reference sites, but one had slightly greater depth and breadth of ECO clients and capability. They were awarded preferred bidder status and, following successful completion of a due diligence process, were appointed as our new supplier for vehicle management and accident management.

Changing leasing supplier can be a big exercise, and at the same time you also changed the way you funded your fleet which would have made things even more complicated. What steps did you take to ensure a smooth transition?

Changing suppliers, or multi sourcing, in a traditional contract hire environment, is relatively easy, and can be managed reasonably well, such that any impact is transparent to employees. However, changing ECO providers is a lot more daunting, all the more so as it has legislative and HMRC consequences. Add to this the fact that we were not just porting a scheme from one provider to another, but changing from a 'classic' to 'new generation' ECO scheme, plus introducing one of the first blended schemes in the country, incorporating contract hire, it was especially important to ensure that everything went as smoothly as possible.

As mentioned previously, we had involved key stakeholders, across the business, at an early stage. It was important for them to become advocates of the new scheme, once it was launched, but equally important to get their critical evaluation of the new scheme architecture as it evolved; what may seem like a great idea from the centre of the business, may present some unforeseen challenges for the actual driver. I cannot stress enough how critical this engagement was to the success of the ultimate launch. Whilst Fleet, Finance and HR could drive much of the project, input from representatives of the driver community, across all types of driver, was fundamental to success; as was our corporate communications department's ability to pull together the comms. Some things only required very minor changes along the way, but their impact and contribution to a successful launch was immense. Equally, the incumbent, now old, supplier was also an important, and valued, stakeholder, as it would be imperative for the old and new suppliers to have a good working relationship, to facilitate a smooth run out of the legacy fleet.

The new supplier appointed a project manager with clearly identified work streams and timelines to work to. There were regular check point meetings, to monitor progress and highlight any issues for resolution; assigning clear ownership for problem resolution being critical. A significant amount of time was invested in mapping existing process and procedural documentation to the new scheme, and designing new ones, where required, once the architecture was defined. In parallel, communications material was also prepared, including branding of the new scheme. Clearly, the wider driver community was getting wind of a change, so high level 'teaser' mails were sent to employees to prepare them for the changes, and the launch of a new scheme, paying particular attention not to set unrealistic expectations.

At this point, we ceased ordering new vehicles from the old supplier, in order to maximise the demand – and cost savings – as we migrated to the new scheme with a new supplier. We also took the opportunity to conduct an electronic survey of all car eligible employees, to capture as much information as we could from them, ensuring that they felt consulted and involved. It was the results of this survey that determined that staff would prefer a launch via a webinar, rather than on-site launch events in each of our major branches, which had been our initial intention. It was important that we communicated with drivers in the manner that they most preferred to be communicated with. The flexibility of this method of communication gave us the maximum reach to the driver population as, so long as they had access to the internet, they could attend the launch from wherever they were. The only concern being that you couldn't see people's reactions.

As we got closer to launch, with more mature presentation documentation, we gathered together a focus group of our more vocal, and challenging, drivers to trial the material on.

The focus group was very open, and the feedback from it dramatically changed the order in which the material was presented, and some of the content; both taking things out and adding other things in. We also gained further employee buy-in; as not only were we giving them advanced visibility of the new scheme, and listening to their feedback, but, importantly, we were seen to be acting upon it. It resulted in the final launch material being far more concise, impactful and designed from the driver's point of view. We had taken all of the points and questions raised and ensured that, wherever possible, they were dealt with within the presentation.

Another benefit of the focus group was that they had not been part of the core stakeholder group, so the terminology of the new scheme was fresh and unfamiliar to them; we quickly learnt that we had used far too much industry language that would not have been universally understood in the webinar.

The webinars were hosted by me, and presented by our new supplier, to ensure a united, company and supplier, launch. They lasted 30 minutes, and were followed by a facilitated Question and Answer session that gave people the opportunity to clarify understanding. There was also an email address to send questions to, for people who did not feel able to ask their question in public (it may have been specific to their circumstances).

Simultaneous to the launch, the fleet pages on our internal intranet site were updated with all of the new launch material, process documentation and links to the new supplier and their on line quoting system. We own our master Driver Support telephone number, so it was also relatively easy to get this simultaneously changed to add in an option to be connected to the new supplier. Once the webinars had ended, a replay facility was added to the intranet site too, so anyone unable to attend could see a re-run at a time that suited them.

One of the measures of success was that the first order, under the new scheme, was placed within 24 hours of the launch!

In all, it took six months from contract award to scheme launch, one day to take the first order and seventeen weeks to generate the first 100 orders.

How have you gone about advising employees on tax and legislative issues?

Our employees were already well aware of the tax and legislative impacts of an ECO scheme, so the education process was not as difficult as launching a scheme from scratch. The beauty of the new scheme is that an employee receives a detailed personal impact statement when they quote for their vehicle. This has been one of the most popular enhancements, within the new scheme, as it makes it very easy for the driver to understand all of the individual cost elements that are associated with their vehicle choice.

This is also an area that has validated our decision to appoint a supplier with a depth and breadth of experience in ECO provision, as they consistently have people manning our driver line who are familiar with the product, the types of questions asked and how best to answer them. As it's a core product for our provider; as and when tax and legislation changes, it flows seamlessly through their processes and procedures, ensuring that we, and our drivers, remain up to date.

Having a blended scheme has also had the unintended benefit of making it clearer to our drivers that there is no cost difference, to them, between contract hire and ECO.

You place a lot of emphasis on CO_2 reduction in your business. What have you been doing and what progress has been made?

Computacenter has a strong environmental policy and commitment to reducing CO_2 emissions in all areas of our business. Fleet clearly has a big role to play. Six years ago we introduced a CO_2 cap, and we have continued to reduce this in order to eliminate the most environmentally unfriendly vehicles, and the cap will reduce further. As our new scheme is based on 'new generation' ECO, where the employee's contribution towards their vehicle is the same as the company car tax that they would have paid had the vehicle been provided under traditional contract hire, it naturally encourages employees to select lower CO_2 emission vehicles; as their contribution towards the vehicle will be lower if they do so. Obviously, they are free to choose less environmentally friendly vehicles, so long as they are below our CO_2 cap, but there is an increased cost for them in doing so.

As mentioned before, we reimburse fuel against HMRC's Advisory Fuel Rate calculation, which take into account the increasingly more fuel efficient vehicles available. So, once again, employees are encouraged to make more environmentally friendly choices when selecting their company car, otherwise their fuel reimbursement will not cover the actual cost of fuel for their vehicle.

Finally, we have been working with the Energy Savings Trust to measure the CO_2 impact of our fleet, and to evaluate ways to sustainably reduce its carbon footprint moving forward. Looking at the first 100 vehicles that our employees have chosen, it's encouraging to see that our CO_2 emissions are reducing.

What are the things that you have done with your fleet that you are most proud of, and that represent best practice as far as you are concerned?

Recognising that to run an effective and efficient fleet requires a team, and not individuals. This is not just the fleet team, but the virtual team of stakeholders, both internally and externally. The best ideas, and the best practice, come from listening to people, finding the common ground, and harmonising the needs of all stakeholders. Though this may seem like you'll always end up with a compromise, with good facilitation you can ensure that the end product represents best practice for your business. And, by actively involving stakeholders, you avoid many of the pitfalls, and some 'own goals', associated with imposing policy and practice on the driver community without consultation.

Fleet impacts so many people, and functions, that best practice can only be a function of the team and not any one individual. The team of stakeholders includes Finance, HR, Insurance and Risk Management, Employee Forums and Driver communities. Suppliers and professional associations are also a great source of information, as is networking with colleagues in other companies.

One of the other cornerstones of our best practice was implementing and enforcing a firm, but fair, Fleet Policy. This meant ensuring that there is ultimately a balance between penalties and rewards, where all drivers are treated equally and encouraged to take responsibility, and be accountable, for their actions, such as paying for unfair wear and tear charges, and the excess on insurance claims where a third party is not at fault. Not only does this mean that the business ceases to incur avoidable costs, but ultimately, and more importantly, it creates a culture where people take more care of their vehicles and their driving. In doing so, they experience fewer accidents, and fewer off road days, which in turn, directly translates into savings on insurance premiums. All good practice when it comes to managing occupational road risk.

Would you recommend that other fleet managers follow the same course you have?

Now that HM Revenue & Customs have published their report on the interaction between company cars, employee car ownership scheme cars and mileage allowance payments, and confirmed that the factors in favour of imposing a new tax specifically on ECOS were currently outweighed by those against, I suspect more fleet managers, with drivers driving significant business miles, will start looking seriously at ECO, as a funding option.

With fleet managers increasing under pressure to deliver more for less from their suppliers, I believe ECO has its role to play in cutting the cost of running a working fleet. With the advent of blended schemes, allowing you to seamlessly channel drivers into the right funding product for the company, my view is that it should be seriously evaluated as an option. Without doubt, a scheme that involves an element of ECO does require a little more administration and communication. However, products and knowledge have matured to a point where it's a lot easier to roll out than you may initially think, with suppliers who offer ECO as part of their core portfolio well equipped to deal with much of this burden.

Do you have any plans to change your current arrangements to improve things even further?

As a business we are committed to continual improvement in order to ensure that we optimise the costs of running the fleet, whilst at least maintaining, and ideally improving, employee satisfaction. The next initiative is to review the level of detail provided to line managers with P&L responsibility, to ensure that they have all of the information they require, and need, to manage costs, and driver behavior, at a local level. Currently we provide them with information electronically, but we're always looking to improve, and enhance the content.

Keith B. Cook Chartered MCIPD
Deputy Financial Controller
Computacenter UK Limited

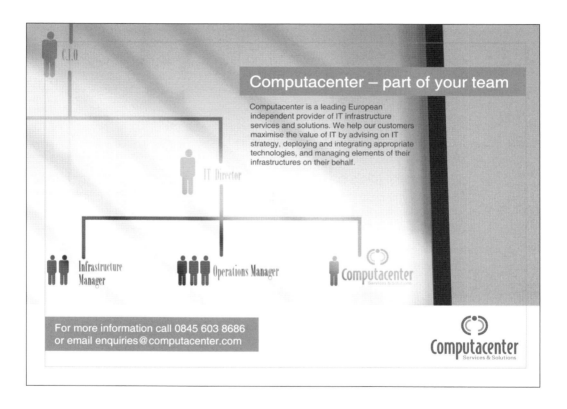

3

REDUCING FUEL COSTS AND EMISSIONS

> **Howard Browning**
> Director for Corporate Responsibility
> James McNaughton Group

Please introduce yourself and explain how you became involved in environmental issues.

I have worked within the paper industry for 30 years, gaining the majority of my experience from the business of national and international paper merchanting.

I have held senior sales and sales management positions within the group culminating with the position of Regional Sales Director.

In June 2006, the McNaughton board recognised the growing importance that society in general and more importantly our clients were placing on environmental responsibility and charged me with the responsibility to analyse and facilitate group wide cultural and environmental changes to deliver environmental impact reductions whilst looking for any financial benefits that might be possible from process improvements around the group.

As a result I was appointed to the newly created role of Director for Corporate Responsibility. Whilst not an expert in the field of corporate responsibility or the environment, I did as a father of two rapidly growing teenagers possess a core personal belief in the need for companies as well as individuals to take much greater responsibility for the impact their actions have on society and now crucially upon the environment.

The subject of corporate and environmental responsibility is complex and rapidly expanding although as an avid reader and analyser of data, I have greatly enjoyed the challenge of building up the expertise and knowledge necessary to help move the company's environmental aspirations forward. I would also point to the significant benefits of having an in depth knowledge of every operational process of the business in terms of being able to effect cultural change within an organisation.

Since that time, the group has seen a dramatic rise in environmental awareness in all of its business areas, and significant improvements in its actual environmental performance have been achieved. As a result, McNaughton now has all aspects of sustainability at the core of its business strategies, and is widely acknowledged as having taken the environmental lead within the paper industry.

During 2007, these group wide environmental initiatives resulted in The McNaughton Group winning two major environmental awards, namely the Environmental Supplier Of The Year in the Print Media awards and taking the top category 'Extra Mile award' at the Mayor of London's 'Green Procurement Code annual awards. Talk Paper, the group's specialist office products supply company received Europe-wide recognition for their sustainable solutions programme when they narrowly lost to 3M in the category finals for Environmental Responsibility in Business. Talk Paper are the UK's biggest supplier of recycled and certified office papers.

In 2007, the group was also runner-up in The Energy Savings Trust Green Fleet awards for the significant fuel and carbon reductions we achieved by implementing a green car policy and in 2008 we went one better when we won the Energy Savings Trust's Fleet Heroes award.

I am very proud of these awards as they recognise the great efforts of all of my McNaughton colleagues in embracing the company's new approach, which is fundamentally about ensuring that we can achieve continued business success without it having a detrimental impact on society and the environment.

My personal approach has been to adopt a very direct and hands on approach to the challenges of introducing and implementing the numerous initiatives throughout every part of the organisation and again I have gained invaluable knowledge and experience in the process.

I am regularly called upon to advise and assist clients and colleagues alike and have presented McNaughton's experiences publicly on numerous occasions. Now, almost 3 years on, I believe more than ever that individuals and companies alike have both a moral and corporate duty to adopt a more sustainable personal and business approach.

Many readers will be unaware of James McNaughton Group. What does the group do and how big is its fleet?

The James McNaughton Group is one of the UK and Ireland's leading suppliers of graphic and office papers, boards, plastics and other substrates. Our divisions offer experienced sales support to clients throughout the printing, publishing, display, public sector and corporate markets.

The group is part of the European Map Merchant Group, which was in Dec 2007 acquired by the Antalis Group, a wholly owned subsidary of the Sequana Group. The Antalis merchant group is now the largest paper merchant in Europe, with a business presence in 30 countries and a combined turnover of 3.74 billion Euros and sales of 3,400,000 tonnes.

There are 680 McNaughton employees, working from our HQ at Erith, Kent and our

Regional Sales Centres in London, Chelmsford, Hemel Hempstead, Tonbridge Wells, Norwich, Nottingham, Gateshead, Warrington, Glasgow, Cardiff, Bristol, Billiericay, Leeds, Dublin, Cork & Belfast. We also have additional distribution sites at Coalville & Woking,

Group turnover is £281,000,000.

We operate 10 vans, 220 heavy goods vehicles, a dozen artics, 2 electric Modec trucks and a car fleet of 170 employee-owned vehicles.

As an organisation, we are committed to becoming corporately responsible for the various environments in which we operate. Through a series of exciting initiatives, we are building upon strong foundations and adapting our behaviour both as individuals and as a business, to make a clear and visible difference to the wider environment around us.

What did you do to win the 'Fleet Heroes' award?

Whilst we had taken considerable steps towards implementing a group-wide policy of environmental responsibility – renewable energy supplies, paper from sustainable sources, a serious attitude towards recycling and so on - when it came to our car fleet, we didn't know where best to start.

I then discovered the Energy Saving Trust's website and was impressed with the range of issues on which it offered help and, in particular, its experience of transport issues, and the offer of a free car fleet review.

From website, to case-study downloads, to phone calls and then face-to-face meetings with an EST client manager, followed by the green fleet audit by an independent consultant appointed and paid for by the Trust. It was all very easy and efficient.

What wasn't so comfortable was the spotlight that the EST reviews turned on the Group's lack of fleet management information.

The EST wanted to study our figures regarding petrol consumption, mileage and so forth, and I was very surprised to discover that we just didn't collate and analyse such information. The only thing we really noticed were the increasing fuel bills being paid by our accounts department.

That was the first and probably the most important lesson we learned from the EST: what you don't measure you don't monitor.

The EST reviews obliged us to look, in incredible detail, at every aspect of the fleet and its operation, and today we can summon up a spreadsheet which displays facts and figures for every car in the fleet; the miles-per-gallon achieved, individual and combined carbon emissions; the number of petrol station stops per month, the price paid at the pumps and the average cost per mile, all with comparisons to previous periods.

Two years earlier we had moved from company cars to an ECO scheme in which each employee is given a car allowance each month to buy their own vehicles. Critically, we retained control over employees' car choice at that time, with token minimum mpg restrictions. Ultimately what the EST showed us was that we could achieve significant financial and environmental benefits by developing a green car policy.

Based on the findings and recommendations of the EST fleet review, we changed our group car policy significantly. We restricted car changes to diesel, hybrid or bio fuel vehicles, with a minimum combined consumption of 37mpg. Restrictions on mileage and age are also applied to used car purchases to ensure the fleet's environmental performance continues to improve.

During 2006/2007, this policy change saw the diesel penetration of our fleet increase from 57.5% to 62.3%, and this improved still further to 68.8% for the year 2007/8.

All car changes, including main board directors' cars, must comply with our green car policy and be approved by me before purchase. The authorisation form requires that drivers report combined mpg and CO_2 values, and we verify these with the VCA database. In addition, we insist that all cars have a park assist system in order to improve driver safety and reduce accidents.

We have created an extensive reporting spreadsheet, which enables us to fully monitor all aspects of the fleet's performance. This delivers accurate data and statistics for mpg, cost, fuel volume, CO_2 emissions, business & private mileage and cost, fill-ups per month, Shell card & expense claim fuel, average fuel price and cost per mile.

The information from this report forms the basis of any policy changes in the coming year, and from 2009 all drivers will receive a personalised year-on-year comparison report.

For the last tax year, our policy changes have resulted in the following savings and statistics.

- The fleet's mileage reduced by 473,571 over the previous year, which reduced fuel usage by 22,829 gallons and saved £60,827 in the fleets fuel costs.
- Our total annual carbon emissions were reduced by 232 tonnes or 20.3% to 1138 tonnes. This was calculated using the Defra GHG conversion factors. Diesel cars used 262,714 litres of fuel x 2.6304 kg CO_2 per litre = 691.04 tonnes and petrol cars used used 193,021 litres of fuel x 2.3154 kg CO_2 per litre = 446.92 tonnes.
- Average CO_2 rating per car; diesels 166g CO_2 /km, compared to 196g/km for petrol cars.
- Average mpg for the fleet improved by 8.6% to 37.3mpg. Diesel cars averaged 41.2 mpg, up 4.8% from 39.3mpg and even our greatly reduced fleet of petrol cars improved fuel consumption by 3.6% from an average of 30.2 to 31.3mpg. Overall our diesel cars were 31.5% more fuel-efficient than the petrol cars, up from 23.2%.
- On average the petrol drivers had to fill up once more per month than the diesel drivers, and
- If all of our fleet had been 100% diesel, we would have saved 10,158 gallons of fuel, 91.4 tonnes of carbon emissions and around £45,000.

In addition, we produce and annually update an extensive 'JMGL Driver's Guide', with 240 points aimed at promoting safer, greener and cheaper driving, as well as reporting the previous years fleet performance statistics.

The key aims of our green car policy going forward remain to:

1   Reduce our total CO_2 emissions by using less fuel.
2   Control and reduce our costs through better fuel consumption.
3   Reduce our total miles through better planning & reduced meeting miles.
4   Annually review all aspects of the fleet's performance and make sensible changes to ensure continued progress needed to achieve the aims of points 1 - 3.

You have also looked at using new technology. Please tell us about this.

During 2008, we have investigated and run trials of fuel optimisation technology. This new technology involves making minor adjustments to some of the settings in the vehicle's engine management unit and offers improved fuel efficiency. The benefits of this technology are:

- Optimises the amount of fuel burnt during the combustion process.
- Improves the volumetric efficiency of the engine.
- Reduces fuel consumption.
- Reduces harmful hydrocarbon emissions.

Receiving 2008 Fleet Hero award from Geoff Hoon, Transport Secretary

- Small power increase usually between 6% -10% according to the vehicle's original specification.
- Produces a smoother torque curve.
- Encourages earlier gear change.
- Encourages driving at lower RPM levels.
- Does not increase vehicle's maximum speed.
- Does not increase the level of risk for insurers.
- Drivers will not notice the power increase; the vehicle will simply be smoother to drive.

Running a trial on my own car a Mercedes E270Cdi over a 4-month period, the average mpg increased from 37.3 to 41.2mpg, which is a 10.4% increase. Based on my last year's total fuel usage, this would save 43.99 gallons of diesel and approximately £220.

We are now looking to roll this out across suitable cars within the diesel fleets, based on selecting the highest mileage and the newest vehicles.

Did you need to do anything to ensure buy-in by staff and senior management?

When we originally changed from providing company cars to opting for an ECO system, the company maintained control over car choice and this enabled us to move to a greener car policy with relative ease, and with the support of the car fleet drivers.

By ensuring that all car changes were into diesels with a minimum combined mpg level, we have seen significant savings coming to both the company in terms of fuel as well as to drivers as they are taxed on the amount of fuel they've used. Of the cars changed in 2007/8, the average projected annual savings per driver were:

92 gallons, £ 400 in fuel cost, 928kgs of CO_2 and £160 in personal fuel tax.

Whilst the 2008 minimum mpg is set at 42mpg, the average combined mpg for car changes this year has been 46.5, further demonstrating the driver's acceptance of the scheme and the potential for the fleet to make even greater savings going forward.

I maintain and monitor the car policy, which ensures that everyone understands these changes are environmentally focussed, but probably the single biggest point to note is that the policy also applies to every member of the senior management team and the main board. We believe strongly that any environmental policies must be backed by senior management and we adopt a strategy of 'top floor led, bottom floor fed'

How have you reduced the number of miles travelled?

We have installed video conferencing facilities at three of our main hubs. However, we experienced some practical problems with VC so today the main focus is on teleconferencing. We have issued managers with their own teleconferencing cards and encouraged them to think about these other options before calling meetings that involve a lot of travel. Personal contact and interaction will remain essential to all businesses, but we have certainly witnessed a willingness of colleagues to embrace these other options, particularly when it can save them 3-4 hours sitting in their cars or traffic jams.

We encourage our sales executives to plan their week much more methodically to ensure they are visiting their customers with an appointment, a specific business reason and at the right intervals. This makes their calls much more productive and of course inevitably reduces wasted journey miles. We have found that a regular phone call can provide a much better relationship link to the customer than a 5 minute rushed visit, especially if the customer is busy.

Have you considered introducing other types of fuel?

We changed our bunker fuel sites over a 5% biofuel mix in advance of the government's Renewable Transport Fuel Obligation (RTFO). However, we haven't sought to communicate this to our customers as an environmental initiative because people do have concerns about the environmental impacts of creating biofuels and whether it can be sustainably sourced. So we are adopting a watching brief at present.

Fuel costs have gone up like a rocket, but our monthly cost of fuel hasn't increased because our overall volume of fuel has gone down. That wouldn't have been possible without the switch to diesel. The widening recent difference between the cost of diesel and petrol is likely to cause us to rethink our diesel only rule and when the policy is revised next year I expect to allow petrol cars back into the fold, as long as they can match or exceed the company's 42 mpg minimum requirement.

In August 2008 our logistic subsidiary GM2 took delivery of its first all-electric delivery truck from Modec. It was painted in a unique and iconic livery that carries a clear environmental message promoting 'ZERO CO_2' deliveries. We were delighted that the CEO of the Energy Savings Trust agreed to officially launch the vehicle at their headquarters in London.

It is used for central London copier paper deliveries and has the unique benefits of being both silent and having zero CO_2 emission. The vehicle replaced a traditional diesel van, and delivers genuine reductions in the environmental impact of paper deliveries, saving over 4,250 litres of fuel and around 12 tonnes of CO_2 emissions each year.

The other advantage is that it is exempt from road fund tax as well as the daily congestion charge, saving the company over £2200 per year.

The Modec is quite a celebrity and has been a big hit with customers and the general public alike.

In London people stop our driver in the street and ask questions about it. Even traffic wardens are pleasant to him! It has all the torque he wants and it's also much easier to drive than the transit van it replaces as it has a similar turning circle to a London taxi.

At £30,000, the Modecs don't come cheap, but longer running life, lower servicing costs, fuel-savings, and exemption from the London congestion charge mean I wouldn't hesitate from choosing Modec when more vans come up for replacement.

Would you recommend that other fleet managers follow the same course you have?

As every fleet manager will tell you, the choice of company cars remains possibly the most emotive and divisive of topics within an organisation, so any change that restricts or directs drivers' choice is never going to be easy to implement and it's even harder to be thanked for doing it!

I hope that our experiences, approach and relative success will encourage any other fleet manager to review their car policies and encourage the change in driver habits and fuel performance, hopefully gaining the financial and environmental benefits we have started to see.

In the troubling financial environment companies now find themselves in, it has never been more important to review every opportunity to reduce costs, and whilst environmental responsibility may be seen as secondary to ensuring financial sustainability, I firmly believe that they need not be seen as mutually exclusive business agendas.

Steering a company through turbulent economical conditions whilst also safeguarding its environmental impact must remain the ultimate objective for all organisations that emerge through these difficult times.

Howard Browning
Director for Corporate Responsibility
James McNaughton Group

4   RUNNING A GREEN FLEET

> **Glenn Ewen**
> Fleet Manager
> Clear Channel UK Limited

Please introduce yourself and tell us a little about your business and your fleet.

I have been involved with vehicle and fleet issues for over 30 years: joining the Army in 1975, aged 18, where I trained as a vehicle mechanic, working on tanks and armoured personnel carriers. I left the Army in 1988 and a spell of HGV driving and music venue security led me into the music industry, and Virgin Records in 1990; eventually becoming Fleet Manager for the EMI Group PLC. I have been at Clear Channel for the last seven years. The fleet consists of:

- 370 light commercial vehicles (LCVs), 340 of which are bi-fuel, running on liquid petroleum gas (LPG) and petrol:

- 160 cars, 75% of them business use and the remainder perk. Of those, 29 are Honda Civic hybrids and six are Vauxhall Astra LPG.

- 3 heavy goods vehicles (HGVs) and

- 3 motorcycles.

Clear Channel is the largest outdoor advertising company in the UK, providing over 70,000 advertising opportunities nationwide on bus shelters, billboards and taxis.

You have won awards for your fleet activities.

Clear Channel was: awarded Private Sector Green Fleet 2005; awarded Energy Savings Trust Fleet Heroes Large Fleet (500+) 2007; shortlisted in the National Energy Efficiency Awards 2008; shortlisted in the Fleet Van Awards 2008 and highly commended in European Green Fleet Awards 2008.

Please tell us about the work you have done with the Energy Saving Trust.

We have worked with the EST for at least six years now, not least has been their involvement in the drawing up of our vehicle policies. We took advantage of a free fleet review several years ago and were gratified to find that we were doing most of the right things. They were also able to offer sound advice and provided the resources that enabled us to improve on our existing practices and to introduce a few worthwhile measures, designed to reduce costs and lower our impact on the environment. The EST had made Powershift grants of up to £1,260 (60% of the total cost) available for the conversion of vehicles to LPG. Until discontinued, Clear Channel made full use of these grants for every LPG vehicle purchased. We used the online EST Powershift Register to determine which vehicle would best suit conversion to LPG and qualified for the 100% discount from Congestion Charging (CC) London. The register also listed diesel equivalent fuel consumption and emissions figures so that we could anticipate fuel consumption for budgeting purposes and calculate CO_2, NOx and particulate reductions. Most resources still are available online, and are free to access. They send out regular email newsletters with relevant initiatives and information and are a valuable source of information and assistance.

Why did you decide to go 'green'?

Clear Channel has always been aware of the environmental impact of their vehicles, so much so that we had been operating 30 bi-fuel Ford transits since 1997, and we acquired a further 70 bi-fuel Vauxhall Astra vans in 2000. In 2001, we began to experience increasing interest from local authorities, who are our main partners in providing bus shelter and street furniture contracts. They wanted assurances that our operations were as environmentally friendly as they could be. It was obvious that this was not the case in many city centres, as most of our van fleet was diesel: a primary source of nitrous oxide and particulates: these two factors alone contribute most to poor local air quality, particularly in urban areas. Both the bi-fuel vehicle types were only of Euro II emissions standard, so were not the cleanest, but were the best available at the time. It was clear that, with the imminent introduction of the London Congestion Charge, none of these vehicles would qualify for the 100% discount (not an exemption) from the Congestion Charge, as they needed to be at least 40% cleaner than the current Euro IV emissions standard. We were facing a £5 per day charge for every vehicle, and with over 100 vehicles based in or around London; we anticipated a potential annual bill of over £100,000.

At the time, other major UK cities were contemplating charging in some form or another and we assumed that they would use the same qualification criteria as London for any discounts/exemptions.

With guidance and support from Clear Channel's Environmental Steering Committee, in late 2001 we began a review of our fleet operations with a simple brief that required us to do three things:

1   Introduce the cleanest vehicles possible
2   Reduce annual mileages
3   Do both of the above without increasing costs

At the time of the review, our fleet was travelling some 14 million miles per annum, producing an estimated 4,990 tonnes of CO_2 yearly and emitting large quantities of nitrous oxide and particulates. The old company car benefit in kind (BIK) tax regime was still in place: encouraging drivers to travel at least 2,500 business miles per annum to reduce their tax liability to 25%; with those doing higher mileage incentivised to aim for 18,000 business miles to reduce their tax burden to 15%.

It was common to see every attendee at a meeting bringing their own car, when some had actually come from the same office. Thankfully, the new tax rules would deal with this anomaly by eliminating the business mileage element and switching to CO_2 as a measuring tool.

With 35 Sales Executives about to start paying 26% when they had previously enjoyed a liability of only 15%, the pressure was on to introduce a more BIK tax efficient company car choice list.

LCV drivers had unlimited private use of their vehicles. This meant that we had little control over van mileage, particularly at weekends. The company was paying the benefit in kind tax on behalf of all the LCV drivers, amounting to over £60,000 per annum.

Two thirds of the LCV fleet were still diesel, and fuel prices and duty were increasing steadily, making LPG vehicles an even more attractive financial proposition.

The review produced the following firm decisions:

1   Switch the entire LCV fleet to LPG, all vehicles must be 100% Congestion Charging discounted

2   Bunker LPG at as many of our operational sites as possible

3   Where practicable, offer an LPG option to all car drivers

4   Introduce route planning for all LCVs and Sales Executives where possible.

5   Company car choice lists should show BIK impact and mpg figures, to encourage drivers to choose more tax, and by default NIC efficient cars

6   All HGVs would be Euro IV diesel, or be retro-fitted to reach at least that standard

7   Motorcycles would be introduced into London initially, with a view to implementing them nationally later

How did you decide which vehicles to use?

We had already made the decision that we would only purchase original equipment manufacture (OEM), rather than any after-fit LPG conversions. Not, however, because we did not trust the converters, rather we wanted to ensure we had manufacturer support and full warranty protection in the event of any possible later problems. At the time of the review, and the introduction of Congestion Charging, the only viable (for us) OEM LPG panel van was the Ford Transit, which was already 100% Congestion Charging discounted. We chose this van, in most of its available formats, for the majority of the LCV fleet and selected the Transit Connect where a smaller panel van was required. Our Team Leaders, who had been using the LPG Vauxhall Astravans, would receive LPG Vauxhall Combos as direct replacements. These were smaller, lighter vehicles and Vauxhall changed from the same 1.6 engine in the Astravans to the more powerful and fuel-efficient 1.4 engines in the Combos mid-order. This actually resulted in a 5% improvement in fuel consumption

Whilst we had calculated that 10,000 annual miles was the average cut-off to ensure that LPG was cost effective versus diesel, several of our centre of London area vans were doing only half that mileage so would potentially cost us more money to run than the diesels had. We could offset some of this extra cost with the potential saving of £5 per day in Congestion charges: and the knowledge that we were no longer polluting to the same degree. The savings made on the rest of the LCV fleet would more than compensate for the extra costs of these vans.

Was LPG readily available and how did you ensure you were well supplied?

The LPG fuel retail network was extensive and had grown to over 1,200 outlets, so coverage was sufficient for the whole country. We already bunkered LPG at two of our sites, so we knew it was possible to make it work.

Bunkering involves placing a 2000 litre (one tonne) LPG tank, called a 'skid' tank because it just sits on its mounting that resembles 'skids' and is unsecured to the ground. You must site the tank a specified distance from an occupied building: if your site is unfenced, you must build a secure compound around the tank. The gas supplier will draw up plans and ensure that the location is safe and suitable: and will not commission a tank until they are sure that you have met all the required safety conditions. All that is then required is a power supply and the unit is up and running.

The next step for us was to go out to tender on five of our operational sites (where we had received the property owner's permission to install a tank). This allowed us to consolidate the supply and reduce costs per litre overall. Bunkered LPG is at least 9p ex vat per litre cheaper than in the retail network.

Please tell us about your experience of running vehicles on LPG. Does it save money?

A bi-fuel (LPG) vehicle is normally a petrol-engined vehicle that has been adapted to run on liquid petroleum gas. Some are designed specifically to operate on LPG alone: but typically, only forklift trucks or other plant machinery will do so. Some vehicles operate on a diesel/LPG blend as a means of increasing power and improving fuel consumption: LPG, introduced into the air inlet, ignites with the diesel: this produces a smoother ignition cycle and ensures that more of the diesel is burnt: resulting in lower fuel bills. The vehicles run more cleanly, with engine oil filters needing less frequent changes. HGVs would occasionally have this system fitted. However, most bi-fuel vehicles will be petrol/LPG. The petrol delivery and ignition system remains in place. Then a gas delivery system is retrofitted. The main idea being that the gas is cheaper to purchase and cleaner burning; this therefore, saves money and is good for local air quality.

In operation, vehicles will always start and run initially on petrol. Once warmed up, they will switch over to LPG: the switchover timing varies by model and the type of LPG conversion kit fitted. Once the vehicle has warmed up, they will switch over to LPG more rapidly, but there is always a small amount of petrol used at each start up. A vehicle operating on a frequent stop/start cycle will use more petrol than one doing longer journeys or making fewer stops.

Clear Channel have the situation, on some city centre main roads, and where bus shelters are close together, when a van will run entirely on petrol, as it does not have time to switch over to LPG before it arrives at the next shelter! An unfortunate side effect, but still cleaner than running on diesel. LPG is 15%-20% less efficient than petrol, but costs around half the price.

In 2001, LPG was around a third the price of diesel. That meant, provided fuel consumption achieved was better than a half that of diesels: it would be cheaper to run LPG vans and the more mileage travelled, the greater the savings. These savings rely on the maximum percentage of gas rather than being used as possible on every journey; not simply using LPG as a means of increasing range (some drivers would merely run on LPG until the tank was empty, switch to petrol till that was exhausted, refill both tanks and start the cycle again!).

We identified the requirement for each bi-fuel vehicle to use at least 75% LPG to ensure they cost less than diesels to run. No effective monitoring had formerly taken place and it was clear that some drivers were simply using petrol continuously as the easy option.

To ensure we were utilising as much LPG as possible, we introduced a minimum quarterly target for each vehicle and produced a monthly report to highlight those drivers who were making the effort, those that were not, and the vehicles that were perhaps not running correctly on LPG. A bonus scheme was set up to reward the Team Leaders whose operatives reached the average each quarter.

We supplied BoostLPG maps to all drivers. These listed all the known LPG fuel stations nationwide, with opening times, telephone numbers and other facility information. We made sure that drivers had the right fuel card, or combination of fuel cards for their area and particular situation. Where appropriate, we opened accounts with local LPG suppliers as generally, they charged less than the retail sites and were convenient to the branches where we could not get permission to site a skid tank. Once 75% LPG usage had become the norm, we raised the minimum to 80% and plan to increase this still further on those vans where we know it is feasible. Some vans are already consistently attaining over 95%.

How did you implement the agreed initiatives?

We concentrated on introducing the new vehicles into London initially; to take advantage of Congestion Charging discount as this was the operating area for almost one third of our fleet. Additionally, the first two LPG bunker sites were already located at the two main London branches, so it made sense to utilise as much of the bulk LPG as possible until the three other sites could be opened up.

As previously stated, all our Sales Executives were in the unenviable position of having their BIK tax rise from 15% to 26% on their current cars, so being able to offer them the chance to reduce that to 14% and lower their Authorised Mileage Rate for their private mileage was a huge incentive to adopt LPG vehicles. We offered LPG cars to all car drivers, with emphasis on the higher mileage users to ensure cost savings. Most of our car drivers receive a fuel card and are recharged their private mileage at HMRC Advisory Fuel Rates. Therefore, their pence per mile would be lower as these rates significantly favour LPG cars.

The LCV drivers were easy to win over. Most lived in the areas where they worked, so air quality was important to them. LPG vans are quieter, cleaner and vibrate less than diesels generally. Add to that the fact that their existing vans were getting old; there was very little resistance to their 'going green'!

All drivers of LPG vehicles are expected to read and sign their agreement to a set of LPG Guidelines. These give clear reasons for our switch to an alternative fuel, as well as instructions on how to use the two types of filler nozzle found at refuelling stations and hints on how best to maintain a high percentage of LPG use.

How did you reduce mileages?

In 2001, our average mileage for LCVs was 20,000 per annum, and for cars 30,000 per annum. A significant and uncontrollable source of unwanted mileage was unlimited private use of LCVs, so we withdrew the privilege. They are not permitted to use their vans for anything other than home to depot, or their designated routes. Withdrawal of private use meant we could negotiate with the Inland Revenue a 50% reduction in the van BIK charge: which Clear Channel had always paid on behalf of the LCV drivers. This lowered our liability by £30,000 per annum as well as our mileages, fuel costs, accident rates and general wear and tear on the vehicles.

As a form of trade-off, we removed the requirement for drivers to pay a proportion of their at-fault accident costs. These had been set on a rising scale: increasing with each accident, to a maximum of four in any three-year period, whereupon the driver paid all the costs of the accident. Interestingly, this seemed to placate the majority of drivers; when in fact, we had never used the recharge facility on any of them!

The latest rule changes regarding private use of vans means that we no longer have to pay anything to HMRC. We have introduced a barcode reader that our operatives use to scan at each site as they arrive and leave. They also input their mileage at each site. This means that we can keep an accurate log of their journeys and have the required paperwork to satisfy any audit by HMRC.

We rearranged some operational areas to reduce the distance operatives travelled to collect posters and cleaning materials from their branch, opened a new branch in Cambridgeshire to provide us with a local base covering East Anglia: an area previously administered from Dartford. The Cambridgeshire branch is also now the base for our HGV tractor unit and trailer. It travels the length of the UK on a two weekly cycle delivering shelter and advertising unit parts to all our branches and some suppliers and contractors. The delivery cycle is Scotland/Northern England on

one fortnight, and Southern England/Wales the next. Before relocation, the truck had operated out of Hayes, in Middlesex. This new base has reduced the mileage of the truck by over 20,000 miles per annum, and the driver does not have to stay away overnight as often as before.

To ensure that we covered the operatives' areas with the minimum mileage, we introduced route planning. The shelters require washing every two weeks, so the vans carry their own clean water supply. Some operatives are on water meters at home, or where they live makes it impossible for them to fill up at the roadside. We fitted 380 litre water tanks on most of the vans so that they do not have to return to the depots as often to refill or to manhandle heavy water containers in and out of the vans.

We have introduced satellite navigation systems to cars on a limited basis: mostly the plug-in type. This has proved very successful and the intention is to ensure that we choose vehicles that have the systems as standard, or can be factory/dealer fitted at a reasonable cost. As an example, several years ago, we needed to survey a large number of sites in London and the South East, with a limited number of people. We drafted-in personnel from other regions and gave them cars fitted with sat nav systems pre-programmed with their destinations. They were able to cover twice as many locations than would have been possible using conventional maps.

How did you cut costs?

Even with the fuel savings from running on LPG, there were concerns that the bi-fuel vehicles would be more expensive to purchase and run, as we expected residual values to be much lower than the equivalent diesel vehicles. The purchase price of a petrol van is lower than for the diesel, but the residual value difference was still a significant factor. We had already established that LPG would be a cheaper fuel option, provided each vehicle exceeded 10,000 miles per annum and used a minimum of 75% LPG. The 60% grants towards the cost of the conversion and the likelihood of congestion charging or road pricing nationwide meant that the gap closed and we were able to predict running costs roughly in line with those of the diesel vans we were then operating.

We knew that we could reduce annual mileages, so contracts could be set at lower mileages, as could rental and maintenance budgets. The majority of lease companies had little faith in bi-fuels, so were writing residuals at very low levels. If, as we hoped and expected, the residuals were better at resale than they anticipated, the lease companies would take the double benefit of the higher rental payments through the term of the lease, and the profit at resale.

We set about negotiating a lease that would allow us to benefit from any increase in residual values over the then pessimistic predictions. We needed the ability to budget, so wanted a lease provider to guarantee residuals, but in return for allowing them to write them down hard, we would take any profits at resale. Mileage penalties and damage recharges would never amount to more than the balloon payment at lease end, so we knew exactly how much each van would cost and we had the potential to make a profit at the end.

The nature of our business dictates that our vehicles are operating in bus lanes and at bus stops for a great deal of their work cycle. In the past, this had meant that we received far more than our fair share of Penalty Charge Notices (PCN). In many cases, there was no facility for lease companies to nominate us, so they had to pay them, or make representations on our behalf: a costly and time-consuming exercise for both parties. With each PCN came an admin fee: regardless of whether the lease company paid it or they nominated us. Immediate payment of a PCN, at the discounted rate, meant there was little or no prospect of successfully making a representation.

We determined that the only way to ensure that we could deal with PCNs correctly and to cut costs was to have the vehicles registered to us so that we got first sight of every PCN as soon as it was issued. We now have formal procedures in place, to send out standard letters with copies of work schedules and extracts from the relevant regulations detailing the exemption that we qualify for and we are now successful with around 98% of our representations. This action resulted in a minimum annual saving of £12,000 in previously uncontested PCNs and associated admin fees. It has helped to reduce mileages and emissions as drivers can now park directly on site instead of trying to find somewhere to park off route.

We switched all new contracts away from budgeted maintenance, where we paid the lease company a fixed monthly fee, to 'pay on use' maintenance. This meant that we only paid for work on the vehicles when we actually needed to. The money sits in our bank, earning interest, instead of in the lease company's account. Even with a particularly busy month for service and repairs, we still pay less overall than we previously paid for budgeted maintenance every month.

Because we are the registered keeper of the vehicles, we are responsible for the road tax, so we are now more aware of the need to get MOT inspections done in good time to ensure that we can apply for the road tax before the end of each month and

issue them before the old disc expires. When the previous vehicles were registered in the lease company's name, they sent out reminders, but were not responsible if a vehicle was not MOT tested in time and it was always difficult to keep MOT dates accurate on the fleet database when we had no direct involvement in booking and paying for the tests. We will not amend the MOT expiry until we have the certificate on file.

We were able to attract significant financial support from manufacturers, as they were keen to promote alternative fuel vehicles: particularly as Congestion Charging was about to start. We negotiated favourable terms, which helped to greatly reduce the monthly cost of all the vans.

In 2005, we increased the standard contract length on all new cars from 36 months to 42 months. This action alone significantly reduced the monthly costs on every lease and cut administration, as we now change cars less often.

Have you introduced any other green initiatives?

In 2003, we introduced the first of the motorcycles, on a limited basis, into Greater London. The rider's task was checking shelters, to ensure build quality, that they were in the right place and were to our specification. It meant he could stop right next to the site, without causing an obstruction, and then go on to the next one quickly, without worrying about traffic or getting a parking ticket.

The initial trial involved sending the same inspector in a car around London to visit 11 sites, whilst someone else (me) rode a demonstrator motorcycle around the same route. Both started with full tanks, and at exactly the same time. Both were to spend 10 minutes at each site before moving onto the next one. The car travelled 85 miles: the motorcycle 69 miles. The car used £8.59 in fuel: the bike only £2.78. The car cost £5 in Congestion Charges: the motorcycle was 100% discounted. Finally, the motorcycle finished 2½ hours before the car. This proved that, when heavy or bulky equipment was not required, a motorcycle was faster, and far more cost effective than a car or van. We have since introduced a further two motorcycles. Both have purpose built panniers to carry cleaning materials. They provide a rapid response to remove offensive or racist graffiti from shelters or advertising panels. They can also get to a site in an emergency to make it safe if damaged by vandalism or if a vehicle collides with a shelter.

In 2004, we needed to replace the two 7.5 tonne trucks that we operate in London and Bristol. They are 24-hour Emergency Response Vehicles, fitted with a crane. Their task is to provide a rapid pull-down facility should a shelter become damaged beyond immediate safe repair. The vehicle carries sufficient equipment to remove the shelter and load it onto the back. They then reinstate the pavement to make it safe. The old 7.5 tonne vehicles were only Euro II emission compliant. We introduced two Euro III compliant trucks, and had CRT exhaust filters retrofitted. These were 75% funded by an EST 'Cleanup' grant. The exhaust filters effectively raised the engine emissions to Euro IV standard. This meant that we would be unaffected by the introduction of the proposed London Low Emission Zone.

Early in 2005, we mandated that only Euro IV emissions standard cars could appear on our car choice lists to ensure that they were the cleanest possible and to take advantage of the 3% BIK reduction for Euro IV cars.

Later in 2005, we introduced Honda Civic IMA petrol/electric hybrid cars. They proved very popular amongst our Sales Executives working in urban areas. Initially, we made them available to all Executives. The cars' extremely low emissions meant that they were 100% Congestion Charging discounted and their fuel consumption was excellent. The specification on the cars was good, providing each driver with leather upholstery as standard. We received excellent support terms from Honda. The Executives also appreciated the much lower BIK liability as the low CO_2 meant that their tax reduced to 11% or 12%.

The only drawback was their higher fuel consumption when used anywhere other than in an urban environment. The small engine (1300cc) and the electric motor assist meant that they were ideally suited to stop/start traffic conditions. The electric motor was not beneficial on major roads, or at higher motorway speeds, so we tried to ensure that we only gave them to drivers who covered mainly urban areas. This was not always possible as it was felt that we should give all Executives the same standard of cars irrespective of where they worked. When they covered high mileage, we still had the LPG Vauxhall Astras to benefit from the better fuel consumption at motorway speeds and the fuel savings generated by LPG. LPG car drivers were not disadvantaged. They paid higher company car BIK than those with Honda Civics, but this could be offset by the lower HMRC Approved Mileage Rates for their private mileage than the Civic drivers received. If we needed them to, they could also enter the Congestion Zone free of charge.

Early in 2006, as part of our desire to reduce CO_2 emissions on the cars, we introduced the first cap on CO_2 for each grade. Starting at a maximum of 189 gm/km and rising by ten grams for each grade up to a maximum of 219 gm/km. This had the effect of immediately reducing fuel consumptions on all new cars, as there is a direct link between lower CO_2 and lower fuel consumption.

We had already produced spreadsheet based car choice lists that showed drivers the List Price for Tax, the CO_2, the Combined MPG and the actual monthly tax payable for each model. That meant they could sort the lists in any order they saw fit and decide how much tax they wanted to pay. Before every car order, we sent out the BIK information and asked the driver to confirm their choice. Within six months, we were able to remove higher CO_2 cars from the lists completely as no-one was choosing them anyway.

In 2007, to reduce our fuel bills, we set minimum mpg limits on the choice lists and removed all cars with a combined mpg of less than 40.

In May of 2008, we set a maximum CO_2 for any new car on the fleet at 150 gm/km. The average CO_2 for the fleet was already low at 154, because we had encouraged lower CO_2 cars. The Honda Civic hybrids and LPG cars were keeping the average down but we still had some cars that were high CO_2 emitters.

It was logical step to try to get the rest of the fleet down as low as possible. Manufacturers are launching new models all the time, with more efficient and environmentally friendly engines. Convincing drivers has not been difficult as low CO_2 is encouraged by the current tax treatment of company cars. Particulate filters and catalytic converters have done a great deal to reduce harmful emissions and particulates, but everyone needs to do more.

Overall, how successful have these efforts been?

We have spent the last seven years reducing our total vehicle mileage by 4.75 million miles per annum, our CO_2 by 1,760 tonnes per year and saving £200,000 per annum on fuel costs and London Congestion Charges. Our environmental performance has been exemplary and we will continue, wherever possible, to maintain the highest standards. Air quality should be the issue for every business that operates vehicles: and not just in urban areas. We have succeeded in achieving a huge reduction in our emissions and have saved money at the same time. Our environmental performance is, in most cases, better than the organisations that ask us if we have an 'Environmental Policy'!

Would you recommend that other fleet managers follow the same course you have?

Undoubtedly, but our model would not suit every company. We operate differently to all but a few similar industry organisations. What suits us would not necessarily work for everyone.

LPG grants are no longer available, so average mileages will need to be higher to achieve payback.

There needs to be commitment and support from the highest levels within the company, or it will fail.

Alternative fuels are not a 'one size fits all' panacea. In some cases, diesel, or even petrol will be the answer, depending on the task required of the vehicle. Our ability to bunker LPG has helped keep costs down. The higher number of vehicles has meant that we could absorb the higher costs on a few vehicles, to ensure that they all stay clean.

Smaller companies may not be able to achieve the manufacturer discounts necessary to make alternative fuelled vehicles a viable option when annual mileage alone is not sufficient to produce the savings required.

Residual values for LPG vehicles have improved beyond anyone's expectations, so should keep lease costs lower in the future (if the lease companies pass the saving on!). There is a greater acceptance of LPG in general.

Cost calculators are available on a great many websites to help decide whether alternative fuels are the answer. Realism is the key. You cannot assume that drivers will use more than 80% LPG from the outset. You may find that they do well initially, but without constant monitoring, their enthusiasm wears off. We have found limited coverage of retail sites in some areas, and have had to make other arrangements with local suppliers. This may not be practical if a company only has one or two vehicles. LPG is particularly suited to companies whose vehicles are depot based, and can refuel on each shift. LPG conversions are becoming more efficient and reliable, but the only thing that makes it viable at present is the lower cost of the gas.

Government policy regulates the amount of duty applied to each litre, so is vulnerable to the whims of a politician. Hybrids are fantastic for use in urban areas, but are not necessarily cost effective unless used in that environment for most of their life cycle. Not all are practical. Currently, there is not a proper affordable hatchback available. This is likely to change within the next year and hybrids will undoubtedly become more popular. They are a clean, efficient means of transport and more convenient for drivers as they do not have the more complicated refuelling process of the LPG vehicles.

We have not touched on electric vehicles yet. The main reason for us not using purely electric cars or vans is that so few of our staff are depot based. Charging is impractical as few of them have access to an outside power supply to recharge the batteries overnight outside their home. This would require a driveway, or a designated parking space. Local Authorities are making charging points available in city centres, but, for us, this is still not viable.

In our opinion, electric vehicles require the following conditions:

1   ready access to a safe and secure charging point

2   a route that is not likely to exceed the maximum range

3   regular schedules that are unlikely to change at short notice

Whilst they are clean, they are not as flexible as standard vehicles. Should a vehicle return to base and need to go out again at short notice, it would most likely not be possible without several hours recharging. Rapid recharging is improving and quick-change batteries would appear to be another option. Refuelling of fossil fuel vehicles is easy and they are ready to go again immediately.

We have looked at the option of making electric vehicles depot based and asking the drivers to collect them each morning. All that will do is transfer the emissions from our van to the driver's transport to and from work. This is likely to increase emissions, as we would have little control over their personal transport.

Do you have any advice to give to other fleet managers about how to amend their policy to reduce costs and emissions?

Get senior management approval and backing if you can. Demonstrate that cutting emissions is also about reducing fuel use, and, by default costs. Try to quantify the savings by possibly showing how much of your company's product you would have to sell to make the same amount of profit. Try not to move too fast. Give people time to adjust to each step and explain thoroughly your reasons for introducing it. Try to include a plus side for each driver as well so that they feel the benefits. Ask drivers to sign an agreement that shows they understand what you are trying to do and why.

Do not try to introduce every measure at the same time. You will need to know which initiatives work, and how well. Either way, monitor each step to ensure that you meet your targets. If you can reduce fuel consumption on each of your vehicles by as little as 5mpg, you will save money. Compare current fuel consumption figures of all your vehicles against what think you should be getting to identify those drivers that may need some form of training, or whose vehicle is not running correctly. Emphasise the need to have vehicles serviced on a regular basis and to check tyre pressure and condition at least weekly. Showing the results to the whole company will highlight those doing well and those who are not making as much effort. Peer pressure will work wonders. Some policies will take longer to show results, so try not to be discouraged if things do not change immediately. Try to keep up with new developments and incorporate them into your plans if relevant.

Make sure you have 'what if' plans in place.

Two examples:

1   There was no cost effective replacement van for the existing LPG Ford Transits, so we started to order diesel vans to replace those most in need of change and extended the contracts on the remainder by 18 months. This gave us the breathing space to persuade another manufacturer to produce a suitably sized petrol van that we can have converted to LPG. At the same time, it will save us in the region of £500,000 in lease payments.

2   Mayor Ken Livingstone had originally planned to remove the 100% discount for alternatively fuelled vans: but only for those not registered to the original keeper or for new vans registered after October 2008. We had intended to move our newest vans into the London area to make sure that we could keep the discount in place for as long as possible. Mayor Boris Johnson has now cancelled the proposed changes.

Do you have any plans to change your current arrangements to improve things even further?

We will keep looking at electric vehicles as they become more efficient and their range increases. If we can change any of our work practices to incorporate them, we will.

We will continue with LPG. We recently started placing orders for petrol vans to replace the Transits. These will be smaller and lighter. We will benefit from greatly improved fuel consumption and will specify the size of the fuel tanks. This will mean that our drivers will not need to refuel with LPG anywhere other than at our own bunker sites or a designated retail site where we have some control over the cost.

We will reduce the maximum CO_2 on cars to 140 gm/km during 2009 and lowering it in the coming years as manufacturers produce models that are more efficient.

By 2010, we will only pay Approved Mileage Rates for the bottom two bands (below 1999cc) even if the car's engine is above 2 litres. This will encourage drivers, using their own cars for business, to drive smaller-engined cars.

We intend to recharge drivers the actual cost of their fuel on a pence per mile basis. That should ensure that drivers choose the cheapest fuel available and moderate their driving to get the best fuel consumption they can.

Glenn Ewen
Fleet Manager
Clear Channel UK Limited

Clear Channel Outdoor
Where ideas take shape

Clear Channel Outdoor is the United Kingdom's leading outdoor advertising company, providing more than 70,000 advertising opportunities across its four premier brands: Clear Channel Pinnacle, Clear Channel Billboards, Clear Channel Adshel and Taxi Media.

THE SUNDAY TIMES

BEST GREEN
COMPANIES
2008

Corporate Responsibility

Named one of the greenest companies in Britain in the inaugural Sunday Times Green List of the UK's Best Green Companies, Clear Channel Outdoor considers the impact on the environment in all aspects of its activities and recognises that its corporate responsibility is to minimise the potential for causing harm to the environment.

CLEARCHANNEL OUTDOOR   33 Golden Square | London W1F 9JT | 020 7478 2200 | www.clearchannel.co.uk

5 MANAGING A LARGE CORPORATE FLEET

Liz Hollands
Car Fleet Manager
DTZ

Some readers may be unaware of DTZ. What does the group do and how big is its vehicle fleet?

DTZ is one of the top four firms of property advisers in the UK and also has offices around the world. We act for clients in all aspects of property for example, investment, retail, management and residential. Our teams are multi-discipline and work with both private and public sector clients to provide innovative and robust property solutions. You should see our DTZ sale and letting boards almost anywhere around the country. Find out more about us at www.dtz.com.

I am responsible for the UK vehicle fleet which has around 430 vehicles, plus another 900 employees taking a cash allowance. All employees above a certain grade are entitled to a company car or allowance. Although we offer a very flexible car policy, in line with our aim to be an employer of choice to attract and retain the best talent in the marketplace, we operate from regional offices predominantly based in city centres. A number of our employees live and work in those city centres and have no need of a car. Some prefer to take membership of a car club for the rare occasions when they need to drive. Others will have disposable income sufficient to fund cars outside the boundaries of our scheme, and so these people tend to opt for the cash allowance instead.

Please can you outline how you fund and manage your fleet.

We operate our cars on contract hire agreements using three suppliers – Lex, Marshall Leasing and Zenith – and they compete on price and service. All three are very good. Marshall Leasing and Zenith are quite different from Lex in terms of size and type of operation but are able to offer a very personal, efficient service. Zenith were inherited when we took over another company in 2007. Unlike most contract hire companies, they made the most of the opportunity to show us what they could do and I was very impressed with the operation. We have been with Lex since 1995 and brought Marshalls on board in 2001 and I think the length of tenure speaks volumes about the service we receive from them. My favourite business reference ever came from a Marshalls customer who, when I called him as a prospect said 'You'll never want to leave.'

Two suppliers would be ideal really; three is a little cumbersome in terms of management reporting. Of course, each of them would like a sole supply arrangement!

Our cars are on full maintenance contracts, and we use the accident management service provided by the contract hire companies. Two of these are based in-house and one is outsourced. It really doesn't matter that some services are subcontracted, so long as they are effectively managed by the supplier. I'm a fan of accident management since I once calculated I spent 15% of my time dealing with accident claims. Fuel cards are provided to a limited number of directors with company cars (more about this later).

You use contract hire to fund your fleet. Why did you choose contract hire?

DTZ uses contract hire to fund its company car fleet, and this has been the case since 1993. We used to take some of the £25k+ cars on contract purchase. These days we do not want to see cars on the balance sheet so outright and contract purchase are not for us.

With outright purchase, although there is flexibility in terms of being able to buy and sell at will, there are considerable risks to be borne on residual value. A company with many employees must offer a strict policy, and all those within specific grades should be treated equally. That means we must offer all employees a car over a fixed term. Anyway, buying and selling cars is not our core business. Contract hire, with its add-on services such as maintenance, accident management and breakdown cover, suits us well. Fixed monthly payments are easier to budget for and in addition, it allows us to benefit from the buying power of the supplier.

We used the services of an independent fleet consultant to carry out an audit a few years ago and he concluded that contract hire was right for DTZ. Neither subsequent legislation nor changes to our fleet have given us any reason to change from this method of acquisition although we have investigated Employee Car Ownership schemes and salary sacrifice.

Do you offer your employees a fixed list of cars to choose from or is it a user-chooser fleet?

DTZ currently operates a user-chooser fleet. As a market leader in our field, we aim to attract the best talent by offering a benefits package which is second to none, and this includes our company cars. However at the time of writing (2009) given the current economic climate we are investigating restricted badge options.

Cars are taken on four year contracts regardless of mileage, but we are not generally a high-mileage fleet. Vehicle quotes are based on four years and 70,000 miles total but contracts are written for the actual mileage required. Mileage is reviewed at the contract mid point and then as required. There is no restriction on the number of times we may review the mileage and I rarely recontract during the first year since drivers always seem to drive more miles in the first twelve months. Strange but true.

Drivers may top up their allowance or trade down, in which case we pay the balance in salary, but they may not change cars at promotion. Car contributions are deducted monthly although I would prefer to see them paid in total at the beginning of the contract, and this is something which is under review. We do not distinguish between perk and job need cars although we are not generally a high-mileage fleet.

Are there any vehicles you would not allow onto your fleet?

The only exclusion is two seat vehicles. Otherwise employees may take four wheel drive, convertibles, people carriers, coupes, coupe cabriolets, from any manufacturer. The original reason for the restriction was that two seat cars were considered to present the wrong image to clients, they were not suitable to take clients as passengers; and there were issues over deciding exactly which two seaters would be allowed (eg Honda S2000) and which would not (Caterham 7).

Although we don't expressly forbid motorcycles in our written policy, we have never actually allowed any. As a keen former biker myself, I appreciate the particular health and safety, training and protective clothing issues which arise when using bikes. There is really no solid business case for anyone using a bike for work as there might be, for example, in a company where an emergency reaction force is key.

As an aside, recently one of our managed shopping centres ordered a Vespa scooter. They wanted scantily clothed agency promotion girls to ride it around the centre. None of the girls had licences, none had ridden bikes before. I insisted that the order was cancelled.

Have you taken any steps recently to reduce your fleet costs?

I am constantly on the lookout for cost saving measures. And of course in order to make savings, you have to know what you are spending in the first place.

Fuel is a major cost and although historically we have offered fuel for private use to directors with a company car, I do provide them with an annual statement showing the likely cost of purchasing their private fuel versus the tax payable on the benefit. As a result, the majority have now realised they were paying more in tax than they were spending on fuel purchase, and have opted out. So we have made considerable savings there.

Business mileage reimbursement to employees is always at HMRC advisory rates, to avoid incurring additional tax on drivers.

In addition, we rarely early terminate leases when employees leave. I have always reallocated cars to new employees, or to newly-qualified surveyors when they first become entitled to a company car. It saves us short-term hire costs whilst waiting for a new car, and reduces our overheads should the employment not continue for any reason. Although there are costs involved in reallocating the cars with some inevitable downtime, and costs for safety checks, valeting and transport, these aren't even a tenth of the costs we would have had if we simply terminated leases.

As I write this the UK is in recession and so we have placed a temporary freeze on ordering new vehicles until we have reallocated those already available.

We don't use telematics as the sort of fleet we operate wouldn't be able to utilise many of the key features they offer – route scheduling for example - and the costs aren't worth paying without being able to enjoy the benefits. If I were using telematics I would be carrying out extensive research into suppliers as I have heard too many horror stories of companies disappearing without trace, leaving expensive systems with no maintenance nor reporting available.

The other area where we are constantly striving to reduce cost is accidental damage and end of term dehire damage, and we have taken various steps to manage these. All drivers, whether regular or occasional, are required to carry out an on-line driver profile provided by our nominated driver training organisation, MAC. Depending upon the result of the profile, an employee may be asked to undertake a half-day's on-road training with MAC, at our cost. We will also ask them to undertake this training if they have had more than one at-fault accident in a year, six points or more on their licence, or drive more than 10,000 miles a year on business.

The training given has been successful in that the number of more serious incidents has reduced. We also ask MAC to call those drivers involved in the bigger incidents, to discuss what happened and how the accident might have been avoided. However carelessness is still a problem and like many other companies, incidents are often reported as 'hit whilst parked'. We now insist that any driver reporting a hit whilst parked incident obtains a crime reference from the police.

We have also reinstated regular checks on vehicles by line managers. Although this is an unpopular task, it serves to remind employees that they have a responsibility to look after the condition and maintenance of their cars in a suitable manner. Employees are given a copy of the BVRLA Fair Wear and Tear booklet when they are provided with a car. At the end of a hire, cars are inspected jointly by the line manager and employee. Any damage beyond fair wear and tear is recharged to us by the contract hire company, backed up by digital photographs, and passed on to the driver. The availability of photographs stops most of the arguments about condition.

How much have you saved as a result of making these changes?

If we had simply terminated leases, we would have spent at least another £180k a year, based on average reallocations. The reduction in fuel cards has been gradual over the past five years or more, with additional savings of about £30k each year. The savings on accidental and careless damage are also substantial.

Some fleet managers have been talking about extending leases, or lease periods, to keep costs down. Do you plan to do this?

DTZ has extended leases on some contracts which were due for change within the next 12 months, but this is for lower mileage cars and after discussion with drivers who have volunteered to keep their cars longer, in light of the current freeze on new vehicles. Our primary focus is on ensuring we don't allow employees to extend contracts which are already well overdue, but encourage them into cars from our reallocation fleet.

A number of employees – myself included – are driving diesels which qualify for the Euro IV three per cent discount, as they were registered prior to 31st December 2005. I'm suggesting we could extend the contracts on those vehicles so that employees continue to enjoy the tax holiday. However, it's important to be even-handed to all employees and consider the effect on staff morale. Recruitment fees aren't exactly minor figures these days.

Overall, our contracts already run for four years and, from the quotes obtained to date, I don't consider that extending them still further will necessarily make us great savings – more a chip than a swathe.

Do you have any advice to give other fleet managers on how to manage supplier relationships?

Cars are not simply another item for procurement. They are extremely expensive items of equipment requiring regular maintenance and proper care. They are physically large and a real nuisance to manage in terms of keeping them somewhere secure and cheap whilst not in use. If you try to be clever and make a name for yourself by being hard-nosed at the front end negotiations, be sure it will come back to bite you when you are in a tight spot. We have chosen suppliers who, like us, prefer long-term relationships.

I have regular reviews with specific contacts I have known well for a number of years. I often alternate reviews between our offices and theirs so that I also meet the back-office staff who carry out the day to day jobs on our behalf. It's important that each of us understands how the other works, and that they know if they are not efficient, our business suffers. Many years ago an employee had a car problem which was poorly managed and he wasted many valuable working hours trying to get the car fixed. I remember his frustration as he said to me 'If I had wanted to mess about with cars all day, I would have trained as a mechanic'. Suppliers must remember that we employ their expertise so that we can concentrate on ours.

How have you gone about advising employees on tax and legislative issues?

I have always given employees as much notice as possible of changing tax legislation. When we changed to emissions-based taxation, I had been notifying employees for at least two years prior, so that they were able to make sensible choices of car. This is important when you have to keep your car for four years.

Under our scheme rules, drivers may top up their allowance. At the point of order I give them a statement showing how much they are paying in tax and additional contributions, to ensure they understand how much the car will cost them. However, at the moment we are switching from simple lease rental rate lists to whole life costs, so that again employees can see the true costs, and the benefit of choosing cars with emissions less than 160 gm/km of CO_2.

There is a simple tax calculator located on our company car intranet too. When new Notices of Tax Coding are issued, I remind drivers that they can check HMRC car benefit figures using our calculator.

As mentioned earlier, every year I provide an individual statement to all those directors who are entitled to private fuel, showing the likely costs versus tax for the forthcoming year. Changes in fuel price and private mileage can affect the calculations significantly.

A number of DTZ employees take a cash allowance instead of a company car. How do you help them to make the cash v car decision?

Software is available on the internet from accounting firms and others, but some of it is confusing to use. People tend to underestimate the costs of running their own car, to forget about depreciation, and not factor in additional expenditure such as punctures and insurance excesses. I prefer to focus on a series of flyers we have produced showing how little one can pay to run a sensible company car. Quite a trickle of employees have tried the cash allowance for a few years but come back into the car scheme at renewal time.

People get hung up on the idea of company car tax, believing that any change means an increase. In fact when the current scheme was implemented and taxation was based on emissions rather than mileage, most of our drivers' tax decreased, because they had made sensible car choices. Sometimes you have to remind them how much of the car allowance they are losing in income tax before they will look more closely at the company car option.

What administrative arrangements have you put in place to manage the allowance?

We are not yet strict enough in setting out what type and age of cars are allowed. We do maintain a register of driving licences, V5 registration documents, insurance showing business use, MOT certificates etc, with scanned copies linked to the database. You need to check Data Protection Act rules when doing this. Maintaining the register and obtaining all details is an ongoing and thankless task. There are agencies prepared to do this for you of course, at a cost. Employees also have to sign a declaration on expense forms confirming their car is legal and roadworthy. Such a declaration is the very minimum, to my mind, that a company should be asking for, if they allow private cars to be used on business.

DVLA mandates are the only sure way to obtain up to date information on driving licences. Although a company will know what penalty points are earned by a driver when in his or her company car (because the Notices of Intended Prosecution are sent to your company via the leasing company), there is no way of knowing what points they incur when driving other privately-owned vehicles. ACFO (Association of Car Fleet Operators) is currently lobbying for an improved and more readily-available service from DVLA.

In addition, I would like to see the MID (Motor Insurance Database) able to provide confirmation of business insurance to employers, where employees' private cars are being used on business. I am told that whilst they are committed to being able to offer customer-facing initiatives in the future, they are not able to do so yet.

For anyone not aware of the MID, it was set up to combat the crime of uninsured driving. Every insured car must be listed on the database. This task may be carried out by your insurer, your broker, or by your company. New cars must be logged on the database and, equally importantly, cars you no longer own, removed. There are specific timescales for making updates. The police are one of the MID's biggest users, cross-checking information listed on it against detail gleaned whilst using their Automatic Number Plate Recognition (ANPR) equipment. Any car which appears to be uninsured may be seized and if insurance cannot be proved, may be crushed. More information is available from www.miic.org.uk.

Of course, some companies will not allow private cars to be used on business and insist on hiring short term rental vehicles instead. This ensures that vehicles are fit for purpose, properly maintained and insured. It is not necessary to drive many business miles before the cost of a rental car will outweigh the financial costs of reimbursing employees in a private car, aside from the risk considerations. It's worth doing the calculations.

Have you considered introducing an employee car ownership scheme or a salary sacrifice scheme?

DTZ did look at one of the market-leading ECO schemes a few years back but the product is not right for us. Most employees do insufficient business mileage and staff turnover is too high. The provider was very honest in their assessment to us and I was impressed with their offering. Similarly, salary sacrifice doesn't work for us but there will be others running a bigger ratio of sub 120gm/km cars, with low staff turnover, for whom the schemes may be perfect. The administration in terms of monthly accounting looks a bit scary though.

Fears about changes in AMAP (Authorised Mileage Allowance Payments, currently 40 pence per mile for the first 10,000 miles per annum, 25 pence per mile thereafter) reducing the value of these schemes have so far been unfounded. But they do remain a potential 'gotcha' given that contracts may be set up for 2-4 years, and the Chancellor's Budget can change the rules year on year with very little warning. Of course, like investments, rates could move either way.

You are very active in ACFO. Some readers may be unaware of ACFO. Please tell us about it and how it benefits its members.

ACFO is the leading organisation representing and supporting the needs of all fleet operators. It is a UK organisation providing information, best practice ideas and networking opportunities for fleet operators to meet up with each other on a regular basis. Fleet managers tend to be office-based and only see their counterparts at manufacturer launches.

ACFO is also a powerful lobbying association and has regular meetings with HMRC, Treasury and DVLA where we are able to offer suggestions on forthcoming policy. ACFO constantly challenges HMRC for more timely notification of forthcoming changes in order that fleets can plan strategic policy changes on a sensible timescale.

There are nine ACFO regions around the country with meetings roughly every two months so there is bound to be one near you. We invite speakers to present on current hot topics and there is ample time for networking and discussion on best practice. The company, not the individual, is the member, and fleet managers are invited to bring along their HR or Finance Directors as well.

We run occasional free seminars and workshops for members – a recent one covered the revised capital allowances due to take effect in April 2009 – and our members are frequent speakers at industry forums and conferences. It's hard to recall a meeting when I haven't walked away without at least one good new idea.

Membership costs are surprisingly low. You can check us out at www.acfo.org.

Do you have any alternatively fuelled cars on your fleet?

DTZ has four Toyota Prius on fleet, but no LPG vehicles. Two of the Prius are pool cars in central London but the other two are drivers' chosen company cars. There have been no issues with the running of the vehicles themselves and obviously we benefit from them being congestion charge free.

However, pool cars are principally for the use of graduates who do not receive a company car or allowance. Think of the scenario of people who learned to drive before they went to university. They didn't drive whilst at university because they had no money. They then went to work in central London and were asked to drive on company business. They were given a Toyota Prius which sounds as though it isn't running when it is, and has an automatic gearbox, and sent off into the thick of Oxford Circus on their own. To be fair, we have had no issues and these are intelligent people who are required to take an on-line driver risk profile and satisfy other scheme requirements before they borrow a car. But still worth thinking about.

No-one has yet taken an LPG car due to nervousness about convenient availability of supply, and not being able to go through the Channel Tunnel should they wish to.

When you try to make changes in the way the fleet is run, do you encounter any resistance within the organisation?

It's very difficult to get any Board to spend money without demonstrating quantified savings first, which is understandable. I am rapidly coming to the conclusion that we fleet managers are our own worst enemies when it comes to getting ourselves heard at Board level. We need to provide frequent written reports to our Board on our activities generally, for example, where our existing policy falls down, the improvements we are making and in particular, the savings we make every day, every week of the year.

I have also found it useful to develop decent working relationships with our Health and Safety Director and our Regional Finance Controllers. As with supplier relationships, a better understanding of the requirements and problems of the other party helps us pull together and achieve our company aims.

You have been DTZ Fleet Manager for 15 years and have been an active ACFO member for more than a decade. How do you think fleet management has changed since you first became involved?

There are far fewer fleet managers than there were when I started, as companies seek to outsource all but their core business. Fleet has become a part-time job for either HR executives or finance people, who in turn outsource to contract hire providers. Good as they may be, those providers do not achieve the kind of savings that may be overseen and negotiated by a proper in-house fleet manager, who has the monetary interests of their company at heart. The savings we make on competitive quoting alone more than justifies an in-house employee salary cost.

There is more quality information available from the internet, the fleet trade press, and of course ACFO. Training courses are available from various providers, ideal for those starting out in fleet or who have been tasked with looking after company cars aside from their main job.

There is more focus on costs and strategic issues, and less about the day to day management of maintenance issues, probably since contract hire became a major player and dealt with those issues on our behalf.

Have you made any significant changes recently to the way you manage your fleet? Or, do you have any plans to change the way you manage your fleet?

DTZ is currently carrying out a strategic review and examining possibilities such as restricted or preferred badge and basing driver quotes on whole life costs – which we should have done before, to be honest. But review is an ongoing process, and I am always looking for ways to improve on what we already do.

Would you recommend that other fleet managers follow the same course you have?

The DTZ fleet will be different from one run by a charity, or a building firm, or a fleet of service engineers and there are things which would be ideal for those fleets (single badge, telematics, vans, motorcycles) which don't make sense for us. All of us will focus on keeping costs to a minimum. For some, outright purchase may be a more flexible route. Others will be in a position to obtain a better rate of finance than a contract hire company. Some will have workshops and be able to undertake their own maintenance rather than subcontracting.

There is no single correct route to follow, and we all have to be constantly ready to change our policies and practices to meet new demands.

Liz Hollands
Car Fleet Manager
DTZ
125 Old Broad Street
London EC2N 2BQ

6 ENCOURAGING EMPLOYEES BACK INTO COMPANY CARS

> **Mark Mardell**
> Supply Chain Director
> VT Education & Skills

Please introduce yourself and tell us a little about your business and your fleet.

I work in VT Education & Skills (VT E&S) which employs approx 4,000 people with a turnover of £250million. Our business consists of five Business Units: VT Flagship (the Royal Navy's training partner), VT FourS (education support services), VT Training (vocational training), VT Careers Management (information, advice and guidance) and Building Schools for the Future (building and maintaining new schools).

VT E&S is the UK's largest training, education and skills company and is part of VT Group (www.vtplc.com) which employs over 14,000 people and has an annual turnover in excess of £1.2billion.

VT E&S supports over 500 schools providing school improvement, education consultancy, ICT solutions, workforce development, training and conferences. It also has two Building Schools for the Future (BSF) contracts which will, in due course, cover about 25 secondary schools. Through VT Flagship the company plays a key role in designing, planning, delivering and assessing 900 training courses across the Royal Navy's training establishments.

My role within VT E&S is the Supply Chain Director reporting to the VT E&S Managing Director. I have held this post for just over two years and my responsibilities include the Procurement function, Property Management as well as a small team (the Asset Management Team) who look after our car fleet and staff 'personal' equipment (e.g. laptops, mobiles, Blackberries etc).

The Asset Management Team looks after 450 VT E&S company cars (VT Group has just under 1300) as well as managing a large 'grey fleet' of staff-owned cars which are used to deliver our product to various customers across the UK.

My involvement with our car fleet started approx 12 years ago when I negotiated the lease car contract on behalf of the group. The relationship with our provider (Godfrey Davis / Lex) has grown over this period and they support various customer contracts and the staff car scheme which allows a choice from a wide range of cars within 5 cost bands / grades.

The fleet, until the end of 2007, consisted of a few vans and pool cars with the rest being management grade staff vehicles. We have approx 65 sites in the UK and the majority of cars are used to travel between sites and cover relatively high mileage. However approx 50% could be regarded as a business perk. A cash alternative is also available which has been taken up by approximately 50 staff.

At the end of 1998 we identified a need for our field delivery staff to also benefit from lease cars and the fleet expanded in a matter of months from 350 to 450.

You changed your company car scheme recently and received a Fleet Heroes award from the Energy Saving Trust and The Guardian newspaper for being a Grey Fleet Champion. Please explain the changes you made and why you made them?

During 2007 we identified the requirement to make changes for three key business reasons. Firstly the competitive nature of the recruitment market covering our VT Training field staff. This is a very competitive market area and we were keen to ensure we retained our highest performing staff. We explored a number of options and introduced staff benefits including changes in our car scheme which would attract and retain high performers and differentiate us from our competitors.

The idea came about as a result of our many discussions with staff (leavers and current employees) about various issues including the cost of running their own cars. This not only included the servicing, tyres, insurance etc but also the purchase cost of their cars which needed to be replaced on a regular basis. To highlight the size of the issue approx 500 staff travel over six million business miles per year in their own cars.

The second reason was the company's desire to ensure our employees operate in a safe environment. The combination of staff generally running older cars, and the high mileage meant we had to do something about it.

Mark Mardell receives Fleet Hero award from Geoff Hoon (Secretary of State for Transport) and Martyn Moore (Editor, Fleet News)

Recent changes in duty of care legislation have highlighted the 'grey fleet' issue, which is about employees using their private cars on business. This is a common practice across British businesses with an estimated four million people involved. However, it's one that severely limits the control an employer can have over the emission levels and condition of privately owned vehicles and this can have both environmental and safety impacts.

This was initially addressed in a number of ways through the reorganisation of the field sales areas and improving the technology they use to deliver the product. We also introduced a management system covering service frequency and MOT checking which again provided further improvement. These changes resulted in fewer and shorter journeys and also gave some reassurance that the cars were roadworthy. However whilst this improved the issue it did not remove it.

A third and, at the time, less significant requirement was the company's drive to reduce our carbon footprint. Efforts had previously been limited to encouragement of low emission cars and this was again relatively successful in reducing the average emissions of the fleet.

An investigation then began which explored whether there was a cost effective way to allow delivery staff to have company cars against a background of a limited company budget to fund the vehicles (which was effectively the mileage costs being paid to the staff), the perception amongst the staff that it cost little to run their own cars and the company's traditional view of who should and should not have cars.

How did you make the decision and who was involved?

The overiding factor for this being a sucess was that HR, Finance and Supply Chain worked together as a team albeit sometimes with different priorities. The business objective of attracting and retaining quality staff together with addressing our need to ensure staff worked in a safe environment, quickly led us to form a team to investigate if it was viable to offer company cars to a group of 500 staff.

We regard ourselves as a responsible employer with strong green credentials, and decided to deal with the problem by introducing a fleet of company owned cars that employees could use both for work and privately. The key was to find a vehicle that was acceptable to the employees, would have a low emissions level, and for which there would be a good national service network that matched VT's own wide geographical spread.

The Corsa was chosen and a trial commenced with 50 of the ecoFlex 3CDTi model. This quickly led to a further 25 being made available, followed by another 25 on order. The scheme has proved popular with employees who see the benefits of having a comfortable, economical and reliable vehicle, with good maintenance back-up available locally through the Vauxhall network, all provided for a fixed and modest monthly outlay.

Together we looked at a number of cars and agreed the cost model which supported the business case. This model considered the cost savings as a result of the reduction

in the fuel pence per mile, the total cost of the car, the practicality of the car to support the job requirements, the cost of the car to the employee and its attractiveness to staff. It also looked at the softer savings of improved sales as a result of the retention of staff and the reduced cost of recruitment.

This needed the support of our lease car provider who looked at a number of options and included manufacturer support. Selecting the right make and model of car on which to base the scheme was critical. Various 'green' models were tested and the eventual choice was the Vauxhall Corsa 1.3 CDTi which was chosen for its fuel efficiency, low emissions of 119 g/km of CO_2, sustainability and low lease cost.

Part of the decision which would affect the lease cost is if a large number of the same models came off lease at the same time. This would have an effect on the residual value of the car and hence the lease cost.

The next step was to consult with staff about the viability of the scheme and to get Board approval. As a result of an extensive study of the market, staff consultation and a robust financial model/business case, this proved to be relatively simple although it still took approx five months from concept to receipt of the first vehicles.

Has the scheme been a success?

From a company perspective it has been a great sucess in that risks to employees who drive on business have been reduced and the ability to retain high calibre employees and to attract new people has been enhanced. Overall costs related to the use of cars on company business are lower, more predictable and can be better controlled. And the low emission level and good fuel efficiency of the Corsa 1.3CDTi is contributing significantly to reducing the company's carbon footprint. It is, as always difficult to forecast actual cost reductions regarding the 'softer' advantages such as lower recruitement costs and improved efficiency by retaining high calibre employees, however we believe the overall benefit is significant.

Overall the staff affected see this as a success although the take up has not been as high as we expected. For staff to qualify they needed to have been with VT for a given period and also to be travelling a minimum number of business miles. We estimate that approximately 30% of the eligible staff have to date been provided with a car. In a recent survey of staff which attempted to identify any barriers to the take up, the main reasons stated were the timing of the availabilty of the car compared to when the staff wanted to renew their car, the size of the car and the perceived cost to staff.

To address these issues we have now opened up the scheme to allow staff to take up the opportunity at any time (it was previously every six months) and we are also marketing the car internally to try and address the concerns regarding perceived cost and the size of car. We believe we will within a year exceed 250.

When marketing of the scheme to employees we include material from Vauxhall and we set out the benefits to the employees, ie:

- reduction in initial outlay of purchasing fuel before monthly expenses are claimed back
- safety has been improved due to the maintenance package which comes with the car
- additional benefit to employees by having a new car not just for work purposes but also for private usage
- private mileage reduction in costs
- reduced worry of unplanned cost due to breakdown or accident
- the release of the capital which was previously held in their own vehicle
- a better vehicle
- no large (sudden, unexpected or otherwise) costs e.g. tyres, accidents, insurance, MOT repairs etc.

From a business perspective the aim was to ensure that the direct costs were at least neutral. This will very much depend on the as yet unknown cost associated with the usual insured losses (damage, accidents and theft), end of lease costs and fuel costs. However we believe we have taken a relatively prudent view and the forecast is currently that the scheme will be at least cost neutral.

From an environmental perspective it is a huge success. Since February, it is estimated that we have saved some 45 tonnes of CO_2. It is hoped that if 70 per cent of the 500 eligible employees join the scheme the saving could eventually reach 340 tonnes a year, equal to the average annual output of 56 homes.

Our partnership with Lex and their relationship with Vauxhall also proved to be invaluable. Choosing the right vehicle was critical and this activity has again proved the worth of the relationship. We set them an objective of finding the right vehicle within our budget and they provided us with a number of options

Have there been any issues?

One of the early issues was that a number of drivers questioned if the pence per mile that the company paid was sufficient to cover the costs. This coincided with the sharp rise in fuel costs and had the potential to become a big issue. The main cause of this was that employees challenged the published MPG as being a sound basis for the calculation.

To investigate this claim I requested a demonstrator for one month. This proved to be a very different experience from driving my own company car; however after a few days of getting used to the change, I found this wasn't an issue. I logged all my journeys, the type of driving, speed, fuel, miles etc. and at the end of the month worked out the average MPG.

To my suprise the average MPG was exactly the same as the manufacturer's figures. This was published to the workforce and a challenge was offered to them; you can obtain higher mpg and reduce the risk of accidents by modifying your driving style. Approximately one month after this exercise was complete the fuel costs started to go down again so whilst the exercise appeared to resolve the issue realistically it would only be tested if prices rise to a similar level again.

Would you recommend that other fleet managers follow the same course you have?

The scheme is undoubtably attractive to VT. However any decision will depend on the needs of the company which will include a number of factors:

- The current cost of your grey fleet – are the costs able to fund the running cost of the lease cars? If not, are you prepared to fund the difference? A major factor will obviously be the number of miles travelled and the cost of this.
- The cost of the lease and running costs of the car – the MPG of the vehicle needs to be carefully considered against the type of use e.g. if your staff intend to travel mainly on the motorway a hybrid vehicle might not be the right choice
- What arrangement have you got in place to ensure the grey fleet is safe? There could also be a cost of your current scheme which would be saved or a cost of the management that you would need to put in place.
- What is your environmental policy? Is it strong enough to drive through a scheme such as this irrespective of the financial position? Is the company willing to fund any deficit?
- Would this be a valuable improvement of staff benefits? Can you put a value against this?
- What image are you trying to portray to the market? Is your brand important?
- What would your aspirations be regarding the vehicle? Clearly the vehicle needs to satisfy the business need e.g. size, comfort etc. However the more expensive the vehicle the more difficult the business case becomes.

Do you have any advice to give other fleet managers about how to amend their policy to reduce costs and emissions?

The main issue that this does not address is the reduction of miles. This has the obvious impact of a significant reduction in cost and emissions. Planning their journeys is one factor and the use of a Tom Tom (or similar) is a very effective way of doing this.

Another way is to monitor the activity closely which will provide some guidance on areas to look at and to consider with regard to more effective planning, changing driving habits etc.

We are currently considering issuing petrol cards to all Corsa drivers. This will allow us to get regular management information on the mileage and MPG achieved which will allow us to quickly look at ways of reducing the overall miles and also to give us accurate MPG figure which, when measured against the published figures, can help idenify higher risk drivers. This could lead us to offer more support to these staff.

Do you have any plans to change your current arrangements to improve things even further?

As previously discussed the use of fuel cards together with a one vehicle fleet could realise great benefits in control and monitoring. However this scheme has also created a realisation of the benefits that can be achieved by a bit of creative thinking in the use of cars.

We have a huge Group spend (and carbon footprint) as a result of our UK coverage and Group global business. We are therefore looking at ways to introduce similar schemes which deliver a similar wide range of company and employee benefits.

One simple example of this is to look at placing hybrid / low emission pool cars at sites with a high mileage / travel requirement and including the potential to car-share.

As a team we are committed to looking for the other improvements as we believe this has been a catalyst for a great number of initiatives which will be beneficial to the employee, the company and the environment.

This is an exciting new initiative for all of us.

Mark Mardell
Supply Chain Director
VT Education & Skills

VT
Education and Skills

Largest Education and
Skills company in the UK

Integrated training and
support services provider

Royal Navy's training partner

Training partnership with
VW Group, BAA, Network Rail,
and British Energy

Winner of Energy Savings
Trust Fleet Hero 2008: Grey Fleet

learning
&
guidance
&
training
&
infrastructure

7

RUNNING A POLICE FLEET

> **John Robinson**
> Fleet Manager
> Cambridgeshire Constabulary

How big is your vehicle fleet?

Cambridgeshire Constabulary's fleet is currently around 490 of which around 53% is marked (ie: carries either full police 'Battenberg' livery or minimal markings such as a force crest) and the remainder is totally unmarked.

Most mainstream manufacturers are represented within the fleet but some in only small numbers. In terms of cars the principal manufacturer is Ford followed by Skoda and Volvo; these three manufacturers account for 70% of the total fleet. About 25% of the fleet are van/personnel carriers; the main supplier of these is Ford followed by Mercedes-Benz and LDV.

There is a small number of executive cars – mostly Volvos – operated by senior police officers.

Finally, there are about 15 motorcycles, mostly of BMW manufacture, and one Leyland double-decker bus converted to a mobile police office.

From time to time, as required, the fleet is supplemented by a variety of hire vehicles and demonstrators.

Please can you explain, in outline, how you fund and manage your fleet?

The fleet is entirely outright-purchased and totally managed in-house by a professional team led by myself. I have overall responsibility for all fleet operations including three geographically-dispersed vehicle workshops, run by Workshop Managers, which carry out the servicing and repair of the fleet along with some commissioning of new vehicles ie: installation of police equipment such as light bars and sirens. Notwithstanding this, at particularly busy times, some maintenance may be outsourced to franchised dealers, the latter also being used for warranty work.

Because of the intensive use many of our vehicles experience, particularly the marked response ones, servicing and inspection is carried out at a greater frequency than recommended by manufacturers.

This is because, in the police environment, components such as tyres, braking materials and lubricants will not always reach manufacturers' designed replacement parameters. So servicing intervals need to be shortened to compensate for this and ensure our vehicles remain roadworthy.

Generally, these arduous use vehicles are serviced every 6,000 miles (some may be covering around 1,000 miles per week). Those used less intensively, such as pool cars and CID vehicles, are generally serviced in accordance with manufacturers' intervals.

All fuel has been purchased with fuel cards for the last 12 years. Prior to then the Constabulary operated a number of in-house fuel installations supplemented by the use of fuel cards for those locations without bulk supplies.

However, many of these fuel installations were well past their best, and a full renewal would have involved significant capital outlay as well as disruption to customers.

I undertook an exercise to evaluate the pros and cons of fuel cards versus bulk supplies from both a financial and operational perspective. The conclusion was that, over time, both systems would cost about the same. However, using commercial outlets gave officers far greater flexibility in where to obtain fuel.

Whilst bulk fuel can obviously be purchased at a lower price than that from commercial pumps, the infrastructure overheads of having in-house fuel installations, together with the fact that the fuel has to be paid for before it is used, must be balanced against paying the higher price of commercial forecourt fuel. The latter is brought on credit, with the cost evenly spread throughout the year, but without the need for administrative overheads such as dipping tanks and reconciling stocks.

In addition, it was considered an unnecessary cost, both financially and environmentally, having vehicles drive to our sites purely to fuel-up, probably passing several petrol stations en route; indeed, the very presence of marked police vehicles on petrol forecourts ties in with the Constabulary's ethos of 'High-Visibility' policing.

I am not directly involved with accident management, this falling within the remit of the force's Insurance Department. However, they work closely with the driving school, divisions and myself to highlight trends in accidents so that preventative action can be taken to address any areas of concern.

The job of police fleet manager entails working with a broad range of suppliers covering a wide spectrum of products and services. As well as the vehicle manufacturers themselves and vehicle converters, there are numerous suppliers of police equipment; these cover areas such as blue lights, sirens, livery materials, black box data recorders, mobile data terminals, load carriers, firearms boxes, police radios etc.

Generally speaking, most of these items are installed in our vehicles by specialist contractors working in the 'Blue Light' market. Over the years we have built up very close working relationships with these organisations and they are effectively part of our supply chain from ordering a vehicle to obtaining the finished product, fully converted to meet our operational requirements.

We find that, because of the breadth of knowledge and experience these contractors have in carrying out vehicle builds and conversions in their specialised market, they are very pro-active in suggesting innovative solutions to the challenges we give them.

What are the special challenges involved with running a police fleet?

Police fleets are notoriously challenging to manage because of their 24/7 operation and the rigours of police vehicle usage. Many police vehicles, particularly those which respond to incidents, are used at the limits of their capability in terms of speed, acceleration and payload so, as already alluded to, this requires a more intensive servicing regime than vehicles in normal domestic use.

Consequently, our workshop staff are highly-skilled and are trained to use highly sophisticated diagnostic equipment. Indeed, because of this intensive use of many police vehicles, technicians are often dealing with technical issues which their counterparts in commercial dealerships will have rarely, if ever, encountered.

In order to maintain warranties, and also ensure that safety and reliability is not compromised, only manufacturers' original parts are used; the potential saving of using lower cost non-original parts could be wiped out in a stroke if a warranty claim was not upheld.

It is critical that not only are the cars fit for the purpose to which they are put, but that their drivers are trained to an appropriate level, often far in excess of that of other professional drivers.

Thus, police officers are highly-trained individuals who are able to maximise the performance of the vehicles they drive in order to ensure they can respond to incidents quickly but with absolute safety, both to themselves and other road users. All our police drivers are rigorously-trained to nationally-defined standards by the force's Driving School. This training becomes even more intensive in order to drive faster and more powerful vehicles such as the Volvo V70s used by the Roads Policing and Tactical Firearms Units.

As information technology becomes more sophisticated and with newly-found applications, police cars are no longer simply a means of transport; they can now act as a mobile office bristling with state-of-the-art IT equipment such as radios, mobile data terminals, video and ANPR (Automatic Number Plate Recognition) systems.

One of the challenges I face is to have this equipment fitted in such a way that it does not pose a health and safety risk. For example, equipment should ideally be flush-fitted so there are no protrusions or hard edges. In the event of an accident, if somebody's head or body came into contact with protruding edges it could cause them serious injuries. Additionally, equipment must be fitted so it does not interfere with the deployment of airbags, is not in the 'swept view' through the windscreen and is ergonomically positioned for ease of use and safety.

The available space within a vehicle (usually around the dashboard area) is quite clearly limited and some of the latest equipment uses a single screen through which several applications can be operated, for example, the light bar switch panel, police radio, video, mobile data etc. This obviously reduces the amount of space the police equipment takes up but the technical challenge to make disparate systems work on one piece of hardware is immense.

More recently, some converters of police vehicle have started to look at using the steering wheel controls (normally used for radio, volume etc) to operate police equipment. With Canbus technology this is apparently now a relatively simple matter of re-programming the buttons. Only a few years ago, when I asked for this facility, I was advised it was not technically possible.

After the police officers themselves, our vehicles represent the public face of the Constabulary, a tangible asset that the public can see. In so doing, they need to project a professional and re-assuring image, contributing to Cambridgeshire's ethos of high-visibility policing.

The nature of police work, where anything can happen (and invariably does) means that for me every day can present different challenges. There is often a need to respond immediately to changing operational circumstances, planned and unplanned operations and the like.

Sometimes this can lead to a requirement to allocate and deploy resources, such as vehicles, at a moment's notice; this might be done through hiring, seeking any available demonstrators from manufacturers, using new vehicles not yet allocated or withdrawn vehicles not yet sold and, where necessary, borrowing from other police forces.

Another part of my remit is responsibility for a team of drivers who operate the internal mail service which transports mail between police stations in Cambridgeshire and also DNA samples to the laboratory for analysis. In addition, the service provides collections and deliveries of urgent court papers and exhibits. The criticality of the latter cannot be underestimated as any delays or loss within the system could jeopardise or delay court proceedings.

The option of outsourcing the internal mail service has been looked into but has always been significantly more expensive than the in-house operation and incapable of responding to urgent demands on the spot; something that I can approve simply by changing priorities at a moment's notice when the situation demands.

As well as being able to respond to front line requirements, sometimes with little or no notice (major incidents and murders cannot be foreseen) it is also vital that we are commercially astute. We have to be very customer-focused at all times to get the most out of our fixed budgets, which after all comes from the public purse, whilst providing the best possible service to support police officers in their frontline duties.

Only by understanding their business thoroughly can we provide a service which meets, and hopefully exceeds, their requirements.

You use outright purchase to fund your fleet. Why did you choose this option?

Our fleet is purchased outright as part of the Constabulary's annual capital expenditure programme, this method of purchase being the norm for many areas of the Constabulary's expenditure.

Leasing of vehicles has been looked at on several occasions including as part of a Best Value Review of fleet. However, after thorough examination and meetings with representatives from some leasing companies, it was not considered a suitable option for us.

The quotes we have received have reflected the nature police fleet operations; the harsh use of vehicles; the need for total flexibility; possibly retaining vehicles longer than planned, even after the replacement has arrived, thus preventing key-for-key changeover; the need to support unforeseen operational requirements, and the need to drill holes in parts of the vehicle (roof, dashboard, etc) to install police equipment. These make us a high-risk proposition for leasing companies.

Adhering to fixed mileage contracts would also be an unacceptable constraint on the way we operate, where flexibility is paramount, and would probably, under leasing, lead to excess mileage charges which would add to our operating costs. Indeed, a number of other police fleets which were into leasing have now moved back into outright purchase for reasons such as these.

What have you found to be the advantages and the disadvantages of this form of vehicle funding?

As mentioned above one of the principal advantages of outright purchase is that I am not constrained by the conditions which would be associated with a leasing contract. This gives me a high degree of flexibility in how I operate the fleet and replace it, without which I believe the level of service I provide to customers would be diminished, with a detrimental effect on front-line policing.

For example, I can buy and sell vehicles with ease to reflect operational requirements and priorities and retain vehicles after planned replacement if there is a need. This might be to expand the fleet size to cope with peaks in demand - such vehicles are known as 'Double Runners' - and will be disposed of in the normal way when the temporary need for them has disappeared.

Occasionally, there have been problems with capital provision in that there are many competing demands on the fixed capital cake such as IT Projects, Estates and Body Armour so that Fleet might not get sufficient funds to cover its entire planned vehicle replacement programme in a given financial year.

When this happens, those vehicles scheduled for replacement are assessed by the workshop managers to determine which can have their replacement deferred until the following year. This process works well and I have managed to maintain an average fleet age of just over 3 years.

For job-use cars, how do you decide which vehicles to acquire?

Selecting vehicles for the wide variety of police roles is a complex process that takes into account many factors. These include, in no particular order, the existing fleet mix, whole life costs, manufacturer and dealer support, parts availability, technical expertise, availability of specialist tools, fuel type, performance, load capacity (both payload and load space), environmental considerations, NCAP ratings and compliance with national framework agreements. To keep abreast of the latest vehicles I regularly obtain demonstrators for evaluation by our Driving School and operational officers; this helps inform future fleet purchasing decisions.

The overall choice of vehicles available to UK police forces is largely decided upon by the NAPFM (National Association of Police Fleet Managers) working in partnership with NPIA (National Policing Improvement Agency) Procurement.

All UK police fleet managers are members of NAPFM, with representatives on various committees such as Procurement, Technical and Benchmarking.

Police fleet managers work very closely with vehicle manufacturers and suppliers of equipment (eg: light bars, load carriers etc) to ensure that safety remains the number one priority when developing police specification vehicles.

NPIA goes out to tender for vehicles every 3 to 5 years against a comprehensive specification of characteristics required in the police environment. These vehicles fall into two categories; 'Restricted Badge' and the others.

Restricted Badge (or Police Specification) is split into Low, Intermediate and High Performance and each of these three groupings contains a small number of vehicles, usually used in a marked and/or response role, from which fleet managers can select.

Others encompass everything else such as vans, 4x4s and the remaining cars (not on the Restricted list) used for more general duties such as CID etc.

Fleet managers do have an element of choice from within the list of vehicles available in these 'Framework Agreements'; in Cambridgeshire, as mentioned earlier, we are largely a Ford-based fleet (including Volvo).

There is an historical element to this in that we have been with Ford for decades, well before I took over, and a lot of our processes and technician training is geared towards Ford. This marque has served us well over the years and it has to be recognised that there is a cost to change so I would not consider such a move without looking at the wider picture.

Having said that, for the last six years I have dual-sourced my response cars from both Ford (Focus) and Skoda (Octavia). This gives a little resilience, were there to be a recall for example, as not all vehicles would be affected. Manufacturer recalls that ground significant numbers of police vehicles are, however, thankfully uncommon.

NAPFM's Procurement and Technical Committees work closely with vehicle manufacturers to assess the suitability of Restricted Badge vehicles for use in the police environment. This covers some of the issues already mentioned such as performance (acceleration, top speed, handling and braking), payload, CO_2 emissions, NCAP ratings etc.

In addition, on the safety side, vehicles have to be checked for electrical emission compliance by NPIA's Automotive and Electrical Section. This department has immense expertise in evaluating the electrical performance of vehicles in relation to EMC (Electromagnetic Compatibility) and radio frequency with regard to both vehicles and specialist electrical equipment such as light bars, sirens and ANPR.

There can be instances where the electrical emissions from vehicle components such as the ECU (Electronic Control Unit) could interfere with police equipment fitted to the vehicle such as the radio, thus causing problems with possibly missing a critical radio message or in evidence gathering. Equally, the electrical equipment installed in our vehicles needs testing for emissions to make sure these do not interfere with the working of the car eg: affect the operation of ABS, airbags etc.

The current contracts reduce the choice of Restricted Badge make/models considerably from those previously available thus getting closer to a 'standard' police car and achieving economies of scale in pricing. All options are now diesel apart from at the high-performance end (such as Roads Policing Unit (RPU) and Armed Response Vehicle (ARV)) where both diesel and petrol options are available.

What replacement cycles do you operate for your fleet?

Replacement cycles vary depending on the role of the vehicle.

For example, the Volvo V70s used by the Traffic and Firearms departments are replaced at 3 years/150,000 miles. Beyond this period the vehicles are out of their (extended) warranty so any major component failures can then become quite costly causing maintenance budgets to overspend; whilst the warranty is in force these costs can more easily be predicted and budgeted for.

Additionally, after three years very intensive work, I would be reluctant to retain high performance vehicles much beyond their replacement parameters from a safety and reliability perspective.

Our Ford Focuses and Skoda Octavias have differing replacement cycles depending on their operational role. Those used as marked response cars are 3 years/100,000 miles whilst plain ones, used in less taxing roles such as CID and the Pool are replaced at 5 years/80,000.

Vans and motorcycles tend to be replaced every 5 years and specialist vehicles such as Protected Personnel Carriers and Mobile Police Stations every 7 years, or even longer, reflecting their relatively low usage.

These replacement parameters are part of the vehicle record on our fleet management IT system, allowing me to run off a replacement programme for each financial year and cost it up as part of my Capital Budget submission.

Replacement cycles influence fleet size. An older, less reliable, fleet would actually need to be larger to maintain a given level of mobility, as theoretically more vehicles would be off the road awaiting repair at any one time. This would, in turn, have a knock-on affect on workshop capacity. At present our replacement parameters, fleet size and workshop capacity are in equilibrium, allowing me to maintain vehicle availability of around 96% ie: at any one time approximately 20 of the fleet of 490 is in the workshop for scheduled or unscheduled repair.

Finally, in order to optimise whole life costs it is important to dispose of vehicles at the right point. They inevitably become more expensive to operate as running costs rise and residual values fall. I aim to dispose of them whilst they still have a reasonable residual value rather than run them into the ground when they would be virtually worthless.

Police workshop

In reality, these replacement parameters merely indicate when vehicles are eligible for replacement and in the final reckoning it is the overall condition of each vehicle, plus the likely cost of future maintenance, that dictates when replacement will actually take place. So, whilst some vehicles will be replaced later than planned, some others may be replaced earlier than planned because their condition warrants this.

Do you offer your employees a fixed list of cars to choose from or is it a user-chooser fleet?

The only allocated cars in the fleet are those operated by the ACPO level officers and the Superintendents. ACPO (Association of Chief Police Officers) is a national association made up of senior police officers from each force (usually Chief Constable, Deputy Chief Constable and Assistant Chief Constable – although the titles may be different in some forces). Other than in clarifying this, my references to ACPO in this chapter relate to ACPO level officers within forces rather than the Association as a whole.

There is some flexibility in the choice of ACPO level cars, but with a price ceiling depending on rank, although the vehicles must be suitable for policing purposes (ie: act as a command platform so be of a sufficient size, payload etc) and fit in with the existing fleet manufacturer profile.

The Superintendents all operate the same type and specification of car which is determined following thorough evaluation of alternatives by the users and recommendation by me in order to obtain force, ACPO and Police Authority agreement. Again, the chosen vehicle must fit in with the existing fleet profile and be fit for policing purposes.

Are there any vehicles you would not allow onto your fleet?

There would not normally be any need for convertibles or 2-seat sports cars etc on the fleet although I know that some other police forces have used such vehicles either in a covert role or, at the opposite extreme, in a high-visibility marked one.

Also, any vehicle with prohibitive whole life costs, where a lower cost alternative could do the job just as well, would probably be difficult to justify unless there was a sound business and operational justification for having that particular type of vehicle on the fleet.

Any police vehicle is simply a tool to facilitate an officer in carrying out their duties so, first and foremost, a vehicle must be fit for purpose and safe for the role expected of it. This in itself helps separate the wheat from the chaff in deciding which vehicle best suits a particular role.

It is inevitable that some of the larger cars operated in the fleet will tend to be luxury marques. Experience has shown that operating vehicles from these prestige manufacturers can create adverse opinion from some individuals; in the past we have received letters from members of the public in relation to such cars which they have considered 'extravagant' and asked 'why don't we buy British?'

The usual response to such comments is that there are now few mainstream British car manufacturers in existence from which we could buy and even if there were, European law requires tendering at a Europe-wide level. In addition, the vehicles have to meet the specifications laid out by NAPFM and NPIA referred to earlier. Ultimately, the question has to be asked whether a Honda built in Swindon is more British than a Ford built in Spain?

Have you taken any steps recently to reduce your fleet costs?

Several years ago I started purchasing silver cars instead of white for marked response use. This was principally due to the better residuals of metallic colours over white and also I thought they looked better. The additional cost of metallic paint was far exceeded by the increase in auction prices over identical cars in white. Our marked Traffic and Firearms vehicles are now purchased in dark metallic blue, although silver is still the chosen colour for most of the remaining response vehicles. Only vans are now purchased in white.

Over the last few years the fleet has moved across from petrol to diesel as part of our diesel policy, the two foundations of which are to provide cost and environmental benefits. A targeted approach has been made with several petrol vehicles being changed earlier than their replacement cycle in order to accelerate the changeover.

Unfortunately, the widening gulf between diesel and petrol prices in 2008 has not helped with the cost issues but I am still committed to diesel and the only petrol vehicles still purchased are those used in high performance roles where a diesel alternative which meets our requirements is not currently available. Thus, the fleet is now about 80% diesel whereas ten years ago the only diesel vehicles were the vans.

With forecourt prices at their current level it is important that officers purchase fuel from the cheapest retailers in their area, referring to fuel price websites when necessary.

There is also, now, a much greater emphasis on measuring utilisation of our fleet. In the police environment utilisation is a combination of hours used and, in some cases to a lesser extent, mileage.

For example, a police vehicle could be parked outside somebody's house whilst an officer takes a statement or collects evidence. In such an instance the vehicle is being utilised ie: helping the officer do their job - even though it is not being driven.

I am currently in the process of implementing a force-wide electronic key management system which will measure key usage, and therefore utilisation, as well as collecting mileage data. It is hoped that this will lead to significant cost savings when it goes live in 2009 as under-utilised vehicles could be disposed of or reallocated to locations where a need for them is identified.

Another development which has provided cost benefits is the installation of IDRs (Incident Data Recorders – 'Black Boxes') to the fleet. This started about five years ago and the majority of vehicles now have them.

The driving force behind the IDRs was Corporate Governance (Duty of Care) and a desire to take a positive stance to reduce police vehicle accidents. As well as reducing the Constabulary's exposure to risk and possible litigation it has added to its reputation as a responsible organisation committed to improving safety not only for its own employees but also for other road users and pedestrians.

Our IDRs collect data regarding speed, acceleration, braking, gravitational forces and whether items such as lights and siren are in use or not. The technology protects officers as it can easily settle disputes when, for example, a member of the public states they did not see the police car because 'its lights weren't on'. This can save hours of investigation and avoid paying out for possibly spurious claims. In the event of a serious collision where injuries or death might occur, the data from the Black Box can provide a picture of the circumstances of the incident at a 'forensic' level which can be admissible in court should the need arise.

The data from collisions can also proactively be used to inform driver training needs and possibly influence future vehicle purchasing strategies.

One of the most recent initiatives I have become involved with is the NAPFM Benchmarking which most police fleet managers participate in. All police fleet managers strive for continuous improvement and by submitting data sets containing fleet costs, vehicle downtime, utilisation and mileage etc some very powerful Key

Performance Indicators (KPIs) can be created. These in turn allow fleet managers to find out from their colleagues, who may have more favourable KPIs in some areas, how they are achieving this. In so doing, everyone's game is raised and the ultimate benefit is to the front line officers using our service and the public purse through greater efficiencies and adoption of Best Practice.

How much have you saved as result of making these changes?

It is difficult to quantify savings against an economic background of ever-increasing costs but certainly if we had not introduced these measures costs would have risen even further.

IDRs have reduced accident costs and wear and tear on vehicles as officers have started to drive less harshly. In their first year of use the number of motor insurance claims reduced by 20% which was broadly in line with what other users of IDRs had experienced.

In terms of the key management system it is anticipated that after paying for itself within 18-24 months, it will lead to further savings in future years through more robust management of vehicle keys and improved, more timely, fleet management data, as vehicle allocations become more tuned in with where the actual demand for vehicles is as demonstrated by key usage.

The greatest savings I achieve are actually those made through using the NPIA Framework Agreements mentioned earlier. As well as vehicles and spare parts, they also cover areas such as replacement glass, fuel, lubricants, tyres, auction services, light bars and the benchmarking consultancy work.

Nationally, police fleet managers spend around £201m annually through these agreements and reap annual savings of over £42m; Cambridgeshire spends about £3m and saves about £500,000 annually.

How do you manage your supplier relationships to ensure you obtain a high quality service?

By and large we have very good relationships with suppliers, often going back many years. The NPIA-contracted Restricted Badge manufactures have dedicated police fleet personnel who keep closely in touch, know our business, and are proactive in finding solutions to our needs. They host police liaison meetings, open days, and there are review meetings between suppliers and NPIA to ensure everything goes smoothly. I encourage equipment suppliers to work closely with the vehicle converters I use to ensure workable and quality finished vehicles provided in a seamless way.

More recently, Volvo have produced a 'Turnkey' solution patrol car where Volvo representatives in the UK, working with their engineering colleagues in Sweden, and in conjunction with the NAPFM Technical Committee and the Police Federation, have developed a factory-equipped and approved roads policing patrol vehicle. This innovative project provides a significant benefit to the UK police service in that the vehicle manufacturer has taken on board a significant risk and responsibility for the commissioning process and delivery of a police car 'out of the box' which has been crash-tested in its finished state.

Other manufacturers, in producing similar factory built police cars, are allowing police forces to reduce their exposure to the risk of corporate manslaughter by knowing that no compromise to the original vehicle build has occurred during the commissioning process. As a significant user of Volvo patrol cars I will be looking to operate one of their Turnkey vehicles on trial at the earliest opportunity.

Although all our vehicles are purchased directly from the manufacturers, rather than franchised dealers, the latter are generally used for PDI (Pre Delivery Inspection) and also to supply spare parts and carry out warranty work. They also provide technical advice when needed and are usually able to provide some priority in turning our vehicles around quickly when in their care.

All our accident repair work is outsourced to a number of body shops within Cambridgeshire and they, too, give our vehicles priority in order that the downtime is kept to a minimum.

How have you gone about advising employees on tax and legislative issues?

Vehicle tax issues are not really applicable in police fleets apart from those cars allocated to ACPO level officers and the Superintendents where there is an element of personal use. However, advice of this nature is supplied by a specialist in our Finance Department when required. This individual also provides similar tax advice to employees using their own vehicles for Constabulary business - the 'Grey Fleet' - although this aspect of transportation does not, for the moment at least, fall within my remit.

In terms of legislative issues, all vehicle users have to follow stringent pre-driving and weekly checking of Constabulary vehicles. These include checking condition of tyres, fluids and any damage as well as ensuring vital police equipment such as signs and cones are all present and in a serviceable condition; it is too late when officers need these at the scene of an incident to find they are not there.

Do you have any alternatively-fuelled cars on your fleet?

We had a couple of Ford Fiesta Courier petrol/LPG vans used on the internal mail service about ten years ago but the LPG conversion (which was an aftermarket one) was not very reliable so the vehicles tended to be driven mainly in petrol mode, therefore providing little data to assess the effectiveness of the vehicles.

In those days we also had problems with LPG availability; there were no mainstream retailers of LPG in the county then so we had to obtain it from sources such as the local council and a caravan centre. Although we were 100% fuel card we found they were not accepted at these locations. This added extra paperwork to the process in terms of invoicing and entering fuel issues to our fleet management IT system so really, overall, LPG was not a success story for us.

Currently, we have four Honda Civic IMA pool cars which are petrol/electric technology. Apart from these our current environmental policy is to use diesel although I am interested in looking at hydrogen fuel cells when an economically-viable solution becomes available, though I suspect this may not be in my working lifetime! I also understand some manufacturers are looking at diesel/electric hybrid technology which, given our mainly diesel fleet, is more relevant to me than petrol/electric hybrids.

I have talked to some other police fleet managers who have suggested that installing police equipment such as light bars, sirens and radios in hybrid vehicles could negate the benefits of the hybrid technology because of the large electrical draw of these items. Partly for this reason, as well as performance issues, I have not so far introduced any hybrid vehicles to front line service.

When you try to make changes to the way the fleet is run, do you encounter any resistance within the organisation?

I have no real problems in this respect. I ensure that Fleet has a consistently high profile within the organisation and the force ACPO team are very supportive of the department and the initiatives I suggest as, indeed, are the vast majority of users, borne out from customer satisfaction surveys I undertake periodically.

The Constabulary is split into Divisions which have Vehicle User Groups (VUG) made up of a spectrum of operational users. However, it is important to manage expectations as officers invariably want the sportiest and fastest cars!

It is also important for me to take a corporate view of the fleet otherwise each Division could end up with its own distinctive fleet profile made up of different makes and models. As well as considerably adding to costs it would detract from the corporate image the fleet strives to portray.

To determine which vehicle is used for a particular role, users provide a specification of what they need in order to do their job eg: performance (acceleration/top speed/handling), payload, load space etc. I then put a badge to this based on what is available through the NPIA contracts and bearing in mind what our Regional partner forces, who we collaborate with on many fleet issues, are using.

One of the biggest changes I have made was the transition from petrol to diesel cars. In the early 1990s, before I became fleet manager here, a number of the response cars were Ford Escort 1.8 diesels, purchased without power steering to save money. Their sluggish performance and heavy steering meant they were universally hated by officers and used as little as possible when alternative vehicles were available. I was even questioned at my interview what I would do to resolve this issue! I suggested that if the cars were that unpopular early disposal and replacement with equivalent petrol Escorts should be considered. I got the job and this is exactly what I did.

Potentially, after these early experiences with diesel, going back to that fuel again only a few years later could have been a difficult concept to 'sell'. However, diesel engines had improved dramatically and evaluation of demonstrators showed the vehicles now 'passed muster'. Since that time, virtually all cars purchased have been diesel apart from the high performance ones and the users have not had cause to complain.

Another potentially difficult situation was when it was decided to install Incident Data Recorders in cars. However, by engaging stakeholders in working parties from the outset, such as officer representatives and the Police Federation, once again the transition went smoothly so that now officers express disappointment if they have an incident in a vehicle which does not have a Black Box installed.

You have been a police fleet manager for 12 years. How do you think fleet management has changed since you first became involved?

In terms of fleet management generally I think the greatest two changes I have seen since I started with Cambridgeshire in 1996, following fourteen years working within the Fleet Department of British Gas, have been in the areas of Duty of Care and the Environment.

At first these new areas were perhaps seen as add-ons to the day job but they have now been assimilated into 'Business as Usual' and are now an integral part of fleet operation.

In addition, In terms of police fleet management specifically, there has always been a need to demonstrate that we are providing 'Best Value' to the force we serve; this does not necessarily mean being the cheapest, as quality of service is extremely important too, and there is an old adage that if you buy cheap you buy twice.

Police departments, including Fleet, are subject to regular scrutiny from bodies such as Her Majesty's Inspectorate of Constabulary (HMIC), external auditors and in-house functions and, as such, always need to demonstrate they are operating in a cost-effective and customer-focused manner.

Whilst we have moved on from the Best Value regime of a few years ago, which was followed by enforced force mergers (these were eventually dropped) the emphasis now is on collaborative working.

Cambridgeshire currently works very closely with the neighbouring Essex, Norfolk and Suffolk fleet management teams in order to realise the benefits that collaboration can bring. An early, ongoing, initiative is to establish a Regional Vehicle Catalogue thus harmonising the vehicles used for each of the roles across the four forces. This includes standardising the fitted equipment such as light bars, sirens and livery so that future vehicles will be identical apart from the force crest and the communications equipment.

This will provide economies of scale when we purchase vehicles and equipment, allow faster replacement of write-offs (as there should be a greater pool of standard new vehicles being commissioned at any one time), and increase driver familiarity. The best practices of each of the forces will be adopted across the region to provide the best possible vehicles for officers to drive.

Have you made any significant changes recently to the way you manage your fleet?

Most changes to the fleet tend to be incremental rather than anything that could be considered significant. However, the collaborative working with our partners in Essex, Norfolk and Suffolk is likely to bring about one of the biggest changes so far seen in the way we operate in terms of setting out to standardise the vehicles used in each role and also, wherever possible, harmonise practices and procedures.

In terms of the past, one of the biggest changes I made when I joined the Constabulary in 1996 was to raise the profile of the Fleet department within the organisation and make it more customer-focussed. This I was able to do in a fairly short timescale making use of the skills and experience I had obtained in my previous 14 years with British Gas.

Would you recommend that other police service fleet managers follow the same course you have?

Although there are a lot of similarities in the way police forces, and therefore police fleets, operate nationally there can be differences based on, for example, geography and demographics so one size certainly does not fit all.

Clearly, the large forces operating in densely-populated metropolitan counties are going to have different policing priorities and challenges than those operating in sparsely-populated rural counties and this will be reflected in the composition of the vehicle fleet. Some of these counties do not have motorways, for example, so there may not be a requirement for high performance Traffic cars. Others have rivers or coastline which means that water-borne craft may be part of the fleet manager's remit.

Other police forces may have significant strategic centres within their area such as international ports or airports or major stadia so this too will be reflected in the fleet make up with, for example, a need for specialist armoured vehicles.

I know that some of the Scottish forces, particularly those covering remote areas, do not have sufficient (if any) coverage of franchised dealers for the vehicles they operate so cannot obtain manufacturers' original equipment parts in a timely fashion. There are also logistical challenges when the nearest police workshop may be over 100 miles away. Thus, some of these forces may have to use independent repairers and non-original parts in order to maintain their fleet operation.

In many respects, what is important in fleet management is the output (ie: the service the customer receives). How it is done (the behind-the-scenes input) is down to the fleet manager, based on the resources at their disposal whilst obviously working within legislation, policies and procedures. All police fleet managers are highly professional and network with colleagues regularly, so often pick up or pass on new ideas and are always seeking best practice.

The reporting lines of fleet managers, and thus where fleet sits within the organisation, also varies between police forces and can have an affect on the amount of freedom the individual enjoys.

In many, such as Cambridgeshire, Fleet is part of the Finance directorate but in some forces fleet managers report to a senior police officer or are part of the procurement department. This can inevitably lead to differences in the way the fleet manager operates (input) but hopefully the service provided (output) will be much the same.

I would, therefore, not necessarily say that other police fleet managers should follow all my courses of action because they might not work or be appropriate in a differently-structured organisation. I know, for example, that in some forces white marked cars are still the norm because that is what ACPO locally insists on.

Having said that, I feel that in any organisation vehicles are always a very emotive issue and every driver thinks they are a fleet manager! It is therefore important to engage stakeholders, including drivers (who just happen to be mostly police officers in my case) in the decision-making process, so even if they don't always get what they want they do understand the rationale for the decisions made and know their views have at least been listened to.

In my 30-year career in fleet I know that whether it is buses, gas vans or police cars, if you give drivers vehicles they do not like some will not show them respect and will do whatever they can to defect them. This makes the job more difficult for everyone and impedes the smooth and effective working of the organisation. In a business as critical as policing this simply cannot be an option.

How do you dispose of your vehicles?

Police forces nationally use an NPIA contract for vehicle disposal which has been awarded to BCA. In Cambridgeshire, BCA have a branch in Peterborough which is not far from our vehicle workshop in the city so we are able to drive vehicles there and save on the collection charge!

BCA provide specialist police sales and provide good management information as part of the contract, showing data such as total and average sale values by month, sale price versus reserve and sale price versus CAP Clean.

Whilst it is recognised that most police vehicles are high mileage and often are peppered with dents and grazes (or worse!) there is actually a strong market for them. Buyers from all over the country attend these sales and, quite frequently, hammer prices are far in excess of the reserves I agree with BCA.

Probably one of the main attractions of police vehicles is that they have been maintained to a strict regime yet sell at lower prices than equivalent vehicles from non-police sources and therefore offer good value for money.

Whilst BCA is our principal outlet for disposals I do send some vehicles to other auctions in order to spread them around (in the hope of keeping residuals higher than if I flooded the market) and to benchmark residual values between auctions.

I am always seeking incremental ways of maximising residual values. As already mentioned, some years ago I moved over to silver then metallic dark blue for high performance cars, and this has increased values above equivalent white cars.

More recently, with some of our more prestigious vehicles, such as Volvo V70 T5s and Range Rovers, I have sent these to the bodyshop prior to auction. Here, any holes left by removal of police equipment, particularly in the roof, can be professionally filled in (rather than just inserting rubber bungs) and re-sprayed. This work costs around £700 but has added around twice this amount to the residual value.

Also, until recently, our vehicles were sold 'As Seen' without service histories, the hammer price reflecting this. Following sale, I would frequently be contacted by the buyer of the vehicle requesting the service history. This was declined on the basis they had purchased the vehicle knowing it had no history (either directly at auction or as a subsequent buyer from a trader) at a correspondingly lower price than if history had been provided.

Recognising that it is relatively easy to print off the service details from our fleet IT system these are now provided when vehicles are auctioned. As well as probably adding a small amount to the residual value they deflect these subsequent enquiries from buyers.

John P Robinson BSc MCIT MILT
Fleet Manager
Cambridgeshire Constabulary
john.robinson@cambs.pnn.police.uk

Creating a safer
Cambridgeshire

8

MANAGING A LARGE FLEET

John Wills FICFM
Fleet Manager
Prudential plc

Please tell us about your vehicle fleet.

I will give you a very short background to the Prudential Group so that you can understand where the UK fleet fits into the Group structure. There are five businesses across the globe. One of these businesses is Prudential UK and Europe whose strategy is to concentrate on those areas of retirement saving and income markets where it can generate attractive returns, capitalising on its longevity experience, multi-asset management capabilities, brand and financial strength.

Within Prudential UK some employees are entitled to receive a company car by way of job role or by way of grade.

The current fleet is made up of 477 vehicles with the majority of these based around the three regional centres of London, Reading and Stirling and the remainder spread over the rest of the UK.

The UK fleet consists of two schemes, a business user scheme for employees who are in sales roles and a status user scheme where the company car is part of the remuneration package for those office based employees eligible through their grade.

The composition of the fleet is very similar to other financial service companies whose head office is in the City of London, in that it mainly comprises of cars and very few LCVs. It is well known that employees of financial services companies tend to choose the makes that combine the perceived brand image and quality especially associated with the German makes. It is worth noting that many of the other non-German manufacturers are now building cars to the same or similar quality and as such it is likely that these cars will become more popular.

The brands of Audi, BMW, Volkswagen and Mercedes comprise over 50% of the total Prudential UK fleet numbers with the remainder made up of nearly every other popular make.

The split between different fuel types is 62% diesel, 37% petrol and 1% petrol/hybrid. There has been a slight change back to petrol driven cars in the last six months with the introduction of more efficient petrol models being made available.

Do you offer your employees a fixed list of cars to choose from or is it a user-chooser fleet?

The question of offering a fixed list of cars or a free choice is one that always comes to light at every annual car scheme review.

The cars on the fleet are not adapted or highly specialised to do specific jobs. There a thousands of cars available in the UK that are fit for purpose for our employees to drive on company business on the national road network in the course of their duties. This makes the task of choosing vehicles to be added to the vehicle list much simpler. There are certain vehicle exceptions but these exceptions are based on other criteria such as financial reasons or passenger capacity.

At Prudential we genuinely believe that our people are our greatest asset. A competitive benefits package is very important in tailoring an individual's needs as those needs are unique and each individual has different priorities.

In the same way that the company allows flexible working practices and offers a flexible benefits package where employees can choose from a selection of benefits such as, extra holidays, private medical or cycle to work scheme, we also offer the employees entitled to a company car a user chooser car scheme. Offering a free choice of car helps to both retain and attract employees to the company.

It is likely that if we offered a single or dual badge scheme, the company could possibly save money on the purchase cost due to higher discounts being made available by manufacturers, but this would have a negative effect on the perception of the company and car scheme overall and the advantages as outlined above of this user chooser scheme. We do discuss on a regular basis the introduction of a fixed choice of just a few different makes and models but the financial advantage would not be enough to dispense with the current free choice (with restrictions).

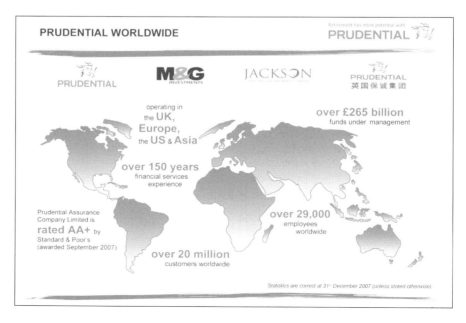

As with most user chooser schemes we allow employees to 'trade up' to a better car by contributing more in the way of a personal use contribution and to 'trade down' by giving a cash balance for those employees who choose a car with a running cost less than their allowance.

The current choice list encompasses the majority of cars available in the UK but with restrictions. There are two main restrictions, one is that no cars with either two seats or two plus two seats are allowed and a second is an environmental consideration.

The reasons for no two seat cars are:

*   Business users would not be able to accommodate more than one client in the car
*   Two seat cars have a very limited reallocation market within the company.

We try to utilise every car on the fleet by reallocating cars from employees who have left, to either, new employees or employees who are due to change their existing company cars. An incentive in the form of a reduction in personal contribution helps to make these returned cars attractive, and the company benefits where the total reduction in personal contribution over the remainder of the car's contract is less than the early termination cost the company would otherwise incur.

The environmental considerations were brought in during 2004, long before the recent price rise in fuel costs and the current popular move towards greener motoring.

We do not allow cars over a certain CO_2 limit for the following reasons.

*   We realised that cars with high CO_2 emissions were not in line with our environmental policy
*   These cars tended to be expensive to run and attracted a very high personal use contribution thereby making them next to impossible to reallocate due to the high costs even after a reduction in the personal use contribution.

How does your allocation policy work?

Some fleets use list price or contract hire rates to determine which car certain grades of employees can choose. This is not really the most accurate method of knowing how much each car is going to cost the company in its life.

We use the method of calculating the whole-life cost for each vehicle which whilst it may not always be entirely accurate due to residual value fluctuations, is far more scientific than the other two methods. Taking industry data plus our historical maintenance data, insurance costs and national insurance contributions we are in the best position to know the total cost of the fleet over its life. You may have noticed that I have not included fuel in the calculation, but this is deliberate as it is classed as a business cost in much the same way as travel on public transport and other associated business expenses claimed by employees.

Whole–life costing therefore enables us to compare every car available on the scheme against each different grade of employee thereby determining a personal use contribution or cash balance for each car.

We have three grades in the Status user scheme and a further three grades in the Business user scheme. They all have the same choice of cars but with each grade given a different car allowance there is a differentiation between the levels of each employee grade.

This broadband grading system gives the employee the ability to choose a car that suits his need and this goes hand in hand with our flexible working policies. So for example any eligible employee can choose an expensive car or alternatively a small inexpensive car. The wide choice of cars is welcomed by all employees.

The administration involved in keeping this choice of cars up to date is minimal as all we need to do is add new vehicles when they are launched and delete old vehicles when they are no longer produced.

Please explain, in outline, how you manage your fleet.

At Prudential we currently perform those parts of the fleet administration where we feel we can add value.

The fleet department is responsible in conjunction with the Human Resources (HR) department for car policy and all operational tasks such as negotiating with suppliers, new car purchasing, driver management, cost centre management and disposals.

It is pointless trying to hold onto some tasks which plainly can be performed more effectively by a 3rd party supplier, so we use specialist suppliers for those different tasks.

Suppliers can offer a different type of expertise or provide technological input which the current in-house set up is not equipped to perform.

We do not automatically appoint one supplier to perform all the outsourced tasks, but appoint the best supplier for each individual element. The advantages are that we are using the best and most suitable supplier for our requirements. If we encounter a major problem with a particular service, it is much easier to cease a contract with that one individual supplier than to be in dispute over one service with a supplier who is still providing other services for us. The disadvantage of not using one supplier for everything is that potentially we may not be benefiting from economies of scale. In our experience provided the individual suppliers are managed effectively this has not been the case.

The tasks that are currently outsourced are:
- Insurance claims handling
- Maintenance management
- Vehicle funding
- Driving licence checking

Insurance claims handling

This is provided by the fleet insurers under a fully comprehensive insurance policy. Claims reporting, assessment of damage, authorisation of repairs, uninsured loss recovery and personal injury administration all require sophisticated systems and specialist knowledge that no small fleet department could fully hope to emulate.

When the insurance policy is due for renewal we have a standard procedure to decide what type of insurance and policy is required moving forwards.

The options are:

- Fully comprehensive with choice of different excesses of £250, £500, £1000 etc.
- Third party only (where we pay for all our own damage).

Criteria that need to be met are:

- Coverage – try to get the best for our fleet structure and claims experience.
- Price – competitive pricing.
- Service – ensuring we receive the best level of customer service.
- Financial stability – although this is unlikely to be an issue, it is something to consider given the current financial climate.
- Flexibility – an insurer who responds quickly to requested policy wording changes and will happily adapt our policy to any change in our circumstances or ad hoc coverage requests.

We have always opted for fully comprehensive cover as it offers the least risk and the best value to the company.

MAINTENANCE MANAGEMENT

The management of the maintenance is something the fleet department used to do in the past. As the cost of maintenance is one of the major components in the cost of running a car, we outsourced this task to a specialist maintenance management company. They employ specialist maintenance controllers who use systems for checking labour rates, repair times and parts prices. They also help with post-warranty claims and act as a 'policeman' using zero tolerance invoice checking.

With a fleet of nearly 500 cars, we chose a 'pay on use' service rather than a fixed price contract per car. We pay less for maintenance than the industry average over the life of the cars on our fleet which are not driven especially hard.

This lower maintenance cost is helped by utilising the reduced labour rates and prices for tyres and windscreens which are negotiated by the maintenance management company using their total customer volumes as a lever to reduce prices.

VEHICLE FUNDING

The company funds the vehicle fleet with the same finance company it banks with. The vehicle finance contract is therefore part of the overall banking contract. Further details of the funding arrangements are given later.

DRIVING LICENCE CHECKING

Licence checking seems a very simple task but it is labour intensive. We use the DVLA mandate system where the company car drivers sign a mandate to authorise the electronic checking of their licence against the DVLA database. We use a supplier to send out mandates to our drivers on our behalf; they then send the mandates off to the DVLA and evaluate the results before putting them into an easily readable spreadsheet. This method highlights any exceptions or licences that should be closely monitored.

What method do you use to fund your vehicles, and why have you chosen this method?

As a financial institution our products are exempt from VAT and therefore we are not entitled to recover any input VAT. Contract hire is therefore out of the question and due consideration was given to other options such as: hire purchase, lease purchase, contract purchase or conditional sale to determine the best method for us.

- Our internal rate of return is high enough to make it more beneficial to finance the cars rather than use our own funds to outright purchase.

- The majority of our cars are classed as 'expensive 'cars for capital allowance purposes, costing over £12,000 and the value of company cars compared to the balance sheet is minimal.

- Conditional sale agreements work on the principle that you must purchase the vehicle at the end of the contract. This was not what we required as we wanted more flexibility.

- Contract purchase includes a maintenance agreement but we already had a maintenance agreement in place with one specialist supplier so that was not appropriate.

- End of contract control was required to give us the flexibility to keep the car for a longer period should the employee not be ready to choose a new vehicle. In this case we would pay the balloon payment at the end of the contract and continue to run what is now our own car.

- We also required the option of being able to return cars at the end of the contract should there be a dramatic fall in residual values, thereby minimising any losses. This return option was available but with restrictions.

The most appropriate method to fund the purchase of our company cars was therefore deemed to be a lease purchase arrangement.

With this option we do hold the residual risk and have the ability to sell the cars ourselves at contract end. Selling cars ourselves is only beneficial where there are good disposal avenues and the sale proceeds exceed the balloon payment after disposal costs.

You use a vehicle finance company to fund your fleet. Why did you choose them?

Historically we always outright purchased company cars but in the 1990s the company decided to complete a sales and leaseback of the fleet in order to release and reallocate funds to other investments.

We completed one of the biggest sale and leasebacks in the fleet industry and sold the fleet to a vehicle finance company owned by a high street bank. This bank had an existing relationship with the Prudential as it supplied the company with banking services.

Have you taken any steps recently to reduce your fleet costs?

It is important to conduct regular reviews as to how car schemes are run in order to keep up with new trends and changes in legislation and to ensure we continue to run a fleet that is cost effective and market competitive.

We have brought in measures over the last few years to reduce the running cost of the fleet, to save the company money and to provide a better benefit to the employees.

OUTSOURCE

As previously suggested it is not always advisable to outsource all fleet management tasks as the loss of control both in terms of service and costs can be a major problem.

Maintenance management was one area that was outsourced and has been a great success. It not only saved money but offered a substantially better service with access to much greater technical expertise and 24 hour cover which a fleet department could never match.

REALLOCATION

The early termination of cars is always a serious cost consideration. Unlike a contract hire agreement, under our finance agreement there is no termination charge because we are responsible for the residual risk.

The loss when selling a car before the end of its contract is really due to the steepness of the depreciation curve early on in the vehicle's life. In essence the sales proceeds are unlikely to equal or be greater than the capital owed to the finance company thereby creating a monetary loss. The average loss is usually between £3,500 and £4,000 with the actual loss dependent upon car, condition, age and mileage.

We have taken this aspect of loss very seriously and actively market on our internal intranet all cars that are returned early when employees leave the business and hand back their cars.

Cars are refurbished and exterior and interior photos are taken, before the car is marketed on the fleet intranet. A reduction in personal use contribution is offered to any member entitled to a company car who is due for a change of car or who currently takes the cash alternative.

The reallocation project has been helped by the change in policy towards more standard family type cars and excluding two seater cars and high CO_2 emitting cars from the car list.

The reallocation rate is now approaching a healthy 85%.

REDUCING CO$_2$ EMISSIONS

The change in policy four years ago to reduce total CO$_2$ emissions of the fleet was an environmental decision and has helped us more recently in a number of ways.

Fuel consumption of higher polluting vehicles is generally greater than those of lower polluting vehicles. The price of fuel in 2004 was 81p per litre and it is now approximately 20% higher.

By reducing the type of cars employees can choose we save on reimbursement of fuel for business use.

Looking forward to April 2009, it is likely that the Writing Down Allowances (WDA) will be greater for those cars emitting below 160g/km of CO$_2$ than above. Our policy will help us to save money as we have more efficient cars on the fleet.

EMPLOYEE DRIVER FAULT EXCESS

We have introduced a personal excess to charge employees who have a driver fault insurance claim in their company car.

The charge was brought in as a deterrent to make drivers think about how safely they drive and to stop the drivers becoming complacent over rising company fleet costs.

Previously the company paid all excess charges without recharging that cost to the driver.

The charge increases if they have more than one driver fault incident in a 12 month period. The policy excess to the company is £250, so the initial charge is £75 rising to £125 for a second incident and £250 for a third.

This method is not usually effective in isolation but must be used in conjunction with end of contract charges.

END OF CONTRACT CHARGES

Much like the contract hire companies, who charge for unfair wear and tear if a car is returned in a condition that is not commensurate with age and mileage, we also reserve the right to levy an end of contract charge on our drivers.

This is very important otherwise there is a great temptation for a driver not to report an incident of damage to the company car, hoping to avoid the driver fault excess.

The maximum end of contract charge we can make is £500, which we feel is sufficient to cover most parking type incidents and is also higher than the driver fault excess.

In the past year the insurance claims ratio has reduced to below 30% giving us a saving on our insurance renewal premium.

It is vital to incorporate any charges such as those above within the company car policy to avoid disputes and financial loss.

How much have you saved as result of making these changes?

It is quite difficult to quantify exactly how much money has been saved by changing policy and processes and even harder to measure the hidden savings of improved service.

As an estimate, the tangible savings per annum on our fleet of c.500 cars have been:

Outsource maintenance management	£100,000
Reallocation policy	£ 80,000
Driver excess and end of contract charges	£ 30,000

And over the last year we have seen our insurance premium reduce by £24,000.

At the time of writing it is too early to calculate what effect the reduction in the number of cars with high CO_2 emissions will yield in savings.

Some fleet managers have been talking about extending leases, or lease periods, to keep costs down. Do you plan to do this?

At the present time we do not expect to extend the car contracts of any company cars. In our experience a good percentage of employees do not insist on replacing their company cars on the last day of their car contract but tend to take a relaxed view during the replacement stage. Many employees like to test drive and take their time choosing the correct car for their needs.

Under our finance arrangements we pay the balloon at the end of each contract so therefore we own the car from that date. Provided the maintenance costs are kept in check all we are paying is the depreciation on a car that is already 3 or 4 years old and this depreciation is smaller compared to a nearly new car due to its age. We therefore avoid having to buy the employee a new car immediately and delay suffering the depreciation of that new car until a later date.

In this situation it holds true that 'A good Fleet Manager invites their employees to replace their cars before the end of contract, but a very good one delays the invitation to help save money!'

In the current market I would expect lead times to increase as we hear of factories changing working patterns to producing only 3 or 4 days a week or shutting one week every month. This will also have the effect of increasing delivery times, which in turn helps the company.

How do you manage your supplier relationships to ensure you receive a high quality service?

Dealing with suppliers is one of the most interesting parts of the fleet manager's job. It is important to have a good relationship with all suppliers whether they are dealers, manufacturers or service providers. This will help to obtain the maximum benefit for the company.

We like to foster a partnership type relationship where the supplier feels they are also gaining as much from the association as the customer.

We use different methods to ensure a quality service is derived from the supplier and this is dependent on the product in question.

New Car Dealers

Dealers provide new cars, so networking with other fleet managers is a great way to find out about current discounts or offers and to get information on service levels.

Once a dealer is on board and supplying vehicles, regular contact with the dealer administration team and not just the sales manager is useful to build up a rapport and to teach them about the company's values and working methods.

After delivery, surveying the company car driver to ask questions about their contact with the dealer and their impressions is a good tool to use.

Manufacturers

Making yourself available seems on the face of it a very basic statement to make but it forms the basis of any dealings with manufacturers.

Once a manufacturer has their models on the choice list, regular face to face contact, three or four times a year to discuss different aspects of whole life running costs, discounts and after sales problems is needed to form a proper business relationship.

More frequent telephone and e-mail correspondence helps to resolve more urgent issues or queries.

Service Providers

Dealings with service providers are usually on a daily basis and service providers tend to have the most interaction with company car drivers. If the service from the supplier is not good, company car drivers are not normally shy in coming forward with their comments. This very quickly gives the fleet manager first hand knowledge of any shortcomings in the level of service.

As part of any contract, a comprehensive service level agreement with realistic key performance indicators (KPI) should be written to avoid deterioration in service. Penalty clauses within the contract if KPIs are not met can help to re focus the supplier to provide the service that was originally agreed upon.

Surveying drivers about service providers is another method we use to find out whether the service is as it should be.

How have you gone about advising employees on tax and legislative issues?

The Cars@Pru intranet site contains comprehensive information about the car policy and contribution and benefit in kind information.

At Prudential we have the ability to collect tax on company cars at source from each employee's monthly pay rather than having to complete P46 forms on a regular basis and P11D forms after the end of each tax year.

The advantages are:

- Less administration during one short period
- Employee's car tax position is always up to date
- The total cost of a company car to an employee is very simple to understand

We offer our eligible population the use of an on-line car selector program. This program includes all models of car available. It calculates both personal use contribution and benefit in kind tax for the model selected for the whole 3 or 4 year contract of the car. The employee is therefore informed of their tax liability on the car before they take delivery.

If new legislation is brought in which would affect the tax position of each employee, usually after a Budget, a letter is sent out to all company car users informing them of the change.

The intranet site and on-line selector system are also updated to inform any would-be company car users.

A number of Prudential employees take a cash allowance instead of a company car. How do you help them to make the Cash v Car decision?

The competitive benefits package gives those employees who are eligible for a company car under the Status user scheme the option of taking a cash allowance instead of a company car. Whilst we were keen to provide choice, we also made a business decision to not to promote car over cash or vice versa.

We realise that not everybody requires a car or they may already have a car at the present time so may wish to use the cash allowance to supplement their income.

We provide information on the intranet to offer advice and guidance on the costs of running a car.

It is a very simple task to show an employee how much a company car would cost per month by using the on-line car selector and taking into account how much car allowance they would forego if they took the company car.

Showing an example calculation really opens the eyes of employees to the true cost of running a car.

We use a calculation program that enables the employee to compare costs. It is however prone to user error as employees do not always know the accurate cost of insurance or their predicted mileage or fuel consumption rate. As a basic tool it is very useful.

Have you considered introducing an Employee Car Ownership Scheme or a Salary Sacrifice scheme?

Employee car ownership schemes (ECOS) have been considered in the past but the projects have never passed the initial stages.

ECO schemes work for some companies but the savings from these schemes are not guaranteed and have never found favour in the company because of the low business mileage travelled by our employees, high start up costs and unpredictability.

The fairness and fixed cost associated with company cars has been chosen over a scheme that is dependent on business mileage travelled, current tax legislation and mileage rates staying favourable.

Salary sacrifice is another topic that is discussed on a regular basis and can sometimes fit in well with flexible benefits systems. At the present time we do not run a salary sacrifice scheme.

Do you have any alternatively-fuelled cars on your fleet?

At Prudential we aim to comply with or exceed environmental legislation requirements at all our locations. We also continuously improve environmental performance and raise awareness among our employees. Part of the environmental policy involves including efficient vehicles on the company car scheme.

The introduction of highly efficient petrol or diesel fuelled vehicles in 2008 has given the company car user a greater choice of efficient vehicles even though they may not be alternatively fuelled. We recommend any cars that are more environmentally friendly than a typical standard car.

The take up of alternatively fuelled vehicles however has been quite low due to the small choice on offer from manufacturers.

Some of the issues citied by our employees as to the reason why they have not chosen these alternatively fuelled vehicles are that they are quite small and the performance of the CVT automatic type gearboxes have not been liked.

When you try to make changes to the way the fleet is run, do you encounter any resistance within the organisation?

Over the past few years we have reviewed many aspects of company car policy including:
- Car allowance
- Cost savings
- Allocation policy
- Contract period
- Company Car or ECO schemes
- Harmonisation of car schemes

In each case we worked closely with line managers and human resources, engaged with Union and employee representatives and took proposals to the Executive Board members.

Where we have implemented significant change, clear communication to employees has been a key part to the success of the rollout of new policy.

Collaborative working and thorough research has resulted in little if any resistance to the changes that have been put forward.

We have not had to engage with Union or Board members to introduce simple changes to the policy such a excluding certain makes/models.

Where there are legislative changes the fleet department works in partnership with the Tax and/or Payroll department to ensure any changes are implemented effectively.

How do you think fleet management has changed since you first became involved?

I have been a Fleet Manager for eight years and have worked in fleet management for nineteen years. Over that period I have obviously seen a lot of changes within the company and the industry as a whole. The following are some of the most significant changes that have happened to our fleet and fleet management generally:

- Fleet management has really changed in the last fifteen years from being just a job dealing with cars to a professionally run part of the company. The fleet department has needed to change due to changing pace of life and the increased expectations of both management and employees alike. There is now more emphasis on providing a better service at a lower cost.

- The Fleet Manager now has to be professionally qualified to obtain the position of Fleet Manager. In the past facilities managers and finance employees may have been given the job of looking after the fleet. Finance Directors now realise that the turnover of a fleet department can be quite substantial and managing the fleet requires specialist knowledge.

- There are more fleet management companies offering to take over the management of the fleet than ever before. Outsourcing can be a positive move if a company's current set up is not managed efficiently. On the negative side it can also cause problems and not be cost effective if the fleet management company is not properly managed.

- The introduction of computer databases to store details of vehicle, maintenance and finance data instead of using handwritten cardboard folios to store information. As you can imagine it is much easier to access data now than 19 years ago.

- Fleets similar to ours employ specialist help such as the maintenance management service. In the very early days we used to turn the answerphone on when we left the office and picked up the messages the next day to listen to the various calamities that happened overnight. Through outsourcing our maintenance management we are now able to provide twenty four hour cover.

- Fleet management generally is becoming more complex with increased legislation and red tape. In truth most of the changes are for the better and will be accommodated by any good Fleet Manager

Have you made any significant changes recently to the way you manage your fleet?

The most significant change to the running of our fleet was the introduction of the on-line car selector and ordering system.

The employees can now choose from a menu of cars that are specific to their grade and that adhere to the car policy.

The system produces quotes in real time giving the employee all the information they need to know about the specified car. Details of standard specification and extras, mpg and CO_2 figures and the all-important personal contribution and BIK tax amount are available at the touch of a button.

Once the car is requested we can send on this request electronically to a supplying dealer or dealers to get the fastest delivery time and best price.

The advantages are:

- Employees spend less (work) time manually calculating the cost of cars and more time performing their own jobs

- The information is current and easily accessible

- The system is easy to use so fewer mistakes are made by the employee and the fleet department

- The fleet department does not have to manually calculate figures for employees thereby saving significant time

- The car choice list can be refreshed in minutes rather than hours using manual spreadsheets

- Electronic ordering saves on paper and provides a good audit trail

- It provides a good reporting tool on number and type of orders and the performance of supplying dealers

Do you think it is essential to obtain professional qualifications and/or to join organisations such as ACFO?

I believe it is essential for any fleet employee to obtain professional qualifications such as those offered by The Institute of Car Fleet Management.

The courses offered by the ICFM give a really good grounding in every aspect of fleet management whether you work for a service provider, leasing company or a fleet management department.

It is not only the professional qualification you gain, although that will always help with future employment, but you also gain a network of contacts that you gradually build up as you pass through the stages of the education programmes. These contacts have been maintained and we regularly discuss the latest issues affecting our fleets.

Another networking opportunity is to join the Association of Car Fleet Operators (ACFO) which host meetings in regions all over the country on a bi-monthly basis.

ACFO usually ask a supplier to host a meeting, make a presentation and provide facilities where people in the fleet industry can discuss current topics.

ACFO also have a very good website for members with a library of interesting topics, links and information for the Fleet Manager.

Please tell us about your approach to risk management.

Since the Corporate Manslaughter bill was passed most companies have felt the need to review their polices to ensure compliance from a risk management perspective.

Our first task was to put in place a risk management strategy for employees driving on company business. In 2005 we completed an initial risk assessment to establish our compliance with legislation.

Since then we have purchased an electronic tool to enable us to collate data from both the company car users and those employees using a private car on company business, also known as the 'grey' fleet. The risk is assessed from both a corporate focus and a driver/employee perspective.

Would you recommend that other fleet managers follow the same course you have?

It is difficult to suggest other Fleet Managers should follow exactly the same course as we have at Prudential largely because each company's circumstances are different. What is more important is that they give due consideration to what is good practice.

Strong technical expertise is paramount and this can be gained both through experience, fleet publications and formal training. It is the publications and the formal training however that provide the more immediate knowledge to fleet employees, which they can use to their advantage in fleet management. These will give a good basic grounding of the principles of fleet management not just in the employee's current business but for all types of fleet that they may be involved with in the future.

At Prudential we have been encouraged to pursue formal qualifications. We have also been given scope to use the knowledge gained to influence decision making and implement changes to policies and procedures.

There are so many options available to a fleet manager with regard to: policy; allocation decisions; administration methods; financing requirements; tendering suppliers; health and safety etc and the list goes on. Each individual component must be right for the company and must gel together to provide the best service at the cheapest cost to the company.

In my experience I believe sourcing those components from suppliers who are at the top in their field is a better way of managing a fleet than using the supplier who offers the one stop shop approach.

John Wills FICFM
Fleet Manager
Prudential plc

Home > Cars at Pru

Cars at Pru

Pru Car Zone

Company Cars

Intranet home

Your feedback and comments

Cars at Pru

CARS AT PRU

At Prudential, we aim to provide our employees with flexibility, personal choice and value in the benefits we offer.

There are two broad categories of car provision within the car benefit:

- A car purchase scheme called Pru Car Zone that uses Prudential's buying power to give all employees in the UK the opportunity to buy their own new or used car at very competitive prices.

- A range of Company car schemes that offer an extensive choice of makes and models, plus associated benefits including fully comprehensive fleet insurance; annual road fund licence; full service and maintenance; UK and European breakdown cover and a 24-hour dedicated driver support helpline.

Click on the links to take you to the detail of the relevant schemes and to find more information to a wide range of related topics from different car manufacturers, model costings, HM Revenue and Customs car tax treatment, routefinder information and congestion charging.

Note on Benefit in Kind Taxation

The Inland Revenue have realigned the CO_2 threshold for benefit in kind tax on company cars from 6th April 2008. This means that the minimum threshold for cars has been reduced from 140g/km to 135g/km

9 FLEET POLICY

Paul Harrop
Sales and Marketing Director
Daimler Fleet Management

We hear a lot about fleet policy. What does it mean?

Fleet policy means different things to different people and, depending on the functional perspective held, can cover everything from financial acquisition method through car type to health and safety policies. In my opinion however, the fleet policy operated by a company should cover all areas and ultimately leave the driver, and the business, with a clear knowledge of their options and responsibilities.

Given this, a true fleet policy will cover what vehicles are allowed and whether any variations can be applied. It should also outline why these variations might be applicable and the sign-off process for authorisation. Trade up / trade down and cash alternative options must be fully documented with ideally some typical benefits examples.

The policy will determine the duration for which a driver will keep the vehicle and how many miles the vehicle can cover. Of less importance to the driver but significant to the company is how the vehicle should be funded and where it should be funded from, what services are to be taken with the funding and how a driver will obtain support for all the operational requirements.

Authorised use of the vehicle, restrictions on time to be spent in the vehicle and recommendations on breaks should all be included in the policy, as well as the fitting of accessories and use of mobile technology. The company's expectations on vehicle condition, both during the life of the vehicle and at the end of the contract should be clearly laid out, not forgetting the charges to the driver for breaches of this part of the policy.

The completeness of the policy is the key to ensuring its consistent application. A policy which is vague or unspecific may seem to offer flexibility to a company; however in the long term it will result in confusion and driver unrest. For a policy to succeed it must place both a level of responsibility and a penalty for failure on the driver.

How should a fleet manager determine an allocation policy?

This is the first stage of designing your fleet policy and comes before whether a company even wishes to offer company cars at all. There are a number of alternatives to the company car depending on tax, mileage covered and the role an employee is performing. However before the optimum solution can be derived a business must determine whether it wants to offer a mobility solution and to whom this solution should be provided.

In general, companies will split their vehicle allocation policy into two broad types, although of course the categorisation criteria can vary considerably.

Job / need employees – as the name suggests these are where mobility is needed by the employee to perform the job they are employed for. A sales person for instance or an engineer whose responsibility is to travel to customers on a regular basis. Vehicles in this category will normally cover a reasonable business mileage and may have specific load bearing / performance characteristics.

The perk / benefit employee – a mobility solution is provided as a result of the grade of the employee. Primarily offered to the employee as an extension of their salary package, this solution is essential in some industries to retain staff.

JOB / NEED EMPLOYEES

In the case of job / need employees it clear that a mobility solution is required and it is vital that this solution is controlled tightly by the business. These employees are representing you and visiting your customers, so the vehicle they arrive in will create an impression of your business. But what determines when an employee role requires a mobility solution? Most consider that a driver covering more that 500 miles per month on business should be included in this category and whilst this is not definitive it offers a good guide.

The requirement for you as a business is to ensure the solution you provide meets health and safety requirements, is cost-efficient and allows the optimum flexibility. Given these constraints most businesses opt for the provision of company vehicles in this category. It guarantees the vehicles are "fit for purpose" and is the simplest way of ensuring the employer's duty of care is maintained.

PERK EMPLOYEES

The perk employee position is not so clear. Firstly, if a driver covers any business mileage at all there is a requirement for you to ensure reasonable checks have been made to ensure the mobility they use is fit and able to satisfy health and safety requirements. However in most cases the need for a mobility solution for perk employees has been established as a historical offering and one that is mirrored within your industry. The solution will be differentiated as a mobility offering and separate from just salary.

Most perk allocations are made on the basis of employee grade although it is reasonable to differentiate further into business functions or skill disciplines as the market dictates.

An interesting extension to the normal mobility allocation policy has been seen recently as a result of employers wishing to offer a flexible benefits package to all employees. In this instance all employees can trade salary for a car allocation, sometimes known as a cash sacrifice. This should be considered separately to need employees.

How should a fleet decide which vehicles should be available for selection?

Once the need for a mobility solution has been identified the value of this solution must be found. The easiest way of determining this value is by identifying the optimum vehicle solution – the "benchmark vehicle". Irrespective of final provision method, identifying the best vehicle allows you to determine the costs and values involved in its provision, or the provision of an alternative. The method and considerations for selecting the best car are the same for both need and perk although the selection weighting will obviously be different.

Most fleets have been operating vehicles for a period of time so the selection of the benchmark vehicle is not that difficult. Clearly the vehicle must be able to do the job for which it is required; for instance you wouldn't give someone who is going to cover a lot of motorway driving a small-engined run-around. Health and safety considerations could include number of doors, load capability, electronic skid protection, and restriction of sports cars. Environmental considerations could include CO_2 emissions, use of hybrids and area of operation.

Type of fuel will have an impact on the costs of operation and the employee's benefit in kind taxation. Diesel fuel offers higher miles per gallon and normally lower emission levels, although petrol has significantly improved. However some drivers still prefer petrol vehicles. The selection of more expensive premium brand manufacturers may offer increased driver satisfaction at a cost to you and the individual.

In determining the optimum benchmark vehicle all the above factors should be considered in conjunction with the emotional effect of selection on your drivers. It is also sensible to take into consideration the needs of your business and the offers made by your competitors. The optimum benchmark vehicle will satisfy all the needs of the business and be an acceptable or even motivational solution for your employees. You can still decide to offer a lesser vehicle once you have determined the provision costs but this will then be an informed commercial decision.

Is it a good idea to have a fixed list of cars?

If a business decides to offer a company car based on the benchmark vehicle determined for the grade, they can offer this in a number of ways. Fixed lists can offer benefits to an employer as they ensure, dependent on how restrictive the list is, that vehicles are similar across that grade.

This has the benefit of budgeting your costs much more accurately and being able to compare running characteristics between drivers. Fixed lists will also drive volume into predetermined makes which may allow you to negotiate improved discounts with that manufacturer. Your staff will be able to understand the process easily and vehicle reallocation will be more palatable should a vehicle be released before its expiry date. The use of a list reduces the time spent by employees on the selection process and removes the chance that a driver may obtain a vehicle which has costs outside of the anticipated parameters.

Fixed lists do have their negatives as well however. The restriction may leave some drivers unhappy with the lack of choice. If costs of the vehicles in the list increase the employer will immediately have to bear these where with a totally free list, based on rental cost for instance, the employer could hold the rate for a period of time.

Fixed lists tend to be operated in need car sectors where motivation is secondary to ensuring that employees are able to perform their task fully. If using a fixed list be aware of the CO_2 values of the vehicles selected and try to offer vehicles which aren't at the top of your price band, so you can maintain the list over a longer period.

Is a good idea to allow employees to choose their own cars?

This is the alternative to operating a fixed list policy and the key to its success is determining the selection criteria to be used. Policies vary hugely and can be based on cost aspects from manufacturers' list price through to true cost to the business. Variations on this theme include CO_2 restrictions, badge restrictions and fuel restrictions.

The main issue in using an open choice based selection system is that the costs to the business are controlled and remain reasonably predictable. The use of any selection system which does not take into account the dealer discount, final purchase price, residual value or the maintenance costs would leave a business extremely exposed. A perfect selection system would take all the costs mentioned into account as well as employer's national insurance and fuel. Unfortunately including employer national insurance is complex and not generally available. The most optimum solution readily available from sources such as "What Car" and all the contract hire suppliers is the whole life cost of a vehicle. This provides a cost per month figure for the vehicle over a fixed mileage and term parameter.

By allowing a driver to choose any vehicle up to the whole life cost allowance, the employer ensures that costs are capped whilst the employee has choice of the vehicle they prefer. The selection can still be restricted, eg no sports cars or two doors, for operational or image reasons, to ensure the vehicle remains appropriate for business use.

The remaining cost fluctuation risks of employer NI can be controlled by restricting the CO_2 emissions. However most businesses believe these are self-controlling. A high CO_2 emission will have high fuel costs and therefore high whole life costs. This would exclude it from choice.

What are whole life costs?

Whole life costs are the total cost that can be associated with the running of a vehicle over a set period and mileage. They are made up of the depreciation, interest, maintenance, service, road fund licence and fuel. Whole Life costs primarily differ from contract hire costs as they include the fuel cost. Fuel is a key cost element which can fluctuate considerably from vehicle to vehicle. To ensure a choice list operates effectively it must therefore include fuel costs.

Whole life costs are generally agreed to be the best, readily available, running cost comparison.

Some companies offer the option to trade up / trade down. How does this work?

The option to trade up or down normally arises when an employer wishes to offer more flexibility to the employee. This allows an employee to pick a better vehicle than the norm and pay for the difference out of their own salary, or to select as lower vehicle and receive the saving.

A trade up / down policy can be operated within a fixed choice list: the driver receives or pays an identified amount to trade between grades. Far more usual however is to apply the option to trade up / down within a choice-based policy. In this instance the employee is already benefiting from the ability to choose a vehicle up to a monthly price. The option to trade up or down simply allows the driver to select a vehicle that is more expensive than the benchmark allowance, paying the difference as a monthly salary contribution, or to take a less expensive vehicle and receive the difference as a positive salary adjustment.

Trade up / down policies are best operated within a whole life cost policy as the costs utilised are total operational costs for the business. A typical policy would normally restrict the amount an employee can move, to a maximum of say 10%-15% of their allowance. This protects the employee from taking a vehicle which proves to

be too expensive for them to operate in future years, whilst protecting the employer in the event the driver leaves and the vehicle needs to be reallocated.

Biodiesel, electric and hybrid. Should a fleet manager think about putting some of these on the fleet?

A number of engine options have recently come to light offering reduced emissions. However one of the concerns for environmentalists is how friendly the entire life process will be, measured from production right through to recycling. It is also apparent that the application of congestion charges will grow and it may be worth selecting vehicles whose characteristics benefit from the legislation applicable.

Currently it is fair to say that the most cost-effective vehicles for fleet operation remain the petrol and diesel alternatives we know so well. Manufacturers have made significant improvements in the efficiency of these power trains with CO_2 emissions continuously falling. The use of whole life costs will allow a business to know when alternatives become cost-effective to take onto the fleet, however this time is not now.

What should be included in the driver handbook?

The driver handbook is a vital tool for ensuring the business delivers on its duty of care and maintains a protected position. It is the key method of communication of all policies and procedures and should ensure consistency throughout the business. The handbook outlines expected behaviour from the employee and the impact/penalty for breaches of policy. Whilst some companies use the handbook as a cut down version of the entire car policy, holding the policy on a separate web site for instance, I believe the driver handbook should be provided in a complete state and signed for by the driver on delivery. Only then will the driver have been given the best opportunity to understand the company policy and the employer will have taken all reasonable steps to ensure they have communicated the policy.

The handbook should provide all relevant details to the car policy including:

- Employee Handbook
- Cash / Car options
- Car selection policy
- Vehicle allocation / term and mileage
- Vehicle selection
- Trade up / down
- Vehicle Maintenance
    - Service
- Repairs
- Vehicle Condition
    - Requirements thorough life
- Return condition requirements
- Duty of Care
    - Hours driving / rest period
    - Use of mobile / Blackberry
- What to do if
    - Accident
    - Puncture
    - Windshield Failure
    - Vehicle stolen
    - RFL out of date
- Key contact points
- Tabular summary of driver costs

What is best practice when a driver returns a vehicle in an unsatisfactory condition?

Best practice would suggest a proven optimum and this doesn't seem to exist. In general most businesses would appear to like the idea of charging the driver if a vehicle is not returned in an acceptable condition, though few seem to actually apply the charges. The key factors in effectively managing vehicle condition is to start from day 1; Communicate in the driver handbook the condition the vehicle should be kept in and include a clear description of what is acceptable. The BVRLA has a fair wear and tear guide which is available and used by most of the contract hire companies. Provide the drivers with clear guidelines on how to get vehicles rectified through the contract life. Confirm prior to vehicle return the expected return conditions and the repair process.

Once all these aspects have been established the driver should not be surprised to be charged for a vehicle which is operated or returned in an unsatisfactory condition.

The charge should be equal to or greater than the cost applied in the event of an own-fault accident, so as to ensure a consistency.

It is worth remembering that damage to a vehicle will cost you, the employer. If the vehicle is owned the cost will be realised in a lower sale value and if contract hired an end of contract damage charge will be levied.

Whilst I have seen a proportion of the cost being recharged, in my experience a £250 charge to the driver for vehicles being returned below standard or for own-fault accidents is reasonable and positively affects behaviour.

How should a fleet manager tailor their fleet policy to reduce costs?

For most businesses fleet costs remain a large part of their operational costs and therefore reducing these costs is a focus point. Balancing this is the effect on morale and the potential costs of staff movement.

Term and mileage are key factors in determining the cost of fleet operation, and extending the benchmark term from 36 to 48 months will see significant changes to the cost of running a vehicle. Moving to more efficient vehicles and reducing fuel costs also offers a significant cost reduction. If you are using fuel allowances the selection of a more efficient benchmark vehicle allows the reduction of the fuel allowance rate resulting in cost reductions.

Choosing the right financial product for the vehicles you wish to operate given your business tax position is vital. A number of organisations can run discounted cash flow models, which compare costs at today's value of money, to determine the optimum funding method. These are only as good as the parameters input however so it is imperative the inputs are correct for your business if the results are to be accurate.

Review the option to operate on limited manufacturer arrangements. The opportunity to reduce costs by restricting supply is available on relatively small fleet sizes.

How can Daimler Fleet Management help fleet managers?

All the above steps can be achieved by a fleet manager and the information required to complete a full policy review is available. The question therefore is why are so many fleets operating a fleet policy which, by their own admission, is out of date and needs reviewing? The answer is that the time required to consider all the options and get the information is restrictive in this period of resource constraints and business pressure.

At Daimler we consider our field managers to be consultants not sales people. They are able to walk a fleet manager through each aspect of the decision process, providing information which is impartial and relevant. The decisions made remain in the control of the customer however the ground work is completed by our professionals.

They can negotiate with manufacturers, develop choice policies and guide the customer through the development of the company handbook ensuring all considerations from financial to legislative are covered. With years of experience and comparisons across industries and fleet sizes to draw on, you, the fleet manager, will feel confident that the guidance has a practical application and will deliver the requirements identified.

Developing the entire fleet policy is important, but unless it is delivered and enforced it remains useless. Once completed our team will develop an implementation plan to ensure complete communication across both the customer touch points and Daimler Fleet Management Ltd to ensure the services offered are understood and delivered on.

Left alone a full review is a daunting task for any fleet manager. Daimler Fleet Management can ensure it becomes a task whose results far outweigh the effort required.

Paul Harrop
Sales and Marketing Director
Daimler Fleet Management

10 A MANUFACTURER'S VIEW OF THE FLEET MARKET

Ian Dutfield

Marketing Manager

Mercedes-Benz UK

Mercedes has a long pedigree in the fleet market, having been the marque of choice for managers for decades. What is Mercedes' approach the fleet market?

At Mercedes-Benz we recognised the growing significance of the fleet market a number of years ago and introduced a structure specifically designed to support the needs of the fleet and leasing market. The Sales, Marketing and After Sales areas of Mercedes-Benz have dedicated resources to act as a conduit between the fleet managers and the manufacturer. On the sales front we have a team of account managers who specifically deal with fleets of 300 or more vehicles, they are backed up by a team of Corporate Development Managers who concentrate on fleets of less than 300 and finally a team who are dedicated to the contract hire and leasing industry.

In addition to this front line support we have a dedicated Corporate Marketing department that is focussing on the production of bespoke materials for the individual channels, digital brochures, newsletters etc. They also act as a conduit back into the product development and national communications teams to provide valuable insight into the market trends. Implementation of specific corporate-biased events and vehicle launches also falls under the remit of the Corporate Marketing team.

Whilst vehicle quality and reliability is now at an all time high, we still support fleet managers with a dedicated After Sales resource, not only to handle customer issues but also to provide technical information and to optimise service, maintenance and repair costs.

Have manufacturers changed the way they deal with the fleet market in recent years?

Consumer buying trends have changed significantly in recent years with a move towards risk-free monthly payments rather than outright purchase This has accelerated the impact of fleet managed vehicles as a proportion of most manufacturers' sales. It is now such a large part of our business that it needs to be treated with the level of professionalism that our brand demands.

The holding cost of a vehicle is decisive in the positioning and purchase process. To achieve this we not only need to maintain competitive list prices but we also need to ensure that our residual values are healthy against our competitors. To assist with this position we have developed much stronger relationships with the whole life cost providers and industry influencers in order to ensure that our products are optimally positioned for the fleet user. We now, as a matter of course, engage this group of specialists at the earliest possible stage in our new product launch activities. Their feedback is used to ensure that price and equipment levels are optimised in order to produce a vehicle that not only appeals to the driver but also one that has attractive ownership costs and is appealing as a used car when it is finally sold on.

The UK market carries some of the heaviest CO_2 based taxes in the world and our recent product development strategy has been very much geared towards optimising CO_2. The fleet market is particularly influenced by this taxation policy so we have to ensure that we are taking their requirements into consideration. In reality, if you get the product right for the fleet market in terms of holding cost, specification and CO_2 /fuel economy then the benefits are also applicable to the retail and used car markets.

What developments have there been in motor design that have been particularly valuable to fleet customers?

A Mercedes-Benz customer is a Mercedes-Benz customer no matter what vehicle they have purchased and through whatever channel they have purchased it. Therefore any development or action that we take for the fleet market is equally applicable to the retail customer as well.

Perhaps the biggest development resulting from the emergence of the fleet market has manifested itself in the packaging and pricing of cars. As we have already seen, the holding cost of a car is a major contributor to the purchase decision so we need

to achieve the best residual value/list price relationship in order to achieve the best holding cost. This has led to an increase in standard equipment to include a decent set of alloy wheels, high quality in-car entertainment and where possible styling touches to achieve the appropriate 'car park appeal' for the driver. If these items add value to the appeal of a new car they will also carry this effect through to the used car market, thus improving residual values as well as optimising the holding cost for the fleet manager.

The high levels of CO_2 based taxation in the UK market has also accelerated the development of technologies for improving fuel consumption and has led us to look very carefully at engine and transmission combinations, tyre sizes and any other elements that influence fuel consumption. Outside of the normal CO_2 debate, Mercedes-Benz is at the forefront of the development of alternative fuel powertrains and technologies that significantly reduce smog-forming gases such as nitrous oxides. Unfortunately, due to the singular focus on CO_2 in our market, we do not have the demand for such products at this stage.

Another key area of focus for anyone providing a vehicle for work purposes is around the subject of the duty of care to the driver. It is no longer acceptable to rely purely on the safety credentials of the car, even though all of our vehicles are Euro NCAP 5 star rated. We need to create a safe working environment for the driver that is fit for purpose and minimises stress and fatigue. More vehicles are used as mobile offices these days so it is important for the driver's technology, be it telephone or e-mail functionality, to be fully integrated into the car. We offer full integration of Bluetooth technology that can be controlled, as standard, through the steering wheel controls and has a full display within the driver's natural field of vision. And there is the option of full voice activation of all telematic functions on our COMAND equipped vehicles.

How should a fleet manager go about deciding which makes and models of vehicle to allow onto their fleet?

The main influencing factors for a fleet manager to consider when selecting vehicles are rational. Factors such as holding costs, service, maintenance and repair (SMR) costs and the CO_2 taxation implications will significantly influence the purchase choice. Another upcoming issue is the revised capital write down allowance that will apply from April 2009. This applies a different financial treatment to cars under 160g/km and will drive businesses to adopt cars below this threshold due to a beneficial write down policy.

Tax benefits are sometimes provided for the early adoption of new emission technologies. In the past we saw the 3% taxation supplement for diesel engines removed in advance of the legal introduction date of EU4 emission regulations. This gave a personal taxation benefit to the company car driver, attracted higher residual values and also enabled the fleet manager to demonstrate support for environmental improvements. The result was that many fleets made it a policy to only specify EU4 cars even though it was not a legislative requirement at the time.

Other considerations are more emotional and relate to the image of the brand itself. Firstly the brand must fit with the business's requirements and needs to reinforce their values. If they operate a single badge policy they must ensure that the product range is sufficiently wide to cover all of their operational requirements at every level. Other companies operate brand differentiation for different grades to allow the product to create the appropriate differentiation. And in some cases the company requires a brand that originates from the same country as their products.

The fleet manager should also consider the emotional impact of a brand on employees. We should not underestimate the perceived value that certain brands can bring to current and potential employees. Without adding any significant cost to the business a company can very often offer a Mercedes-Benz in place of a standard volume fleet model. The value to the employee is significantly greater than the cost to the business.

What features of motor vehicles should careful fleet managers specify as standard?

With Corporate Responsibility becoming more prevalent it is important that the vehicle provides an appropriate environment for the driver. A variety of safety systems are now offered as standard on the majority of cars. ABS, airbags, power steering and some form of electronic stability system are considered mainstream in cars of today, so the fleet manager should be looking at convenience functions such as navigation systems, cruise control/speed limiters, Bluetooth connectivity and voice activation - all of which are designed to ease operation and reduce fatigue.

As previously identified, enhancing driver safety both passively and actively is central to our brand philosophy. During 2009 Mercedes-Benz will bring a number of their class-leading safety innovations into models accessible to fleet users. Some notable developments are DistronicPlus, which is a radar controlled cruise control that is enhanced with an active braking system that will automatically bring the car to a complete standstill if required. The car will genuinely drive itself. Once the speed is set the car will maintain a safe distance from the vehicle in front, if that vehicle slows down or if the gap reduces the DistronicPlus system will reduce power or brake automatically.

Attention Assist is a feature that monitors up to 70 inputs by the driver. If it detects any unusual patterns in the driver's behaviours it will activate visual and audible warnings to gain the driver's attention and advise that a break from driving is required.

Another feature is the Adaptive High Beam Assist that automatically optimises the headlamp range and intensity. It monitors road conditions, speed and vehicles on the road ahead and adapts the light beam accordingly. This ensures the optimum illumination of the road ahead but prevents any dazzling of oncoming vehicles.

All of these developments are not gimmicks but have been developed to significantly improve the driving environment, improve attention and reduce driver fatigue. Of course, all of the vehicles across our range carry the renowned Mercedes-Benz qualities of safety, comfort and balance between an enjoyable and dynamic drive and class-leading levels of comfort and noise-suppression.

What recent developments have there been in manufacturers' thinking that has been particularly valuable to fleet managers?

We have already mentioned several times that CO_2 based taxation has made this subject front of mind for both the driver and the fleet manager. Some competitors were early to market with energy-saving features such as start-stop functions and also active management of generators, power steering and water pumps. Mercedes-Benz is now introducing all such measures on our latest products.

Our range of BlueEFFICIENCY vehicles not only incorporate all of the latest engine developments to reduce friction and wasted energy but also incorporate weight-saving measures, aerodynamic optimisation and the latest in low rolling resistance tyres. These developments not only achieve a lower tax bill but also deliver significant improvements to fuel consumption without compromising performance.

Some manufacturers offer volume related bonuses to fleet buyers. Please explain, generally, what these are and how they work.

The volume related bonuses offered by a number of manufacturers are exactly what the name suggests. These incentives are offered to a fleet buyer who commits to purchase an agreed volume of a particular model. The motive behind these incentives will vary from company to company. They are often used towards the end of a product lifecycle as a tactical tool to ensure orderly disposal of soon-to-be-replaced vehicles. The mechanism for payment of this support depends on the requirements of the individual fleet manager and it is usually negotiated with the account manager from the manufacturer.

And sometimes there are specific 'tactical' deals available. How do these work, in general?

Tactical offers can take many forms and are usually determined by market conditions and the model lifecycle. They can be used to improve the relative attractiveness of a particular model in the marketplace or they can be used to achieve an attractive position within a fleet listing. The support packages can consist of numerous measures and are structured to maintain, or achieve, specific positioning of particular vehicles. Typical tactical measures include supporting the holding costs of a vehicle or adding value through service packages or equipment upgrade packages.

If you were to advise a fleet manager on the best practice when it comes to selecting their vehicles, what would that advice be?

The fleet manager must ensure that the product is financially viable in terms of holding and running costs, attractive to the driver in terms of taxable benefit and the product must reflect their business needs in terms of functionality and brand image. They should also consider the range of products on offer from the manufacturer, because dealing with one manufacturer for all of their requirements will not only simplify the management of the fleet but will also create greater consistency for the drivers and the company.

What should fleet managers be doing to reduce the CO_2 levels of their fleets?

Reduction of CO_2 is an important factor for all of us and intensive development continues in all sectors in order to reach stringent legislative targets. This ongoing development delivers a natural reduction in CO_2 through more fuel efficient cars. The effect of personal taxation encourages the driver to consider CO_2 as part of their purchase process and the forthcoming introduction of revised writing down allowance restrictions will encourage businesses to consider vehicles with emissions below 160g/km. However, consideration must also be given to the wider environmental impact of a vehicle. CO_2 emissions are only a small but easily measurable element of the overall environmental impact of a vehicle on the planet. Design, manufacturing, in-life servicing and end of life recyclability are all major factors that have an impact on the environment. Mercedes-Benz was the first manufacturer to obtain the highly regarded TUV Environmental Certificate on a number of its vehicles. This certification considers the cradle to grave impact on the environment. The fleet manager should also consider other potentially harmful tailpipe emissions. Particulates and smog-forming nitrous oxides are also emissions that can be reduced through technological solutions although at this stage there is no taxable benefit in these areas.

Should a fleet manager have a direct relationship with a manufacturer, or should this relationship be handled by a franchised dealer or leasing company?

A strong relationship between a fleet manager and manufacturer is mutually beneficial. A good understanding of the business needs and products available the beter the fit. The complexity is more than just the broad range of vehicles and technologies available, it also includes a range of financial solutions, delivery options and post delivery support solutions that can add value to the process of buying cars. The relationship with a manufacturer ensures that the latest and most appropriate information is available. The account manager will also ensure that any transaction is structured in the most appropriate way for the business and include, where relevant, the leasing company, the retailer and the manufacturer.

This relationship also opens up access to specific events such as early previews of new models and technology. This ensures that customers are aware of the positioning of new products and services to enable them to make informed and pro-active decisions that are to the benefit of their business and users.

Have there been any recent manufacturer-led developments that have changed the landscape for fleet managers?

As previously mentioned, the key factors for fleet customers are equally applicable to the retail market. Focus in these areas has accelerated developments that influence the total ownership costs of a vehicle. Mercedes-Benz are well positioned with current and future models to meet today's market requirements but also being leaders in the development of technologies such as BlueTEC diesels, hybrids, fuel cells and full electric vehicles we are well placed to embrace future legislation and tax initiatives.

Ian Dutfield
Marketing Manager
Mercedes-Benz UK

Mercedes-Benz

11 SHORT TERM LEASING

Mel Goodliffe
Managing Director
Flexxilease

What is short term leasing?

Short term leasing provides vehicles on a contract rental basis for periods of 3 to 18 months. It fills the space between a plethora of daily rental products and the heavily populated market of two and three year lease providers.

Is it a product for private individuals or companies?

The product serves both private individuals and companies.

The motivations of the private individual are numerous. Recent times have seen an increased shift to short term leasing by former company car drivers (opt out drivers) who have tried the used car option, chosen to drive the five year old, high mileage executive vehicle only to regret the cost implications associated with service, maintenance, repairs, tyres and depreciation.

Many opt out drivers have never bought a car in their life and find it difficult to assess the many options available to them, be it purchasing a new or used car, what to buy, where to buy, when to sell, whether to lease and for what period, whether to buy a warranty or an all inclusive lease product etc.

As well as the opt out driver short term leasing also appeals to individuals with changing circumstances such as new babies, employment of a nanny, short term employment contract and imminent emigration all being cited as reasons. Of course there is also the driver that loves the appeal of driving particular 'high maintenance' cars without long term commitments or significant investment and finally, those that enjoy the kudos of a new car in their driveway every year.

There has been an increased take-up of short term leasing by companies as the economy has slowed, commercial uncertainty has grown and the appetite for long term commitments has dwindled. It is clearly still important to ensure the motivation of employees and Flexxilease provides the best of both worlds with its mix of price, commitment and product. That said, some corporate clients have specific requirements such as sporting seasons, seasonal promotions and product launches that require unique product and periods that neither outright purchase nor long term lease can deliver.

Can fleet managers get short term leasing from their daily hire companies?

The majority of mainstream daily hire companies offer a short term leasing product. These products tend to feature a restricted product proposition in line with the daily hire companies' typical product offering, and specific vehicle availability can be difficult. Depending on the vehicle choice and period of hire required it may also be that the vehicles are used and may have to be changed during the contract period.

What's included in the short term lease?

This depends on the supplier. All Flexxilease contracts include road fund licence, collection and delivery. Contracts of less than 11 months are also fully supported maintenance, repair and tyres (SMRT). Customers are responsible for the SMRT costs on contracts of 12 months and above but with a typical mileage allowance of 10,000 miles per annum the exposure to such costs is minimal given the service intervals and requirements of new cars.

Why would a fleet manager want to lease a car for a short period?

The needs and requirements of fleet managers vary dramatically. The more mainstream reasons for using a short team leasing company such as Flexxilease include new employee probation periods, internal or cross-border secondment, awaiting delivery of a long term lease vehicle, and ad-hoc projects requiring short term support and management.

Can short term leasing provide savings for fleets?

Most definitely. Outright purchase and long term lease commitments expose fleets to potential accounting losses and early termination penalties if they need to sell or terminate a vehicle or contract early. Additionally the buying and utilisation model employed by companies such as Flexxilease can demonstrate real like for like monthly cost reductions dependant on the vehicle, its contract period and mileage. Collectively, short term leasing represents a real and viable alternative to purchase and long term leasing.

Can you give some examples of typical cost savings

See table overleaf.

Figures based on:

- 8% interest rate
- Vehicle valuations taken from CAP Monitor
- Number of lease payments - 15
- Monthly least cost £352.49 inc VAT at 17.5%
- Figures accurate as of November 2008

	BMW 3 Series, 320d Coupe 2.0 SE 2dr	BMW X5 Series, 3.0d SE 5dr Auto	BMW 6 Series 630i Coupe 2dr Auto	Mercedes Benz S Class S320 Cdi Saloon Auto	Mercedes Benz B-Class B150 Sport 5dr	Land Rover Range Rover Sport TDV6 S 5dr
Cost to buy						
Vehicle valuation	£26,761	£38,963	£47,080	£52,721	£17,665	£36,550
Value after one year	£19,725	£29,375	£27,175	£33,300	£10,425	£21,050
Vehicle depreciation	£7,036	£9,588	£19,905	£19,421	£7,240	£15,500
Interest on finance	£2,141	£3,117	£3,767	£6,327	£2,120	£4,386
Total cost of vehicle - year one	£9,177	£12,705	£23,672	£25,748	£9,360	£19,886
Cost to lease						
Total cost of lease	£5,287	£8,813	£13,160	£14,100	£4,935	£13,513
Interest lost on initial payment	£85	£141	£151	£170	£60	£353
Interest lost on lease payments	£184	£306	£489	£804	£282	£670
Total cost of lease - year one	£5,556	£9,260	£13,800	£15,074	£5,277	£14,536
Total saving	£3,621	£3,445	£9,872	£10,674	£4,083	£5,350

What are the advantages of short term leasing?

The advantages will always be cost and commitment without compromising product. The added benefits of transparent pricing and the ability to flex the vehicle, mileage, payment profile and geographical location further enhance the attractiveness of the proposition.

Would it be as attractive to small companies as for big ones?

Arguably it is more attractive to smaller companies as they tend to have greater flexibility in terms of vehicle choice, allocation and use. The ability to react to changing general business and economic circumstance appears more fluid within the smaller company community and short term leasing with companies such as Flexxilease dovetails perfectly with these circumstance and demands.

And what are the disadvantages?

There are no clear disadvantages. Short term leasing companies can supply a wide range of vehicles in each of the recognised segments over a variety of periods and mileages. If a client wants to specify a colour, specification and protracted delivery schedule, they could be disappointed. But our experience suggests that the high specification, premium marque, readily available, low cost stock compensates for any such compromise.

Do regular contract hire companies offer short term leasing?

Most of the regular contract hire companies market a similar offering to support their clients' interim and pre-contract requirements. Although a small number of these companies use their own fleets to provide this service the majority outsource service provision to daily rental companies as the utilisation and logistics management is unique to the short term lease and daily rental sectors.

What happens if the car is involved in an accident?

This may vary between suppliers but if the car is leased from Flexxilease the accident and claims would be managed by our parent company Car Crash Line Group, one of the best known accident management companies in the UK. Dependant on the customers' insurance arrangements a replacement vehicle can be provided whilst the contract vehicle is being repaired.

What happens at the end of the lease?

A good supplier will maintain regular contact with its customers throughout the lease period and will speak with each client ahead of their contract end date to establish the client's requirements. Dependant on the vehicle age and mileage the supplier will extend the contract or offer another vehicle from their current fleet.

In our case, all collections and deliveries are undertaken by our staff operating from 9 locations across the UK. They use a state-of-the-art PDA system to record the mileage and condition of all vehicles and any charges on damage are calculated using the BVRLA's industry recognised fair wear and tear guidelines. Excess mileage is charged at a pre-agreed pence per mile rate.

Can a fleet pay monthly or is an up-front payment normally required?

As with any customer the payment profile is one of the items the lessor's underwriting team will consider. For example, we partner with the top two UK credit agencies to assess all applications. Typically lessors' payment profiles require between one and three months' initial payments on contracts from 3 to 18 month.

Are there any 'hidden' costs, such as delivery or excess mileage charges?

This again depends on the supplier. The Flexxilease pricing proposition is 100% transparent. A wide range of payment profiles are offered to reflect the budgeting preferences of our customers whilst our policies on excess mileage, SMRT obligations and vehicle damage are documented throughout our website and customer communications.

All legislative charges such as parking fines and traffic penalties are paid and recharged with a predetermined administration fee in the event that they remain unpaid by the customer.

Can fleet managers still choose the cars they want or is there a restricted choice?

Most suppliers offer a select range of cars and always feature a choice of vehicle within each of the various segments. Demand for the product is continually strong and the onus tends to be on clients to choose and execute their choice in a timely manner to secure their vehicle requirement.

Will the cars be new?

This depends on the supplier. All our cars are UK sourced through appointed manufacturer dealerships. Typically all 12 month contracts are new cars whilst our 3, 6 and 9 month contracts will be no older than 9 months and by the nature of our fleet, can also be brand new.

Are fleets more likely to use short term leasing during an economic downturn?

I'm sure any opportunity to reduce expenditure and increase cost control will be grasped by every fleet manager. The volatile costs and issues associated with fleet management – taxation regimes, fuel, residual values, SMRT – tend to exaggerate during downturns and can have a dramatic impact on fleet strategies across the spectrum. Short term leasing provides a low cost, low commitment, high value, big brand breath of fresh air to any downturn.

How can short term leasing help a fleet manager run a corporate fleet?

Short term leasing fills the gap between daily hire and long term lease or ownership. Until now fleet managers have looked to shoehorn this gap into either daily hire or their longer term procurement choice. This goes someway to delivering but it is costly, inflexible and doesn't always work for the fleet manager or their driver. Surely a tailor made solution would be preferable?

Please tell us about your company.

As far as we are aware Flexxilease is the only 3 to 18 month vehicle lease supplier. We provide a wide range of cars from top of the range brands like BMW, Audi and Mercedes to popular runarounds like VW, Vauxhall and Ford. Our honest pricing, exceptional customer care and efficient delivery service make us the driver's choice for flexible low cost motoring.

Simply choose from our extensive range of vehicles, select your contract length and preferred mileage and let Flexxilease do the rest.

We offer:

- Low up-front payments
- Fixed monthly rental rates
- Wide range of vehicles

- 3 to 18 month flexible contracts
- Nationwide delivery
- Road fund licence, manufacturer's warranty & breakdown cover
- Personal & business customers

At the end of the contract period you can choose to:

1 Change to a new vehicle and a new contract
2 Extend the contract on that vehicle on a month by month basis
3 Hand the vehicle back to us and walk away

The Flexxilease website gives you all the information you need including an extensive Frequently Asked Questions section, detailed vehicle specifications plus payment schedules and details of the substantial savings our customers enjoy through leasing compared to purchasing their vehicle.

Case Study

Justin Garlick: Aged 39. Profession: MD School Business Services

Vehicle: Audi A4 Avant 2.0 tdi s-line multitronic

Length of lease: total time of leases (36 months+)

Justin Garlick is a successful business man, and always looking for a good deal. As the MD of School Business Services Justin is often on the road meeting and greeting, and needs a reliable and smart looking car.

Justin stumbled on Flexxilease after running a 'short term lease' Google search, and today is on his seventh Flexxilease vehicle. Opting for 6 month contracts, Justin has leased a Mazda RX-8, Peugeot 307cc, Subaru Impreza WRX, Grand Jeep Cherokee, Chrylser 300c, Mitsubishi Outlander 2.0D Elegance and today whizzes around in an Audi Avant 2.0TDi s-line – and loves it!

Justin says this about Flexxilease: "They offer great value for money and have some fantastic vehicles for as little as £160 a month - what you see on the website is actually what you pay. The site is clear and easy to navigate and the customer services team are always available to help, even to offer an opinion (if asked!) on a particular model of car and colour. Their input and support makes the application process so much easier. They may not always have the colour you want but I am yet to be disappointed!"

Justin also argues that in times of an economic slowdown and the rising cost of owning a car, Flexxilease is smart thinking for both the SME and consumer. "I didn't want to spend money on a new car that would lose much of its value. I wanted a short-term and flexible solution that offered me choices, was simple to engage and, of course saved money. Had I owned any of the cars for the time that I have leased them from Flexxilease I shudder to think what I would have suffered in deprecation; I would reckon at least 3 times what I have paid in lease charges (I pay on average £300 per

> month +VAT). What's more the cars all come inclusive of road tax & breakdown cover and I've yet to pay for a service as I don't keep them long enough! I regularly find myself browsing the site wondering what my next selection may be…and I only have to wait 6 months!"

Why lease through Flexxilease?

Cash purchase or long term lease commitments can impact on a business's budget, restrict its borrowing capabilities and expose it to increased servicing and maintenance costs. Combine these factors with spiraling depreciation values and car purchase is no longer the obvious choice. (Used car values fell 11% between September 2007 and September 2008).

Since 2004, Flexxilease has become a way of life for thousands of cost conscious UK motorists and businesses. Not only do they benefit from the flexibility and savings offered by Flexxilease they can be certain they are using cars featuring the latest fuel, engineering and emissions technologies helping to limit their own carbon footprint.

Mel Goodliffe
Managing Director
Flexxilease

12 TYRES

Andrew Guile
Key Account Manager
Michelin Tyre Public Limited Company

What is your role within Michelin and how long have you been in the industry?

My current role is as a Key Account Manager within the National Car Fleets team. My portfolio of customers includes Lloyds TSB Autolease, Lombard Vehicle Management, ING Car Lease, Pendragon Contracts and Arnold Clark Vehicle Management. I joined Michelin back in 1988 and worked in one of the regional sales offices dealing with telephone sales, technical queries, stock ordering and other related issues. After a few years and a 16 week training programme I joined the external sales force selling car/van/truck/ agricultural/ two wheel and earthmover products in the Yorkshire Area. I then moved onto a more specialised sales role looking after key independents who concentrated on car tyre sales in the North of England. The next move was to become a Regional Sales Manager with a team looking after the North and Midlands part of the country. Then there was a move to become the Customer Training Manager of the Michelin Training and Information Centre which was based in Watford but then moved up to the Company headquarters in Stoke-on-Trent. After about five years I then joined our Original Equipment Department looking after our European business with Honda and Toyota which was extremely interesting. I then moved to my current job in 2005 looking after some of the fleets mentioned earlier.

Michelin is one of the best known tyre manufacturers. How does it operate in the fleet market?

Michelin as a global player in the world tyre market has relationships with the largest fleets worldwide. We also service a number of pan-European fleets, liaising with their headquarters wherever that may be. In the UK there is a dedicated team to call on the key car/van fleet customers. The team's portfolio covers mainly the FN50, but also extends to some smaller regionally based accounts. The team is headed up by Dave Crinson who is Sales Manager Car Fleets UK&ROI, and consists of four Key Account Managers and a Regional Fleet Specialist.

Michelin sees the fleet market as a key area of business which delivers a high volume of unit sales and a rich mix of higher end tyre sizes and speed ratings. One of the key missions is to ensure that the Michelin product isn't seen as just a commodity, but that customers realise the value of a very highly engineered product.

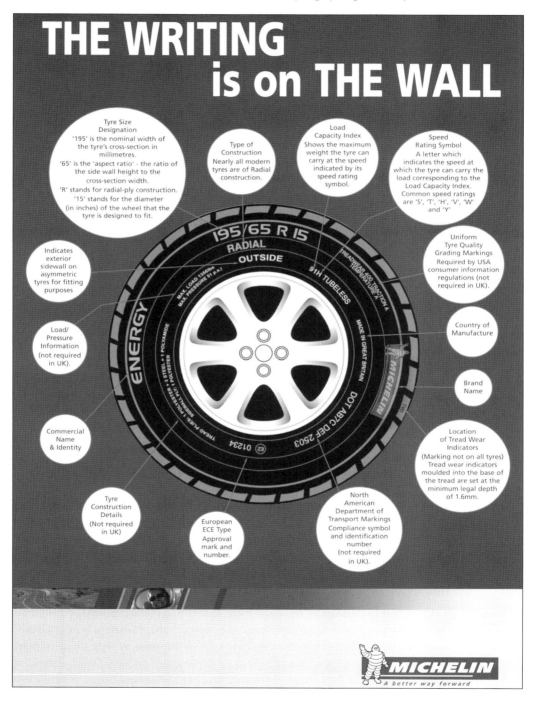

THE WRITING
is on THE WALL

Tyre Size Designation
'195' is the nominal width of the tyre's cross-section in millimetres.
'65' is the 'aspect ratio' - the ratio of the side wall height to the cross-section width.
'R' stands for radial-ply construction.
'15' stands for the diameter (in inches) of the wheel that the tyre is designed to fit.

Type of Construction
Nearly all modern tyres are of Radial construction.

Load Capacity Index
Shows the maximum weight the tyre can carry at the speed indicated by its speed rating symbol.

Speed Rating Symbol
A letter which indicates the speed at which the tyre can carry the load corresponding to the Load Capacity Index. Common speed ratings are 'S', 'T', 'H', 'V', 'W' and 'Y'

Indicates exterior sidewall on asymmetric tyres for fitting purposes

Uniform Tyre Quality Grading Markings
Required by USA consumer information regulations (not required in UK).

Load/ Pressure Information (not required in UK).

Country of Manufacture

Commercial Name & Identity

Brand Name

Location of Tread Wear Indicators
(Marking not on all tyres) Tread wear indicators moulded into the base of the tread are set at the minimum legal depth of 1.6mm.

Tyre Construction Details (Not required in UK)

European ECE Type Approval mark and number.

North American Department of Transport Markings
Compliance symbol and identification number (not required in UK).

MICHELIN
A better way forward

Fleet Managers, operational staff, key directors and decision makers are called upon and updated on current and new products, industry innovations and developments both within Michelin and the tyre business in general. Literature on tyre safety, tyre care, environmental developments etc can also be provided. Support is given to assist the fleets with promotional ideas, branding and any other areas where our expertise can be useful. We also, uniquely amongst the tyre manufacturers, host a twice yearly Fleet Panel made up of key decision makers and influencers from the UK's major car fleet companies. This gives Michelin an opportunity to address, debate and present new developments and innovations in the market. It is also an important chance for the attendees to meet and discuss this fast changing industry. We are also involved with sponsoring fleet awards and regularly advertise and sponsor articles in the fleet press.

Does a Fleet Manager really need to know about tyres? Can't they just defer to the advice of the fast-fit outlet or garage when deciding which tyre to fit?

In these days where duty of care and corporate responsibility are key issues, it is vital that a fleet manager knows sufficient about the tyres fitted on his vehicles so that he feels confident about his drivers and their welfare. There are so many different tyre makes, tread patterns, speed ratings and loadings that it is possible that an incorrect fitment could be made. Therefore some basic knowledge backed up with literature, and access to tyre information websites such as www.michelin.co.uk, will provide both knowledge and reassurance.

A basic understanding is necessary of specific regulations such as the Road Vehicles (Constructions and Use Regulations) 1986. It is worth remembering that the ability to monitor, check and understand the data from a fast-fit or garage is also a key management function. The tyre distributor also needs to be aware that they are dealing with a fleet manager who is both proficient and vigilant in policing what they are doing. It may be that a certain distributor has a leaning, for what ever reason, towards a certain tyre manufacturer. The fleet manager needs to know and understand this, so they can ensure their drivers are receiving both the best advice and the correct fitments on their vehicles. It is also important that the fleet manager is fully aware that all tyres are not the same; they may all look similar but there are premium, second line and budget tyres of many different makes. Taking into account the different performances these products will deliver, the manager must decide his policy and know and understand the reasons for that decision.

Have tyre manufacturers changed the way they deal with the fleet market in recent years?

Certainly within Michelin we have over the last 20 years developed a closer relationship with   our fleet customers. We feel it is vital to have a team calling to negotiate, assist, and give technical advice. Over this time, vehicle developments have meant tyre sizes and speed ratings have increased and the range of tyres on offer has grown enormously. Cars which 20 years ago would have been on a 13 or 14 inch wheel, are now on a 16, 17 or 18 inch wheel fitted with tyres with a high speed capability. We have also seen developments in tread patterns with directional, asymmetric, and fuel saving tyres now offered. There has also been the introduction and growth of the run-flat or Zero Pressure tyre, which has been seen mainly on BMW models.

The fleet manager has had to increase his awareness and knowledge of these developments and manufacturers have had to provide more comprehensive information for them. Additionally, the fleet sector has polarised, with many of the smaller fleets being taken over or absorbed into huge fleets operating many thousands of vehicles. It is critical for us to understand who the key decision makers are, and establish a relationship with them, so that when a tender or an opportunity to bid for business arises, we know the fleet and the people involved. With recent developments within the industry suggesting that some of the largest companies are getting larger, we need to be able to meet any challenges that are presented.

What developments have there been in tyre design that have been particularly valuable to fleet customers?

There are a number of tyre developments in recent years that have meant increased benefits for fleet customers. These include our Energy Saver range, for which specific rubber compounds have been developed to reduce the rolling resistance of the tyre without sacrificing the other factors such as grip and comfort. Less fuel consumption, lower running costs, fewer CO_2 emissions, and fewer tyres to dispose of all help the environment and benefit the fleet customer.

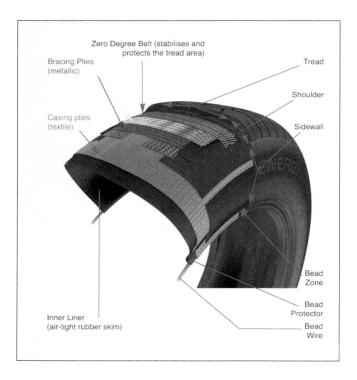

The development of Michelin Zero Pressure tyres, (run flat technology), with a self supporting reinforced sidewall that allows a driver to continue a journey for 50 miles at 50mph has allowed for continued mobility and control. These allow drivers to get off a motorway or find a safe convenient place to stop and get assistance. These sorts of tyres, fitted to a limited range of vehicles, mainly BMW, need to be used in conjunction with a Tyre Pressure Monitoring System in the car which alerts the driver of an issue.

Van tyre design has moved on leaps and bounds over the years as vans have become more powerful and developed car-like ride and handling. The Michelin Agilis tyre has evolved to meet these demands as well as having to provide the sturdy construction traditionally required by this sector of the market.

Additionally the huge growth in the fleet market of the 4x4 type of vehicle has meant tyre manufacturers have had to design and build new ranges of tyres suitable for the different applications. The more traditional off road vehicles have been joined by a host of on road cousins requiring different products to meet new applications and challenges such as the motorway and the supermarket car park.

Tyres are generally categorised as premium, second line and budget. How should a fleet manager decide which category of tyre to fit? And, having decided which category, how should they decide between manufacturers?

Certainly in the market today there are manufacturers who make tyres which can be classified as premium, second line and also budget. The first thing a fleet manager should realise is that there are differences in performance between these products and they will not all last as long as each other, grip as well as each other, or offer the same levels of comfort, noise reduction and fuel economy.

Premium tyres are also likely to give fleet vehicles improved dynamics, as vehicle and tyre manufacturers dedicate a lot of resources to ensure that the tyre and vehicle are developed to be well matched. This development leads to a technical approval (or homologation) from the vehicle manufacturer and original equipment supply. The fleet manager must therefore take his driver's satisfaction and safety into account when considering whether fitting a cheaper option is the best solution. Part of the decision making process needs to be the achievement of the best value for money option for a business, and the cheapest initial purchase price rarely delivers the best long term solution. Overall running costs taking into account the price, fuel efficiency, the environmental impact including CO_2 emissions, and the longevity offered all need to be analysed before a final decision.

It is worth noting that some high performance vehicles such as Porsche use specifically developed tyres which can be identified by specialised markings (N marked tyres in the case of Porsche). These high performance vehicles are particularly sensitive and require these specific premium tyres to be fitted.

Once a manager decides which quality of tyre will be fitted, he then needs to determine which manufacturer offers the most benefits for the business and the driver. Virtually all the major fleet companies opt for tyres from the premium end of the market. These decisions may well be taken after discussions with the major national tyre distributors, and with the tyre manufacturers themselves. It is up to the tyre manufacturers to try and convince the manager of the benefits of fitting their products from longevity, comfort, fuel saving etc, as well as the level of technical support that is offered. Some fleets choose to work with a very established tyre brand because they realise there are additional benefits of major brands working together in a very competitive market. Michelin for example will endeavour to bring its resources from marketing, communications, and research and development to benefit the fleet and then work with them to bring added value to the driver themselves.

The tyre retread industry promotes retread tyres as being environmentally sound because the main part of the tyre is simply used again. What is your view of retread tyres? Are they safe?

There are very few retreaded car or light van tyres on the market today in the UK, and there are no major fleets using them. However in the truck market, over 17.5" wheel diameter, retreads have established themselves as a cost effective solution used very successfully by almost all operators. The truck casing is designed with retreading in mind and is capable of many many thousands of miles of effective and durable service.

The retreading of a car/light van tyre is not always cost effective with the cost of materials, processing and logistics outweighing any possible end cost benefits. Additionally there are budget car and van tyres available which provide a cheap alternative to a retread tyre.

There has been some comment in the automotive press about using low rolling-resistance tyres to reduce fuel costs. Should fleet managers specify these tyres? How much fuel do they save and how much extra do they cost?

There have been low rolling-resistance tyres on offer in the market since the 1990s. Research and development by the major tyre manufacturers has resulted in tyre designs and rubber compounds that reduce the amount of energy consumed by the tyre as it rotates. This means that the engine has to work less hard to power the vehicle which reduces fuel costs and also means that less CO_2 is given off into the atmosphere. The Michelin Energy Saver tyre for example saves about 0.2 of a litre per 100 kilometres compared to an average of the premium competitors, and reduces CO_2 emissions by about 4 grams per kilometre.

The majority of Michelin tyres now have low rolling resistance properties to reduce fuel consumption. The very important point to note is that these developments have been made without a trade off in performance in other key areas such as wet braking and longevity.

To ensure that fleet mangers benefit from this fuel saving technology, they should investigate whether the tyres they purchase from the manufacturers are in fact low rolling-resistance tyres.

Should a fleet manager have a direct relationship with a tyre manufacturer, or should this relationship be handled by a dealer or fast-fit company?

Earlier I talked about some of the reasons that a fleet manager needs to know about the tyres that are fitted to the vehicles under his responsibility. The most knowledgeable people to talk to about any product are the people who make that product. With the developments and innovations in the premium end of the market, the tyre manufacturer has the most up to date and accurate information. If a fleet manager has a direct relationship with a tyre manufacturer, this gives him the opportunity to negotiate any discounts if the volumes available are appropriate. He can also be kept directly up to date with any tyre related issues and the direction the market is moving, which will ensure he has the support needed to make informed and accurate buying decisions. If the manager's relationship is only via a dealer or fast-fit company, messages can become distorted and more time consuming as parties wait for questions and then responses via a 3rd party.

Michelin has always worked to spread the message of the importance of the tyres on any vehicle, and to help customers maintain them to get the maximum mileage and by using the correct pressures and care. Literature is produced to help managers generate the awareness amongst drivers of correct tyre maintenance, and with a direct relationship this can be delivered direct to where it is needed.

What advice would you give to a fleet manager regarding tyre maintenance?

The tyre is the only point of contact between the vehicle and the road surface so it plays a hugely important role. The maintenance of the tyre is key to getting the best performance from it. Below are some of the key areas to pay attention to:

a   When fitting replacement tyres ensure they are the same size and load index, and have the same speed symbol as recommended by the vehicle manufacturer. When tyres are not fitted in complete sets of four, we advise that tyre types are not mixed across an axle. It is important to contact your tyre dealer or a leading manufacturer to check any details. Special care needs to be taken with 4x4 fitments where tyres should be used in identical sets of four, bearing in mind any specific recommendations from the vehicle manufacturer.

b   Encourage a regular visual inspection by the driver or fleet manager to check for tread wear, nails or stones, and cuts or bulges. These preventative measures can stop a potential tyre failure and possible roadside breakdown.

c   Ensure a regular tread depth check by a professional tyre dealer who will respect the UK 1.6mm legal limit. This means the car or van tyre should have at least 1.6mm of tread across the central three quarters of the tyre breadth and around the entire circumference of the tyre. Most tyres nowadays have tread wear indicators set into the main tread grooves which show when the tyre is worn to 1.6mm of remaining tread. When these indicators become level with the tread surface, the tyre is ready for immediate replacement.

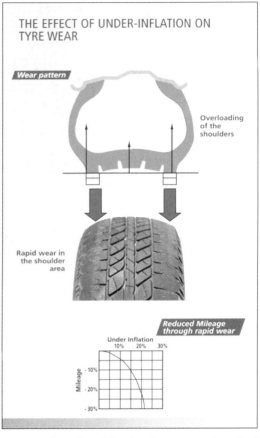

THE EFFECT OF UNDER-INFLATION ON TYRE WEAR

Wear pattern

Overloading of the shoulders

Rapid wear in the shoulder area

Reduced Mileage through rapid wear

d   Maintaining the correct tyre pressure is an important factor in both the safety and longevity of tyres. Too little or too much air could adversely affect the vehicle handling and the tyre's performance and durability. Also keeping the tyres at their correct pressure and using energy-efficient tyres reduces your engine's workload. This means you will save fuel and reduce CO_2 emissions too. Someone driving 7psi under-inflated (at 23psi rather than 30psi) will increase their fuel consumption by around 2 per cent. Over a year, 2 per cent on an individual's and then a fleet's fuel bill is considerable. CO_2 emissions will also be increased unnecessarily so damaging the environment. Pressures should be checked using an accurate gauge and can be done by the driver, or at a local service station or tyre dealer. Advice on the correct operating pressures will be contained in the vehicle manufacturer's handbook or be marked on the vehicle. Pressures should be checked monthly and before long journeys when the tyres are cold. If appropriate they should be adjusted for full loads or towing.

e   When replacing tyres the ideal situation would be to replace all four tyres together. However as vehicles wear their front and rear tyres at different rates this cannot always be done. In this case Michelin's recommendation is to fit new tyres to the rear and move the part worn rear tyres to the front. The reason for this is to maintain the best stability of the vehicle in extreme conditions of hard or emergency braking and cornering, particularly in wet or slippery conditions. For 4x4 vehicles always refer to the vehicle manufacturer's data on changing tyres.

f   If the correct alignment on a vehicle is not correctly maintained it can result in rapid and irregular tyre wear. This can affect costs and the handling and safety of the vehicle. On a vehicle with 15 inch wheels, if the suspension is misaligned by 4mm (just 2mm per wheel), then for every mile you travel the tyre is being forced sideways by 8.4 metres!

If all the above points are followed, this will help a Fleet Manager and his/her drivers get the best out of the product that they have purchased.

If you were to advise a fleet manager on the best practice when it comes to choosing their tyres, what would that advice be?

The first choice for a fleet manager should be for a premium quality tyre, the adage of the more you pay the better product or service you get generally works here. A premium quality tyre is what is technically approved by the vehicle manufacturers as being most suitable for use. The internet will give a lot of helpful advice for a fleet manager to start to formulate a policy, and discussions can then take place with tyre manufacturers and with tyre distributors to again help in making a decision. The key points to remember are to look for a brand that offers safety, value for money, fuel saving, good product information, technical backup, a strong brand image, and good environmental credentials. Value for money is something that is sometimes missed by the fleet manager when deciding what brand to choose; he should take into account whole life costs rather than just the initial purchase price.

Andrew Guile
Key Account Manager
Michelin Tyre Public Limited Company

Michelin is a major player in the world tyre industry with a sales network covering 170 countries.

It has more than 121,000 employees, and its 68 production plants in 19 countries produced 191 million tyres and 17 million maps and guides in 2007.

As the world's leading tyre manufacturer, Michelin has a long history of innovations aimed at making driving more economical, safer and more pleasurable. To highlight this commitment to advances in tyre performance, Michelin spends around four per cent of its annual turnover on research and development – more than any other tyre manufacturer.

To control its environmental impact, Michelin conducted a global assessment of its operations and products and this led it to focus on developing technologies aimed at: reducing its tyres' rolling resistance: increasing tyre life to reduce the number of end-of-life tyres to be processed: and using raw materials that have a low environmental impact. At the end of 2007, 99.5 per cent of output in volume terms was carried out in ISO 14001-certified plants.

In addition to tyres, Michelin runs local initiatives to keep drivers informed about the importance of checking their tyre pressures, not only for their own safety, but also to reduce fuel consumption. The Company's Fill Up With Air road show runs throughout the UK and Europe annually, and offers fleet and private drivers free tyre pressure checks and advice on tyre maintenance.

On the global stage, Michelin continues to actively encourage advances in sustainable mobility through its bi-annual Challenge Bibendum rally. These events take place in different countries, and are supported by car, truck and motorcycle manufacturers from around the world along with component manufacturers, scientific institutions and non-government organisations.

13 GLASS

Steve Greenway
Partnership Manager
Auto Windscreens

Please introduce yourself

I am a Partnership Manager within Auto Windscreens' fleet sales team. I have been with the business for 27 years in both my current role, dealing with national contract hire, leasing and rental companies, and formerly in a local sales role, managing the glass needs of small fleets.

Regardless of the role and size of fleet, I believe it is important, as a Partnership Manager, to build multi-level partnerships with customers to ensure Auto Windscreens provides the services that meet their fleet's needs.

Please give us an overview of the windscreen market.

The windscreen repair and replacement market in the UK is worth around half a billion pounds. It has three key national players, Auto Windscreens, Autoglass and National Windscreens. Together they account for around 75% of all automotive glass repaired or replaced in the UK each year – roughly three million incidents. Small, independent automotive glazing companies handle the remaining 25% of the market.

The larger players in the industry offer nationwide coverage with a network of fitting centres supported by a fleet of mobile technicians. The geographical spread and resources of national automotive glazing services companies makes them an ideal business partner for insurance companies and contract hire and leasing companies, whose customer base tends to be UK-wide.

The primary activity of most automotive glazing services companies is the repair and replacement of vehicle glass. Auto Windscreens, however, also manufactures windscreens. It is the only company of its kind to do this. Producing windscreens gives Auto Windscreens greater control over the supply chain and market forces. It also has the added bonus of being able to make any unusual windscreens if they are not able to be easily sourced through the usual channels.

The customer base for the automotive glazing services sector is primarily drawn from three main groups – insurers, fleets and direct consumers. Direct consumers represent the smallest customer group. They are typically consumers with third party insurance which does not include glass cover, or those with specialist requirements, such as classic car restorers.

Are the majority of damaged windscreens replaced at fitting centres or by mobile service units?

Fleets favour a mobile service. Using a mobile service can help fleets get their vehicles back on the road more quickly, particularly if the automotive glazing services company has the specialist tools and equipment to ensure that weather conditions do not compromise its mobile service. If a customer does not have adequate cover at their premises, then a windscreen replacement cannot be undertaken when it's raining, which will ultimately result in the job being cancelled and rescheduled until better weather.

Auto Windscreens, has developed a Wet Weather Canopy Van to ensure there are fewer rain-related job cancellations. Taking this further, the company has also worked in conjunction with Dow Automotive – the world's number one automotive glass chemical company – to develop a new primer for use in sub-zero and damp conditions. The primer is so revolutionary that Dow Automotive is making it available worldwide.

Are all replacement windscreens supplied by the original manufacturer or are non-original windscreens available too?

There are only a handful of windscreen manufacturers – primarily Pilkington and Saint Gobain.

Auto Windscreens also manufactures windscreens and is the only automotive glazing services company to do so. Producing its own windscreens enables Auto Windscreens to be less at the mercy of market forces and more in control of the supply chain.

Regardless of the manufacturer, it is important to ensure that replacement windscreens carry either the UK standard – BS857 Safety Glass for Land Transport – or the European e-Mark. Either of these standards ensures the replacement windscreen has been manufactured to the highest quality standards.

Is it good practice for fleet managers to specify that they prefer an OEM windscreen or doesn't it really matter?

As long as the windscreen carries either of the recognised quality assurance marks – BS 857 Safety Glass for Land Transport or e-Mark – there is absolutely no difference in quality between an OEM windscreen and one manufactured by another supplier.

Asking for an OEM windscreen could delay the automotive glazing services provider obtaining one quickly. If the vehicle is brand new to market, for instance, then windscreens and other replacement parts will be in short supply which could mean that the windscreen company is unable to get your vehicle back on the road quickly

Additionally, if you select an automotive glazing services company that uses quality-tested materials and follows a recognised fitting process, then a windscreen replacement will return a vehicle to equivalent OEM specification.

When can a windscreen be repaired and when must it be replaced?

It is possible to repair chips and very small cracks on windscreens. A successful repair, however, is very much dependent on the size of the damage and the area on the windscreen it is located.

If you are not sure, then visit an automotive glazing services' fitting centre for a free windscreen check and they will be able to advise whether a repair is possible. Alternatively, visit Auto Windscreens' website – www.autowindscreens.co.uk – which provides visitors with an interactive tutorial to identify whether minor windscreen cracks and chips can be repaired.

If you notice a chip in your windscreen, get it repaired as soon as possible as, eventually, it will become a crack and you will require a more costly windscreen replacement.

Are repaired windscreens as strong as replacement units?

A windscreen is given its strength by the PVB interlayer which is sandwiched between two pieces of glass. If a chip or small crack does not pierce the PVB interlayer then the windscreen will be returned to its full strength with a resin repair. To ensure the quality of the repair, choose a company that follows the BSAU242a code of practice for glass repair.

Other than the cost-saving, are there any other benefits of a repair compared to a replacement?

The cost-savings of a windscreen repair over a replacement cannot be underestimated. For fleets there can be the difference in hundreds of pounds. Better still, for fully comprehensively insured drivers a repair is usually free and there is no loss of no claims discount.

Other than the enormous cost savings, there are also numerous other benefits to having a windscreen repaired. Repairs are far quicker to do than a replacement. They usually take around 30 minutes whereas it is a minimum of two hours for a standard windscreen replacement.

Repairs are also very environmentally friendly. Do you know that: 'The waste from 40 windscreen repairs will fill the palm of your hand, whereas the waste from 40 replacements will fill a skip'?

Several glass supply/fit companies operate in the fleet market. How should a fleet manager choose between them?

With the current focus on corporate manslaughter, health and safety should be top of every fleet manager's list. While price is always a primary consideration, it is also advisable to choose a supply/fit company that has good health and safety practices and procedures, particularly if you are inviting them on to your premises to carry out work.

With so many different types of vehicles, it is essential that automotive glazing technicians have the right training, experience and knowledge of both the vehicle and the glass before they undertake work. For example, failure to reconnect an airbag sensor during a windscreen replacement could have tragic consequences for the driver.

A commitment to health and safety should be a 'must have' for fleet managers choosing a supplier. On the next page is a checklist that fleet managers can use as a starting point for appointing an automotive glazing services partner.

Does a fleet manager really need to know anything about glass?

It is not necessary at all for a fleet manager to know about glass. The vehicle's registration number should tell a glass company all they need to know about the replacement glass needed for the vehicle. Even the insurers rely on the glass companies to be the experts.

Auto Windscreens' contact centre agents are trained to ask the right questions about the vehicle, its glass and the damage to ensure we get the correct information. Additionally, they can advise if windscreen damage can be repaired rather than replaced, which will save the fleet manager both time and money.

To ensure the best, most streamlined service possible, it is advisable for the fleet manager to provide the appointed supplier with all its fleet's vehicles' VRN data upfront as well as any other information, such as non-factory fitted amendments.

Automotive Glazing Services Provider Checklist	Yes/No
Technicians undergo ongoing, industry-recognised training and development?	
Relevant and up-to-date Quality Management systems?	
All repairs carried out to BSAU242a?	
All replacement glass fitted carries BS857 Safety Glass for Land Transport or e-Mark?	
Guarantees on all glass repairs and fitting?	
Pre and post inspection procedures?	
Service provided in areas we require it?	
UK-based contact centre?	
24/7/365 contact centre?	
Freephone job booking number?	
Online booking facility?	
Option to have work done mobile or fitting centre?	
True all-weather mobile service provided?	
Fitting centre with comfortable waiting areas?	
Bespoke response system offered?	
Out of hours repair and replacement service?	
Good stock levels and stock distribution facilities?	
Account facilities available?	
Nominated Account manager?	
Relevant monthly Management Information (MI) supplied free of charge?	
Fleet cards supplied free of charge?	
Commitment to 'Repair before Replace'?	
Quotes provided before job commenced?	
Customer Services Department?	
Customer testimonies available?	
Recognised brand?	

A checklist as a starting point for appointing an automotive glazing services partner.

This will enable the service provider to deal with things more quickly and efficiently throughout the process.

Should fleet managers have a direct relationship with a windscreen company or should they leave this to the insurance company?

It is entirely up to the fleet manager whether or not they choose to have a direct relationship with an automotive glazing services company or leave it to their supplier – whether it's a contract hire and leasing company or an insurer.

If your business needs will not be met by the service level agreements in place with the insurer or leasing company, then it is advisable to talk directly to the windscreen company and establish a direct relationship.

Having a direct relationship can help speed up the glass repair and replacement process. Some windscreen companies, like Auto Windscreens, will supply fleet cards, free of charge, to fleet drivers. The cards contain information which helps speed up the job booking and invoicing process.

What services should a fleet manager expect to receive from a windscreen company?

First and foremost a fleet manager should expect to receive the service they have been promised!

Quality and safety should be top of a windscreen company's list. To ensure that your vehicles' windscreen repairs meet the highest safety and quality standards, ensure you choose a supplier that follows the BSAU242a code of practice for glass repair and uses replacement glass that carries either the BS857 Safety Glass for Land Transport or the e-Mark.

As a minimum, a fleet manager should expect a windscreen company to meet the needs of their drivers, take into account driver situation, have good parts availability, be committed to minimising downtime and have a seamless billing process.

It is advisable to develop a partnership with your automotive glazing services provider – whether this is with an account manager or direct with a fitting centre. Having this relationship will enable you to ensure that your windscreen services provider is well informed to meet the needs of your fleet.

How can fleet managers ensure they pay the right price for a windscreen?

If a fleet manager has an account with an automotive glazing services company, then the likelihood is that they will receive considerable discount on the cost of a replacement part.

An automotive glazing service should not just be measured on price, rather value for money. For example if you have a large mixed fleet that requires a national, mobile service, it is likely that a large automotive glazing services company would have to provide this. One of the benefits of choosing a national windscreen replacement company is that they have greater buying power.

Please tell us more about Auto Windscreens

Auto Windscreens is a leading independent automotive glazing services provider in the UK and was voted No. 1 supplier to fleets. It has a dedicated freephone, UK contact centre (0800 999 8000) and online booking service which is available 24/7/365 days a year. Additionally the business operates a network of 98 fitting centres which are supported by a fully equipped all-weather mobile service. We provide a glazing service for virtually any vehicle or equipment – from cars, lorries and coaches to rail, marine, agricultural and plant equipment.

Having a national fitting capability, coupled with a 38-year history, has enabled Auto Windscreens to develop relationships with a vast proportion of the UK's fleet companies, whether large or small.

Every year, more fleets choose Auto Windscreens as their preferred automotive glazing services provider for five key reasons:

- We have industry-leading tools, equipment and systems to ensure we are responding to our customers needs accurately and getting their vehicles back on the road more quickly.

- Making our customers' lives easy is at the forefront of our thinking and enables

us to provide great service. Whether it is customer-facing or behind the scenes, we are always looking at how we can do things better and more efficiently for the benefit of our customers – whether they are the fleet operator or the end user – the drivers.

- Continuous improvement and innovation in all areas of our business means we are able to reduce our bottom-line costs and pass these savings onto our customers through highly competitive pricing.

- We innovate and invest in our service provision at all levels to ensure that we deliver what we say we will do and keep our promises to our customers.

- Working in partnership is key. We work closely with, and listen to, our customers to ensure we provide the most appropriate service to their business.

Have windscreen suppliers changed the way they deal with the fleet market in recent years?

Auto Windscreens has invested a lot of time in listening to its fleet customers to find out what they really want from a windscreen supplier. The overwhelming feedback was that they wanted more jobs to be completed by mobile service units, fleet checks and the provision of meaningful management information (MI).

The implications of duty of care have really changed the way fleet managers deal with windscreen suppliers. Prior to this, windscreens were regarded as a necessary inconvenience. Now, fleet managers are more conscious of the health and safety implications of damaged windscreens and are welcoming free fleet checks from windscreen suppliers. Fleet checks have the added bonus of helping fleet managers better manage their glass costs by identifying and repairing chips before they become cracks resulting in a costly windscreen replacement.

Fleet managers are also asking for more meaningful MI to help them actively forecast and manage their glass costs. In response to this, Auto Windscreens has developed an industry-leading MI report, Template 10. It enables fleets to:

- Understand the operational performance of their glass service provider
- look inwardly at their business and identify what may be causing them pain
- Support or influence fleet buying decisions
- Monitor spend
- Have information in one place that is already analysed

What developments have there been in your sector that have been particularly valuable to fleet customers?

Glazing is playing an increasing role in the overall design of vehicles as manufacturers seek to enhance the driver experience with the overall use of glass.

While this was once confined to the prestige end of the market it is now filtering through to more mainstream vehicles. Panoramic windscreens, for instance, are now appearing in mass production cars, the Vauxhall Astra being one of them – which is excellent news for fleet drivers.

Windscreen sizes have increased dramatically and as such, health and safety regulations require that many windscreens must not be lifted by a single technician. Many windscreens companies have had to invest heavily in lifting equipment.

A robotic lifting device, known as SUMO 30, is the latest piece of groundbreaking technology to be introduced to Auto Windscreens' national network of fitting centres and mobile service fleet.

Designed in-house, SUMO 30 can be used on any terrain, including grass, lorry parks and workshops to lift glass weighing up to 30kg. It is portable, safe and easy to use. More importantly, it allows the technician to undertake no manual handling of the glass.

Lifting devices like SUMO 30 significantly reduce the amount of time it takes a mobile technician to replace glass.

Similarly, many windscreen companies have had to improve the capability of their mobile service offering in line with fleet customer demand. Rain is very much the enemy of the mobile windscreen replacement. If there is not sufficient cover available when it rains, then a windscreen replacement cannot be completed. In 2007 the Wet Weather Canopy Van was introduced to Auto Windscreens' fleet of mobile service units.

Since its introduction, the Canopy Van has proved a huge success with technicians and customers alike. It enables more mobile windscreen replacements to be completed in damp conditions if the customer doesn't have the required covered facilities. It has led to a dramatic reduction in the number of mobile windscreen replacements we are forced to cancel in damp and cold weather conditions.

Also helping to reduce cancelled mobile jobs in cold and wet weather, is a new primer we have developed in conjunction with Dow Automotive.

It can be used at sub zero temperatures and also in damp conditions. It is so revolutionary that Dow is now making it available worldwide.

If you were to advise a fleet manager on the best practice when it comes to choosing their windscreen supplier, what would that advice be?

With so many developments in automotive glazing, it is important that a fleet manager chooses a windscreen company, regardless of size, that continually invests in training and innovation to ensure they can deliver their service commitment. If the company does not have the right tools, equipment and training then this will lead to them breaking their service promise to you, which could result in your vehicles being off the road longer than they need to.

Think carefully about what service level your fleet requires and choose an automotive glazing service company that best matches this at a fair price.

Steve Greenway
Partnership Manager
Auto Windscreens

Beware the
chip on the shoulder

auto
windscreens™

For immediate assistance, call us free on
0800 999 8000
FIGHTING THE ENEMY ON THE GROUND

Calls may be recorded and/or monitored

14 DAILY HIRE

Kathleen Whittam
Regional Sales Director
National Car Rental

Please introduce yourself and your company.

I have over 25 years' experience in the vehicle leasing and rental sector. As Regional Sales Director at National Car Rental, I head up a team of key account directors, territory sales managers and the telesales team looking after key fleet and corporate customers.

National's consultative approach means I spend a lot of my time meeting with customers, working with them to identify where greater efficiencies can be made and how specific business targets and travel policies can be met.

National Car Rental is part of Europcar UK Group, the UK's leading vehicle rental organisation with an industry-leading fleet of over 60,000 vehicles from over 200 locations nationwide.

Europcar in the UK is a subsidiary of Europcar, which was founded more than 50 years ago in Paris and now serves business and leisure customers throughout Europe, Africa, the Middle East, Latin America and the Asia-Pacific region through 5,300 rental outlets in 160 countries.

What sort of vehicles can be rented?

Whatever the journey, the rental industry today has a vehicle to match.

Within National alone, there are over 100 different models from 26 manufacturers. Cars range from small city run-arounds to larger hatchbacks, saloons, MPVs and hybrids. All rental cars are maintained to manufacturer's specifications and covered by 24-hour breakdown assistance for added peace of mind. This is a crucial factor in supporting duty of care responsibilities for businesses.

The vehicle rental industry offers a wide choice of 'green' solutions to meet environmental targets. In fact, because rental cars are relatively new, capitalising on advances in tackling CO_2 emissions, they can be a greener choice than driving an older vehicle. For example our fleet has an average CO_2 of 157 g/km compared to the average UK car parc which has 164.9 g/km CO_2 (source: SMMT 2007).

LCVs are also a critical element of any rental fleet, ranging from smaller vans such as the Ford Connect to the large LDV Maxus equipped with a tail-lift, which makes even the biggest tasks easy to handle. The main rental organisations also offer long term van rental with the option of decals, tow bars and other customisations to meet customer demand.

When specialist transport is needed, services such as National's Specialist Vehicle Management Centre come into play. From refrigerated vans, 12 and 15 seater minibuses, motorcycles, Lorries to restored World War Two tanks.

And finally when impressions count, renting a prestige car can be the solution. From the fun Mini Cooper S to the seriously sporty Porsche Boxster up to luxury 4x4s such as the Range Rover Vogue, prestige rental fleets offer a first class service in luxury car rental plus the opportunity to drive some of the world's most coveted performance cars on the road today.

Presumably the daily rental market offers different services for the managers of small and large organisations. What services are available?

While the core service – the right vehicle in the right place at the right time – is the same regardless of the business size, the rental industry now offers an enormous amount of flexibility to businesses to help support cost control, duty of care responsibilities and environmental concerns – whether they rent one car a month or 100.

The key point is that the rental industry has evolved to become service-led so that no matter how large or small an organisation, there will be a solution to fit – whether it's based on a personal relationship with a local branch or an international contract covering multiple global locations.

But first, looking at the basic services available to all businesses:

1 hour to 6 months or more

The term 'daily rental' is now a bit of a misnomer. Vehicle rental can be for an hour, a day to six months or more, meeting demands from businesses for short to longer term transport solutions. Longer term solutions are particularly useful for businesses affected by seasonal demands, working on short term-contracts or needing to supply transport for temporary staff. The beauty of longer term rental is that there's no early termination fee – the business just has the vehicles for the time they are needed.

At the other end of the scale 1 hour rentals ensure businesses have access to vehicles to support those quick jobs that arise, helping to manage costs.

Choice of Reservation Routes

A choice of reservation routes is offered for all businesses – whether online through rental management systems, phone or fax or at the local branch. The client's travel policies can be applied at the point of booking and driver profiles created to speed the booking process.

Online reservation systems can allow bookers and drivers to place and amend reservations at any time including authorising, extending and terminating rentals, viewing and monitoring reservations.

Keeping an eye with MI

Management information helps identify where cost-savings can be made and to support duty of care responsibilities. This can be delivered online or in hard copy reports.

Online Invoicing

Keeping tabs on invoices and expenditure is also supported by delivery of invoices direct to the desktop.

Payment Methods

Businesses can also benefit from a choice of payment facilities including payment by credit card.

Flexible Rates

Rates can be negotiated based on the volume of rentals and any ancillary services required such as delivery and collection. Customers may choose a rate that includes zero excess on rentals so there's no need to worry about damage costs or use their company's own insurance, making rental rates more cost-effective than ever.

Once a rate has been agreed it should remain static for the period of the contract regardless of market dynamics.

RESPONDING TO THE NEEDS OF MAJOR CORPORATES

Technological advances have driven cost-efficiencies throughout the rental process – from booking a car to issuing an invoice and management information – and all customers benefit from these developments. However where large volumes of rentals are concerned, specialised services are utilised to bring even greater efficiencies and control over the provision of temporary transport solutions. These include:

- **Dedicated customer reservations, sales and customer support teams** – Specifically focused on the requirements of fleet & corporate businesses and their drivers, with market-focused teams ensuring services meet specific sector needs.

- **Systems Integration** – transparently linking the customer's and rental operator's systems providing enhanced control on the entire vehicle reservations process.

- **Tailored Product Development** – In response to specific customer requirements, including customer-branded vehicle rental websites, designed, hosted and managed by the rental provider

- **SMS service** – To extend a rental at the press of a button on a mobile 'phone. This creates an accurate record of the request which means fewer queries at the end of the rental.

- **Complete Outsourcing Solutions** – Including 'ring-fencing' of fleets, branding of vehicles, full systems integration and customer-branded on and off-line marketing and sales support.
- **Affinity Products** – Tailored programmes for customers' employees and the employees of fleet customers' customers.
- **Bespoke Fleets** – Including diesel and eco fleets to meet specific customer requirements.
- **Pool Car Fleets** – Operated at a customer's own premises, removing the burden of fleet management and duty of care issues and freeing up capital assets.
- **Automated Claims** – Designed specifically to support fleet & corporate customers' administration and reporting of insurance claims.

How can daily hire companies help fleet managers to reduce costs?

Businesses should be demanding cost savings and efficiencies from their rental company that go beyond having the right car in the right place at the right time – that's a given. We're living in an era of heightened health and safety legislation and greater awareness of green issues and both these issues have a direct impact on costs. Businesses need to work with a vehicle rental provider who will help them meet their corporate and social responsibilities in a cost-effective and efficient manner – from monitoring the use of vehicles driven, to cutting down on paper wastage.

The good news for fleet managers is that the sheer competitiveness of the rental industry combined with its maturity have made this, beyond all doubt, a service industry. Businesses such as National are constantly striving to develop innovative solutions that make the fleet manager's job easier and bring them cost savings into the bargain. And this is where the application of online technology has had such a massive impact for rental providers and their customers.

E-BUSINESS IS TOUCHING EVERY PART OF THE RENTAL PROCESS

From reservations in line with company policy through to online management information, e-billing and query resolution, e-business now touches every aspect of the rental process to make it smoother, quicker and more efficient. Just as importantly it also gives fleet managers greater control over bookings, costs incurred and valuable information to help support duty of care responsibilities.

Forget paper, we are in an age now when every aspect of the process can and should be managed online. If a rental company isn't exploiting these technologies it isn't being efficient in its own business and is therefore unlikely to be able to offer any worthwhile cost-savings.

AUTHORISATION OF RENTALS

Of course as a cost control measure and with the strengthening of corporate manslaughter legislation, fleet managers may wish to authorise the rental before the booking process is completed. Rental Management systems such as carhirebooker.com from National now offer a workflow function ensuring that when a driver or booker raises a reservation, the details of the vehicle group booked, the duration and the cost are automatically emailed to the fleet or travel manager responsible for authorising the rental. They can then check that the vehicle type being booked is appropriate for the task and keep a record of the cost of the rental.

E-BILLING

Looking at the invoicing process, millions of invoices are issued by car rental companies annually, wasting resources from paper to postage. However, the process of e-billing means that invoices may be queried and corrected on-line with duplicate invoices produced and management data provided straight to the customer's desktop. Any additional copies of the invoice can also be sent electronically, meaning same day delivery anywhere in the world.

CONTROLLING USAGE IS KEY TO MANAGING COST AND RISK

Finally, online management information is a crucial tool for fleet managers, enabling them to work with the rental provider to monitor vehicle usage on an ongoing basis. This helps to identify areas where travel policies may need to be tightened whilst also finding areas where cost savings can be made.

For example, National provides extensive reporting on rental fuel usage for corporate customers, helping fleet managers to spot where savings can be made through driver training, better route planning and generally through more efficient use of vehicles. Certainly fleet managers should be demanding this information from their rental supplier if this isn't currently being offered.

FLEXIBLE RENTAL

Of course, the sheer flexibility of rental can help reduce unnecessary journeys and save fuel and costs. Hourly and one way rentals for example, backed up by delivery and collection cut down miles incurred and cut fuel use. Conversely, the longer the rental, the more cost-effective it can become.

In an increasing unpredictable economic climate, businesses need solutions that offer cost control without cutting corners in terms of staff health and safety. Vehicle rental does just that, providing immediate and longer term solutions to get staff from A to B whilst supporting duty of care responsibilities.

Presumably clients can carry out much of their rental management by using rental company's online services?

The entire rental process – from reservation in line with company policy through to e-billing and query resolution - can be conducted online. This not only improves efficiencies but gives fleet managers greater control over bookings and costs incurred, as well as valuable information to help support corporate and social responsibilities.

ONLINE RESERVATIONS AND RENTAL MANAGEMENT

Systems such as carhirebooker.com - National's self service online rental management solution - offer complete control of the reservation & rental process. Fleet managers, bookers and drivers can obtain quotations, place, amend, confirm, extend, terminate, cancel, view and monitor reservations.

When a vehicle is booked all of the emails generated contain full details of the hire and any extra information that the customer wants to capture. The customer can receive their booking confirmation, whilst the email confirmation to the fleet manager may also include the cost of hire and any additional information they may require. Up to 11 customer-specific data fields can be captured from the booker, enabling fleet managers to manage costs and understand the reasons for hire.

When a driver or booker raises a reservation, the details of the vehicle group booked, the duration and the cost are automatically emailed to the fleet or travel manager responsible for authorising the rental. They can then check that the vehicle type being booked is appropriate for the task and keep a record of the cost for the rental.

If they approve the request, the system sends the reservation to the branch and generates an email to confirm the booking to the driver or booker. If the request is declined an email is generated to the driver or booker to confirm this.

These systems also offer the facility to customise the car groupings to match a company's own classification, rather than using the rental provider's. This makes it easier than ever for drivers and bookers to identify the right car group. In addition, customers can enter an address for delivery or collection and the system will calculate the distance from the nearest branch, which is particularly beneficial for companies who are charged by the mile.

Feedback is clearly crucial to the ongoing development of rental management systems so the key systems include the facility to receive automatic feedback on service quality – both the rental process and the vehicle.

Finally, rental management systems can be tailored or personalised to a customer's brand including logo and message of the day.

SMS MESSAGING

SMS rental services simplify the notification of rental extensions and vehicle mileages to enhance billing accuracy and support duty of care. Drivers have the option to provide a mobile number as the key point of contact to be held on the rental agreement. Text messages are then sent to remind the driver of overdue vehicles or imminent return dates. Each message includes an option to extend the rental by simply responding by text. For longer rental periods of 25 days or more, vehicle mileage is requested via text, so drivers can respond instantly. This means more accurate mileage information for businesses, and importantly, raises awareness of high mileage vehicles to fleet managers.

BYPASS THE COUNTER AND GO STRAIGHT TO THE CAR

The development of key lockers at key airports in the UK by organisations such as National means that drivers arriving to collect a vehicle can bypass the rental counter, swipe their credit card through the key locker and have the vehicle keys and rental agreement automatically dispensed.

CAR RETURN

Just as important as car collection, is the process of car return and this has been automated with quick check-in systems. Rental agents employ hand held devices at key locations so drivers can simply had over their keys and get on with the rest of their journey. Quick check-in systems link directly with the central reservation systems and some such as National's also include automated damage pricing. This uses cost information obtained directly from motor manufacturers and independent parts vendors to enable an instant calculation of the repair cost of any damage that is identified when the car is returned.

INVOICE AT THE END OF THE RENTAL

Providing total online access to invoices, e-billing enables customers to manage the use and costs of vehicle rental. Invoices are provided direct to the customer's desktop within 24 hours of the rental completion.

ONLINE MANAGEMENT INFORMATION AND REPORTS

Online management information gives businesses instant access to vehicle rental usage data, at any time, providing the facility to assess every aspect of vehicle usage and cost. Reports are accessible on vehicle usage to suit an organisation's requirements, with total flexibility over the level and frequency of reporting. The reports are also extremely comprehensive, allowing extensive comparison and trends reporting for a business. National's systems allow reporting to go back as far as 2004.

E-SERVICE FOR CUSTOMER SERVICE ENQUIRIES

Even customer service is supported through online developments such as E-service from National. This is an online customer service tool, enabling customers to register and report service issues for a more streamlined issue resolution process.

At National we have brought together this complete suite of online and counter-bypass products to create one integrated 'self-service' solution for fleet managers and drivers. This is designed to improve business and traveller efficiency and experience; reduce business costs and, importantly, assist companies to meet their duty of care responsibilities. Once the initial reservation is made the customer doesn't need to provide any further information or have any further contact – unless they wish to.

FLEET INDUSTRY SYSTEMS INTEGRATION

Of course, major fleet organisations require systems integration to give them full control of their rental requirements. National is the only daily rental company to fully integrate its reservation system with the 1Link hire network, operated by Epyx. Used by a number of major fleet companies, 1Link provides a single interface with suppliers, reducing administrative tasks and improving business efficiency and accuracy.

There are so many rental companies out there, how is a fleet manager to choose between them?

There are a number of factors to consider when choosing a rental company:

- **Full service rental company**

  Check that you are dealing with a full service rental company that can provide a complete range of flexible services, a wide choice of vehicles – cars, vans, specialist and prestige - and a good network of locations, including airports. Make sure that if you need a car at 3am in the morning, they have the infrastructure to meet that need.

- **Fleet and size of network**

  The fleet and size of network is an important consideration but check that the fleet can be moved if necessary between locations so that your needs can always be met. Make sure there are locations near to your key sites too.

- **E-business**

  Appoint a supplier who has the capability to deliver e-business solutions to cut costs and improve efficiency. For example, online reservations, e-vouchers, e-billing, online management information, even online customer service for swift query resolution.

- **Choice of reservation routes**

  A good vehicle rental organisation will offer a choice of reservation routes, online, phone, fax, email, Implant team – or a combination of all to suit your needs

- **Support Travel Policies**

  Make sure the rental provider can implement a system that ensures you're your corporate policies and guidelines for vehicle rental are adhered to, in order to support duty of care responsibilities, environmental concerns and, of course, cost controls. Rental policies should be automatically applied and driver profiles pre-filled for online bookings – speeding up the booking time and ensuring accuracy of information

- **Delivery and Collection**

  Check that delivery & collection covers home or business address and is available inside and outside normal branch hours.

- **One-way**

  Ensure vehicles can be collected from one location and returned to another for one-way trips. Many smaller providers cannot offer this service.

- **One day to as long as you need**

  Some rental companies offer attractive and flexible options for medium-term rental for both cars and commercial vehicles. This may be a more cost-effective option in the case of new recruits and employees on fixed-term contracts.

- **Preferential Leisure Rates**

  Your staff probably rent cars privately when on holiday. Pick a rental partner who can provide them with competitive holiday rental rates for all the top tourist destinations. This is a great staff benefit at no cost to you.

Choosing the right vehicle rental supplier really has to be a two way process. Any potential supplier will need a good understanding of the volume and profile of your business such as what vehicles are rented, how many rentals you generate, the average length of rental and use of ancillary services such as delivery and collection. Give them details such as how many airport rentals you use, how many rentals bookings require delivery and collection, and the split between home and business delivery and collection. Often the charges vary. Also tell them your requirements for specialist or prestige vehicles. Do the same insurance terms apply to all your rentals?

Providing them with this level of detail will help ensure that the tenders you receive are realistic, deliverable and sustainable.

Produce a shortlist of financially evaluated companies from a selected group of potential suppliers, and then have face-to-face meetings to make the final selection. With the sums out of the way you can focus time on ensuring the chemistry is right. During this process ask for previous experience of your type of business including testimonials.

Finally ensure you select a supplier who will work alongside you to deliver bespoke transport solutions to meet the needs of your business. Check they have access to the skills, expertise and technology to provide services beyond the provision of core

daily rental and that this expertise comes as part of the contract – not as an extra cost.

When it comes to typical cost, there are many variables to consider such as volume, the profile of the business and reservation method used. Rental businesses will agree a standard rate for rentals for the groups of vehicles used based on these factors and may provide separate rates for ancillary services used such as delivery and collection and one-way rentals. Alternatively, inclusive products may be provided if customers prefer.

Judge how the rates stack up by price-checking a number of providers in line with what services, commitments and products they offer in return, and then negotiate a deal with your preferred provider. At the end of the day make sure you are on the same wave-length as the people you will be working with – it's this human element that makes the real difference to the service.

How can rental companies help multinational companies?

Multinationals have an enormous challenge in terms of managing transport costs for drivers as well as ensuring they are supporting the duty of care they have to their staff worldwide. However, by working with one rental provider covering all the business's locations, they can gain a clear understanding of the vehicle rentals undertaken, allowing them to control costs more effectively as well as take advantage of tools to tackle the very important corporate responsibilities that every business must address.

As European business travel continues to expand, many rental operators such as National are expanding to meet the demands of corporate customers.

- **Global expertise**

  Working with a global rental provider means customers benefit from expert knowledge at both a local and global level and also ensures a consistent level of service is offered. A dedicated international sales team will support the account, working with a centralised procurement department along with local country travel management departments.

  This means fleet and travel managers, travel buyers and travel agents of international businesses can gain a true understanding of the local markets they operate in.

- **Fleet**

  Businesses have the assurance that their drivers have access to a quality fleet of vehicles, generally less than six months old and covered by roadside assistance. This also includes one-way rental, as well as delivery and collection in many countries.

- **Central Reservations**

  Online booking systems mean drivers and bookers can make reservations 24 hours a day, regardless of their global location and pre-filled driver profiles make booking fast and accurate.

- **Fast Track**

  Global businesses also benefit from frequent renter programmes such as Emerald Club from National which means:

  No queues
  No forms to sign
  No fuss
  Chosen vehicle ready to collect at the Emerald Club desk
  Vehicle held for up to three hours after agreed pick-up time
  Member status

- **Preferential Rates**

  Rental providers may also offer competitive rates for employees of corporate customers when they rent privately in global destinations. For example, National's unique international affinity programme offers corporate customers car hire at the best daily rental price in the market.

- **Frequent flyers**

  Rental operators are committed to bringing added value benefits to corporate customers. Business travellers can make the most of the frequent flyer partnerships offered by their rental provider. Customers just have to present their airline Frequent Flyer membership card at the rental counter when they arrive to collect their car.

- **Pointing the way**

  Time is precious for business travellers, which is why rental operators are investing in technology to help customers get to their destination as quickly and easily as possible. GPS units are now widely available to hire across key business destinations globally to help smooth the journey.

What are the benefits of setting up a corporate account?

Setting up a corporate account for vehicle rental services offers many benefits to the fleet manager.

For a start, the business can set its terms and service levels required from the outset of the contract. Rates can be agreed based on the volume and profile of the business, ensuring and the agreed rate will then remain static for the duration of the contract so that the business is able to budget accurately for travel costs. Discounted rates for overseas leisure travel for staff may also be negotiated, as a valuable employee 'perk'.

A dedicated account management team will be assigned to the account to ensure the rental service runs smoothly and any teething problems are ironed out quickly. This team will invariably have solid experience of working with businesses on their travel management needs and will provide invaluable support and advice for the duration of the contract.

Of course access to a wide fleet of quality vehicles, often within 2 hours of a request is guaranteed along with all the back up support required in terms of rental management systems, online management information and e-billing.

Accounts also benefit from tailor-made services including:

- In-house rental teams
- Bespoke microsites for ease of booking
- Delivery and collection services
- A tailored fleet to company requirements

Finally, rental providers recognise individual business needs and offer loyalty programmes that can be tailored to all business travellers from the occasional renter to the more frequent traveller.

What developments have there been in the daily hire market in the last few years that have been particularly valuable to fleet managers?

Changes in the daily rental sector have largely been driven by the challenges facing customers in terms of cost management, strengthened corporate manslaughter legislation and the environmental agenda.

'Control' has been the watchword – control of drivers, control of fuel use, control of vehicle use and control of costs.

Through advances in technology, fleet managers now have the power to manage and monitor rental use and costs much more closely than ever before. Rental Management systems allow automated mandating of rentals in line with travel policies and authorisation of rentals by line managers can be made part of the process. Every part of the rental process can now be conducted online through to the invoice at the end of the rental.

Online management information now provides detailed understanding of rental use, allowing constant review and evaluation of where costs are being incurred – right down to miles driven, fuel used and repair costs. This also helps inform fleet managers about the need for driver training and supports duty of care responsibilities.

In fact the strengthening of corporate manslaughter legislation in April 2008 has seen many small and medium sized concerns currently operating 'grey fleets' (private cars used for business) start adopting rental as part of a business travel policy. This offers peace of mind that a vehicle being used for a business trip is in good condition and covered by roadside assistance. Rental providers have responded to that demand with services tailored to smaller businesses to make access to rental as easy and cost-effective as possible.

The focus on vehicle emissions has changed the profile of the rental fleet too. Fleets now include a good choice of fuel-efficient vehicles including hybrids such as the Toyota Prius. Specific 'eco' fleets have been developed for businesses, not just in the UK but overseas too – demonstrating the increasing focus businesses today have on cutting emissions. Corporate customers now also have access to much more information on the average CO_2 emissions of vehicles on fleet. For example, National now offers this information for each of its vehicle groups.

Is anything happening now, or will anything be happening soon, that is likely to change the daily hire landscape for fleet managers?

The rental industry is bracing itself and its customers for change. While we are seeing an increase in rental business from some sectors, fleet managers should be aware that prices are likely to rise across the industry unless the current economic situation improves.

This is primarily because the motor manufacturers have been particularly hard hit by the economic turmoil we are all experiencing. And the truth is, whatever affects motor manufacturers has a direct impact on the rental sector and we are already starting to experience the shockwaves.

Some stark facts; this year - cars imported into the UK have seen a cost increase of between 15% and 17%, used car values have dropped by as much as 25% and next year new car sales are predicted to drop below 2 million. This could see manufacturers simply cutting back on production, moving to a three-day week and/or temporarily shutting factories.

Not surprisingly, these conditions are forcing motor manufacturers to become much more disciplined about the way in which they work with rental operators. The challenge of remarketing rental cars will drive holding costs up or may even force manufacturers to step away from the rental market altogether. Rental operators taking the residual risk themselves won't be immune either. These businesses are already experiencing the higher costs caused by poor residual values. Manufacturers wanting more control over the value at which their vehicles are being sold, may decide to reduce the volumes they put into the rental market.

Needless to say, relationships between the rental industry and manufacturers have never been more important.

When you take all this into account then consider the proposed tax changes that come into effect in April 2009, the rental industry in the UK is facing an immense challenge to contain costs.

If you were to advise a fleet manager on the best practice when it comes to daily hire, what would that advice be?

There are two elements to best practice – the relationship with the rental provider and the relationship with drivers.

First looking at rental providers – the key to best practice is to agree service levels from the outset of the contract. Typically these can include:

- **Booking Channels & Call Centre Standards**

  You should ensure rental vehicles can be booked via a number of different channels so that you can make a reservation on-line (through carhirebooker.com for example), book through a travel agent, use a real-time desktop system or book over the phone.

When booking over the phone, the car rental company should use its best endeavours to ensure that all calls are answered within an agreed time.

- **Delivery Service**

  As a corporate customer, the delivery service should cover home and business addresses and should be available inside and outside normal branch operating hours.

- **Abortive Delivery**

  As part of the delivery service contract, agree whether a fixed charge should be made if a car is delivered and is no longer required.

- **Delivery Time**

  Whilst a car rental supplier should use its best endeavours to ensure that vehicles are delivered on time, in extreme cases this may not be possible. Under such circumstances a scale of compensation may be agreed.

- **Collection Service**

  As a corporate customer, collection services should cover home and business addresses and should be available inside and outside normal branch operating hours.

- **Abortive Collection**

  Within the agreed collection service agreement, ensure there is a clear policy regarding charges if a vehicle's keys are not available at the agreed collection, time.

- **Collection Time**

  Whilst the car rental company should use its best endeavours to ensure that vehicles are collected on time, in extreme cases this may not be possible. As with deliveries, a compensation scale should therefore be agreed.

- **One-way rentals**

  Customers should be able to collect a car from one location and return it to another. This service should be available on request.

- **Queries & Complaints**

  The car rental company must use its best endeavours to ensure that customer complaints are kept to a minimum. However, on the rare occasion where customers have a query or complaint regarding a product or service, the car rental company should use its best endeavours to ensure that such issues are resolved within agreed timescales, dependent on the type of query.

- **Upgrades/Downgrades**

  Car rental companies divide their vehicles into groups, with several models available in each. They can't usually guarantee a particular make or model, but under normal circumstances they should provide you with a vehicle from the group for which you have been quoted.

  Whilst every effort should be made to provide customers with a vehicle from the group that they have booked, on some occasions this may not always be possible.

Under such circumstances the car rental company should use its best endeavours to provide a vehicle from the next group up.

Under exceptional circumstances it may be necessary to provide customers with a vehicle of a lower group than the group stated in the confirmed reservation. Naturally, the customer should only be charged the appropriate rate for the lower car group.

- **Invoicing**

  The car rental company should strive to ensure that invoices are correct and that customers (under normal operating conditions) are charged the rate they have been quoted. Any additional rental days or services that fall outside of the rental agreement such as fuel, child/baby seats, additional drivers or satellite navigation equipment are extra and should be paid for if these services are taken at the time of rental.

- **Cancellation policy**

  There should be an agreed cancellation policy which will enable you to change or cancel your reservation within a pre-agreed time limit. This policy may alter according to the reservation method used. If you don't cancel or change your booking within the agreed period then fail to take up the rental, the car rental company may reserve the right to charge you a fee.

  With regard to best practice for drivers, this needs to start with a robust travel policy. This should include the car groups that can be requested, the ancillary services such as delivery and collection that can be utilised and the authorisation process that needs to be in place for rentals to be booked. It should also provide clear guidance on the service standards detailed above so that drivers and bookers are aware of the agreements in place with their rental provider. Finally, clear guidance should be provided to drivers on what they should do in the event of an accident or damage to a vehicle while it is on rent.

How can National help fleet managers?

There's nothing that National can't do when it comes to daily rental services. No other company can offer the breadth of service and support. With National, fleet managers can be assured of access to the UK's largest rental fleet of over 54,000 cars and over 6,000 vans as well as prestige and specialist vehicles from over 200 locations across the UK including all major airports, 24 hours a day, 365 days a year.

Our relationship with motor manufacturers means we have access to some of the newest, most fuel-efficient vehicles on the road today. Every vehicle is covered by 24 hour roadside assistance and our unique FirstCall service ensures that should an accident happen, all appropriate parties are informed without delay.

We are committed to ensuring the right car is in the right place at the right time for our customers with delivery often within two hours of a request. Rentals can be for 1 hour up to 6 months or more, with no early termination penalties, offering businesses the ultimate flexibility.

Reservations can be made via the web, telephone and fax, 24/7 and online management information provides complete control of every aspect of vehicle usage, right down to fuel consumption. We also offer a range of tailor-made solutions for fleet managers with integrated systems and branded websites.

In summary, everything we do is focused on the needs of corporate and fleet customers, providing consistent and knowledgeable support at every level of our organisation.

Kathleen Whittam
Regional Sales Director
National Car Rental
Aldenham Road
Bushey
Watford
WD23 2QQ
Tel: 0845 600 0540
email: business@nationalcar.co.uk

15 FAST-FIT

Mike Wise

Head of Kwik-Fit Fleet.

Please give us an outline of your career in the fast fit market

I started in the tyre business at fourteen years old! Fast-Fit as we commonly call it these days had only just begun: Kwik-Fit started in 1971. At that time tyres were purchased at the franchise dealers or petrol service stations.

I worked at one such service station, and was asked one day to work in the tyre bay. Within hours I was fitting tyres using a bar on a static tyre machine, and a bubble balancer. Only six tyre sizes were needed, Ford Anglia, Ford Cortina, Austin Cambridge, Morris Minor and the original MINI. The answer was always yes to a telephone enquiry, a far cry from today where Kwik-Fit sell around 600 tyre types brands and sizes.

I progressed through the industry and found my niche at Kwik-Fit Fleet. Sales driven, dealing with B2B customers on a long term partnership basis. No single B2B customer has the same product; our bespoke product offerings are as unique as the fleet customers who buy them.

How has the fast-fit business developed?

Fast-fit grew up in the 1970s around three products – tyres, batteries and exhausts – but in the 21st century they are now a one-stop shop for all routine company car and van service, maintenance and repair requirements.

The expansion in the range of services now offered by fast-fits in the 21st century has put companies such as Kwik-Fit – Britain's largest – in the fast lane to securing corporate business.

Fleet decision-makers and company car and van drivers have increasingly turned to fast-fits for a number of reasons: cost savings in comparison with franchise dealers, flexibility as a result of longer opening hours linked to a business culture of long hours' working, the availability of 'come to you' mobile tyre repair and replacement; and, crucially, the relaxation of the European Union Block Exemption, which opened the door to vehicle servicing.

More recently, the focus on occupational road risk management with the April 2008 implementation of the Corporate Manslaughter and Corporate Homicide Act and the January 2009 introduction of the Health and Safety (Offences) Act has resulted in hundreds of fleets nationwide turning to Kwik-Fit for help to ensure vehicles are in tip-top condition.

Has your industry's move into vehicle servicing been a success?

There is no doubt that the fast-fit industry is booming and much of that business success is at the expense of inflexible franchise dealers. The lifting of many of the rules in October 2003 that made vehicle servicing, typically the preserve of the franchise dealer network, was lifted.

Couple these rule changes with the trend for manufacturers to increase service intervals, in some cases to 20,000 miles, which did not take account of the need for drivers to change friction items such as brakes and oil in between major services, and the door was opened for fast-fit developments.

At Kwik-Fit, the capability to undertake the majority of routine service work such as oil changes, brake pads/discs and fluid checks was quickly added to our portfolio and more recently we have added servicing in accordance with manufacturer schedules.

The manufacturers' service initiative enables customers to book a service at a minimum 48 hours notice, which is significantly more convenient than franchise dealers where up to 14 days' notice could be required.

Initially, Kwik-Fit's existing all-makes fixed price menu-driven vehicle servicing offer had been a largely retail initiative. There are eight price bands based on vehicle engine size, fuel type and oil type.

There was significant fleet demand for Britain's largest independent fast-fit company to undertake servicing on company cars and vans, but in some quarters there was concern that such a move could breach manufacturer warranties.

That was overcome earlier this year with the introduction of new computer software at the 400 centres currently offering vehicle servicing that enables technicians to download each vehicle manufacturer's exact service schedule on a model-by-model basis. The cost of each service is individually calculated by adding together ICME service time, hourly labour rates and spare part prices.

While the cost of a service is commensurate with model-type and mileage, Kwik-Fit estimates that the cost of a service is up to 20% less than at a franchise dealer. In addition, because the service can be completed on a 'while u wait' basis, vehicle downtime will be cut.

Vehicles are serviced using long-established service procedures and even if warranties are in place they are not impacted. Our database details point-by-point every single aspect of all vehicle manufacturers' service schedules.

Time is money and for that reason fleets want a fast and efficient service that is convenient for their company car and van drivers. Kwik-Fit's seven-day-a-week

extended hours opening and its ability to offer a service promptly rather than the 14 days of some franchised dealers makes vehicle servicing very attractive to fleet operators and drivers.

And, it is not just on vehicle servicing where fast-fits have a price advantage over franchise dealers. Whether requiring a new tyre, glass repair, brake adjustment or air conditioning recharging, the cost of having the work completed at a fast-fit will be less than at a dealer. In fact, some franchise dealers will even ask a fast-fit to carry out the work and charge a mark-up for the privilege!

In the UK, fast-fit companies come in all shapes and sizes. How should a fleet manager choose the right one for their fleet?

Fleet decision-makers need to be certain that their vehicle is being serviced, maintained and repaired in accordance with best practice and manufacturer recommendations. One of the key best practice recommendations in the Health and Safety Executive/Department for Transport 'Driving at-work: Managing work-related road safety' document, which provides benchmark guidance for businesses to manage the occupational road risk posed by their at-work drivers, is that companies must be 'satisfied that vehicles are maintained in a safe and fit condition'.

In addition, the guidance says that:

- Maintenance should be carried out to an acceptable standard
- Planned and preventative maintenance should be carried out in accordance with manufacturers' recommendations.

Put simply, legal compliance means that all fleet decision-makers must be able to follow a comprehensive audit trail detailing every aspect of work carried out on any vehicle driven on business – including 'grey' fleet vehicles.

Not only that, but maintaining and repairing a vehicle is a major cost so fleet chiefs and drivers need to be assured that their car or van is in the hands of a skilled mechanic employed by a reputable organisation.

So, for example, at Kwik-Fit Fleet, our authorisation processes build a complete 'picture' of a vehicle's health during the fleet cycle. A computer print out of a vehicle's maintenance history can be sent to the fleet operator.

In addition, our centre and mobile technicians are trained to the highest standard. This year, an inspection by OFSTED, the Government's Office for Standards in Education, Children's Services and Skills, declared Kwik-Fit's multi-million pound staff training programme to be 'outstanding'.

Kwik-Fit's annual training budget totals more than £3 million and the glowing report placed the business in the top 5-10% for corporate training provision in the UK.

The OFSTED report said: 'The overall effectiveness of Kwik-Fit's provision is outstanding. This is the third inspection of the company's training in the last 10 years and they have consistently improved the grades for their motor vehicle provision and for leadership and management.

'Quality improvement is high on the company's agenda and the company invests heavily in training and developing their people. The company training centres are very well equipped with excellent up-to-date industry standard equipment. Training in the training centres and in the workplace is particularly good.'

The inspectors singled out Kwik-Fit's key strengths as: high training programme success rates; good teaching, learning and skills development; excellent training resources; good progression; very effective quality improvement processes; a strong company commitment to training; a particularly well planned and managed training programme; good partnership arrangements; and good initiatives to recruit female apprentices.

The training and development of Kwik-Fit staff is crucial to the company's on-going crusade to continually raise standards not only in the fast-fit sector but also in the motor industry as a whole.

Kwik-Fit has three dedicated training centres in Derby, Harlow, and Gloucester. Staff from apprentices upwards work through a series of qualifications overseen by NVQ and City and Guilds.

Additionally, Kwik-Fit (GB) Ltd has gained PAS80 accreditation from the British Standards Institute for its range of services supplied through its Broxburn, Scotland, headquarters and its 670 centres and 220 mobile units across the UK.

In addition, the company's headquarters and centres have once again been accredited with ISO9001, the BSI quality management standard which Kwik-Fit has had in place since1992.

This therefore is the Gold Standard of the fast-fit industry and we invite you to use these standards when deciding which fast-fit to choose.

Competitive pricing, flexible opening hours, the range of services, consolidated invoicing and its corporate social responsibility ethic (see below) are all reasons why fleet chiefs should opt to use a fast-fit to keep their vehicles on-the-road. However, in differentiating one fast-fit from the other service quality and staff training is key and that puts Kwik-Fit in the fast lane.

What else do fast-fits offer fleet managers?

Corporate social responsibility (CSR) has become part of the language of business in recent years. It means taking a responsible attitude and following best practice principles whatever the size of your organisation.

In the fleet sector, CSR particularly applies to occupational road risk management and environmental management.

So, for example, at Kwik-Fit Fleet we recognise the importance and the impact of CSR on all motorists and we support our business customers by providing the tools needed.

An example of our pro-active approach to occupational road risk management has been our long-standing free five-point winter safety check as well as our mobile technicians carrying out thousands of tyre health checks in company car parks across the UK. More recently, the company has added brake checks to its safety portfolio.

Road casualties peak in the winter months with many crashes caused by vehicles not being in tip-top condition – the exact reason why Kwik-Fit offers its free winter checks and urges fleet chiefs and company car drivers to call in at a centre for the no-appointment work to be undertaken.

The free checks cover:
- Tyre check – pressures, tread depth and general condition (including spare)
- Battery check – using electronic test equipment
- Exhaust check – condition and fitment including hangers and brackets
- Tracking check – visual check to determine if the tyres show related wear
- Glass/wipers check – condition of vehicle glass and wipers

Meanwhile, as the importance of managing occupational road risk has risen up the corporate agenda, demand for tyre safety checks has increased.

This year more than 250,000 checks will be undertaken in company car parks or at a driver's location of choice.

The worrying aspect of the checks is that initially our technicians find that about 25% of company vehicles inspected require attention – usually tyres being replaced because they are illegal. Extrapolated across the UK's three million-strong company car and approximately one million van parc, up to 800,000 vehicles could be running on at least one unsafe tyre.

Typically tyres maybe under or over inflated; tread maybe below, or close to the 1.6mm legal minimum across the central three-quarters of the breadth of the tyre and around the entire circumference; tyre wear maybe irregular which may indicate a wheel alignment or vehicle loading problem; or the wall of a tyre may be damaged.

The current fine for driving on illegal tyres is £2,500 per tyre and three points per tyre on a driving licence.

At 70 mph the stopping distance of a car fitted with a new tyre with 8mm of tread is calculated to be almost 100 metres; with 3mm of tread remaining a car's stopping distance increases to 150 metres; with 1.6mm of tread remaining a car's stopping distance is 200 metres – double that of a vehicle fitted with a new tyre – and with just 1mm of a tread remaining a car's stopping distance is 250 metres.

In 2008 a survey by fleet consultants Total Motion reported that of almost 6,000 company cars and privately-owned vehicles used on business, 70% of vehicles had tyre-related problems.

This was highlighted by the National Tyre Distributors Association (NTDA) and NTDA director Richard Edy commented: 'This is yet another damning indictment on the lack of interest in tyres, which are such a safety critical component of all vehicles.'

Tyres are the only part of a vehicle that are in contact with the road so it is essential that they are in tip-top condition. Ensuring tyres meet the legal requirements is a vital part of any corporate risk strategy.

In the event of a crash involving a vehicle being driven on business, tyre condition will be one of the issues looked at by investigating police officers. A failure to ensure checks are being carried out and to have a record of those checks could leave companies wide open to court action.

A case study might be useful here:

British Gas

Tyre safety checks on almost 9,500 British Gas Home Service light commercial vehicles driven by the organisation's engineers who provide a range of services, including installing and servicing domestic boilers, remain a major feature of the organisation's fast-fit contract with Kwik-Fit Fleet.

Kwik-Fit Fleet's mobile technicians undertake regular tyre wear and tear and pressure checks, to assist British Gas comply with its at-work driving duty of care responsibilities.

British Gas fleet operations manager Colin Marriott said: 'Our customer-focused operation means that there is little time for vehicles to be off the road. Consequently, we expect the majority of vehicles to be serviced by Kwik-Fit Fleet's mobile technicians to ensure downtime is kept to an absolute minimum.

'It is also vital that we meet all our at-work driving health and safety obligations and the unique tyre inspection service that Kwik-Fit is providing will help achieve that aim.'

Mobile phone company, the 20:20 Mobile Group

Kwik-Fit Fleet has a long term relationship with 20:20 Mobile Group. They told us 'We ensure that all vehicles are checked and any remedial work is then carried out and that gives the company a complete auditable report.

'Not only is that vital from a duty of care perspective, but there is no lost time with staff having to go to centres to have the checks carried out. Additionally, employees who are not aufait with how to check tyres for pressure and wear and tear have nothing to worry about; and we ensure that qualified and fully trained technicians carry out the checks and any repair and replacement work.'

How often on average would a fast-fit organisation expect to see a fleet client's car?

I can give you Kwik-Fit statistics. On average our centres see a company car twice a year and by default when the tyres are off the technicians will undertake a visual brake check. A free and comprehensive brake inspection will be carried out with fleet approval and if any work is required that will only be completed after gaining fleet operator confirmation.

Technicians are fitting an increasing number of company vehicles with new brake pads, with work being driven by a combination of extended vehicle service intervals and the growing importance of at-work driving safety that means regular brake inspections are more critical than ever.

Additionally, drivers are detecting brake-related problems in their company cars with some vehicles now fitted with warning lights 'flashing up' a potential problem and advising that maintenance is carried out immediately.

The average company car driver can expect to replace the brake pads on their vehicle once a year. However, due to their design and usage, many vehicles may require brake inspections as often as four times a year.

A free brake inspection at a fast-fit centre can prove to be a major cost saving for fleet managers. A few minutes spent inspecting brake pads could save a hefty bill for brake disc replacement if the pads are allowed to wear down to the metal. It is false economy not to have brakes inspected for wear and tear.

Can the fast-fit industry be 'green'?

In tenders from Britain's major fleet companies, including Motability, contract hire and leasing organisations and vehicle rental providers, fast-fit companies such as ours are increasingly being asked for our 'green' credentials.

Speaking once again for Kwik-Fit, for many years we have been at the forefront of ensuring that tyres collected from our centres are reprocessed and not sent to landfill sites. As the company's range of services has extended in recent years to embrace brake replacement and vehicle servicing and MoT work, so Kwik-Fit has worked with waste management companies to dispose of all waste products.

In fact, we view worn out parts not as rubbish, but as the raw product for something else.

The fleet industry – suppliers and their fleet customers – must work together to ensure tyres, exhausts, batteries and other vehicle parts and fluids are not being illegally dumped or stockpiled. Fleets need to be sure that waste is being disposed of in the correct way and, where possible, recycled to create other resources.

In 2008, the company's 'green' ethos was significantly increased with the opening of Kwik-Fit's £10 million National Distribution Centre in Corby, Northamptonshire.

The 245,000 square feet complex – the size of 10 football pitches – stocks up to 300,000 tyres across up to 650 different sizes with the guarantee of next day delivery to our 670 centres and 200+ mobile fitting units.

Previously it could take up to three days for tyres to be delivered depending on suppliers, but now online ordering by high street centres, mobile control centres as well as dealers who use us for tyre replacement, means stocks are replenished and customer requirements met daily.

The proliferation of tyre sizes has made it a necessity for us to have our own distribution operation rather than being reliant on tyre manufacturers to deliver to centres, which can take several days. Ensuring tyres are in tip-top condition is vital for road safety. While customers are prepared to wait overnight, if necessary, for a replacement tyre they do not want to wait a few days. We are now masters of our own destiny.

Simultaneously, a process of 'reverse logistics' has been introduced meaning that the new 69-vehicle truck fleet – having delivered tyres to five distribution hubs across the UK or the centres – returns reloaded in just eight minutes with removed tyre casings and scrap catalytic converters. This industry first 'one-for-one exchange' results in trucks travelling fully-loaded thus saving up to three million miles a year and an estimated 3,000 tonnes of carbon in reduced emissions.

Tyres and catalytic converters are returned to the National Distribution Centre, in Corby, Northamptonshire. Some tyre casings are remoulded and others are shredded on site for use as fuel in cement kilns and aggregate in landfill engineering projects and for use in artificial sports pitches, to make carpet underlay and roof tiles and in producing portable rail crossings equine surfaces and children's playgrounds. The steel cord in casings is extracted and re-used in steel making. Catalytic converters are collected by contractors and sold on the worldwide scrap metal market.

More than six million tyres and almost 40,000 tons of tyre casings are removed from cars and vans annually by Kwik-Fit.

Other material recycled includes:
- Around 1.5 million exhausts removed annually are collected by contractors and sold on the worldwide scrap metal market along with spark plugs, shock

absorbers, zinc balance weights and hundreds of thousands of brake pads, brake discs and hydraulic cylinders. Brake callipers are re-used by manufacturers.

- Precious metals such as rhodium, palladium and platinum are extracted from more than 650,000 old catalytic converters removed annually.

- Thousands of batteries are reprocessed with the lead extracted and re-used, battery casings are reprocessed as plastic and acid is treated and disposed of in line with hazardous waste regulations.

- Almost 500,000 litres of waste oil is reprocessed and used as marine oil and as fuel in a number of factories including steelworks.

- Aluminium from oil and fuel filters is compacted and sold to aluminium smelters and the waste oil reprocessed and sold as industrial fluid along with waste brake fluid.

- Thousands of litres of anti-freeze are sent to specialist chemical extraction processors.

- Air filters are disposed of with general waste via local authority wheeled bin collections. Paper and cardboard waste is separated for reprocessing.

Have there been technological developments in the fast-fit market?

Yes. Underpinning the way that fast-fit companies have advanced over the years has been the advent on sophisticated web-based management reporting and invoicing.

Without doubt, the range of products now available at fast-fit centres has been invaluable in ensuring that SMR work is undertaken swiftly and cost-effectively so that vehicle downtime is kept to a minimum – ever-crucial in today's 24/7 world.

However, at all times fleet decision-makers – whether at end-user fleets or at leasing and fleet management companies with outsourced responsibilities for end-user clients – must be kept fully in the picture to know exactly what work is being carried out on which vehicles and the cost and timeframe of that work.

Taking Kwik-Fit as an example, the range of technology available – in our call centre, our centres as well as our mobile units – means that staff have access to a raft of individual vehicle and fleet data, stock availability and product ordering to further improve customer service.

As every fleet manager knows, a driver who requires more frequent tyre replacement than the norm could in fact be a 'high risk' employee whose driving skills may improve with driver training. Data recorded by Kwik-Fit Fleet would, in this instance, reveal operating above-average costs and trigger management intervention.

Automated authorisation is crucial to any fleet authorisation. The fleet operator can specify his own rule sets in the system; for example brand preference, cost, number of tyres per transaction, or ring fence sub-fleets. If the service provider does not meet a specific criterion this would create a referral, at which time human intervention would occur in order to discuss the circumstances. Otherwise electronic authorisation would be given automatically.

How is the recession affecting your business?

The current economic recession is in its infancy, but is already triggering change with increased fleet replacement cycles perhaps being the most significant along with the obvious: improved cost management across businesses.

That is playing to the strengths of the fast-fit sector. If companies realise that they can extend vehicle replacement cycles from, for example, three years to four years or 60,000 miles to 80,000 miles without significantly increase operating costs then it is unlikely that those lifecycles will be reversed when the tough times ease, perhaps in 2010.

With vehicle holding periods lengthening, fleet demand for fast-fit services will increase. Meanwhile, coupled with the breadth of services now offered – currently it is difficult to see where an additional service could be added to Kwik-Fit Fleet's portfolio – and the ultra-competitive pricing of those services, the outlook is bright.

Please tell us how your company can help fleet managers

Kwik-Fit Fleet provides the corporate sector with a complete one-stop motoring shop. From the initial fast-fit provision of tyres, batteries and exhausts, the company now offers through a nationwide network of 670 High Street centres, a fleet of 220 mobile units, a call centre in Scotland and a recently-opened tyre National Distribution Centre: tyre repair and replacement, exhausts, batteries, brake repair and replacement, all-makes vehicle servicing, MoTs, oil and filter changes, air conditioning recharging and glass repair.

The core services include:

Business Drive Card – a procurement card that offers large fleet benefits to fleets of any size. The card allows for petrol purchases via the All Star network, fast and slow fit, car hire and recovery, all through an auditable and manageable route. Kwik-Fit Fleet has around 40,000 drivers using the card.

Fleet Safety Products – Kwik-Fit offer a free of charge winter safety check to ensure vehicles head into the winter months in a good condition. This is supported by Kwik-Fit Mobile, which offers regular car park tyre safety inspections. In 2008 a record 250,000 tyre safety checks were carried out.

Tyre Management – Kwik-Fit offers the definitive industry outsourcing solution for tyre authorisation, management and billing. For smaller fleets which may not attract volume incentive schemes from tyre manufacturers, Kwik-Fit Fleet pools their spend with major fleets to offer incentives on all premium tyre brands therefore helping keep costs down. Around 1.2 million company cars and vans are on tyre management.

SOS TyreSource – is Kwik-Fit Fleet's specialist business which holds and locates rare tyres or tyres in short supply.

Fleet account – is Kwik-Fit Fleet's standard product with over 7,000 businesses holding accounts with the company. Managed by a regional account manager and supported by named staff at the company fleet headquarters in St Albans, the product is the mainstay of the UK fleet offering. Every account has access to detailed management reporting to ensure we are delivering the goods as promised.

Service Booking – web-based service booking available to outsourced customers

Cover 24 – 24-hour call handling so Kwik-Fit Fleet's customers' offices are never closed when drivers call for assistance.

Mike Wise
Head of Kwik-Fit Fleet

We're geared up to keeping your fleet moving

The largest network of fast-fit sites in the country, the longest opening hours and the widest fast-fit product range from servicing to MOT, air conditioning to windscreen repair.

Kwik-Fit Fleet really has everything to keep your fleet on the road.

Simply call 0800 222 111 for your nearest centre or 0871 22 22 888 for our mobile tyre service

www.kwik-fit.com/fleet

16 BROKERS

Mike Lloyd
Managing Director
Central Contracts

Please introduce yourself and your company.

Central Contracts has been a vehicle funding specialist since February 1998. We operate on a brokerage basis and this means that we maintain multiple relationships with finance providers and motor vehicle manufacturers and are able to take advantage of special terms and offers as soon as they arise, thereby providing our clients with an extremely flexible and cost effective means of sourcing their vehicles.

I have been in the industry since the early eighties in roles that have encompassed retail sales, fleet sales and vehicle funding. Having been made redundant in January 1998, my co-director Marc Hallsworth and I founded Central Contracts with relationships with just two funders. We now represent all of the major finance providers in this market place and I am Vice-Chairman of the BVRLA's Leasing Broker Committee.

What products are available from brokers in the fleet market?

Whilst many brokers operate a simple business model that offers just contract hire for business users and private individuals, a number of the more established companies, such as ourselves, offer virtually any type of funding from outright purchase to full maintenance contract hire, as well as hands-on assistance in the day-to-day challenges that arise from operating business vehicles. Examples of these services include; assistance with establishing workable fleet policies, assistance in the monitoring of driver and vehicle activity, and the capacity to not simply acquire new vehicles but also to dispose of existing cars and vans. Some providers offer a full fleet management service, charging on a car by car basis, which can help not only reduce operating costs but also to meet the exacting duty of care requirements currently in force. Most of the established brokers are more than happy to provide help and advice free of charge on matters such as merchantable quality claims, driving whilst abroad, cherished number plates and will also provide a liaison point between the end user, the franchise dealer network and finance providers, as and when required.

Are brokers mainly there to help SMEs or should the manager of a large fleet also consider doing business with a broker?

All sizes of business can benefit from doing business through a broker. Brokers started out serving just small fleets, but many now have the ability to look after the needs of larger fleets too. For example, if a large fleet offers a car allowance instead of a company car to some of its employees, a broker can offer extremely competitive rates, as well as assistance on benefit in kind implications and ensuring that vehicles are fit for purpose. A number of brokers specifically target larger fleets and offer bespoke packages encompassing full vehicle-by-vehicle fleet management, driver profiling, duty of care management and vehicle supply. These brokers tend to be well established and more than happy to invest both time and effort in ensuring that the end user receives exactly the service that fits their needs.

Why might a fleet manager choose to arrange funding via a broker, rather than going direct to a funder or a dealer?

The better brokers consistently offer low leasing prices because we negotiate with the car manufacturers and shop around a number of funders to find the most competitive prices. No funder or manufacturer is able to offer the best deal on every car all of the time. A broker with strong relationships will be able to find the most cost-effective offering available at the point of purchase. By dealing with a broker a fleet manager can have the best of both worlds; enjoying excellent deals on all makes and models of vehicle from multiple funders whilst the broker provides a single point of contact so the fleet manager does not have to worry about maintaining those multiple relationships. We have all experienced the press button '1' for sales '2' for administration '3' for finance response to our urgent enquiry. For most of us this is one of business life's most frustrating experiences. A good broker will insulate the fleet manager from this frustration by handling the challenge directly and promptly and using their strong relationships to find the shortest route through to a successful conclusion.

Are there any disadvantages for a fleet manager in choosing a broker rather than going direct to a funder?

Obviously I am partisan, however, given that by definition we offer all of the services that any funder would offer and that we are far more highly motivated to maintain individual relationships than a major financial institution might be it is difficult for me to see any disadvantage in offering a broker the opportunity to quote for your business. Most brokers maintain a level of personal relationship with their clients that the mainstream funders are simply too big to be able to do. With us you are not simply a number you are the very means of our commercial survival!

There are many hundreds of brokers in the UK fleet market; some are large organisations arranging thousands of leases a year, others are tiny businesses run from spare bedrooms. How can a fleet manager be sure they are dealing with a well-established broker?

It is extremely important that a fleet manager chooses a broker whose business model meets their own requirements. It is always tempting to scour the internet and pick the offer that looks the most sensational, only to be disappointed when either the offer turns out to be bogus, or the broker is unable or unwilling to deliver the service to match the fleet manager's expectations. The old adage that if the price looks too good to be true, it probably is, definitely holds true here.

Fortunately, it is relatively straight forward to ensure that you are dealing with a well established broker. The British Vehicle Rental and Leasing Association has a specific committee for representing the broker delivery channel. This is known as the Leasing Broker Committee. It operates in exactly the same way as all of the BVRLA Committees, meeting quarterly to discuss best practice and future market place developments. In addition to the representation enjoyed by brokers on this committee, a number of the major funding partners are also permanent members and this means that the brokers and the funders work very closely to develop operational policies that ensure best practice is enjoyed by the fleet managers, whilst meeting legislative responsibilities.

In order to become BVRLA accredited a broker must demonstrate they are well established. Both a physical inspection and independent references are undertaken, financial probity is investigated and the newly-accredited broker automatically agrees to abide by a code of conduct and acknowledges the BVRLA's position as arbiter in the event of any dispute arising between the broker and client.

A fleet manager takes delivery of 10 new cars

Another key indicator as to the quality of a broker is their association with the Financial Services Authority. I would expect to see any serious broker enjoy at least appointed representative status. This means that they have been appointed by a company regulated by the Financial Services Authority, usually for insurance mediation purposes. Comfort can be drawn by the fleet manager on the basis that if the broker were to fail to meet the rigorous audit standards laid down by the FSA this would not only result in their own loss of status, but would also adversely affect the position of their principle.

It is very easy to check whether your chosen broker partner has taken steps to achieve accreditation in these two areas. The BVRLA logo should be clearly displayed on any headed paper or website belonging to the broker, as will their status as an appointed representative. Achievement of both of these accreditations should give fleet managers confidence that the broker has a long term business strategy and actually intends to be around to provide the future service they are promising. Ask your broker; do you operate from proper business premises?, do you own those business premises?, how long have you been established?, do you have dedicated administration staff? These things are easy to forget when we have been offered what appears to be an unbeatable deal, but will readily spring to the fore should you encounter challenges at a later stage.

What developments have there been in the broker section of the fleet market in the last few years that have been particularly valuable to fleet managers?

Over the past few years the broker delivery channel has become both recognised and respected by a strong cross-section of the major vehicle finance providers in the UK. Regulation by the Financial Services Authority and the creation of the Leasing Broker Committee by the BVRLA, together with the recognition of the sheer volume of contracts being written by the broker channel have meant that brokers have enjoyed a more positive profile than had previously been the case. Many of the major manufacturers and funders have now decided that there are a number of well-established, well-motivated, properly-run organisations that operate as brokers, that have long term aspirations and can be trusted to help develop a long term sales strategy. For some funders broker activity accounts for a third or more of their overall registrations. This has become simply too large a slice of their business for them to ignore. They naturally want to write as much business as possible whilst exposing themselves to the least commercial risk possible, and this has led to the growth of a strong contingent of professionally-run brokerages from which a fleet manager may buy with confidence. These brokers recognise that the best business model is to maintain a strong relationship with their clients and to provide added value services designed to ease the pain of running a vehicle fleet and provide operational efficiencies. Such brokers are offering a wide range of services that can be tailored on an individual basis, thereby providing a singular solution for each customer.

What advice would you give to a fleet manager who is setting out to choose a broker?

There are a number of simple ways to make sure that you are dealing with a broker capable of meeting your requirements:

- Is the broker accredited by the BVRLA?
- Does the broker enjoy any FSA accreditation?
- Which funders support the broker?
- Does the broker operate from proper business premises?
- Does the broker own these premises?
- Does the broker have a dedicated administration team?
- Does the broker have a clear management structure?
- What is the broker's business philosophy?

Is anything happening now, or will anything be happening soon, that is likely to change the landscape for fleet managers, in their dealings with brokers?

Now that a significant number of funders are represented on the Leasing Broker Committee of the BVRLA significant strides are being made towards providing a best

practice framework for the broker industry. Increasingly the BVRLA is seen as the natural conduit for change within our industry as it acts as a forum where the manufacturers, the funders and the brokers can all express their views and be advised as to the best way forwards. The most tangible evidence of this is the decision by Network Vehicles Limited to make BVRLA membership mandatory for all of its brokers. This has the immediate affect of significantly increasing the number of members and both the reputation and reach of the BVRLA within the broker market place. I for one certainly expect to see much more emphasis on BVRLA membership from the other funders in the near future. This will boost the pool of accredited brokers from which fleet managers can choose the most appropriate partner to meet their needs.

How can Central Contracts help fleet managers?

The most obvious response to this question is that Central Contracts enjoys strong relationships with all of the major funders represented in the broker market place. Therefore we are normally able to offer extremely competitive pricing whilst increasing our customers' credit facilities and spreading their risk amongst a number of funders. I would like to feel, however, that we go much further than this. Marc and I started the business with the simple premise that we would like to offer a good service at a good price, combined with transparency. This would hopefully enable us to build strong relationships with people who felt they could trust us to look after their interests in the long run and this has certainly borne out by the fact that around 60% of our business is generated by repeat and referral orders.

Over the years we have invested in quality administration staff whose function is not simply to process contracts, but also to provide a range of support services designed to give our clients a one stop shop for help and advice on how to operate their vehicles on a day-to-day basis. If we are asked a question and don't know the answer, we say so and then use our extensive network of contacts to obtain the right answer.

Along the way we have developed Transfer Contracts, a service designed to provide our customers with the means of advertising unwanted contract hire vehicles whilst simultaneously providing other clients with an opportunity to purchase shorter-term contracts.

Additionally we have developed Fleet Monitor, a service that majors on assisting our clients to meet the health and safety demands arising from running business vehicles. Our appointed representative status allows us to offer best advice to our clients on how to insure against the losses that could potentially arise from transacting vehicle contracts.

Since moving into our own premises in April 2008 Central Contracts has established an Associates Programme, to ensure that new entrants into our industry have early exposure to the best practice and training facilities that will ensure that they grow into strong, responsible and profitable businesses in the future.

We have also recently been appointed as the funding partner for the Cars 4 Fans Programme. Currently going through the pilot stage, this programme potentially offers an opportunity for sports fans all over the country to support their chosen team whilst enjoying the competitive benefits that Central Contracts has to offer.

In short we like to treat people as we ourselves like to be treated. Please feel free to visit our website or call us to learn more.

Mike Lloyd
Managing Director
Central Contracts

CENTRAL CONTRACTS IS AN INDEPENDENT VEHICLE FUNDING SPECIALIST COMBINING THE PROVEN KNOWLEDGE AND SKILLS OF STAFF WHO ARE EXPERTS IN THE FIELD.

The company offers a full range of facilities and services to cover virtually every aspect of acquiring, maintaining and disposal of vehicles. The fundamental principle is that we take care of the motoring headaches leaving our clients to concentrate on living their lives.

The principal advantages offered by the company are as follows:

- All types of vehicle supplied
- Door to door delivery
- Full fleet management is available
- Nearly new vehicles are a speciality
- Vehicle disposal arranged
- Accident management is available

Without wishing to squeeze the life out of a hackneyed phrase, 'Big enough to cope, small enough to care' describes the Central Contracts approach perfectly.

Our aim is to use the national resources of major high street funders in combination with flexible, approachable and experienced staff to provide the total service you require.

Central Contracts (SOT) Ltd is an appointed representative of Premia Solutions Ltd, who are authorised and regulated by the Financial Services Authority.

- Personal contracts on new and used cars
- All types of funding methods available from outright purchase to contract hire
- Bespoke racking and conversions undertaken for commercial vehicles
- Dedicated account managers

Central Contracts (SOT) Limited

Phone 01782 644388

info@centralcontracts.com

Fax 01782 659330

www.centralcontracts.com

Central House
Trentham Business Quarter
Bellringer Road
Stoke on Trent, Staffordshire ST4 8GB
United Kingdom

17 TELEMATICS

Adrian McMullan
Director
L & A Consultants Limited

Please introduce yourself and your business

Welcome to the world of telematics.

I have over 25 years experience in working in the fleet management environment. My career includes roles such as Head of Fleet Management at the Metropolitan Police, managing over 4,500 vehicles, and more recently Principal Lecturer at the Centre for Automotive Industries Management (CAIM) at Nottingham Business School, specialising in fleet management. I keep my links with the fleet world as a Visiting Fellow at the Centre for Automotive Management at the University of Buckingham.

My world seems to always seems come back to fleet management, despite moves into related fields. It is a profession which has always had to be innovative and forward thinking and my association with L&A Consultants now uses new technology to enhance the fleet management role further.

L&A Consultants is a consultancy practice specialising in organisational change and business improvement. In recent years, L&A has been involved in optimising fleet profiles and fleet operations. Our involvement in telematics came about as a by-product of our work in advising organisations on how many vehicles they need in their fleet to meet their customers' requirements and whether savings could be made without adversely affecting the business.

However unfair, fleet management is often seen as an 'overhead' to the business. During my time at CAIM I worked with Professor Peter Cooke on his Business Car Expectations surveys which have now been running for over 10 years. Each year the number one key business driver for fleet managers has been cost or as I would prefer 'the ability to show value for money and cost effectiveness'.

Telematics can be a real cost-cutter. Aligning fleet resources to an organisation's key priorities can deliver real value and show in cash terms how the fleet department can add value to the business aims of a company.

Please explain how telematics can work within a fleet environment

First let's deal with the basics.

There has been an explosion in telematics systems over the last decade. Most systems offer similar basic features which can assist the fleet manager in key aspects such as asset management. But how do such systems work?

Most systems use Global Positioning System (GPS) technology to identify the location of a vehicle. This uses a series of satellites to calculate position. The satellites talk to a 'black box' installed in the vehicle.

The location of the box, and hence the vehicle, is sent to a central computer using mobile phone technology such as Global System for Mobile (GSM) network or the later variation (GPRS). Typically this information will include the longitude and latitude of a vehicle, together with the time at which the data was collected.

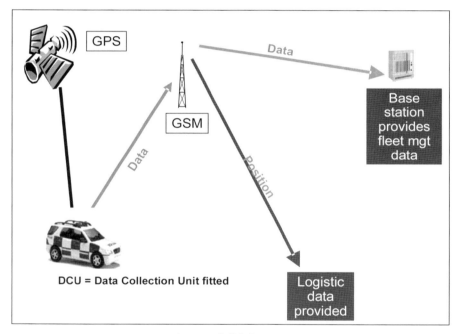

A typical AVLS set up

The vehicle location is then manipulated by software and placed on a map. By taking location signals from the black box over a period of time, ranging from a few seconds to several minutes, the software is able to show not just where a vehicle is, but also the direction of travel and speed.

Collectively the systems are known as Automatic Vehicle Location Systems (AVLS), and using AVLS a fleet manager can determine how vehicles are being used and how long they are spending at key locations, and can replay journeys and analyse speed.

However as technology improves, satellite navigation (Sat Nav) systems are providing a 'connected' service. Not only is the vehicle tracked and management reports provided, but the company can send the driver text messages such as changes in a schedule or appointments and send revised routes to the Sat Nav unit.

When AVLS is linked to Sat Nav, it can also allow the fleet manager to send information to drivers or to operations managers which may affect their use of vehicles – such as utilisation, fuel consumption, servicing, etc.

Telematics, linked to other business systems, enables the fleet manager to support his/ her operational colleagues in providing a number of key features. For example, real time vehicle tracking can show where a vehicle is at any time. This can have important safety value for people working in vulnerable environments such as social care, probation services and other such sectors. It can pinpoint where their vehicle is in case of an incident.

What are the benefits?

From a cost-effectiveness perspective, it can also show how vehicles are being used and report on whether that is effective. One interesting example from our work is the utilisation of vehicles. As many fleet managers know, fleets tend to evolve. New company initiatives require vehicles and the fleet grows. But is providing a vehicle the most cost effective way of providing transport when there are numerous other forms of transport available?

One client of ours had seen a significant increase in the number of fleet vehicles as well as a significant increase in daily rental. Initial analysis suggested they had too few vehicles. However using telematics and our software we were able to show that the utilisation of the fleet vehicles was rather poor. Because daily rental was a 'soft alternative', drivers who needed occasional transport had just been booking hire cars.

By giving operational managers a tool, via the company intranet, which showed them which fleet vehicles were not being used, they were able to re-distribute vehicles to

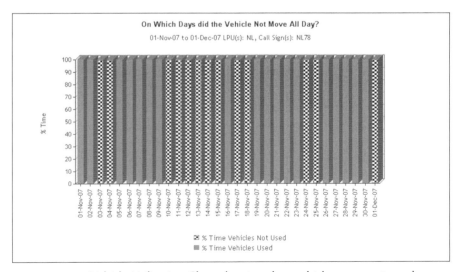

Vehicle Utilisation Chart showing days vehicles were not used

more appropriate departments and only use daily rental when necessary. Not only did this improve the utilisation of the core fleet vehicles, it also reduced daily rental by over 50%.

In our experience, the productivity gains and cashable cost savings from using an appropriate telematics system are significant. An example with one client shows that if telematics are used in conjunction with the in-house systems, it should be possible to achieve a 20% saving in fleet costs.

This can be achieved by optimising the fleet to meet the organisation's requirements rather than having vehicles 'just in case', reducing unnecessary miles and re-focusing where vehicles need to be. Indeed in several client organisations we have worked with, we were both able to show 20% cost savings and also improve the productivity because fleet resources were more focused on the operational needs.

Two examples come to mind: one is a sales department whose staff were driving over 75,000 miles a year because of the make-up of their sales territories. Sales executives were spending a lot of time driving and less than 15% of their time engaged with customers.

Telematics were able to show the ineffectiveness of this and suggest a re-definition of sales territories. Sales staff were then driving fewer miles, saving costs and spending more time in front of customers. Equally in the emergency services environment, by linking telematics to incident data, ambulances and police vehicles have been strategically located to respond to an emergency more quickly. This again not only saves on fleet and fuel costs but improves productivity and response times.

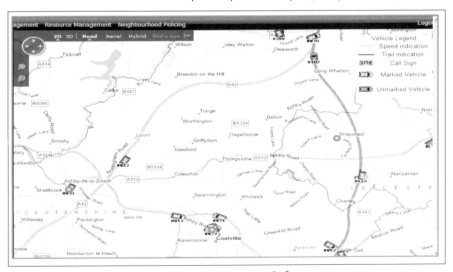

Location using Mapping Software

Recent advances in system integration allows telematics systems to link into other fleet management systems to provide the fleet manager with reports which are more focused on fleet-specific issues.

One obvious example is the ability to integrate accurate mileage data, the bane of every fleet manager's life, into other systems to give accurate servicing forecasts – also becoming more important as a duty of care issue. Telematics can also integrate with workshop data. It can show when a vehicle was delivered to and collected from a workshop, ensuring that vehicle downtime is minimised. Also, by integrating accurate mileage data with fuel figures, it can assist in managing fuel consumption.

Is there a risk of information overload?

One of the early concerns with some telematics systems was the wealth of reports which were available. Research showed that some early adopters of telematics felt overwhelmed by data and reports. Unfortunately key analysis was missed, leaving the fleet managers querying the effectiveness of such systems. Since then, many systems have been refined to allow user-defined reports or exception reports which provide the fleet manager with only the relevant reports.

Using our experience of the business improvement world, we spend quite some time with clients to determine which reports would be useful and informative to them, what value they will derive from them and how they can be used to deliver not only fleet but operational savings and productivity gains.

We recognised early on that telematics systems should become an integral part of any fleet operation for both fleet management and operational effectiveness and we worked with a number of clients to develop a 'Benefits Realisation Framework'. This helps to implement the changes required to achieve the desired results. It also shows both to Finance Directors and Operations Directors how the telematics systems have delivered benefits in the form of savings and productivity gains.

This has ensured that the data and reports are relevant and can be used to derive real benefits. It also ensures the system is used well beyond any 'honeymoon' period and is integrated into the fleet and operational elements of the company over the long term.

Clearly, as part of the Benefits Realisation Framework, once one benefit has been achieved others may become apparent and may require other reports. So keeping a close relationship with your telematics supplier should enable you to introduce other reports as the system develops and the organisation's ability to use the reports matures.

An example of this from our police experience was the development of a basic report which showed vehicle utilisation from which operational police managers could see how vehicles were used and therefore determine whether their use was effective. This led to a more refined report which showed in more detail how vehicles were used, e.g. one sector of the report showed when vehicles were parked up away from their home base. This was seen as a positive action as the vehicle was being used to engage in the community while it was parked up – the officers would be speaking to the public, patrolling a known crime hotspot on foot, taking statements or giving advice to the public.

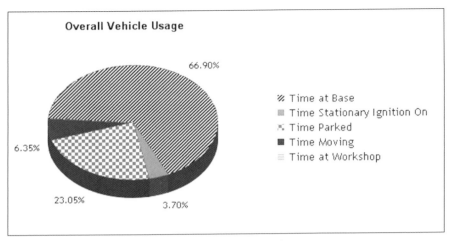

Vehicle Utilisation Pie Chart

By linking the telematics to the tasks the officers had been allocated, we were able to report on the precise work undertaken. This gave their managers a greater understanding of how resources were being used and enabled them to re-direct resources to meet changing priorities.

In a non-emergency service environment, a similar scenario would be the ability to break down the time spent at specific jobs and then analyse whether this was effective, whether improvements in productivity could be realised or indeed whether the type of vehicle used was appropriate.

Are many car fleets now using this sort of system?

The use of telematics has been very much pioneered in the logistics and distribution markets where vehicle tracking and the need for responsiveness to changing circumstances is an important feature. The advent of more sophisticated telematics linked to engine management systems has also allowed fleet managers to predict servicing and maintenance requirements and so ensure HGVs were being serviced in low demand times, minimising the impact on the operational side of the business.

Today, telematics have a role in any fleet – car, van or HGV – where vehicles are used as a 'utility' or working tool in support of the company's core activities. This could be sales, service delivery, technical support, maintenance, or any activity where an employee uses a fleet vehicle to carry out work on behalf of the company.

In the past, telematics were not installed in 'benefit in kind' vehicles which were seen as part of an individual's remuneration. However recent legislation relating to 'duty of care and corporate social responsibility' has seen some companies including all vehicles in their AVLS schemes.

So why has there been a migration of telematics into the more general fleet vehicles? As previously mentioned the ever rising costs of fleet operations have led to a number of organisations reviewing their fleet costs and seeking ways in which to reduce costs without compromising the efficiency of the fleet.

The core fleet operations such as procurement, maintenance, support services and administration are usually well managed. If any savings can be made the percentage savings is comparatively small, say 5%-10% of the total budget. However, in our experience, when companies use telematics to assess how well the fleet requirements meets the business needs, the savings can be in excess of 20%.

These savings have been achieved by assessing the 'supply and demand' characteristics of the fleet operation and then using telematics software to balance them. In this way, unnecessary miles are reduced, idle time is greatly reduced and indeed in a number of organisations the number of vehicles required is significantly reduced.

In one example, we were able to show how to reduce a vehicle fleet of 500 vehicles by over 80 vehicles saving the organisation nearly £800,000 in capital costs and over £300,000 in annual running costs.

Additionally, the software enabled the organisation to ensure its vehicles were in the right place to meet customer requirements, which led to an increase in customer satisfaction despite the reduction in fleet numbers. So it gave 'soft' benefits as well as the cash savings.

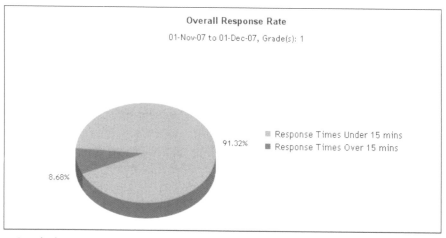

Graph shows improvements in responsiveness from a target of 85% to over 91%

Duty of Care is a major topic at present. How can telematics help?

Increasingly fleet managers have being given the remit of managing the fleet aspects for 'duty of care' or 'corporate responsibility'. In many cases, fleet managers have introduced schemes such as driving licence checks and insurance cover checks where employees use their own cars.

However when a vehicle is used as part of an employee's core role, as a working tool, then the requirement to ensure the vehicle is being used responsibly is more onerous. Many fleet managers feel they have limited ability to monitor and manage how vehicles are used in the field. Telematics can be a useful tool to assist duty of care initiatives, so long as the data and information are used in a responsible and proportionate way.

The latest telematics systems include a device known as an 'Incident Data Recorder', a clever device either within the AVLS black box or alongside it, which detects when a vehicle has suffered a severe deceleration (normally triggered between 1.2g and 2.0g) depending on the vehicle use. The IDR device constantly monitors key data such as;

- Speed
- Direction of travel
- Brake pressure
- Engine speed
- Whether the wipers were on
- Whether the lights were on
- Whether the horn was sounded

When the vehicle decelerates severely, the black box retains the 30 seconds immediately before the incident and the 5 seconds after activation. This can be sent back to the fleet manager as an 'IDR alert' so he/ she can enquire whether the driver is injured or needs accident assistance. It can also be used to determine how the employee has been driving, leading up to the accident, and this can be very beneficial in defending a potential claim.

Graph shows where the accident occurs and the speed of the vehicle (28.10 mph)

It also can lead to significant decreases in insurance premiums as driver behaviour improves leading to a reduction in the number and severity of accidents. Some insurance companies give a reduction in insurance premiums when an organisation fits AVLS with IDR technology, as it provides information which can assist them in assessing who is liable for the claim.

One of our clients saw their insurance premium reduce by £40,000 per annum and saw a 50% reduction in accidents within the fleet.

Another aspect of duty of care is the duration of journeys for some employees. Industry guidelines suggest that a driver should have a break at least once every 2 hours for a minimum of 15 minutes and that drivers should not drive continuously for over 120 miles without a break. But how does a fleet manager, say controlling 100 vehicles, know whether employees are abiding by these guidelines?

Telematics can provide the solution; the software can monitor journeys and provide exception reports when an employee has exceeded the 2 hour or 120 mile limits. The limits can be varied by the fleet manager if the company decides that a more rigorous requirement is needed. The exception reports can give fleet and operational managers information on which employees are more prone to long continuous journeys and therefore ensure 'at risk' individuals are not overlooked. An example of a typical report is given below;

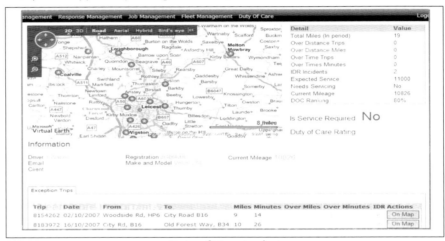

Duty of Care Analysis

This also has a 'knock on' benefit in that the information provides an electronic log book of the journeys undertaken, enabling an organisation to automate its vehicle journey expenses system.

The driver can use the organisation's intranet to review the journeys he/she has undertaken and then submit an expenses claim. The telematics software can replay journeys if the driver is unsure whether a journey was related to the business or not. An example is given below.

From a corporate responsibility perspective, the software can also demonstrate that the organisation is acting responsibly in managing the fleet, It can show that it is only paying for journeys undertaken as part of the business and that the expenses claimed accurately reflect the cost incurred.

Whilst this may be seen as a little over- bearing, in today's economic climate many companies are looking to reduce costs and this is an automated way of ensuring travel expenses are accurate.

Trip	Date	From	To	Miles	Minutes	Trip Type	Actions
8160940	05/10/2007	Woodside Rd, HP6	City Road B16	4	8	⊙Business ○Private	On Map
8160957	06/10/2007	City Rd, B16	Old Forest Way, B34	3	12	⊙Business ○Private	On Map
8162907	07/10/2007	Old Forest Way	B34 Lymes Road, ST5	1	6	○Business ⊙Private	On Map
8164687	08/10/2007	Woodside Rd, HP6	City Road B16	0	1	⊙Business ○Private	On Map
8173633	12/10/2007	Lymes Road, ST5	Woodside Rd, HP6	11	20	○Business ⊙Private	On Map
8181586	16/10/2007	Woodside Rd, HP6	West Rd, BS3	1	1	○Business ⊙Private	On Map
8184295	17/10/2007	Barnwell Rd, BS24	Pinksmoor Lane, TA21	3	7	⊙Business ○Private	On Map
8188784	18/10/2007	Pinksmoor Lane, TA21	Woodside Rd, HP6	7	11	⊙Business ○Private	On Map
8188808	19/10/2007	Woodside Rd, HP6	Heathside Park Rd, SK3	18	34	○Business ⊙Private	On Map
8192919	20/10/2007	Heathside Park Rd	Parkside Lane, LS11	3	43	⊙Business ○Private	On Map
8192920	20/10/2007	Parkside Lane, LS11	Collier Lane, LS32	3	4	⊙Business ○Private	On Map
8202590	26/10/2007	Collier Lane, LS32	Mill Lane, NG23	2	5	⊙Business ○Private	On Map
8202594	26/10/2007	Mill Lane, NG23	Burrowfield, AL7	0	1	⊙Business ○Private	On Map
8204839	27/10/2007	Burrowfield, AL7	Woodside Rd, HP6	0	1	⊙Business ○Private	On Map
8204841	27/10/2007	Woodside Rd, HP6	Blakelands, MK14	5	10	⊙Business ○Private	On Map
8206970	27/10/2007	London Road, SL3	Mill Lane, NG23	13	24	⊙Business ○Private	On Map
8206974	27/10/2007	Blakelands, MK14	Tongwell, MK15	0	25	⊙Business ○Private	On Map
8184301	17/10/2007	Tongwell, MK15	New Road, HP12	17	39	⊙Business ○Private	On Map

Journey Reporting

Trip	Date	From	To	Miles	Fuel PM	Cost (£)
8204841	27/10/2007	City Rd, B16	Old Forest Way, B34	5.30	£0.07	£0.37
8206970	27/10/2007	Old Forest Way	B34 Lymes Road, ST5	12.76	£0.07	£0.89
8206970	27/10/2007	Lymes Road, ST5	Woodside Rd, HP6	12.76	£0.07	£0.89
8206976	27/10/2007	Woodside Rd, HP6	West Rd, BS3	19.53	£0.07	£1.37
8202590	26/10/2007	Barnwell Rd, BS24	Pinksmoor Lane, TA21	1.61	£0.07	£0.11
8202593	26/10/2007	Woodside Rd, HP6	Heathside Park Rd, SK3	7.82	£0.07	£0.55
8202585	26/10/2007	Heathside Park Rd	Parkside Lane, LS11	11.57	£0.07	£0.81
8202576	26/10/2007	Parkside Lane, LS11	Collier Lane, LS32	9.87	£0.07	£0.69
8202576	26/10/2007	Collier Lane, LS32	Mill Lane, NG23	9.87	£0.07	£0.69
8192932	21/10/2007	Blakelands, MK14	Tongwell, MK15	10.70	£0.07	£0.75
8192940	21/10/2007	Tongwell, MK15	New Road, HP12	15.15	£0.07	£1.06
8192955	21/10/2007	New Road, HP12	Woodside Rd, HP6	20.43	£0.07	£1.43
8192919	20/10/2007	Woodside Rd, HP6	City Road B16	3.43	£0.07	£0.24
8192920	20/10/2007	City Rd, B16	Old Forest Way, B34	2.99	£0.07	£0.21
8192923	20/10/2007	Woodside Rd, HP6	West Rd, BS3	6.45	£0.07	£0.45
8190990	20/10/2007	Pinksmoor Lane, TA21	Woodside Rd, HP6	3.11	£0.07	£0.22
8190971	19/10/2007	Parkside Lane, LS11	Collier Lane, LS32	4.94	£0.07	£0.35
8190967	19/10/2007	Collier Lane, LS32	Mill Lane, NG23	14.27	£0.07	£1.00
8190969	19/10/2007	Mill Lane, NG23	Burrowfield, AL7	5.52	£0.07	£0.39
Totals:						£12.47

Journey Cost Profiling

How can telematics be used to reduce a fleet's carbon footprint?

A topical subject at the moment is the fleet's contribution to reducing the company's carbon footprint and how fleet managers can use innovations such as telematics to assist this process. Of course, most fleet managers would have already considered the move to more fuel efficient cars, the use of less polluting fuels and advising employees on how to reduce their individual carbon footprint by more measured driving, but once all of those initiatives have been put into place what more can the fleet manager offer?

Telematics have been used in several organisations to help reduce the carbon footprint even further, linking telematics to other fleet systems.

In one organisation we have been working with, they have reduced the number of 'unnecessary miles' by nearly 500,000 miles a year, without reducing service delivery, which equates to a saving of nearly 180 tonnes of CO_2 per annum – a significant reduction.

Other initiatives include monitoring when the most fuel efficient vehicles have been used, especially where drivers may be using different types of vehicles. When they have a choice of vehicle, do they choose the most fuel efficient?

Telematics can show whether fuel efficient vehicles have been used and indeed encourage the use of more fuel efficient vehicles. Interestingly, in one organisation the drivers initiated a scheme whereby vehicle keys were colour coded – green, amber and red – to show their fuel efficiency and this enabled the drivers to contribute to the cost reductions. The drivers saw it as a way to help the company with cost efficiencies and at the same time help in a small way to secure their jobs.

Telematics linked to fuel management systems can help in improving fuel consumption by showing comparative fuel usage within a class of vehicles. In one

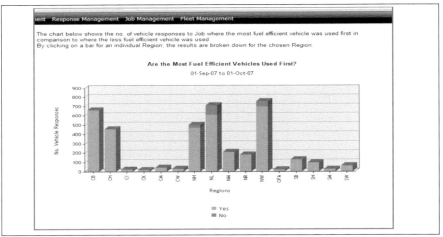

Graph of Fuel Efficiency

Fuel Consumption Reporting								
Date From: 01/01/2008				**Date To:** 07/01/2008				
Reg No.	Location	Make and Model	Fuel Type	Mileage in Period	Fuel Used (litres)	Fuel Consumption (mpg)	Average MPG for Role	Compare with Average MPG
YR07ABD	AB	Ford Transit	Diesel	681	85	36.4	33.6	Above
MG56LOU	BS	Ford Transit	Diesel	243	40	27.6	33.6	Below
PY05KNF	CD	Ford Mondeo	Diesel	164	20	37.2	33.6	Above
GT04JKT	NL	Vauxhall Vectra	Petrol	44	6	33.3	33.6	Below
MM55JHT	NH	BMW 530	Diesel	1121	123	41.4	36.3	Above
DF06MHT	CS	BMW 530	Diesel	159	26	27.8	36.3	Below
DS06NHG	GF	Toyota Auris	Diesel	131	15	39.6	36.3	Above
JG06KHE	GF	BMW 530	Petrol	111	21	24.0	30.1	Below
NB55OGR	AS	Vauxhall Astra	Petrol	29	4	32.9	30.1	Above
MM06HJY	NB	Ford Mondeo	Petrol	22	3	33.3	30.1	Above

Table of Fuel Consumption

organisation they monitored fuel using telematics and the impact was a significant saving in fuel of over £180,000 per annum – managing fuel consumption using tables as shown on the opposite page.

Can you give an example of a project you have worked on?

In 2005, L&A were asked by a leading UK police force to assist them in reducing their fleet costs by at least 20% (over £1 million) but without compromising operational effectiveness and efficiency. It seemed a tall order. However, by combining our knowledge of the fleet world, business improvement processes and with the advent of cheaper more sophisticated telematics solutions, we not only demonstrated the £1million cash saving but also improved how the fleet supported the core business. So how was it achieved?

The initial part of the project was to assess the 'supply and demand' characteristics of policing and how vehicles contributed within the supply side, i.e. getting officers to incidents, patrolling and general transport. From this we soon realised that the supply and demand scenario was very dynamic and to enable us to assess this accurately we would need a more sophisticated analysis using real time data. This required us to know where the vehicles where and what they were doing and hence the development of a telematics solution. With AVLS on board, we could assess;

- how well police vehicles responded to incidents
- whether their patrolling was as directed
- whether sufficient or too many vehicles attended incidents
- whether police vehicles were in the right place at the right time to prevent crime, as well as responding to it
- and whether the fleet was being utilised in a cost effective way

From the initial AVLS analysis, we were able to show not only a £1Million saving but also show how telematics could improve the way the police worked and responded to incidents and patrolling needs.

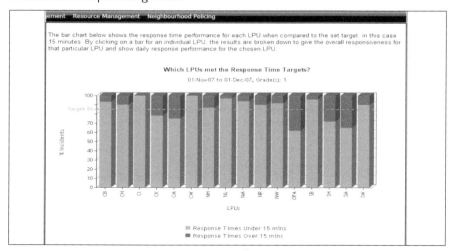

Responsiveness by Region

L&A worked with the police force to develop a series of other reports which helped them to identify crime hotspots, set targeted patrols and ensure that vehicles and officers were in the right place at the right time.

A typical example of this was the location of dog vans nearer to areas where typically they were needed to carry out searches etc.

This developed further into one version of our current iR3 product, a telematics solution which aids police managers to make decisions on how their resources are deployed, whether they are meeting their response targets and whether they are using their vehicles effectively. The ongoing savings have been significant, giving an investment return of over £3 for every £1 invested in the software.

Today L&A have also developed a private sector version which will enable company fleets to determine how they balance their supply (vehicles) and demand (work) to ensure their fleet composition is appropriate and that it is fit for their business's needs.

What features should a fleet manager expect to see in the most highly developed telematics systems?

Telematics like all IT systems is constantly evolving and the most sophisticated systems can offer the fleet manager an abundance of features and functionality to align a telematics solution to his/ her requirements. Typically the most highly developed systems can offer reports on the following;

- Real time vehicle tracking
- Tracking high value items
- Delivery forecast times
- Re-scheduling analysis
- Vehicle idle time
- Vehicle utilisation analysis
- Current speed
- Work demand analysis
- Current direction
- Fuel efficiency analysis
- Journey replay
- Under utilised vehicles
- Journey speed / time
- Responsiveness analysis
- Engine revs
- Driver behaviour analysis
- Fuel consumption
- Electronic Log Books
- Intelligent Satellite Navigation
- Predictive Servicing analysis

- Traffic Congestion
- Duty of Care analysis
- Accident data collection
- Corporate Responsibility analysis
- Mileage Capture
- Driver Identification
- Expenses claims
- Carbon Footprint analysis
- Workshop downtime analysis
- Whole life cost analysis

The list above is not exhaustive but it does give a flavour of where the most developed systems are going. However, to reinforce the point, the important aspect for the fleet manager and their company is to understand which reports and analysis are essential for their operation, which are desirable and which are not really appropriate. When you consider that each of the above features can provide analysis at a company, divisional, regional, local and individual vehicle level, the potential for information overload is very apparent.

The more sophisticated telematics suppliers will work with the fleet manager and his/ her colleagues to determine what report and analyses are important, and how they will derive benefits in both cost savings and operations. The benefits realisation aspects are very important when trying to 'sell in' telematics technology within the company, especially to senior managers and directors who will want to be assured of the benefits.

Are these systems expensive?

The very basic systems can cost as little as 79p per vehicle per day. In many cases the AVLS black box will be required which can cost upwards of £150 per unit, depending on the functionality required. Most telematics companies will lease their boxes over a three or five year period so that the capital costs are spread over the rental term.

The more sophisticated systems which integrate into other fleet or company systems will probably cost double the basic systems, at around £1.50 per vehicle per day. However they have the ability to adapt to the needs of the business and offer a greater opportunity to realise cash savings and productivity gains quickly and in a sustainable fashion.

What do you see as the next steps in the evolution of these systems?

Future developments in telematics will see the use of more data and information to advise on how assets such as vehicles are being used. The use of technology to link into the vehicle's computers and diagnostic software will enable telematics systems to report on how an engine is performing, whether it needs a service in advance of its prescribed service interval and whether the correct fuel is being used.

Not only is it now possible to link into the latest satellite navigation systems to send SMS and text messages to drivers via their Sat Nav units, but also to allow drivers to interrogate the company intranet via fast data links such as GPRS and 3G. They can be re-directed to higher priority jobs, advised of traffic delays on their proposed route and have delivered to them data about the area in which they are driving, which can be constantly changing as they proceed along their route. Such systems can also advise fleet managers and job schedulers whether a driver is likely to meet his/ her proposed delivery time, can keep customers advised of any potential delays and can also assess driver behaviour to ensure the vehicle is being driven appropriately, economically and efficiently. Latest developments will alert fleet managers if a vehicle is involved in a collision and some can also ring remotely the emergency services to request assistance so protecting what are, after all, valuable company assets – the driver and their vehicle.

It may all seem like future technology but such systems are emerging today into the telematics market and they will be able to combine current features with the forthcoming additional functionality to provide a very comprehensive management system to aid both the fleet manager and his/ her operational management colleagues.

Another key development is the delivery of such systems which traditionally have been PC based and often have been restricted to a few users. The emerging use of intranet and web enabled technology means applications and functionality can be accessed from the Web, as can secure data storage.

The internet model will provide a more open access system, allowing individual drivers to view their information, automate expenses, update their driver records, etc. It will allow the fleet manager to access information on fleet issues such as servicing, accidents, fuel consumption, duty of care, utilisation and whole life costs. It will enable operational managers to manage their fleets more effectively, determine how the demand side will affect their fleet profile and also engage with duty of care and corporate responsibility.

So where is the development of telematics going to take us? In the near future, telematics hardware will get smaller and cheaper so enabling it to go into more novel applications such as logistics, scheduling, service delivery, etc.

The advent of Automatic Resource Location Systems [ARLS] will enable personnel to be located using GPS cellular phones or PDAs. This would enable companies to know where personnel are as well as vehicles. It may sound like a 'Big Brother' scenario but imagine if you are a lone worker, or work in vulnerable situations, or work in an environment where you are required to be responsive to quickly changing demands, then the ability to be located would be essential from a health and safety or operational perspective.

Perhaps the biggest future development will be the further integration of telematics with other company systems. The benefits to the company and fleet managers could be considerable. Linking future telematics functionality with company systems via web enabled software would allow the fleet manager role to develop into a more sophisticated role as 'Mobility Manager' whereby he/she managed all aspects of the company's mobility requirements and not just the vehicle or fleet aspects.

As Mobility Manager, the fleet manager would be responsible for ensuring all transport requirements were met in a cost effective way and which also minimises the company's carbon footprint. This could combine transport alternatives and link up key interfaces such as train, taxi, car hire or air travel.

This may sound fanciful but if government objectives for reducing congestion and reducing dramatically the country's CO_2 emissions are to be achieved, then the economics of using a company car may become questionable. It is not unimaginable to suggest that in the next decade sophisticated road pricing will be introduced and companies will have to use carbon offset tariffs to pay for their carbon usage. In that scenario, company vehicles will have to be justified far more than now, and usage will have to be closely monitored to ensure they are cost effective for the company. Telematics could achieve this.

The future of telematics, and its ability to assist the fleet manager further, may be demonstrated by the following scenario. It's 2015, variable road pricing is in place, the M25 costs £3 per mile during rush hour, other roads vary between £0.01 per mile in rural locations and up to £5 mile in central London. The average carbon offset for a company van is £0.25/mile.

Using telematics the driver can be directed to the most 'green' but cost efficient route. If traffic congestion increases on a specific road, telematics will advise the driver to re-route to a more cost effective option, ensuring the delivery is made on time without incurring additional congestion or carbon offset costs. The linking of telematics with other technologies would enable this.

From a mobility management perspective, the fleet or mobility manager could use telematics to assist his/ her colleagues.

Again picture the scenario, a sales manager is based in Reading and has a meeting in Aberdeen. How might a future telematics linked to mobility software assist him?

It could plan his route to minimise road charging costs and link to the electronic car parking system at the train system to book and pay for his car parking space.

En route it could advise him of a slight delay to his train.

Once on the train, the telematics within his PDA will download any updates to his schedule advising him that a taxi has been booked for his planned arrival at Aberdeen and that the fare has been paid.

As he nears the station, the telematics know this and so advise the taxi company of his imminent arrival – so the taxi is ready and he arrives at his meeting on time and with the minimum of fuss.

It may sound like science fiction but in reality it is simply the integration of a number of existing technologies to give a more joined up approach to transport in the 21st century.

So how might a fleet manager set about obtaining the benefits you have outlined?

Our advice would be to start in simple terms and understand what benefits can be achieved by implementing a telematics system. Are there key questions or issues which the fleet manager or company needs to address? These might be;

1   Are our fleet costs in line with our competitors or with recognised best practice?

2   If not, where are our areas of weaknesses?

3   Have we followed all the recognised fleet good practice guidelines which are outlined in other chapters in this book?

4   Do we know how vehicles are utilised and where potential savings could be found?

If not, telematics could be of real benefit in delivering cashable savings.

Telematics will enable the fleet manager to work with his/ her operational colleagues to ensure the right number and mix of vehicles are available to ensure company requirements are met in a cost effective way.

It can also assist in pure fleet management performance measures such as workshop downtime, ensuring vehicles spend as little time as possible off the road, ensuring vehicles are serviced only in periods of idle time and making sure the appropriate level of vehicles are available when required.

Other areas for consideration would be;

*   Duty of care – are we managing our fleet in an effective way which protects our employees and the company? Telematics can assist in ensuring an organisation's guidelines are met.

*   Environmental Issues – have we undertaken all the environmental steps we can and if so what more can we do? The use of telematics to analyse scheduling, unnecessary journeys, vehicle utilisation, fuel consumption, etc would assist in an effective environmental strategy.

*   Corporate Responsibility – are we using our vehicles effectively and efficiently, are drivers being reimbursed appropriately, and are the overall costs of the fleet being managed effectively?

The most important step in determining whether telematics will work in your operation, and how any savings or benefits will be achieved, is to develop a benefits realisation strategy. No doubt, in many companies the fleet manager will have to write a business case for the purchase of a telematics system. Analysing how key benefits and savings can be realised will certainly strengthen the case, as will showing how the fleet manager will deliver the benefits.

In our experience this approach provides confidence in the system, its benefits and in the investment required. It also helps to raise the profile of the fleet manager and demonstrate that the company's strategic goals have been considered in developing the need for a telematics system.

And how should they go about implementation?

Once a fleet manager has determined the need for telematics and how it will assist in providing benefits, the implementation of the system will be important. Our experience would suggest that fleet managers start with a small number of core features and, as they become more experienced at using the system, incorporate more functionality as it fits with the overall strategic fleet goals. In practice this may involve the following steps;

- Initially use exception reports to analyse utilisation, service delivery performance and core fleet management activities such as fuel consumption, servicing forecasts, etc. This will give the fleet manager a good understanding of where vehicles are not fully utilised, where potential over resourcing is occurring, and where potential under resourcing is causing a deterioration in service delivery.

- From this, the fleet manager can provide more detailed reports on the possible problem areas, such as reviewing utilisation at an area or local level, comparing service delivery performance and how it is impacted by resources, and make recommendations to his/ her colleagues on how a re-distribution of vehicles could save resources and improve customer satisfaction.

- After taking some vehicles away or re-distributing them, the fleet manager will need to have in place alternative transport methods such as public transport, pool cars, daily rental, flexi–lease or contract hire and have the systems and processes in place to ensure that ad hoc or occasional transport requirements can be met.

- As a parallel phase, the fleet manager can introduce the duty of care and environmental reports which will ensure that operational managers are aware of any breaches in company guidelines, assist in modifying driver behaviour and act as a catalyst in reducing accident rates and reducing environmental impact.

- Finally, the fleet manager could integrate the telematics systems with other fleet management and company systems to provide a true mobility management solution which will provide on-going and sustainable savings and develop the fleet function into a more integrated mobility operation.

How can L&A can help fleet managers?

L&A have been successful in helping a large number of fleet operations achieve real savings and improved productivity benefits by taking an innovative approach to the use of telematics in the fleet environment. We have years of fleet management experience and understand how IT systems can help (and hinder) fleet managers.

Our approach in developing our telematics solution, iR3, was to work from the ground up and work with fleet practitioners to develop a product which will give real value and enable fleet managers to deliver savings as well as productivity gains.

We see our offering as not just an IT solution: indeed we work with fleet managers and their colleagues to understand how their business works and then suggest which reports would have the most impact early on and which would be useful for the on-going stages. Our tried and tested method is to link the use of telematics such as iR3 with an advisory approach so that through a benefits realisation framework we can help the fleet manager to realise the benefits over the long term.

Adrian McMullan
Director
L&A Consultants Limited

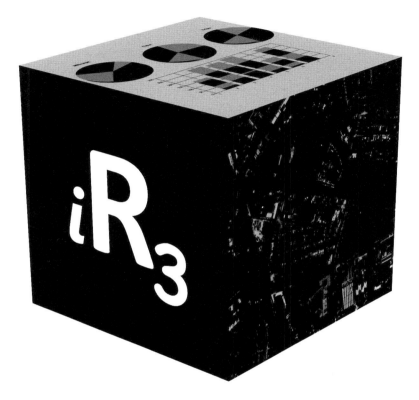

New angles on fleet managment with iR3

www.landaconsultants.com

18 ROADSIDE ASSISTANCE

Steve Whitmarsh

Senior Partnership Manager, Fleet

RAC

There cannot be many people who have not heard of the RAC, but please introduce your company

RAC has been providing breakdown services since 1897, with the formation of The Automobile Club of Great Britain.

Patrols were introduced in 1901 and, over the years, RAC has gone through a number of significant changes. These include the introduction of the Advanced Computer Aided Rescue System in 1987, acquiring the British School of Motoring in 1997, being purchased by the Lex Group in 1999, and more recently in 2005, being purchased by Aviva Plc, creating RAC Rescue.

What are the different types of fleet breakdown services?

Every fleet has different needs and therefore the level of cover available can usually be tailored to suit each fleet's individual requirements, whatever its size.

For example, RAC has agreements with fleets that require no more than roadside rescue and a short tow, (typically a maximum distance ranging from 10 to 50 miles). Under this contract, if the vehicle can be fixed at roadside by the patrol, the fleet driver can be on their way. If not, the patrol will tow the vehicle to a place of safety or to a repairer within the agreed recovery mileage range and then the fleet manager has the responsibility to make arrangements to repair the vehicle.

Under a Recovery agreement, there are different levels of service available for fleets, relating to the distance a business would potentially need their vehicles towed if they were to break down. For example, if a company doesn't want to be exposed to the possibility of higher costs for a long distance tow, they can choose a maximum of 20 miles to a garage. Maximum distances of 30, 50 or 100 miles are also available.

At Home cover is for when a fleet driver breaks down at home. This is often if the car won't start or it has a flat tyre. RAC will attend the driver at home and try to fix the problem or recover the vehicle to a place where it can be fixed.

Onward Travel is another service that is attractive to certain fleets. In the event of a breakdown that cannot be repaired at the roadside, the driver will be provided with a hire car, or will be covered for use of public transport or taxis to get to their destination. Or, if necessary, hotel accommodation will be provided.

What are the different ways that fleets can cover the cost of breakdowns?

There are a number of ways to pay for breakdown cover, but they generally fall into two categories:

- **Pay-on-use** – where the fleet pays for each event as it occurs, and
- **Subscription** – where the fleet has an insurance policy to cover the risk of any breakdown.

There are positives and negatives associated with each of these options that fleets should be aware of.

With the first option, the fleet bears the risk of each individual instance of a breakdown. With a subscription contract, the supplier takes this risk. Fleets should also be aware that there are certain bespoke contract structures, which are tax efficient methods of underwriting the risk associated with pay-on-use contracts.

A pay-on-use type of agreement attracts VAT as it is a provision of service; however VAT is a recoverable tax for the majority of fleets. With a subscription scheme however, a fleet will have to pay insurance premium tax (IPT) which is a non-recoverable tax. This is worth bearing in mind as, if a fleet wishes to underwrite a subscription scheme, there will be an additional cost due to this tax.

Paying per vehicle, per month under a subscription scheme is a good way of spreading the cost of breakdown recovery, but there is also the option of paying in advance on an annual basis. Theoretically, if the subscription scheme is set correctly, this can assist a business with budgeting.

Fleet managers must weigh up the options and make an informed decision on which agreement would be the most suitable dependent on their organisation's appetite for risk and budgeting requirements.

How can a fleet breakdown service make life easier for fleet managers when vehicles break down?

One of the major problems facing fleet managers if a vehicle breaks down is downtime, which can be expensive for a business. In simple terms, breakdowns prevent a fleet driver doing their job, whether it is the distribution of goods or provision of a service.

Fleet breakdown services can lessen the risk of downtime by helping drivers as quickly as possible, either through repairing the vehicle, taking it to a place where it can be fixed, or getting the driver to their destination.

There are a number of ways to make this happen, and whilst speed of attendance will obviously contribute to the reduction in downtime, of far more importance is the ability to attend with the right resource. If we can do this the driver is only waiting for one resource rather than for multiple resources such as a patrol and a recovery vehicle – which extends the overall length of vehicle downtime.

Therefore, RAC Breakdown Assistance Centre staff have questions and answers which they take the customer though before a resource is despatched to the scene. These are non-technical, symptom based questions, such as asking if the vehicle is making a particular noise or is emitting smoke of a particular colour. These questions are put to customers who don't necessarily have technical knowledge, but when combined with the reported fault, produce technical answers about the problem with the vehicle. This enables our Customer Solutions Team to determine the most appropriate resource required to attend the vehicle and therefore increase the chances of the fleet customer being able to drive away.

Another way that RAC is attempting to cut the time a fleet driver is stuck at the roadside, not to mention cutting CO_2 emissions, is through its Fix without Resource initiative. Technical specialists are on hand to speak to the driver of the broken down vehicle to try to diagnose the problem by asking them a set of questions. If this is possible, they can then determine whether the problem can be fixed without the driver having to wait for a patrol. Not only does this service mean that the driver is back on the road again quicker, meaning less downtime, but this service is charged at a greatly reduced rate compared to the full cost of sending a patrol for pay on use customers.

RAC can also provide fleet customers with vehicle fault analysis data, which can potentially help reduce time lost through breakdowns. It helps to identify the causes of breakdowns and fleet managers can use the data to determine the necessary steps to avoid, or at least reduce, the risk of future breakdowns.

Driver training is one example of a requirement identified by the vehicle fault analysis, particularly if it shows that breakdowns are often the fault of the drivers themselves.

Changes to purchasing patterns are another possibility, such as changing the type of vehicles available on a fleet choice list to more reliable models.

Downtime is not the only concern of a fleet manager when a vehicle has broken down. Health and safety is another issue that should be considered carefully, as they have a duty of care responsibility to their drivers. And, since the introduction of the Corporate Manslaughter and Homicide Act 2007, this has become an even greater priority.

It may seem unlikely, but if a vehicle is broken down at roadside, particularly on a motorway or dual carriageway, there is a greatly increased risk of the vehicle or the driver being hit by another road user.

RAC provides reassurance to fleet managers as the contact centre staff will take customers through a safety briefing in the event of a break down. This could include, for example, advising the driver to get out of the car and go to a safe place away from the road, even if this means sitting on a wet verge at the side of the motorway in the rain. After all, it is better to be cold and wet than run the risk of being hit by oncoming traffic.

There is no particular rule whereby small fleets go for one type of breakdown service and large fleets need another. There are different levels of cover that can be tailored to suit the needs of any sized fleet.

RAC does have a relatively standardised set of products that have been developed over many years to meet the requirements of smaller fleets. These are:

- **RAC Select Premier** – includes Roadside, Recovery, At Home;
- **RAC Select Premier Level 1** – includes Roadside, Recovery, At Home and 24 hour Onward Travel; and
- **RAC Select Premier Level 2** – includes Roadside, Recovery, At Home and 48 hour Onward Travel.

Where fleets have specific requirements, this can be tailored accordingly and a bespoke service can be devised, as required, for fleets of any size. This tailoring tends to be around onward travel and recovery requirements. For example, some very large fleets have their own specific agreements with a network of repair outlets.

There is also specific cover for taxis and minibuses. Minibus Assist is a special package for minibus operators. Cover includes onwards travel, where in the event of a breakdown, drivers and passengers can continue their journey with the minimum disruption possible. Taxi Assist is the same cover as RAC Select Premier but is sold to customers who use their vehicles for hire or reward.

How extensive is your European breakdown cover for fleets?

RAC European Cover is a service delivered through RAC France, based in Lyon, which ensures that you and your drivers are supported whilst travelling abroad with assistance for breakdown, accident or fire across mainland Europe. The service is provided from RAC's multilingual facility where all operators speak English.

European cover can be added to any RAC agreement but it is only available as a subscription product. So, if added to a pay-on-use fleet agreement, a separate European Subscription account would be set up.

Other variations of European cover are based on the number of vehicles included. It can obviously be purchased for a whole fleet, where the premium is payable per car to cover travel abroad within the policy year. But it is also available as a selective vehicle subscription, where fleets can pay an annual premium to cover certain vehicles that travel abroad.

A single trip product is also just about to be launched, which will allow a fleet customer to purchase European cover for the duration of a trip, rather than annually.

RAC's European cover currently provides service in up to 47 countries, which are split into two zones, but the extent of cover you receive is subject to the policy type. For example, under certain policies, a fleet would pay a supplement to cover Zone 2.

RAC Provides Assistance in 47 Countries	
Zone 1	
Andorra	Republic of Ireland (*plus Northern Ireland*
Austria	*for residents of Great Britain*
Belgium	*travelling from the mainland)*
Denmark	Netherlands
Finland	Norway
France	Portugal
Germany	San Marino
Gibraltar	Spain
Italy	Sweden
Liechtenstein	Switzerland
Luxembourg	*and offshore islands of above*
Monaco	
Zone 2	
Albania	Latvia
Armenia	Lithuania
Azerbaijan	Macedonia
Belarus	Malta
Bosnia Herzegovina	Moldova
Bulgaria	Poland
Croatia	Ukraine
Cyprus	Romania
Czech Republic	Russian mainland (west of Urals)
Estonia	Serbia and Montenegro
Georgia	Slovakian Republic
Greece	Slovenia
Hungary	Turkey

What about large haulage firms, with articulated vehicles? They must suffer badly if one of their container-carrying vehicles breaks down or has an accident. Is there an RAC service applicable to them?

Large Goods Vehicles (LGVs), which are classed as over 3.5 tonnes, require a different type of service to normal, car-derived breakdown services. There are a number of specialist commercial vehicle breakdown companies in the UK, one of which is RAC Commercial Assistance.

LGV fleets have access, via RAC Commercial Assistance's state of the art Assistance Centre, to our network of specialist agents who can recover and repair vehicles of any weight category, typically up to 44 tonnes, but often up to and exceeding 100 tonnes.

Having this division as part of RAC offers customers the best of both worlds. It complements our own patrol force, which cannot recover LGVs, but does have the capability to carry out many simple repairs at the roadside. For instance, RAC Patrols can jump start any vehicle, with either 12V or 24V electrical systems, if the problem is a flat battery. If this is the case, the patrol will attend instead of the contractor and the customer will not have to pay the increased price for the special recovery agent call out.

RAC Commercial Assistance is only available on a pay-on-use basis. In fact, there are no providers of LGV breakdown cover on subscription in the UK. The normal way of charging is on an hourly basis; ie, the amount of time it takes to either attend and repair or recover the vehicle. This is due to the amount of skill and time often required to get these vehicles into a state they can be recovered.

RAC is in a good position to monitor developments in the motoring world. How have vehicles and driving habits changed over the years?

The RAC Report on Motoring 2008, a study of how motoring in Britain has changed over the last twenty years, found that motoring has changed significantly, with more drivers, more cars and more traffic on the roads generally, yet less road space. In fact, 92% of motorists think we are much more dependent on our cars and more car-focused than in 1988.

Motorists think that the single biggest change over the past twenty years has been the increased cost of motoring. However, our research has shown that the real cost of motoring has actually fallen by 18%, even when rising petrol prices are taken into account. The increase in aggressive driving is also something that has become apparent over the years with one-in-three motorists saying they have fallen victim to road rage or aggressive driving, to the extent where they have felt physically threatened.

Motorists see themselves as law-abiding drivers, but over the last twenty years, motoring offences, particularly speeding, have increased significantly. Motorists are much more willing to drive within the speed limit in built up areas than they are on motorways, where they call for the limit to be raised to 80mph.

In relation to cars themselves, these days they are much safer and we tend to feel a lot more comfortable in them. This has been brought about largely by improvements in safety and technology and the fact that cars are generally more reliable.

What has RAC done to better serve its increasingly car-dependent customers?

I have already mentioned two recent innovations: the questions posed by call centre staff (to ensure that the correct resource is despatched to the scene), and RAC's Fix Without Resource initiative (where our technical experts instruct the customer on what to do to fix the problem quickly).

One initiative that RAC is rolling out in 2009 is called Repair and Go. A network of 180 RAC-approved repair centres across the UK will be on stand by to get people back on the road as quickly as possible. Where a vehicle can't be fixed at roadside, RAC will take it to one of these centres where the problem will be resolved and the driver put back on the road within, for example, a couple of hours.

One increasingly common problem where this could be useful is for the misfuelling of vehicles. Often a driver would have to return the vehicle to a franchised dealer to tackle this. But instead, the car can be drained and back on the road within two hours, avoiding the need for the driver to be without their vehicle for a potentially long period of time.

Another big change has been the introduction of the Rapid Deployment Trailer which is now fitted across the patrol force. It folds out of the back of the patrol van, allowing the patrol to recover vehicles themselves. Previously, customers either had to be straight bar towed, which can be an unpleasant experience, or to wait for a recovery vehicle, which greatly increased the time taken to resolve the customer's situation.

For those times when the car cannot be towed, another development was the introduction of Flat Bed Recovery Vehicles. We now have 90 RAC-branded flatbeds on the roads, helping reduce the reliance on contractors for recoveries and providing extra assurance for customers.

All of these developments are helping car-dependent fleet drivers keep moving and minimise interruptions to their working day.

To continually gauge whether RAC is meeting customer requirements, at the end of a breakdown customers are asked to complete a satisfaction survey, which is now completed on a mobile PDA system. This questionnaire gathers feedback on the service they received and forms the Electronic Customer Satisfaction Index (eCSI). Previously, there was a paper-based system in place which had an 18% response rate, whereas with this new system, 60% of customers provide feedback, enabling RAC to constantly monitor the service to improve it and deal with any issues.

What new technology have you introduced recently?

In terms of dispatching patrols, RAC's Intelligent Computer Aided Dispatch (iCAD) was implemented approximately five years ago. In around 90% of cases, the computer will automatically determine and then dispatch the most appropriate and fastest resource to a customer, based on data being entered by the Breakdown Assistance Centre team. This cuts out the amount of time it would take for staff to determine and action this themselves, reducing the waiting time for customers.

Regarding technology for the patrol vans, they are all equipped with the latest generation Patrol Vehicle System (PVS). This uses the latest 3G mobile phone network, enabling patrols to download the latest diagnostic information to their vans, 24 hours a day and to have more information regarding each breakdown. With the rapidly evolving and increasingly complicated technology of modern vehicles, this greatly increases the chances that vehicles can be fixed at roadside.

What are the top five faults you come across, and how might fleet managers reduce common problems?

Wheel changing appears to be the most prominent problem for fleet drivers. Frequently, RAC attends vehicles that don't have a spare tyre or where drivers have not repaired a previously punctured tyre. It seems many fleet drivers are unwilling to make an attempt at changing them or are reluctant to have the spare fixed. Although RAC will continue to attend breakdowns of this nature, it has developed a solution to the problem when the tyre cannot be repaired at roadside. Patrols are now equipped with a multi-fit wheel which allows around 80% of vehicles to be taken straight to the nearest tyre repair agent, avoiding the wait for a secondary recovery vehicle. Locking wheel nuts can also pose an additional challenge to the driver when changing wheels, especially when the key has been left at home. RAC are equipped to deal with this also, but an unnecessary delay can be avoided by ensuring the key is with the vehicle at all times.

The condition of tyres, including the spare, should be checked regularly including tyre pressure and legal tread depth. The current minimum legal tread depth for cars and light commercial vehicles is 1.6mm. However, it is generally acknowledged that the greater the tread depth, the more efficient the tyre is at clearing water in its path, making driving conditions safer.

Failing to check tyres regularly could, of course, lead to road traffic accidents or multiple collisions. RAC suggests that the tread depth of a tyre should not fall beneath 3mm.

Fleet managers should ensure that drivers are aware of the wheel replacement procedure, which should include the tools/jack, locking wheel nut locations and spare wheel access. Advise drivers to avoid hitting tyres against kerbs, especially when parking, as this can weaken the tyre sidewalls without showing external damage.

Fleet vehicles have become like mobile offices with more and more current-hungry gadgets, such as mobile phones, PCs and navigation systems. So flat batteries rank as the second highest reason for fleet call outs, and data suggests that 33% of breakdown call outs could be avoided, as such problems are preventable.

Forgetting to switch off interior and exterior lights is a bigger problem with cars today as modern batteries are designed for a high discharge of power when starting the car, but not for a constant, steady current drain as in the case of lights or charging mobile equipment. To tackle this, it's good to run the engine and replenish the charge of the battery or get a garage to fit a larger capacity battery.

On average, RAC anticipates a 20% increase in flat battery call outs following daylight saving periods, due to vehicle lights being left on. The longer hours spent driving in the dark increases the need for exterior lights, and, in the morning rush, people often forget to switch them off. Heaters, heated screens and seats can also drain a vehicle's battery, so it is important to avoid using these types of devices any longer than necessary, especially when the vehicle is idling in traffic. Fleet managers should advise their drivers to turn all electrical gadgets off when the vehicle is parked. Vehicles that are stored or parked for a long period should have a battery charger/optimiser connected, so that the battery is fully charged when handed to the driver.

The cost of an accident can be far reaching for businesses. It includes at least two hours to arrange repair during which the driver is probably off the road, a minimum one day for a replacement car at an average of £23 per day, loss of excess and, if the fleet driver is self-insured, a bill to pick up for the whole repair cost, which could be between £1,000 and £10,000.

Misfuelling is another problem. Fleet drivers, who may be pre-occupied when filling up, thinking about their next meeting, the journey ahead or rushing to keep their appointments, could well be at risk of filling their vehicle with the wrong fuel. RAC data shows that diesel contamination – petrol in diesel – counts for almost a quarter of the top 20 fleet 'driver induced' faults, and the impact of misfuelling could cost fleets needlessly thousands of pounds a year to put right. Not only do fleet managers lose the value of the fuel, but also costly vehicle repairs are involved.

If a vehicle is misfuelled, the car should not be unlocked and the key should certainly not be put in the ignition. Damage can occur as some cars now incorporate 'easy start systems' which begin to pump fuel around the engine as soon as the door is unlocked. Under no circumstances should the engine be started, since it could result in a repair cost of around £200 to have the fuel tank drained and between £3,000 and £6,000 to repair any damage to the engine. Fleet managers should clearly mark the fuel type on a vehicle with a sticker/label, close to the filler aperture and on the instrument dashboard. In addition, fleet managers should fit anti-contamination devices to diesel vehicles and make drivers aware of the correct procedure to follow in the event that the fuel becomes contaminated.

What is the key message that RAC would like to give to fleet managers?

RAC estimates that over 40,000 fleet breakdown call outs a year could be avoided if fleet drivers were to conduct basic maintenance checks of their vehicles and undertook driver training.

Drivers can help prevent a breakdown by carrying out basic weekly 'forecourt checks' on vehicles, such as checking engine oil and coolant and water levels. Failing to conduct such checks could result in a need for a replacement engine costing the business £3,000 or more, as well as the cost of a replacement car whilst the vehicle is being repaired. In fact, a work vehicle should be checked every time before use and it would be a good idea for fleet managers to introduce a driver log book to record all the details of these vehicle checks.

If a fleet driver becomes aware of abnormal noises or a lack of performance, they should know to have the vehicle checked or inspected immediately. Robust procedures should also be in place to have fleet vehicles independently inspected at least every three months to improve their general condition, and to demonstrate mitigation in the event that an accident lands their company in court.

How important is it for fleet vehicles to be professionally inspected, either on purchase, resale or during their ownership?

It's easy to forget to check the tyres, top up the oil and refill the screenwash. With the increasingly long intervals between servicing fleet vehicles, it is no surprise that many company cars only get checked once a year. There are no guidelines about how often fleet vehicles should be inspected, but we suggest companies check vehicles with the help of an independent third party.

Vehicle inspections can save fleets valuable time and money and reduce many of the risks fleet drivers face, as well as exposure to legal action. A regular schedule of fleet inspection will help with businesses' early identification of vehicle faults and help to prevent further problems. This results in fleets being able to cut repair costs, while helping them to improve residual values when a fleet vehicle comes to the end of its life, especially since the value of vehicles significantly diminishes without a service history.

Furthermore, the cost of an inspection is far less than the cost of bent metal if a vehicle is involved in a collision and certainly less than the cost of prosecution should a fleet manager be liable for an incident.

The RAC carries out inspections for fleets. One fleet we inspected recently had 140 cars less than two and a half years old. 31 of these would have failed an MOT test and 11 had faults which would have put the driver on the wrong side of the law. More worryingly, 19 had dangerously faulty brakes or steering – which could easily have put the driver on the wrong side of the road!

Drivers are particularly poor in carrying out routine maintenance checks. According to RAC data, 53% of inspections identify failures in routine maintenance carried out by fleet drivers. Thorough checks by a fleet manager or by an independent third party can help to identify those fleet drivers who fail to maintain their vehicles.

Although it is a fleet driver who is faced with a fine or a driving ban if their vehicle fails to comply with the law, it is the fleet manager who has a corporate duty of care to ensure regular inspections are carried out. Inspections limit a company's exposure to a Health and Safety Executive investigation, should an employee be involved in an accident. For those companies that don't have a fleet maintenance department, RAC's duty of care inspections service is one risk management solution.

What is RAC Inspections?

RAC Inspections is one of the UK's largest and most experienced providers of inspection services, carrying out over 190,000 inspections each year. Besides duty of care inspections, RAC offers a wide range of inspection services for the fleet market, including:

- **Cause and Fault Inspections** – provides an independent check of a leased vehicle to find the cause of its faults, so costs can be assigned correctly, for example, to the driver or warranty.
- **Fair Wear and Tear Inspections** – provides an independent check of end-of-lease vehicles and an estimate of costs that you may have to pay your provider.
- **Service, Maintenance and Repair Inspection** – Spot checks and workshop audits to independently assess the service, maintenance and repair suppliers that fleet managers deal with. This enables fleet managers to track and benchmark a service supplier's performance.

What are the advantages of using RAC Inspections compared to competitors?

Since RAC engineers aren't trying to sell repair and maintenance services, their only concern is the roadworthiness of fleet vehicles and the safety of drivers. All RAC examining engineers have a recognised industry qualification under the British Vehicle and Rental Association, are members of the Institute of Road Transport Engineers or Institute of the Motor Industry, and have at least eight years' motor trade experience.

RAC engineers also continue to receive training and to be aware of ever-changing legislation that affects fleets. Examining engineers are able to access RAC breakdown and management information data on recurring faults on the fleet vehicles our patrols attend. Fleets can then be advised to claim on their warranty to rectify any problems, instead of paying for the fault to be fixed by a service provider.

Finally, no work is ever sub-contracted to other parties to complete, so fleets have peace of mind that an inspection is conducted by examining engineers from start to finish.

Statistically, fleet drivers are more likely to have an accident than other drivers. Why is this? What are the legal and moral implications for a fleet manager and their business?

The Road Casualties in Great Britain 2007 statistics from the Department for Transport, show that out of approximately 3,000 deaths on Britain's roads each year, a third are drivers who are "at work" at the time. RAC's own data also shows that fleet drivers are twice as likely to be involved in a road traffic accident as other road users.

It's true that the road fatality figures have decreased in recent years, but by nowhere near enough.

Companies are still failing to address the number one issue that could improve the situation: the behaviour and competence of drivers. By ignoring the person holding the steering wheel, they are leaving themselves wide open to corporate risk while not gaining any of the benefits of properly assessed and trained staff.

Lack of knowledge is a problem, as is the commitment from senior management to get things done. Often, those responsible for fleet vehicles are wearing a number of hats, and may actually work in human resources or finance. And even where the fleet manager role does exist, the responsible person needs to persuade others to enable investment and co-operation with road risk initiatives to happen. Yet when insurance companies are offering to part-fund driver training, firms are still reluctant to act, citing business pressures such as the inability to release drivers to undertake training. And where there's no external funding, or managers can't see the return on investment, the impetus to take action reduces further.

But the impetus to get a grip on occupational road risk needs to come from the highest level in an organisation; it's not something to deal with when an accident happens.

So where are companies running fleet vehicles most vulnerable? It's best to split the issues into three distinct areas:

- The driver
- The vehicle
- The journey

In terms of drivers, they are rarely provided with training beyond having a licence and are simply let loose on a vehicle. This can sometimes mean putting a young, inexperienced person in a high powered car: a recipe for potential disaster.

The business driver – in some ways – should be accustomed to the dangers of using UK roads, as they are exposed to their worst elements more often.

However, driving at work brings a wealth of distractions that don't necessarily affect the private motorist, such as mobile phone conversations that may require greater concentration; the stress of getting to an appointment on time and the use of satellite navigation systems to get there.

And risk is increased when the person behind the wheel isn't always the person you expect. Employee's spouses and children are sometimes allowed access to company vehicles, often without managers having any knowledge of their eligibility or capability to drive.

Regarding the risk presented by vehicles, manufacturers have now ensured that many safety features are built in as standard, thus increasing the protection for drivers. But with brand new, leased vehicles there is an increased interval between services – sometimes 20,000 miles – and this places a greater onus on companies and their drivers to conduct basic car maintenance, such as checking fluid levels, tyres, lights and windscreens. The condition and safety of a car that is used regularly for business can change a lot between services and needs to be monitored.

Finally, journey types for fleet drivers present a major health and safety challenge, with the number of miles they are likely to do in a day far exceeding those of the ordinary motorist. This, clearly, can involve leaving home early in the morning, driving somewhere in a hurry and returning late at night.

With such an array of risk factors, businesses simply must have systems in place that are foolproof.

Which raises the question, how should a fleet manage risk? The Health and Safety Executive's *Driving at Work* document (reference INDG382) – available from the HSE website – provides a comprehensive framework, based on existing legislation, for approaching fleet risk management.

At the very least, anyone responsible for company vehicles should have a documented driving at work policy. This needs to cover all company and driver-owned vehicles and should be read, understood and signed by all staff.

Once that is in place, it is necessary – under the requirements of the Health and Safety at Work Act 1974 – to carry out risk assessments.

This extends the definition of the "workplace" to include the vehicles staff are using as part of their job, which is often the most dangerous place they could be.

Other legislation has bolstered the demands of the 1974 Act and needs to be taken into account, including the Corporate Manslaughter and Homicide Act 2007, Management of Health and Safety at Work Regulations 1999, and the Road Traffic Acts.

In addition, new sentencing guidelines have been introduced, which increase the penalties if it's proven that an accident was caused by in-car distractions such as the use of a mobile phone.

Risk assessments can be carried out in various ways. RAC has a risk assessment process that can be done either online or via hard copy, which involves a 10-minute multiple-choice questionnaire to help identify occupational road risk levels in an organisation.

Management information from the risk assessments can be used to pinpoint what has created the risk level and determine the appropriate response. Consequently, online training and seminars can be provided for low to medium risk drivers. However, for those drivers deemed high risk, the only real option is to use on-road driver training in the vehicle normally used for business.

In addition, risk management workshops aimed at company managers can help to cascade good risk management information throughout the organisation. This can be supplemented with managers themselves being trained as "task observers", qualified to assess and mentor drivers on an on-going basis.

For new drivers, risk management should become part of the induction process where they are risk assessed and trained accordingly. Ideally, human resources procedures need to be put in place for every employee who might be driving on business.

'Grey fleet' drivers – those receiving a cash allowance or providing their own vehicle as opposed to having a company vehicle – equally need risk assessments and training. But you also need to know if they have proper business insurance, an MOT certificate and carry out adequate maintenance.

Something that can help manage both fleet and grey fleet drivers is having a system of driver permits. After putting a driver through the risk assessment and training process, you can issue an internal driving permit which shows the person is eligible to drive on company business until something changes that status, such as an accident or road traffic conviction, or even simply a change of vehicle.

A practical tactic – simple but beneficial – is issuing all drivers with safety packs they can keep in their vehicles. These should include everything they might need in the event of an accident either in the UK or abroad, such as a first aid kit, high visibility jacket, camera, etc.

Ensuring that drivers are interviewed post–accident doesn't always happen, despite the essential lessons that companies can learn. To guarantee that this does take place, RAC can conduct post–accident driver interviews on behalf of employers to help identify what might have been done to reduce the impact of the accident and make recommendations for preventing future problems.

Any organisation using vehicles should have a driving at work policy, check driving licences, carry out risk assessments and implement driver training. And fleet managers should be under no illusion: these are not 'nice to have'; they are legal requirements and the absolute minimum you should be doing.

You are active in the warranty market. Please tell us about how fleet managers can use warranties to improve the bottom line.

When times are tough – which they undoubtedly are right now – every bit of revenue helps.

Companies faced with off-loading vehicles know that the used car values they once achieved at auction have plummeted, which has started to have an impact on businesses' profit and loss accounts.

Companies need to find new ways of getting rid of vehicles while maximising the returns on them. One way of doing this is selling vehicles back to staff members instead of going via the trade. This can potentially attract more value for the company, while providing an opportunity for employees to obtain a vehicle without paying dealership prices.

But when company vehicles are disposed of at the end of their term, they tend to be outside the cover period for manufacturers' warranty. This isn't a problem when managing vehicle disposal through the trade, as dealers become responsible for the on-going condition and maintenance of the vehicle under a warranty agreement, and there is no come-back for the fleet manager.

So, when selling ex-fleet vehicles to staff, it becomes necessary for companies to provide that warranty cover. Having branded cover, such as through RAC, gives the employee peace of mind that the vehicle purchased is fully serviced and maintained, and is covered for full parts and labour costs on any mechanical and electrical faults that may occur. Having comprehensive warranty cover also increases the perceived value of the vehicle itself.

And for the company, whose core business expertise is unlikely to be dealing in motor vehicles, the warranty is the best form of protection. If the car goes wrong, the warranty kicks in, deals with the customer's problem and means fleet managers don't have to face discontented staff coming back months later with complaints and issues.

Under Financial Services Authority (FSA) regulations, businesses shouldn't offer warranties with vehicles. But a maintenance and repair warranty is considered a service contract and does not have to be FSA regulated. In addition, the fleet provider can claim back VAT, therefore making it a tax-efficient option.

Overall, it's a win-win situation. The employee gets a new car – often with a generous specification – that has been well-maintained, at a reasonable price and with the support and benefit of a warranty, while the company obtains a better residual value with no ongoing risk exposure.

But this is an area where some fleet managers need help, as selling warranty-covered cars to staff isn't always considered an option. Nevertheless, others have woken up to the benefits of disposing of vehicles in this way, rather than giving profit to a used vehicles trader or selling via auction when that route isn't delivering the value that's needed.

Steve Whitmarsh
Senior Partnership Manager, Fleet
RAC

There when you need us

At RAC we have a wide range of solutions to help you keep your fleet moving smoothly, from breakdown cover to vehicle inspections.

Call us today on the numbers below and find out how we can help you and your fleet.

Roadside Assistance	**08000 156 638**
Commercial Vehicle Assistance	**08000 159 976**
Fleet Inspections	**08700 109 506**
Risk Management	**0870 606 2606**
RAC Warranty	**0844 871 8228**

Calls may be recorded and/or monitored

RAC

Rob Barr
Group Communications Director
Manheim UK & Europe

Why should a fleet operator use an auction to dispose of their vehicles?

Auctions have long been regarded as the most efficient method of disposing of cars and commercial vehicles at the end of commercial contracts or periods of use on a fleet. The more reputable auction houses such as Manheim Auctions and BCA have well established sale programmes for the fleet market, delivered through national networks of auction centres. This means that there is nearly always a suitable auction on your doorstep. It's worth looking at the huge variety of organisations who use auction as the primary route to remarket their vehicles or those reputable dealer groups who buy vehicles for their retail forecourts at auction.

What are the advantages of using an auction over other methods?

Selling vehicles by auction will usually provide the quickest and most reliable way for fleets to turn their unwanted vehicles into cash. The larger auction houses cater for all types and values of vehicles from the cheaper, higher mileages ones right up to the luxury end of the market. From start to finish the entire process is generally handled by the auction company and there is little involvement required on the part of the fleet operator. The most obvious advantage that auctions have over other methods

is that they can attract thousands of trade buyers which ensures a fair market price for your fleet vehicles. By using auction you do not have to get involved in advertising vehicles or dealing directly with dealers and traders. By keeping the sale at arm's length through a reputable auction company, you will also minimise the risk of selling vehicles to somebody who may not fully honour the payment.

How can fleet managers find out how an auction works?

Generally all auction companies produce useful guides to buying and selling at auction and these can be obtained across the counter at most of the larger locations. Alternatively, the leading auction houses have websites which publish this summary information online.

As an example, Manheim Auctions have comprehensive information for those customers who are thinking about using auction for the first time. If you want to know more about selling, check out www.manheim.co.uk/sell and then choose 'Guide to Selling' from the list of information available. Virtually every question you are likely to have will be answered in this section, including details of the selling process, how to get a vehicle valued, how to offer vehicles to best advantage, a really useful Top 10 Tips To Selling and even a 'jargon buster' which makes sense of all the terminology used. If you are considering buying vehicles at auction for your fleet, then go to www.manheim.co.uk/buy and choose 'Buying at Auction' for all the advice you'll need.

Additionally, it is very important to request a copy of the terms & conditions of entry and sale from the auction house. They are legally obliged to produce these and should also have them prominently displayed at every location. This provides the full detail of the legal obligations placed on the seller, the buyer and also the auction company. The major auction companies also provide this information and other disclaimers online through their websites.

How can fleet managers ensure they are dealing with a high-quality auction company?

All reputable auction companies belong to the Society of Motor Auctions (SMA) which is part of the larger trade association, the Retail Motor Industry Federation. Members are bound by the SMA Customer Charter which promises to:

- Promote 'Best Practice' in the industry
- Be fair to both seller and purchaser
- Protect the purchaser against defect in title
- Commit to the SMA Code of Practice
- Ensure all staff are familiar with customers' rights under the code
- Have an easily identifiable procedure for the handling of complaints
- Provide access to an independent arbitration facility

The SMA has over 70 members who between them sell in excess of 1.5 million vehicles per annum and their research suggests that over 60% of all fleet vehicles are sold by auction. A good yardstick as to whether or not to use a particular auction is to simply look at which other fleet operators are selling their vehicles through that auction. It is fairly safe to assume that most of the larger operators will have conducted rigorous checks before sending their vehicles there for sale.

Additionally, fleet operators may wish to consult with a newly formed organisation IARA UK (International Automotive Remarketing Association) which, as an affiliate of the Society of Motor Manufacturers and Traders (SMMT), has been formed to represent this huge industry and in particular promote best practice.

What services should a fleet manager expect from an auction company?

The range of products and services available from auction houses, particularly the larger ones, is surprisingly comprehensive. There should be very little that an auction company cannot provide a fleet operator to ensure ex-fleet vehicles are sold at maximum market value in the shortest possible time. Most services are available on a clearly priced menu basis and all the fleet operator needs to do is to pick those which are most likely to fulfill their specific requirements.

The main services provided by the leading auction companies relating to vehicle remarketing at auction are as follows:

YOUR CHOICE OF AUCTION CENTRE

Manheim Auctions and BCA between them have a combined national network of 40 auction centres that cover the length and breadth of the UK, holding more than 120 auctions every week for cars and commercial vehicles. There are two different types of auctions held -

'Open' Auctions: these are open to all-comers, trade or private buyers and make up the vast majority of auctions.

'Closed' Auctions: these are for authorised trade buyers or dealers only and are not open to all-comers. They mainly cater for vehicles coming directly from the motor manufacturers and represent less than 10% of all auctions.

VEHICLE COLLECTION

An essential part of any auction service is their ability to collect vehicles promptly within a short period of time from anywhere in the country and deliver them into the chosen auction centre.

Auction logistics can collect single vehicles or full loads of up to 11 vehicles at a time. They offer a highly responsive service which should see all collections undertaken within three working days from initial request or even quicker using a number of premium 'fast track' propositions.

The leading auction companies all have access to large fleets of in-house or contracted vehicle transporters, plus huge teams of trade-plate drivers and these combine to provide the capacity and responsiveness required.

VEHICLE INSPECTION

In today's market it's essential to know what condition fleet vehicles are in, for a number of very good reasons. If the vehicle is in a remote location, and inspection enables the fleet operator to fully understand how the driver has looked after it during its life. This information might be used to penalise a driver for causing undue damage over fair wear and tear. It is also used to assist in ascertaining a vehicle's likely value and of course to provide more information to buyers who might be using the internet to search for vehicles they want.

Generally, inspection services are available throughout the UK, providing flexibility and onward vehicle logistics solutions. Inspections undertaken by the main auction companies are carried out by trained inspectors deployed in company vehicles. Drivers can also be teamed with the inspectors to provide a simultaneous uplift of the inspected vehicles (inspect and collect). This service is usually available from any location in the UK with delivery into nominated auction centres or other defleet locations.

In today's modern remarketing environment technology plays a key part in the vehicle inspection process. For example, Manheim Auctions deploys the latest hand-held technology with either wireless or GPRS connectivity for both on-site inspections and those done at off-site locations. This enables timely and accurate electronic transfer of vehicle data back to the main database, which customers can access using a web browser. The technology is actually developed by Manheim's own specialist inspection software company and is also used by a number of the UK's well known logistics and recovery organisations.

Vehicle inspection

VEHICLE RECONDITIONING

Not surprisingly, buyers are more likely to seek out those vehicles which are in better condition than those that are damaged. This doesn't mean to say that dents and scratches make vehicles unsaleable, but they certainly reduce the level of interest and highlight the value of pre-sale reconditioning.

Significant investments have been made by the remarketing industry in reconditioning and smart repair services. Generally available at any of the major UK locations, these are designed to assist vendors to derive the maximum value from their fleet by ensuring ex-fleet vehicles are presented to the market in a condition most likely to optimise the sale price.

Reconditioning, using smart repair methods, is a very effective way of enhancing a vehicle's value and can be done very efficiently, as all work is carried out on-site on a 'just in time' basis. Smart repairs include paintless dent removal, localised paint refinishing, cosmetic refurbishment of trim and upholstery and repairs to chipped or scuffed alloy wheels.

VEHICLE PREPARATION

Perhaps one of the simplest and most cost-effective ways of attracting interest in your ex-fleet vehicles is to ensure they are properly cleaned at the time of sale. Don't let buyers wonder what a vehicle might be like when it is clean – let them see for themselves and present it to it's best effect, inside and out.

All auction companies offer a comprehensive range of valeting services throughout the country, from a basic wash and leather through to a high retail-standard package, all at surprisingly reasonable prices.

Time and time again, customer surveys confirm that buyers have greater confidence in a vehicle – and also the vendor – when vehicles are presented in excellent condition. Attracting more buyers means better first time sale conversions and higher prices.

ENGINEERS MECHANICAL REPORTS

Vehicles sold in auction are all subject to statements about their mechanical condition, which are particularly important as buyers are not able to drive vehicles before bidding on them. These statements may range from 'sold as seen', where the vendor does not wish to offer any opinion on the vehicle's mechanical condition, through to specific declarations by the vendor which may include a statement such as 'no major mechanical faults'. When any such opinion is given it must be based on a reasonable knowledge of the vehicle, because a buyer will have recourse should it be proven to be inaccurate.

It is quite common for fleet vendors not to have physically seen their vehicles prior to them being collected and entered into auction. As such, an extremely effective method of creating buyer confidence is to instruct the auction company to produce an engineer's report on a vehicle on your behalf. This service is generally available from the leading auction companies.

An example of this is Manheim Assured, which provides a guarantee to the buyer, based on a basic 15-point vehicle check undertaken by Manheim Auctions' vehicle inspection team. Each vehicle undergoing an Assured check is backed by a 3-day, peace-of-mind promise which provides much needed confidence for buyers in the auction hall. This assurance generates greater interest from more buyers, in turn maximising the sale price.

Who buys vehicles at auction?

Every vehicle sold by a fleet operator requires a buyer and the leading auction houses have well-established relationships with thousands of them. Generally speaking, vehicle auctions attract trade buyers but, with the exception of 'closed auctions' the halls are also open to members of the public.

There are literally thousands of trade buyers, comprising franchised dealers, independent retailers and wholesalers who buy stock at auction. The great majority of vehicles, easily exceeding 85%, are sold to motor dealers who bid against each other in the auction for the stock they require. This combination of a broad spectrum of wholesale trade buyers, coupled to an increasingly significant number of private consumers, creates strong buying power from which the fleet operator benefits. Dealers who are regular attendees at auction often buy a number of vehicles in one sale, sometimes buying hundreds of vehicles each year. On the other hand, members of the public are usually only going to buy a vehicle every two or three years.

It's worth looking at how the auction companies market their sales locally, regionally and nationally through mailshots, catalogues and increasingly through website promotion. Check out the main websites and look in particular for online information services such as 'What's On Guides' and 'Sales Calendars'. These show how the overall sales programme is marketed by the auction companies to buyers, often categorised by vendor source and the type of vehicles on offer.

There's much talk about selling vehicles over the internet. How can an auction company help with this and does it work?

Selling goods using the Internet is well established and this now also applies to used vehicles, although where cars are concerned online transactions are generally restricted to the wholesale market and not a main channel for consumer retailing as yet.

Over recent years there have been a number of independent online vehicle remarketing propositions brought to market but none of them have really taken off. However, sites such as e-Bay do offer cars, amidst the plethora of everything else on show. But this still means that the vendor has got to physically keep custody of the vehicle and do all the work in liaising with potential buyers etc.

Apart from convenience, the real key to successful online selling is exactly the same as exists for physical auction i.e. established and trusted relationships with buyers. So it's not surprising that the best online solutions are those which have been developed by the traditional major auction companies. These include electronic real-time auctions,

bid and buy auctions and a very effective service, offered by both Manheim Auctions and BCA, which enables registered buyers to bid directly into the physical auctions competing head-on with those buyers attending in the halls. Importantly, online buyers who are bidding without seeing the vehicle need access to accurate condition reports, vehicle images and of course reliable mechanical statements, which is where the trust element is vital.

In the last few years since the introduction of these technologies, the growth in online bidding has been exponential. This does not mean that the buyers who attend the sales in person will disappear. It simply means that auction companies can offer stock to a wider group of buyers, and buyers are able to bid at a number of different sales across the country without leaving their offices. Whilst the number of vehicles sold online is still relatively small compared to those sold in the auction halls, it is now estimated to be around 7-8% of the total. It will undoubtedly continue to grow and, even at these current levels, is extremely effective in maximising buying power and prices.

How can a fleet manager ensure they are getting the right price for their vehicles?

Ascertaining the right price is for a used vehicle has always been the hardest challenge facing any seller. The price offered by a prospective purchaser will often depend on whether they actually really want the vehicle or not or more likely who wants it the most. So offering it in an auction is an excellent way of establishing fair market value on the day. The more buyers attending the auction the better the price, providing of course the vehicle is presented in its best light.

All the leading auction companies would expect a seller to place a 'reserve' selling price on each vehicle entered for sale. This 'reserve' is the minimum price which the seller will accept but it does need to be realistic. Optimistically high reserve prices will often make a vehicle unsaleable but all the auction houses will be pleased to provide advice on a fair reserve price beforehand. The leading auction companies

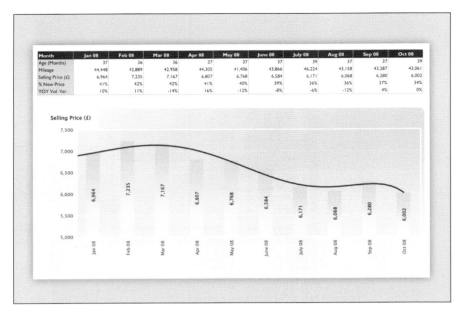

Month	Jan 08	Feb 08	Mar 08	Apr 08	May 08	June 08	July 08	Aug 08	Sep 08	Oct 08
Age (Months)	37	36	36	37	37	37	39	37	37	39
Mileage	44,448	42,889	42,958	44,305	41,406	43,866	46,224	43,158	43,287	43,061
Selling Price (£)	6,964	7,235	7,167	6,807	6,768	6,584	6,171	6,068	6,280	6,002
% New Price	41%	42%	42%	41%	40%	39%	36%	36%	37%	34%
YOY Vol. Var.	10%	11%	-14%	16%	-12%	-8%	-6%	-12%	4%	0%

Average selling price

also publish their own online sale price guides which report on actual sale prices achieved by make and model over the past month. This service is generally available to regular trade and corporate customers at no charge. There are also the leading vehicle price publishers, including CAP and Glass's Guide, who will allow bonafide fleet operators and dealers to subscribe to monthly used vehicle price data.

It is important to remember that market conditions change throughout the year, with peaks and troughs reflecting market demand at the time. This was particularly so during 2008 where prices for used vehicles simply reflected the broader economic downturn. The charts provided by Manheim Auctions, show data from their overall vehicles sales and clearly illustrate what a tough market we have seen during the past 12 months. They show the reducing average sale price over this period, the decreasing % retained of the original 'cost new price', together with the average age and mileage. The lesson from this is simply to keep in touch with the prevailing market conditions at the time and take as much advice as you can on likely sale values.

What can fleet managers do to maximise sale values?

There are a number of essential things which a fleet operator can do to further enhance a vehicle's value when selling at auction. Firstly take full advantage of the services offered by the auction company which clearly add value, namely reconditioning where relevant, a good standard of valeting and the mechanical inspection report. Additionally, the following actions will also ensure that vehicles are offered to the market in the best way possible:

- The V5 registration document should be present and with the auctioneer at the time of sale
- The up-to-date service records should also be with the auctioneer
- Any MOT certificate with less than 3 months to expiry should be renewed for a full 12 months
- Warrant the mileage, wherever you know this to be correct

When is a vehicle actually sold and what happens if the bidding does not reach the reserve price?

When your vehicles are entered for sale the resulting bidding should hopefully exceed your reserve prices but there is no guarantee of this. The auction company cannot sell your vehicle outright unless the bidding has reached or exceeded the stated reserve. On the fall of the hammer a binding contract of sale is established between the seller, the buyer and the auction company. This is subject to both the seller and the buyer conforming to the auction's terms & conditions of entry and sale.

However, should the bidding not reach the reserve price, but be close enough for the auction to think you should be offered the option of accepting a lower price, the vehicle will be sold 'provisionally' and the auction company will refer back to you very shortly thereafter. Under these circumstances you should consider this provisional bid promptly and let the auction company have your decision as soon as possible. There is always some room for negotiation on provisional bids and you should endeavour to establish whether the buyer may be prepared to increase the bid. This is quite normal practice and regular buyers expect it. It is important to note that the auction company is under no obligation to either the seller or the buyer under a provisional bid arrangement and either party is free to withdraw or refuse the bid at any time up to the point an agreement is reached.

When should the seller expect to receive their sales proceeds?

You should normally expect to receive the net proceeds from the sale of any vehicle in auction within three working days following its sale. Net funds are the hammer price less the auctioneer's commission and fees for other services which you may have requested, plus VAT on all charges. If you are an occasional vendor the proceeds may be sent to you by cheque accompanied by a statement of sale Alternatively, more frequent users of auction can arrange to have funds transferred electronically post-sale with supporting online statements. This is normal practice for the leading auction companies. Arrangements can also be made for multiple vehicles to be paid in one transaction, where required.

How will the auction company handle fleet managers as customers?

To an extent, this is up to you and will depend on how much support you require from your auction company. If you are only likely to use the auction on rare occasions then you should receive as much help as you need from the general customer services function. However, if you are intending to use auction more frequently then it is advisable to speak to the corporate account management team and to get a local or regional representative allocated to your fleet. The larger auction houses have well established sales teams who will be able to handle all your requirements and manage all aspects of the process of getting your vehicles successfully entered into sale and sold.

What information should a fleet manager expect to receive from an auction company?

Again this will largely be influenced by what you feel you need. Even for the most basic of requirements you should expect to be kept informed of the progress of any vehicles you may have with the auction company. Typically this will include being informed about when your vehicles have been collected, which sale they are being entered into, liaison on any provisional bids and post-sale advices on sold and unsold vehicles. They will naturally be keen to discuss any unsold vehicles, usually the day after the sale and why they didn't generate the interest or reach the reserve price. This gives you the opportunity to revisit details concerning a vehicle's condition and maybe adjust your reserve to make it more attractive.

If you frequently use an auction to sell multiple vehicles, you should request some consolidated sale reporting. The larger vendors all benefit from substantial monthly reports which provide detailed analysis on both operational and sale performance.

Manheim Auctions even offers a real-time online reporting service to larger corporate sellers. This is securely accessed over the internet and provides a comprehensive reporting package which can present the vehicle data in any format required using flexible report writers.

How much should a fleet operator typically expect to pay when selling their cars at auction?

All auctions companies publish standard terms of business which detail the charges for both sellers and buyers but these tend to be for single transactions. Auction sale commission fees for sellers are generally based on a % of the sale price. Depending on how many vehicles you may have and the likely value of those vehicles, there is always room for negotiation. Additionally, all the valued-added services are usually menu priced and therefore very easy to quantify before deciding to proceed.

Typically the sale commission chargeable to a fleet company would probably range from 2% to 4% of the hammer price, plus VAT. In cases of extremely low or high likely vehicle sale values, it is not unusual to see a minimum and/or maximum fee capping applied.

Are sellers liable for the vehicles they sell at auction?

Put simply yes, as auctions are governed by statutory British law. However the seller's liability is restricted to matters which are entirely reasonable and these include (but are not limited to) having full title to any vehicles being sold, not declaring major accident damage or previously written-off vehicles and mileage warranty statements later found to be incorrect. You should also not make false declarations about the mechanical condition of vehicles at the time of sale. Full details of seller and buyer liabilities and obligations are contained in the standard terms & conditions of entry and sale, available from all reputable auction companies.

Might fleet operators also consider buying vehicles at auction?

This is certainly becoming increasingly popular with fleet operators and there are examples of some smaller fleets which source all their vehicles - cars and commercial vehicles - at auction. The range of vehicles sold in auction, in particular those such as Manheim Auctions and BCA, is very broad with entries coming in from many sources including manufacturers, daily rental operators and the major leasing companies. These often comprise quite young vehicles (under 12 months old) with very low mileages and the trade prices, at which they are offered, make them extremely attractive to the cost conscious fleet operator. Even some of the larger fleets source their pool cars in auction, to great effect.

The advice to fleets looking to buy in auction has to be firstly, do it with plenty of research beforehand and retain a degree of caution. There is undoubtedly great value to be had in this process but selecting the right vehicles to suit your needs and ensuring you have checked them out thoroughly beforehand is vital. You should expect to receive assistance with this from your local auction centre and remember that most auction companies list all the vehicles going into sale in online catalogues on their websites.

What recent developments have there been in the auction market that have been particularly valuable to fleet managers?

Probably the most significant recent developments in auction which provide the greatest benefits to fleet sellers are those which have been facilitated by the use of technology. It is the investment in systems and general IT infrastructure which today really does drive the modern auction process and differentiates the leading auction companies from the smaller ones.

Typically this might include –

- CRM systems to drive the huge marketing programmes and effectively target the thousands of buyers, with the right vehicles being promoted to the relevant audience.
- Hand-held inspection technology to capture vehicle condition details in a robust process and send that information quickly to central databases for instant visibility

by the fleet operator. Combined with an 'inspect and collect' service this provides further major advantages to fleet owners.

- Highly functional websites which not only provide comprehensive information on general services but also access to the online sales channels and vehicle pricing data.

- The pure electronic auctions and online stock locators which allow vehicles to be offered to audiences other than those who attend the physical sales. Perhaps the most notable development in this area is the introduction of web-based bidding into the live auction halls, providing the best of both worlds. This is the ultimate way of maximising buying power for fleets.

- Online stock management systems which allow the fleet operator to view the status of all their vehicles in the auction process, plus a suite of comprehensive reporting tools detailing the sales performance of their own stock.

- Regular online market reports providing vital intelligence on the state of the market and influencing those key decisions which face all fleet operators.

What is the future for auctions? Are they likely to be around in 10 years?

The auction industry is in extremely good shape to face the challenges ahead. Unlike some other industries, it has not stood by and just watched the market and its emerging new entrants overtake it. On the contrary, it has continued to do what it does best and has enhanced this with a range of value-added developments which have positioned it very well against any competitive threats.

Auctions have been around for many years throughout the world and it was once said that 'if auctions did not exist, they would be the next invention' which, to a great extent, underlines what a natural fit they have with open markets and fair trading.

The corporate sector, including the manufacturers, leasing companies and fleet operators have been relying on them to responsibly remarket their inventory since the 1980s. During this time they have become mutually dependent and have worked closely together to develop an extremely effective proposition which definitely fits today's requirements.

There is no doubt there will always be alternatives to auction, but none to date has been able to provide the consistency in performance and scale to match them. Auctions will certainly be around in 10, 20 and 50 years time – the only question is perhaps the balance between how many vehicles will still be sold to buyers attending the physical sales and those who choose to bid online. One thing's for certain though - the vehicles will still be physical and will continue to require collecting, reconditioning, preparing, securely storing and then offering for sale. After all, that is the domain of the modern auction business!

How can Manheim help fleet managers?

Manheim Auctions are a company going places and with an impressive pedigree. Part of the world's largest automotive services provider, Manheim Inc, they have over 140 auction locations spread across 5 continents, selling more than 5.5 million vehicles each year. Employing 35,000 staff they offer an unparalleled range of products and services, all designed to help their customers sell vehicles in the shortest time and for the best returns.

Established in the UK in 1996, Manheim Auctions today works in partnership with a very broad customer base of leading company brands and smaller local businesses to assist them achieve their remarketing objectives.

Since 2005, Manheim Auctions have been voted Best Remarketing Company by the Fleet Industry for three consecutive years and have also won many other awards in recognition of their achievements. These include Best Website, Best Internet and Best Innovation, reflecting the substantial investment and commitment the company has made in this sector.

There is very little which Manheim Auctions cannot provide a fleet operator, no matter how large or small. The list of services is huge and is best viewed on their website – www.manheim.co.uk. There is a host of information on this award winning site – of particular relevance to fleet operators are the section tabs 'Sell', 'Products & Services' and 'My Manheim'.

Rob Barr
Group Communications Director
Manheim UK & Europe

Trust Manheim Auctions to maximise your residual values

You do the Maths...

- Access auction buyers for your cars, vans, trucks, bikes or plant, through our nationwide network of 19 dedicated centres.

- Reach new buyers through the UK's premier online sales channel, Simulcast.

- Make sense of a rapidly changing market, through Manheim Intelligence.

- Discover why Manheim Auctions has been voted Britain's best remarketing company for the last 4 years.

Listening to partners, understanding the market...
...helping our customers succeed!

20 DRIVER RISK MANAGEMENT

> **Steve Johnson**
> Director of Communications
> DriveTech (UK) plc

Please introduce yourself and your company

So what makes me qualified to talk about this topic?

Well I guess as I've had responsibility for communicating the benefits of driver risk management for some of the largest brands in the business over the last 15 years, I have made it my job to keep abreast of facts, figures, research, trends and news on all aspects of occupational driver safety.

I've also attended numerous conferences, launches, exhibitions and special interest group meetings on the topic over the years, so I've tried to act as a sponge for information of all sorts, which hopefully gives me the sort of pragmatic, balanced view of things which might be of value to this readership.

Additionally I'm passionate about driving…particularly good driving. Before I became enmeshed in the fleet industry, I had the privilege to work alongside a raft of race and rally champions and I've sat alongside many of the finest, observing from close quarters what sets them apart from us mere mortals.

And to complete the picture I guess I'm a bit of an anorak, starting life as a chassis development engineer, becoming a certified test driver for three big industry names, and then taking every chance possible to have additional training behind the wheel thereafter. I've also been responsible for managing a thirty vehicle fleet in my time too.

These days I'm the Director of Communications for DriveTech, arguably the leading provider of driver education schemes in the UK. Apart from providing all manner of interventions for some 400 fleet customers of all sizes, DriveTech also delivers training for nearly 30 different police driver education schemes across the country and also has a truly innovative learner driver programme which is expanding rapidly from its Home Counties roots.

There seems to have been much more focus on implementing driver risk management programmes in recent years. Why is this?

There are many reasons but top of the list must be the maturity of the market. The sector we're talking about used to be referred to as 'driver training', and sadly this misnomer is still bandied about today in some quarters, but we've all moved on. Practical, in-vehicle driver training still has its place but should now form only one part of a suite of measures that a supplier should offer to meet the needs of customers. And those needs first and foremost must be business driven.

Of course duty of care and health and safety compliance are important considerations but the service we're talking about here has to make sound business sense for the customer if it's to be of true value and therefore have ongoing appeal.

Changes in the law obviously play a part too and few in the industry can be unaware of the media exposure that relevant pieces of legislation attract on introduction (I'll summarise the current applicable legislation later), although some of the resulting advice on offer from some suppliers is sadly misguided.

The media also pick up on the bad news stories too of course and those involving on-road incidents seem to attract more than their fair share of coverage…sometimes to the detriment of the employer involved. Despite being essentially negative reportage it nonetheless helps raise awareness of the issues and they're hard to ignore.

Finally we mustn't discount the corporate social responsibility and environmental impact effect. There is no question that there has been a significant cultural shift in the UK in this respect. The majority of organisations now understand how improving the behaviour and responsibility of their business drivers can have a major effect on how their company, brand or service is perceived by their various audiences. Whilst 'going green' doesn't do it for everybody, few organisations would risk turning their back on an opportunity to demonstrate responsible citizenship, particularly where they've principled stake-holders to appease.

What sort of services should fleet managers be considering?

You're in no position to determine the type or intervention that is appropriate for your organisation until you know the size and nature of your problem. A crucial consideration of course is how the fleet is made up. Is it all fully-funded company cars or a mixture of company cars and cash opt-outs? Do you have a mixture of cars and vans? Are there any specialist vehicles that need accommodating? The challenges will be different in each case.

Usually the most obvious pointer is escalating vehicle damage and associated cost but it isn't always the case. Some fleets appear on the surface to have few incidents and nothing to worry about but is there a hidden danger here, waiting to catch them out and possibly cost them dear?

At the very least, whoever is responsible for the fleet needs to check if the drivers in their employ have legal driving licences and this cannot be done effectively by just looking at a hard copy at appraisal time or during the quarterly sales meeting. Not only is driving licence fraud now very sophisticated but drivers can also make quite innocent mistakes which render them driving illegally without their knowledge. Only a proper driver licence check involving the DVLA will resolve this issue so this is a crucial start point. There are for instance 30,000 photocard licences due to expire in the coming year and many drivers will choose to ignore the reminder. Could some of your drivers be amongst this group?

Based purely on our own driver licence checking experience we've come across the following outcomes of checks on active drivers:

- Employees who did not have a valid licence at all
- Employees who only had provisional entitlement to drive
- Employees whose provisional entitlement to drive had expired
- Employees who had 12 points on their licence and were on the verge of being banned
- Employees who had been disqualified under totting up
- Employees with live drink/driving offences
- Employees with recent periods of disqualification
- Employees who had failed to inform their employer of a serious, live motoring offence at the time of recruitment
- Non-UK licence holders who had not complied with the rules of driving in the GB as a resident/temporary visitor

You would have thought that most responsible employers would want to know these details, even if the employee was not driving for business purposes, as it tells them a lot about their possible suitability for work.

Another crucial service to consider is a mechanism to ensure that any vehicle used for business purposes is legal in all respects. Even with a fully funded company vehicle on contract hire, the driver cannot assume he or she is absolved from responsibility for regular checks and inter-service maintenance. Front tyres for instance could easily wear out during the service interval and there have been many reports of expensive engine blow-ups because the driver didn't believe the need for checking the oil level. The latter is not just expensive either – it's a serious safety issue, particularly if it happens at high speed on the motorway.

If vehicle damage is an issue, you need to analyse the problem with detailed and reliable data from your insurer or accident management provider. This should be compared to industry benchmark figures so that you work out where you are now and then work out where you want to be.

There are all sorts of products and services available in the UK fleet market, which we will come on to look at in more detail later, but clearly, irrespective of what you chose to do, there will be some form of up-front financial commitment to consider. It's really a question of working out what you will be gaining from introducing various measures against what they cost to implement, but most targeted and well thought through driver risk management programmes should actually show a visible return on investment. Most quality suppliers should be able to help you with this calculation.

Effective driver risk management programmes need to be holistic, adaptable and run over a period of time…but then, given my background, I would say that wouldn't I! But seriously, if you tackle it piecemeal it's unlikely to work and could in fact have a negative effect.

What is your advice to a fleet manager who needs to impress on senior management the need for action?

Your key message must be that introducing a driver risk management programme makes good business sense. Have all the facts and figures at your fingertips and create a persuasive win/win argument. Although you can play the 'corporate manslaughter, get-out-of-jail-free card' I would advise against it. By all means refer to it in the small print but don't go overboard. (If you want more detail on this see my legislation appendix at the end of this chapter).

The second message must be about compliance with duty of care and health and safety responsibilities, because they are enshrined in law and non negotiable. There is lots of good guidance on this and a good start point is The Motorists Forum report (www.cfit.gov.uk), the Department for Transport's dedicated website www.dft.gov.uk/drivingforwork and the website of another DfT-supported initiative 'Driving For Better Business' www.drivingforbetterbusiness.com.

Don't underestimate the power that Personnel or Human Resources can bring to the party either. If you have a colleague in that role, get his or her buy-in to the proposition. In HR terms a driver risk management initiative can only be a good thing. The training provided free of charge by the organisation is a life skill and applies both inside and outside work. In fact I've come across dozens of instances where trainees have said that they've passed on advice and techniques to friends and family…all courtesy of the employer.

Once you've assembled your facts, figures, support and argument, you need to create a powerful presentation that succinctly gets to the point and illustrates the benefits of embedding a safety culture within the organisation. Often your driver risk management or accident management supplier will be able to help with ammunition for such a presentation so take advantage of their knowledge and experience.

It's absolutely crucial that you get at least one board member or senior director to fully commit to the project and undertake to be the champion for your cause. All too often, motivated fleet managers put forward a powerful case for a driver risk management programme and receive a positive reaction, for it to all fall apart once implementation starts through lack of management inertia and belief.

An important role for the champion is to ensure that middle managers believe in the programme too. Without their support your programme is dead in the water.

What exactly should the programme involve?

1. BENCHMARKING

To have any hope of ending up where you need to be you have to work out where you are to start with, something that can only really be done by carrying out a benchmarking exercise. The parameters for this will come from various sources;

a   The fleet industry accepted averages for incident and claims rates, accidents per 1000 kms etc.

b   Data that is specific to your industry or market sector

c   Parameters that your organisation sets for itself and are relevant to this programme

2. SETTING OBJECTIVES

Once the benchmarking is complete you need to decide what are acceptable and achievable targets for the programme. Don't expect results overnight. A professionally deployed, targeted driver risk management programme will yield results but for a large organisation it might take three years to realise its full potential in terms of savings. It's not something you can switch on and off and expect to pick up where you left off.

However, all things being equal, it would not be unreasonable to expect savings/reduction in incidents/improvements in the order of 20% in year one, a further 25% in year two and another 15% in year three.

3. CHOOSING A SUPPLIER

There are a number of reputable driver risk management suppliers in the UK but you need to select one that can provide a wide range of interventions and is willing to tailor a specific programme to your needs. There is no 'one size fits all solution' in this business and you should certainly shy away from anybody who suggests practical in-vehicle training for all.

There are a few *must haves* though.

If practical training is likely to be one of the requirements you should ensure that this will only be carried out by fully qualified Approved Driving Instructors who are on the DSA Fleet Register and there must be geographical coverage to meet your needs.

The supplier should be able to demonstrate good customer retention and be happy to provide references. Evidence of trade recognition in the form of awards is re-assuring but not essential, whereas a recognised ISO accreditation should be considered vital.

The supplier should be willing to sign up to a service level agreement, which should be far more than just a set of terms and conditions. If they are not willing to formalise the arrangement in this way it suggests they don't have the courage of their convictions and there are going to be all sorts of excuses for non performance to come.

But, as with so many things in life, the final decision will be mainly influenced by the 'chemistry' between the individuals involved.

4. Policies

Apart from the fact that your drivers have to have some guidance on what is expected of them when they are driving for business purposes, the authorities would take a very dim view if they had cause to investigate an incident and found that you had no duty of care-related policies in place.

Your risk management provider should be able to help ensure that you cover all the salient points but the most important consideration of all is to have a mechanism that demonstrates that each driver has been given access to the policies and accepts that it is their responsibility to comply.

5. Getting the message across

There's something odd about refresher driver training for business drivers. Suggesting you need training is like touching a raw nerve. For many it's one step short of being labelled as a rubbish driver. And in most cases the reason they think like this is because they were never fully apprised of the raison d'être in the first place.

It just isn't enough to send an email out saying 'A decision has been made and like it or not, we're doing it'. You need to spell out why you're implementing the programme, exactly what's involved and how it will affect the people in your employ. You will almost certainly need to separately motivate line or departmental managers to support you and you'll also need the overt enthusiasm of the Chairman, CEO or Managing Director.

You will also most certainly require face-to-face meetings or workshops to fully get the point home, perhaps supported by demonstrations from the supplier, and these should backed up by dedicated information pages on a secure area of the company website or intranet, together with regular information updates in company or departmental newsletters.

You just can't communicate enough when it comes to the sensitive subject of driving ability but, however you do it, you must emphasise that nobody is singled out, nobody is being criticised and the benefits are both company-wide and for the individual. Driving is, after all, a life skill.

6. DRIVER ASSESSMENT OR PROFILING

It's a mandatory requirement of Management of Health & Safety at Work Regulations 1999 to carry out a 'suitable & sufficient risk assessment of every risk to employees' and this includes driving for any work purpose.

There are many different types and styles of risk assessment, and as yet no British standard for them. Some are psychometric based and some merely factual. Some include attitude to risk scenario assessments and some are merely jumped-up hazard perception tests, little better than the one in the driving test. Some are worth so little that the suppliers give them away.

Whichever one you chose at least you've fulfilled the requirement and, providing you have documentary evidence to support that, you're halfway to doing enough to appease the authorities should there be an investigation following a serious incident involving one of your drivers.

The better assessments divide drivers into risk bands so that the highest risk group can be identified and given the appropriate support as a priority.

7. APPROPRIATE TRAINING

The point of the assessment is to identify those who are likely to be more at risk than others, so that you can apply the most appropriate form of training to reduce that risk. As I said earlier, this does not always need to be relatively expensive in-vehicle practical training. A lot of very worthwhile training can be delivered via online modules, particularly those involving multi-media, and they are invariably good value, particularly as the driver can complete the modules when and where he or she pleases.

Group workshops or seminars are also effective and represent good value on a per head basis. The advantage here is that there is as much, if not more, interactivity than there would be if the training was provided in-vehicle.

8. ONGOING PROJECT MANAGEMENT

Whatever the exact nature of the programme, it needs monitoring and managing if it is to be effective. Your supplier should be providing you with regular reports on who has been assessed and who has been trained. Your insurer or accident management provider should be providing you with before and after incident data. In fact some systems combine all these inputs so that all the information is available on screen with just a couple of mouse clicks.

For bigger fleets, where the programme is not only complex but could be developing all the time, it's not unreasonable to expect the supplier to attend regular review meetings to discuss performance and modifications to the programme.

What should the organisation be doing to ensure that, whatever programme they implement, it has the best chance of success?

Communication, communication, communication. We've already talked about how essential this is but it's equally important to respond to people's concerns and comments as a result of that initial burst of communications activity.

Canvass people's opinions about the assessment or training they've had, respond to any inputs and make them feel genuinely part of the process.

If you're able to, why not make the driver risk management programme a constituent part of any incentive or reward scheme? Conversely, allotting vehicle damage costs to individual department budgets, where they can potentially influence sales target achievement, does wonders for focussing the mind!

Whatever you do, the aim is to make the organisation become risk averse when it comes to the welfare of its driving staff.

How can a fleet manager improve their company's procedures so as to reduce risk and what sort of information should they be keeping to help manage and control this area?

In an ideal world a fleet manager needs to know who is driving what, where and when. They also need to establish, as we've referred to earlier, that both the driver and vehicle are fit for purpose. All this information should be kept up to date and in one place, so that you have the makings of a classic audit trail of risk management activity, should you ever be called upon to provide evidence.

There are clearly many different types of fleet management software packages available to enable you to manage this information in a fairly painless way but you do need to have in place a robust mechanism that will inform you about any change of data. This may sound a lot of work but needn't be with the right system, ideally one that can talk to your existing sources of data. After all, you have to make Motor Insurance Database notifications in good time whenever there is a vehicle or driver change so you may as well have everything else you might need at your fingertips as well.

One important but often overlooked piece of information, which employers should be seeking to establish if they are really concerned about efficient risk management, is the driver's health. When it comes to driver safety there is, understandably perhaps, a lot of emphasis placed on the vehicle's mechanical state but what about the driver? There is increasing academic evidence to suggest that some prescription and even over-the-counter drugs can have detrimental effects on driver judgement and reactions but most employers are unlikely to be a position to know if their employees could be affected in this way.

It is of course impractical to have a notification system in place for this eventuality and no doubt there would be considerable resistance anyway, on the grounds of human rights. However it's not unreasonable to demand that drivers sign a declaration that they will not take any medication that might affect their driving. At least that way you will have taken a reasonable step to contain the risk from this particular source.

We've already mentioned driver and vehicle policies but it's worth reiterating that these must be updated when company policy or legislation changes, and once again, there must be a mechanism for ensuring that drivers have read and understood the implications of the changes.

One essential ingredient in the driving policy must be reference to the maximum length of time that employees are allowed to drive between breaks, as fatigue plays a huge contributory part in crashes these days. Crucially, drivers need to know that if they cannot continue to drive due to fatigue they can book into a hotel, safe in the knowledge that the company will not only pick up the tab but also not penalise them for not completing their work schedule for the day.

One effective way of controlling and managing risk, and which is gaining in popularity, is the issuing of 'Permits to Drive'. Essentially an employee cannot drive on behalf of the business unless he or she meets the criteria for issue. This is particularly useful for the 'grey fleet' drivers over whom fleet managers traditionally have had far less control due to the vehicle funding arrangements. One can build in declarations of adherence to service schedules and other maintenance items, such as tyre status, which can be otherwise difficult to monitor accurately.

Talking of tyres brings me to the sometimes controversial topic of spot vehicle checks. Sadly the threat of one really is the only way to get many drivers to take vehicle safety seriously. On several occasions I've been involved in driver safety events where we've done spot checks on cars in the car park. I can remember one occasion where nearly 30% of the vehicles checked, all fully funded company supplied cars, had at least one illegal tyre. Quite why the drivers would leave themselves exposed to a £1,000 fine and points on their licence, when one phone call to the fleet manager would have fixed it, is beyond me!

POST-COLLISION REMEDIAL ACTION.

Even in the best managed fleet, crashes of some sort are inevitable and you'll never eliminate them entirely. Look upon them as an opportunity to learn something from the experience and to reduce the risk of something similar happening again.

A crucial first step in making this process worthwhile is to let it be known that there will be no 'blame culture' allowed in your department. The unfortunate driver concerned (it's a harrowing experience for even the most hardened campaigner) will only open up and reveal the true circumstances if you engender trust and a genuine willingness to understand how to avoid future occurrences.

Once the post-incident interview is completed, send the report to your driver risk management supplier for analysis and an assessment of any training needs or other support that are highlighted.

Let the driver know the outcome of the meeting and the steps you intend taking and, if this does involve driver training of some kind, make every effort to emphasise the support you are providing and that it in no way is a criticism of his or her abilities per se.

Once whatever training or support has been delivered, bring the driver back in for another chat to ascertain that the outcome has helped the situation. Assuming that this has been a positive experience for all concerned, you could consider using it as a case study internally to encourage others to come forward to discuss the collisions that so nearly happened, the so-called 'near misses' that can provide such valuable information for pro-active, pre-emptive training.

In these financially straitened times, if a fleet manager wants to make progress along the risk-reduction road but has little budget, what can you recommend?

It's often said that it's almost worse to identify a driver risk management problem and do nothing about it, than to do nothing at all in the first place. Having said that, most of us in the risk management industry realise that money doesn't grow on trees and, despite the fact that you should see a return on your investment, finding the budget for a programme of risk reducing activity is not always easy.

Assuming you've implemented your mandatory driver risk assessment, you will probably have between 15% and 25% of your drivers in the 'high risk' category, not because they're bad drivers but because of the types of roads they're spending most of their time on, the times of the day they're travelling and their historical predilection to involvement in incidents.

If your budget is stretched you really must throw what you do have at this group, for they will be your biggest headache in the future. If you don't have the funds available for the best solution - one-to-one, in-vehicle, practical defensive driver training – the next best thing is a group workshop where the moderator can really engage with the audience, find out what makes them tick and then persuade them to think about their driving in a whole new way. At DriveTech, for example, we use a keypad-based electronic voting system to liven things up and get people talking, as well as multi-media AVs and role playing.

If you can't get a group together in one place, and budget is still tight, why not consider an online workshop or a so-called 'webinar'. Here delegates can be at home, in the office or even in a hotel. All they need is a laptop and web access via broadband. Essentially the same thing happens as in the face-to-face version, except that the moderator is remote and will run the workshop by activating things on screen by his mouse clicks.

As all the delegates are connected via an audio link up, they can ask questions at any time and respond to the moderator's remarks accordingly, ensuring that the webinar proceeds at a pace that is suitable for all involved.

Not all suppliers can provide webinars but at DriveTech we have a number of different ones, on such topics as Eco Driving, The Cause of the Most Common Road Incidents, Winter Driving Tips, UK Familiarisation and Journey Planning.

What other types of driver training should fleet managers be aware of?

Driver Certificate of Professional Competence (Driver CPC) training is already with us for PSVs and this will be extended to LGVs in September 2009. Training will need to tracked and recorded rigorously, as without valid certificates professional drivers will be driving illegally. All working professional PCV and LGV drivers will need to complete 35 hours of Driver CPC training every FIVE years in a minimum of seven hour blocks. Upon completion of the 35 hours within the five year period, a driver will receive a Driver Qualification Card, which will validate their licence. A good source of further information is: http://www.skillsforlogistics.org/en/jaupt/jaupt/

The Safe and Efficient Driving (SAFED) for Vans scheme, devised by DriveTech for the DfT, is nearing the end of its subsidy period now but has proved a great success, demonstrating that one can achieve a 16% fuel consumption reduction without any measurable affect on journey times. With a 33% reduction in gear changes, and tips on reducing the need for harsh acceleration and braking, SAFED training can bring big reductions in wear and tear costs too. There's more on SAFED at: http://www.safed.org.uk/

The Minibus Driver Awareness Scheme (MiDAS) is for those, largely non-professional, drivers who have the daunting responsibility of taking, often vulnerable, passengers in minibuses. For those wishing to take the DSA minibus test, it's D1 minibus training that you require.

More information about MiDAS training can be obtained at the Community Transport Association website www.ctauk.org/index.aspx?id=150

The licence and training requirements for those wishing to tow a trailer are now quite a minefield and many an occupational driver has been found to be driving illegally unbeknown to themselves or their employer. The entitlements are quite different depending upon whether you passed your test before or after January 1, 1997. More information on this at: www.direct.gov.uk/en/Motoring/DriverLicensing

Some fleets, particularly those working for the utility companies, have a requirement for 4x4 off-road training and this is a largely unregulated area, so be cautious who you entrust this training to. If your provider already has other DSA-accredited courses you probably have nothing to worry about but, if not, you should choose one that can at least demonstrate that their instructors are members of the British Off Road Association (BORDA) and abide by its code of practice. For more details of BORDA see: www.borda.org.uk/

Organisations that co-opt foreign nationals for periods of time would do well to consider a UK Familiarisation course, as having a valid licence and being mechanically proficient at starting, stopping and turning clearly isn't sufficient. Rules, regulations and signs are not even consistent yet throughout the EU, let alone the rest of the world, and the potential for confusion is high with this group so they must be considered high risk in the first instance.

For those organisations with big fleets it may well be more cost effective to have a permanent in-house assessor, who could be on hand to give a verdict on aptitude at an early stage in employment, ideally during the induction process. The specialist provider could still be called in for the training itself – the function we're talking about here would be to assess need in a consistent manner and in line with the specific requirements of the employer.

Although all modern training for qualified drivers should be principally aiming to improve drivers' anticipation and awareness of risk, there is still a place for the refinement of control skills, provided the trainer understands very clearly the objectives of the course. Using suitable off road facilities, most drivers benefit from feeling what it is like to exploit ABS to its full potential, understand how ESC is far smarter than most drivers or to catch a skid before it actually becomes one. DriveTech is one of a number of specialist suppliers who can offer such courses and these must be viewed as an integral part of the risk management programme, as opposed to a fun day out for the lads.

Is anything happening in this area of fleet operation that is likely to change the landscape for fleet managers soon?

Partly because they have an obligation to under the revised ACPO Road Death Investigation Manual procedure guidelines, the police now have to establish if any 'at-work' vehicles are involved in serious on-road incidents. This is because where fatalities, or injuries that may lead to fatalities, occur these now have to be considered as crime scenes until determined otherwise. We've all seen the road closures, police no entry tape and the tent over the immediate crime scene.

Take the incident I referred to earlier, where a vehicle with an illegal tyre is involved in a serious incident. Yes, the driver DOES get the fine (assuming he lives to tell the tale) but there is still a good chance that, if that vehicle had been involved in a serious collision resulting in a fatality, you, as the provider of the vehicle, would be liable for its mechanical condition.

If that condition was a contributory factor to the crash the police will want to investigate further, which could involve early morning office raids, business disruption, confiscation of PCs or hard drives, lengthy interviews of those involved in the management of the fleet and ultimately maybe even court appearances, leading to an outcome that doesn't bear thinking about.

Now, this particular scenario hasn't happened yet and I do not subscribe to the school of scare-mongering, but it could. The Police have the powers, renewed interest in the topic and a desire for the fleet industry to take its responsibilities seriously, and paradoxically the much talked about Corporate Manslaughter Act of 2007 is a bit of a red herring here, as there is plenty of other existing legislation in place they can bring to bear.

Another development which has had a low profile in the media but could have significant implications for the fleet industry, is the increased powers of the Coroners' courts to determine blame for management failures that lead to deaths in the workplace. Whilst they cannot impose custodial sentences, such courts pronouncements are obviously widely reported and attract the attention of the police and other regulatory bodies.

Another ever-changing dynamic is the way that vehicles are funded and therefore the perception of where responsibility for the actions of drivers lies. Depending upon which piece of research or opinion poll you read, the UK fully-funded company vehicle fleet is either expanding or contracting. It flits back and forth like a yoyo. As it contracts, so the 'grey fleet' expands, and visa versa. As I hope is now clear from this chapter generally, in the eyes of the law the way a vehicle is funded is irrelevant when it comes to the actions of an employee driving for purposes directly connected to the discharge of his or her duties whilst at work.

Although some offences will always be the direct responsibility of the driver (speeding, drink/driving, dangerous driving etc.) there are clearly others that can be laid at the corporate door (mobile phone use, texting, driving whilst tired, maintenance-related defects) and without doubt there is a gradual responsibility shift coming about in the UK…to the detriment of the body corporate.

The fitting of tachographs has transformed the LGV industry and one can see these being fitted to some vehicles weighing less than 3500 kgs GVW before long. Despite regular reports of tampering and fraud, there is no question that the fitting of these devices has helped immeasurably with road safety, so hopes are high that a similar influence will be exerted on the Sprinter set.

Mandatory driver training for business car drivers looked like pie in the sky five years ago but has now re-appeared on the agenda as a real possibility within the next decade, as the momentum for driver training gains favour within the EU as a means of reducing casualty rates.

Intelligent Speed Adaptation (ISA) has now evolved from science fiction to become science fact and the fleet manager of the not too distant future is going to have to cope with all sorts of attempts to over-ride the system in the interests of human and/or employee rights. The jury is still out amongst the road safety community on this topic but it's becoming increasingly hard to argue against as more and more of the technical challenges are resolved.

Hybrid cars are starting to become a viable choice for business drivers and in fact their take-up by the UK fleets is amongst the highest in Europe. Whilst they do require different driving techniques to get the best out of them, there is no requirement for drivers to have any form of additional training to cope and this will have to be addressed as the vehicles become more complex.

Finally that old chestnut….insurance. The insurance industry seems to have paid lip service to driver risk management over the years, with some well known names advocating its wholesale adoption and others barely acknowledging its influence. I've certainly seen enough verified data from major insurers to convince me that, if insured and insurer work together and keep talking, the claims plummet and the benefits are there for all to see. This must be good news, as your crystal ball will no doubt reveal only one direction for insurance premiums to go…inexorably upwards!

What developments have there been in your part of the fleet market in the last few years that have been particularly valuable to fleet managers?

Clearly the advent of more sophisticated web-based management and information tools has increased the number of products and services that can be made available online. A potential customer can research the market relatively easily from the comfort of their own office with a couple of clicks of the mouse and a log-in code.

One thing that fleet customers need more than anything is accurate reporting of supplier activity, and data can now be uploaded on the web in a far more user-friendly way than the old paper-based systems of days gone by. Online booking and direct uploads of post-training critiques have transformed the fleet manager's ability to monitor progress and react to changing circumstances.

Another change is that the larger risk management suppliers have led the way in finding a way to make training more financially palatable, by categorising drivers by risk band and then offering a suite of interventions matched to individual need. High risk drivers are likely to be offered the highest value product – practical on-road training. Those considered to be medium risk can benefit from a less expensive solution, such as completing e-learning modules or a workshop, and low risk drivers quite frankly need nothing more than a periodic re-assessment (definitely if their driving circumstances change) and regular hints and tips via something like a newsletter or intranet posting.

If you were to advise a fleet manager to do one thing to reduce the risk of work-related driving, what would it be?

Document everything! I've mentioned it before in this chapter but an audit trail of information and actions is the Holy Grail of driver risk management. Ensure all updates are entered promptly and that the system can be interrogated remotely via a secure access, allowing you to monitor activity wherever you happen to be.

If you can demonstrate to any investigator that you have taken all reasonable steps to reduce risk then you'll be home and dry.

Please summarise the relevant legislation

All of the pieces of legislation listed below contain stipulations and requirements that are relevant to the vehicle fleet industry:

- Health & Safety at Work Act 1974
  [See www.opsi.gov.uk/RevisedStatutes/Acts/ukpga/1974/
    cukpga_19740037_en_1]

- Management of Health & Safety at Work Regulations 1999
  [See www.opsi.gov.uk/si/si1999/19993242.htm#3]

- The Provision and Use of Work Equipment Regulations 1998
  [See www.opsi.gov.uk/si/si1998/19982306.htm#7]

- The Road Safety Act 2006
  [See www.opsi.gov.uk/acts/acts2006/ukpga_20060049_en_1]

- The Health Act 2006
  [See www.opsi.gov.uk/si/si2007/uksi_20070765_en_1]

- Corporate Manslaughter and Corporate Homicide Act 2007
  [See www.opsi.gov.uk/si/si2008/uksi_20080396_en_1]

- The Health and Safety (Offences) Act 2008
  [See www.opsi.gov.uk/acts/acts2008/ukpga_20080020_en_1]

What are the key elements a fleet manager should consider when building the business case to introduce a driver risk management programme?

- Reduced direct cost of collision (substantial if third party cover only)
- Potential for reduced insurance cost (particularly excess levels)
- Reduced fuel consumption (expect between 10 and 15%)
- Reduced non insurance claim damage (usually hidden in expense claims)
- Reduced staff absence due to post collision injury; replacement vehicle cost
- Reduced vehicle wear and wear cost (e.g. tyre and brake wear can be reduced by 25%)
- Improved vehicle residual value due to enhanced mechanical sympathy applied
- Improved Corporate Social Responsibility
- Reduced carbon footprint/environmental impact
- Less stressed, more productive driving workforce
- Reduced chance of negative publicity resulting from a serious on-road collision (now more likely under mandatory publicity orders within the CMCH Act 2007)

Steve Johnson
Director of Communications
DriveTech (UK) plc

ECOS, CASH FOR CAR, SALARY SACRIFICE, TAX & NI

> **Alastair Kendrick**
> Director, Employment Tax Services
> Mazars LLP

Please introduce yourself and your company

I am a director at Mazars LLP an international firm of auditors involved in audits, tax and advisory services. For many years I have specialised in company car tax and am involved in working with clients in shaping their car policy and structuring their car procurement arrangements with leasing concerns. I have experience of not only the UK market but also Europe. My particular expertise is in employee car ownership schemes and I am often called upon to give advice or speak on this topic. Before joining the accountancy profession in 1989 I was an inspector of taxes.

It seems that the tax treatment of company cars is constantly under the government's spotlight. Please give us a thumbnail sketch of how tax affects company car fleets, and the upcoming changes.

Yes. It is the present policy of the UK government to use the taxation system to encourage employees to take cars which are good to the environment having low CO_2 emissions. It is fair to say that a similar approach is now being adopted by many other countries across Europe.

We saw a significant change in benefit in kind rules in 2002 to link the level of benefit in kind to the list price of the vehicle and its CO_2 levels. This basis was later extended to attach a similar arrangement to fuel provided for private use. Given that the level of Class 1A National Insurance paid by the employer is set by reference to the benefit in kind then again the National Insurance is also largely geared to CO_2 emission levels. These changes have been heralded to be a significant success and in view of this we are unlikely to see any major re-write of the rules for a number of years to come. We are likely to see the levels of benefit revised to further incentivise greener vehicles

In relation to corporation tax we will be seeing a significant revision to these rules at April 2009 when the basis of calculation will be easier to understand and will be on the following basis:

- Capital allowances which can be claimed by the owner of the vehicle will depend on the CO_2 emission of the vehicle. Vehicles with a CO_2 emission of 160gms or greater will be pooled together and a writing down allowance of 10% permitted. For cars above 110 gms but below 160 a writing down allowance of 20% will be permitted. In regard to cars below 110gms a first year allowance of 100% will be permitted.

- If the vehicle is leased then the lessee will from April 2009 be in a position to claim full tax relief against their profits for the leasing costs if the vehicle provided is below 160gms CO_2 emissions. For cars of 160gms or over 85% of the relief can be claimed.

It should be noted that these new rules apply to all cars acquired after 1 April 2009 in the case of a limited company or 6 April 2009 for an individual self employed person or partnership.

It is fair to say the use of CO_2 emission levels to determine the level of taxation is seen to be a carrot and stick to be used with car manufacturers. The manufacturers have recognised that employees will be interested in buying cars which have reasonable CO_2 emissions and many car policies prepared by employers have been revised to get employees to take cars that meet these criteria. It is very clear we will see the CO_2 emission levels lowered on the benefit table to incentivise the taking of lower CO_2 emission vehicles.

The VAT rules are not straightforward but as a general rule, the VAT incurred on the purchase of a car is not available for input VAT credit. However, input VAT incurred on cars acquired *wholly for business use* can be recovered in accordance with the normal rules on input VAT recovery.

Contract purchase and hire purchase arrangements are generally regarded as outright purchases because title of the car will eventually pass and, therefore, VAT recovery is blocked as above. With regard to lease or hire charges, i.e. where the title of the car will not pass, there is a blanket 50% disallowance of input VAT where the car is available for *any* private use.

Only expenditure on the purchase/hire/lease of the car itself is blocked or restricted and, provided there is some business use, input VAT can be recovered on the whole cost of servicing etc without any disallowance for private use. Input VAT credit on accessories is also allowed provided there is some business use. If, however, something is fitted to the car when it is first purchased, it is deemed to be part of the car and input VAT credit is disallowed.

If a business buys road fuel and allows private use of it by an employee, it has three choices:

1 claim all the input VAT and apply a scale rate to determine the output VAT liability for the private use of the fuel. The fuel scale rates are given in the VAT legislation and from 1 May 2007 have been based on CO_2 emissions;

2 claim no input VAT on any fuel purchased by the business; or

3   keep detailed records to demonstrate the split between business and private mileage and only recover VAT in relation to business use.

The general rule is that business must retain invoices to evidence the input VAT credit on fuel expenses incurred by employee for business purposes, unless an employee purchases fuel using a fuel card, credit card or debit card provided by an employer.

Many companies now allow employees to choose between a company car and a cash allowance. What advice would you give to a company thinking about implementing a cash allowance scheme?

It is a matter of fact that many employers have moved to offer employees a cash alternative to the company car. In addition there is a growing number of employers who have decided to stop providing a company car altogether and have instead totally moved to a cash alternative for all the workers who previously had been eligible for a company car. Many employers have revised their policies without taking proper advice or without ensuring that their proposals work and deliver what they are expecting.

There are major concerns within the leasing industry over how employers who permit employees to opt out can satisfy themselves over the 'duty of care' legislation. These drivers are often now called the 'grey fleet'. This is an aspect that many employers have considered and have managed to introduce procedures which mean that they are satisfied that these responsibilities are met. It is important though that those employers who are looking at offering a cash alternative take this fact into account. It is important also to bear in mind that employees' duties can change and it is possible that a low mileage driver who you have permitted to take a cash allowance can under a new role be required to travel high levels of mileage. You will need to consider whether there are rules in place to review the car policy for these drivers to possibly fit them back in to a company car.

It is my experience that, when setting the level of cash to provide to employees in lieu of a company car, many employers often get their calculations wrong and this results in an excessive allowance being paid. This clearly leads to additional costs for the employer. It is the case that often once the allowances are fixed these are set in stone and I have seen many cases in which employers have been paying excessive amounts because vehicle and associated prices have reduced. These employers are then faced with having to ring fence the allowance, with a lower allowance being paid to new employees.

It is often the case that HR departments determine the level of cash allowance to be paid, by working from data in technical publications showing what their competitors pay. It would be better to work out what it currently costs to provide each employee with a vehicle in order to ensure that the level of cash being offered does not increase cost.

It is here in my experience that many employers go wrong. Even if an employer tries this exercise, it is easy for some costs to be overlooked as costs are scattered across a number of nominal accounts. I have found that most employers have no accurate indication of their total fleet costs.

A common mistake is to forget that if the employee is no longer provided with a company car, they will cease to be taxed on a benefit in kind. Clearly in any calculation the tax saving to the employee needs to recognise that the amount saved by the employee can be used towards the cost of any vehicle. There is also a saving in Class 1A National Insurance for the employer.

If the employee is currently provided with free private fuel, will this continue to be offered to those taking the cash alternative? This is relevant because the benefit in kind on fuel (the fuel scale charge) does not apply to employees who no longer have a company car whereas the benefit for cash takers is determined by reference to the cost of private fuel provided. This cost needs to be modelled but to do this you clearly need to have some indication of the private mileage of the employee.

It may be sensible to use this change in contract in any event to buy out the benefit from the employee. Many employers find it difficult to decide on the amount of the 'buy out'. It would be unfair if this buy out is individually calculated as this would lead those who drive higher levels of private miles receiving a bigger allowance than employees who have been frugal with the use of this benefit. It is worth remembering if the fuel card is not provided, employees will be required to provide details of their business mileage in a form which would satisfy any review by HM Revenue & Customs. This will need to show not only the mileage covered but the location visited and from where the journey commenced.

It should also be remembered that employees taking cash are unlikely to be able to enjoy the same discount levels as their employers were offered by dealers and manufacturers. It is also the case that the cost of insurance will vary depending on the age of the employee, their driving history and the postal code of their home. Employers need to consider how to deal with these when producing a financial model to determine the cash allowance.

There are two financial methods adopted

1   The most common is to offer a cash allowance which on paper would be adequate to enable the employee to buy the car hey would have previously been entitled to under the company car scheme.
2   The alternative methodology is to offer a cash allowance which leaves the employer cash neutral to the former company car scheme.

It is often the case that the employer will change their methodology during the course of any project to review this area. This can lead to additional consultant time and cost, so it is sensible to try to decide which method to use at the outset and get this approved by the main stakeholders prior to the project commencing.

It never ceases to amaze me what an emotive subject cars are in most organisations and many main board directors will be anxious to ensure that any change in policy will be acceptable to employees and will be considered attractive to those looking to join the organisation. It is the case that any proposal that does not meet these criteria will never get adopted.

I have been involved in a significant number of projects which have just died because they are not considered workable by the main stakeholders.

There is a technical issue also about approved mileage allowance payments (AMAPs). These are the amounts an employer can pay to their employee free of income tax and National Insurance to cover the cost to the employee of running their own vehicle on business. It is the case that in setting the cash allowance it is likely the employer will have taken some of those same costs into account so we land up double counting those costs.

We have seen a number of examples which leave employees getting the cash allowance and then the approved mileage allowance payment. The employees soon work out that they are making money using their cars on business and soon the employer's costs are going through the roof. It may be that the employer should not pay the full approved mileage allowance payment but instead only the cost of fuel but then take account of the fact that the employee can make a personal tax claim for tax relief on the difference between the approved mileage allowance payment and the amount paid.

There are a number of providers who operate software which enables a reconciliation to be performed to use the approved mileage allowance payment against the cash allowance and fuel paid. This reduces the employer's cost and is worth considering if an employer has cash allowance takers doing significant levels of business mileage. To try and do this without specialist software is difficult and may result in a significant tax and National Insurance exposure. I would suggest those considering doing this take advice and get HM Revenue & Customs approval to what is being done.

Many organisations that provide company cars have discovered that running a car fleet is expensive and the benefit is not always appreciated by employees. This is particularly the case if the employee is not an essential car user. I suspect that the changes to the capital allowance rules which will defer the relief to those owning the vehicle will lead to cars costing more to provide (particularly cars with CO_2 emissions in excess of 160gms.). This could lead to many more employers looking to implement cash allowance arrangements.

So in conclusion it is essential for employers to consider this further and, if a cash allowance is provided, is provided to ensure this is set at a reasonable level when comparing against the cost of providing a company car.

In recent years we have heard quite a lot about how some large companies have used employee car ownership schemes (ECOS) to make significant savings. Please explain how these schemes work.

Employee car ownership schemes (ECOS) have been with us for a number of years and they are popular in particular industries like the pharmaceutical and construction industry. There are many different ways in which these schemes are designed and different providers have adopted their own names for them.

Some schemes are provided to employees instead of a traditional company car (a formal scheme). Other schemes form part of a staff benefit package to allow employees to acquire a vehicle (often called an affinity arrangement).

ECOS require the employee to purchase a car with finance provided by a third party funder. For these schemes to work for tax purposes it is necessary to ensure that title to the vehicle transfers to the employee at the outset of the agreement. If title does not transfer at the outset it is likely that HM Revenue & Customs will consider that the vehicle is a company car until title transfers. They would then seek to charge the employee to benefit in kind in this period on the basis that this was a company car.

It is generally the case that the employer will have negotiated discount terms with car manufacturers/dealers and that these rates are made available to the employee. The employer will have also agreed finance terms for the vehicle loan and maintenance, as well as a guaranteed buy back price on the vehicle at the expiry of the loan period. The employer would also generally permit their car insurance policy to be extended to cover these vehicles. Therefore to the driver the arrangement seems similar to their previous experience in a company car.

One of the major issues is determining what happens if an employee leaves the employment of the company. Given that the loan exists with the employee there are tax issues which need to be considered. Some scheme providers offer insurance to cover the costs of early termination. However, this insurance is of course an added cost and there are likely to be limitations over when a claim can be made. Therefore employers looking to introduce ECOS need to consider whether they wish to take the insurance. Alternatively if an employee leaves then a benefit in kind would arise on any loss arising on the vehicle, and tax and National Insurance would need to be accounted for in this respect.

The employee would be expected to meet the repayments on the loan for the car finance and would be reimbursed the employer's contribution. The employer's contribution is normally considered to be the cost of the repayments, less the tax saving the employee will enjoy from no longer having to pay benefit in kind tax on a company car. The employer would hope to meet part of their contribution in the form of approved mileage allowance payments (AMAP) and pay any balance needed by way of a cash allowance.

There are a number of ways in which providers deal with the payment but there are complex income tax and National Insurance rules which need to be followed. Failure to comply with these rules can lead an employer to facing a significant tax exposure. It is important to take proper advice and not simply rely on a scheme provider who may not be tax trained.

An example of how an ECOS arrangement may work is as follows:

An employee is currently in a company car with a list price of £15,000 and a taxable benefit of 17%. The employee travels 12,000 business miles on average per year and is currently reimbursed at 15p per mile for the cost of business fuel. The employee earns £45,000 per annum and is therefore a 40% taxpayer and above the upper earnings limit for National Insurance. The company car is leased and the cost of contract hire is £225 per month net of VAT but inclusive of maintenance. Insurance costs £75 per month. The employer pays corporation tax at 21%

The employee opts to join the company ECOS arrangement and takes an equivalent car to that previously provided by the company. Using the company discount terms with the manufacturer he secures this vehicle for £14,000. His monthly repayments are £350 per month which includes the cost of maintenance and insurance cover. The car's anticipated residual value is £3,500 at the end of the loan period

Monthly costs for the purchase of the motor vehicle £350 x 12 =		4,200
Employee contribution =Tax paid on a company car		
£15,000 x 17% x 40% =		(1,020)
Balance of funding required =		3,180
AMAP due 10,000 @40p	4,000	
2,000 @25p	500	
Total AMAP	4,500	
Less petrol costs 12,000@ 15P	(1,800)	(2,700)
Balance of funding required		£480
Engrossing the £480 balance for tax and National Insurance		
(NI) will be 480 x 41/59 = tax and Employees NI =		£333
Employer's NI 480 +333 @ 12.8% =		£104
Total tax and NI =		£437

Note that calculating the NI would need to be done by reference to the earnings period of the employee. It is also worth noting that 40p per mile applies for NI on all mileage (it does not reduce after 10,000 miles like with tax).

Some employers use an interest free loan of up to £5,000 to help fund the scheme for the employee. The tax rules permit an employer to provide a loan of up to £5,000 to an employee without a tax liability arising. If an employer considers adopting this then they must:

1   Ensure they are not already providing an interest free loan to an employee eg season ticket loan

2   Ensure that the amount of the loan does not exceed the anticipated residual value of the vehicle, given that the loan will be settled using the sale proceeds.

If the employer offered the above employee an interest free loan then this will be limited to the lower of £5,000 or the anticipated residual value of the vehicle at the expiry of the car loan. In this example the anticipated residual value is £3,500. Therefore the interest free loan will be limited to the amount of £3,500.

Therefore on this basis the figures will be revised as follows:

Car cost after discount	£14,000
Less interest free loan based on	
Lower of £5,000 or anticipated residual value	£3,500
Balance of funding required	£10,500
Loan from third party	£10,500

Note. The interest free loan will not be repaid by the employee but from the finance generated by the disposal of the vehicle at the end of the loan period.

It is essential that those introducing ECOS walk HM Revenue & Customs through their proposed scheme and share with them all the scheme documentation. This is to ensure that at some point in the future the scheme rules do not get challenged which could leave the employer facing a significant tax bill.

Are they successful in reducing the costs?

Yes, subject to the scheme having been properly designed to make sure that the anticipated spend is achieved and that, when the anticipated costs are calculated, all the major areas of risk are considered.

I have seen a significant number of schemes that have been poorly designed or sold by an inexperienced salesman to an employer who would never be in a position to benefit from the promised savings. ECOS produce best savings when used by an employer whose drivers do fairly high levels of business mileage and when staff turnover levels (in the car population) are relatively low.

The sort of issues I have experienced are as follows:

1   When introducing the scheme the company had not considered their staff turnover levels and when the cost of early termination was taken in to account ECOS was no longer beneficial. I have seen a number of employers who had been led to believe that cars could be simply reallocated to new employees but this is not straightforward given the tax rules and in any event proves difficult to implement when the new employee is required to buy a used vehicle possibly not at a commercial value

2   That in modelling the scheme employers have not taken accurate levels of business or total mileage into account which then means that there is insufficient approved mileage allowance available, so more of the payment provided to the driver needs to be engrossed for income tax and National Insurance

3   That the rate of mileage allowance paid encourages employees to use their cars more and adds to scheme costs

4   That the scheme was not tax robust and did not take account of the complex mileage allowance payment rules which apply to income tax and National Insurance. (It should be borne in mind that there are different rules for income tax and National Insurance).

5   That the finance provided to the employee means that title to the vehicle does not transfer at the outset of the loan agreement

I believe that employers looking to introduce ECOS need to carefully consider what they are doing and take proper advice from a relevant professional firm and not simply rely on what their fleet provider tells them.

What is the future of ECOS?

Over recent years there have been a number of reviews by HM Treasury of ECOS and in particular the interaction of these schemes with the approved mileage allowance payment tax rules. The decision is to not challenge these schemes but it is clear that HM Revenue & Customs will want to ensure that going forward these schemes comply strictly with the income tax and National Insurance rules.

ECOS will always be attractive to a particular population of employers. I expect that, with the introduction of the new capital allowance rules at April 2009, many employers will look again at ECOS particularly for vehicles supplied to senior employees whose vehicles have CO_2 emissions exceeding 160 gms. ECOS vehicles do not attract capital allowances so the rule changes do not impact on them.

The last year or so has seen the re-emergence of a new tax saving arrangement, salary sacrifice schemes. How do these work, and do they achieve savings?

Salary sacrifice schemes are not new and I came across my first scheme more than 15 years ago. Salary sacrifice arrangements have been used in other areas like nursery care, computers and bike to work schemes. They are viewed by HM Revenue & Customs to be fairly tax-aggressive and if not properly set up can leave the employer exposed to significant income tax and National Insurance. It should be borne in mind that the introduction of a salary sacrifice arrangement will not only have a tax impact but needs to be considered for employment law and pension arrangements.

The arrangement works by the employee sacrificing part of their salary which is then used by the employer to meet the cost of providing a company car. In some cases the sacrifice may be set to cover the costs of the employee being provided with a company car that exceeds the benchmark vehicle to which that employee is entitled.

The employer saves from not having to pay employer's Class 1 National Insurance on the amount of the sacrificed salary but they will have to meet Class 1A National Insurance on the benefit in kind arising on the vehicle.

In addition to sacrificing a proportion of their salary the employee will also have to meet the income tax arising on the company car they are provided with.

In reality these schemes will only be attractive to employees wishing to take a vehicle on which the benefit in kind is low, because the figures do not work out if the employee is left with a significant salary sacrifice and a large benefit in kind on the vehicle. My experience is that whilst a number of employers have looked to introduce these arrangements, the number of employees looking to take a car is very low.

The major difficulty for an employer entering in to a salary sacrifice arrangement is to determine what happens if the employee leaves part way through the term of the contract. Seeing the vehicle is leased under a company contract the employer will be required either to meet the early termination costs or to try and get another employee to take over the arrangement. I know that a number of providers offer early termination insurance but when these costs are taken in to account the arrangement becomes more complex.

It is important that the employee's contract of employment is correctly revised to reflect the salary sacrifice and a failure to do this will leave the employer liable to income tax and National Insurance on the earnings prior to the sacrifice being introduced. It is also not possible to revise a salary sacrifice for a period of 12 months. If this approach is not followed HM Revenue and Customs are likely to seek income tax on the sacrificed amount under 'monies worth' rules. There is a further problem in that if the employee is in a company pension scheme and the contribution to that scheme is calculated by reference to earnings then that employee's pension pot may be reduced because of the sacrifice. Some pension schemes have rules that permit the pension contribution to be calculated by reference to a notional salary; this would be the earnings before sacrifice. The problem though is that HM Revenue & Customs may not give permission for a notional salary to be used.

In addition to the above it should be remembered that a sacrifice cannot take an employee's earnings below the National Minimum Wage and may impact on student loan repayments. Working family tax credits become relevant here as do credit applications the employee makes to a bank or building society.

Many employers who operate a flexible benefit arrangement need to consider how a salary sacrifice car scheme can fit in and how they can manage the possibility of the car being supplied on a date other than the anniversary of the scheme. This in practice can be a major difficulty and leads many HR teams to decide that this arrangement is unworkable.

Therefore in my view salary sacrifice car schemes will have a limited appeal and will be considered by employers who wish to enable employees to take low CO_2 emission cars in their flexible benefit package. There will also be the employer who wishes to offer the perk driver the ability to flex up into a higher value vehicle and take a salary sacrifice to permit the additional costs to be collected in a National Insurance efficient way.

It is essential that those looking to introduce a salary sacrifice arrangement take proper advice from a tax specialist and also involve their employment lawyers. It is the policy of HM Revenue & Customs not to give clearance on such schemes so employers need to be comfortable that what they are proposing to introduce is tax robust.

An example of how this works is as follows. I have used the same data in regard to the ECOS example with the details as follows:

An employee currently has a company car with a list price of £15,000 and a taxable benefit of 17%. The employee travels 12,000 business miles on average per year and is currently reimbursed at 15p per mile for the cost of business fuel. The employee earns £45,000 per annum and is therefore a 40% taxpayer and above the upper earnings limit for National Insurance. The company car is leased and the cost of contract hire is £225 per month net of VAT but inclusive of maintenance. Insurance costs £75 per month. The employer pays corporation tax at 21%

The employee is offered a car via a salary sacrifice arrangement through the company's flexible benefit scheme. The sacrificed amount is equal to the cost to the employer of leasing the vehicle.

The employee is therefore offered the car with a salary sacrifice which is £3,802 (£225 + £75 + VAT on 50% of rental of £16.87 x 12 months)

Employee Position

Therefore the employee's contracted salary is reduced from £45,000 to £41,198. This costs the employee the lost salary net of income tax and NI so

£3,802 x 41/59 =	£2,642

Plus income tax to be paid by the employee on benefit in kind;

£15,000 x17% x 40% =	£1,020
Total cost to employee =	£3662 or £305.16 per month

Employer position

The employer loses the corporation tax relief on the on the sacrificed salary but gains the corporation tax relief on the leasing payments and cost of insurance. From April 2009 this will balance out (assuming the car is a less than 160gms CO_2).

The employer is no longer liable to Class 1 NI on the earnings sacrificed which are:

Sacrificed salary £3,802 x 12.8% =	£486.65
Instead the employer is liable to Class 1A NI on benefit	
£15,000 x 17% x 12.8% =	£326.40
Net Gain	£160.25
Less Corporation Tax Relief on the difference at 21%	£33.65
Net saving to employer	£126.60

Notes. The example ignores the fact that the employer will be liable for the lease payments in the event that the employee leaves part way through the agreement. It also assumes that the employee is not in a company pension scheme or, if he is, that his contribution will not be amended by the sacrifice. Clearly the employee is earning in excess of the minimum wage and the sacrifice will not create difficulty.

The employee will need to decide whether the net cost for the vehicle of £305.16 per month is reasonable compared to what a similar vehicle may cost on say a PCP deal.

If a fleet manager approached you and said they wanted to reduce the overall level of tax burden arising from company cars, what advice would you give them?

This is not normally what happens. I would generally be approached by the Finance Director or Managing Director who had concerns over their spend on company cars. It is generally the case that company cars is the second largest item of employee spend with salaries being first and pensions third. In my review of that fleet's current costs there would be the need to consider the taxation costs.

In answer to the question though I would look at the funding method which the employer had chosen for the particular cars and and see, given the tax position, whether this was appropriate. It may be that the employer should have more than one funding arrangement with the method used being dependent on the cost of the vehicle. In suggesting a change of funding method though it would be important to bear in mind whether the employer wanted the vehicles to be on or off balance sheet and whether they wanted to bear the residual risk. In my experience this is something that fleet managers should consider. I do have concerns that when employers get the calculation performed by their lease provider the provider may load the residual values on one of the funding methods simply to make this look less attractive.

It is also worth looking at the cars that employees are eligible to drive to see if these achieve good CO_2 emissions against their competitors. It may be better to shift to another model of car but of course whilst this may save tax it could be that the discounts and whole life costs of that car will not make the proposition viable. It is therefore important not simply to look at tax in isolation; it should be considered with all other costs.

National Insurance is a significant cost to employers and employees but it is often overlooked. How might a fleet manager go about reducing the level of NI being paid?

The answer is similar to that of the previous question. National Insurance can be saved by reducing the CO_2 emissions of the vehicles provided to employees. There can be also significant National Insurance savings by using a salary sacrifice arrangement but I have spelt out the risks of this earlier in the chapter.

There is an opportunity to reduce National Insurance paid on fuel if the advice given in the Overdrive case is followed: when acquiring fuel the employee should make the petrol station aware that he is going to be acquiring the fuel by use of a corporate fuel/credit card. This means then that National Insurance under Class 1A applies only on the fuel scale charge. If this step is not taken then HM Revenue & Customs can seek Class 1 National Insurance.

There are some important rules to follow over how the calculation of National Insurance in respect of an employee car ownership scheme and failure to follow these can lead an employer facing National Insurance on the contributions paid to fund the car in total without any relief for costs on business travel.

How can your firm help reduce tax for employers and employees?

We have considerable experience of undertaking projects to assist employers to analyse their fleet costs and generally our clients would expect that work to include a review of the car policy. We would use that review to benchmark the current costs (including tax costs) and to consider ways in which the car policy may be revised and the financial impact of those recommended changes.

Alastair Kendrick
Director, Employment Tax Services
Mazars LLP

22 FUEL AND FUEL CARDS

Eric Fanchini
Fuel Card Manager
TOTAL UK

Please tell us about yourself and your role.

I've been the fuel card manager of TOTAL UK since 2006. My background is in sales and IT. I worked for 10 years in sales in various countries such as Canada, Kazakhstan, Russia, the UK and France, where I managed commercialisation of hardware and software.

In my previous role at TOTAL UK, I was the Head of UK Information Systems and managed the roll out of Group solutions, such as cards, ledger, service station infrastructure and optimisation of truck deliveries.

Fuel card is a good combination of IT and sales skills. Customers are looking for excellence in customer services, including technology, to monitor their expenses and optimise their costs.

Many companies allow their employees to pay for fuel and reclaim the cost through expenses. What added benefits do fuel cards give?

All fleet managers have a lot of responsibility. This is linked to three main duties: Health and Safety, cost control and environmentally sensitive monitoring.

We believe that a fuel card is a good solution to address these three points. Firstly, from a health and safety point of view, drivers should not carry cash or worry about potential bank card fraud. The fuel card industry has made significant progress to secure transactions. With TOTALCARD, for instance, all transactions are PIN verified and users can choose to have a maximum amount and number of transactions per card and per day.

In addition, fuel cards providers offer an online management solution. These reports provide precious data, and can help fleet managers to better control drivers' behaviours and habits. We should never forget that in 2006 more than 3,000 people were killed on UK roads.

Secondly, the cost of fuel is a growing concern for companies – especially for the transport industry where fuel is a third of their total costs. The volatility of the product and variation, from $50 to $140 a barrel, make budgeting difficult.

Nevertheless, according to Fleet News, expert assessments estimate that up to 35% of fleets are burdened with additional costs of more than 20% due to lack of proper cost monitoring. Again, the fuel card is a good way to reduce fuel spending to the minimum required for company activity. The online tools give clear pictures of spending – featuring miles per gallon analysis, reports on daily transactions and e-mail alerts for any abnormal usage.

Thirdly, business awareness of their environmental impact is no longer up for debate. Transport is the largest end use category of emissions in the UK, accounting for between a quarter and a third of UK carbon emissions. More and more senior managers and board members ask for reports on carbon emissions. Clearly the government's approach and fiscal incentives have played a key role in this change of behaviour. We are convinced that a fuel card is a good way to assess this carbon performance. Combined with premium fuels, it is proven that businesses can reduce CO_2 emissions by 5% and carbon monoxide by 10%.

How should a fleet manager decide which fuel card is right for their fleet?

Fleet managers should balance the benefits of each fuel card by considering the following factors:

- What is an acceptable network size? Convenience is a key element, as there is no point driving extra miles and burning potential savings. Fuel buying habits show that in 55% of cases forecourt choice is based on proximity and most drivers only ever use one site. It explains why oil distributors put in place cross-acceptance agreements (for example TOTAL with BP/SHELL). Therefore, fleet managers must request mapping analysis to identify the best network to meet their needs. For local businesses, the average distance should be around two miles. For national businesses, an average of three miles is acceptable.

- What is the best price? The pricing policy of each brand should be carefully analysed to measure potential savings against the UK national average. Extra costs, such as card re-issuing or card fees, must be discussed and understood to assess each offer. Finally, payment terms and the impact on cash flow are also essential elements.

- What is the value of the management information offered? Fleet managers need easy access to the data, the capacity to run reports – especially in order to measure abnormal usage. Management information is the key tool to address operational issues, such as how to detect fraud, correct drivers' bad habits or the poor performance of a vehicle. Fleet managers should also obtain the average time to process transactions.

- How secure is the product? The PIN is a pre-requisite to avoid fraud and card cloning. Fleet managers need to understand the processes in place when fraud occurs and the limit of their liability. During tenders, fleet managers should ask how fraud is investigated. They should also make sure that the fuel card provider offers a 24/7 helpline to stop lost or stolen cards.

- What should be expected from customer service? Fleet managers will save time and money if they define the right criteria to measure the performance of customer service. How long does it take to open an account? How easy is it to order new cards? How quickly can you deliver the cards? Is there an express delivery process in case of an operational emergency? Can the cards be delivered to the driver's address? What is the process to cancel a card? What type of product can I purchase with my fuel card and can I change this? When can I obtain my monthly report? When do you invoice, and is it in line with my internal accounting timetable?

These subjects should be reviewed during the implementation plan and be part of an agreed Service Level Agreement to validate roles and responsibilities.

For large accounts, a kick off meeting should always take place and should cover the following subjects:

- Implementation planning: timescales and card requirement dates
- Review of the agreed commercial conditions
- Validation of account structure, cost centres. The cost centres will structure the invoice and reflect the organisation of each customer
- Communication plan: designated contact points, account management review, structure, checkpoint dates, prospective dates
- Validation of card embossing. The card can be linked to a driver or to a vehicle. Some cards also offer optional fields that can be useful as they will be part of the invoice data

- Validation of management reporting needs
- Validation of documentation
- Site locations and mapping
- Online tools: user guidance, training, set up
- Interfaces with customer ledgers for large accounts
- Review and validation of a Service Level Agreement and customer service arrangement (KPI, escalation process, customer's log).
- Finally, for large businesses, a good understanding of the provider's business continuity plan gives a guarantee – number of days of fuel stocks at sites; IT disaster recovery plan, back-up procedures. It will minimise operational impact and drivers blocked at sites in case of failure.

How is the price of the fuel determined when a fuel card is used? Is it generally better for a fleet to pay pump price or a fixed price?

A fuel card transaction is linked to a pricing structure as the driver does not pay at the site.

Pricing can be pump price – which is a good offer for local businesses – or fixed price for large accounts. Large accounts, such as hauliers, have an interest in opting for a fixed price as it is set weekly.

Businesses should always compare the pricing proposals for a period of 12 months, and measure the difference of each offer. It is easier to work net of VAT. Whether VAT should be included or excluded should be specified in the weekly price notice.

How does the EU Sixth VAT Directive impact fuel cards?

Some employees still claim VAT using till receipts. This Directive stops the reclaiming of VAT on invoices that are not in the registered company name. Therefore, fuel transactions have to be made with a company credit card or a fuel card. A fuel card offers more advantages as each transaction is recorded per product (fuel, shops, wash) and the level of risk is lower.

For international transport business, all transactions are consolidated with a different view per country. All international fuel providers offer options to claim VAT in express mode and are fully compliant with the EU Sixth VAT Directive.

What sort of reports can a fleet manager expect to see from the fuel card company?

Firstly, fleet managers should expect: a summary turnover report in litres or in sterling; a turnover report per network; a yearly comparison; and card activity report. This can be provided on a monthly basis.

Flexible systems mean all reports can be downloaded in csv format or Excel. TOTAL, for instance, offers a converter to extract all data and create personalised reports.

For large accounts, these reports facilitate reconciliation between invoice file and transactions file.

In addition, the management information must give an accurate mile per gallon (MPG) of each vehicle.

Obviously, the quality of the data depends on the drivers. When the driver keys in a wrong mileage at a service station, the MPG information will be false.

The fleet manager should be given the MPG calculation rule and be able to correct the wrong mileage in the system in order to automatically correct the MPG consumption. The system should store the wrong mileage in case the fleet manager wants to restore this data, e.g. if the vehicle is changed the mileage will be significantly different from the previous one but this isn't the driver's mistake.

Fleet managers also require the option to select various criteria to monitor their fleets. Once a transaction is processed, the fuel card provider can email an alert if an exception has occurred.

Examples of these criteria include:

- Excessive filling: this will monitor the tank capability of each vehicle and will create an alert when it has been exceeded
- Timeslots: to customise cards for use on certain days or between certain times. Transactions attempted outside of these times will be flagged as abnormal
- Mileage per gallon can also be monitored: unusual consumption patterns can then be flagged.

Finally, fleet managers are also keen to calculate their fleet's carbon footprint, based on fuel consumption. Fuel cards can help them to follow up the CO_2 emissions reduction plan.

Have there been any recent developments in the fuel card market that will be of particular interest to fleet managers?

Security is always a key area and constant progress is being made by the industry to avoid fraud. PIN is obviously a 'must have', while velocity checks – the maximum amount per card per day – is the latest valuable initiative.

Regarding email alerts, new criteria, such as regional control, can be useful to monitor vehicles that are attached to a geographical perimeter.

The other area of progress is the range of available geomapping services, which include phone service station locator, text locator, and the chance to download service stations into a sat nav device.

Looking into the future, how do you see the fuel card market developing?

The fuel card market is well established, and the UK is a mature market. A lot of offers from the oil majors or resellers are available. We believe that there is still a growing market for the product, as fuel cards are easy to roll out and are the most secure way for businesses to pay fuel and claim VAT.

Looking forward, onboard equipment and M-payment are areas to keep an eye on, but the associated costs can still dissuade fleet managers who expect simple and cost-effective solutions.

The price of fuel has fluctuated wildly in recent times and fleet managers are looking for ways to reduce their fuel bills. What is your advice to them?

Fleet managers should identify the best network at the best price. The needs of a haulage company, a national car company or a local plumber van are all different. The pricing offered will vary depending on their needs and the volume at stake.

In any case, the calculation of the average distance from a forecourt is important. Obviously, operational needs, such as 24/7 requirements, quality of the sites or HGV acceptance, have to be considered in the decision process. The quality of sites is particularly relevant for hauliers as, for instance, they have to make sure that goods are secure when they stop abroad.

Regarding expenses, the intensive use of the online system helps monitor and reduce spending. This is useful in monitoring drivers' habits, vehicle comparisons, the network used and also monitoring mileage to avoid concealed personal purchases. Driver training will help to reduce insurance premiums, and the cost of training should be offset by fuel consumption reductions.

Another major purpose of setting up a fuel card account is that it allows reallocation to other departments, depots and so on, depending on the customer's organisation. The savings on administrative tasks is significant, and key accounts require an interface download to their accounting ledger to simplify their internal Finance process.

Some fleet managers pay attention to the loyalty scheme in order to avoid unnecessary miles. However, most fuel card providers have a way to stop the reclaiming of loyalty points if deemed necessary.

Fleet managers usually review the basics such as:

- Tyres inflated to the correct pressure, as this can improve fuel consumption as well as safety
- Maintaining the correct level of oil to improve engine efficiency;
- The use of equipment such as racks, which increase fuel consumption when attached to a vehicle
- Speeding, which also increases fuel consumption.

Finally, for international transport, a 'one card in hand' approach can help. This is because it avoids non-essential stops and simplifies the management of fuel. For instance, Eurotrafic cards can be used in all European tolls, Euro tunnel/Mont Blanc/Frejus (standard) and for breakdown/fine services and VAT recovery (optional packages on customer demands). A good understanding of European VAT claims will also help with savings, as options exist to have the VAT amount credited on the following invoice.

Other than moving to low CO_2 cars and vans, is there anything the environmentally-aware fleet should be doing to reduce its environmental impact?

TOTAL has invested in EXCELLIUM, an advanced range of fuels that decreases fuel consumption. As a result, TOTAL EXCELLIUM offers its users an average 4% reduction in fuel consumption.

EXCELLIUM is also proven to clean the most sensitive parts of modern engines – in particular the areas involved with petrol injection and high pressure diesel injection. In addition, it cuts carbon dioxide emissions by up to 5% and carbon monoxide by up to 10% in new cars, and by up to 25% in cars more than five years old.

In addition, the higher Cetane index of EXCELLIUM DIESEL reduces noise inside and outside the vehicle by up to 37% when starting the engine from cold.

Finally, our new economy-focussed ranges of engine lubricants for diesel and petrol engines are proven to reduce engine friction, resulting in 50% less wear and providing a significant fuel economy improvement of 3-4%.

What recent fuel-related developments should fleet managers be aware of?

There are lots of debates in the press about energy in the future. TOTAL is obviously involved in many projects across the world that are developing and researching alternative energy.

In parallel, we are making significant investments in our refinery capacity. For example, work is in progress to install a €300 million hydro-desulphurisation unit at our TOTAL Lindsey Oil Refinery in North Lincolnshire. This unit will remove sulphur from fuels, allowing TOTAL to both meet European Union fuel directives and to respond to changes in the crude oil supply market.

Rather than using petrol stations, some companies buy fuel cheaply in bulk and have it delivered to their own storage installation, i.e. bunkering. Is this practice growing? What are the advantage and disadvantages?

Some companies who require larger amounts of diesel opt for delivery to their own installations. This decision requires an accurate understanding of environmental legislation. Health and Safety rules with oil products and oil storage regulations are strict and must be applied.

In addition, there is a strong need for pricing analysts to take the right decision for delivery and stocks management. In a volatile market, it is not the easiest choice but can represent some saving, but equally, if the market goes the opposite way it can present some additional costs.

Another point to be considered is the capacity for drivers to be able to return to their nearest depot for a refuel. It can make sense for transport organisations, but can be less relevant for vans or fleet business.

Finally, storage requires security measures at site to avoid spillage or theft, and security arrangements will represent additional costs.

Therefore, decisions on storage installation and a fuel card solution depend on the company, the capacity to optimize price, to know legislation, and to manage storage in the most efficient way possible. In some situations, a fuel card solution and a bulk delivery can be complementary, offering a range of savings and transport options.

What is your advice to fleet managers on how best to reduce fuel-related costs?

At the initial stage, fleet managers must make sure that they opt for the best price and coverage, with a good understanding of the management information offered.

The saving will come from the capacity to manage the exceptions. What are the average miles per gallon for your fleet vs worst vehicles? Are drivers' motoring habits causing a problem? Is it the vehicle at risk? All the controls at stake (tank capacity, region etc) help to reduce the total spending.

In addition, fleet managers should follow the European Petroleum Industry and the European commission advice:

- Keep your car well serviced and check the oil level regularly: correctly maintained cars can operate more efficiently and help reduce CO_2 emissions.
- Check tyre pressure every month: under-inflated tyres can increase fuel consumption by up to 4% according to the International Energy Agency.
- Remove unnecessary weight from boot or back seats. The heavier the car, the harder the engine has to work and the more fuel it consumes.
- Close your windows, especially at higher speeds, and remove empty roof racks. This will reduce wind resistance and can lower your fuel consumption and CO_2 emissions by up to 10% according to the European Commission.

- Use air conditioning only when necessary. Unnecessary use increases fuel consumption and CO_2 emissions by up to 5% according to the European Commission.

- Start driving soon after starting the engine and turn off the engine when stationary for more than one minute. Modern engines enable drivers to just get in and go, thus reducing fuel consumption.

- Drive at reasonable speeds and, above all, drive smoothly. Every time you accelerate or brake suddenly, the engine uses more fuel and produces more CO_2.

- When accelerating, change up gears as early as possible. According to the European Commission higher gears reduce fuel consumption.

- Try to anticipate traffic flow. Look at the traffic as far ahead as possible in order to avoid unnecessary stopping and starting within the flow of traffic.

- Consider car sharing for work or leisure. It helps reduce congestion and fuel consumption.

How can Total help fleet managers reduce costs and increase control over fleet expenditure?

TOTAL is the fourth largest petrol company in the world. Our operations cover the entire energy chain, including oil exploration and production to trading, shipping and refining, as well as the marketing of petroleum products, as well as chemicals. The Group has operations in over 130 countries and employs more than 95,000 people worldwide. It has the second highest capitalisation in the Euro zone. Our rules of behaviour and business principles include Ethics, Development, Corporate Philanthropy, and Health and Safety.

The diversity of the Group's worldwide business is reflected in the UK with activity in all three key areas: Exploration and Production, Refining and Marketing, and Chemicals. TOTAL UK is the fourth largest oil company in the UK and employs more than 5,000 people. Our refinery is based on the east coast at Killingholme, Lincolnshire, where thousands of barrels of oil are refined every day and turned into a wide range of products, from different types of liquid fuels to gas, special fluids and bitumen. Once the finished products leave the refineries, they are distributed around the UK by road, rail, sea and underground pipelines. TOTAL has oil storage terminals at strategic locations around England, Wales, the Isle of Man and the Channel Islands. From these terminals, products are transported to commercial customers and the company's network of 830 service stations.

TOTALCARD and EUROTRAFIC are the fuel card solutions of TOTAL UK Ltd. Both products were awarded 'Fuel Card of the Year' in 2008 for the innovative approach taken by TOTAL.

Indeed, these products are part of the TOTAL long-term strategy to provide effective and comprehensive solutions for professionals with a suitable network and a high level of customer service. For national usage, TOTAL offers TOTALCARD, the first PIN approved fuel card in the UK with management information, which can be used in TOTAL, BP and SHELL filling stations.

For customers who have needs outside the United Kingdom, TOTAL also offers Eurotrafic, our international card accepted in 16 countries and 13,000 service stations and on most motorways in Europe.

From a pricing point of view, we offer various flexible solutions such as pump or weekly price depending on customers' needs and preferences.

As our aim is to develop a long-term partnership with our customers, we have in place a dedicated account management local programme. Each customer has a designated back office account manager who assists your team in all aspects of managing your account, including account creation and structure, card ordering and modification, reporting and any operational questions encountered.

In addition, TOTALCARD provides customers with a web-based account management solution that provides a clear picture of your spending and includes miles per gallon analysis, spend summary analysis and simple, but effective, control of card management and email alerts.

Our fuel solution is simple and secure. The product is easy to roll out and invoices are VAT approved. This is why TOTALCARD is recognised by the market.

Institute of Transport Management

UK Fuel Card of The Year Awards

Birmingham 12 March 2008

Against a backdrop of ever decreasing fuel margins, stabilised demand and well established markets, the UK and European fuel card industry is growing, albeit at a slightly decreasing rate.

Growth opportunities for fuel card operators largely centre on European countries such as Switzerland, Ireland, Spain, Portugal and Italy, which are lagging behind the most highly penetrated markets of Austria, Denmark and Finland.

Yet even in the markets, where fuel card penetration is high, there is a significant number of motorists in both the commercial and fleet segment that have never had a fuel card.

In the UK and beyond, good network coverage is the core reason for choosing a fuel card provider. The smaller fleet size manager is usually less willing to move provider than his counterpart operating the larger fleet – so customer retention is not a big motivator for these companies.

As a result, efforts by fuel card operators to increase market share usually focus on marketing and awareness of the benefits of their service to customers, to attract new business, and, at the same time, develop products which reward loyalty.

TOTALCARD has been singled out by the Institute of Transport Management for its 'UK Fuel Card of the Year 2008' Award as a result of its superior product, service offerings and geographical reach.

Commenting on the award for TOTALCARD, Patrick Sheedy, Media & PR Director for the Institute, said: "TOTALCARD is a leading integrated fuel management service, which offers the fuel card as a means of a practical, innovative and effective management solution for fleets of all sizes.

"The scheme provides a highly flexible structure for account control, with a range of configurations and online access. The card accounts can be controlled through the internet, which also enables more immediate and easily accessible fleet management. The web-based system allows cards to be ordered, replaced, and cancelled at the click of a button, and for transactions and invoices to be accessed and downloaded.

"Each company was judged on a number of areas, which we identified as extremely important. We looked at the range of services provided, the importance of innovation, the security in place, and the importance placed by the company on customer relations.

"It became clear that TOTAL OIL's TOTALCARD excelled in all these areas, separating the company from its competitors and making TOTALCARD the UK's premier fuel card."

Sheedy continued: "It is my pleasure to announce TOTALCARD as the 'UK Fuel Card of the Year 2008', in recognition of TOTAL OIL's sterling development of the card and also the extensive range of surrounding support services, which will make fleet operators more cost effective.

"Effective security is a must when dealing with fuel cards and TOTALCARD was the first to offer a PIN service, and is widely considered to be the safest fuel card in the UK. Fleet managers not only benefit from this impressive security, they can also ensure simple and effective fuel management through the use of TOTALCARD. Through TOTAL's partnership with SHELL and BP, the card is accepted at a huge number of service stations across the UK.

"TOTAL provides excellent support services to back up TOTALCARD, making fuel account management even easier. These online services include TRACKER, PERFORMER, and TOTAL BUSINESS. Through using TOTALCARD and the accompanying services, fleet managers can receive updates about their account and their vehicles' daily levels of fuel consumption, and also select specific criteria that TOTAL will monitor and inform them about.

Sheedy continued: "The TOTALCARD is an easy-to-use, VAT-approved management tool that will ensure that users are able to manage and control fuel spend in a more professional and cost-effective way. The benefits of a fuel card far outweigh those of paper payments – but that message must be communicated to the target market through any possible means.

"In the past, direct mailing and telesales have proven successful in acquiring customers from competitors and from the alternative payment market. However, these means are proving more and more ineffective. In today's more sophisticated market, companies like TOTAL are showing much more innovation and flair in getting the message across.

Sheedy concluded: "The Institute is delighted to welcome TOTAL back to the awards table in respect of its excellence in Fuel Card services. This is a crucial sector in the overall fleet management picture, and it is very important to the Institute that its members receive the best recommendations when it comes to fuel card use. I would like to take this opportunity to officially congratulate TOTAL on this success."

Eric Fanchini
Fuel Card Manager
TOTAL UK

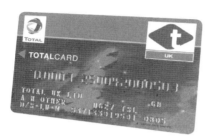

23 FLEET SYSTEMS

Jason Francis
Managing Director
Jaama Ltd

Many companies manage their fleets quite well just using Excel. At what size of fleet does it become essential to use fleet software?

It is difficult to get exact numbers when trying to determine the size of the UK fleet market. The government estimates that there are currently 1.1 million company cars on the UK's roads but the British Vehicle Rental and leasing Association disagrees, saying that their members have a total fleet size of 1.8 million business cars. We estimate that there are approximately 41,000 organisations with 'fleet' vehicles. The majority of these fleets are very small comprising just a handful of vehicles or less.

Even if these numbers are marginally out, what is clear is that the vast majority of company car fleet operators do not use specialist software and therefore the fleet size is the most significant factor when determining whether to use fleet software or not, though it is not the only factor.

In addition to size, other major factors which determine at what point it becomes essential to use specialist software are the type of vehicles, the use of those vehicles and the fleet policy. The more complex the fleet operation becomes – acquisition method, specification, vehicle purpose - the more likely it is that fleet software will be in use.

In the past there have been 3 barriers to implementing fleet software: it's specialist nature and perceived complexity, the ease of implementation and general availability awareness. In the last decade, like most management systems, fleet software has changed to become more accessible to small businesses and more appropriate to operators of smaller fleet.

Systems that used to be installed on a single PC or office network are now provided through an online web-based connection and referred to as 'fully-hosted', which means all you need to do to operate them is type in a web address and you're away. These simple to use systems allow multi-user access to constantly updated secure information which is continually backed up for you. These systems cost around £250 per annum including 24/7 support and provide all the functionality necessary to manage a small to medium size fleets.

You don't have to have a large fleet to operate fleet software. The smallest fleet customer of Jaama currently has 2 vehicles!

Fleet managers are interested in managing their duty of care risks as well as the day-to-day activities of the fleet department. In your opinion what issues should be handled by a modern fleet system?

These issues can broadly be grouped into 2 categories: actions that are required to keep the driver safe and legal and those that are required to keep costs as low as possible. Detailed records enabling the management of processes, monitoring of costs and measuring of efficiency are vital for any fleet operation.

The recent introduction of the Corporate Manslaughter and Corporate Homicide Act 2007 and the Health and Safety (Offences) Act 2008 has been a catalyst for many company directors and senior managers to implement robust fleet and driver risk management systems. They now face a heavy fine or can be jailed for up to 2 years if a driver on a work-related journey is killed or seriously injured as a result of gross corporate or individual failures.

Duty of care risk management should be an active and integral part of the fleet management process and a modern fleet system will provide the necessary framework to enable this to be achieved on an ongoing basis from the data collected with little additional effort.

The extent to which you require fleet software functionality and the functions you need it to perform will depend upon many factors such as how many vehicles and drivers you have, and the capabilities of your company's existing finance, payroll and HR software systems. What follows is a summary of areas where information can be collected and managed by modern fleet software. The type of vehicles you use, their purpose and your fleet policy will determine which of these areas are relevant and to what level:

DRIVER MANAGEMENT
- Personal information and contact details
- Grade or category, allowable vehicles, nature of use and usage restrictions
- Vehicle allocation dates and allocation history
- Cash allowance, trade up or down variances and driver personal contributions
- Valid driver's licence held, endorsements, restrictions and periodic monitoring check frequency
- Training, planning, qualifications and history
- Journey logs, mileage history and driver hours
- Expenses, cost allocation to departments and driver recharges
- Fuel usage, management and reimbursement
- Insurance cover and Motor Insurance Database notifications
- Benefit-in-kind taxation (P11D, NIC)
- Allocated equipment

- Congestion, parking and traffic offence fines and driver recharges
- Document management

DUTY OF CARE RISK ASSESSMENT

- Expected annual mileage, monthly mileage and driving hours
- The number and cost of blameworthy incidents or accidents
- The number of traffic offences
- The driver's attitude to risk (determined via driver risk profiling questions)
- Age and experience
- Medical history, impairment and eyesight tests
- Driver handbook/fleet policy issued and confirmation notification returned
- Drivers' own vehicles used for work-related journeys; document checks

VEHICLE MANAGEMENT

- Inventory, technical specification, fuel type, capacity and CO_2
- Purchase price, cost for P11D tax, depreciation
- Accessories and special equipment allocated
- Replacement term, distance and ordering details
- Routine service, MOT, maintenance authorisations and cost management
- Breakdown, recovery and vehicle off-road management
- Warranty claims
- Defects and safety checks
- Road fund licence
- Disposal mileage, V5 and SORN sent to DVLA
- London Transport exemptions and low emissions
- Document management

LEASE COMPANY MANAGEMENT

- Lease type for finance management
- Start date, end date and distance allowed
- Advanced, regular and final settlement payments
- Cost management, allocation and effective rental VAT calculation
- Maintenance, recovery, relief vehicle services
- Payment history
- Excess mileage charges and other out-of-contract charges
- Realignment and adjustment history

ACCIDENT AND REPAIR MANAGEMENT

- Incident type, location and description
- Cause, speed, weather, visibility
- Injury, days off work and estimated cost
- Police notification, reference and attending officer

- Claim date, type, status and insurance details
- Third party and witness details
- Uninsured loss recovery claim and claim amount
- Damage details, repair status and estimated costs
- Cost estimates, purchase order management and recharges

The difference between a simple database or spreadsheet and a comprehensive fleet software package is the functionality that surrounds the collection of this data. Pressure in business today is forcing down the 'cost of control'. By this I mean that you no longer have the luxury of time to personally check and manage information using traditional monitoring and reporting controls.

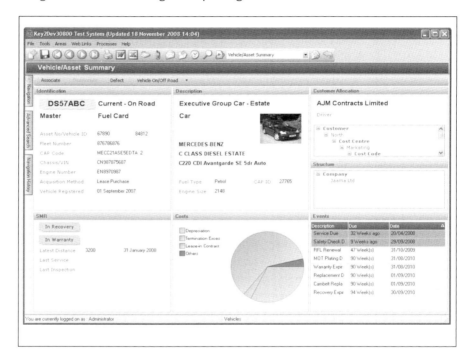

What are the key reports that a fleet manager should expect to get from a good fleet system?

Let me start my answer with what the basic tenets of a good fleet system should be:

- Where possible data should be collected and validated at source, once, with no duplication or re-keying
- Seamless integration with other internal software systems
- Automatic on-event processing and workflow management
- Tolerances set and monitored for exceptions
- Reporting triggers based upon exception rather than manual checks
- Information widely available and 'pushed' to the appropriate people and systems

A modern fleet software system will help to reduce the amount of time spent on fleet administration by enabling information to be entered once and usually at source. For example drivers enter their expenses, mileage and journey logs or these are captured from some other system and imported automatically. Fuel data and maintenance transactions are imported from service providers or electronic invoices. Driver details are taken electronically from the company's HR system; you get the general picture.

A modern fleet system will take all this captured information and analyse it against the criteria you set. List-based reports produced by selecting the report type from a menu and printing it out are virtually a thing of the past. With today's systems you decide what information you need to be informed of. For example, you may want to know some or all of the following:

- Which contract hire vehicles are doing more mileage than your contract allows?
- Your worst 10 drivers for fuel MPG consumption
- You most expensive 'whole life cost' vehicles
- Drivers who are most at risk
- Vehicles which are likely to exceed their maintenance budget
- Drivers who are not servicing their vehicle on time
- Rogue vehicles
- Routine events not completed on time
- Drivers with new licence endorsements
- Drivers not complying with routine safety checks

These reports would usually be emailed to you automatically by the system when appropriate, helping you to reduce operational costs and to monitor and control risk. The system should also enable you to effectively implement and manage your fleet and risk management policy and further reduce costs through driver education and enforcement. I refer to the old adage that if you can't measure it you can't manage it.

According to recent research conducted by the RAC, nearly a fifth of pool fleet cars may not be roadworthy, leaving businesses exposed to extra costs and possible legal action. In 2008 they conducted checks of over 21,370 pool cars and deemed 16% to be unroadworthy. Almost 8% of vehicles did not have correct fluid levels, 14% did not have the correct tyre tread or tyre pressure and 19% did not have a full service history.

Fleet drivers are causing unnecessary breakdowns, increased maintenance and repair costs due to a lack of basic car maintenance leading to vehicles being off the road for at least 11,757 days a year. This warning came following the RAC estimate that over 40,000 fleet breakdown call-outs could be avoided if fleet drivers conducted basic maintenance checks of their vehicles.

A good fleet system should make it must easier to proactively reduce problems like this.

The DVLA's licence-checking system is valuable to fleet managers but many fleets don't use it. Is there any technology available that can help automate this task?

It is calculated that there are up to one million drivers on the road without a valid driving licence. The Department for Transport and the DVLA estimate these drivers are nine times more likely to be involved in an accident than a qualified licence holder.

The full weight of criminal law is being applied to organisations and individuals whose standards and attitude towards risk and health & safety are far below what could be reasonably expected. Investigators will look into management systems, practices and attitude towards risk, and organisations and individuals that have not assured themselves that they have proper corporate governance of safety in place will be prosecuted.

Regardless of how small the fleet, licence-checking should be the most obvious basic risk management step for all businesses as they get to grips with ever-tougher legislation targeted at improving driver safety and removing dangerous drivers from the UK's roads. Modern fleet management software will incorporate integrated risk management functions that will enable a holistic duty of care approach to be taken. Such software systems will provide automated on-line licence checking with the DVLA at a frequency determined by the 'risk profile' of the driver.

All employees who drive on company business should have their licences validated and any endorsements put on file whether they drive company-provided vehicles or their own. In the past, driver licence checking has always been the Achilles' heel for many fleets. There have been frequent examples of drivers who have shown their employer a paper copy of their licence when they have in fact been banned from driving. In the past, prior to the availability of the on-line link to the DVLA, these rogue drivers were difficult to spot.

For checks to be carried out with the DVLA database, employers must obtain permission by getting the employee to sign a 3 year mandate. Checks can be carried out on-line as frequently as deemed necessary by the company's risk management policy. An initial licence check should be carried out on all employees. Industry best practice then suggests that checks should take place during the new starter recruitment process and follow-up checks should be carried out at regular intervals: 0-3 points annually; 4-8 points every three to six months; 9 points or more monthly.

These periodic checks are carried out automatically by the management software with the following details being returned:

- Licence commencement date
- Expiry date
- Categories
- Restrictions
- Conviction dates
- Offence dates
- Offence code
- Points
- Disqualification until date

The DVLA licence data then updates your records and notifies you immediately of any exceptions or irregularities.

I believe that companies should make it a condition of employment that driving licence checks will be carried out. Companies should ensure that contracts of employment make it clear what actions could be taken against the employee if policy rules on point accumulation are broken. Having undertaken licence checks, the information uncovered should be used by companies to put in place driver information and training programmes.

Today, more driving offences incur points not just fines. Tougher new laws on the use of hand-held mobile phones whilst driving, and penalties for offences such as failing to provide information about the identity of a driver, have increased from three points to six points. With the government also planning to double the penalty for excessive speeding to 6 points the likelihood is that employees who drive on business are ever more likely to have points on their licences.

As a result of increasing legislation, driver audit trails encompassing best practice processes such as driving licence checks will ensure that companies are not only safeguarding themselves against possible prosecution but are introducing a good and caring environment in which their staff can work.

Licence Checking

Do you have any facts and figures showing how much time a fleet manager could save by moving from Excel and a diary system to using a good fleet system instead? And can a good fleet system help reduce the cost of running a car fleet, other than admin costs?

To answer these questions I would like to use a real example of one of our customers. 20:20 and their subsidiary company Phones 4 U is a good example the efficiencies that modern fleet management software brings if it is sourced from the right supplier and implemented appropriately.

Phones 4 U has a fleet of 800 vehicles and 300 cash-for-car drivers. Prior to implementing Jaama's Key 2 Vehicle Management software they were relying on no fewer than 30 spreadsheets and things were slowly grinding to a halt.

In the past Phones 4 U had to register a new employee with the HR team and than manually re-input the details on the payroll. The same details were then added to the fleet database. In addition to the administration cost of repetition, this caused a significant time delay which affected decision making. For example, cars were hired for new starters when spare vehicles were sat around not being used.

Phones 4 U tendered for a fleet software provider whose system focused on automating and cutting out this repetition. Jaama's Key2 Vehicle Management system was chosen as it was simple to integrate with the company's existing HR and payroll system, enabling management to be devolved to subsidiary companies. This put an end to the company-wide 'paper chase' and enabled information to be captured at source from drivers and suppliers who input it themselves online.

Jaama's fleet system now provides the technology at the centre of the company's car fleet management. Phones 4 U are saving many hours of administration time every month as well as thousands of pounds in overall costs. They claim to have cut invoice queries from around 150 a month to almost zero.

In the words of their pensions and benefits manager, "Our move to web-based software has reduced an almost impossible workload and all departments, including fleet, HR and payroll, as well as the fleet administrators in our subsidiary companies are benefiting. The technology is enabling us to capture more information on our fleet so we can be far more proactive and analytical in our management. It is improving operating efficiencies and ultimately reducing costs still further."

I believe that this is an excellent example of a company that understands the importance of choosing fleet technology that can fully integrate with systems operated by external suppliers and other company departments, such as HR, payroll and finance, and that can also be accessed by drivers to enter critical information on-line.

This is rather a large fleet and therefore the savings are significant and not just in terms of administration hours. Phones 4 U are no longer hiring temporary vehicles for new starters when existing vehicles sit unused. Vehicles are being returned to leasing companies on time, reducing contract hire charges. Drivers' vehicle allocations and tax details are recorded immediately meaning Benefit in Kind, P46 calculations and HMRC submissions are less time-consuming. Fuel expenditure has been significantly reduced and driver fines and driver recharges occur quicker and are not overlooked.

Whilst this is a good example of how a large fleet can make savings, much smaller fleet operators can also benefit. Pressure to reduce fleet administration and manage risk was the driving factor behind Abingdon-based Smeg UK opting for Jaama's web-based fleet software. Smeg UK, a leading supplier of prestige domestic appliances, operates a leased fleet of 24 company cars and 14 commercial vehicles. The vehicles are managed from the company's headquarters but are located nationwide and are driven by sales people, product trainers and delivery drivers.

Before implementing a system from Jaama, all the information on vehicles and drivers was held in spreadsheets. Information was often written out by hand and keyed-in to more than one spreadsheet. There was considerable duplication on files.

Smeg UK's assistant accountant who is responsible for the fleet said "Managing the fleet was a significant administration task and the problems increased if I was asked to provide information on either a vehicle or a driver, as the only way I could find it was by trawling through paper files and spreadsheets. It was becoming increasingly difficult to keep track of all aspects of the fleet. Instead of searching through paper trying to find information, I can now access the required information in seconds. Often I'm not even asked for the information as it can be accessed directly by those who require it. It's difficult to quantify the amount of money saved but the technology has contributed to all-round fleet and time-saving efficiencies."

In companies such as Smeg UK it is common for the role of fleet manager to be combined with other corporate responsibilities. Smeg UK is a typical example of companies that contract hire vehicles but still have to manage their vehicles, drivers and duty of care on a daily basis.

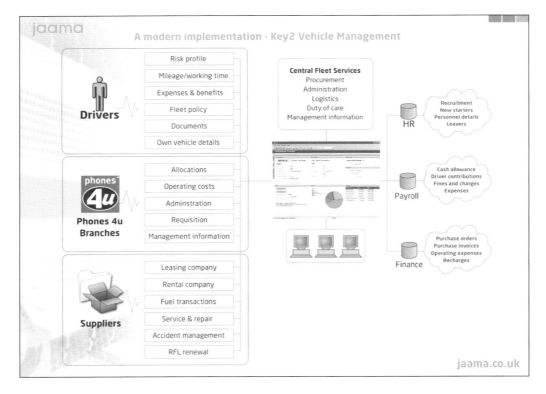

How can a good fleet system help with setting and monitoring management controls and how can 'workflow' technology help a fleet manager do his job?

Fleet software should be much more than a 2 dimensional record keeping system. It should provide a proactive work-flow management tool that performs actions based upon the data held. The better systems will have this functionality built-in and without being too complex they will allow you to configure it to match your own fleet policy and corporate requirements. What follows are examples of these in-built work-flow functions which will help you in automating the management of processes, monitoring of costs and measuring of efficiency.

OPERATIONAL CONTROLS

A good fleet system will let you set operational controls and tolerance levels for exception reporting. They will monitor the information and provide reminders to make sure your fleet is operating as you expect it to. Not only will it remind you when routine tasks and scheduled recurring events are due, it will also let you know when these have not been carried out when expected. Modern technology will send notifications by email or SMS text.

Let me give you an example of how software should manage a vehicle's service, MOT or any scheduled event for a typical fleet. The software will automatically check the due dates recorded on the system and when they are within 30 days, it will send a notification to the driver by email informing them of the date the vehicle must be serviced and the location to be used. The system then sends a further reminder 7 days before the service date.

All being well the driver has the vehicle serviced and confirms the service date on your company intranet but in this example the driver forgets (clearly, that never happens in real life!). The system sees that it has not had this confirmation from the driver nor has it had any associated costs, so 7 days after the expected service date it notifies the driver by email and SMS text that the service is now overdue and that their expenses will no longer be paid. A week later the system again notifies the driver and at this time it informs the fleet controller so they can take action. Notice that this is the first time the fleet controller has had to become involved. This saves valuable management time and means that you only need to get involved with the 'exceptions'.

Eventually, our driver complies, the service is carried out and their expenses are taken off stop. The system calculates the next service due date and the process continues.

My example can be used for any date-driven event and the notification process and response times could be changed to suit your own preferences. Using a combination of the appropriate data and your own policy criteria, fleet software will notify drivers when they are expected to carry out regular safety checks such as tyre tread depths or routine safety inspections. This sort of proactive fleet management is becoming even more important as vehicle service intervals lengthen and they enter the workshop less frequently.

These functions mean that fleet managers are doing everything possible to ensure that maintenance is carried out and that, crucially, they can show in an auditable manner from the software's records that they have managed their fleet in a responsible fashion. This would be a valuable defence in the face of any possible legal action.

These control and notification mechanisms are relevant to all aspects of vehicle management and a good fleet software system will enable you to:

- Monitor cost against budgets
- Track monthly mileage against contract allowances and accrue for variances or suggest you realign your contract
- Identify the most inefficient drivers
- Identify fuel fraud
- Manage risk against a risk assessment strategy
- Identify missing documents
- Predict costs
- Identify unacceptable vehicle downtime

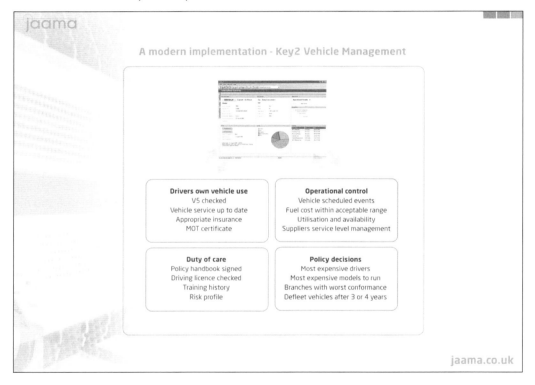

What steps should a fleet manager go through when considering the introduction of a fleet system for the first time?

I have listed below the steps I consider to be relevant and that will need addressing when considering the introduction of a fleet system. You will quickly be able to answer many of the following points if your fleet size is very small but some of them will require greater investigation if you are to make the most of your investment – in both time and money:

- Identify the catalyst(s) for change
- What problems do you currently have, which can be fixed?
- What priority and level of importance do you give to fixing these problems?

- What impact will fixing these problems will have on company departments?
- How will you get buy-in from those affected, including those who will be using the new system and those who won't?
- Identify where the relevant data is currently held, what problems disparate data locations will have and how these need to change
- How will processes and procedures need to change?
- How will the new fleet system's data be loaded initially?
- How integrated can the system become with other software systems?
- How integrated can the system become with data providers?
- Could its implementation impact and improve service from your suppliers?
- What information do you currently receive which could be collected at source and therefore input for you?
- What information do you want to get out of the new fleet system?
- Are there any additional procedures or processes which could also be improved?
- Do you have sufficient resource to undertake the project?
- Will the implementation need a project manager?
- What is your timeframe for completing the implementation?

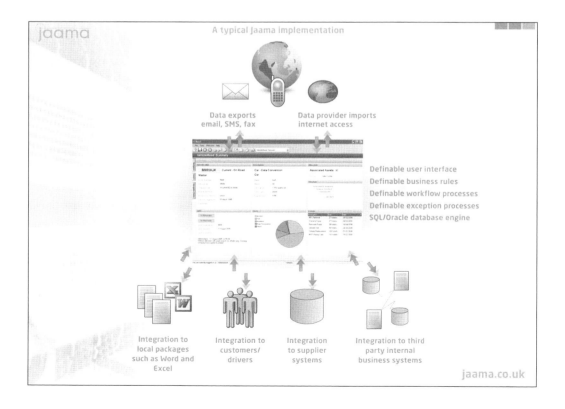

There seems to be a lot of different technology underlying the fleet systems that are available in the market at present; Oracle, SQL, .NET, XML, etc. What do all these acronyms mean?

There are dozens of software acronyms which can be confusing to the uninitiated. Some software companies forget that not everyone is as geeky as they are and tend to pepper conversation and documentation with terminology which is difficult to understand. The acronym examples given above refer to three areas: databases, software development tools and type of data communication.

Like most industries, in recent years the software industry has become more standardised. That's not to say that there is only one standard as that would obviously be far too simple.

Oracle and SQL are types of databases and have each become an industry standard meaning you will likely opt for one of the other. Give any fleet system a wide berth if it doesn't use one of these.

.NET – pronounced dot net – from Microsoft, has become the industry standard web software development programme language. There are different types of .NET but these should be irrelevant to you when choosing fleet software.

XML defines the type of data communication between software systems and has itself become an industry standard. There are others but they are rapidly becoming outdated modes of data transfer.

When choosing a new fleet software system, try not to get too concerned with technology terms. If you only shortlist providers of modern web based systems you will be sure to be investing in the right technology.

Internet solutions seem to be developing fast in many areas of business. Is there a role for these in the management of a car fleet and, if so, what is that role?

Web based internet solutions are not a panacea to all that's wrong. I often overhear sales people saying that 'they can be accessed anywhere in the world'. So what? What's the benefit? That is what I ask. Why would you want to access fleet software from a beach in the Caribbean?

Well let me tell you why.

The benefit of web based internet management systems is that they can be easily accessed without the need for any special software to be installed on your PC, and this provides access mobility. Now the benefit of access mobility is not that you can access your fleet from anywhere in the world; the benefit is that you can open up the collection of data. The collection of data is what modern technology and the internet has revolutionised in recent years and I don't often use the overused word 'revolutionised'. Consider how much money companies are now saving by getting you to do their work for them. Internet banking, internet shopping, on-line tax returns, etc. Each time you sit at your PC or laptop and type in your personal details you are saving someone else the time and money. It is this collection of data which has been revolutionised.

Now imagine your operation and the information you collect. How can you change this collection process so that rather than you being sent bits of paper, emails or faxes, you capture it at source? Information can be captured via a laptop, mobile phone, Blackberry, vehicle black-boxes, and so on. This is the true benefit. So information that used to be sent to a fleet or HR department via paper or email can now be entered once and captured at source. For example, drivers can complete their mileage returns on-line via a company intranet. This will actually be the fleet system which has pages published on the company's intranet which have been configured to match the company's intranet style. The data is validated as the driver types it in. It is checked to see if the mileage entered corresponds to the tolerance level which has been preset and any other validation the company needs. Once the driver has finished and saves the entry, it's in the fleet system and is already triggering the next process which may be an expense claim or management authorisation approval.

Now that's the benefit!

No fleet manager wants to invest in technology that will be obsolete soon. How should they decide which to go for?

There has been a shift in recent years for media to be rented or licensed. Music, TV channels and games are good examples. Most leading suppliers of fleet systems now license their software to customers rather than sell it for a one-off fee. Like all technology, fleet software constantly evolves and the advantage of using it under licence is that most providers will periodically update it to the latest version free of charge. This type of arrangement should eliminate the possibility of the software becoming obsolete.

So if the software itself looks like it will always be up to date, what other areas should you consider when deciding which system to go for? I've listed below in no particular order what I consider to be the key areas you should evaluate:

- Quality – of product and services
- Functionality fit – to your requirements and your culture
- Supplier – capacity, capability and after-sales support
- Service – people and processes
- Value – competitively priced
- Innovation – appropriate use of the industry's latest technology
- Risk – terms and conditions, financial status, contingency
- Software technology platform – modern and industry-standard

What impact will the implementation of a fleet system have on other departments?

Operating in today's global economy brings intense pressures for companies to continually operate their businesses more efficiently and effectively. They must continually improve operation controls and information reporting to meet the conflicting demands of higher quality products, better levels of service and lower costs. Meeting these challenges is difficult and the greater the fleet size the more difficult the task becomes. The good news is that the greater the challenge, the greater the opportunity.

The impact a fleet system implementation will have on other departments depends entirely upon the return on resource investment. Earlier I gave two very different examples of fleet system customers. The first, Phones 4 U, rolled out a fully integrated system whereby a new employee's details including start date and job grade would be entered into a HR system. These would then be passed electronically to the fleet system which would automatically trigger either an existing vehicle on fleet to be allocated or a requisition to be approved for an appropriate hire vehicle.

To achieve this level of automation, a business workflow process had to be drawn up and then analysts had to specify the flow of data and trigger-rules on how to manage the exceptions. Clearly, this took time and the involvement and agreement of many departments. The end result was impressive and turned many dozens of manual processes into automated electronic events. The resultant annual cost saving far outweighed the investment required, making the exercise worthwhile.

In my second example of Smeg UK, their fleet has only a handful of vehicles so there would be no point in trying to achieve the same level of departmental integration. However there would still be an impact on other departments because no department operates in isolation. Where interactions between departments exist – usually communication and information exchange - thought will need to be given as to what will be affected and what can be improved.

So the impact that a fleet software system implementation will have on other departments will depend upon the desired end result, the likely benefit of resource investment and the current and desired communication and information exchange between departments.

What consideration needs to be given to how a fleet system will interact with other software systems?

Even the smallest fleet operators are unlikely to require fleet software which interacts with no other software system. For example, most new fleet software users will import vehicle and driver data from Excel.

Fleet software can import and export data in many different formats and modern systems will be able to achieve this as a scheduled service or by on-event processing, without any manual intervention. This information data exchange can occur between both internal and external systems. For example, vehicle ordering and delivery details with suppliers, submissions from drivers, telematics data from vehicles and so on. These data-flows enable information to move around company systems with them in effect 'talking' to each other.

What follows are some examples of typical data imports and exports:

Data imports:
- Fuel transactions
- Maintenance transactions
- Driver information
- Vehicle orders
- Contract hire charges
- Driver's mileage and journey log
- Driver's hours
- Vehicle telematics data
- Supplier invoices
- Road Fund Licence renewals
- Finance rates
- Vehicle make, model and financial data
- Tyre charges

Data exports:
- Purchase ledger transactions
- Approved invoices
- Cost accruals
- Driver vehicle allocation movements
- HMRC on-line P11D submissions
- Motor Insurance Database vehicles on/off insurance submissions
- Payroll deductions
- Driver vehicle contributions
- Accident claims

How can Jaama help a fleet manager automate the fleet department?

To achieve automation, fleet software needs to have the ability to capture the necessary information, the functionality to process it accordingly and the ability to produce the required outputs. For example, to automate the 'vehicles that require servicing' process, it must capture the service date, check whether it is due and then provide an alert notification to the driver or fleet manager at the appropriate time.

Successful systems will achieve this through a simple design requiring the minimum amount of initial configuration and understanding. They will offer many choices when it comes to when and how notifications are received and who receives them.

Jaama's Key2 Vehicle Management software achieves this by using the latest web-based technology. This delivers widespread usage availability, flexibility and industry standard communication methods such as automated email, SMS, fax, Microsoft Word and Excel. Our software does not just hold data records and produce list-based reports on demand. It has been specifically designed by fleet industry experts to provide a platform to allow fleet operators to choose the level and method of automation required. Automation is at the centre of our software system's design and is driven by condition-based workflow process management. For example, if the vehicle is allocated to a driver and is within a week of its service due date, notify the driver by SMS text. These condition types are preset, so in most cases there is no complex set-up need. You simply select the required functionality from configuration menus. Communication can be with drivers, other departments, managers, suppliers, customers and even other software systems.

There are many areas of running a fleet that involve managing scheduled events and tasks. Jaama's Key2 Vehicle Management software is developed around an active event and task management system which enables scheduled events and tasks to be processed with minimum manual intervention. This functionality enables fleet operators to implement and run best practice fleet and risk management policies with minimum time, effort and cost.

Jason Francis
Managing Director
Jaama Ltd

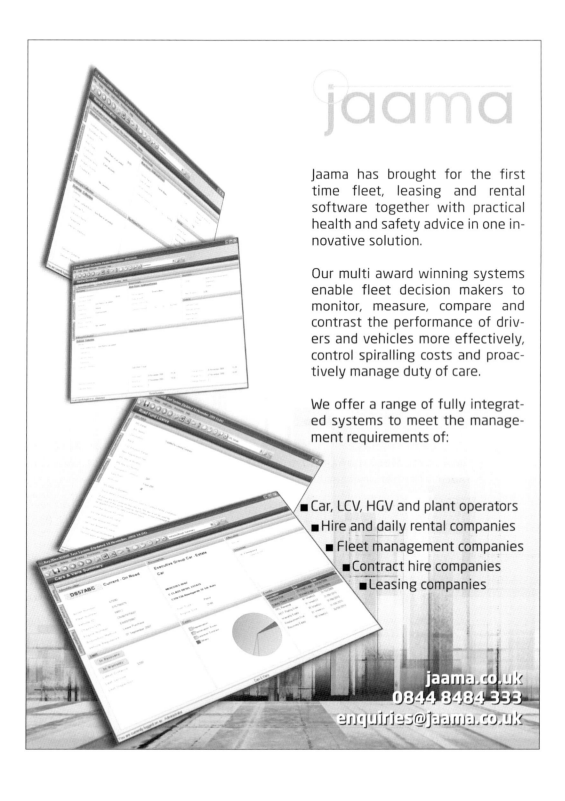

CREDIT HIRE AND ACCIDENT MANAGEMENT

Chris Ashworth

Head of Sales and Marketing

Drive Assist UK

Please introduce yourself and explain the services your company provides to business fleets.

I am Head of Sales and Marketing at Drive Assist UK one of the UK's largest accident management companies. I have worked in the accident management industry for 15 years, the last 6 with Drive Assist. My role involves dealing with all aspects of the business relationships and development thereof and I am fortunate to work with a wide range of companies from insurers, brokers and repairers to fleet managers and individual companies.

Accident management services have been available for decades but some fleet managers may not know much about these. What is accident management?

For me, accident management is a service that complements a traditional insurance relationship to provide something that best fits the needs of an individual fleet manager or company.

Accident management comes in a number of different forms and guises; as such there is no 'off the shelf' solution, just like the needs of an individual following an accident almost all of the accident management solutions that currently exist are different.

Typically, accident management solutions can comprise some or all of the following services:

· Claims notification, sometimes referred to as FNOL (First Notification of Loss)

· Vehicle repair management

· Replacement vehicle hire

· Credit hire

· Third party capture

· Uninsured loss recovery

· Legal services and personal injury claims handling

The scope of services provided will depend on a number of variable factors including but not limited to the capability of the service provider, the size and needs of the individual fleet, whether there is an existing fleet management function and the type of insurance cover held by the fleet. (For example, third party only fleets have a much bigger gap in their insurance cover that needs to be complimented by an in-house or outsourced accident management function).

One thing I would say is that however robust the current arrangements or in-house offering, every single fleet out there would benefit from assistance in some or all of the areas mentioned.

What are the benefits to a fleet manager of using an accident management service rather than just leaving it up to his insurance company?

Like the range of services offered, the benefits derived by the fleet manager are varied and dependant on a number of factors, not least the existing arrangements they have in place.

However, I believe the main benefits a fleet manager should be looking to create or improve are:

- Improved cost management and control leading to lower insurance premiums
- Improved work-force mobility - keeping the team mobile is key to sustaining earnings
- Reduced vehicle down-time and loss of use
- Generation of revenue streams to off-set against the cost of fleet ownership

The most significant benefit a fleet manager should be looking for is flexibility in a provider so that a solution that is bespoke to their exact requirements can be created to deliver the right balance of cost v service and seamless integration with the existing process.

Credit hire arrived on the UK fleet scene nearly 20 years ago but here again it may be unknown to some fleet managers. What is it and how does it work?

Essentially, credit hire is the provision of a replacement vehicle following a non-fault accident, with the charges being recovered directly from the negligent party's insurer under agreed terms.

As you say, credit hire has been around for over 20 years, however it has not really penetrated the fleet market to the same levels as other areas of the insurance market.

I believe that this is due to a number of factors which include the fact that fleets have access to pool cars / spare replacement vehicles or are accustomed to simply paying for hire cars as and when required. Additionally, the more traditional fleet brokers have been slow to offer accident management solutions to their fleets, favouring instead the insurer's one size fits all solution.

As we know, there is also a school of thought that suggests fleets only ever have fault accidents and whilst this is clearly not the case, data suggests that fleets are still much slower to report accidents, so it is more difficult to make the best of the situation.

What are the benefits to a fleet manager of using a credit hire service rather than just leaving it up to his insurance company?

The primary benefit should always be that your employee, the fleet driver, will be mobile quickly and in an appropriate vehicle to ensure they are able to continue their business with minimal inconvenience.

In addition to this there is a clear opportunity to save current expenditure on replacement vehicle hire.

Depending on the service provider, there may also be referral fees available from credit hire operators which are usually absorbed by the insurer or broker if not controlled by the fleet manager, and these can be used to further reduce fleet costs.

The credit hire industry has fought a long battle with the insurance industry. What is the current position?

This is true, however the industry has matured to it's current size and level of acceptability by reaching agreement / protocols with the majority of the insurance companies, the most common of which is known as the ABI General Terms of Agreement for Replacement Vehicle Hire (GTA).

The protocols typically set out a way of working and fee structures to ensure claims and associated costs are managed appropriately and that insurers settle claims promptly.

The very high level of acceptance of credit hire by major insurers can be seen by the fact that they offer credit hire to their own policyholders when presented with the opportunity to do so.

Like many industries there are still, however, less ethical operators who do not operate under protocols such as the GTA and look to unecessarily inflate the costs of claims, which is clearly not beneficial to the consumer in any way.

How big are the accident management and credit hire industries?

Accident management is a broad description for a service that comprises of a number of different products and solutions, so it is very difficult to provide a precise answer to this question. Accident management services can literally be applied to any motor vehicle accident (of which there are several million per annum).

Credit hire as a stand-alone service is currently provided to around 500,000 customers per annum, and this figure has grown exponentially over the last 3-5 years as the market has become saturated and the majority of insurers have adopted the services of the major credit hire players.

The credit hire market itself is a little like the UK motor market, with a relatively small number of large providers and a large number of smaller operators.

As with the motor market the top 3-5 companies have in excess of 65% market share. However there are at least 70 companies that currently subscribe to the 1st tier of the GTA where nation-wide coverage is a requirement.

In truth many of the smaller operators will outsource the service outside of their own local catchment area, in what is a highly competitive market.

What other services does your industry offer?

As credit hire is provided after a non-fault accident, many of the services traditionally provided by credit hire companies focus on these claims, typically involving credit repair, uninsured loss recovery and personal injury compensation.

The larger credit hire organisations have evolved their propositions to include all of the above along with the comprehensive accident management solutions as described previously.

In essence, companies in this sector differentiate themselves from traditional insurance claims handling service by being flexible, and reacting quickly in a rapidly changing environment.

I can honestly say that across our top 20 blue chip clients, no two solutions are identical. Equally, constant evolution means that none of these solutions are the same today as they were at inception.

Our approach is to build a suite of services that fit your exact requirements in the most financially attractive manner, it's not a case of service at any cost but more the service you want at a price you want to pay.

In actual fact many of the solutions we provide are income-generative and you would be amazed at the level of additional service you can obtain on a cost-neutral basis in comparision to those offered by a traditional insurer.

It seems like this industry must produce a mountain of paperwork!

The entire motor claims process is very cumbersome in terms of process duplication and associated paperwork. Replacement vehicle provision in general is also burdensome on the environment.

Whilst we are working at an industry level to eliminate duplication and find smarter ways of exchanging information to reduce cost and improve the customer jouney, we have also taken a good look at our own business to see where improvements can be made.

In 2005 we invested in, and developed a bespoke hand-held delivery software solution which has eliminated over 1.5million sheets of paper from our rental process and reduced annual mileage by c3 million miles.

This system is still unique in the rental industry today and as well as providing the benefits outlined above there have been obvoius environmental benefits, along with an ability for us to get the right car to the right customer more quickly, something that is key to the fleet operator.

What developments have there been in the accident management or credit hire sectors in the last few years that have been particularly valuable to fleet managers?

The most significant development would be acceptance / adoption of our services by insurers. This has legitimised the provision of credit hire services such that it is now a viable and appropriate service for the fleet operator.

Equally, the expansion in the range of services provided by the leading accident management companies has meant that solutions are more ideally tailored to the needs and demands of the fleet market.

On a similar note, expansion of these companies' vehicle fleets in terms of the range of vehicles available has made the services more attractive and appropriate for the needs of the fleet manager.

Is anything happening now, or will anything be happening soon, that is likely to change the accident-related landscape for fleet managers?

One thing that is consistent within the motor claims industry is change; however for the fleet manager I do not see any changes that should detract from his key focus of cost containment and optimum vehicle utilisation.

In fact, it is probably more the economic climate that is driving change with increased premiums and higher costs of ownership being more key than ever as businesses are subjected to increasing financial pressures.

Adoption of an accident management solution that will help a fleet operator achieve these objectives more easily has never been more important.

If you were to advise a fleet manager on the best practice when it comes to accident management, what would that advice be?

My advice would be to select a partner that understands the needs of your business and is flexible and adaptable enough to produce a solution that fits your exact requirements.

Scale, nation-wide coverage and financial stability should also be key selection criteria but this should not detract from the requirement that they must be able to provide you with the highest levels of service and attention, even if your fleet is relatively small.

Also look for companies that actually provide some of the core services directly rather than a company that just brokers a number of different outsourcing arrangements on your behalf. That way you will typically get better value for money and improved financial returns.

Finally, I would always ensure you chose an ethical company that looks to work within the industry agreements that currently exist, such as the GTA. Whilst there may be more money on the table from other companies, it is important that your accident management solution works in harmony with your insurance provider otherwise delays and additional costs will be incurred.

And if you were to advise a fleet manager on the best practice when it comes to the use of a credit hire service, what would that advice be?

In actual fact my advice is similar with the additional requirement of ensuring the supplier has a substantial and appropriate vehicle fleet that suits the needs of your particular business.

Other than that, all of the above principles apply to ensure appropriate partners are selected.

How can Drive Assist help fleet managers?

Drive Assist is ideally placed to help fleet managers achieve a number of key objectives including but not limited to:

- Reduction in costs
- Improved utilisation of vehicle fleet
- Income generation
- Reduction in number of claims made against insurance policy to help maintain / reduce premiums.

The business is currently handling in excess of 400,000 claims per annum and we have a vehicle fleet in excess of 19,000 vehicles.

With 19 locations around the UK and our unique vehicle delivery software, we can delivery vehicles promptly to any location across the UK.

Our call centres have the latest systems and telephony solutions to ensure our dedicated operational teams can deliver the highest levels of service and customer satisfaction.

Our approach is simple: we listen to your needs and provide no cost / obligation recommendations based on our findings.

We then work closely with the fleet operator to ensure a seamless delivery of the solution along with KPIs and Management Information to ensure quality of delivery

In conclusion, there is no cost involved in asking us to consider a solution and if we are unable to improve on the current service, we will say so.

Chris Ashworth
Head of Sales and Marketing
Drive Assist UK

25 FLEET ANALYTICS – A VIEW FROM AUSTRALIA

> **Mark Bernard**
> Director
> Fleet Software & Services Pty Ltd, Melbourne, Australia

Please introduce yourself and your business

I own and operate a fleet consultancy business called Fleet Software and Services Pty Ltd based in Australia (and happy to work internationally). I have spent about 25 years working in organisations involved in the Automotive and Fleet Industries. My career commenced with Shell and BHP and I worked with a small team to introduce LPG as an alternative automotive fuel for taxi and fleet operators in Australia. After Shell, I worked with Hertz Rent a Car, running their Franchise Operations in Australia (and parts of Asia) and then as General Manager, Hertz Car Leasing. I then took a year off to study in Switzerland (MBA-IMD) and worked in the United Kingdom with Nortel for a couple of years, before returning to Australia to start a new fleet leasing company, InterCity Lease Management, backed by Australia's largest franchise dealer group.

On the sale of InterCity Lease Management, we operated as the Kerridge Systems Master Distributor in Australia and New Zealand for most of 1990's and in the later 1990's as the distributor for David Henley Systems. During the Internet boom, I temporarily left the fleet industry to be CEO and director of a number of small ASX-listed technology and telecommunications companies for 5 years, before returning the fleet industry as an independent Fleet Consultant in late 2004.

How did you develop your interest in fleet analytics?

I have been operating as a fleet management consultant for the last 4 years having spent 20 years working in various corners of fleet management business.

We thought it might be time for some fresh thinking on a couple of thorny old chestnuts that have been around the fleet management industry for a long time.

So, we have looked to develop some new approaches to some common challenges in fleet management. As a result we initiated a number of research and development projects with the University of Melbourne, initially on vehicle replacement modeling (and optimisation) and then building vehicle valuation models, optimal reserve setting models and new vehicle valuation software.

In the last 3 years we have developed expertise in data mining and predictive analytics. We have used these new and innovative techniques to develop new approaches to two long term fleet industry issues; optimum replacement cycles and optimal vehicle remarketing strategies.

Why should Fleet Managers be interested in fleet analytics?

The practice of fleet management generates a lot of data. However, our observation was that this data was never properly 'mined' to generate a better understanding of fleet management problems, business and cost models and perhaps generate new knowledge or even possibly 'fleet intelligence' on vehicle cost behaviors. You could argue that the purpose of fleet analytics is to find out what other people do not know.

In the end, the benefit of fleet analytics is to predict what will happen in the future and decide the best decision to make right now.

Fleet analytics seeks to answer some previously unanswerable questions in the practice and processes of fleet management. We are using fleet analytics to find, and model, interesting relationships buried in the sea of fleet management data currently resident in fleet management systems the world over.

For example, we have used fleet analytics to improve the quality of vehicle remarketing decisions. We have isolated and quantified the value of vehicle colours and certain vehicle options on used vehicle values. We can now detect small differences in auction house sales value differences in 'head to head' auction house performance 'shoot-outs'. We have modeled and quantified successive best bids for vehicles in subsequent auction appearances and we are currently modeling sale value differences created by different sales methods (internet sales, fixed price sales, auction sales, etc).

We also use our vehicle valuation model as an important component to predict vehicle depreciation for our vehicle replacement model.

How can fleet analytics help fleet managers and fleet operators?

Fleet analytics can help fleet managers make better decisions about vehicle selection, vehicle replacement; vehicle remarketing (getting more money for off lease or used company vehicles), electronic vehicle use analysis and vehicle use pattern recognition.

More generally, we think it can be used to tackle the common, but challenging fleet management decisions, with fresh thinking and innovative approaches.

The latest data mining and predictive analytics software can be used to explore and discover new and interesting relationships in the ocean of fleet management data.

We also like to try and implement our new approaches with software applications (prototypes) that allow people to automate fleet business processes and improve and automate their fleet management decision making processes.

More recently, we have used in-vehicle telematics devices to determine the optimal fleet size for pooled or shared vehicle fleets running between 800 to 1,000 pool vehicles.

Let me explain how fleet analytics can be applied to three issues in fleet management:

- Optimal replacement cycles
- Optimal vehicle remarketing strategies
- Optimal fleet size for pooled fleets

We outline below the story of our journey into fleet analytics, what we discovered along the way, and what we would still like to know, and do.

In my life as a fleet management consultant there are always two recurrent questions that I am frequently asked. These could be called the two 'R's'

- Replacement: When is the best time to replace my vehicles?
- Remarketing: How do I get the most money for my used vehicles?

On the courses we run in Australia and across Asia, there are always two topics that people always want from the course content:

- Fleet optimisation
- Fleet utilisation

We have tried to find new ways to think about fleet replacement decisions, fleet utilisation (or vehicle use efficiency) and more generally fleet optimisation decisions. The major fleet optimisation challenges are to arrive at decisions about:

- Optimal fleet size
- Optimal fleet mix
- Optimal vehicle use
- Optimal vehicle allocation

How did you start your journey into fleet analytics?

The first place to start was to see what the academic research (papers, journals and publications) had to say on 'approaches' to these issues and whether these approaches and methods could be easily applied to practical fleet management problems.

While we reviewed a number of 'theoretical' approaches in journal articles, we could not find (and our student contractors and senior lecturers could not find) any academic material that had any real or applied practical benefit to making optimal fleet management decisions.

So we had to start, and invest in, our own applied fleet management research.

We even thought of starting a not for profit Fleet Research Foundation to undertake this work The Foundation could be tasked to find practical solutions to common fleet management problems.

These fleet management problems could include:

- What is the optimal fleet supply to meet my mobility and transport requirements in terms of optimal fleet size and optimal fleet mix?
- What is an optimum replacement cycle and how would you determine what it is?
- Why are vehicle replacements cycles fixed in terms of time and distance (at the beginning of the vehicle life)? Is there a case for variable replacement cycles set dynamically during the term as vehicle use changes and changes in used vehicle markets occur?
- What can we do to monitor, measure, manage and ultimately improve vehicle use efficiency (utilisation) and what is the business case for using in-vehicle telematics devices to achieve this objective?

We will briefly touch on parts of our journey and findings in four areas:

1 Optimum replacement cycles
2 Variable replacement cycles
3 Vehicle remarketing decisions
4 Vehicle use management

1 Optimum replacement cycles

The choice of vehicle replacement cycles has a major influence on the capital required to finance a fleet operation and determines the future costs of vehicle operation.

The good thing about vehicle replacement decisions is that they can be easily changed with the stroke of a pen.

When we are asked to review replacement policies of various fleets, we are always surprised at the variation of replacement cycles in terms of time and distance. Why is that similar fleets being used in similar applications have such different replacement cycles? We always ask for the rationale for this replacement rule and we seldom find an evidence-based answer.

We propose the reason is that there is no underlying 'theory' of vehicle replacement. And because there is no theory of vehicle replacement, fleet managers have no 'guiding light' or decision framework as to the best replacement policy.

There are two critical costs that determine the optimal replacement cycle decisions; the marginal cost of future depreciation and the marginal cost of service, maintenance and repairs.

The economic perspective (rule) is that you should replace the vehicle at the bottom of the average cost curve or where marginal cost will start to rise with future use. This will occur when the marginal cost of service, maintenance and repairs exceeds the change in vehicle value (depreciation) over the same time period.

When we calculated this point for a typical fleet vehicle doing 20,000 kms pa we found the economic optimum replacement period to be about 8-9 years or about 160,000 to 180,000 kms. Where vehicles are used in more severe operating environments the term may be shorter, due to a higher rate of maintenance expenditure. Whilst this might be the optimum it is hard to see people applying the optimum replacement rule.

However, we have seen very cost-conscious companies running vehicles to 150,000 to 180,000 kms (about 100,000 miles) where vehicles are doing 30,000 kpa and above. Essentially their replacement rule is 5 years or 150,000 kms. This will produce the lowest cost per month or year or the lowest cost per distance (km). So, why do firms use an average replacement cycle of between 2 to 4 years? The current replacement practice (theory?) seems to both increase the cost of vehicle operation and increase the amount of capital required to finance the fleet. But, why do organisations do this?

Having researched this area we have come to the view that a reasonable case exists for new replacement rules (rather than just time and distance based rules).

We would like to suggest a new replacement rule and to encourage you to think about variable replacement cycles that reward reduced vehicle use, better vehicle selection and capital conservation.

2 VARIABLE REPLACEMENT CYCLES

We have been increasingly thinking about how to think about replacement cycles. Our view is that organisations will not adopt the optimum replacement cycle or the lowest average monthly cost rule. So, the challenge was to see if we could come up with a new and better replacement rule. We think we have. We call it the minimum depreciation rule.

Depreciation is the largest and most manageable vehicle cost, followed by maintenance costs. Depreciation typically represents 30-45% of total operating costs. Therefore, the focus should be on depreciation and more specifically depreciation per month and depreciation per distance travelled.

The normal vehicle replacement rules can be described as:

- Time only
- Distance only
- Time and distance
- Time or distance (whichever occurs first)

The vehicle replacement strategy defines when an organisation should replace its fleet vehicles. Most organisations currently use time or distance vehicle replacement rules.

Vehicle depreciation is one major vehicle cost that can be actively managed by appropriate vehicle selection in conjunction with 'optimum' replacement rules. Why not make vehicle replacement decisions change dynamically as 'things' change?

We think the logic for using the minimum depreciation rule is as follows:

- The cost of vehicle ownership (and use) to an organisation is its real deprecation cost over the time of its ownership. Therefore, the aim should be to minimise the deprecation cost over the required use period.

- The deprecation cost per period is a direct linear function of purchase price and disposal value divided by the replacement time period (term). Mathematically it is defined as

$$\frac{\text{Purchase Price less Disposal Value}}{\text{Term}}$$

- Therefore, a lower purchase price or higher disposal value relative to the purchase price (ie a higher residual value ratio) or a longer term will result in a lower deprecation cost per period.

In the end, the organisation wants to be able to accurately budget for depreciation and know future cost of vehicle ownership.

The result of the minimum depreciation rule is that:

- vehicles with lower purchase prices are replaced relatively sooner than vehicles with relatively higher purchase prices – you can have a more expensive vehicle you just to drive it for a longer period

- vehicles with high residual value ratios are replaced sooner than vehicles with lower residual value ratios – if you select a low depreciation vehicle you can change your vehicle more frequently

In practice, better vehicle decisions are rewarded with a new vehicle and a more frequent vehicle changeover.

We believe the benefits of the minimum depreciation rule are:

- Simple accurate vehicle cost budgeting – depreciation cost never exceeds the budgeted depreciation (no surprises and no profit and loss on sale).

- Minimises discretionary vehicle use – the lower the vehicle kilometres per period the sooner the vehicle can be replaced (compared to the current situation that rewards distance travelled with a new vehicle sooner).

- Everybody is focused on cost minimisation – the vehicle custodian is focused on minimising depreciation in the vehicle selection process and vehicle use processes – rather than getting the most expensive vehicle often with the lowest retained value.

We propose the introduction of this simple new rule to change the current 'replacement policies' and to change the focus to managing and monitoring depreciation on a regular basis.

The running depreciation rule rewards good vehicle selection with early replacement, accommodates opportunities that arise in a changing used vehicle market (see remarketing modeling) and substantially improves the accuracy of vehicle cost budgeting. (A table of high variations in book profit and loss normally shows the weakness in the standard approach.)

We would also propose the introduction of another simple rule; that depreciation should not exceed $250/1,000km.

Our preferred dual replacement rule for passenger vehicles is that yearly depreciation should be capped at $5,000 and depreciation should not exceed $250/1,000km.

When these two tests are met the vehicle can be replaced and these replacement parameters will vary by vehicle type.

We would like to see organisations adopt our new minimum depreciation rule. Our recommendation is to consider adopting the $5,000 per year (or $400 per month) minimum depreciation rule for all passenger and light commercial vehicles. The vehicles' depreciation cost per month can be calculated regularly and when the depreciation cost per month reaches a minimum of $400 per month then a new vehicle replacement request can be raised.

However, in order to (mathematically) model future replacement cycles, you need to be able to calculate the value of a vehicle at any time in the future for any vehicle age and vehicle distance (odometer) combination.

This led to us to develop software that could calculate a vehicle value and to investigate what determines a current vehicle value. We call this the vehicle valuation model.

3 VEHICLE REMARKETING DECISIONS

There are about 20 vehicle, vehicle use and sale attributes that determine the value of a used vehicle. We have been progressively building more variables into the model to get increasing levels of vehicle value accuracy.

The predictive analytics model and software is currently able to value a fleet (high-volume) vehicle within 2.5% of the actual sale value. This is about as accurate as a vehicle trader (wholesaler) and on some vehicle models the vehicle valuation software is more accurate than a trader.

The one variable we would like to incorporate into our vehicle valuation model is a standardised measure of vehicle condition. Currently this does not exist (at least in Australia) and we have encouraged some major sellers and auction houses to consider this vehicle condition metric as part of the disposal process.

Our vehicle valuation model allows us to isolate and quantify the differences in vehicle value caused by different vehicle attributes and different sale attributes.

Some of the vehicle (static) attributes that affect vehicle resale value include:
- Vehicle body type
- Vehicle transmission type
- Vehicle drive type
- Vehicle colour

And there are many more!

The vehicle use (dynamic) attributes that affect vehicle resale value include:

- Vehicle age
- Vehicle odometer
- Vehicle condition

These are also the variables we use to determine depreciation in our replacement modeling.

In addition, vehicle resale values are affected by when you sell, how you sell, who you use to sell and what sale method you use to sell the vehicle. These can be summarised by:

- Sale timing (month)
- Sale agent
- Sale location
- Sale method

In addition, you would also want to set an 'optimum' vehicle reserve value to maximise used vehicle sale values; so you don't reject a best bid 'never to be repeated' or to achieve a particular clearance rate.

We use the latest neural network (machine learning) modeling, prediction and self training software to build these vehicle valuation models.

We have used this newly developed valuation model to develop vehicle valuation software (VVS) and we have used the VVS on a number of recent consulting projects.

We also use these valuation models to undertake a number of consulting assignments that had not been possible before the use of this advanced machine learning (predictive analytics) software.

We used our vehicle valuation software on one government department to address these questions from our client:

> Quantify the effect of each vehicle colour on vehicle value (all other things being equal) and determine the total improvement in vehicle sale values if we banned the 5 colours with the worst resale values and replaced them with the 5 colours with the best resale values.

The result was a revenue improvement exceeding $0.5 million per year.

The chart below shows the effect of vehicle colour on used vehicles sale values (all other things being equal). The analysis shows the price effect of a vehicle colour across three related, but different vehicle models.

The most interesting aspect is the price effect of vehicle colour on different vehicle models. Heron (White) receives about $500 less than the average of all colours on an Executive Sedan, but 'White' reduces the price of a V8 Sports Model by over $2,000. However, Yellow Devil (Bright Yellow) increases the used vehicle value by $700 (above the average of all colours) and commands a premium of nearly $3,000 over a white version of a V8 Sports Model.

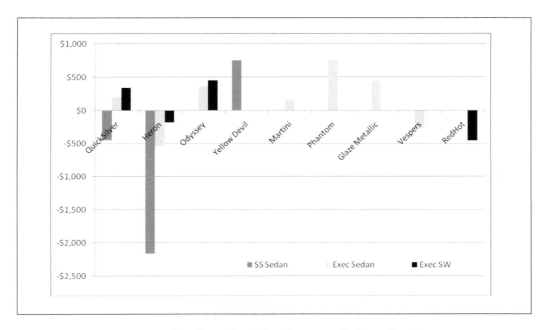

Figure 1: The effect of vehicle colour on vehicle resale values

Everybody is aware of the seasonal influence on used vehicle value. We used our vehicle valuation software to estimate the seasonal effect of sale month (for each month) for each vehicle model.

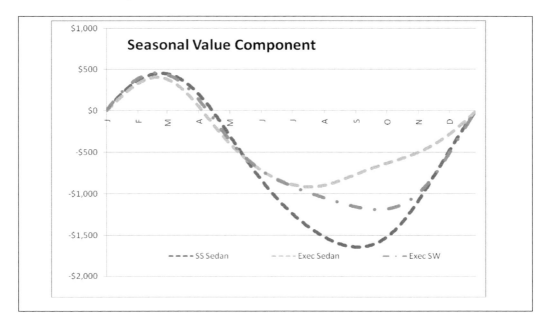

Figure 2: The effect of Sale Month of used vehicle values

This chart shows the effect of sale month on different vehicle models. The vehicle valuation model can quantify the difference, by model, by month and shows that the difference between the worst sale month and best sale month is $1,500 on Executive Sedans and $2,200 on the SS Sedan (all other things being equal). We have used the seasonal valuation component and the volume effect valuation component (see below) derived from our vehicle valuation software to model and optimise the sale timing and disposal volumes for a fleet with 4,000 disposals per year.

We then investigated a number of vehicle replacement scenarios.

The first was take 30% of the vehicles sold in the lowest seasonal sale value months and sell those vehicles in the 3 months with the highest sale value.

This required us to select the model that had the highest relative seasonal effect on vehicle model (the worst seasonal impact in $ terms) and sell it in the month where its value was the greatest.

In other words, the software would select the optimum number and type of vehicles to maximise the revenue from the 130-odd vehicle sale month changes. The software also made adjustments for different vehicle age and kilometres when moving the vehicles sale month forward and backward in time. This essentially modeled the benefit of variable replacement cycles. We found a net benefit exceeding $0.85 million per year.

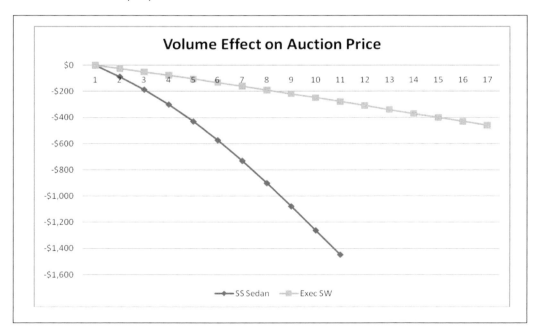

Figure 3: The effect of vehicle sales volumes on the used vehicle value at auction (volume effect)

This chart shows the effect on resale values of increasing sales volumes for two different vehicle models. The SS sedan is a V8 Sports vehicle where vehicle demand is limited and relatively elastic and increased supply has a significant negative impact on used vehicle auction prices – the 7th vehicle sale will get a value $1,000 lower than the 1st vehicle sale.

However, the demand curve for a fleet station wagon is relatively inelastic with the 15th sale at the same auction only reducing the vehicle price by $400. We have used this model to maximise vehicle resale values for organisations with highly standardised fleets by optimising the distribution of vehicles across sales agents (Auction Houses) and sales methods.

The point is that we can now predict and quantify these differences so we can compare the financial effects of different remarketing decisions and undertake programmed and predicted volume balancing.

In another project, we recently worked for a finance company that sells about 4,000 repossessed vehicles per year.

Our client gave us the challenge to increase sales revenue by an extra 5% from the sale of their repossessed vehicles using our 'smart software'. The agreement required us to prove (using an independent statistical control) that we could get a premium over and above what they would normally get for their vehicles (all other things being equal) using vehicle valuation software (or what we like to call our intelligent remarketing service).

The commercial agreement said we would share the additional used vehicle sale revenue on 30%/70% basis. We agreed and the project has started.

We back-tested their current auction allocation strategy against a random allocation (an allocation of vehicles to auction houses and sales agents by random numbers). We found the random allocation generated gross sales revenue 2% higher than the finance company's current auction allocation strategy. This indicated that their existing remarketing strategy was basically delivering less sales revenue than a random allocation across their sales agents.

We then showed that by isolating and quantifying auction house performance differences by vehicle model, vehicle age, vehicle age odometer and predicted vehicle value we could improve used vehicle sales revenues.

We showed that our vehicle valuation software could generate additional returns over and above the random allocation by in the region of 2.0%-2.5%.

This result has got us close to the target 5% and this result is worth well over $1.0 million extra sales revenue per year and we now trying to finesse the sale method to get up to an extra 1%.

In conclusion, these changes are relatively easy to implement and in our view represent quick easy wins for a finance company or corporate fleet operator.

Our current research is to investigate the effect of sale method (Retail, Internet [Online], Direct Client Sales, Auction, Dealer or Wholesaler) on used vehicle values.

As part of this research we are also looking at the effect of simultaneous internet sales on auction prices.

Another issue we are currently investigating is the answer to the question: What is the return on investment (higher sale values) on vehicle pre-sale preparation?

There also are three areas we plan to research in the coming year.

- Setting of optimal vehicle reserve values for auction sales
- Detection of vehicle trading arbitrage opportunities
- Automated used vehicle trading strategies and software

4 VEHICLE USE MANAGEMENT

The traditional focus of fleet management has predominately been on vehicle management. We would argue that future gains in fleet management will come from vehicle use management.

Over the years, we have been asked to undertake a number of fleet use reviews, more often called 'utilisation studies'.

Traditionally, the only existing source of vehicle use data has been vehicle logbooks. This required keying data from paper logbooks initially into EXCEL and then verifying and consolidating these records in a SQL database.

We then developed software to investigate unauthorised (non-complaint) vehicle use, vehicle use ratios (utilisation) and vehicle use patterns (trip distance, trip duration and location analysis) and we then determined the optimal number of vehicles required to meet the current demand for vehicles.

After undertaking a number of these projects, we looked for a better way to monitor vehicle use.

We have monitored the recent developments in telematics and have watched the quality of these services improve and the range of services increase over time and most importantly the cost of commercial telematics services decline over time.

We have now undertaken a number of projects on what we call vehicle use management using the latest telematics (GPS) devices to better understand how vehicles are used. We now use this electronic journey data to calculate the maximum and optimal number of vehicle required to meet a certain vehicle demand.

Recently, we have used these telematics services as a consulting tool for undertaking fleet (vehicle) use reviews to better understand vehicle use patterns and to derive the optimal fleet size.

A recent project involved renting 20 telematics units from a telematics service provider. We selected two representative samples of vehicles and electronically monitored vehicle use for a two continuous 45 day periods on the two 20 vehicle samples.

We designed and developed a vehicle use analysis framework and employed two PhDs in Computer Science to develop vehicle use analysis software.

The purpose of vehicle use analysis software is to take raw electronic trip records and convert them into management information (intelligence) that can be used to make better evidence-based fleet size decisions and to investigate vehicle use patterns.

Unfortunately, we are unable to reproduce, in this book, the colour 3D visual vehicle use analysis we have recently developed.

However, this software now allows us to automate the vehicle use analysis process and deliver a set of vehicle use analyses based on real time 100% accurate electronic location vehicle trip records. We have developed the following:

- Optimal fleet size analysis – determines the optimal fleet size for a given vehicle demand profile
- Vehicle demand and use profile – details vehicle use by day, by hour, by location and by vehicle
- Journey and trip analysis – details journey types, journey destinations, locations, times at destinations, trip durations, trip distances and trip locations
- Vehicle use efficiency analysis – details the time-based vehicle use ratio on each vehicle each day

We have also looked at modeling a flexible vehicle supply model.

This software looks at each vehicle trip-including start time, trip travel time and distance, destinations, location and time at destination (stationary time), and calculates whether it is more economical to use a taxi or a rental vehicle for a journey (defined as a combination of trips) and calculates the impact of the proposed transport mode substitution on optimal fleet size.

The purpose of the transport mode substitution analysis is to determine optimal fleet supply, as opposed to optimal fleet size.

The flexible vehicle supply analysis tries to determine the most cost-effective supply solution for a given level of vehicle demand.

The chart on the opposite page typically shows the result of our vehicle use efficiency analysis.

The vehicle use efficiency analysis typically finds a fleet reduction opportunity of at least 20% and often up the 30%. We think this is a surprising result.

We have recently undertaken four fleet use reviews. We have consistently found that fleets typically have more vehicles than they need.

This is always a surprising result because when we conduct the initial user interviews they nearly always complain of 'vehicle shortages'.

The vehicle use efficiency analysis is an evidence-based approach (particularly when using data from electronic vehicle use monitors) and it is always interesting to provide (and present) the vehicle use efficiency analysis and see what happens when 'fact' meets 'opinion' in the fleet manager's Use Review Workshop.

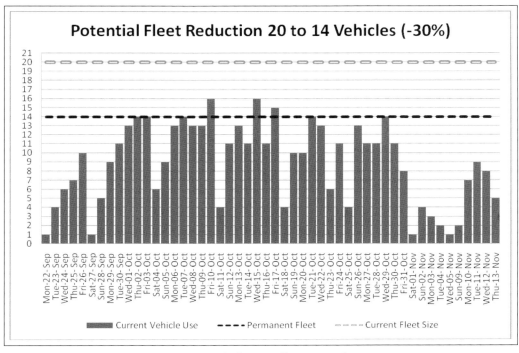

Figure 4: Vehicle use efficiency analysis

How you considered any other uses for telematics?

We are very interested in using vehicle use monitors as a platform for delivering more innovative vehicle use models based on a variable pricing and billing model.

We would allow employee use of employer supplied/operated/owned vehicles for non-business purposes and bill them a rate that is slightly higher than the marginal (variable) cost of vehicle use. This is a very attractive time and kilometre rate for employees and reduces the total cost of vehicle use to the employer.

Typically, the non-business demand for vehicle use always has very little negative impact on work time vehicle use efficiency. It seems that everybody wins.

The vehicle use monitors platform could support a fully automated vehicle use billing solution that would remove any issues surrounding administration (presumably one the current 'roadblocks'). More importantly, you can use variable pricing models (in the same way the airlines do) to improve vehicle use yields and reduce the employer cost of vehicle provision. We are very excited about this possibility and are just waiting for a fleet client to allow us to pilot this flexible vehicle supply model and variable vehicle use pricing model on a pilot project. These are the two final 'keys' to the path to optimal vehicle supply, optimal use and the minimal cost per vehicle use (the ultimate measure of vehicle use cost efficiency). However we also see vehicle use monitors being used in two other key areas; driver behaviour management and vehicle emissions reporting by vehicle (and by driver!)

Vehicle use monitors bring vehicle use transparency. This transparency brings a certain 'self-policing' of vehicle use.

What is the future of vehicle use management?

We believe most of the gains to be made in the traditional areas of fleet management have already been realised. We believe there are significant cost and efficiency gains available from vehicle use management. And the business case for the telematics technology to deliver vehicle use management is compelling. This technology is now quite mature and available at a commercially attractive cost. There is also the new generation of telematics devices arriving from China that has halved the cost of the 'black box' hardware.

We are trying to find innovative ways to use this new vehicle use 'data' service to build 'value added' services to help organisations use their vehicle resources, more efficiently, and more effectively, and in a way that respects the environmental consequences of vehicle use. In the final analysis, it is drivers that drive vehicle use, vehicle costs and vehicle damage.

The advantage of this technology is that it makes a direct real time transparent connection between vehicle use decisions and vehicle cost and CO_2 consequences. It is similar to having a taxi meter in a vehicle showing cost and CO_2 metrics for each vehicle trip.

We see vehicle use management being the next generation of professional fleet management.

How can your company help fleet managers?

We believe we have three strong capabilities in fleet analytics: data modeling and data analysis; new solution and strategy formulation, and strong software and application development prototype capability.

We have used these three strong capabilities in three specific areas: vehicle replacement modelling; vehicle valuation modeling and remarketing strategy development, and vehicle use modeling and management

Our Software Services:

We have developed the following application software for consulting and client use: fleet replacement service; vehicle valuation service; intelligent vehicle remarketing service, and vehicle use analytics and management service.

Our Project Experience:

We have undertaken over 35 consulting assignments for government and commercial organisations.

Our projects with government organisations include Department of Defence (multiple projects), Department of Treasury and Finance Victorian Government (multiple projects), NSW Department of Commerce, Queensland Government (Q-Fleet), Tasmanian Government (DHHS), ACT Government (Treasury) and Department of Human Services, Victoria.

Our commercial projects with fleet lease and fleet management companies include GE Money, Custom Fleet, Ford Credit, Swan Insurance, ORIX Corporation, PL Lease Management, RACQ, FleetPartners and Toyota Financial Services.

Our commercial projects with corporate fleets have included AWB (Australian Wheat Board) Ltd, RailCorp, Price Waterhouse (PWC) and Caltex Petroleum.

The projects assignments have included: Australian Fleet Industry Study, Fleet Reviews, Vehicle Remarketing Improvement Strategy (x2), Fleet Systems Requirements and Selection (x3), Fleet Lease Systems Architecture & Design, Vehicle Use Management Review, Optimal Pool Vehicle Size, Optimal Pool Vehicle Size and Mix, Vehicle Telematics Requirements and Vendor Selection (x2), Vehicle Size and Use Efficiency Review (x2), Optimal Pool Vehicle Size and Use Efficiency Review using In-Vehicle Telematics Devices (a consulting first).

Our 2 Day Seminars:

Our recent 2 day seminars conducted with Paul Lauria, President Mercury Associates Inc:

- Fleet Management Master Class – Melbourne and Sydney, Australia-October 2007
- Fleet Management and Transport Management-Shanghai, China – September 2008
- Fleet Management, Transport Management and Fleet Optimisation – Bangkok, Thailand, November 2008
- We have presented in the Australian Fleet Management and Annual Conference and Breakfast Series
- Fleet Systems – The Lessons from 20 Fleet Systems Implementations
- Intelligent Vehicle Remarketing-Reviewing Remarketing Myths and Mistakes
- The next presentation will be Electronic Vehicle Use Management – The Next Generation of Fleet Management

Fleet analytics capability:

Fleet Software & Services Pty Ltd has developed a strong capability in data modeling and data analysis. Over the last 5 years we have used a number of statistical and mathematical techniques to explore relationship between independent variables and a dependent variable. We have also used a number of optimisation techniques in vehicle routing and scheduling.

Our recent modeling has focused on building a vehicle valuation model (VVM). This models the relationship (and inter-relationships) between 12-20 independent variables and their impact on vehicle values over time.

This unique modeling capability has been used by the Victorian, NSW, Queensland,

and West Australian governments to make decisions on vehicle selection, vehicle disposal, selection of sales agents and choice of sales methods. These clients have acknowledged our work and our ability to model a large number of complex changing continuous and discrete variables from large 'challenging' datasets. We understand we are the first company to achieve the accurate computer prediction of vehicle values and this work has attracted international interest. We are current applying this modeling and data analysis expertise to vehicle use patterns for use, cost, fuel, driver and emissions management for the Tasmania Government and AWB Ltd. This innovative approach is based on our modeling and software development capability.

The methods we have developed seem ideal for the modeling of transport energy use. Energy use is a function of a significant number of inter-related variables and we believe this more sophisticated approach can throw new light on energy use reduction opportunities. We are now responding to the challenge of modeling vehicle use in real time where we have mobile assets in different locations, different use profiles and different operating environments.

Our other unique approach is that we often develop software prototypes so our client can easily use the developed capability in making their day to day decisions.

We have just completed a data modeler and automated data conversion system to take 'dirty' real world data and automatically covert this data to a common schema to be used for management (automated) decision making.

We employ 5 PhDs on our team to undertake innovative 'research' in modeling and data conversion work. We currently have two PhDs writing new vehicle use analytics software to take real time vehicle use data and provide summary data on vehicle use such as vehicle use efficiency. We see direct parallels in this approach and tracking vehicle use through time (and analysing patterns of use) in vehicle, cost and energy use modeling.

Our view is that historical use data only has a limited value for today's decision making. Our view is that you must make vehicle (and energy) use visible in real time (or near time) to raise awareness and visibility at the point of (management) control. This measurement makes a direct visible link between energy use decisions and energy use consequences in terms of use and cost. We are developing software to support this approach. We also have close relationships with senior lecturers in engineering, computer science and software engineering and mathematics and statistics faculties where we share and develop our modeling capabilities.

Mark Bernard
Director
Fleet Software & Services Pty Ltd
Melbourne, Australia

Fleet Software & Services Consultancy Services

Fleet Systems Consultancy

We provide services on the selection, implementation and modification of vehicle quotation, vehicle leasing, fleet management and pool management systems for professional fleet lessors and corporate and government fleets. Our services in new fleet systems acquisition, and fleet systems replacement projects, include:

- Requirements and Gap Analysis
- Software Selection and Vendor Evaluation
- Software Implementation and Project Management

Fleet Analytics Consultancy

Fleet analytics and software development project capacity and software:

- Vehicle Remarketing Strategy and Software (Vehicle Valuation, Optimal Reserve Setting)
- Fleet Replacement Capital, Cost and Emissions Reduction Strategy and Software
- Vehicle Use Analysis, Vehicle Use Management and Optimal Fleet Size Software

Fleet Research and Development

We would like to start a not-for-profit International Fleet Research Institute (IFRI) to undertake collaborative, syndicated research into fleet industry issues. IFRI could be funded on a subscription basis and IFRI members could suggest and sponsor research into new and innovative solutions to common problems and issues facing the vehicle leasing and fleet management industry. Our first projects could be:

- The Green Fleet Challenge - design, development and deployment of a greener fleet operation
- Fleet Cost and Emissions Optimisation - strategies to simultaneously reduce vehicle use, costs and emissions

Contact Details

Mark D. Bernard
Fleet Strategy & Systems Consultant
Fleet Software & Services Pty Ltd
10 Monaro Road, Kooyong, Victoria, Australia 3144
Phone: +61 (0) 419 59 59 00
Fax: +61 (0) 3 9824 8640
Email: mark.bernard@fleet.com.au
Web: www.fleet.com.au

26 SETTING RESIDUAL VALUES AND MAINTENANCE BUDGETS

> **Stephen Dilley**
> Country Manager
> FleetData UK Limited

Please introduce yourself and your company.

My role is that of Country Manager of FleetData UK Limited, part of the FleetGlobal Group. Established in 2003, we currently operate in 13 countries worldwide. The business provides technical market intelligence to the automotive industry and all vehicle operators – data for new vehicles, residual values, service, maintenance and repair costs and used car values, plus a range of software tools.

FleetData has won the confidence of some of the biggest worldwide players, particularly in the fleet management segment.

I have worked in the automotive industry since the mid-1970's, predominantly in senior management positions with contract hire and leasing companies and was, for many years, Managing Director of Motorconsult, offering pricing and data management tools to the leasing industry.

Does that mean your company's clients are mainly leasing and fleet management companies, or larger end-user fleets run by fleet managers?

Our spectrum of clients stretches from the top vehicle leasing companies, through motor manufacturers to small end user fleets – all have a need for the data we offer. It is fundamental to each organisation's commercial decision-making – big or small.

There are about 8000 vehicle models and model derivatives available in the UK market at present. This makes it very difficult to keep on top of the likely used values of vehicles or the amount it will cost to maintain them. Everyone says whole life cost represents the best possible fleet allocation policy.

In your view, given the huge amount of data, how should a fleet manager go about calculating whole life costs?

To start with – some clarification. I know that Whole Life Cost is a commonly used term, but I prefer to use 'Total Cost of Ownership' (TCO). Call it semantics, but when looking at the cost to your company of operating a vehicle, it is not relevant whether the whole life of that vehicle is 8, 10 or 20 years, the cost you are concerned with is that which will be incurred during the period from acquisition to disposal, hence TCO.

It is easy to be intimidated by the scale of choice available in the UK market. That said, it is only the companies that offer an 'all manufacturer' choice of product that need concern themselves with managing such volumes of vehicle data. In other words, the leasing and fleet management companies.

So let us consider them first, before moving on to the end user fleet.

A. The Leasing and Fleet Management Companies

In order to provide their customers and prospective customers with price quotations on any vehicle currently available in the market, the leasing and fleet management companies must be in control of the following technical data:

1 New vehicle prices, specifications and options

2 Service, maintenance and repair (SMR) cycles and costs

3 Other running costs – fuel, insurance, vehicle excise duty

4 Future values (residual values)

(In addition, there will be finance costs included in the packages, although the broad mechanism for calculating such costs will generally be common to all vehicles.)

Of the four types of data listed above, the first, new vehicle prices and options, is factual data and therefore the easiest to work with. The second, SMR costs, is strongly based on fact, but requires clever calculations and some experience and assumptions on things like wear rates in order to produce a budget. The third, fuel, insurance and taxes is fairly easy to compute – although, of course, actual fuel consumption will vary according to usage and driving style. The fourth, residual values, represent a set of forecasts which anticipate the market in used vehicles up to, say, 5 years ahead, adjusted for distance travelled as well as age. (By the way, to define the term residual value: it means the value of the vehicle remaining at a given date and travelled mileage – what is left of its original cost.)

For the purpose of this section, we will concern ourselves with the two types that are hardest to assess – SMR and future values.

Service, Maintenance and Repair Budgets

SMR costs can be split into three segments:

1 Servicing and service parts

2 Wearing parts – such as tyres, brake pads, brake discs, clutch plates etc.

3 Component failures – the necessary replacement of items, not covered by warranty and therefore at a cost to the operator

To be able to predict accurately SMR costs for a given vehicle, you need data – without it you can only guess. So let us go for another list – a little daunting this one, but it will help illustrate what is involved:

Element	Action	Issues
Service intervals	To determine how many services the vehicle will require over a given time and distance	Fixed service intervals – no problem (60,000 miles, 12,000 mile service intervals = 5 services), but remember on low mileage vehicles to allow for time-based service intervals (normally annually)

Variable service intervals – alter according to driving style and use. One driver will get, say, 18,000 miles between services, another only 12,000 miles. |
| Service type | To assess what goes into each service – an A service may be just an oil change, a B service adds plugs and filters, a C service may require a cambelt change – and the order of each service. It may go something like A, B, A, C, A, B. You need to know the order so that you may to correctly forecast the costs. | Extra items – manufacturers' schedules will determine additional jobs within a service 'on inspection' – which means the dealer will take a look and decide whether something extra needs doing. Generally, you would cover this as described under the Wearing Parts section that follows. |
| Wearing parts | Here, we are talking about the replacement of both consumable parts due to wear and those parts that fail after the expiry of any warranty period under which they would have otherwise been covered.

What falls into consumable parts? This can be a long list, but certainly includes tyres, brake pads and linings, brake disc plates, clutch plates. Tyres represent the largest part of most SMR budgets. Trying to assess tyre life is always tricky – 2 identical cars, both travelling the same mileage, can wear tyres at very different rates. If one spends most of its life on motorways, turning few corners and with little stopping and starting, it will achieve much less tyre wear than the car that is based in, say, an urban environment like Milton Keynes with over 100 roundabouts, stopping, starting and leaning on tyre shoulders (and that is without the effect of differing driving styles).

Do not forget things like wiper blades – they can be expensive and, if changed annually, can easily add between £100-£250 to the SMR budget.

As for parts that may fail and not be covered by warranty, some are predictable on especially high mileage vehicles. Others, especially electronic components, do not wear as such, but will fail nonetheless, although not because they have necessarily travelled high mileages or are especially old. In such cases, you must make provision for some replacement costs, but it is unlikely that you will be able to identify each component. In such cases, common practice is to build a basket of components and replacement costs and apply a proportion of that total by way of provision in your SMR budget. | Getting hold of wear rates – a tough one if you do not have viable data for your own fleet. What does 'viable' mean? It means wear rate data based on a substantial spread of vehicles. Data for a handful of common vehicles is not a good basis. If you use an SMR tool, you will probably be provided with a set of wear rates that will form a good basis from which to proceed.

If you are setting SMR budgets on vehicles for which you pick up all the costs, remember that tyre replacement must include those ruined through damage. Be realistic about tyre replacement costs – tyres are very susceptible to commodity prices (components include steel, rubber, synthetic rubber, silica etc.) At the time of writing, tyres prices had increased by c.20% in the UK within a 12 month period. |

To repeat, you cannot accurately budget SMR without data. Use of a top level SMR budgeting tool is fundamental to doing the job right and extremely cost effective.

This single screenshot will give you an idea of just some of the data available from an SMR budgeting tool:

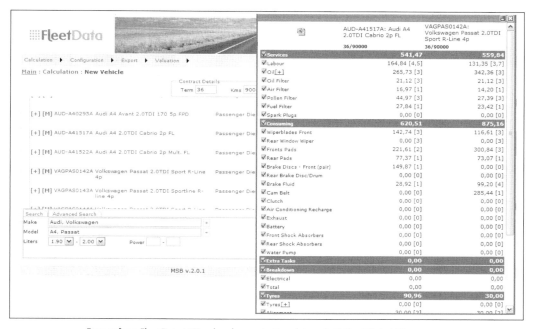

Extract from FleetData MSBook – demonstration data only © FleetGlobal SA

RESIDUAL VALUES

Forecasting residual values is a combination of historic activity, market intelligence and economic performance.

Let us start with simple used car values – the value of a car on the day it is for sale. For the moment, let us ignore differences between models, even differences between specifications on particular models. Imagine you have two identical cars – same model, specification and registered on the same day (let us call it the 'SidebySide' test). What will make one of those cars more or less valuable than the other? Here is a shopping list of criteria that will affect the future value of a vehicle:

1 Age
2 Mileage
3 Condition
4 Service history
5 Colour
6 Geography

Obvious stuff – an older car will be worth less than a younger one, the same applies to mileage. A car in good condition will be worth more than one that has been less well cared for. That includes things like tyre wear, too. If the tyres need renewal on one car and are nearly new on another, that could affect the sale price by several hundred pounds.

The service history of each car is important too. If you have visited an auction, you will have heard the auctioneer saying something like 'this car comes with a fully stamped service book' or 'this car has a full manufacturer service history'. That means the car has been regularly serviced and it makes a difference by whom the servicing has been done. Work by a franchised agent of that car's manufacturer is viewed as being more valuable than work carried out by an independent garage which perhaps lacks the expertise and specialist tools to do a proper job.

Then there is the colour of the car – until it became the 'cool' colour recently, white was a value-losing colour and remains so on certain models. What is known as 'doom blue' – a solid, dark blue body colour, can take several hundred pounds value off a car. Many dealers will not buy a green car because of superstitious customers.

Geography can impact the value of a vehicle, because certain models will sell better in one area than in another. Knowledge of sales performance in different locations can be very valuable.

All these criteria will make a car more or less valuable than the next. Do not forget that 'saturation' (over supply of a certain model) can also adversely affect the value of that car. More on that later in this section.

Then other factors come into play – those that can apply irrespective of manufacturer, model or specification:
1 The Economy
2 Running costs
3 Taxation
4 Saturation

Again, some of these are self-explanatory. The general economic situation – the financial health of businesses, consumers and buyers – will naturally impact the market's 'enthusiasm'.

The higher the running cost of a car, the lower will be its used car value in relation to its price when new. Often you will be able to buy an expensive car for less than a more 'run of the mill' car, same age, same mileage, because it will cost substantially more to run in fuel, tyres, insurance and repairs.

I have separated taxation from running costs because, even when buying a used car, it is an element of cost that is not necessarily fixed. Changes in road fund tax (VED) linked to emissions mean that taxation can go up disproportionately to other costs.

Finally, another element that can affect prices. We call it saturation. Essentially, saturation means greater supply than demand. This could be across the market in general, a certain over availability of one model (sometimes seen when manufacturers 'force-feed' new car sales of a particular model, for it to arrive in the used car market in high volume just a few months later), or an excess of high mileage vehicles when the market is looking for low mileage.

So all the above are factors that will impact the value of a used car on the day of its sale and all must be considered when projecting a future residual value.

The effect of the period between these 2 points – today's value and a future disposal date, say, 3 years ahead – must then be accommodated.

Again, let us list the criteria that may influence the transition from today's value to that future value.

1   Model and specification obsolescence
2   Technology and design
3   Desirability
4   Tax and legislative changes
5   Inflation and other economic factors

Model obsolescence is a continuing consideration – manufacturers regularly update their product range. Sometimes it is simply a small change in specification that will have only a minor impact on the future value of the car. Remember the 'SidebySide' test? Would you pay more for the car with the revised specification – and if so, how much?

Often put forward by a manufacturer as a 'new model' will be the 'face-lift' – essentially the same car, but with cosmetic changes: new lights, a new grille, change of wheel style etc.

Then there is the real model change – a new engineering platform, different body styling and new panels throughout (even if it looks similar in an evolutionary sort of way). VW Golf is a good example – now on its 6th incarnation since being introduced in 1976.

What impact will a new model have on the value of an existing one? If the change is substantial (especially visually), it will have a greater impact. The more evolutionary the change, the smaller the value impact.

How can I see it coming? In other words, when I try to predict a value, say, 3 years ahead, how can I tell if a new model is likely to be launched before then? All manufacturers work in product cycles: they have a design phase, an engineering phase and a tooling phase, all of which dictate a lead time between the launch of one model and its successor.

Look at previous model change times. Of course, if the previous model is a notable failure, the manufacturer will try to change it as soon as is practical, but generally, 3-4 years is a good yardstick.

Very closely linked to model obsolescence must be technology and design. The push towards much more fuel efficient and eco-friendly vehicles drives changes in technology. Our need for safer cars has changed the way we design them and today many new small cars are safer in a crash than much larger, older–design cars. Perhaps they are less visible, but these changes are demanded by the discerning used car buyer and therefore will impact future values.

Desirability is a bit of a chameleon – a changing thing. Large 4 wheel drive vehicles were very desirable not too many years ago, yet today have lost large chunks of value and are viewed as 'bad' except in rare circumstances. Everyone has a different view – this is perhaps the most subjective of all areas.

Which takes us straight into tax and legislation – using the same example, could we foresee that the large, fuel guzzling four wheel drive would be penalised by higher levels of VED and congestion charging? Maybe, in which case we should reflect that in our future value forecast. What else will Whitehall and local government invent by way of vehicle taxation? Work that out and you can predict part of what will influence future values.

Finally, inflation and other economic factors. As a rule of thumb, a future value is set as a percentage of the original (new) price of the car. As prices for new cars change, so they will impact used car values. Inflation is the most consistent, but other economic factors will certainly come into play, affecting the spending power of the potential used car buyer and thus the price for which the car can be sold in the future. As an example, in the period between September 2007 and September 2008, when the economy was in turmoil, sales of off-road and luxury cars both fell by over 40% and the only area of growth in sales volume was the city car.

As you can see, there are myriad elements that need to be considered. So, to summarise, these are the elements to consider when forecasting residual values:

Vehicle Specific:
1   Age
2   Mileage
3   Condition
4   Service history
5   Colour
6   Geography

Market Specific:
7   The Economy
8   Running costs
9   Taxation
10 Saturation

Future Specific:
11 Model and specification obsolescence
12 Technology and design
13 Desirability
14 Tax and legislative changes
15 Inflation and other economic factors

So, the person who takes all the above into account when setting future values will be sure to get it right? I am sure you can guess the answer to that! There are no guaranteed outcomes but if you consider all of these you can have confidence that you are basing your projections on sound principles.

Is that the end of it? By no means. Regular, periodic review is essential – your future commitments can rapidly shift from apparently risk-free to positively dodgy. Then the skill of managing disposal performance starts – long before the vehicle goes on sale.

B. The End User Fleet Operator

An end user fleet operator can use the above techniques, if appropriate to his/her acquisition method. However, it should not be necessary to concern oneself with such large volumes of vehicles.

For the end user operator, even of the larger fleet, your vehicle policy will inevitably select a range of vehicles appropriate to your business needs and your ability to manage that fleet. It will not take long to weed out the 'non-starters'. By which I mean those vehicles that simply do not meet minimum criteria.

1) Clear away the chaff

    Let us try it out: a common company car policy will have a set of exclusions. Let us take just four: no petrol cars, nothing with an insurance rating higher than group 12 (or 30 in new money), maximum CO_2 emissions of 160 g/km and no 4x4s, no sports, no cabriolets or convertibles. This will still leave quite a large choice.

2) Macro manage the rest

    In other words, you must define what will represent a manageable choice list. This may mean restricting brand and/or model choice or, setting financial limits by policy category if you lease/contract hire your vehicles. Care here – remember special deals from the manufacturer or lease/contract hire company could allow someone into a car above their intended specification. Set both rental and list price limits.

Correctly structured, you should now have a manageable fleet selection from which you can build your final company vehicle list.

Which brings us back to Whole Life Costs or, in my preferred terms, Total Cost of Ownership (TCO). Once you have established the residual value and SMR budget for a vehicle, you can apply the other elements to produce the TCO:

*   New vehicle price on the road (including VED, registration charge, delivery charges etc.) including any options, *then add*
*   Service, maintenance and repair (SMR) costs *and add*
*   Other running costs – fuel, insurance, vehicle excise duty *then subtract*
*   Future values (residual values)

(You may wish to include financing costs, if appropriate)

The result will be your TCO for that vehicle. Applying the same to each vehicle in your fleet selection will then give you a clear indication of the best choices for your fleet policy.

So that covers all the complex elements of achieving a TCO for a vehicle. There is, of course, a simpler approach for the end user operator – get contract hire quotations for all of the vehicles in your fleet selection, add fuel and insurance costs and use the result as your TCOs. You may wish to source vehicles from several suppliers, rentals may differ from supplier to supplier, but remember what you are trying to achieve – a finite list of vehicles for inclusion in your company vehicle policy – TCOs will vary over time (remember the changing cost of tyres due to commodity prices? Manufacturers will change prices, fuel will cost more…) so you must work in 'Differentials'. In other words, it is the relationship – the difference – between TCOs that will dictate your choice, not the level of TCO itself. If you try to work in any other way, you will never deliver because the horizon is always moving.

How does market intelligence fit into this picture?

Without market intelligence, your view of TCOs, as a whole or individual elements, will be at best restricted and very possibly non-existent. The point of market intelligence is that it provides a view based upon a substantial sample of data – the larger the sample, the better the view. This does not mean that you use market intelligence without applying your own experience (if you have it). Market intelligence can tell you what the bigger world is doing – but yours may not be the 'average' fleet. To get the best results, applying your experience onto market intelligence will get a 'bespoke' result, relevant to your needs.

Most fleet managers will be familiar with the little pricing books carried by motor traders and dealers. In your view, are these books an accurate representation of market prices?

This is simple to answer – yes and no. It is true that the value view expressed in the books can often influence rather than reflect the market. This is a natural outcome of such a guide – a guide should contain a reflection of the market. However, if the user applies the values from the guide, then the guide must, by definition, set the market values. That is not a problem provided the guide accurately carries market values (even if those values were created through the use of a guide). The risk is when the guide presents values which are the creation of the authors, not factual numbers from the market. How can you tell? To be blunt, you cannot necessarily – but if you see a big shift in the valuation of a vehicle without explanation, or with an explanation that seems shaky, you may have spotted something that does not reflect the market. In our own products, we only reflect the market – it is the soundest basis of valuation.

How should a fleet manager go about assembling the fleet data they require in order to make decisions?

Be realistic in your choice of fleet data. Nobody wants to spend money if it can be avoided, but do not fool yourself into believing you can guess the answers. Think how the leasing and fleet management companies do it – they buy in new vehicle pricing data, service, maintenance and repair data, used vehicle and residual value data – normally with data management, budgeting and forecasting tools, too.

For the smaller end user operator, this is likely to be a budget-busting investment and, realistically, not necessary. Do the ground work first, as described above, fine tuning your selection of vehicles, then consider purchasing a TCO dataset (covering your selection of vehicles) from a reputable automotive data supplier. Whatever your method of acquisition, this will provide you with an objective means by which to finalise your company vehicle policy.

What would be your advice to a fleet manager who wishes to manage and control fleet costs whilst still providing cars that are attractive to employees?

Retention and recruitment of employees are important factors for any employer. For the employer, you may consider your primary (selfish) need is to run an effective and cost efficient fleet. However, if that means a fleet of sign-written vans for your sales force, you may find it difficult to employ the right people. At the same time, do not go overboard in accommodating each driver's every whim. It will cost you a lot of money and you will very soon discover that anomalies (or too much flexibility) in your policy will make management very difficult.

Certainly consult company vehicle drivers when you are defining your policy, but you must take the final decision, no doubt ending up in the middle ground, which gives a good mix of financial and operational efficiency and an attractive recruitment and retention package.

And what would be your advice to contract hire companies that want to set accurate and reliable residual values and maintenance budgets?

Look to the automotive data providers that can offer transparency, consistency and a preparedness to listen. Also, consider the expertise of their personnel, the robustness of their data production systems and the scope of their offerings (international coverage, client base, product range, etc.)

Some operators take data products from multiple sources – great if you have the budget. Over time, it will certainly help you develop a view as to which is best for you.

Then, your data provider selected, use that data intelligently. Yes, you can subscribe to data and use it 'straight from the box', but you also have your own fleet experience. Apply what you know with the market intelligence you have bought.

What about tyres and insurance costs?

Tyres are a substantial part of the running cost budget. As described above, they are difficult to budget for and their replacement cost can vary quite substantially over time. For FleetData, detailed collection of tyre data by brand, as well as size, speed rating and profile, is important to ensure we offer the client the right intelligence not only to budget accurately but also to achieve supply efficiencies.

Insurance is a harder one to deal with. Yes, FleetData does carry both pan-European and global insurance data, but it is important to remember that each fleet, big or small, will have its own unique set of conditions, track record (claims history) and usage profile. We always recommend that you have detailed discussions with insurers to ensure you achieve the right level of cover matched to reasonable cost.

What developments have there been in your part of the fleet market in the last few years that have been particularly valuable to fleet managers?

More than anything else in this millennium it has been the motor manufacturers' grasp of the need to provide data for establishing the total cost of ownership (TCO). This shows that they understand what the fleet operator needs. Increased service intervals, greater warranty cover and the like have all shown this understanding – to everyone's benefit.

Have there been developments that have been particularly valuable to contract hire companies?

The same ones, really. Data, intelligence, is critical to good management and accurate costings. The relatively easy availability of data also enables powerful applications: tools to revalue contracts and to enable automation of job authorisation and e-billing are a couple of good examples.

Is anything happening now, or will anything be happening soon, that is likely to change the landscape for fleet managers when it comes to setting accurate maintenance budgets and residual values?

Well, I could tell you, but then I would have to kill you.

However, I guess the thing to watch out for is legislation that forces a more rapid transition to eco-cars (hybrid, fuel cell and electric). The impact on residual values could be quite extreme.

If you were to advise a fleet manager on the best practice when it comes to setting accurate maintenance budgets and residual values, what would that advice be?

Be prudent, apply the recommendations that I have made earlier in this chapter and be consistent.

How can your company help fleet managers?

FleetData UK has an enviable record in the provision of the kind of data and tools that fleet managers need. FleetData is also the chosen partner of other major worldwide market intelligence companies – a major accolade in itself. The strength of our product range means that we can satisfy all of your requirements, thus ensuring consistency of use, presentation and application. Our personnel have the strongest background and experience currently available and our reputation of listening means that you can be sure your needs are given the highest priority.

FleetData UK is happy to offer advice whatever your requirements, so, if this chapter has been valuable, do contact us; let us take you the next step.

Whatever you do, do not underestimate the value of data – it empowers.

Stephen Dilley, Country Manager, FleetData UK Limited

27 INTERNATIONAL LEASING AND FLEET MANAGEMENT

Matt Dyer
Managing Director
LeasePlan International B.V.

Please introduce yourself and your company

LeasePlan International B.V. is a separate company established within the LeasePlan Group specifically to develop and manage relationships with multinational companies who wish to manage their fleet requirements on an international basis.

LeasePlan is a global provider of vehicle leasing and fleet management services to the corporate sector. Present in 30 countries around the world, they are the market leader in Europe. The company is owned by three shareholders; the Volkswagen Group, Mubadala Development Corporation and the Olayan Group. LeasePlan has been actively involved in the international market sector since 1996.

At the end of 2007, LeasePlan managed over 1.3 million vehicles worldwide, employed 5,800 people and delivered annual profit of € 255 million.

I have been with the LeasePlan Group for 13 years and worked in roles at a national, corporate and international level. In my current role as MD, I am responsible for managing the international team (new business, account management, finance, legal, HR and ICT) in the seven regions around the world; UK, US, Germany, France, the Netherlands, Australia and Brazil.

Wholly owned subsidiaries
in **30 countries**

Strategic alliances in
•Baltic States
(Estonia, Latvia , Lithuania)
•Canada
•South Africa

This means I spend my time with the LPI teams around the world, the 30 LeasePlan countries around the world and multinational companies wherever they may be around the world!

What do you define as an international deal?

International deals come in all shapes and sizes. When a company has 1500 vehicles or more in three or more countries, we are typically talking about the scale and mandate to truly make an impact with an international deal. This is also the scale at which it makes sense for leasing companies to deploy their international teams to take ownership.

The scope for international deals can vary. There are companies with a strong corporate ethos and mandate who can apply deals across many countries and several continents. For example, LeasePlan have specific international customers covering upwards of 25 countries across four continents.

It has become very common for European based multinationals to conclude pan-European agreements especially as individual leasing companies are present in all the relevant markets and have the control over these countries through a wholly owned subsidiary model. This brings major benefits in an international deal as it ensures that the pricing, product, service and reporting tools committed as part of the agreement can be delivered throughout the countries involved. It also allows one point of contact as well as the confidence to know that systems, processes and date sit together in the same way in each country.

Some companies work with alliance or joint venture partners to provide the necessary geographic scope. This allows a wider market of potential international leasing suppliers but has drawbacks in terms of commitment to contractually agreed terms and consistent service and product delivery. With different companies participating in an alliance there can often be difficulty in agreeing one pricing approach, harmonised product features and services, consolidated reporting and consistent service levels for the drivers.

It is now also becoming relatively common for companies to agree transatlantic deals. There are quite big differences between the European and US approaches to the company car. However at the end of the day, the requirement is still to look after a driver, buy a vehicle, maintain it, fuel it and sell it. The way the lease is delivered may be different but the cost components and service requirements involved are the same. This mindset allows companies to consider one fleet leasing supplier for their transatlantic needs.

Whilst scale is important, smaller international deals do take place. They can be very important especially when using one larger country to provide scale and leverage benefits to a handful of smaller countries. It is typical for leasing companies to use their local networks to manage these types of requirements rather than employing the mandated international team.

How do international deals start?

Experience to date suggests that an international approach develops according to the organisational approach and culture of specific companies. It all seems to hinge on the magic word: mandate.

Mandate means different things in all companies however it is very rare that it is used in extreme black and white terms. In reality, mandate reflects the degree of influence that can be applied in order to direct or encourage different operating companies or subsidiaries to follow an agreed international approach.

In reality the mandate needs to be earned and this is often based on a business case of what could be achieved by taking an international approach to a particular product or service category. In the case of fleet management, this business case should cover the key country fleets (those that have the scale) and the smaller fleets (those that will benefit most from using the scale of others).

It should then look at three specific areas:

1   Direct Leverage: what are the possible benefits on interest rate and management fee of conducting and delivering an international approach?

2   Indirect Leverage: what are the benefits in terms of key cost categories through working on an international basis? These would include depreciation (improved vehicle manufacturer terms), maintenance and tyre management, fuel management, insurance. I will cover these later.

    These are all categories where costs can be reduced through concerted action. A key factor that often dictates the level of saving available is the type of driver included within the international scope. If the bias is towards drivers who view the vehicle as a part of their compensation package or are part of a sales team, the level of savings available through restriction of policy is reduced. If, however, the majority are tool of trade drivers, then the degree of direction to a specific policy is greater as are the savings available.

3   Process Improvement: one of the consistent benefits that come from companies working together in an international approach is through the use of demonstrated good practice.

    The starting point for an international approach is for individual operating companies to be open about their current approach and the reasons behind it. This discussion is hugely valuable because it opens the eyes of everyone involved to the possibilities and it invariably highlights a number of opportunities for improvement. This is especially true in the degree of outsourcing and direct driver contact that can be achieved within a customer – international fleet supplier relationship.

    This focus on implementing good demonstrated practice provides numerous savings opportunities for relatively limited investment. These are often captured as ongoing productivity savings within a specific deal.

You will notice that I referred to good demonstrated practice not best practice. It is important within an international project, especially in the early stages, to maintain as much objectivity as possible. This phrase best practice assumes too much. In reality, all subsidiaries and individuals involved in a project have reached their current approach through a mixture of legacy, culture, organisation and individuals. It is not right to judge one against the other and state that one is better than all others; one may not work for all companies involved. It is best to share the approaches of all involved and agree amongst the team which are the good practices and then to use this as the pool from which a move to an improved approach can be selected.

What are international decision makers looking for?

Often there is one leading decision maker within an international team when the project begins. This is usually the person with the key international role – Chief Procurement Officer, International Purchasing Manager, International Fleet Manager – or it can also be the person from a leading subsidiary who has used their experience to build agreement and support for an international approach using a business case. In both situations, the person taking responsibility will have used an overall sponsor to get the show on the road. This sponsor is key for approval, influence and escalation in the future.

Once the international decision maker is in place, the first step is to build a team of key stakeholders and influencers that can be used to determine the current situation, assess the key objectives of the approach, evaluate potential suppliers and then make a decision on the way forward.

This committee will include various levels and functions from the relevant countries. For example, in a transatlantic deal it would be normal to see a senior team member from the key European countries (DE, UK, FR) as well as the US. Countries with particularly significant fleets will also be included along with one or two representatives from the smaller countries involved. The functions involved can vary; procurement, human resources and fleet are the most usual though finance, treasury and facilities can also be involved. It is essential that a broad spectrum of countries and functions are included to ensure that decisions are stress-tested from as many sides as possible and ensure that the decision team itself has strong credibility and stands up to scrutiny.

How should fleets go about selecting the right partner?

The objectives of an international fleet project are predominantly geared towards control; reduction in the supplier base, reduction in cost, a stronger international approach, data consolidation, a reduction in FTEs involved. All of these require the selection of an international fleet supplier that can offer the control to achieve these objectives as well as the commitment and expertise required to make them happen and to keep delivering.

Finding this supplier requires a relatively broad market assessment from the project leader in which the key international fleet suppliers with the necessary scope are all involved. This usually means a list of about five companies. It is possible that well established local suppliers may also be included in order to reflect their contribution in the past.

These initial deliberations can lead to a shortlist of most suitable suppliers and discussions then usually move quickly to contractual issues with one, maybe two, specific suppliers. If that is the view of the team, you can then start to use this supplier to build the awareness on the current situation using data consolidation and to test the quality and cost level of the current local suppliers through a market by market assessment. The time saving made from avoiding an RFP can be used to start to deliver cost savings and control. However, as mentioned, these would need the support of those involved within the international fleet committee.

The alternative approach is through a tender using a Request for Information and then a Request for Proposal in order to select the most suitable supplier. This process can often take more than nine months to conduct and does involve considerable amounts of detail when you need to assess quotes from different suppliers across several countries.

It is important to keep it as simple as possible in a number of areas but especially in the service descriptions and the quotations. It is not unusual to see tenders that ask questions on the service approach covering well over 100 pages. Similarly the quotes can run into thousands in each stage of the RFP. At this stage, the project team is important. Use the key stakeholders to truly define their key requirements and to commit their most likely make, model, term and mileage requirements. This ensures that you can keep the RFP simple. Without these commitments, you are using the scatter-gun approach of ask everything and ask for quotes for everything. This does not lead to a good result as the complexity behind the analysis and lack of focus on the really important aspects mean the final outcomes become unclear.

An RFP with clear and direct focus will deliver a result that recommends the way forward. As you can imagine there are no set results as to what this will be as each company has specific factors that are unique. However the resulting picture usually sees one sole international supplier being appointed for all countries (the overall most competitive suppliers across all markets) or two suppliers are appointed across the international scope though they are appointed on a sole supply basis within each country.

Sole supply on a national level is important as it demonstrates that the benefits from increased outsourcing and direct contact between the driver and the leasing company are a growing source of savings. It also reflects the fact that it is almost impossible to expect one supplier to be the most competitive across all countries at all points in time. An international supplier will commit to be most competitive across the whole international scope however it not realistic to expect a deal that delivers absolute competitiveness in each and every market.

This is often due to the fact that residual values and MRT (maintenance, repair and tyre) budgets can evolve over time. A supplier will commit a harmonised interest rate mechanism, interest surcharge and management fee across all countries. However the same cannot take place with RVs and MRT. These are priced locally according to the specific market conditions and forecasts by the national division of the leasing company. Therefore differences can appear. Obviously different customers and different drivers can reflect a different proposition and this can lead to some limited fine tuning from the leasing companies to reflect reality. However, RVs and MRT budgets need to be carefully assessed during an RFP to ensure an accurate comparison is being made. This is why the specific selection of make, model, term and mileage combinations is important; as much as possible it should reflect the future buying patterns.

The selection in terms of supplier model has both positives and drawbacks. One sole supplier offers benefits in terms of additional leverage of interest and fee and provides considerable productivity and process improvements. At an international level, it also allows a commitment to one supplier and their international e-business solutions. If you select two international suppliers in order to accommodate variations in RV and MRT pricing, all these benefits can be diluted and there is considerable complexity added by needing to work with two international suppliers especially when clear ownership of cost reduction targets is required.

How is the agreement documented?

After selection and negotiation, the key document for the future is an International Co-operation or Framework agreement (ICA). This is a contractual commitment between two companies to work together on an international approach.

This contract sits over the local master leasing agreement (LMA) and individual leasing agreements (lease schedules) and will clearly state that it takes precedence. This allows a rapid implementation since the local master leasing agreements can either continue or be concluded as normal, safe in the knowledge that the commitments made internationally will be included in the ICA. All that needs to happen is to insert a schedule locally stating that the international agreement takes precedence.

An international co-operation agreement is not a leasing agreement. The complexity of building an international agreement that covers all the necessary fiscal and tax issues required for all included countries is far too heavy.

The LMA remains the key document to determine the specifics for leasing in each country.

It also remains the key document to define the specifics of the local product and service approach. In the world of international fleet, one size does not fit all. It would therefore be wrong to assume that all elements of product and service should be defined and set within the international agreement; there will be the need for local specifics and these should be discussed and agreed locally. At the end of the day, strong national agreements will always underpin a successful international agreement. If the country agreements do not flourish, the international approach will be restricted.

So, there should be the flexibility required for product specifics (early termination, reconditioning, over / under mileage, tax reporting, mileage pooling) as well as local services (driver solutions, reporting, renewal process). With this in mind, the following are the key elements of the ICA:

- Geographic scope and volume commitment (numbers of vehicles by country)
- Product selection (what is included, degree of transparency, settlement features)
- Pricing (interest rate mechanism, interest surcharge, management fee)
- Term and termination (including escalation processes)
- International Guarantee (to ensure that local credit decisions do not restrict the benefits)
- Implementation Process and Governance (including country phasing)
- International Service Delivery (reporting, cost savings, consultancy)
- Minimum standards for local service delivery (driver and fleet manager SLA)

A number of companies have assessed the use of cross border leasing. Please explain this approach.

These deals have looked to take advantage of lower or fully reclaimable VAT in certain European markets by leasing from one country into another. Though possible this model was complicated and the loophole on which it was based will close from 2010 onwards.

Cross border buying in Europe has been equally challenging as the possibility to buy a specific local model from another country is pretty much non-existent. On top of that issue, it is extremely difficult to set residual values and maintenance budgets for models that do not have a track record or precedent in a particular market. As such, specific negotiations with the vehicle manufacturers at an international level by customers, supported by their chosen leasing partners, are used to ensure that the buying price is as competitive as possible based on volumes. This process is very often co-ordinated by the international fleet leasing supplier as part of their ongoing cost savings and TCO responsibilities.

I have heard you say that "International total cost of ownership for fleet is a quest for enlightenment". Can you enlighten us?

Increasing leverage and reducing expenditure in the area of indirect procurement is a key challenge for many organisations. The impact of financial and process benefits achieved in these areas – travel, PCs and peripherals, temporary staff, facilities services – can have a significant impact on the bottom line. However, for indirect procurement teams, the need for a clear and accurate understanding of the total cost of ownership for a fleet of vehicles can be a true quest for enlightenment! The key themes and measures regarding TCO are relevant on both a national and international basis.

As people in procurement teams will testify, contribution to the bottom line in any of these expenditure areas is often the light at the end of a long and twisting tunnel. This tunnel can move from purchasing to HR, to employee benefits, to operations, to finance and back to purchasing again. However, the common thread for any of these projects is the need to have a clear and accurate picture of the current service expenditure – the current international total cost of ownership (TCO) – before any improvement initiatives can be introduced.

In no other area is this more relevant than in corporate car fleets. Very often, this will be one of the top two indirect expenditure items for companies. It is also one that needs a delicate balance between finance (the vehicle cost), HR (the benefit to the driver) and operations (the service to the customer). To complete the picture it also requires a large number of services – vehicle purchase, maintenance, fuel, tyres, breakdown cover, insurance, replacement vehicles – the list continues. With this change has come an increase in professionalism and transparency from suppliers, so that a clear understanding of the total cost of ownership is not only possible but essential.

There is a clear differentiation between two types of cost. The first are the direct costs – those directly related to the company car – depreciation, fuel, insurance, maintenance, etc. These can be analysed and understood in detail.

Then there is the hidden cost of time spent on fleet-related items by people in the company who are not directly managing the fleet. This would include driver time, accounts receivables, HR time to implement the fleet policy and secretarial time to liaise with fleet service providers on behalf of drivers. In terms of cost impact, this hidden category can be huge and should never be overlooked in terms of process and savings opportunities

But there are no rules about the scale of these hidden costs, as every organisation differs in style, structure and approach. Therefore, most companies initially focus on the direct total cost of ownership.

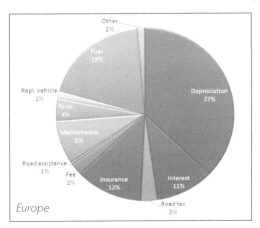

Europe

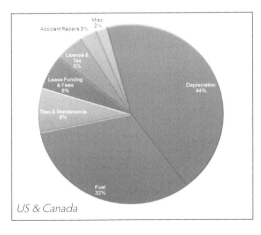

US & Canada

As the pie chart clearly shows, the largest international cost factor is depreciation, the reduction in value over the life of the vehicle from purchase (investment) to resale (the residual value). The scale of depreciation cost is directly linked to the type of vehicle (the depreciation on a Mercedes S class will differ to that of a Fiat Multipla) as well as the term and mileage for which the vehicle will be in economic use for a company. In reality, the depreciation curve is steep in the early life of the vehicle and flattens the older it gets.

There is also the interest cost to fund the investment required for the vehicle. This will be incurred regardless of whether the company purchases its vehicles outright or leases. The difference is how the funding cost is determined; from a leasing company this will be derived from the external money markets, whereas for companies who buy their own vehicles this will be determined by the company's own internal cost of borrowing.

Fuel costs are the second biggest element in fleet international TCO and, as recent developments in oil prices have shown, these can be highly volatile. Fuel costs will obviously vary depending on the mileage driven as well as the fuel economy of the vehicle. However, significant improvements can be made when considering the type of fuel for the vehicle (petrol vs. diesel) and by channeling expenditure to a limited number of fuel suppliers.

Maintenance, repair and tyre costs represent a significant slice of the total cost of ownership. These are determined by the routine servicing required, and the expected cost of technical breakdown and tyre replacement. Improvements in scope from OEM warranties and reliability over recent years have reduced costs in this area, although they are still sizeable enough to require clear understanding. This is especially true given the impact of driver behaviour, model choice and mileage. A key point to understand is the degree to which technical breakdown and repair is covered in the budget set by the leasing company or fleet department.

Insurance and damage management has become increasingly important. In fact, most fleet operators are now more likely to manage a vehicle through a damage repair process than routine servicing.

Insurance costs can impact companies in many ways – Third Party Liability premiums, Own Damage premiums (if insured), Own Damage direct costs (if self insured), replacement vehicles, excess or CASCO amounts and vehicle downtime. The scale of the cost in these areas is heavily dependent on driver behaviour, insurance provision and the quality of the damage or accident management service.

Then there are two other areas which make up the remainder of the direct fleet TCO pie chart. The first are taxes – road taxes, radio tax or road fund licence, call it what you will, they represent the tax payable to local or national government to keep the vehicle on the road. Toll fees and congestion charges are growing in importance for TCO and there is no doubt that emissions and environmental impact will hit vehicle taxes more in the future.

Finally, there is the direct resource – the internal fleet team and the fleet management company fee – to carry out the tasks required, such as vehicle purchase, disposal, technical control of the running costs, damage repair, arranging replacement vehicles, roadside assistance and fine management. These all require expertise and service excellence for the fleet to be managed efficiently.

This list completes the main elements of a fleet's total cost of ownership. Once you have completed the picture by vehicle, you will have a clear view of the total cost of ownership. However, this is just the start of the journey.

Next, you will have to take into account the importance of vehicle make and model selection to the overall TCO of the fleet. As we have already identified:

*   Each model will have a different depreciation profile
*   Each vehicle will have a different fuel economy
*   Each vehicle will vary with regards to technical repair
*   Each driver will vary with regards to driving style and behaviour

All of these need to be considered in the TCO calculation, along with the impact of the mileage for which a company will operate a vehicle. In simple terms, more miles lead to more depreciation, more routine servicing and less fuel economy. However, on balance, the cost per mile could decline as you reach the optimal term and mileage combination for a specific vehicle. This is where a proactive international fleet management company can truly add value for its customers.

How will these cost elements differ if a fleet is operated across multiple countries?

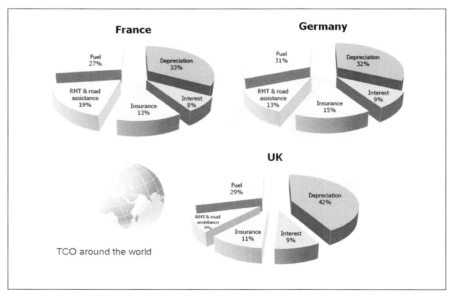

Through experience with international companies, it is clear that there are many factors involved, making an understanding of TCO quite complex but also increasing the opportunity and potential benefit of an international deal

As you would expect, there are some major differences between countries. First, the list price and investment required to buy a vehicle will vary by country. For example, an Opel Vectra 1.8 costs a lot less in Spain than in Germany.

Also, the expected resale value for the same vehicle over a given mileage will differ by country due to local economic conditions, resale channels and consumer availability. These two factors create a varied picture of the depreciation cost for a similar vehicle on a country by country basis.

The same principle holds true for fuel where different prices and driving infrastructures create variations in fuel costs for the same vehicle, along with the differing impacts of diesel compared to petrol.

Overall, the road to determining the total cost of ownership for an international fleet will be complex, but ultimately rewarding. It will provide the insight and transparency that is the starting point for delivering significant and sustainable improvements to the bottom line of the company, as well as delivering an essential business tool and employee benefit mechanism.

What international developments have there been in the last few years?

1   A move from a solely 'Green' focus to a more comprehensive CSR (Corporate Social Responsibility) approach for global fleets
    In the past couple of years many companies have started developing and implementing Green policies for their fleets driven from an international level. Green measures range from offsetting CO_2 emissions to a more comprehensive carbon footprint measurement and management programme. These programmes typically include driver training and effective car maintenance. They have a positive impact on employee safety. In future we will see more corporations taking a more comprehensive CSR approach to the management of their fleet. This will include balancing the environmental impact of their fleet with employee safety whilst keeping a close eye on the cost related impact of these measures.

2. Further reduction of involvement in non-core activities
    Due to increased competitive pressures in many markets and industries, more companies are focusing their internal resources on their core activities and competences. They need to be able to rely on business partners for non-core processes. Companies are increasingly expecting leasing suppliers to provide an end-to-end fleet management service; managing all fleet related activities on behalf of the client including elements such as fleet policy development, direct driver communication and TCO control.

3   Continued international expansion of client organisations
    Many companies are continuing to grow internationally across the world and expect their business partners to grow with them. In order to manage their international expansion in an operationally efficient and cost-effective way, there will be a continued focus on process and policy harmonisation in fleet management. This means that geographic expansion by fleet suppliers to reflect the global presence of key companies is essential whilst ensuring that the set-up and way of working in these new countries reflects the success factors that have been previously applied.

Is anything happening now that will change the international leasing and fleet management landscape?

Going green is a major fleet challenge for international companies.

From about 2006 we've seen a steady increase in the number of inquiries from multinational companies on how to make their fleets greener. This is part of a wider focus by companies on environmental issues and the need to manage their businesses in a sustainable way but driven from the corporate centre.

The changing climate is now a widely accepted phenomenon. The Intergovernmental Panel of Climate Change recently concluded that the warming of the climate system is unequivocal.

CO_2 is one of the major gases responsible for bringing about this change in climate. Transport globally contributes 13.1% to the overall CO_2 emissions from fossil fuels.

If we look at the statistics since 1970 there's been a stable and sometimes even declining emissions trend for some greenhouse gases but the level of CO_2 emitted by burning fossil fuel has continued to increase during the past 30-40 years.

In addition, the transport industry is growing rapidly. If you combine this with the fact that there is an ever-increasing number of cars being put on the road every day, you start to realise why there is such a need to address the 'green' issue.

The high price of oil and raw materials is another reason companies are starting to take a conscious approach to their usage of fuel resources. If we talk in terms of fleet management, on average, fuel accounts for 22% of the costs for running a company car. In the US this percentage can be as high as 32%. With fleet costs being in the Top 3 of non-direct costs for many companies, a reduction in a company's fuel consumption will produce substantial cost savings as well as having a beneficial impact on the environment.

A third important reason why companies introduce green or sustainable business practices is a commercial one. It's becoming increasingly common for companies with well developed green approaches to require that their business partners and suppliers also adhere to certain green requirements.

How might an international company start the process of greening their fleet?

The first place to start is for a company to get an accurate picture of what the current situation is: 'How green am I? How much CO_2 do I currently produce?' This will then provide a good benchmark against which a company can measure the impact of any new 'green' measures it introduces.

Analysing a company's overall fleet composition and its carbon footprint country by country provides a good insight into where its biggest polluters are. By this I mean not only in terms of fuel consumption of the car but also in terms of mileage driven and even the driving behaviour of the company car drivers.

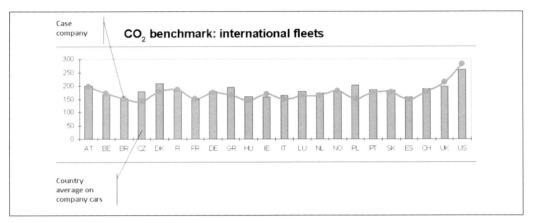

With today's level of information it is possible to benchmark against other companies' functions and industry peers. There might be some business best practices to find.

Once the current situation has been evaluated, the company then needs to set itself international targets: what does it want to achieve? By when? The target then needs to then be widely communicated within the company in order to get buy-in.

Establishing a project group to lead the environmental effort is important as the group will be instrumental in building an eco-conscious yet cost-effective fleet policy for the company; a policy that balances fleet costs with driver mobility and satisfaction as well as reducing the fleet's environmental impact.

For international companies there is also the added challenge of having to manage the fleet across multiple countries with different tax regimes and different attitudes towards cars and driving. Having widespread local country input is therefore very important to ensure that the all the relevant information is known so that informed choices can be made.

In order to make the decisions about what green initiatives should be introduced, it can be very useful to develop scenarios showing what the impact would be. By carrying out cost / benefit analyses the right mix of 'green' initiatives that suits the company's profile and environmental objectives can be chosen. In general there are 4 main groups of environmental actions a company can choose to implement:

1   Vehicle selection is a key tool in managing a greener fleet:

   Consider the cost of fuel in a monthly leasing budget to allow the most economic & greenest fuel choice

   Incentivise / penalise drivers to choose vehicles with a lower CO_2 emission

      Through a CO_2 threshold

      Through energy labels

      Through fiscal incentives

   Consider the use of alternative fuels like bio-ethanol

   Optimise the engine choice within the car policy based on CO_2 emissions and power.

2   Addressing driver behaviour can help reduce emissions whilst also reducing cost:

By ensuring drivers undergo training such as eco-driving training companies can actively impact driver behaviour helping to reduce fuel consumption and CO_2 output – which in turn also reduces cost

Promote the ecological importance of preventive maintenance and regular vehicle servicing.

Simply by providing drivers with tyre pressure gauges and making them aware of the need to regularly check tyre pressure a company can not only help reduce fuel consumption but it is also safer for the driver.

3   Reducing the total mileage driven also reduces the CO_2 output as well as the fuel costs.

Simple measures such as encouraging drivers to car pool where possible can effectively reduce fuel consumption & mileage driven.

Promote the use of in-car systems like cruise control, sat-navigation, and telematics for journey planning.

Use technology such as web or phone conferences to cut down on the need for long-distance travel for brief meetings.

There are a number of key success factors that will help ensure the success of green fleet initiatives:

- Communication is extremely important. Good communication and a clear understanding of what the company is trying to achieve with its environmental targets will help get the buy-in needed to implement new green initiatives. This buy-in needs to be throughout the international organisation from senior management through to the company car drivers.

- Effective consolidated international reporting means that after implementing new green measures, the impact on the level of CO_2 emissions as well as the costs can be tracked and shown. This measurability allows for the successes to be identified and celebrated and the level of progress towards the overall targets tracked.

- Ongoing driver training combined with driver incentive programmes will help stimulate driver cooperation in achieving the environmental objectives.

- However, by far the biggest key success factor is having a multidisciplinary approach to the project! By having senior representatives from HR, Finance & Fleet Management on the project board as well as Environmental representatives, the board can more easily get buy-in from across the organisation. It will also be better able to develop initiatives that will best fit the organisation.

- Create a CO_2 baseline assessment for fleet and compare it with your overall CO_2 foot print

- Check your fleet composition including anticipated renewals

- Set yourself an international target to reduce CO_2; why not ask your employees for an individual target?

- Know your biggest polluters; mileage, driver behaviour, vehicle choice

- Identify opportunities reduce to your CO_2 including vehicle selection and policy
- Work out the cost/benefit of initiatives and decide on which initiatives to implement
- Implement the revised car policy and approach from an international level

Can you give us an example of an international deal you have worked on?

Yes! I will explain how a particular company found the right balance between local and global needs. They are one of the world's leading pharmaceutical companies. Their business performance is driven by a motivated and mobile global sales force. The company car is an essential business tool and effective fleet management is critical in sustaining business success. Fleet represents one of the largest areas of cost to the business. Ensuring that these costs are minimised without compromising the role of the company car is a major challenge.

This challenge came into sharp focus as the company set about integrating the acquisitions of two sizeable companies. The integration almost doubled the sales force and brought a variety of car policies. A robust international framework was needed.

For success, support would be required in two key areas. The first was the full engagement of the company's senior management to gain endorsement and sponsorship to launch a global fleet management programme. The second was support of a suitable international fleet supplier to supporting the company's fleet management country by country.

With over 10,000 vehicles, Europe was the logical place to start, and it quickly became clear that major differences existed in the fleet landscape from country to country. Everything from the characteristics of the local labour market through to fuel preferences, vehicle specifications, tax and even the road infrastructure had an impact on the way fleet was run. Fleet management was carried out differently in every country and responsibility for various elements was often spread around departments with no central point of overall control.

It was apparent that unique local conditions would always remain, so the role of the international team should be to bring resource, discipline and expertise to bear in such a way that common value could be created for the local teams to utilise.

One of the clearest opportunities was to maximise the company's global purchasing power. Whilst seemingly simple, the reality was somewhat more complex. The total cost of ownership needed to be analysed. This had to be coupled with a clear understanding of the role of the company car in the compensation and benefits strategy for each country, so that attracting and retaining the right talent was not adversely affected.

Extensive analysis resulted in the development of a fleet 'dashboard' for monitoring and measuring the fleet costs in each country. Importantly, it also helped to create a benchmark from which future changes could be forecast and assessed for impact when implemented. The international fleet supplier helped to generate buy-in to the new approach in each country, and the local teams helped by running roadshows around the company's European offices. This approach transformed the capability of the local country fleet management. They did not try to impose a solution on them. Instead, the local needs were carefully considered, included in the local solution and by working together with the global approach, they achieved true local ownership and empowerment within a global fleet framework and approach. Over four years, fleet costs have reduced by more than 13%.

What is best practice when aligning car policies internationally?

Just as the car you drive says something about your personality, so a company's vehicle fleet represents an outward expression of its corporate culture. However, harmonising fleet policy should go beyond simply improving brand image or motivating employees; it should deliver significant benefits to the bottom line. Of course, for multi-national organisations, achieving a common fleet policy in the face of cross-border variations represents a considerable challenge. Driver preferences, the availability of different makes and models in each territory and long-standing local arrangements all present potential obstacles. Despite this, if implemented effectively, global fleet harmonisation can deliver significant returns through reduced costs and simplified company vehicle provision.

International policy harmonisation does not just emphasise a common culture. It ensures that all employees get the same benefits no matter where they work. Moreover, greater economies of scale have a significant impact on a company's bottom line. Cross-border procurement increases buying power and creates greater leverage with manufacturers and suppliers. Standard management processes around a common fleet policy reduce administration. Detailed planning, clear communication and co-operation between different departments in different countries are essential if these benefits are to be maximised. It is therefore important to define what we mean by an aligned international fleet policy and consider its component parts.

First, it is critical that a policy should clearly outline the rights and responsibilities of the employer and employee. It effectively forms a contract between them and should clearly set out the agreed system for choosing, using and returning company vehicles. Vehicles designated for business use are seen as an extension of the workplace. Therefore, businesses should enshrine their health and safety responsibilities within the policy as well as considering corporate social responsibility (CSR) objectives. This could include guidelines on appropriate vehicle usage, driver training requirements or even establishing the means to reduce carbon emissions. In this way the car policy becomes a valuable business tool as well as a working document.

Choice lists are central to most international fleet policies. These provide employees with a choice of vehicles and monthly lease rates that relate to their job grade. However, policies should be designed so that even drivers with no vehicle choice (such as essential business users or service based staff) should still need to refer to the policy document to check other rights and responsibilities. Hence, from an HR point of view, no employee is left out.

A structured approach to developing a policy will usually yield the best results. The suggested steps for introducing such important changes will now be considered.

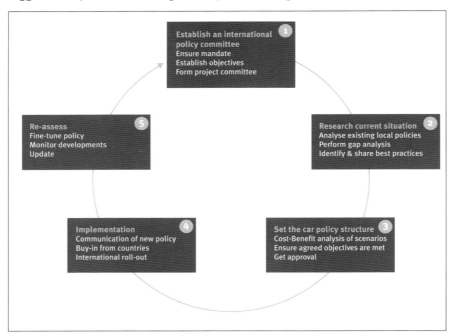

STEP 1: ESTABLISH THE RIGHT TEAM

It is vital that the right people are selected to manage the process from the outset. When choosing a steering group, the following factors should be taken into account:

- Mandate: The team must be empowered to move things forward. They must secure the support of senior management and be seen to be acting with the appropriate authority.

- Profile: The team should have the right mix of people in order to provide support and insight from a local level and develop a clear global vision for the aligned policy. Furthermore, because co-operation between different departments is vital, the committee should include representatives from finance, HR, legal, fleet and procurement. This will help to ensure the right balance between reducing total cost of ownership and maintaining employee satisfaction.

- Scope: The committee must decide whether to establish a few essential guidelines for individual countries or to provide a comprehensive set of rules covering all aspects of cross-border fleet management. It also needs to agree the parameters of international company car use, from a full user-chooser policy to a more restrictive one for essential users only or something in between the two. Finally there needs to be agreement from the outset on the objectives and implementation timelines for the alignment process.

STEP 2: BENCHMARK EXISTING POLICIES

Comparing existing fleet policies across each country will allow the steering group to establish common good demonstrated practice. It will also highlight current car choice across different territories and enable benchmarking of different makes and models. Moreover, working with an international fleet provider can provide a more extensive benchmarking opportunity, as policies can be compared across different companies and industry sectors. There are a number of considerations at this stage:

- Understanding the reasons behind vehicle provision for different driver profiles
- Ensuring vehicles on choice lists are fit for purpose from a health and safety point of view
- Measuring annual mileage and lease term to achieve accurate forecasting of residual values
- Analysing the impact of different degrees of car choice and the additional implications of allowing drivers to customise choice through optional extras
- Examining fuel choice and the likely costs based on predicted mileage rates
- Reviewing environmental considerations from both a CSR and financial perspective, especially given the trend towards emissions-based tax regimes

STEP 3: AGREE THE STRUCTURE

Having established which elements of the current national policies will remain at a global level, these must now be combined with the introduction of new procedures based on the latest industry practice.

An experienced international fleet management supplier can be especially helpful at this stage in providing this insight. The following factors represent some of the more important considerations:

- Setting parameters for employees to contribute towards the cost of their vehicle (eg upgrading to a higher spec or model) as a way of increasing choice without additional expense to the company
- Developing a choice list that strikes the right balance between cost and employee satisfaction
- Harmonising guidelines on private usage of company vehicles in the context of national fiscal implications such as benefit in kind taxation
- Clarifying rules on fair wear and tear so that drivers are aware of their responsibilities when it comes to the condition of returned vehicles
- Setting guidelines for newly-promoted employees and considering the implications for mid term leases if they are allowed to take a higher-grade car immediately
- Establishing a pool of vehicles for common business use by employees who do not qualify for a company car, or to provide cover during changeover periods, breakdowns etc

Detailed cost-benefit analysis in each of these areas, allied with the sharing of best practice, will support decision making at this stage.

STEP 4: IMPLEMENTATION

By this stage, careful research and planning should have created the foundation for a successful implementation. Once the policy has been agreed and signed off at a corporate and national level, it should then be disseminated throughout the wider organisation.

The importance of clear, effective communication at this stage cannot be overstressed. Company vehicles are an emotive topic and matter greatly to employees. There could be resistance to change, especially if it is felt that new conditions are simply being imposed without a clear rationale. By explaining the thinking behind any changes to national fleet managers and drivers, resistance or dissatisfaction can be mitigated and the objectives behind aligning international fleet policy can be successfully met.

STEP 5: RE-ASSESS

Implementation should not be seen as the end of the harmonisation process and the fleet policy should continue to evolve. Further development will inevitably be needed at a national or global level as legislative and fiscal changes occur and new vehicles are released to the market. Moreover, the wider financial, HR and CSR objectives of the business will inevitably change over time and the policy must remain in step with these.

Any fleet policy should be reviewed regularly to ensure it continues to keep pace with the latest industry developments, best practice and corporate strategy. A static policy will soon become irrelevant and will no longer achieve the benefits identified at the outset.

In conclusion, developing, implementing and managing an aligned international car policy is a complex but ultimately rewarding process. It requires considerable investment in time and resources to achieve global corporate objectives and ensure sensitivity to local conditions and driver needs. However, the payback for the business can be significant.

Communication at every stage is vital to the success of the scheme. Rather than see them as obstacles, successful harmonisation should embrace national variations in fleet operations to create a common set of guidelines that are fair, transparent and consistent and universally applicable.

In this way, the aligned policy will reflect corporate culture and provide company vehicles in a way that maximises the benefits for both the organisation and its employees.

How can LeasePlan International help fleet managers?

LeasePlan International is the world leader in global vehicle leasing and fleet management solutions with a growing network of offices in 30 countries worldwide.

We provide an unparalleled cohesive global coordination and support structure to our global customers. Using our experience and expertise, we offer a truly consistent added value service and harmonised product range designed specifically for today's multinational organisation. We work in partnership with you to create a solution that is right for your needs of today and the opportunities of tomorrow at both a national and international level.

LeasePlan International is a wholly owned subsidiary of LeasePlan Corporation. We provide the mechanism for global companies to realise the economic and qualitative benefits of a global vehicle management solution. We are committed to achieving our clients' business objectives and work in partnership with them to accomplish this.

We add value

At LeasePlan International we believe that only through an open and transparent partnership can we truly add value to our customers' business. We have developed a tailor-made portfolio of products and services that enable this open partnership. Through our range of products and consultative services we provide added value to our customers in a number of key areas:

Cost Saving

Many companies need to reduce their fleet costs. So LeasePlan International helps customers maximise economies of scale. We enable them to reduce their spend on non-core assets through structured and tailored cost reduction programmes. Total Cost of Ownership is a concept which has dramatically evolved in recent times. A clear understanding of TCO is essential for companies striving to manage an optimised fleet.

Streamline Fleet Policy

Managing a global fleet is a complex process. LeasePlan International works in partnership with customers to help them streamline their fleet policies in order to maximise efficiencies whilst maintaining a competitive fleet policy.

Insight & Control

In managing international fleets, insight and control is an essential element. LeasePlan International's best in class reporting tool, International Fleet Reporting, is a user-friendly e-tool providing consolidated reporting whenever you want it. LeasePlan has been offering consolidated global reporting to its customers for more than five years. We can deliver the complete global picture in easy-to-understand consolidated reports. Supported by a dedicated global account management structure you get the global picture with a local touch.

Streamlining global fleets is about managing them optimally, maximising efficiencies whilst retaining their competitiveness. Global fleet management is a complex process and streamlining your fleet requires insight and clear understanding of fleet policies. The areas involved range from examining current fleet policies to gain insight into the current position, measuring policies, benchmarking them against peers and industry leaders and then aligning these policies to corporate strategy.

OUR CONSULTATIVE APPROACH

LeasePlan International has developed a range of consulting modules that target different aspects of global fleet management. These modules form our consultancy suite of products, ConsultPlus. A number of our consultative modules can be used to increase the effectiveness of your global fleet policy.

Our fleet policy advice module, Policy+ reviews opportunities to make your fleet policy an effective business tool for your organisation. By incorporating best practice, we can jointly ensure your policy is compliant, market competitive and aligned with your company's objectives.

Benchmarking + is our consulting module that compares and evaluates your company's fleet profile against industry peers and market leaders. We provide a detailed gap analysis and make recommendations to customers based on their key strategic objectives and competitive environment.

The consultative module Brand+ provides the expertise and focus of LeasePlan International to our multinational customers to establish international vehicle manufacturer agreements. With LPI guiding or running this process, significant reductions can be achieved in depreciation cost and all opportunities for additional support from the vehicle manufacturers can be explored.

 In essence, LeasePlan International offers the control, commitment and expertise to support a multinational company on its journey to realise major benefits in using an international approach to fleet management.

Matt Dyer
Managing Director
LeasePlan International B.V.

28 REDUCING BUSINESS MILEAGE

Julian Feasby
Head of Internal Environment Management
The Environment Agency

Please introduce yourself and your role

I work for the Environment Agency as Head of Internal Environment Management. My role is to support my fleet management colleagues in their efforts to make our fleet use more sustainable. I have experience of fleet management as I was previously Head of Customer Services at Arval.

The Environment Agency is the leading public body for protecting and improving the environment in England and Wales. It's our job to make sure that air, land and water are looked after by everyone in today's society, so that tomorrow's generations inherit a cleaner, healthier world.

We have around 12,000 members of staff and a budget of around £1 billion. We were set up under the Environment Act 1995 and given certain duties and powers.

We are a public body – around 60 per cent of our funding comes from Government, and most of the rest comes from various charges schemes. We are independent, but we work closely with Government to get the best possible results for the environment.

Although we work across England and Wales, we have regional offices working closely with other regional bodies to develop the right solutions for local environments. We also have area offices that work with local authorities and others to tackle the immediate environmental issues in your area. Our work includes:

- **Protecting people from floods** – last year we increased flood protection to around 30,000 properties by building or improving our flood defences
- **Working with industry to protect the environment and human health** – since the mid 1990s we have reduced the amount of sulphur dioxide released into the air by 75 per cent. Sulphur dioxide can create acid rain and damage people's health.
- **Concentrating our effort on higher risk businesses** – those that run potentially hazardous operations, or whose performance just isn't coming up to scratch.

- **Helping business use resources more efficiently** – currently less than half of the waste produced by the businesses we regulate is put to productive use such as recycling and producing energy.

- **Taking action against those who don't take their environmental responsibilities seriously** – every year we bring hundreds of offenders to justice, leading to millions of pounds of fines.

- **Looking after wildlife** – we complete around 400 projects every year to improve the habitats of threatened species. Over the last 25 years there has been a six-fold increase in the number of places where otters can be found in England.

- **Helping people get the most out of their environment, including boaters and anglers.** We sell over a million rod licences a year, many to young people coming into the sport for the first time. All the money we raise goes straight back into improving the places people fish.

- **Working with farmers** to build their role as guardians of the environment, tackling pollution that we cannot see as well as adding to the beauty of the countryside.

- **Helping to improve the quality of inner city areas** and parks by restoring rivers and lakes.

- **Influencing and working with Government**, industry and local authorities to make the environment a priority.

I have worked for the Environment Agency for two and half years and my current role can be summarised as covering three main things:

- Leading and co-ordinating the work to make the Environment Agency as 'green' and sustainable as possible

- Leading the work to communicate our successes internally and externally

- Leading our efforts to ensure we are complying with all the relevant regulations that we all have to abide by

My role is particularly interesting as we are an organisation with very high levels of scientific expertise. This means that decisions and policies are robustly challenged internally to make them as solid and factually based as possible. This is particularly true of our 'green' agenda where we have many people at the cutting edge of climate change science.

As a subset of a wide ranging Internal Environmental Strategy, we have set some very challenging five year targets. These include:

1   To reduce our overall mileage by 20% from 2005/6 levels

2   To reduce water use by 25% from 2005/6 levels

3   To reduce energy use in our main buildings by 30% from 2005/6 levels

4   To reduce our overall carbon dioxide footprint by 30% from 2006/7 levels

5   To recycle 80% of our office waste by 2012

Clearly the first target is of particular relevance to this chapter.

Within our organisation we have a fleet management team which manages the strategic and tactical elements of vehicles and their use. As our role is very geographically spread and covers a huge range of operational activities, our fleet managers have involvement in:

·   lease cars

·   light commercial vehicles

·   4x 4 vehicles

·   HGVs

·   heavy plant

·   boats

·   trailers

·   hire cars

We even need to hold a small fleet of off-road quad-bikes which are used when inspecting landfill sites, as regular vehicles are not practical in those circumstances.

The Environment Agency has creatively brought fleet management and Internal Environment Management under the same line management. Graham Ledward is the Director of Resources and he leads on Human Resources, Accommodation, Fleet, Information Technology and Internal Environment Management. Aligning these functions has meant that there is a much closer practical relationship between the behavioural changes needed to help drivers and the efforts of fleet management to green the fleet.

What motivated you to embark on a mileage reduction programme?

As mentioned above, as part of the sustainability agenda one of the agreed business targets is to reduce our overall mileage by 20% from 2005/6 levels by 2012. Being a regulatory organisation as well as one carrying out a lot of geographically spread flood risk management work, we recognised that reducing our mileage levels would be a particularly difficult challenge. However, we know that transport plays a major role in the emission levels of any organisation like ours, so we chose to tackle the issue head on.

We were very aware that we had a role to play in leading private business and the public sector in this way as mileage reduction is a thorny nettle to grasp at the best of times. We were keen to walk the talk regarding the government's messages on climate change and to set an example which others will hopefully follow. We are keen to share our experiences on our mileage reduction work too.

A lot of organisations provide greener cars for their fleet and consider they then have a green light to travel as much as they have always done. They find it difficult to challenge people to give up their cars or use them less, because you really have to do this face to face.

We decided that despite the Environment Agency being a "travelling" organisation, travel had to be minimised wherever possible.

How did you go about this?

Setting the strategic imperative

As any manager worth their salt will tell you, the first, most useful step in seriously changing an organisation's behaviour is to get the buy-in of your most senior managers. In our case the Board of Directors and our own Directors Team were 100% behind the concept of reducing our mileage and the benefits this would bring.

In some organisations, perhaps in many, it will not be easy to persuade senior managers of the benefits of reducing mileage. It may need a creative approach to remind them of the financial benefits as well as the environmental ones, not to mention the enhanced credibility and public relations benefits.

The overall level of ambition and reasons for reducing mileage could therefore be woven into our business planning activities and performance management framework. This helped ensure that the targets were firmly embedded in the core management practices of the organisation. Directors could eloquently describe what we were trying to achieve, alongside the many other elements of our activity. This helps avoid the perception that mileage reduction is somehow 'on top' of the day job. Embedding it like this means that mileage reduction becomes a part of the day job.

COMMUNICATION AND DISSEMINATION

Having agreed the national level targets it is clearly crucial to ensure that people across the organisation know that the targets exist. This needs to happen in a variety of ways to ensure your messages land with people in ways which they respond to best– as everyone is different of course.

Using an internal intranet site and e-mails can be useful for describing a bit more as to what is behind the thinking. However, in a heavily field-based organisation it is important to remember that not everyone has easy access to e-mail. For these kinds of teams you need to plug into the existing communications structures, which may be cascaded through team meetings, managers' briefings or posters and fact sheets. Staff magazines can also be useful ways of getting your message (and justification) out there.

At the Environment Agency we have used some less standard methods of spreading the word, such as inserting messages into payslips. It is crucial to remember that not everyone absorbs communication in the same way, so you must try to flex your approach to maximise your impact.

CAPTURING DATA

It is obvious to say that without some existing measurement of mileage you are going to struggle to show that you have improved. We have been tracking all elements of mileage for a number of years using a variety of sources. These include mileage claims from payroll; data from fuel card systems; and fuel usage data from our hire car provider.

Each of these sources needs regular verification to ensure that the data capture process is robust and the information being generated is meaningful and accurate. This is no mean feat with a fleet as diverse as ours.

SPLITTING TARGETS

Once national targets had been set we began the process of allocating five year mileage reduction targets to all of our major business areas. This included our head office functions as well as our operational regions. The existing data was crucial here as it gave us a starting point for setting targets. We also needed to remain firm when departments challenged us, as most business managers want to see a good reason for embarking on such a difficult and new type of challenge. We had no experience of introducing formal mileage reduction targets so we needed to take a firm stand – and have continued to do so.

Below the top departmental level it is important that central teams should not try to split targets any further. To get a true sense of ownership it is useful to allow others internally to divide their mileage targets themselves as part of their business planning processes. This means they can be realistic and use their knowledge of what is really happening on the ground and how their other business plans will impact their need to drive.

If possible it is also useful not to set a central profile on how to reach a five year goal. We allowed our sub-departments to set their own reduction profile year on year which they then communicated to us centrally to track their performance. As time progresses our departments and regions provide regular commentary on how they are achieving their target or what they are doing to improve.

This allows to us share good practice throughout the organisation. There is also the added benefit of an informal competition between departments to meet their targets faster than the others.

Reporting of progress

To truly embed mileage reduction targets, you need to report progress in the same way that you report your performance against other business targets. This may be by a scorecard, performance reports, graphs, pictures, whatever works for you. As before, this helps to ensure that your senior staff will review progress as a matter of course rather than as an 'add on' measure that they may only review infrequently.

A multi-pronged attack

It is not possible to hit difficult mileage reduction targets just by setting targets. It is necessary to set up some practical tools that people can use to help them to reduce mileage. You also need to support local initiatives to gain further buy-in, because centrally-dictated processes may fail quite quickly.

Transport Hierarchy

One way of helping staff is to create, publicise and embed a 'travel hierarchy'. This is a simple tool that reminds people of the things they can do to avoid jumping in their car. It needs to be written in a clear, unambiguous way and made easy for people to access whether or not they have computer access. You may chose, as we have, to have local 'green champions' who can act as influencers within normal business.

On the next page is a copy of our transport hierarchy, clearly showing the steps we expect people to go through when deciding whether or not to make a journey. It is now the norm for our staff to use this tool, and it is even included in our induction of new starters, to ensure they are aware of what we are expect of them.

Minimising our footprint in ⊗ Transport

Greening the Agency's miles – Hierarchy of Decision making

As 'Champion of the Environment' the Environment Agency is committed to reducing its total emissions from business travel (by car) by 20% using a baseline of 2005/2006 by end March 2012. Part of Agency policy to work towards this is that all casual journeys greater than 100 miles should be done in a hire car. This will have both economic and environmental benefits. All staff have a role to play in reducing their emissions by choosing the lowest emission option for travel.

Purpose: Staff and line managers to consider the following travel options prior to making a business journey.

1) **Is the journey necessary or can video, web or audio-conferencing be used instead?**
(Video conferencing intranet link.)

 Our use of audio and web conferencing is saving around 1 million miles per month. During the petrol strikes, utilisation of videoconferencing trebled, showing we could do more.

2) **Is public transport viable and effective?**

 Public transport can be more business efficient when taking into account such issues as ability to work, road delays etc. Interest free loans are available for season tickets, and rail travel cards will be paid for by the Agency.

NB. For short journeys the Agency offers a business mileage allowance for bicycles, interest free loans for bicycle purchases as well as the tax free bike to work scheme.

✈ Plane journeys should only be considered when the corresponding rail journey is greater than 5 hours. These journeys require Director approval before travel.

3) **If no, what car should be chosen to undertake the journey?**

🚗 *To reduce our emissions the lowest emission vehicle should be driven. Car sharing is to be considered where appropriate. In order of preference the lowest emission vehicle options are pool car, lease car, hire car (where suitable miles are undertaken) and finally casual car.*

- **Is a pool car available for use?**

The Agency aims to maximise the use of its pool fleet. Environmentally, the typical Agency pool car has much lower emissions than that of a typical casual car. Financially pool cars are more cost-effective.

- **Is a lease car available for use? (this may involve borrowing a lease car from colleagues)**

The Agency aims to maximise the use of its lease fleet. The typical average emissions for a new lease car are currently 128g/km compared to 165g/km for a casual car. Financially, lease cars are more cost-effective

- **Will a hire car be cost effective?**

Environmentally, a typical hire car will not be more than 2 years old and have lower emissions than a typical casual car. Financially, a hire car will normally become cost effective if the journey distance is more than 70 miles.

- **Finally, having exhausted all other options, a casual car can be used**

On average, casual cars are significantly more polluting than alternative car options detailed above. Casual miles should not be undertaken for journeys greater than 100 miles. Annually, individual casual mileage must not exceed 10,000 miles.

As you can see, the best way to avoid mileage is to challenge the need to travel at all. So, for example, you may decide that it is not necessary to attend a meeting yourself, or that other people can attend on your behalf whilst travelling fewer miles to get there.

We have made alternatives to driving as easy as possible for our staff. We have a healthy approach to remote working whereby some staff are able to work remotely from their normal base. Technology is widely available for this approach and most other organisations could easily adopt this approach.

Teleconferencing is widely used in the Environment Agency and it does not take long to work out how to make the most of the approach .This usually amounts to keeping discussions short, having clear agendas and keeping attendance to manageable levels. It is still important to remember that you still have a business to run and face-to-face meetings must not be frowned upon if they save the need for a series of phone meetings.

Our monitoring shows that we are avoiding around 1 million miles per month by utilising this approach. This is in addition to our 8.9 million mile reduction in the last two years.

Videoconferencing is also a useful tool but it has not seen the huge take-up that many mangers expected when it was first introduced. New versions of the technology may improve things in the future.

The principle throughout has been to avoid travel where necessary and then chose the greenest option.

Public transport

It is a much-debated fact that just transferring driven miles to public transport to hit targets is not entirely straightforward. For one thing public transport can take longer, can be stressful, can be more expensive and can involve multiple journeys if your destination is not near a transport hub.

It needs a sensible and sensitive approach to overcome some of these challenges, not least an attitude that sometimes it is perfectly acceptable to drive by car. We are still running businesses after all. However, there is much you can do to make the alternatives more palatable and accessible. For us this has involved working with an online train booking company to make finding and booking train journeys painless and quick, with plenty of easy ways to reduce ticket costs. We have even set up facilities to print tickets in the receptions of our main buildings.

You can also remind people of the benefits of public transport in a work context – you can work on a laptop, read business papers, write reports, make phone calls safely and even hold meetings if you plan these in advance with your colleagues. By using public transport rather than cars in the rush hour you are less likely to be affected by delays.

Promoting the use of car share schemes is a good way to remind people how they can reduce mileage and save money. We have gone a step further by adjusting many of our car parks to cater predominantly for those who car share to get to work and to get around. We have developed an award winning car share database to encourage and incentivise staff to share journeys.

The Environment Agency has recently won an Energy Savings Trust/Department for Transport 'Fleet Heroes' award for reducing business mileage. How successful were you in reducing business mileage?

The results of our approaches have seen us reduce the number of miles driven by our lease and grey fleet over the last two years by 8.9 million miles. This represents a 25% reduction. This has resulted in around 2,200 tonnes less CO_2 emitted into the bargain.

YEAR	MILES DRIVEN	CO_2 EMISSIONS (tonnes)
2005/06	35,835,369	8,833
2006/07	30,082,258	7,348
2007/08	26,868,902	6,630

We find that success breeds success and it is good to hear staff expressing pride that their efforts are being recognised externally by awards such as this. Hopefully this will lead to greater innovation by teams to perform even better against our targets.

Did you encounter any problems in motivating your staff?

People are really passionate about cutting their mileage, partly because we are an environmental organisation, but mainly because we've made it achievable and relevant to their work. It has helped that we see a high level of awareness of climate change, as one would expect from an organisation such as the Environment Agency. However, the subject is now sufficiently main-stream to change the behaviour of most people in most organisations. Fuel price rises have similar impacts

Many of our staff have gone a step further and chosen to target mileage reduction within their individual performance (and pay award) assessments.

Those who fail to get the message are quickly identified: three times a year managers are provided with a list of the 100 staff who clock up the most miles. The idea isn't to name and shame but to alert managers to the staff who need the most help to go green. Helping them may involve asking for a plan to reduce miles or discussions about how to re-shape their jobs, perhaps by making use of other resources in other teams.

Advice such as checking the travel news before embarking on a journey can save miles circumnavigating traffic jams. Most people don't drive miles unnecessarily, they just need help from the systems we have in place.

A longer term plan is to maximise the benefits of route planning systems for operational staff. These systems are useful for optimising driving routes for staff on the road, but there is still nothing better than a serious think about your working day before setting out.

HUMAN RESOURCES POLICIES

In addition to the practical things already mentioned, there is an element of behavioural change that can be facilitated by a willing Human Resources department. So, for example, we regularly review our mileage allowance rates, making them increasingly less attractive, to encourage our staff to take public transport rather than drive a car.

If you give staff higher allowances for travelling with colleagues, this will encourage car sharing, and if you pay higher allowances for bike miles than car miles this will have a noticeable impact on those office-to-office runs in the same city or town. Reducing the mileage rate for drivers who exceed a certain threshold can also help to focus their minds on seeking alternatives.

The selection of your fleet vehicles themselves can have an impact. We have been bold and offer a very limited choice for lease drivers and almost no choice for our 'badged' fleet. If drivers cannot have their dream car they will not be tempted to spend more time in it. This has had the added benefit of markedly reducing the cost of running our fleet and the simplicity of maintaining it.

Do you have any final points you wish to make on how fleet managers might best go about reducing work-related mileage?

I hope this relatively brief summary has helped to give an indication of how the Environmental Agency has managed to make some good progress on reducing its mileage.

My key messages are that you will not achieve anything unless you tie mileage reduction targets into your main business performance methods to make them a part of 'business as usual'. You also need to ensure that you communicate what you want to achieve in an engaging and relevant way. Staff get over-loaded with messages, so make sure you do not just rely on one standard way to get their attention and buy-in.

Finally, make sure you are not overbearing about your mileage reduction programme. Your plans will flounder if you stick doggedly to your target at any cost. You need to be able to eloquently describe the benefits of doing it and acknowledge the trade-offs. In airing the difficulties I hope you will find, as we have, that drivers are resourceful and will come up with helpful ideas you would never have thought of.

Julian Feasby
Head of Internal Environment Management
Environment Agency

29 LEGAL ASPECTS OF RUNNING A CAR FLEET

Graeme Heaton

Asset Finance Counsel

Morton Fraser LLP

What legislation does a fleet manager particularly need to be aware of?

There is the old adage that ignorance of the law is no excuse. But, these days, the amount of legislation pouring into the statute books makes it almost impossible to keep up with it all. So, the main laws for a car fleet manager to be concerned with are:

i   Consumer Credit Acts 1974 and 2006 and the Regulations under them

ii   The Financial Services (Distance Marketing) Regulations 2004

iii Road Traffic Acts 1988, 1991 etc

iv   Exhaust Emissions Directives

v   End of Life Vehicle Regulations 2003

vi   Consumer Protection Act 1986

vii Sale of Goods Act 1979

viii Unfair Contract Terms Act 1977

ix   Data Protection Act 1998

x   Health and Safety at Work Etc Act 1974

xi   Carriage of Dangerous Goods by Road Regulations 1996

xii Road Vehicles (Construction and Use) Regulations 1986

xiii Motor Vehicles (Designation of Approval Marks) Regulations 1979

xiv Motor Vehicles Tyres (Safety) Regulations 1984

xv   Passenger Car Fuel Consumption Order 1983 and the Passenger Car Fuel Consumption (Amendment Order) 1996 and

xvi Petroleum and Spirit (Motor Vehicles Etc) Regulations 1929.

In outline, what does the new corporate manslaughter legislation say?

The new corporate manslaughter and corporate homicide offences were introduced by the Corporate Manslaughter and Corporate Homicide Act 2007 which came into effect in April 2008. This Act changed the criminal law approach of requiring a person with a guilty mind (the so-called 'mens rea') who commits an act causing death.

As companies and other organisations are a conglomeration of people it has proven difficult to identify any one person who has the 'directing mind' which gives the guilty mind, the intention to do the act. The Act changes the approach to corporate criminal liability by looking at the conduct of senior management in an organisation (it does not apply only to companies) both individually and collectively to see if there is a system in place to prevent deaths. Whether this Act is going to be more effective than the Health and Safety at Work Etc Act 1974 is still open to debate.

The offence is committed by an organisation '…. if the way in which any of the organisation's activities are managed or organised by its senior managers causes a person's death and amounts to a breach of a relevant duty of care owed by the organisation to the deceased'. Under section 1(4)(c) of the Act, a 'senior manager' of an organisation is one who plays a significant role in the making of decisions about how the whole or a substantial part of the organisation's activities are to be managed or organised or the actual managing or organising of those activities.

Car fleet managers are not often on the main board but they will be senior enough to set the agenda with regard to car policy in their organisation and do not forget that, basically, a car is a ton of metal containing combustible liquids that can hurtle into things and people causing damage.

What can a fleet manager do to ensure their company does not fall foul of this legislation?

For a car fleet manager the policies and practices in the company (or organisation) regarding the use of company cars will be crucial. The employee user of the car, in both their professional and personal use, must:

i   be required to drive within the rules set by the Highway Code;

ii   not carry more than the load or passenger limit of the car or vehicle.

The company itself should have documented policies and procedures in place:

i   to require employees to comply with the Highway Code;

ii   that provide some sort of review of conduct or use of cars which is outside the Highway Code.

What responsibility does the fleet manager have for ensuring that the employee/driver complies with road, car and user safety legislation when using the car?

Employers generally have a duty of care to ensure that their employees operate the machinery that is provided safely and that any machinery that is provided in the course of their employment is safe to use. The fleet manager would be the main point of contact for these issues as they relate to employees using cars in the company car fleet. The fleet manager would not normally incur personal liability but the policies and instructions that they issue to corporate car users would be the measure by which the employer would be gauged.

The policies and instructions regarding use must be sensible. They should be as a minimum that the driver should comply with all the rules of the Highway Code when driving the vehicle, such as observing speed limits, not using a mobile phone and installing child seat belts etc where appropriate.

As part of the employer's duty to provide a safe workplace, the cars must be properly maintained. So, the car fleet should be regularly maintained and serviced, at least in accordance with the manufacturer's guidelines.

When reviewing a lessor's or finance company's standard lease or finance agreement, of what issues should a fleet manager be particularly aware?

Most lease and hire purchase agreements contain very similar provisions. They expect the lessee to pay rentals or other instalments on time and in full, to look after the vehicle and to insure it, exclude the lessor from any liability for the quality or performance of the car and set out at length what events can be used to terminate the lease and the consequences of that termination. Financiers generally do not like to have to re-negotiate the terms of their leases but will consider reasonable changes for the circumstances of the lessee.

Some items to consider in particular are:

i   payments – does your company or organisation only pay by invoice or standing order? If so, change the requirement to pay by direct debit and the administration charges they seek to levy for not paying by direct debit or for changing the method of payment after signing the lease;

ii acceptance – check to see if you have to sign an acceptance certificate and how much time after delivery you have to inspect and test the car; ensure that you are not deemed to have accepted the car before you have had a chance to inspect it and preferably test it;

iii tax variations – check to see if you can have a 'two-way' clause, such that if tax rates change favourably to you as lessee you can have a rental reduction; check to see if there are any matters in the lessor's control that are to be disregarded when reviewing the rentals;

iv insurance – see what the lease requires and what you actually have in your car fleet policy to see if there is any mis-match and have the lease varied to ensure you will not be in breach, though there might be a requirement to meet any shortfall in insurance proceeds;

v   right of early termination – often leases do not give this but you may be able to negotiate the right and the terms of that right and return a vehicle at some point during the lease period;

vi breach and default
   •   these might be varied to suit the type of organisation that is entering the lease and to delete irrelevant events and to try to extend the days of grace (but lessors may try to use that as a reason to reprice the rentals); the discount rate or the amount of the termination payment may be negotiable;

- check to see what cross-default provisions may be covered (that is, default by associated companies in your group);
- check that default cannot be triggered for non-material default

vii for Scottish or Northern Ireland lessees it would be reasonable for the leases to be governed by local laws;

viii maintenance

- who is responsible for the maintenance of the vehicles?
- how far does the maintenance extend?
- how is it to be paid for?
- if the finance company is to supply the maintenance then enquiries could be made as to who will actually carry out the work and how much of each rental will be for the provision of maintenance
- have you any right to withhold the payments for poor provision of the maintenance? It is unlikely that the finance element of the payments can be withheld but what about the maintenance element?

ix return conditions – are there any? How full are they in their description of the car?

xi exclusion clauses and indemnities – how widely are these drafted? What do they include and/or exclude?

Some leases include tax variation clauses. Please explain what these are and how enforceable they are.

Tax variation clauses may be included in leases as cars and other motor vehicles are assets for which capital allowances can be claimed by the owner, with the rentals paid by the lessee being taxable in the hands of the owner. The allowances for motor cars are quite restricted and from April 2009 are based on CO_2 emission.

Before 1 April 2008 the allowance is 100% in the first year for new cars with CO_2 emissions below 110 grams per kilometre and for other cars costing less than £12,000 the allowance is 20% of the original cost; these cars are to be in the general pool of assets. For cars costing over £12,000, the allowance remains at 20% and is limited to a maximum of £3,000 per annum.

From 1 April 2009 the allowance will be based solely on emissions and will be 100% for cars emitting 110 grams of CO_2 per kilometre or less and 20% for cars emitting 110-160 grams and 10% for cars emitting over 160 grams per kilometre. 15% of the lease rental payments will be disallowed for these cars.

The rentals are subject to corporation tax for the lessor at the applicable corporation tax rate. They pay tax on the profit element in each rental they receive.

When pricing the lease of the car, the lessor will assume that the various tax rates and allowances will remain constant for the period of the lease of the car. If there is a change in those rates or allowances, usually such that the lessor's net after tax rate of return (their expected profit) reduces, then the rentals will be increased to ensure that the lessor can maintain that expected level of profit.

The enforceability of these clauses has not been much tested by the court. However, they have been around for many years and have been invoked at times when corporation tax rates have changed or when writing down allowances have been reduced. As they are common in business leasing contracts, there is a presumption that businessmen know the terms of the contracts that they enter (see, for example, the comments of the court in the case of Watford Electronics Limited v Sanderson CFL Limited ([2001] EWCA Civ 317).

It is becoming more common to refer to arbitration in lease agreements. Please explain what arbitration is and how binding it is on the parties.

Arbitration is an alternative form of dispute resolution. It is very formal in the way that it is structured and conducted. In England, Wales and Northern Ireland arbitrations are governed by the Arbitration Act 1996 and in Scotland by the Arbitration (Scotland) Act 1893 (though this is likely to be replaced by a new Act). Indeed arbitration is quite similar to court litigation in its formality and cost. Arbitration is just one type of alternative dispute resolution. There are other more informal ones, for example, mediation. Judges these days encourage the use of alternative dispute resolution.

Parties can agree in a contract to pursue a more informal dispute resolution process and refer to disputes between them to a different person for that person to decide. There are a number of organisations and bodies that will act as adjudicators in disputes, and the parties can agree in contracts that such organisation or body will decide disputes between them. Often, the disputes that arise in the course of a contractual relationship can be more quickly and more cheaply dealt with by an alternative dispute resolution process. These processes are usually more consensual than the courts which are adversarial. Indeed, it is often said that businessmen prefer arbitration or mediation and lawyers prefer litigation.

The awards and decisions from these processes are usually expressed to be final and binding on the parties but with the additional wording along the lines of 'except in the case of manifest error'. This leaves an opening for the parties or, at least, the disgruntled one to take the matter to the courts of law claiming some such error or that the arbitrator's procedure has been deficient or he has misdirected himself in law.

In practice, arbitration offers little advantage over litigation unless there is an international element to the dispute. Most likely, it will take just as long and be just as, or even more expensive. However, for disputes other than failure to make payment, mediation can offer genuine advantages and may be worth considering, particularly in a long term contract where there may be a need to keep some decent relationship between the parties.

Bear in mind that some differences of view in a contract may be referred to an expert for determination. This is not alternative dispute resolution. It is just a way of resolving a factual position.

If a lessor wishes to make a charge for something, perhaps for extending the agreement, can they do this if the agreement is silent on this matter?

The rights and obligations of the parties are set out in the contracts that they make between them. Lessors, these days, usually set out in some detail the services or items for which they can make charges, and often the amount of those charges. However, a lessor seeking to levy charges where a contract is silent on the matter does have to be careful as there is no right to levy or a corresponding obligation to pay on the lessee.

So, for example, if a lessee wished to get a copy of a rental invoice it would be unreasonable for a lessor to require anything more than a nominal administration fee. If the lessee requests a change to an existing contract, such as extension of time or a rescheduling of the rentals, then this is something for which a lessor could legitimately make a charge. If the lease requires the return of a car at the end of the lease period but the lessee wishes to keep the vehicle and extend the lease period then this will require a rescheduling on the lessor's system and the preparation of documentation for that. The lessor may well have to come to consequential re-arrangements with other parties. The level of the fee would be negotiable. As bank charges are currently in the spotlight, albeit those levied on a bank's ordinary personal customers, any additional controversy would not be welcome to the finance industry.

The Data Protection Act 1998 allows a customer to request a copy of the file (either proper or electronic) that his lessor has on payment of £10 only, but this only relates to the personal information of the fleet manager and would not usually be relevant to the fleet manager.

If a driver wishes to take his leased company car with him when he changes employer, and the new employer agrees to take on the lease, can his employer insist that the leasing company transfers the lease obligation to the new employer?

Usually, a lease agreement does not allow a lessee to transfer or assign the contract to any other person. However, in the circumstances mentioned above, a request could be made for consent for such a transfer, which would be by way of a novation of the contract. (Novation is the ending of the first contract and the creation of a new contract in the same terms as the first contract.) Unfortunately, a lessor cannot be forced to take on a lessee that they do not like, or want. If the new employer is, in the view of the leasing company, a worse credit risk then they would be acting quite reasonably to withhold any consent to a transfer.

If the car is subject to an employee car ownership scheme then the issue for the original finance company remains the same. The employer is changing and the old employer would be the one paying the sums that are due under the employee car ownership scheme albeit by way of arrangements in the ECO scheme with the employee.

Many leases say that the vehicle has to be returned to the lessor at the end of the lease 'in good condition, fair wear and tear excepted'. What are the contractual rights of the parties if the lessor claims the vehicle was not in reasonable condition and the lessee disputes this?

At the commencement of the lease period the lessor in an operating lease or contract hire agreement will have assumed a residual value for the car at the end of the lease period. If the car does not achieve that residual value or if the lessor believes that the residual value will not be achieved and the lessor believes this is due to the mileage or the condition of the car rather than a downturn in the second hand vehicle market, then the lessor is likely to claim that the car was returned with more than 'fair wear and tear' and that this has caused him loss. The amount of the loss would be either the shortfall in the sale proceeds or the cost of the repairs and work to put the car into the required condition. The lessee has a right to oppose any such claim for compensation.

The car fleet manager should inspect the car when it is about to be returned. The lessor should make an inspection on collection of the car and have a checklist to set out the defects and have the lessee sign that form. This would be crucial evidence of the condition of the car at the time of re-delivery.

However, the best way to mitigate is at the start of the relationship. When agreeing the form and wording of the lease agreement the lessee should try to include some sort of redelivery conditions. These could be either by reference to a standard, such as a condition by reference to the CAP Black Book or Glass's Guide – or, indeed, a lessor or lessee may have a standard set of descriptive terms for the conditions that could be incorporated into the lease contract.

If there is a dispute over the condition on return to the lessor and the lease says nothing about return conditions then the terms of the lease will be looked at to see how maintenance and repair was dealt with in the terms and whether the lessee has observed and performed the obligations that it agreed. The maintenance and repair records will be examined. The standards mentioned above would not be of much use in these instances.

Excess mileage charges are also applicable at this time. As the mileage will be shown on the odometer it is difficult to argue against those charges. The car fleet manager could try to have pooling of cars included in their master leases to mitigate this, so that overuse and under use can balance each other out as far as possible.

What are the circumstances in which the Consumer Credit Acts can become relevant to a fleet manager?

The Consumer Credit Acts are wholly irrelevant if a company, such as the employer, is the lessee.

For employers who operate car fleets through employee car ownership schemes the fleet manager will come across the Consumer Credit Acts 1974 and 2006 and the Regulations made thereunder. The finance agreement will be most usually a credit sale or loan agreement between the finance company direct with the employee. The employer may have arrangements with the finance company and the employee by which the actual payments are deducted from the employee's salary and paid to the finance company, but the Act will govern the credit agreement between the finance company and the employee. The employee's obligations may or may not be guaranteed by the employer, depending on the type of the scheme. This guarantee will not be governed by the Act.

Where the Act does govern the employee's credit agreement, very strict requirements have to be met in completing the agreements. The finance company may require the employer's help in having such agreements marketed to the employees and then completed by them. If so, inevitably the finance company will control what form that marketing will take and how the agreement is completed, with indemnities if the employer fails in any way. Depending on the circumstances, the employer may prefer to stay out of the picture as far as possible because of these potential liabilities.

To whom and what does the Consumer Credit Act apply?

The CCA applies to hirers and debtors who are defined in the Act as being individuals. These individuals include ordinary individual people and sole traders and partnerships of two or three persons, not all of whom are bodies corporate, and unincorporated bodies of persons which do not consist of bodies corporate and is not a partnership (for example, a golf club). It applies to all consumer credit agreements and consumer hire agreements that those individuals enter unless they are exempt agreements. There used to be a limit of £25,000 but that has now been abolished. All agreements with individuals are caught by the Act unless they are exempt.

The main exemptions are:

i   where the amount of credit or rentals exceed £25,000 and the goods are to be used for business purposes;

ii   high net worth individuals;

iii where local authorities enter credit agreements.

For car fleet operating companies entering lease agreements or other forms of finance agreements with lessor or finance companies, the CCA will not be relevant.

If the Consumer Credit Act applies to a fleet transaction, what does a fleet manager need to do to ensure that he, and his lessor, has complied with the legislation? What rights does that fleet manager have if the lessor has not complied with the CCA?

The fleet manager should ensure that if the lessor provides CCA regulated agreements, that the lessor holds the appropriate licences under that Act. Lessors will be able to supply copies of these or they can be inspected on the OFT website at http://www2.crw.gov.uk/pr/Default.aspx.

Where it is relevant due to the nature of the car scheme, the form of the agreement should be checked to ensure compliance with the CCA. The format and content of CCA regulated agreements is set out in the Consumer Credit (Agreement) Regulations 1983 (as amended).

However, the fleet manager should still be careful when looking at agreements. He would not want to be seen to be giving any detailed advice or guidance to employees regarding these issues in case he is found to be giving legal advice or other professional advice to the employees and so possibly holding himself out as being an expert and making the company liable under the laws of negligence if he is wrong in what he tells the employee.

The employer would have to get a consumer credit licence in the appropriate category or categories if the employee car ownership scheme involves the employer in promoting or organising the scheme to employees. The categories will depend on the level of involvement with the scheme.

If the lessor has not in the view of the fleet manager complied with the CCA in setting up the scheme or in the preparation of the agreements, then there is no legal obligation on him to do anything. However, in the interests of good commercial relations it would be helpful to the lessor if these issues were pointed out to them.

For the employee who has entered the credit agreement, the finance agreement is no longer automatically unenforceable (as was sometimes the case until 6 April 2007). If the lessor has not complied with the requirements of the Act and the Regulations then the lessor will have to get a court order to allow enforcement against the employee/lessee/debtor.

What are the circumstances in which the Distance Marketing Regulations can become relevant to a fleet manager?

The Financial Services (Distance Marketing) Regulations 2004 (the 'Distance Marketing Regulations') apply to financial services (which includes providing credit or hire purchase, but not lease or hire) supplied to consumers under organised distance sales or service provision schemes run by a supplier, or an intermediary, and making use of one or more means of distance communications up to the time the contract is concluded.

If the car fleet scheme is in the nature of a ECO scheme where the employee enters the credit agreement and the lessor uses post, e-mail etc to conclude the contract, then the contract will be not only regulated by the Consumer Credit Act 1974 but also by the Distance Marketing Regulations.

The Distance Marketing Regulations give a consumer a right of cancellation of the contract which lasts for 14 days after the conclusion of the contract. Hence, cars might not be delivered to employees until after that period has expired due to there being uncertainty as to whether or not the agreement with the employee will finally proceed. This right cannot be waived.

How can the Distance Marketing Regulations impact upon fleet-related transactions?

Other than in setting up the original scheme with the employee there should be, as with the CCA, only limited impact from the Distance Marketing Regulations.

However, if the car fleet manager wishes to ensure that cars are delivered by the lessor (or the original supplier) as soon as possible after acceptance by the employee of the credit agreement; then in setting up the fleet arrangement the fleet manager may have to get his board's approval to give an indemnity to the lessor/finance company to make good any loss that the lessor/finance company may suffer if the car is delivered during the 14 day cancellation period and the employee does decide to cancel that contract.

The Consumer Protection (Distance Selling) Regulations 2000 might be relevant depending on the type of employee car ownership scheme that is operated. These apply to contracts for the sale of goods and services to consumers using distance communications. The supplier is required to give the consumer details of the supplier and the goods; their characteristics, price and arrangements for delivery. There is a right to cancel the contract that endures for 7 days after delivery and if that is exercised any related finance contract will terminate as well. So if the employee buys a car and uses a finance agreement and then cancels, both agreements would be terminated.

What rights does the fleet manager have if a car is not of satisfactory quality or fit for purpose when it is delivered or if the car is delivered late?

The requirement that a vehicle that is sold or supplied on finance is of satisfactory quality is set out in various statutes and this requirement is by law included as an implied term in every sale contract or finance agreement.

What is 'satisfactory quality'? The Sale of Goods Act 1979, section 14, provides:

(2)   Where the seller sells goods in the course of a business, there is an implied term that the goods supplied under the contract are of satisfactory quality.

(2A)   For the purpose of this Act, goods are of satisfactory quality if they meet the standard that a reasonable person would regard as satisfactory, taking account of any description of the goods, the price (if relevant) and all the other relevant circumstances.

(2B)   For the purposes of this Act, the quality of goods include their state and condition and the following (among others) are in appropriate cases aspects of the quality of goods –

(a)   fitness for all the purposes for which goods of the kind in question are commonly supplied,

(b)   appearance and finish,

(c)   freedom from minor defects,

(d)   safety, and

(e)   durability.

(2C) The term implied by sub-section (2) above does not extend to any matter making the quality of goods unsatisfactory –

(a)   which is specifically drawn to the buyer's attention before the contract is made,

(b)   where the buyer examines the goods before the contract is made, which that examination ought to reveal, or

(c)   in the case of a contract for sale by a sample, which would have been apparent on a reasonable examination of the sample.'

These terms are implied in all sale contracts and that includes conditional sale and credit sale. This is substantially followed in the wording of section 10 of the Supply of Goods (Implied Terms) Act 1973 which applies to the supply of cars under hire purchase terms, and also in section 4 of the Supply of Goods and Services Act 1982 which applies to goods supplied on lease.

There are quite a lot of decided cases about what might be an 'unsatisfactory' car.

For example:

i   Bernstein v Pamsons Motors (Golders Green) Limited [1987] 2 All ER 220, where the engine on a new car seized within three weeks and 140 miles due to a manufacturing defect. The judge said that although a purchaser must expect some teething troubles, this was beyond what could be expected.

ii   Jackson v Chrysler Acceptances Limited [1978] RTR 474, where a new camshaft, exhaust, radiator and clutch were required in the first few months, this made the car un-merchantable (ie, unsatisfactory).

iii Rogers v Parish (Scarborough) Limited [1987] 2 All ER 232, where a brand new Range Rover car was unsatisfactory and returned to the dealer and replaced. The replacement had faulty oil seals and defects in the engine, gearbox and bodywork. This was held not to be of merchantable quality given the description and expectations associated with this brand of car.

The status of the manufacturer's warranty was also given consideration in that third case. This warranty is something that is additional to the customer's right to reject for unsatisfactory quality. However, if the car is of satisfactory quality then the right to reject for minor defects is lost and the customer will have to rely on the manufacturer's warranty to make good any repairs or replacement work that may be required.

For how long after delivery is there a right to reject a car?

Three weeks was too long in Bernstein but in Rogers, six months had elapsed and the customer had not lost the right to reject. There are a number of other cases that have given consideration to the period after delivery in which a car can be rejected:

i   Farnworth Finance Facilities v Attryde [1970] 1 WLR 1053 – a motorcycle being the subject of finance. It was found to have numerous defects and although four instalments had been paid, the condition was such that the customer could reject it.

ii UCB Leasing Limited v Holtom [1987] RTR 362 – a car was delivered in August 1980; it had serious defects. The hirer paid instalments until November but the car was not returned until March 1981. By this time, they had lost the right to reject.

The courts have not given definitive guidance as to when a car may be rejected. But the Sale of Goods Act 1979 requires that there is a 'reasonable time' to inspect the vehicle and discover faults. It is one of those situations where the courts will look at the circumstances in the particular case to see if there has been a reasonable time.

In the case of rejection of a car by a fleet manager, the remedies available for that will depend on the nature of the breach by the supplier and the terms of the hire or credit agreement. A fleet manager will be a non-consumer for the purposes of the Sale of Goods Act 1979, section 15A, so if the implied term of quality is breached in a way that is slight and it would be unreasonable to allow rejection, then the vehicle may still be rejected but the supplier's breach is not a breach of condition, it has the lower status of a breach of warranty and the claim will be for damages only. (Breach of condition is a fundamental breach of the contract that goes to the root of the contract and allows a person to claim for restitution, which is restoration of the person into the position they were in previously, or allows damages to be claimed but for the greater loss that a breach of condition allows.)

The implied terms cannot be excluded in contracts with consumers. They can be excluded in their application to contracts with businesses where the lessee is the employer company. This is dealt with in the next question and answer.

The use of acceptance certificates by finance companies is an attempt by them to reduce the likelihood that any customer complaints will be made regarding the quality of the vehicle. However, whilst they are evidence of the satisfactory quality of a vehicle at the time they are signed, it is only at that time. If there are latent defects that are not apparent on inspection or after short testing but which come to light after a period of time, the car could still be rejected if those defects are sufficiently serious.

Does the Unfair Contract Terms/Unfair Terms in Consumer Contracts legislation have any impact on lease contracts for the fleet manager?

The Unfair Contract Terms Act 1977 is most relevant in relation to the exclusion clauses that are common in leases and other finance agreements. Those are the clauses that say the finance company or lessor is not responsible for the vehicle and has not selected the vehicle and is not responsible for its fitness for purpose or quality.

The Act prohibits the excluding or restricting of liability by a party for a breach of an obligation arising out of an implication of law from the nature of the contract where the breach has caused death or personal injury and, unless the exclusion is reasonable, likewise prohibits exclusion of liability for any other breach. So, in the case of a lease, it is only possible in the case of a business lessee entering a lease contract for a lessor to exclude liability for quality or fitness for purpose of a vehicle if that clause in the lease agreement is reasonable. (Companies operating car fleets are not likely to be consumers in relation to whom it is not possible to exclude those obligations.)

The legislation also applies to other contractual provisions such as those which purport to exclude or restrict liability of the lessor or exclude a particular remedy such as set-off. Other clauses, such as indemnity clauses in leases, also have to be reasonable and it is up to the lessor or finance company to show that those clauses which restrict or exclude their liability are reasonable in the circumstances. On the other hand the lessee might boldly take the view that the more unreasonable the lessor's exclusion clause, the better, as it may be all the more unlikely that a court will uphold it. This is risky route to take, though, as the court decisions swing between them deciding that lessors should not be able to hide behind blanket exclusion clauses, on the one hand, and that business people should be held to contracts they make, on the other, depending on the exact facts. Perhaps the best that can be said is that, if the lessor sticks with its exclusion clause, as it probably will, the lessee may still, in a dispute about a defective vehicle, question the validity of the relevant exclusion of liability for that defect.

In short, when looking at the terms in a finance company's lease or other finance agreement, those clauses that exclude liability should be reviewed to see if they are too wide and the lessor may well make some changes to ensure that they remain reasonable in the circumstances.

The Unfair Terms in Consumer Contracts Regulations 1999 do not apply to fleet operating companies as the definition of 'consumer' in those Regulations is a 'natural person who in making the contract... is acting for purposes which are outside his business'. However, once again, if the car scheme involves the employee entering finance agreements with the finance company, the legislation will apply to those contracts and the individual employees. The effect is to require that the terms of the contract with a consumer have be fair and reasonable in the way that they are written. The terms have to be written with the requirement of good faith in mind. This requires consideration of factors including the strength of the parties and whether the goods or services were supplied specially and whether the supplier has dealt 'fairly and equitably' with the consumer. Also consumer contracts are increasingly expressed in plain English to ensure that these requirements are fulfilled.

A lot of car fleet schemes use undisclosed agency structures. What rights does a fleet manager have if the maintenance is not being provided properly or the finance company goes bust?

In the days before the credit crunch this question would probably never have had to be asked.

The finance company will have made arrangements with maintenance suppliers or the manufacturers to ensure that the cars are maintained from time to time. As they have the principal contract with the maintenance supplier then the lessee company is in some risk of not having maintenance provided should the finance company go into administration or otherwise go bust. However, it is likely the maintenance supplier would be prepared to negotiate with the company to ensure that the maintenance is continued. However, any payments that have been made by the finance company to the maintenance provider would still have to be honoured. That is, if there is maintenance that has been prepaid then the cars that are subject to that prepaid maintenance would still be eligible for that. If there are maintenance payments outstanding then the maintenance supplier would have a lien (which is dealt with in the next section) over the vehicles concerned.

The rental payments may include a finance element for the repayment of the finance for the acquisition of the car and a maintenance element for the provision of the maintenance. If the maintenance is no longer being provided by the finance company then withholding that element of the rentals would be reasonable. The maintenance provider would be willing to negotiate but the costs may be different and the maintenance element of the rentals might not be enough.

It may also be the case that the agency arrangement does not extend to the supply of maintenance, which might still be a direct contract between the maintenance supplier and the lessee. In this case the demise of the finance company will leave the maintenance unaffected.

If a car is sent for repairs, what rights does a repairer have if they are not paid for those repairs?

If a repairer is not paid for repairs and improvements that he has made to a car then he has a lien over the car and the owner will not be able to recover the car until the cost of the repairs is paid. The costs must relate to improvements, not just routine servicing or maintenance of the car. This may be quite a difficult distinction to draw, but has been recognised by the courts over the years.

Where the lessee or hirer with possession and use of the car does not pay for repairs then the situation is little more difficult. The owner must authorise or agree the repairs. This has been implied from the obligation in hire purchase agreements to keep a vehicle in repair. The person claiming the lien is entitled to infer that authority unless any limitations on that authority that are given in the contract are communicated to him.

Ultimately, by virtue of the Torts (Interference with Goods) Act 1977, in England and Wales the repairer can sell the car provided that notice is given to the owner of the car of the intention to do that. For a fleet company, this notice would be sent to either the finance company or the employee if they are the owner of the vehicle (depending on the nature of the car scheme).

What can Morton Fraser LLP do for businesses in the fleet world?

For lessors

We have unrivalled expertise in asset finance and leasing agreements, and have handled transactions with values ranging from £3 million to over £200 million in the past year. As well as drafting standard form agreements that will be used in small and middle ticket deals.

We can offer extensive experience in the vehicle lease sector. For example, we recently advised the funder in a £167.5m syndicated multi-option asset finance facility for a publicly-quoted vehicle provider

A number of our clients in the fleet industry are car fleet management companies which provide cars to employers and employees through various types of employee car ownership schemes.

Based on our experience, we can advise on issues such as setting up employee car schemes, vendor finance schemes and the range of end user and other contracts that is required to implement them.

FOR END USER FLEETS

We act for lessors and funders who provide finance for car fleets and other assets, so based on our knowledge of acting for financiers, we can advise on the scope and content of the agreements that finance companies expect their customers to sign and advise as to where they can be amended and how best to go about that.

Car fleet operators need to be aware of their responsibilities as the employer of the user and the obligor under the finance agreements. We can help with issues that may arise during the life of the finance agreements and in relation to employee issues.

We understand that fleet managers will need advice and support in a number of additional areas over and above finance agreements. These could include obtaining advice on health and safety law from our experts, who can train fleet managers on the key legal issues surrounding corporate manslaughter and the employers' responsibilities for health and safety when they are providing vehicles to their employees.

ADDED VALUE FROM MORTON FRASER

Access to unique expertise: Morton Fraser has a nationally-renowned asset finance and leasing practice, headed by Bruce Wood who is regarded as the leading asset finance lawyer in the UK based outwith the City. Our Corporate team is the current Corporate Firm of the Year, and the Corporate Lawyer of the year Austin Flynn is part of that team. Innes Clark, who heads up our Employment team was recently named Employment Partner of the Year.

Training and coaching for people in the industry in a whole range of legal issues associated with the leasing of fleet vehicles including employment advice, information on directors' responsibilities and health and safety advice.

Graeme Heaton
Asset Finance Counsel
Morton Fraser LLP

MORTON FRASER
SOLICITORS

Morton Fraser is a major commercial law firm based in Edinburgh with offices Glasgow and London with a leading asset finance and leasing team. We deal with small, middle and big ticket work for lessors and vendors and advise fleet operators and equipment users and borrowers in relation to their finance contracts.

The setting up of car leasing and employee car ownership schemes is an area where we can help in advising in all the aspects that are briefly mentioned in the foregoing chapter.

The asset finance and leasing team comprises 4 partners and 5 solicitors with wide ranging skills in drafting and negotiating all types of finance and security contracts and also in relation to the enforcement of rights and recovery of money under those contracts.

Phone Bruce Wood 0131 247 1026
Graeme Heaton 0131 247 1291
Bev Wood 0131 247 1324

30 WORKPLACE TRAVEL PLANS

Heather McInroy

Programme Director

National Business Travel Network

Please introduce yourself and your role

My involvement with travel planning, both as a practitioner and as a researcher, has spanned almost 15 years. During that time I have held various posts with BAA Heathrow related to surface travel and transport involving the reduction of the negative financial, environmental and social impacts of both. As a practitioner, my roles included Heathrow Express Liaison Manager in which I had responsibility for ensuring the smooth interface between the new Paddington to Heathrow rail service and the airport; as Change Manager in the Planning and Environment Team I researched, published and delivered BAA Heathrow's first travel plan 'Travel Choices' (2000) and I was joint lead of 'Project Unity' (2001), an ambitious award-winning project to encourage hot-desking and teleworking amongst the management team (which reduced annual accommodation costs by £400,000 and delivered measured productivity improvements) and as Head of Research and Travel Management I was responsible for 'Changing Direction – Heathrow's Travel Plan 2004-2008' which included Airport Carshare, Airport Commuter, Airport Conference and Airport At Home – all schemes designed to reduce the impact of employee travel to and from the airport as well as on business. These schemes delivered significant business benefits including the deferred building of a multideck staff car park at a saving of £8 million and an initial investment of £100,000 in videoconferencing being recouped within 6 months. Additionally, Airport Carshare remains the largest single-site car share scheme in Europe and won the ACT Travelwise Marketing Award in 2002.

As a researcher I have written reports including 'The Barriers to Reducing Employee Car Dependency' and 'Sustainable Development Versus The Car Culture: The Organisational, Cultural and Structural Factors Necessary for Success' whilst studying for an MA in Change Management. My research continues with a part time doctorate focusing on the business efficiency benefits to be derived from car use reduction and how these can be achieved.

I joined the National Business Travel Network in April 2008 as Programme Director and it is an ideal role in which to use my previous experiences to help influence businesses to reduce their employee travel impacts. Coming from the private sector I can understand why travel planners in organisations find the work challenging and also why senior managers do not instantly see its benefits. Many managers overestimate the costs associated with implementing travel plan measures and underestimate the business benefits. Unless we sell the business benefits first and foremost, business leaders will not be convinced. NBTN helps travel planners make the business case for their work.

I work closely with organisations, academics and government on travel planning issues. My role is to convince business of the benefits of travel planning and to encourage and facilitate behavioural change. It is a delicate subject because cars remain the overwhelming method of travel in the UK today both for commuting and travelling on business. Our attachment to the car and the freedom it offers us are great and the alternatives often seem unattractive by comparison.

Only a minority of organisations have developed and implemented full travel plans. A recent British Chambers of Commerce (BCC) survey 'The Congestion Question' (November 2008) indicates that only 6% of businesses have these in place although other measures associated with travel planning and reducing work-related car use increasingly feature in business life. Nearly two thirds of businesses surveyed indicate that they have implemented at least one measure in response to environmental issues with two out of five businesses having introduced home working strategies and one in three having implemented IT and e-business solutions. The same report advises that the cost of congestion 'has risen by a staggering £5.7 billion to a total of £23.2 billion' yet despite this 98% of businesses describe the road network as important to them including 76% who indicate it is essential.

So perhaps the time is right for increased momentum in travel plan development with traditional travel planners working along side fleet managers and business travel managers. Economic pressures, fluctuating fuel prices, congestion and their increasing costs to businesses may be just what are needed to shake us out of our car comfort. Cars are vital, they have their place but there are ways we can make sure that they are used effectively and efficiently for financial, environmental and social benefits.

What is NTBN?

The National Business Travel Network (NBTN) is a business-to-business network which enables companies to share best practice and promote the rationale for travel plans and Smarter Choices. Through research and practical case studies, NBTN is developing and demonstrating the strong business case for workplace travel planning. A Department for Transport (DfT) funded initiative and part of the government's ACT on CO_2 campaign (http://campaigns.direct.gov.uk/actonco2/home/on-the-move.html) NBTN works in partnership with and supports many existing organisations and networks such as the BCC and The Confederation of British Industry (CBI). NBTN was established in February 2007 and its remit is to encourage businesses – with a specific focus on the FTSE 350 whilst including SMEs – to consider, and act on reducing the financial, social and environmental impact of their employees' work-related travel.

The NBTN Membership Offer includes free attendance at all events, access to research, best practice documentation and knowledge base, business-to-business networking and a two way communication conduit between members and the DfT. There is no charge for joining NBTN as it is viewed as essential by government to communicate the importance of sustainable travel and transport to businesses in order to support the government's CO_2 emissions reductions targets. The network now has over 200 full member organisations – including key businesses such AstraZeneca, BSkyB, BT, E.ON, IBM, Orange and Vodafone.

NBTN also funds research which is carried out by some of the UK's leading travel and transport planning academics and consultants. The purpose of this research is to provide real and up to date business case evidence of the effectiveness of travel plans. This research can be downloaded from NBTN's website.

Fleet managers today are increasingly being asked to take on the role of 'mobility managers', responsible not just for company cars but for all types of work and business travel. We are beginning to hear a lot about Workplace Travel Plans. What is a Workplace Travel Plan and why is it necessary?

It is good to hear that fleet managers are being asked to take on the role of mobility managers and become involved travel planning. The more that fleet managers, travel planners and business travel managers communicate or indeed take on joint roles, the more likely it is that organisations will see the business benefits to be derived from reducing the impact of all work related travel.

Workplace travel plans are plans that are put in place to reduce car use associated with work, which includes both commuting and business travel. They are necessary for many reasons – increasingly congested roads; ever increasing transport related carbon emissions; fluctuating fuel costs; land take associated with car parking; driver stress; social equality and so on.

The Eddington Report on transport, carried out for the government, makes clear links between a high-performing transport system and sustained economic prosperity and argues that a 5% reduction in travel time for all businesses and freight travel on the roads could generate around £2.5 billion of costs savings – which equates to 0.2% of GDP. Eddington also argues that the rising cost of congestion will have a considerable impact on the UK economy if left unchecked and estimates that it would cost an extra £22 billion in terms of time wasted in England alone by 2025 when 13% of all traffic will be subject to stop-start travel conditions.

Finding ways to make the best possible use of transport infrastructure and minimising loss of time and economic damage is a clear priority and an activity that the DfT is encouraging all businesses and sectors of the economy to engage in. Travel plans offer one proven methodology for bringing about this change by making best possible use of transport infrastructure. The DfT has concluded that, on average, travel plans can reduce the number of single-occupancy vehicle trips to a destination by 18%. Reductions in traffic levels of this magnitude at peak time can significantly ease traffic flows, increasing the reliability of journey times and improving the commuting experience.

To understand the problem in more detail it helps to start at a national level. Figure 1 shows the CO_2 emissions in the UK by sector. Transport related CO_2 emissions are 29% of the total with 20% being road sector related and 9% air transport related. Transport emissions are second only to emissions from the energy industries. Transport remains the only sector in which emissions are growing and it is important that government, organisations and individuals all work together to reduce this, not least because the UK Climate Change Act (2008) stipulates an 80% reduction in CO_2 emissions against 1990 levels by 2050.

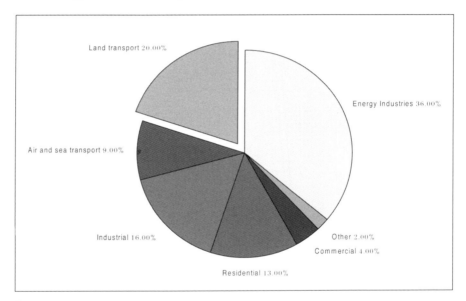

Figure 1
Source: NETCEN (National Environmental Technology Centre) 2006

Figure 2 (over) shows UK CO_2 emissions from transport and reveals that the percentage of CO_2 emissions from cars is over 52.5% of the total whilst railways are 1.7% and buses 3.7%. Car use has a major impact on emissions.

Figure 3 (over) takes car use and breaks it down into the type of journey cars are used for. This is of specific interest to managers with responsibility for reducing the impact of work-related travel as it shows that, of the emissions from passenger cars, 24% are from commuting and 13% from travelling on business. Therefore 37% of passenger car emissions result from peoples' activities in relation to their work – and these journeys have the highest proportion of single occupancy car trips at 91% and 87% respectively. This is the area workplace travel plans are focused on.

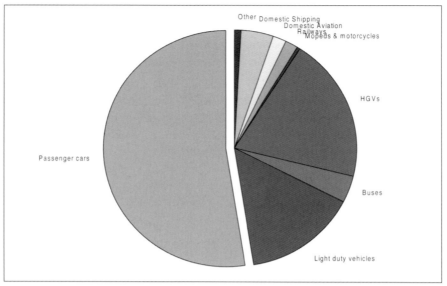

Figure 2. Source DfT

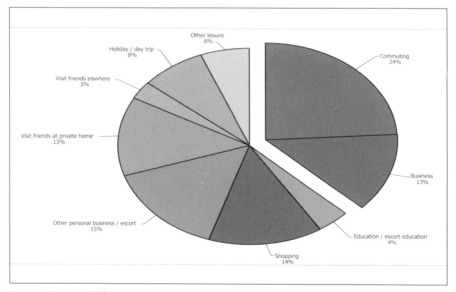

Figure. Source: DfT

Travel Plans have been called by a variety of names including Employer Transport Plan, Green Travel Plan, Site Based Mobility Management, Green Commuter Plan and Site Based Transportation Demand Management. Essentially these are all one and the same thing. The official description of a travel plan is 'a package of measures tailored to meet the needs of individual sites and aimed at promoting greener, cleaner travel choices and reducing reliance on the car. It involves the development of a set of mechanisms, initiatives and targets that together can enable an organisation to reduce the impact of travel and transport on the environment, whilst also bringing a number of other benefits to the organisation as an employer and to staff' (EEBPP, 2001).

A travel plan is a long term strategy for managing the travel generated by an organisation. It can be applied to a workplace, school, university, hospital and superstore, indeed anywhere that attracts travel to or from it, whether it is by employees, customers, visitors, residents or deliveries. Its aims are predominantly to reduce single occupancy car use and to extend travel choice by encouraging more cycling, walking, public transport use, car sharing, flexible and home working. Increasingly travel planners are also turning their attentions to reducing business travel and providing attractive alternatives such as video and audio conferencing to replace non-essential journeys. Reducing car miles not only benefits the environment but can produce financial benefits and productivity improvements, saving both the business and its employees' money and time.

Most workplace travel plans are based on Smarter Choices – a major piece of research commissioned by DfT and published in 2004 (Cairns, S., Sloman, L., Newson, C., Anable, J., Kirkbride, A. & Goodwin, P. (2004) Smarter Choices – Changing the Way we Travel. DfT www.dft.gov.uk/pgr/sustainable/smarterchoices/ctwwt/). Smarter Choices are 'soft' interventions as opposed to 'hard' interventions. 'Soft' measures address the psychological motivations for travel choice as well as economic ones and involve behavioural change, communication and marketing. 'Hard' measures are physical improvements to transport infrastructure or operations, traffic engineering, control of road space and changes in price.

Smarter Choices influence people's travel behaviour towards less carbon-intensive alternatives than the car, such as public transport, walking and cycling, by providing targeted information, opportunities and facilities to consider alternative modes. Smarter Choices can include workplace and school travel plans, personalised travel planning, travel awareness campaigns, public transport information and marketing, car clubs and car sharing schemes and teleworking, teleconferencing and home shopping

This research evidences that travel plans are 'good for business'. A good workplace travel plan can improve the efficiency and environmental credentials of an organisation – and save it money. The table below summarises some of the business benefits:

Finance
<ul><li>Cost savings from reducing the costs of car parking and office accommodation, reduced business mileage and general travel and subsistence costs</li><li>Increased profits – from the above plus proven employee productivity improvements, recruitment and retention benefits</li><li>Greater business efficiency – streamlined business, less waste</li><li>Reduced expansion requirement / possibility for consolidation</li><li>Corporate Social Responsibility benefits</li></ul>

Facilities

- Improved office space efficiency due to flexible working, hot-desking
- Reduced car parking requirement / possibility to turn land to other use
- Improved movement in and around site

Human Resources

- Improved staff retention
- More attractive recruitment package
- Reduced sick leave
- Improved staff health, motivation and morale
- Improved health and safety benefits

Environmental/Corporate Social Responsibility

- Supports accreditation of Environmental Management Systems and Quality Assurance
- Making positive contributions to carbon emissions reduction targets
- Improved staff awareness of and involvement in environmental issues
- Increasing transport sustainability
- Improvements for local community
- Increasing stakeholder engagement

Is there a recognised way to introduce a Travel Plan?

In March 2008, DfT and NBTN published 'The Essential Guide to Travel Planning' which can be downloaded at http://www.nbtn.org.uk/essentialguide.pdf. This is a best practice guide to travel planning which is highly regarded in the travel planning community. It features in the recently published BSI PAS500 Travel Plan Standard and is recommended as a key source of information for organisations developing travel plans and for those wishing to attain the BSI standard.

NBTN was among key stakeholders, including ACT Travelwise, Transport for London and independent experts who all collaborated to produce this BSI-endorsed Publicly Available Specification (PAS) that has all the functionality of a British Standard for the purposes of creating management systems, product benchmarks and codes of practice. PAS500 is intended for use by any organisation planning or developing a workplace travel plan whether it is initiated as part of a CSR policy, planning application or air quality strategy. It defines the requirements for developing and implementing a workplace travel plan, including public availability, resources and claims of conformity. The specification aims to establish a formal process through which all travel plans should be developed although it does not intend to suggest specific targets or measures that should be included in a travel plan, which can be decided by individual organisations.

Launching PAS500, Project Developer Paul Henderson from the London-European Partnership for Transport (LEPT) said: "The development of a national standard for our industry will improve the quality and effectiveness of travel plans and provide a valuable resource that travel plan professionals can rely on."

The PAS500 can be accessed at www.bsigroup.com/en/Shop/Publication-Detail/?pid=000000000030180397

Is the government pushing companies to introduce Travel Plans?

At present there is no legislation requiring an organisation to develop and implement a travel plan with the exception of certain conditions associated with the planning approvals' process. Voluntary travel plans are motivated by financial, environmental and social factors and there is growing evidence of the business benefits of travel planning. The government is keen to influence businesses to introduce travel plans and supports and encourages their introduction as a key way of responding to and reducing the 37% of work-related transport CO_2 emissions.

See www.dft.gov.uk/pgr/sustainable/ for more information.

The government sets out its approach to transport and reducing transport impacts in two key documents. The first is 'Supporting Economic Growth in a Low Carbon World – Towards a Sustainable Transport System' (TaSTS -October 2007). Its main goals are to:

- Support national economic competitiveness and growth
- Reduce transport's emissions of greenhouse gases
- Contribute to better safety, security and health
- Promote greater equality of opportunity
- Improve quality of life

The more recently published 'Delivering a Sustainable Transport System' (November 2008) takes this one stage further and:

- Explains how to put TaSTS into action
- Outlines key components of national infrastructure
- Lays out the difficulties of planning with uncertainty surrounding future demand
- Sets up a new National Networks Strategy Group

This report calls for government to promote travel plans more vigorously to businesses. The findings from the research highlight that whilst travel plans are being implemented with varying degrees of success by many local authorities, NHS trusts and academic institutions and to a lesser extent by businesses, they are far from 'mainstream' in the UK. High profile successes aside, this research indicates that travel plans are often developed on an ad hoc basis without strategic direction and suggests they exist in a policy vacuum, are marginalised, lacking in resources and monitoring and hence are not as effective as they could be.

Whilst there are undoubted environmental and social benefits to be gained from reducing car use, businesses also stand to gain from business efficiency benefits and reduced costs and it is this message that the NBTN is focusing on – particularly given the difficult economic situation. NBTN therefore aims to raise awareness of the high and often overlooked financial costs of these activities and encourages organisations to review how they operate and to consider alternative options that will deliver business efficiencies across the board whilst boosting their CSR credentials.

Can you give us some examples of organisations that have introduced best practice and the benefits they have obtained?

The NBTN website www.nbtn.org.uk has a selection of best practice case studies from a variety of sectors including retail, pharmaceutical, telecommunications, aviation, financial services and energy. Four case studies have been selected for inclusion below – BAA Heathrow, BT, Vodafone and HBOS.

Case Study One: Better Travel Choices at BAA Heathrow

"Our aspiration for the travel plan is that every member of staff should have access to a sustainable transport journey to the airport at all times of the day."

Theo Panayi, Surface Access Strategy Manager

Location and overview

Heathrow is the UK's largest employment site with more than 315 organisations employing 72,000 staff. Over 75% of staff are operational and their work patterns are mainly shift based. 95% of all movements at Heathrow are visitor based with some 68 million passengers per annum. The challenge is to provide high quality alternatives to traveling by car for all staff and visitors, throughout the airport, 24 hours a day. Occupying nearly 12 square miles in the London Borough of Hillingdon, West London, the site is bounded by several major roads including the A30 and A4. An extensive cycling network is rapidly being improved.

Strategic context

BAA's 'Changing Direction' Travel Plan has been in place since 2004 and has recently been rebranded as 'Better Travel Choices: Heathrow's Travel Plan 2008-2012'. The Travel Plan has key interfaces with the Rail, Bus & Coach Strategy, and all projects are under the overall programme of the Airport Surface Strategy 2008-2012.

A Clean Vehicles Programme has also been set up which looks at four key areas:
- Improving fuel economy;
- Reducing vehicle mileage;
- Introducing cleaner vehicles and fuels; and
- Staff travel for commuting and business

Measures / policies in place
- Free travel zone around the airport perimeter
- Airport Staff Travel Card giving up to 50% discount on some routes coming into the Airport
- Earlier running and a new 24 hour local bus services for staff

- Airport Carshare, the largest car share scheme in Europe with over 4,700 registered users
- 40 companies who employ 75% of Heathrow's staff have signed up to the Travel Plan
- Some 20,000 conference calls have been made between BAA airports over the past 4 years

Benefits realised

Primary benefits

Heathrow is on track to achieve no more than 65% of all airport staff coming in by single occupancy car by 2012. This is from a baseline of 72% from 2004

Two years after implementation of the travel plan, demand for parking fell by 500 spaces. The construction of an £8 million multi-storey car park was deferred

Hot-desking has allowed the release of accommodation savings of £400,000 per year

More passengers are choosing to use public transport, increasing from 25.5% to 38.6% between 2003 and 2007. Current figures for the first two quarters in 2008 are even higher and the airport is on track to meet the following target: To achieve 40% of air passengers travelling to and from the airport by public transport by the end of 2012, with an objective of 45% in the longer term with the introduction of new strategic public transport infrastructure such as AirTrack.

Employee Modal Share 2012 Targets		
	Mode 2004 (% actual figures)	Mode 2012 (% target)
Car driver	72.13	65.00
Public bus/coach	10.77	14.00
Underground	4.58	5.00
Car passenger	4.47	6.00
Air	2.39	2.39
Motorcycle	1.37	1.37
Work bus	1.24	1.24
Bicycle	1.16	1.35
Heathrow Express	0.64	0.64
Walk	0.49	0.49
Other rail	0.48	2.23
Taxi	0.28	0.28

Secondary benefits

Reduction in fleet management costs for businesses

Reduction in staff travel and fleet CO_2 emissions. The Heathrow Car Share scheme saves an estimated 247,820 kg of CO_2 per month.

Costs

Staff costs – 2 full-time equivalents (£90,000 per year with on-costs)

Public transport improvements – £2 million per year

Travelcard scheme – £40,000 per year

Free travel zone – £500,000 per year

Future initiatives include an increasing reliance on strong communications as staff are relocated to different terminal buildings, continuing to promote an increase in the use of technology to reduce business travel and developing a support network for other businesses on Heathrow to help them develop their own action plans that will feed into the overall travel plan strategy.

Additional reference material

BAA Heathrow (2008): Sustaining the transport vision: 2008-2012, A Surface Access Strategy for Heathrow.

BAA Heathrow (2008): Better Travel Choices: Heathrow's Travel Plan 2008-2012

With thanks to Theo Panayi, Surface Access Strategy Manager, BAA Heathrow

---

Case Study Two: BT Flexible Working and Workstyle

"At BT we have implemented flexible and home working at scale across the organisation, allowing people to work in the way that best suits them, their job, their personal circumstances and our customers. As a result we've been able not only to make large financial savings and productivity improvements but also to create a more sustainable organisation through reducing travel and CO_2 emissions and by increasing people's levels of satisfaction. Flexible workstyles are now business as usual, helping us to meet the demands of the market, attract and retain the right people and cut out unnecessary cost and bureaucracy."

Neil Mellor, Director Intelligent Transport

Summary

Believed to be one of the largest flexible working projects in Europe with 89,500 BT employees now involved in the BT Workstyle Project. BT Workstyle is not only a set of policies and procedures but also a complete technical architecture in itself. This example goes beyond the traditional travel plan model towards one of complete organisational behavioural change. Demand for home working remains high with around 1,500 employees switching each year.

Strategic context

Senior managers at BT promote ICT as a mode of transport to support travel behavioural change both internally for employees and to external companies. By engaging in the workstyle programme, BT can promote the technological benefits that can be unlocked by other business customers.

Other corporate objectives that are met include:

- To drive down office costs (operational)
- Allows market agility and the ability to respond to change quickly
- The Corporate Social Responsibility benefit – drive down CO_2

The working population

There were approximately 105,000 BT employees worldwide in 2008 with 92,000 based in the UK. In terms of Workstyle, employees are assigned to three distinct bands defined in Table 1 below.

Table One: Working Population

Workstyle employee type	% of total workforce
Contractual home workers	14%
Flexible (mobile, no fixed office but not full-time home workers)	71%
Primarily office based	15%

Measures / policies in place

- Home working
- Local working – relocating to BT premises nearer to home
- Job sharing
- Teleconferencing coupled with a business travel reduction policy
- Internal car sharing scheme
- Staff shuttle from Adastral Park site to Ipswich station

Benefits realised

Primary benefits

- The reduction in office space between 1993 and 2006 saves BT nearly £950 million per annum
- Within that figure, BT's 11,600 home workers (2006) saved the company over £136 million a year in accommodation costs, and were on average 20% more productive than their office-based colleagues. For example, home working BT call centre operators handled up to 20% more calls, giving comparable or better quality response than their office-based colleagues. The remainder of the cost saving was down to office space rationalisation & hot-desking
- There has also been a 20% reduction in business travel between 2006 and 2008
- Telephone conferencing is eliminating 859,784 meetings per year, reducing CO_2 emissions by approximately 97,628 tonnes, making £135 million in travel savings and £103 million per year in productivity gains. (May 2007). Table 2 below shows how these savings are calculated.

Table 2 Financial Value of Avoided Meetings Resulting from Conferencing

	Value Per Meeting	Total Value for BT
Time (Opportunity)	£120	£103,174,092
Travel (Profit & Loss)	£148	£109,788,379
Overnights (Profit & Loss)	£30	£25,793,523
Total Value	£298	£238,745,994

Secondary benefits

- BT home workers are taking 63 percent less sick leave than their office-based counterparts.
- Flexible working has reduced absenteeism to 3.1% (the national average is 8.5%).
- 99% of women return after maternity leave, compared with a national average of 47%.
- Home based workers record 20% less absenteeism
- A reduction of commuting from homeworkers has resulted in over 7.5 million kg of CO_2 emissions being avoided – the calculations for this are shown in Table 3.

Table 3 – Avoided CO_2 emissions from commuting amongst registered homeworkers

Daily kg CO_2 emissions avoided by non-commuting	7.814
Average number of days per week at home	1.9
Weekly kg CO_2 avoided by non-commuting	14.847
Annual kg of CO_2 avoided by non-commuting, per person, per year (of 46 weeks)	682.962
Number of registered homeworkers	11,104
Annual kg CO_2 avoided by non-commuting, all registered BT homeworkers	7,583,610

Setup costs for home workers

These are variable depending on equipment already issued to individuals. In most cases, BT staff already have a laptop, hence the only additional items are a home broadband connection, phone, mail redirection facility (PO Box) and office furniture (desk, filing units, etc.) the cost of which is limited to £600. Health and safety assessments and technical support are also carried out by internal support services.

Annual running costs for home workers

Reduced annual office running costs are sustained: annual cost to support an office-based worker in London is £18,000 per annum, cost for a home worker is less than £3,000.

Additional reference material

- Case Study, BT Workstyle, (2006) Flexible working provides a better work life balance, reduces environmental impact, cuts costs and improves customer focus.
- Professor Peter James, University of Bradford and SustainIT (2007): Conferencing at BT – Results of a Survey on its Economic, Environmental and Social Impacts, Final Report.
- Professor Peter James, University of Bradford and SustainIT (2008): Homeworking at BT – The Economic, Environmental and Social Impacts

With thanks to Neil Mellor, Director Intelligent Transport, BT

Case Study Three: Vodafone

"Our employees are very aware of climate change and expect Vodafone, as a responsible business, to take firm action. The travel plan toolkit provides an innovative solution to meeting the daily transport challenges for staff and contributes to the wider CSR and ISO14001 agenda."

Chris Hopkins, Company Travel Plan Manager

"In our major business areas, our Company's strategy and our CR strategy are inseparable. We have just 'one strategy'. Growth both in emerging markets and through "total communications" are closely linked to responding to society's challenges."

Vodafone One Strategy (2008)

The Vodafone Travel Plan is a toolbox of measures used where necessary to achieve the required modal shift to support the business need. Home working and videoconferencing are extensively encouraged throughout the company. Vodafone's original motivation for videoconferencing was reducing air travel and thereby the cost of air travel, however it also reduces business travel by car.

Use of the videoconferencing facilities has increased by 300% over the last two years with the number of failed conferences one-tenth that of two years ago, which shows that today's videoconferencing is very different technology from its poorly-viewed early predecessor. Today over 80% of all calls are over IP compared to less than half two years ago.

Vodafone is one of the few companies that still operates a sustainable allowance scheme for staff who do not use the car park, helping to achieve a 40% modal shift reduction in staff car use over the last 8 years. Employees are offered up to £85 per month for not parking.

Strategic context

In 2008 Vodafone announced that by 2020 they will reduce their CO_2 emissions by 50% against the 2007 financial year baseline of 1.23 million tonnes. They aim to achieve this principally through operational changes and technological innovation to improve energy efficiency. In terms of cost savings the use of technology helps to reduce expenses claims, maximises productivity and optimises the time front line staff spend on customer relations. In order to realise these goals, Vodafone needed to encourage employees to change their behaviour: instead of travelling, they needed to use videoconferencing. The factors important in delivering this change were:

- **Availability** – There had to be facilities widely available for videoconferencing, and they had to be available when and where people needed them
- **Quality** – Ensuring quality and reliable ISDN videoconferencing is right first time
- **Convenience** – Vodafone makes using VC as convenient as booking flights
- **Awareness** – Making users aware of the benefit to themselves is vitally important

The working population

The travel plan covers 11,000 employees across the UK with 3,400 staff based at the head office in Newbury. 40% of staff now work as full or part-time homeworkers from Newbury. There is only a small 24/7 Network Monitoring Team based in Newbury of about 80 people, all other call centres are in other locations around the country.

Measures / policies in place

- Parking cash-out scheme for sustainable transport users
- Business travel discouraged in favour of videoconferencing
- Flexible working policy covering home or remote working and full time home-based working
- Offering the 5p per mile allowance for car sharing
- Pay 20p per mile allowance for business trips by bike
- The site shuttle service runs every 10 minutes with 25,000 passenger journeys per month
- Interest free loans on sustainable measures
    - Bicycles – up to £500
    - Motorbikes up to 500cc – £1,500
    - Rail season tickets – up to £5,000
- Car sharing is encouraged at all offices. They also run free shuttle services at some of their regional offices

Benefits realised

Primary benefits

- Modal share has reduced by 20% from 85% to 41% since the travel plan has been introduced on the Newbury site.
- Travel reduced by use of videoconference calls at Vodafone. They have avoided approximately 3,000 business trips by using 412 existing videoconferencing facilities
- The main beneficiary was the route between London and Dusseldorf, which has seen an average drop of 33% in the number of trips over two years

Secondary benefits

- Contributes towards CSR/ISO14001 audited by the BSI
- Demonstrates videoconferencing potential to wider business community
- Caps existing car parking and office space to avoid new costs
- Annual running costs £1.3 million in 2008/9 operating costs plus incentive payments currently running at approximately £300 per employee.

Future initiatives

- Ongoing rollout of further measures where needed and the development of a designated Travel Plan for a new call centre in Stoke
- Real time for bus shuttle services
- Needs-based criteria for car parking
- Vehicle number plate recognition system

With thanks to Chris Hopkins, Company Travel Plan Manager, Vodafone

Case Study Four: HBOS Green Travel Case Study

"HBOS is totally committed to increasing awareness of climate change and acting responsibly to reduce our environmental impact. Innovative, flexible travel options for colleagues are an important part of this."

Liza Vizard, Head of Corporate Responsibility

Summary

This case study provides an overview of the green travel strategy at HBOS detailing the measures, initiatives and benefits realised across its UK sites.

Strategic context

As part of its commitment to have a positive influence on the environment, HBOS has developed travel plans and improvements at many of its major employment sites across the UK. HBOS considers this essential to the way it does business and an integral part of its Climate Change Action Plan.

HBOS is associated with the West Yorkshire Travel Plan Network, which brings together Metro, the five local authorities of West Yorkshire and the Highways Agency. The aim of the network is to support employers from West Yorkshire in promoting more sustainable ways of travelling to work and reducing the number of people who drive alone.

The Environment and Travel Coordinator works within the Group Property team. He liaises with the Estate Surveyors in respect of travel planning requirements and with Facilities Management in respect of improvements in facilities that will support green travel.

The working population

HBOS has 66,000 employees working across the UK, of whom approximately two thirds are based at major employment sites with the others based at local branches.

Measures / policies in place

Walking and cycling:
- HBOS Walk-It initiatives, part of the HBOS Colleague Health and Well Being campaign, encourage staff to walk to work by giving out free pedometers.
- Active travel campaigns initiated by the Travel Plan Network.
- Introduced the government's Cycle to Work scheme in 2006 via 'Flex Rewards' enabling staff to purchase bikes at a discount.
- Regular participation in national events including Bike Week.
- User groups have been set up including HBOS Bike User Group and HBOS Motorcycle Club.
- Cycling activity days, discounts on cycling products and training.

Public transport:
- In West Yorkshire an interest free loan has been offered to staff enabling them to purchase a Metrocard (a travel card) with a 15% discount for travel on buses or trains throughout West Yorkshire.
- Promotions including free 'taster' tickets given by local bus operators on 'In Town Without Your Car Days'.
- Dissemination of travel information including the distribution of public transport timetables at many sites.

Car sharing:
- Internal car sharing schemes operate at many sites alongside Liftshare.com.
- Preferential parking for car sharers is available at many sites.

Business travel:
- Introduced a Green Miles scheme in 2007 to encourage staff to use video- or tele-conferencing as opposed to business travel.
- Introduced a carbon calculator to show CO_2 savings if travelling by air, rail or road to various sites.
- A Green Angels initiative has been launched providing advice on how to reduce business travel.

Fleet vehicles:
- Essential company car users are only offered diesel or hybrid vehicles.
- Detailed information is provided on the company website on how to choose a greener car and how driving style and car maintenance affects emissions.
- Lex, HBOS's vehicles leasing business, offers a package of measures for clients to reduce the impact of their fleet including environmental analysis, carbon neutral options and evaluation of hybrid and low CO_2 vehicles.

Flexible working:
- Flexible working practices have been incorporated into the property strategy.
- Working options include homeworking, compressed working and term-time working.
- Flexible working and work-life balance initiatives are combined to provide a high quality and high performing working environment.

Benefits realised

The mode share of all green travel modes is improving whilst the share of single occupancy vehicle travel is decreasing.

The following changes in Key Performance Indicators (KPI's) have been realised:
- The percentage of staff walking to work group-wide in 2008 rose to 7.6%.
- The number of staff taking up the cycle scheme rose from 144 in 2006 to 522 in 2008.
- The number of applications for the Metrocard interest free loan has increased in each of the past 5 years rising from 136 in 2004 to 736 in 2008.

- 23 million business miles have been saved since the launch of the Green Miles scheme in 2007.
- The carbon emissions profile of HBOS's car fleet has improved from 172.56 grams CO_2 per km in January 2006 to 163.77 grams CO_2 per km in December 2007.

Corporate Social Responsibility Benefits:

- The Dow Jones Sustainability Index rated HBOS as the highest UK bank and one of the world's top 5, based on its Corporate Responsibility.
- HBOS is the only UK high street bank to have achieved the highest possible rating (AAA) in Innovest's global review of banks' social and environmental impacts.
- HBOS recently came top (in Scotland) in the Sunday Times' Best Green Companies.
- HBOS support other travel related projects including Calderdale Council's 'seat belt on' initiative which resulted in a 30% reduction in car occupant casualties in 2007/8.

Costs & funding

Costs associated with the travel planning programme include:

- A two year funding programme to improve cycle facilities at £180,000.
- A budget of up to £5,000 is available for attendance at conferences and for workplace initiatives (e.g. incentives).

Costs associated with the upgrading of facilities are incurred incrementally when budgets are available.

Funding:

- Since April 2007 the West Yorkshire Travel Plan Network has received funding from Yorkshire Forward to create the 'Travel for Work' project – to reduce greenhouse gas emissions from journeys to work and business travel in West Yorkshire.
- Extra staffing and resources have been provided to the Network who have assisted HBOS with a number of promotions and initiatives.

Future initiatives

Future initiatives include:

- Undertaking annual monitoring using staff travel surveys.
- Continuing to improve cycle facilities.
- Extending opportunities for car sharing.
- Exploring the possibility of having a green travel rating at major employment sites (similar to Energy Performance certificates).

With thanks to Richard K. Lodge, Environment and Travel Co-ordinator, HBOS

What can NBTN offer fleet managers?

Although we live in an age of internet communications and increasing environmental awareness, the business car remains an important tool and is still a popular employee benefit. Running a clean, environmentally friendly fleet offers businesses many benefits. It can reduce transport costs, cut vehicle emissions and improve corporate social reputation. NBTN can give you best practice information on reducing CO_2 emissions associated with your fleet.

Additionally, if you have been asked to become involved in mobility management or travel planning, NBTN can offer you all the help and support you need to influence your company's board to support your business case for workplace travel planning. You will have access to information from companies already excelling in this area and you will be able to network with their managers at high-quality quarterly events at prestigious conference centres around the country. Case studies, advisory notes and leading edge research will all be at your disposal. There is no cost and you will save your company money whilst reducing the negative impacts of work related car use.

Heather McInroy
Programme Director
National Business Travel Network

National Business Travel Network

Under pressure to cut company car costs and emissions?

Join the Network that can help

The National Business Travel Network (NBTN) understands that cars are an important part of your business. But we also know that fleet managers are under pressure to cut costs and reduce vehicle emissions. That's where we can help. The overwhelming majority of people use their private or company car for commuting and whilst travelling on business. This contributes to congestion which is estimated to cost UK businesses £23.5 billion per annum and is responsible for 37% of the UK's passenger car carbon emissions. As a fleet manager, it costs you too.

The Network has helped a range of businesses from global corporations to small companies to cut running costs, mileage and carbon emissions whilst increasing productivity and efficiency by reducing the need to travel and changing the mode of travel.

We can show you how to do this through developing your own tailored company travel plan with best practice case studies, information and guidance as well as opportunities to develop partnerships through regular meetings and seminars.

Membership is free so why not join our growing list of Network members?

To find out more about how sustainable travel can benefit your business and to sign up for our free newsletter email info@nbtn.org.uk or visit www.nbtn.org.uk

NBTN is a Department for Transport funded initiative

31

PURCHASING CARS

> **Robert Mills**
> General Manager, Operations
> Daimler Fleet Management UK Limited

Please introduce yourself and your role

I have worked in the leasing industry for over 20 years in both sales and operational roles and in my current position I am responsible for the procurement of all our leased vehicles.

Whilst we are part of the Daimler Group we are a multi brand contract hire and fleet management company so we have direct contact with all the other vehicle manufacturers and therefore negotiate purchasing terms directly with them and their dealer network.

Many smaller businesses give the driver the authority to order a vehicle up to a certain price, then leave them to get on and select, find, test drive and order it. Do you see this as a good approach?

There is a trade off here between delegating the time and resource to negotiate and order the car versus ensuring your company has obtained the most competitive terms available.

Empowering staff generally can be very motivating and rewarding and this in itself would have its benefits and for some staff the challenge of negotiating between dealers would ensure that you obtained the best prevailing terms.

A potential downside however would be that for some this could be a daunting task or perceived as a burden, so a car might have been acquired within set financial guidelines but it may not have been acquired on favourable terms. Another factor to consider is how much time they might spend on this activity and whether this is time well spent.

A possible compromise would be to delegate the activity to the driver up until the point of vehicle order and to leave the final price negotiation with you, the fleet manager.

Is it generally better for a fleet manager to place orders through one dealer or is it better if they shop around for the best deal across many dealers?

The value of good reliable customer service should never be underestimated, especially if the dealer will also carry out the servicing. Dealers will generally also provide better terms the more vehicles you buy from them and if the relationship is perceived as more long term, queries and technical issues will tend to get resolved far more efficiently.

That is not to say that you should not benchmark on a regular basis to ensure you are obtaining competitive terms and this will ensure your regular dealer does not become complacent.

Is there a big difference between the prices paid by end-user corporates and leasing companies?

In recent years more and more of the manufacturers have sought to structure their discount structures around the end user customer and not the size of the leasing company. Yes, there are terms that are made available to the leasing companies that are not always available to a small business but if the customer is pre-qualified, additional customer-specific terms will normally be available regardless of whom the customer chooses to fund their cars.

A fleet manager could maximise this opportunity by restricting their car list to a small number of brands thus guaranteeing a minimum annual volume to trigger additional discount.

It does seem that there are a lot of different discounts available to fleet buyers; dealer discounts, manufacturers' volume related bonuses and tactical support. How do these different bonuses work?

The discount structures do vary between manufacturers and can vary during a calendar year so it is advisable to keep abreast of market changes.

Several manufacturers now look to manage the fleet market centrally by offering agency terms to all the leasing companies and customer-specific terms (volume related bonus) as appropriate. The supplying dealer receives a fixed % from the manufacturer so is removed from the negotiation process and therefore can be chosen based on service rather than price.

Other manufacturers operate the more traditional model whereby they will offer standard leasing terms and customer-specific terms (volume related bonus) but will allow their dealer network to offer further discounts as they see fit. The fleet manager can either negotiate this additional dealer discount and nominate their selected dealer to the leasing company or rely on the leasing company to perform this task and select the dealer.

In addition to the above the manufacturer may also offer tactical support from time to time to support sales campaigns. The discounts tend to be only available for a fixed period of time and the vehicles have to be registered by a certain date.

In these financially troubled times, fleet managers will be looking to reduce their vehicle purchasing costs. How do you suggest they do this?

There has never been a better time to buy a new vehicle, with manufacturers and dealers offering significant discounts. However, consideration to whole life costs still needs to be the order of the day and the changes to legislation governing capital allowances and the change to a CO_2 based taxation scheme mean these factors should be the basis of a fleet's company car policy. An apparent price advantage on one vehicle over another could be more than offset by higher running costs.

So the best advice for fleet managers is to review their acquisition and funding policy with their tax advisors to ensure that it remains tax efficient after considering whole life running costs and changes to legislation.

If a fleet manager decides to allow nearly-new vehicles onto his fleet, how do you recommend they should source them?

A fleet manager has two main options which would be either from auction or from a dealer.

Auctions provide an opportunity to acquire vehicles at a trade price but it takes time and resource to purchase via this route and it will not be easy to meet your drivers' exact requirements.

By utilising your existing dealer relationships you can secure discounted nearly new cars and enjoy the same level of service including after sales service that you would receive by buying new. If the relationship is good you would be able to specify the car required. They will be able to source used cars nationally as they will have access to stock lists across the country.

If you buy at auction you can get the car at trade price and can pick up some real bargains. Would you recommend that fleet managers buy relatively young cars at auction?

The key to buying any used car is to be confident that it has been serviced and maintained in line with the manufacturers' recommendations. A relatively young car may not even have been due its first service so the risk of a poorly maintained car is minimal. You will also still enjoy the benefits of any remaining manufacturer's warranty so the newer the car the longer this warranty would be valid.

If you do decide to purchase an older vehicle make sure it has a full service history. An ex contract hire vehicle is more likely to have been serviced regularly than say an ex leased car and this can be checked beforehand.

The Sunday newspapers and motoring magazines contain adverts for imported cars. Is it a good idea for a fleet manager to buy these?

There are two types of imports which are referred to as either parallel or grey.

Parallel imports are vehicles built to a UK specification but available to buy in Europe. They became very common and were often mentioned in the press 5-10 years ago when vehicles manufactured in the UK were exported to the Benelux countries and were still cheaper to import back into the UK than to buy in the UK. The change in Block Exemption rules has largely mitigated this benefit and whilst vehicles may still be advertised they are not as common.

Vehicles purchased via this route still enjoy the benefit of manufacturers' warranty and whilst it has been claimed that resale values would be lower for parallel imports this has not been substantiated. However, you need to weigh up the amount of time you would spend on sourcing a suitable vehicle versus the potential cost savings. You might not receive the same level of after sales service and you would need to be confident you were negotiating with a bona fide dealer.

Grey imports are a different proposition as they are cars built to a different country's specification. This is not just whether the car is left or right hand drive but other specification differences. For example, cars built for the Far East will have a specification suited for different climatic conditions. The other fundamental issue will be that the manufacturer's warranty will be invalid and so what is an apparently cheap vehicle could become very costly.

What developments have there been in the last few years that have been particularly valuable to fleet managers seeking to buy new cars?

The growth of the internet has made most markets more transparent and opened up new opportunities, and the car market has been no exception. It is far easier now to compare prices across models and different suppliers and this makes the benchmarking exercise a far easier task.

This has brought new players into the market, especially the growth of the broker network and whilst there are many who are well-established and offer an excellent service there are some who might prove to be less reliable. Established dealers have also embraced the internet and can be accessed this way and, as mentioned previously, can provide additional value and assurances in addition to a purely monetary transaction.

Is anything happening now, or will anything be happening soon, that is likely to change the vehicle purchasing landscape for fleet managers?

The changing economic climate is certainly affecting most aspects of the vehicle industry in line with other markets but the vehicle market also faces additional challenges. In addition there are legislation changes that have either been implemented or are due to be over the coming years.

Taxation rules on both capital allowances and vehicle excise duty are now geared to the vehicle's CO_2 emissions and this is set to continue. The current price differential between petrol and diesel also needs to be considered because the historic running cost differential between the two fuels has been eroded. Whilst the benefit of diesel over petrol is probably still prevalent for high mileage vehicles (15,000+ miles pa) it is debatable whether this still applies for lower mileage vehicles.

If you are responsible for disposing of vehicles you should be aware that there has been a marked shift towards smaller cars with lower VED and CO_2 rates and with better fuel consumption. So if you want to maximise resale values you may wish to shape your company list towards this market sector.

It would also be advisable to seek advice from your tax advisors to ensure you have a company car policy that is appropriate for today's tax environment.

If you were to advise a fleet manager on the best practice when it comes to buying new vehicles, what would that advice be?

To maximise your buying power I would restrict your company car list to no more than 3-4 manufacturers and if this provides an opportunity to be purchasing 10 or more vehicles from any single manufacturer on an annual basis it is worthwhile negotiating with them directly. If you deal with only a handful of manufacturers you will secure better terms and find the relationships easier to manage.

I would also look to build a relationship with a single dealer per brand. If you are able to secure terms direct with the manufacturer then shopping around between dealers does not make sense. If your annual purchasing requirements are not big enough to secure direct terms there is still a benefit in building the relationship with a single dealer (2 max) but undertake a benchmarking exercise at least twice yearly. Most dealers will now deliver to most parts of the UK at no additional cost.

Quality service is still a key consideration and poorly delivered cars can soon upset your staff and create additional problems for you to manage. Shopping around for every car is time consuming; you have a growing supplier list to manage and marginal price differences can soon be eroded.

How can your company help fleet managers to buy new vehicles?

We work with customers where either we select the supplying dealer or where we work with a customer's preferred dealer. You can take advantage of our buying power and we can also negotiate with your nominated dealer if they are not offering the same terms available elsewhere.

We monitor dealer service levels to ensure anticipated delivery dates are managed and your drivers' expectations are met. Once an order is placed the status is tracked all the way through until delivery and any complaints are dealt with in a timely and efficient manner. This can be fed back to you to enable you to manage KPIs.

We can also arrange demonstration vehicles for your drivers to drive prior to placing orders, as well as presentations from manufacturers to ensure you are aware of new models and technologies

Robert Mills
General Manager, Operations
Daimler Fleet Management UK Limited

32

BUSINESS CAR
INFORMATION FOR SMEs

Ralph Morton

Editor

BusinessCarManager.co.uk

Please introduce BusinessCarManager.co.uk

This book is crammed full of fantastic advice for fleet managers: from managing fuel to writing company car policy. These great fleet management insights are all aimed at large organisations, and the often several hundreds of cars or vans that a fleet manager has under his or her jurisdiction.

But what about small businesses? After all, of the 4.9 million enterprises in the UK, small businesses account for a staggering 4.7 million of that total: a lot of small businesses, contributing between them some 50% of UK turnover and employing 13.5 million people.

But who was providing business car advice and information for them, specifically designed for the small business owner, the sole trader, the professional partnership, and the directors on a small business board?

Quite. No one.

There is, of course, plenty of advice out there. This ranges from the number one consumer publication, What Car?, which I used to edit, to weekly titles such as Auto Express. And there are trade publications, like Fleet News, for the fleet industry.

At the time I was contemplating the idea of Business Car Manager, I was a contributor to what was then Fleet Week, and which subsequently became BusinessCar (no relation). Surely, I thought, small businesses deserved a title providing business car advice? From that thought, Business Car Manager was born, going live in early summer 2006, before launching in August of that year.

Business Car Manager is a B2B website for micro and small businesses. A micro business is defined as a business with between 1-9 employees. A small business has 10-50 employees. A medium-sized enterprise has 51-249 employees.

The magazine's aim is to provide expert information about the issues associated with running a business car. (Those businesses running vans or pick ups now have a bespoke sister site called, well you've guessed it, Business Van Manager.)

A small business fleet can range from one owner-driver vehicle to a more complex sub-50 vehicle set-up. But actually, a small business would never think of itself as having a fleet. That's for larger companies. Company-run business cars, whether one, five or 15, is how a small business would see it.

As that company's business grows, it can find itself running a bunch of business cars – a 'fleet' – almost by default. And often with little structure because it's grown in a haphazard fashion, meeting that firm's immediate requirements. There are few places to turn to for practical help. That's where Business Car Manager comes in.

It's a valuable web-based resource dedicated to helping small businesses run their cars effectively and efficiently – which in turn should save money. It also uses plain English that every business can understand: fleet jargon has no place here. Because there are no fleet managers. The person responsible will be the business owner in a micro business, or possibly the finance director in a small business. But essentially, it's the people making the business happen who will also be making everything else around them…well, happen. That's the way small businesses work: there's no office support structure. Running a small business means rolling your sleeves up and getting on with it.

However, you won't see the magazine in print. It's web based; written for the web (not copy transferred from printed page to web page); pages are easy to navigate; and quick to load. Why? Because small business owners are always pressed for time. They need information; and they need it now.

What sources of information had small businesses been using before Business Car Manager came along?

Interesting this. There really wasn't much out there.

Take my case study while I was doing research for the launch of Business Car Manager – a company local to my office and a very successful publishing company.

The company was started as a bedroom business by two colleagues who had found themselves redundant but full of great ideas. Through their hard work and endeavour it had since grown to the point where it now owned premises on a business park and had 18 staff producing five titles each month and a combined print run of 130,000.

However, although the company had nine field staff, it had no company car policy and no company cars. The nine field sales staff covered 8,000 miles a year each on business. It was a condition of their employment that they had business insurance on their vehicles. Beyond that there were no further standards.

That meant no fleet policy; no policy on in-car mobile phone usage; and no policy on drink/drug driving. All of which could leave the company open to prosecution were staff to be involved in an accident while on business-related driving.

To be fair, the owner said the company realised it needed a stronger focus on health and safety with the move to new premises. But they still had no knowledge of how health and safety issues might have serious implications for their business and the company's field staff which were using their own vehicles.

The owner said he would welcome advice and information on running a fleet that was directed at small businesses through a business-to-business medium.

I think this makes the point that, while the fleet industry is well served by informed comment, the small business sector is not.

Still, small businesses were getting their information from somewhere. So who was it?

The prime source of business-related information was the accountant. A trusted adviser, the accountant has provided the authoritative voice on all financial matters concerning the car or van for the sole trader and small business.

However, the accountant's knowledge was often limited anyway. Traditionally, accountants pointed a small business towards private ownership and purchase. Any business mileage could be reclaimed using the Authorised Mileage Allowance Payment scheme of 40p per mile.

While this clearly works for many small businesses, there are now other issues – such as duty of care, for example – that means this approach has to be more considered. And for many businesses, spending a large lump of capital on a devaluing asset is not necessarily the right thing to be doing with the company's cash – or, indeed, the owner's private money – when other sources of finance are out there and available.

What about other sources of information? The daily newspapers always take a consumer viewpoint. *What Car?* is a marvellous source for deciding on a car, but again its business buying and finance advice is limited.

Other magazines such as *Auto Express* or *Autocar* are product oriented, while *Top Gear* takes its own entertaining approach to the market. But none of these gives advice to the small business.

Fleet News, BusinessCar and *Fleet World* are all aimed at larger fleet operators – and Colin Tourick's own well-researched 'bible' on fleet management, *Managing Your Company Cars*, is aimed more at the professional, rather than the small business part-timer.

Which leaves the odd advice-type article in magazines such as Human Resources or Business Network from the Federation of Small Businesses. But not on a regular basis and frequency to keep small businesses ahead of the legislative, tax and new model news relevant to running and planning a cost-effective range of business cars.

How do you decide what topics to include?

Editorial intuition and knowing your reader are the two key answers to this one. I receive about 50 stories a day unsolicited or through the newswires. Maybe one or two will make it onto the web page as being suitably relevant. So how do I decide what's relevant?

The first is basing information on best practice. If small businesses follow established best practice they can often do things more efficiently. And that's where most of the commissioned articles come from.

Otherwise, I base it on a few simple observations that a small business owner would want to know (and don't forger I'm a small business, too), depending on the story:

- How will it affect my tax position? Good or bad.

- New legislation – how will it affect my business? Could I end up in jail or be fined? Why should I take notice of it?

- What's the deal? Small businesses always like a deal, but they're astute enough to realise it must bring value too.

- Will it save me money? Will it boost the bottom line?

Many stories just don't make the grade. But if a story provides genuinely useful information that could make the operation of a small business more efficient, then it's much more likely to be published.

So what are my most popular pages, read by the 24,000 monthly small business visitors? Let's give you the usual monthly top six, although the order of 3 to 6 does vary. But road tests and news are always top:

1 Road Tests
2 Latest News
3 Editor's Blog
4 Special Reports
5 Advice Centre
6 Home Page

Road tests are an interesting area. There are certain manufacturers that generate plenty of interest. These, in no particular order, are Audi, Mercedes-Benz, Ford, Jaguar and MINI. The new Vauxhall Insignia has also proved highly popular.

But it seems to me that if a car has image and prestige, it needn't matter what size – Fiat 500, MINI, Toyota iQ – then it always attracts interest from readers.

I think it's also worth noting how Ford has moved its image. Business buyers are seeing Fords as credible, well-rounded alternatives to prestige cars.

The award, though, for the most googled car goes to the Mercedes C-Class C220. It is, perhaps, no coincidence that when the Institute of Directors ran a survey of members a couple of years ago, the Mercedes C-Class was the vehicle of choice for the small business director.

The other aspect I think that's valuable to understand is how much good advice and information small business readers want. There are two areas where readers can download information at no cost: the Advice Centre downloads area; and the Knowledge Bank, which features relevant chapters and sections from Colin Tourick's original *Managing Your Company Car*, all available as pdf downloads.

Each month there are 800-1,000 free downloads performed from these sections, all featuring good advice to help small businesses make better business car decisions. These sections, but particularly the Knowledge Bank and the advice within, will be updated, improved and broadened in 2009. Because these advice-based downloads quite clearly hit the sweet spot with small businesses.

Can you give us an example of the sort of information you have included recently?

The news section covers a broad range of topics, from services to new products, and from tax updates to law changes.

Nearly-new leasing launched by Motorpoint. This is a story on the car supermarket's bespoke small business offering that provides cheaper contract hire rentals on nearly-new cars.

Skiing holiday in your car? Then get form VE103. This is a timely news item on the business car documentation required to travel abroad prior to the winter holiday season. I'll run a similar story in the summer.

Businesses lose over £100 on 'soft tyres'. With the credit crunch small businesses need to make every saving possible. Here's some research from Continental highlighting how much money can be wasted simply because tyres are under-inflated.

Fuel duty goes up but no change in AMAPs. While the Chancellor reduced VAT in his Pre Budget Report, he also put up fuel duty. And HMRC has not moved on the AMAP rates, so the cost of running private cars on business is increasing.

Tax-efficient Audi A5 coupe launched. New car product stories are important, especially when they have a money-saving business angle.

New approval standard for Network car brokers. Brokers play an important role in providing good advice and securing good deals for small businesses. But not all brokers share the same standards. Business Car Manager encourages readers to use BVRLA-approved car brokers because of the higher standards they can expect from them. Hence the importance of this story, covering LeasePlan's 200 Network franchised brokers.

Jail or £20k fine for health and safety law breakers. This is a critical piece of information for small business owners. In many ways, this new legislation – the Health and Safety Offences Act 2008 – is far more relevant than corporate manslaughter.

Personal contract hire is Pre Budget Report winner. While economic experts debated the efficacy of a 2.5% cut in the rate of VAT, we took the angle that this was a brilliant opportunity for small businesses to take advantage of a personal contract hire lease.

With a bit of luck, this cross-section of stories has provided a good, broad overview of the breadth of the news coverage, and the sort of angles the magazine takes.

And can you give some examples of the general information you provide?

There are two types of general information provided in Business Car Manager. The first is to be found in the Special Reports section. This covers mainly news-based items or issues that could provide useful advice on running business cars.

Typical examples of Special Reports include the following.

Driving offence fines now linked to earnings. Written by Sean Joyce, a partner at law firm Stephensons Solicitors LLP and a specialist in road traffic and transport law, the article outlines how fines for driving offences will be linked to ability to pay. So a high earner will be fined more for the same offence than a low earner. It's the sort of useful motoring-related information that's hard to find elsewhere.

£1bn to accelerate key transport projects. Transport Secretary, Geoff Hoon, outlines the government's plan for transport investment in 2009.

Save fuel costs by driving efficiently. Written by Frank Reynolds, Europcar's small business specialist, the article reports on how small businesses could save money by more efficient driving techniques – with potential fuel savings in the region of £800.

Capital allowances: should you still buy high emission cars? Written by Nigel Morris, a senior tax manager with Deloitte, the article explains the workings of the new capital allowance system for 2009.

The second type of general information can be found in the Advice Centre. Here the information is based around better, and more efficient methods of running business cars, or simply offering straightforward explanations to the different aspects of business car management. All are written by specialists in their respective fields.

There are five sections: general advice; small business case studies; top tips on practical advice; what is? (which answers those nagging questions); and the Download Centre.

GENERAL ADVICE

In here you will find articles on a broad range of issues, from checking your tyre tread to remain road legal, to fuel cards and the savings available to businesses that use them.

SMALL BUSINESS CASE STUDIES

Everybody likes knowing what someone else does. Shared experience can help a small business pick up tips on more efficient travel management, new ideas on running business cars, and so on.

The case studies include firms that have no company cars, but use public transport and daily rental cars; how a self-employed driving instructor finances her car; why a small business converted to contract hire; and a small consultancy firm that uses private cars for business and repays business mileage with AMAPs.

TOP TIPS

These articles are full of practical advice – ideal for a busy small business when they need information quickly. Typical examples include: Buying a used business car; How to use a leasing broker; What to do if you put the wrong fuel in the car; and How to understand the new Corporate Manslaughter Act.

WHAT IS...?

Simple but not simplistic is the mantra for these useful advice features. These provide answers to all those business car management areas you possibly should know…but don't. So in here you'll find: What is a personal lease?; What is contract hire?; What is HP?; What is daily rental?; and What is a hybrid?.

ADVICE CENTRE DOWNLOAD CENTRE

Finally, the Download Centre features factsheets and useful documents provided by the partners of Business Car Manager – or produced in association with Business Car Manager – that can be easily downloaded by readers in pdf format.

Typical factsheets include: How to maximise transport strategy; Tax Pack: a pocket guide to business car tax; Emissions: CO2 and the future; and Funding your company cars.

You also include a blog. What sort of items have you covered recently?

I started the blog initially to provide greater reporting scope on my own business cars – like my current Audi A4 2.0 TDI SE – and the test cars I drive for the magazine.

Our road tests only provide a quick snapshot a car's ability, so it's useful to have somewhere to write in greater depth about their distinctive qualities, or the brilliant touches the engineers have introduced that surprise and delight.

And while the above still holds true, I now use the blog to comment on a wide range of issues, some of them related to news stories that the magazine runs, others on areas that just interest me – and might prove a useful discussion point for other small businesses.

It seems readers rather like it. When it was first launched, the blog languished down the bottom of the most popular pages but started working its way up the list this summer. First sixth; then fourth most visited; and now third. I guess readers like it because it gives behind-the-scenes glimpses of life as a journo; and has a more relaxed, informal feel.

Today I uploaded an item on Motorpoint's new contract hire offering for nearly new cars – the headline: deal or no deal? It gave me a chance to compare the deals and comment on whether they were good value or not. Motorpoint's deal on a Ford Focus did save money, for example. But its rates on my Audi were out of bed – you could get a brand new diesel A4 from a contract hire company for less.

Talking of Audi, another piece was on the new V10-engined R8 mid-engined coupe. Now, this sports car is not the stuff of normal business car contract hire quotations – unless you're a very successful entrepreneur – but some of its technology is interesting. Like the world-first LED headlamps. These are lighter in weight than conventional units, and consume less power – which helps this astonishingly quick, 5.2-litre V10 engined sports car to achieve over 20mpg (along with some lighweight aluminium construction, of course).

Other entries include tips from the Federation of Small Businesses to beat the credit crunch – and how these could be applied to both general business advice and business car advice.

Or interesting snippets from business meetings – the sort of items that help build a more rounded view of what's going on in the business car market.

And you also include a jargon buster. Do readers find that valuable?

Very much so. It's surprising how much industry professionals take for granted with fleet jargon.

Owners of small businesses are experts in their own field; but not in business car management. They need plain English explanations that are free of jargon and not full of fleet industry shorthand.

So a jargon busting explanation of what a 'balloon payment' is – "A large one-off payment made at the end of some finance agreements, such as contract purchase. Also known as lump sum or final amount to pay" – is really quite necessary.

And would you really expect a business owner to understand that dilapidation was not something his wife received at the beauty spa but: "Also known as 'end of contract charges' and 'dehire damage charges'. It's when the lease company has to carry out repairs to a vehicle at the end of its contract to make it saleable. Allowances are made for fair wear and tear, but lease companies charge for excessive wear, abuse and neglect. Dilapidation rates can vary significantly between different leasing companies. Make sure you understand what condition you are expected to return the car in, and what the charges are if you don't."

How much does it cost to sign up for the website?

Absolutely nothing. Access is free and all content is free. That's the way it has to be for small businesses.

Anything that stops them getting at vital information – and particularly the barrier of yet more form-filling – is just not on.

The website is financed by advertising partners who can contribute articles, downloads and take part in the website's expert panel to answer reader questions. But that doesn't preclude stories on rival operations or products if the stories are valid and pertinent to the audience.

The only item that requires a subscription (just name and email address) is the twice monthly Business Car Manager e-newsletter. Currently there are 50,000 small business subscribers.

How can your online magazine help small businesses?

One of the great things about the small business market – and it's the bit that gives me the biggest buzz – is its sheer variety.

Small business owners can make decisions quickly. They are not constrained by big business bureaucracy. That's why they can start looking for a Ford Mondeo and end up in a Mercedes C-Class – because if the deal's right, the deal can be done. Quickly. Which is one reason why car leasing brokers enjoy such a close relationship with small businesses.

In many ways the small business owner is a hybrid: part consumer; part business. They will often act like a consumer but require the business element of the funding and car management to go with the car acquisition decision.

And while the car market is split into three sections – private, fleet and business – I reckon the small business owner touches all three of these: the private market through personal cars used on business; the fleet market thanks to cars supplied through leasing companies via brokers; and also the business sector for those bigger small companies operating with car dealerships.

Like I said, the small business owner is a wonderful hybrid, a collection of different, fragmented facets.

For this very reason there is no one correct answer for a small business, either. Contract hire might be perfect for one firm, while another would prefer to buy secondhand. Another might use personal contract hire to fund a private car that can be used on business. While other firms still prefer to buy their business cars outright.

All solutions are correct. As long as they remain correct for that business and there's not a better, more efficient, and more cost-effective way of providing business travel.

My job at the helm of this mag is to service that great variety of needs with good stories, sound advice, knowledgeable articles, and acknowledged best practice.

What a great job!

Ralph Morton
Editor
BusinessCarManager.co.uk

MEETING THE NEEDS OF DISABLED DRIVERS

33

Jon Reynolds
Managing Director
AVH Ltd

Please introduce yourself and say how and why you started your business.

'I'm very sorry Mr Reynolds but nobody does it' was the reply from the Motability specialist I was talking to when our family Motability car was involved in a non-fault accident.

The question was – *'Who provides adapted replacement vehicles in the light of the recent changes to the Disability Discrimination Act of 2005, part 3 transportation?'*

It became blatantly apparent from the conversation I had with the Motability specialist that with the change in the DDA, many UK vehicle providers, insurance companies, major daily rental companies, credit hire companies and fleet vehicle providers were unclear on their 'duty of care', and what they should do if approached by a disabled person for a service they already provided to an able bodied person. The new DDA legislation requires that they should not discriminate. Clearly there was a problem.

In Feb 2005 after a few months' research, committing my life savings (with the reluctant agreement of my darling wife) drawing up a business plan with two of my close work pals and convincing them to part with their children's inheritance, Adapted Vehicle Hire Limited – or AVH Ltd as we are more commonly known – was incorporated, to provide replacement adapted vehicles for disabled drivers and wheelchair passengers.

We initially marketed to the insurance and credit hire arena, as this is where we had identified that the 'lack of understanding' towards the change in legislation seemed to be. Also the mention of the words 'adapted vehicle or disabled vehicle' seemed to become a 'hot potato' as it was passed around to various departments for them to try and sort out.

What AVH Ltd did was to become the 'proverbial dumping ground' for the hot potatoes. We knew about disability, we understood about adaptations for disabled drivers and we would go out of our way to make sure the client had as near as possible a like-for-like replacement. We always said 'yes' even if we had to source a vehicle through other channels if we did not have one ourselves. We found a niche, and we very quickly became the largest supplier of adapted replacement vehicles in the UK. The fleet still grows...

Before we move on and look at fleet managing disabled vehicles and how the fleet industry in general will be affected by the DDA Legislation change, let's get some of the 'statistics' out of the way.

There are around 10 million disabled adults in the UK (source DWP Family Survey 2002/2003). There are about 6.9 million people of working age with a long-term disability according to the Labour Force Survey spring 2003/2. Long-term disability is the measure used for the DWP's Public Service Agreement on employment and disability, and consists of people who have a disability that affects the amount or type of work they could do (work-limiting disability) and people with a disability likely to be covered by the DDA.

There are approximately 14m Blue Badge holders in the UK. This number is steadily rising as more medical conditions are recognised (ie cancer sufferers, the terminally ill, MS sufferers and other degenerative diseases have been recently added). Why does this figure differ from the one above? Well you have to take into account  the number of children that meet the Blue Badge criteria. The Blue Badge scheme provides a range of parking concessions for people with severe mobility problems who have difficulty using public transportation. The scheme operates throughout the UK. One interesting point is that the Blue Badge is applicable to the named person on the badge, not to any one vehicle, but it can be transferred by that person to another vehicle that is carrying them or they are driving.

What is the legal position if a disabled driver joins a company?

This should be a simple scenario for fleet managers ....but is it?

A large blue chip company places a recruitment advert in The Grocer (other good advertising publications are available) for a number of field sales agents. The package offered is fairly standard, basic salary, commission with a company vehicle.

The company has a number of suitable applicants who are invited for interview. One of those candidates only has one arm but is considered extremely suitable for the position and is subsequently offered the job, subject to a successful 3 month probationary period (standard company practice). As part of the advertised package a company car is offered.

Now I'm fairly certain that alarm bells will be ringing with many fleet managers at this point from a number of perspectives: How does anyone drive a car with only 1 arm, how do they turn and indicate at the same time, what about insurance, is our claims record about to get worse, where do I get a vehicle for the 3 month probationary period, surely it's going to cost a fortune? These are just some of the thoughts and comments that will be going around your head.

Well your recruitment team made the decision that the candidate is capable of doing the job and during the course of the interview I am sure the subject of the person's disability would have been approached and discussed. It is now down to you as the fleet manager to provide the candidate with one of the necessary tools to complete the job ... a suitable adapted car. Where do you start?

Well firstly having an understanding of the DDA legislation is pretty essential and making sure that the rest of the fleet team are also aware of their responsibility towards a disabled request is also paramount, as they will usually deal with the initial requests for vehicles before you get involved.

This is an extract from DDA 2005 part 5.

Duty to make reasonable adjustments

As to the transport provider's duty to make reasonable adjustments, all transport providers offering services in relation to the provision or use of a vehicle have a duty to take reasonable steps to change a practice, policy or procedure which makes it impossible or unreasonably difficult for disabled people to make use of those services. They also have a duty to provide an auxiliary aid or service if it would enable (or make it easier for) disabled people to make use of those services.'

The basic requirement can be met by having a company like AVH Ltd at the end of the telephone when you need advice about a requested adaptation or vehicle. In the scenario above, what should the fleet manager be doing to make sure the candidate has a suitable adapted vehicle?

Even if you have come across disability within the fleet industry before, it is extremely worthwhile building up a checklist of questions for you and your team to ask. These can be pretty exhaustive but the main areas of questioning needs to be along the lines of:

1   What adaptations do you require in order to be able to drive?
2   How long have you been driving?
3   When did you have your last assessment for driving with adaptations?
4   Could I see a copy of the assessment report?
5   Do you have any restrictions on your driving licence?

These are some basic questions which are extremely relevant if taking on a disabled person for a job in which they are going to be using a company vehicle in their everyday work.

When I refer to the assessment report, this is an assessment that all disabled drivers take at one of the Forum Of Mobility Centres around the UK. There are 17 main centres and a number of smaller ones. The Centres determine what adaptations are required to enable the driver to drive a vehicle comfortably and safely on the road.

From this initial assessment report the driver can purchase a suitable vehicle and have the necessary adaptations fitted by a qualified Motability Accredited fitter. They may need a combination of 2 or 3 adaptations to enable them to drive. I will go into more detail about adaptations later.

So you have asked your questions of the driver and he or she has supplied the necessary reports and information to show that they can drive with certain adaptations and that their licence is or is not restricted by the DVLA. You now have the task of finding a vehicle that will fit the bill for the probationary period and potentially for up to 3 years after that.

Where do you start looking for adapted vehicles for a driver with only one arm? Well I guess your first port of call would be your current daily rental or interim vehicle provider. You ask, 'Can they help?' The answer is 'No'. Where do you go next? Aha! The internet. If you type '**adapted vehicles**' into your search engine and press 'go', ...please let there be ..... Aha! ....your search page reveals a list of potential companies. You scroll down and then realise that you forget to tick the 'search UK only' button. Doh!... Let's try again, this time the page appears with companies listed in the UK fulfilling your search criteria. Now were getting somewhere. Adapted Vehicle Hire Limited is on the list; now that sounds promising. After looking at the website you contact the company and explain your requirement. If you tell us the adaptations the driver says they need, we will tell you what vehicles we can supply to meet the driver's requirements. For your particular driver the solution is an automatic vehicle adapted with a Lodgesons Infa Red unit. A company that can take away my 'hot potato' my search has ended…

Or has it? What about cost, what about insurance and am I getting value for money? – questions that are important to every fleet manager.

It is generally accepted that adapted hire vehicles can cost a little more than standard cars as the adaptations can be quite expensive, so expect to pay slightly higher daily rates than you have negotiated with your current daily rental supplier. As with everything you get what you pay for, and depending on what you and your company prioritise when sourcing vehicles from outside companies – ie, customer service, price, value for money, good communication throughout transactions, politeness – you should be able to identify the right supplier for you.

Let's say you have now successfully sourced an interim adapted vehicle for the probationary period. Now what about a long term solution for the 3 years? There are two possible options:

1   Source a standard vehicle through your normal leasing or purchase channels and find somewhere to have the adaptations fitted. There are many Motability Accredited fitters on the internet, and many provide a mobile service. If you usually lease, you will first have to make sure that your leasing company is aware that there may be some cosmetic damage to parts of the vehicle when the adaptations are fitted. Different adaptations will leave different amounts of cosmetic damage. Replacement parts may have to be costed in to the hire charge.

Also the leasing company should be made aware that a vehicle is going to be used by a disabled driver and there may be some additional marks on the vehicle which might usually fall to be treated as 'unfair wear and tear' under the BVRLA guidelines. We will cover this area in more detail a little further in the chapter.

2   The second option is to lease a suitable adapted vehicle for the duration from a leasing company that specialises in this area. There are now a number of companies that offer longer term leases on adapted vehicles, but again check with them first that they can provide the level of adaptation that your driver requires; some only provide basic hand controls or left foot accelerators. Also check to see what their schedule is for adaptation servicing as this is crucial to the driver being able to use the car and keep it on the road. Find out what provisions they have in place for breakdowns, replacement adapted vehicles etc – all the things you will have already sorted and battened down with your current suppliers.

What sort of adaptations are available?

Well this is where it can become a minefield and perhaps having a specialist company to call upon pays dividends. There are so many adaptations in the market place these days. What I have done below is to list the most widely used adaptations and the ones fleet managers regularly ask for. Developments in adaptations go hand in hand with technology; as technology moves forward so it is applied to other areas, like driving controls. The basic driving controls remain fairly constant and are based on simplicity. The more complicated driving controls that use fly by wire and wireless systems benefit from technological advances made in other areas.

Single Lever Push Pull Hand controls – Fixed to the steering column and to the brake and accelerator by rods, these are by far the most common 'lower limb' driving controls. Combining this with a steering ball attached to the steering wheel means a person who uses a wheelchair can transfer into the driving position, stow their wheelchair and safely drive using these basic controls. You use the controls by pushing to brake the car and pulling to accelerate. Can be mounted either on the left or right hand side of the column. The centre picture is another variation of the hand control, called a Brig-Ayd electric trigger throttle system. The third picture is of the Kivi electric accelerator ring. It sits behind the steering wheel and takes very limited pressure to accelerate, ideal for drivers with arthritis or poor strength in their hands.

[Thank you to Brig-Ayd Controls Ltd, Lodgesons and Autochair for allowing me to use their pictures.]

Steering Aids – simple things to look at yet essential to allow disabled drivers to steer more easily. The first one we have pictured is the quick-release steering ball. As its name suggests, the ball can easily and swiftly be removed if required. The second is called a glove and peg. The third is a combination of a steering ball and a key pad wired into the car's wiring loom to give the driver all they need to operate the auxiliary functions of the car.

 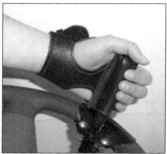 

Left Foot accelerator – here are a couple of versions of the left foot accelerator, both manufactured by Brig-Ayd Controls Ltd. The first is the more commonly used, a Brig-Ayd 'twin flip' style. The original accelerator pedal is cut off and the twin flip is fitted. It can be driven by right-footed drivers. Then if the left pedal is pulled down and used, the right hand pedal disappears into the upper reaches of the footwell until required again. The second pedal is a 'quick release' left foot. There is a heavy mounted plate in the footwell and the left foot accelerator fits into this. When not required it can be released quickly and stored in the vehicle. This second one is temporary, whereas the twin flip is a permanent adaptation.

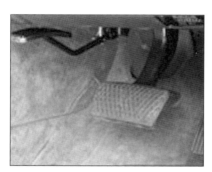  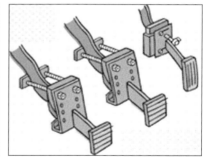

Pedal Extensions – designed and manufactured by Roland Kerr Ltd to extend the existing pedals so that shorter drivers can use the vehicle. These fit onto any vehicle and come in kit form for manual or automatic vehicles. Very simple yet effective, with minimal damage to original pedals.

Brig-Ayd Rear Mounted Boot Hoist – This space age contraption is used by disabled drivers who have some mobility, and who generally use a scooter or electric wheelchair to get around. The hoist allows the driver to stow their scooter or wheelchair in the boot of a vehicle either by a 2-way (up and down) or 4-way (up, down, in and out) hoist that is mounted on one side of the vehicle floor. Once this is stowed safely, the driver then makes his or her way around to the driver's position, and then drives with or without driving aids.

Manual Ramps – Another method of getting a scooter or wheelchair into the back of a vehicle is to use manual ramps. Ramps represent excellent value but the person using them has to be fairly mobile as the process involves some carrying, bending down and pushing the scooter or wheelchair into the back of a vehicle.

Wheelchair Top Box – If the driver has limited mobility and strength then another way of stowing a wheelchair is to use the Autochair wheelchair top box. It is quite a large piece of machinery just to stow a manual wheelchair but it does it very well. It is fully automatic, so the driver can be in the driver's seat when operating the machinery. You can stow manual or small electric wheelchairs though the battery pack may have to be disconnected first. The fuel consumption on the vehicle will increase from the manufacturer's specifications; these are not the most aerodynamic pieces of equipment when fixed to a car roof.

Those are the adaptations that are fairly commonly requested by fleet drivers. Next I have listed the less common adaptations that may be requested. I have put a brief description next to each one. This is not a definitive list, there are too many to list.

- Alfred Bekker Floor Mounted Hand Controls
- Lynx Hand controls – quick release, ideal for holidays
- Accelerator ring – light and simple to use
- Knee and other accelerators – accelerators that are worked by pressing one's knee against a pad. These controls can be custom built to be worked by other parts of the body.

- Easy gear release
- Easy handbrake release
- Electric handbrake
- Push button clutch
- Swivel seats – usually in the front passenger position for easy access and exit
- Bev Turney seat – replaces passenger seat but looks like a car bucket seat
- Carony car chair system – as above but its base forms part of a wheelchair system

If an able-bodied driver's car is off the road, perhaps after an accident, the employer or their insurer will normally arrange for a hire car to tide the driver over. Presumably it's a bit more complicated if the driver's car had been specially modified?

Well under the new DDA Legislation the disabled driver must be offered a replacement vehicle with the necessary driving controls within the same SLA timeframe that a standard vehicle would be provided to able bodied driver's...in theory anyway.

The truth of the matter is that *depending* on the level of adaptations required it might be 24-48 hours before a suitable vehicle can be sourced for the driver...or longer in some cases. If the bodyshop that is repairing the vehicle provides a courtesy vehicle to able bodied drivers they are bound by the DDA legislation to provide an adapted vehicle. (This is where the protocol would be called). The fleet manager's current daily rental protocol may provide temporary Lynx hand controls on a standard vehicle, but if a more complex level of adaptation is required a specialist company would normally be contacted to supply a vehicle. This can be done via the daily rental company or via the insurance company (if they know where to go to get one). However, as more fleet managers become aware of their duty of care under the transportation part 3 of the DDA legislation, I'm confident they will research and find a specialist company that can meet their own high standards and needs and can be called upon confidently to provide adapted vehicles when required.

The mention of an adapted vehicle makes most people draw a sharp intake of breath. It really should not. Adapted vehicles are fast becoming commonplace and will become a mainstream revenue source for many transport providers in the future. The statistics prove that this is a growing area and deserves full attention by fleet managers as no doubt you will be dealing with this area at some point in your career. On your next trip out or up and down the motorway make a conscious note to look at other vehicles on the road and I will be amazed if you don't see an adapted vehicle or two. (But please be careful....perhaps it will be safer if you look when taking that much needed break at the M6 Sandbach services!!)

Most insurance and credit hire companies have a protocol in place if they are asked for a replacement 'specialist' vehicle. In many cases this is because AVH Ltd pressed them to introduce one. We do not currently know how many other fleet companies are unsure of their responsibilities under the DDA and whether they know where to go to find this type of vehicle. Some may have protocols already in place, some not. If you don't you could fall foul of the law and face prosecution.

The most recognisable adapted vehicle on our roads today will no doubt be a wheelchair accessible vehicle (WAV), probably a Renault Kangoo, Fiat Doblo or VW Transporter or similar. Easily recognisable as it will be the vehicle doing 40 in the slow lane or 80 in the fast lane! Again this type of vehicle is something that fleet managers need to consider when looking at fleet vehicles in today's climate. WAVs are basically an office on wheels to some wheelchair-bound clients and I could name 2 or 3 famous people who use their WAVs just so.

The WAV comes in all shapes and sizes, manual or automatic, with or without driving adaptations. The list of adaptations you can make to a WAV is pretty exhaustive. Each client and wheelchair will be different, so there is quite a bit to learn about WAVs and their users. As the manager of a fleet that solely comprises vehicles adapted for disabled drivers and wheelchair passengers, it has taken me quite a while to build up my knowledge of these vehicles and the variations we are asked for.

We recently did a survey for one of our larger clients and the results were jaw-dropping. In the space of 12 months we had provided 284 variations of wheelchair-accessible Renault Kangoos. And that's just one make and model of a WAV. We were very surprised.

Just like we did for the adapted cars, it is extremely beneficial to build up a checklist to ask the client, especially if you are in the insurance or accident management arena. You will be providing a replacement vehicle on the strength of a phone conversation so you had better cover all bases. What are those bases? Well let's look at those in more detail now.

The first and most important question to ask any wheelchair user is 'what is your own vehicle?' This will ensure you start off by eliminating a number of questions. If it is the first time that the person has requested a WAV then let's start at the very beginning and work through. One of the most important areas is the 'wheelchair' itself. It could be manual, electric, 4 wheels, 6 wheels, twin battery pack, extra wide, have an attendant controller on the left or right hand side, headrest, extra long foot rest for a fused leg, oxygen tank holder, the list goes on... Basically there are hundreds of wheelchairs on the market today. So it is important to find out which one is being used.

Once you have ascertained the make, model and dimensions of the wheelchair, the next step is to find out how tall the wheelchair passenger sits when in their chair. This will allow you to cross off unsuitable WAVs that do not have sufficient rear door aperture to allow safe entry and exit. Does the wheelchair passenger carry any special equipment when they travel? (eg oxygen, personal hoist etc). How many other seats are required within the vehicle? Does the vehicle have to be manual or automatic?

I think we are getting somewhere now. We have the dimensions of the wheelchair, how tall the wheelchair passenger sits in their wheelchair, we know what equipment needs to be catered for and we know the preferred transmission of the vehicle. One question that needs to be asked is whether the client has any special adaptations on their own vehicle that need to be replicated on the temporary vehicle. Now this is the leading question, as this is where the 284 variations on our Renault Kangoos came from.

These are just a sample of the variations we provided:

> lowering suspension, flat floor, fully automated rear doors, blacked out windows, easy gear or handbrake release, left foot accelerator, single lever hand controls, Lodgesons Infa red auxiliary controls, panoramic rear view mirror, passenger swivel seat, electric winch, 3 seats, 4 seats, 1 seat, no passenger seats, Oxygen holders, large roof mounted grab rail, automated side door, gas ring, lightened power steering ... and the list goes on

This list really is the worst case scenario a fleet manager might have to deal with. The basic questions we identified above will provide the necessary information to provide a suitable WAV in most cases and can be dealt with by the fleet management team.

There are different entry methods on WAVs of which the two most common are (1) manual rear ramp aided by an electric winch mounted in the vehicle and (2) either a side or rear electric lift. I have provided some photographs to show the difference. The first is of a converted Chrysler Voyager with a manual rear ramp. The second is of a Renault Kangoo with a manual ramp.

WAVs come in all shapes and sizes, and each conversion company stamps its own mark on each conversion. Most, not all, WAVs start life as a commercial vehicle and are then converted by the specialist to provide space for 1, 2, 3, 4, 5 or more wheelchairs, as can happen with the large Community Bus converters.

This is a picture of an electric Ricon lift.

Electric lifts can be fitted on the side, rear or underneath a vehicle to allow access either from the side or rear. These offer an excellent way of getting a wheelchair passenger into a vehicle safely. With undefloor lifts the driver needs to be particularly aware of the speed humps that seem to appear on our roads overnight! There appears to be no uniform size to these piles of leftover tarmac and extreme care is needed when using a vehicle with an underfloor lift.

A major consideration for fleet managers looking to put WAVs onto their fleets is the cost of servicing the adaptations that are put on the vehicles. You have the regular servicing costs for the vehicle itself and these do not change from the manufacturer's servicing schedule. However, electric lifts require servicing and weight-testing every 6 months and if there are hand or other controls on vehicles then these too need to be regularly checked for wear and tear with parts being replaced if required. I would recommend that a regular service of any adaptation on a vehicle be done at least every 6 months. If you are a hire company then every time the vehicle is returned from hire, it needs to be checked and tested. Short term hires can take their toll on adaptations.

One area that every fleet manager has to look at is fair wear and tear on their fleet. The exact same rules apply to adapted vehicles, especially if they are used for hire. The key document here is the Fair Wear and Tear Guide issued by the BVRLA. If the letter of the BVRLA law were to be administered for one of our hire cars, we would need to recharge every customer after every hire. Obviously, I am talking 'literally' here and in the real world, common sense must prevail. Disabled drivers and wheelchair passengers enter and exit vehicles in different ways. Over the few years we have been operating we have identified areas on vehicles being used by people with certain disabilities that are like hot spots for scratches, marks and scuffing. For these disabled drivers and passengers, if you were to look at their own vehicles you would see the exact same areas with the exact same marks. It is unavoidable damage, but should they be penalised just because they enter and exit in a different manner to able-bodied drivers? I certainly don't think so. Speaking with the BVRLA a while ago I discussed the possibility of them producing a guideline for 'fair wear and tear' for disabled drivers and wheelchair passengers. It was deemed at the time I approached them that the current guidelines were adequate and that it was down to the fleet or hire company's discretion of what should be considered fair wear and tear for their own vehicles. Another chapter for another book, I think.

What developments have there been in your part of the fleet market in the last few years that have been particularly valuable to fleet managers who have to meet the needs of disabled drivers?

Over the last few years we have seen developments within the disabled sector of the fleet industry, particularly from an insurance replacement and credit hire point of view. Due to the change in legislation it has become necessary for fleet managers to look at their current protocols for the provision of an adapted vehicle.

Change has also come about because disabled drivers and wheelchair passengers are more aware of their rights to services these days.

I believe this is an area that will continue to be serviced by specialist companies for the foreseeable future, as they have a high level of understanding of the requirements of disabled drivers and wheelchair passengers.

Is anything happening now, or will anything be happening soon, that is likely to change the landscape for these fleet managers?

The future is looking rosy for disabled people. As far as I can see, more and more disabled drivers and wheelchair passengers are aware of their rights. This means that more requests will be placed with transport providers in the UK. More specialist companies will inevitably spring up catering for the needs of this evolving market. Fleet managers will need to be looking for an adapted vehicle protocol if they don't already have one. This is an evolving market, still in its early stages. As it grows, fleets and fleet managers will have to respond positively to benefit from it.

For a fleet manager in today's climate, part and parcel of running a fleet of any size involves having reliable suppliers and backup resources, forging strong relationships and trusting suppliers to do their job in the agreed timescale. Setting standards, boundaries and SLAs from the outset ensures that your suppliers will be keen to fulfil their part of the agreement every time: Because they know that if they don't, you will look elsewhere. They know that and at the end of the day there is always someone else out there willing to tender for the business.

In summary, operating and running a fleet of adapted vehicles and wheelchair-accessible vehicles is a lot like running a fleet of regular vehicles in many ways. You have to look out for and control the same running costs. You still have driver training issues that arise time after time. The fundamental difference is the additional costs for maintaining the adaptations on each vehicle. Some people wonder why hiring an adapted vehicle is more expensive than a standard vehicle. Well, fitting the initial adaptation can be quite expensive but it is the maintenance of those adaptations that adds the cost to the hire, which many people don't see. With some disabled drivers' vehicles costing in excess of £75,000, we are talking about a big investment that requires looking after, and that is why sourcing a specialist company that can assist you from start to finish is the best way forward.

How can AVH help fleet managers?

At the start of this chapter I explained how and why I started AVH Ltd. I am also the proud parent of my 10 year old disabled son, who was the real reason AVH Ltd was started. To this day he is still the inspiration behind what AVH Ltd does.

How can we help you as a fleet manager? There are a number of ways that we assist fleets. Firstly, we can offer our services to become your adapted vehicle 'protocol', should you not have anything in place. Our main services include:
- accident replacement
- daily rental
- short term hire
- 3 and 5 yr contract hire
- flex-able leasing, designed specifically for the rehabilitation and legal arena
- try before you buy scheme and
- credit hire

As an adapted replacement vehicle provider we are Motability Accredited for fitment of adaptations to vehicles. We act as consultants to fleet managers to inform them of their 'duty of care' under the new DDA legislation and last but not least we sell adapted vehicles.

Also we are happy to be an information provider and soundboard should you have any questions relating to vehicles and disability.

AVH Ltd can deliver nationally from its sites in London and Chorley. We have experienced drivers who undergo extensive training to ensure they have a good level of understanding on the adaptations and vehicles they are delivering.

Professor Peter N C Cooke summed up what we do in an article printed in the Mobilise Magazine in May 2008 and we have reproduced that article in full here.

Three Wishes of a Disabled Driver

Professor Peter N C Cooke

University of Buckingham

My wife reckons my three requirements as a disabled driver are probably knowing the location of the next accessible loo, finding an unoccupied disabled parking space on a Saturday – and an adapted vehicle to park in that space. I would add a wish to that list – 'access to a replacement adapted car when mine is off the road'. Simple? 'Yes – but no'.

The first three are the family's problem. The real challenge is the fourth – availability of a replacement adapted vehicle, or even better, a rental programme that can offer the 'occasion vehicle' – one that can take one or two disabled passengers, whether in wheelchairs or needing special access or driving controls.

Have you ever tried to find an adapted, replacement vehicle? It's tough.

Jon Reynolds and his team at Adapted Vehicle Hire Limited or AVH Ltd as they are more commonly known, have a fleet of vehicles that can be adapted for short term hire; amazingly, they can set those adaptions to meet your specific requirements; you can explain the adaptions you need and they can replicate practically anything on a hire car to match your usual vehicle. Well maybe not the colour! More importantly, the team understand adaptions, and is Motability Accredited for the fitment of adaptions, so you will not be embarrassed by controls put together by someone trying to be 'helpful'.

Jon has received a huge and growing file of letters of thanks from people who have used the service.

It's a growing company, well worth contacting if you don't know them, whether you need an adapted rental vehicle, a modified people carrier to take wheelchairs – or are a dealer or rental company looking to widen your service offering, especially in the light of recent changes to government legislation.

Jon Reynolds
Managing Director
AVH Ltd

:: DDA   :: News   :: Vehicles   :: Adaptions   :: Support   :: Contact   :: Links

Contact

Adapted Vehicle Hire Ltd
Poplar House
Cowley Business Park, Cowley Road
Uxbridge, UB8 2AD

Tel: 0845 257 1670
Fax: 0870 131 4529

Email: admin@avhltd.com

View a map of where we are here:

MAP

34 THE DIFFERENT WAYS FLEET MANAGERS CAN DISPOSE OF VEHICLES

Peter Rosie
Miles Turner Associates

Please introduce yourself and explain your background and experience in vehicle remarketing

I have worked in the fleet and contract hire industry for the last 30 years as a senior manager responsible for the management and disposal of large mixed vehicle fleets primarily with outright ownership then latterly in contract hire and leasing.

Back in the late seventies long before the discipline of remarketing was even thought of, believe it or not fleets still had to dispose of vehicles at the end of contract or more likely then at 3 years old at the end of the fleet life cycle. The term 'remarketing' somehow evolved as a new science for selling vehicles but the truth is that for as long as there have been cars as a business resource then the function of selling them has been around. Simply called 'disposals' or 'vehicle sales' the process has evolved into the current discipline but the rules have always been very much the same, get it sold for the most money in the shortest possible time.

My career in remarketing started in the construction industry with George Wimpey PLC as General Manager of the Plant and Transport company fleet making sure that the best possible value was extracted from vehicles which had been consistently subjected to high demands supporting a workforce scattered throughout the UK. After nearly 20 years of selling all types of vehicles from cars to vans to specialised commercial vehicles I moved to contract hire and took up a role as Disposals Manager with Dial Contracts looking after the sale of more than 12,000 vehicles a year which was my intro to volume remarketing. When Dial was acquired by LeasePlan I became Head of Remarketing responsible for the sale of 30,000 vehicles annually.

Now remarketing was firmly established as a discipline and after two years with the LeasePlan Group I was given the opportunity for some real remarketing with Motability, responsible for the effective disposal of 130-150k vehicles annually using both physical and electronic sales channels. So from relatively small volumes by comparison I was responsible for the asset disposal of the biggest fleet in the UK, if not the western hemisphere. After nearly 5 years with Motability I now run my own consultancy specialising in automotive remarketing solutions and have carried out a number of assignments for various companies in the volume disposal market. I also have been involved in related activities including electronic sales channels, vehicle refurbishment and logistics.

Over these next few pages I hope to give you some insight to my views and experience of remarketing and a flavour of the issues that really matter. Being able to maximise the benefit of a consistently commercial approach to the volume sale of vehicles in an effective time frame can make the difference between profit and failure, success and survival. Remember the guides are just that: they can indicate values not achieve them; it is up to you to make the difference!

More than half of UK company cars are funded on contract hire where the leasing company takes care of the vehicle disposal. What disposal routes are available to fleets that have to dispose of their own vehicles?

The funding profile of corporate fleets has changed substantially over the last 20 years so that now rather than using liquid funds to purchase vehicles outright an increasing proportion of organisations now source their transport needs through contract hire and leasing. Over half of the corporate fleet market is now funded by finance based organisations taking the residual risk on company vehicles.

However that still leaves a considerable volume of cars and commercial vehicles to be disposed of by fleet managers. Ex fleet vehicles are a sought after commodity in the motor trade and for that reason it is worthwhile developing a strategy which allows you to create a market where your vehicles can attract buyers because of their desirability. There is no reason why this methodology cannot be used with both trade and private buyers to successfully maximise the sales value.

From a commercial viewpoint, once the vehicle has completed its active fleet life speed is of the essence in turning the asset into cash. The longer the vehicle remains unsold the more the risk of damage, abuse and loss of value. It is very tempting to retain time-expired vehicles as back up but this can be an expensive commodity if not carefully managed. Additional costs can accrue all too easily and force a view that the value needs to be recovered. During that time the vehicle is depreciating and the net sale benefit is being eroded.

Let's consider the options available for selling ex fleet vehicles, the advantages, disadvantages, pitfalls and benefits of exploiting the available markets and the crucial need to research both your vehicle potential and disposal alternatives. Whatever route you decide to choose there are some overriding rule sets that need to be observed. The vehicle provenance is critically important, requiring open disclosure of known faults, structural damage and anything which may be detrimental to the perceived value. The other major consideration is to observe company governance policy to protect both personal and corporate integrity in all dealings.

Reputations take a long time to build but can be lost very quickly when trying to squeeze the last grain of benefit out of a deal or conveniently forgetting to advise pertinent detail. Integrity and credibility are fundamental in building a reputation in an industry which punishes non conformity.

Available routes to market for fleet managers can be summarised as auction, sale to dealer or trader, part exchange, agreed buy back, direct sale or sale to the driver's friends or family. There are more derivatives of the main options and we will cover those in the detail. No matter which route you choose the critical issue is to know how much the car is worth. Many a deal has foundered because the target price was too high or condition and specification were not optimal. Research the market, consult the guides, talk to dealers but most importantly be informed.

Car buyers are more knowledgeable than ever before about car values and the desirability of any car is driven by what the buyer wants and this sets the achievable price level irrespective of sales channel. All elements of the vehicle and specification and condition have a bearing on value. Condition is obviously the key issue and a car 'up on its toes' or in simple language, in good condition will attract more interest. Mileage is becoming a more important factor and whereas 10 years ago a 100k car would still fetch good money buyers are now looking predominantly at lower mileage options.

Colour and specification are also key issues and the overriding majority of buyers are looking for metallic finish and will avoid garish, fashionable and solid colours. Specification is also very relevant and must be in keeping with the model. So superminis need aircon, anything over 2 litres, 4wd and luxury must have leather and auto and sat nav are essential on any luxury model. Additional equipment which makes a car more attractive will make the car much more desirable and consequently worth more.

The message therefore is to be aware of what you are selling and also what triggers the added value generator. The eventual second generation buyer of an ex fleet car is prepared to pay a premium to stand out from the crowd and that represents an additional profit opportunity for the dealer. As a fleet manager you have to make sure that you use that knowledge to optimise the return for your company when you have unusual cars to dispose of.

Finally, on vehicle provenance, all documentation needs to be available at the time of sale. Service history and a dealer stamped service book will give the buyer confidence and handbooks should be with the car. The V5C and MOT are essential at the time of sale and although most dealers will retest a vehicle with less than 6 months remaining it is still worthwhile being able to show the buyer the documents. If a vehicle is registered on a cherished plate plan the changeover or retention well in advance because there is a stigma amongst virtually all dealers in accepting a V5C/2 and this is another reason to 'chip' the price.

Disposing of ex fleet vehicles can be time consuming so establishing a core policy from the outset will inform interested parties and should clearly define alternative channels available. For simplicity most fleets favour a policy of sale to staff or friends and family as a first option, then trade or auction for unsold vehicles. This methodology can work well in giving staff first refusal but there are pitfalls which need to be avoided and potential cost traps which can erode any price benefit. Remember your responsibility is to sell the car at a price which is reflective of a fair market value irrespective of sales channel.

What are the advantages and disadvantages of selling to staff?

From a logistical view selling a time-expired car to the driver or his family is an ideal solution. The advantages for both parties are tangible and ideally the car is sold very shortly after defleet. This will mean that the asset is liquidated quickly and proceeds are in the bank without having to incur additional depreciation and selling costs. There are some potential disadvantages which need to be considered and also should be factored into the pricing policy.

If a driver is looking to buy his ex fleet car for himself, friends or family it is because it is perceived that the purchase price will show a saving and as a fleet manager you have to protect the interests of your company in making sure that any advantage to the buyer is balanced with the level of return. Vehicle price is a key driver to a successful sale and whilst staff will have an advantage in knowing what they are buying, staff sales need to demonstrate compliance to HMRC in charging a fair market value. In other words sale prices need to be realistic in that the car is offered for sale at a price between trade and retail.

There are different methods of calculating sale prices i.e.

- Percentage of mileage adjusted CAP value, say 110%
- Average of 3 dealer valuations
- Auction valuation + 10%
- Sealed bids with a minimum reserve price of best trade bid +5%

The desired result is to achieve more than you would from trade sources and to save the costs of selling at auction. Selling to staff is a good way of fostering good relationships but care has to be taken not to introduce emotion to the deal. The pricing policy must be consistent, transparent and auditable to avoid criticism and to protect negative feedback.

As a precaution vehicles coming to the end of their fleet life should be monitored more carefully at least in the final 3 months to avoid unnecessary expenditure perhaps calculated to covertly enhance the value to a potential buyer. Areas that are obvious are new tyres, last minute major service, cosmetic repairs etc. In short the car should operate in the normal accepted fashion and not be subject to a refurbishment programme prior to sale.

There are some potential pitfalls in selling to staff in that there is, in addition to statutory obligations, a moral responsibility if a major fault develops in the short term. For that reason it is worth considering the addition of a warranty package to any private sale. The cost of this can be added to the sale price and gives the buyer some comfort in knowing that he has a degree of cover in the event of failure.

To summarise, selling cars to staff can be advantageous for both parties but you need to exercise caution by having a clear policy. As a guideline all the major contract hire fleets encourage staff sales as an improved income stream, most include warranty and few, if any, sell more than 6-8% of their end of contract vehicles to private individuals.

What are the advantages and disadvantages of selling to a dealer/trader?

Many fleet managers have established relationships with local retail dealers and traders which operate very successfully. There is strong demand for ex fleet cars and particularly if they can be bought direct from the fleet. For the dealer the advantages are clear in that the added cost of buying at auction can be avoided and there is a much better dialogue regarding the condition and history of the car. Acquisition is usually immediate so the delay in logistics of getting the car back is dispensed with and also from a sales viewpoint the known provenance of the vehicle can be a strong advantage in customer negotiation.

If the dealers are keen to buy direct from fleets then can this be turned to advantage for the vendor? There are distinct advantages in having relationships with local or regular buyers but the relationship must not be perceived as an easy way out of a difficult problem. Most dealers are prepared to take the rough with the smooth but we must not forget that a dealer's main objective is to maximise profit. Therefore he may be prepared to compromise in accepting rough cars but the loss or lost profit has to be supported.

This brings us to the crucial point of how the vehicles are going to be priced. Both parties have an objective to maximise benefit so this inevitably creates potential conflict on pricing policy if the negotiation is direct between buyer and seller. There are various ways in which this can be avoided and most revolve around a tender or sealed bid system. Typically cars for sale are available to view for a few days before sale and dealers are invited to inspect and form a view of the value. A bid is then made and these bids then compared to establish the top offer. A decision can then be made whether or not to accept.

The point of this exercise is essentially to determine the maximum achievable value. How will the fleet manager be able to determine that this is the case? Whatever methodology is used the common factor is that it takes time and can only be classed as subjective. The bottom line is that the car is worth as much as a dealer is prepared to pay for it and that is determined by the number of interested parties, their willingness to bid and the avoidance of collusion between bidders.

From the fleet manager's perspective one thing is clear the process of selling to dealers and traders direct from fleet can be very time consuming and open to criticism unless there are well defined policy guidelines. The cost saving and benefit analysis needs to be carefully weighed to justify this method of sale. That is not to say that sale to dealers is not an effective solution, far from it but with the current emphasis on corporate governance the additional justification is time consuming, stressful and may be difficult to justify.

The number of traders buying ex fleet cars has dropped considerably over the last 10 years and very few can trade profitably unless a retail outlet is available to them. In contrast to the market as it was 20 years ago, sale of used cars is intensely competitive and increased price awareness prevents the ability to build in another trading margin to support buyers who are not going to retail the cars that are bought from fleets.

The whole issue of achievable price is determined by supply and demand and competition in the used car market. Demand is fuelled by a number of factors which are market based and include model, specification, condition and desirability. The competitive element is provided by the number of interested buyers and their willingness to compete with each other to buy your cars at the highest price. Creating these conditions selling relatively small volumes of cars is difficult and time consuming but rewarding if executed properly. If you favour this method of disposal be sure to establish and agree your policy with a clear audit trail and a transparent easily understood negotiation methodology.

What are the advantages and disadvantages of part exchange?

An easy and clean method of disposing of a car at the end of life is to part exchange it against a new replacement. The clear advantage is that there is a seamless transition and a net cash outflow to the company. The downside is that both transactions are blurred and whilst the net benefit can be seen, in accounting terms the two cars have to be treated separately in the accounts. To evaluate the commercial benefit of a part exchange deal both elements of the deal need to be benchmarked and as fleet manager you need to apply the same rule set as you would use in separate purchase and disposal transactions and satisfy yourself that you have secured the best deal for both. That being the case then this is an efficient way of replacing the vehicle, minimising holding costs and avoiding sale and logistics cost.

What are the advantages and disadvantages of dealer buy-back?

Agreeing a buy back deal at the time of purchase is not as common as it used to be primarily because of the increasingly volatile used car markets. Buyback deals work very well for short term life cycles up to 12 months where the combination of attractive front end discounting and a relatively low mileage car at the end of term represents an attractive retail proposition for the dealer or manufacturer. In addition a buyback deal is usually agreed on a set period which will enable pre termination marketing of a known product to promote interest.

Buy back deals are generally linked to percentage of guide value at the end of term and this calculation is based on historical experience of the specific model taking into account supply and demand predictions, desirability and market potential. All buy back deals are subject to condition and mileage parameters and these will have to be agreed at the outset. Excess mileage over the agreed limit normally reduces the agreed sum by an amount per thousand miles, determined by the movement in guide prices for higher mileage examples. There is the facility to pool mileages or average over a number of vehicles to equalise over and under limit.

The condition of the vehicle is a much more contentious area and parameters have to be clearly defined from the outset. In the majority of cases it is better to apply a recognised standard that everyone understands and can refer to. The BVRLA Fair Wear and Tear Guide is recognised across the industry and reduces potentially subjective judgements. If you do choose to create your own condition standard make sure that it is easily understood and minimises the possibility of misinterpretation and subjectivity.

Buy back deals in essence have few draw backs but because of their very nature dealers will be cautious in setting projected residuals in money terms and will be looking to buy back vehicles at less than guide value to mitigate risk and exposure.

What are the advantages and disadvantages of selling ex-fleet cars through a retail dealer?

As a means of getting specialist help in selling your cars you can enlist the help of a dealer. The perception is that achieving retail value for a car will give an enhanced net return to the company. However this may not always be the case as the dealer will expect to retain his margin on the sale. Expenses such as VAT and warranty will have to be covered and preparation costs have to be factored into the net proceeds.

This method can be successful but there are a number of grey areas particularly pre sale preparation which require clear definition from the outset. You must always set a price expectation and timescale and agree this with the dealer. What happens if the car does not sell? who will covers the preparation costs? who will insure the car while it is on offer? – these are all areas that must be agreed beforehand to avoid disagreement later. Also establish whether the arrangement is SOR i.e. sale or return and what happens if a car remains unsold.

Fleet managers will look for a higher return from this type of sale but you must look at the bigger picture and accept that the dealer has to make a margin and where there are no stocking costs will there be the same incentive to maximise return for the owner? There is no such thing as a free lunch!

What are the advantages and disadvantages of direct retail sale?

Selling the car direct to a retail customer using the internet or press is also an option to be considered. Although you may be able to achieve retail money for the car you have to be aware that dealing direct with the customer is a time consuming process. Unless you have a particularly saleable car in good condition this sale method is not a preferred route to sale.

There are obligations as a seller that you will have to take into account and in addition to making sure that the car is in good working order you risk negative feedback in the event of breakdown or failure. Make sure that the car is accurately described in the advert and that the contact details are with someone who can handle the enquiries. Always arrange viewings strictly by appointment to suit your commitments and restrict visitors to avoid timewasters.

Payment terms have to be clear and the car should only be released on receipt of cleared funds. Be aware of your obligations to notify DVLA of change of ownership or you may find yourself responsible for parking or speeding fines!

What are the advantages and disadvantages of sale by auction?

Having originally operated a policy of selling to dealers I have adopted an almost exclusively auction based policy during the last 15+ years of my active remarketing career. The basic auction process has not changed radically over the years but the concept has been developed extensively to offer a complete solution to fleet managers. The sale of ex fleet cars is the cornerstone of the auction sale programmes of the major auctions and is the main draw for trade buyers looking for retail stock.

The combined effect of this situation is to create a market place auction which almost every major fleet in the UK uses as a primary disposal channel. Because of this virtually every motor retailer in the UK uses the auctions to source cars in varying degrees. Buyers will compete with each other for stock to create a free market situation where the value of cars is determined by demand. The internet has become increasingly influential over the last 3-5 years andmore buyers have become attracted to in auctions since sale catalogues became available online. This has the effect of marketing cars across the UK to dealers who may otherwise not have known what is on offer.

With developments in technology it is now possible to take part in a physical auction on an interactive basis over the internet. With web cam technology the car can be viewed online and buyers can bid simultaneously without buyers actually attending the auction. The benefit for vendors is that this increases the number of potential bidders and enhances competition.

There are a number of auction companies in the UK. The two major players have multi site operations nationwide and offer cars at regular sales throughout the week. There are also a number of effective independent auction companies running regular sale programmes for ex fleet cars. Details of individual auctions are available from the internet, price guides and various fleet publications. All the recognised auctions offer solutions for fleet managers and will offer solutions tailored to individual fleet requirements.

Realistically the major fleets will have better negotiating power than the smaller vendors but auctions are keen to attract regular supplies of fresh product so will offer a competitive package in line with the volume of cars offered for sale. As a norm the sale commission is charged on a successful sale and the proceeds are paid to the vendor on a net basis within 5-7 days. All vehicles can have a reserve price set by the vendor so that you are in control of your asset disposal.

There are some basic rules which fleet managers need to take into consideration in setting reserves. The market will essentially dictate what your car is worth so setting an unrealistic reserve will only result in the car remaining unsold which is undesirable from both auction and vendor perspectives. Take advice from the auction on how much the car is worth and apply a pragmatic view to their advice.

That is not to say that the auction will always get it right but their experience is informed and based on actual results in a continually fluctuating market. So take a view which is realistic and remember that you can reduce the price if your aspirations are too high. If the reserve is slightly higher than the market is prepared to pay then the auction will take a provisional bid which means that the vendor can then decide whether to accept or perhaps try to agree a sale price somewhere between the offer and the reserve.

The objective is to maximise the sale price as soon as possible but to be aware of the prevailing market influences affecting sale values. If you are selling a low volume high specification car then bidding will inevitably be brisker than that for a high mileage volume model in a poor colour with damage. All fleet managers want to maximise return but be aware that consistently hanging out for more than the car is realistically worth will result in lower sale conversion and extended days to sell as well as eventual lower prices.

Auctions will offer a complete package of services and the more you use the more you pay. However you can decide what suits your needs and have the comfort of knowing that the car can be collected, appraised, valeted, marketed, sold and paid for without you having to leave your desk. For the process to give the best results a relationship based on mutual trust needs to exist between auction and vendor. It is in neither party's interest for cars to remain unsold and fleet managers need to be aware that cars remaining unsold will probably attract a charge for collection and valeting to cover costs incurred.

Buyers are very aware of vendor product and attitude whilst they will avoid poor cars from a difficult vendor they will be very competitive and pay strong money for the right cars where the vendor takes a realistic attitude. There is a view with some vendors that auction is the last resort for selling cars but in reality competition will drive prices for the right cars to levels that are far in excess of what the car would sell for in a negotiated deal.

Presentation is a key element of achieving top prices and although the car will be valeted prior to sale any damage, poor paintwork, mechanical defects and interior damage will obviously reduce the sales value. Make sure that all relevant documentation is with the auction prior to sale as the trade will not bid for cars which have questionable credibility.

From a governance perspective selling cars at auction using reputable companies demonstrates that assets are being offered in an open market environment and will achieve their true value in a competitive market. The use of auction companies as a sales intermediary reduces exposure to risk and removes the issue of direct buyer dealing by the fleet manager. It also means that the car is on offer to any interested party on the same terms and at almost every auction private individuals can bid for cars against trade buyers. This means that a car can be bought for less than retail but that there is the advantage for the vendor that increased competition may increase the sale price. The end result is that cars will find their true value and satisfy the finance managers.

As a sales channel auction offers the cleanest solution and surplus vehicles can be disposed of quickly taking all the negotiation and administrative burden away from the fleet manager. As with any convenient solution there is a charge in commission but the benefits will outweigh the cost by managing the disposal in a much wider market than is available locally. There has to be input from the vendor to get the best results but in a well run fleet this will be already covered in operating practice so that when the vehicle is offered for sale it is in good condition for age and mileage with all relevant documentation available.

Is it worthwhile spending money to prepare a car prior to sale?

Condition is the most important factor in determining the saleability of an ex fleet car. Price is important but this is critically dependent upon the saleability of the car which in turn is driven by the cost of bringing the car up to retail standard. The great majority of ex fleet cars will need some level of refurbishment prior to resale in a retail environment. As a rule you should take the view that minor cosmetic repairs up to £150 in total are acceptable but where repairs will exceed this then the sales value will possibly be subject to reduction. Dealers are very particular about the quality of repair and there is no point in spending money having a cheap job done prior to sale as this will have the opposite effect and be detrimental to the sales value.

Minor cosmetic work which can be repaired on a SMART (small to medium area repair techniques) basis may be beneficial but dealers will be able to have the work done more cheaply and they prefer to control their own work quality. Paintwork is an area which causes huge concern to dealers and rectification of poor previous repair is expensive. Short of ensuring that damage is correctly repaired in the first place there is little point in getting involved in paint rectification prior to sale. The buyer will take account of any repair when bidding. Interior damage is also a high cost area and again replacement of damaged trim and carpets is rarely commercially viable for vendors.

If the car is being sold direct to a dealer the cost of repair will be taken into account in the price offered and the effect on the sales value will normally be less than the cost of rectification. However there is every reason to make sure that all the original equipment is present and that the car is clean inside and out before being offered. If the vehicle is being offered at auction a valet is usually part of the deal and all auctions will offer various cosmetic services to improve the appearance at extra cost. These include machine polish, PDR (paintless dent removal), deep interior cleans and minor repairs. You need to take a common sense approach to give the sale the best chance and simple things like making sure that if the car has a puncture it is not offered with a space saver fitted, making sure the load space cover is fitted, and removing the roof rack can make that crucial difference when the car is offered.

The message is to use common sense and spend minimally to make the best presentation of the car. There is no point in trying to disguise defects and unless repairs to bodywork are going to be done properly don't do it. Yes you can have bumper corners blown in using air dry paint in the car park but the paint will bloom within a short time and look very obvious. Better to leave it alone and spend the money on a good quality valet.

There will always be exceptions to the rule and there may be instances where repairs have to be carried out to make the car saleable but where this is needed it is better to agree a budget price with the repairer so that you know the extent of your liability before committing yourself to an open ended cheque. Always get bids on a damaged car before making a decision to repair and take a commercial decision which gives you the most effective solution.

If you have a regular disposal programme it may be worthwhile considering refurbishment and there are specialist companies who will offer a defleet preparation service. Usually a menu price basis is available but by working volumes of cars using SMART processes high standards can be achieved at competitive prices. The calculation then needs to be made to establish whether or not the investment creates an improved net return. There is an argument that where steady volumes of vehicles are generated the improved presentation is recognised by buyers as an advantage that will command a premium sale price based on being able to retail the car in a shorter time frame and save cost.

When selling via an auction the auction house will advise on the likely sale price. How should a fleet manager set a sale price when selling via a different disposal route?

The major price guides are published monthly for trade customers only. Both guides give indicative values for individual models dependent on age and mileage. CAP tends to be the benchmark for fleet and contract hire operators and Glass is primarily used by the motor trade. There is some synergy between the two but individual models can vary, sometimes significantly. There are also consumer guides such as Parker's and What Car available on the high street. As mentioned throughout this chapter sale price is determined by condition desirability. Selling to a dealer will inevitably achieve a lower value than to a private individual.

Using CAP as a benchmark, a car in good condition and in keeping with the condition criteria stated in the guide should fetch in the range of 95-102% mileage adjusted value from a dealer. The achievable sale price depends on many variables not least the current market and the supply available. From a dealer perspective the car has to make a profit on resale and this margin is affected by model, mileage, colour, specification and not least demand. It pays to be streetwise when selling cars and if you want to get the best prices you have to keep up with the market. Inevitably this takes time and resource and when selling to a dealer play the price high because you can always come down. There needs to be an element of competition to extract best value and inviting bids is one way of establishing the price.

When selling to staff, CAP show values for clean and retail which can be mileage adjusted. I suggest using a value based on midway or somewhere around 110% of clean trade. Be aware that private buyers are looking to save money but inevitably are drawn to the more desirable models so you have to maximise the advantage without appearing to be too greedy

Also be aware that some manufacturer options can dramatically affect the sale value. Leather trim, automatic gearbox, satellite navigation and upgraded alloys are expensive when new but show little value on resale from a guide perspective. The reality is that certain options that make all the difference. Try selling 2 litre manual petrol with cloth and no sat nav and you surely struggle but the same car as a fully specified diesel auto will fetch strong bids.

Pricing is subjective and open to interpretation so fleet managers need to make use of all available intelligence in conjunction with the industry standard price guide information to extract the best value for each car without compromise.

What recent developments have there been in the disposal market that have been particularly valuable to fleet managers and are there any in the pipeline?

The biggest single influence in selling cars in recent times has undoubtedly been the advances in internet technology. Information can be made available to buyers without having to move cars, and transactions and administration can be carried out remotely be carried out remotely. Images and descriptions can be published online and there are numerous organisations offering sale facilities targeted at private buyers to enhance residual value.

Auctions too have benefitted from internet advances and they can now run physical auctions on an interactive basis on an interactive basis allowing remote bidders to participate in physical sales. Vehicle details can be exchanged over the internet and records can be updated to be instantly accessible. Vehicle inspections can be carried out at the driver location with a PDA and detailed reports including images can be used to value or pre sell cars.

All of these elements help to streamline the sales process, increase accessibility to information but importantly increase the market visibility of cars. By widening the market potential, increased competition should improve time scale and values. Although development in selling electronically has been rapid the number of cars sold online represents a relatively small proportion of the total fleet market. There is still reluctance for the trade to wholly commit to electronic trading. This is partly due to inconsistency in vehicle description and a desire to touch and feel the car before buying.

The private buyer is more aware than ever before largely due to the internet and uses this knowledge to search out the right cars. You can take advantage of the power of the internet by using one of the emerging sellers who sell online with very effective graphical and descriptive packages targeting private buyers but be aware that this is considerably more expensive than auction. Again you have to take a commercial view based on the net return to evaluate the benefit.

In time I am sure that we will evolve to a situation where the internet will facilitate the coordination of physical channels to accumulate the vehicle data available to create a market place for vendors and buyers alike where cars can be bought and sold. The technology is available but the main obstacle remains that we are dealing with an infinitely variable product in a used car, and until a standard code of practice is evolved where the product is accurately described then progress will be a lot slower than we would all like to see.

What is your advice to a fleet manager on best practice when it comes to vehicle remarketing?

Remarketing is the key part of completing the life cycle of a fleet car and is critical to minimising overall cost to the owner. Best practice in remarketing is a combination of achieving the best net sale price in the shortest time with good governance and avoiding reputational risk.

Ideally, selling the car to the driver who has lived with it during its life and knows the vehicle intimately is the best solution. There will never be a longer road test and comeback is rare after the car is sold. As mentioned previously keep an eye on maintenance and replacements in the last couple of months but abuse is not normally an issue. The car should always be in good repair and fully roadworthy in any case and the driver will ensure that he is not compromised.

Selling to the driver, relatives or friends will result in a better return, saving selling and logistics costs and ensuring a quick conclusion. The number of cars able to be sold in this way will be relatively small and will vary according to fleet circumstances. For all remaining cars I recommend that you strike a deal with one of the auction companies to manage your disposal. Volume of cars available for sale will dictate the rate but you will be able to negotiate a competitive deal to have the car collected and sold with your involvement being limited to instruction, documentation and reserve.

All the reputable auction companies offer a high service level and are aware that a successful ongoing relationship is dependent on good customer service and performance. There is no point in entering into protracted negotiations trying to sell cars to different dealers when the whole process can be managed for you at arm's length allowing you to concentrate on the overall management of your fleet.

How can your company help fleet managers?

Miles Turner Associates can offer a range of expertise in the complete spectrum of large fleet operation. We have extensive experience in remarketing, maintenance, logistics and vehicle refurbishment developed over 30 years experience in fleet management. We can draw on a team of highly motivated professional managers with specific skills able to deliver solutions to clients in providing a platform for successful transformation and increased efficiency. Services are available for short and medium term assignments at competitive daily rates. This way we ensure that you get what you pay for without the additional cost of full time employment

Peter A. Rosie FIMI
Miles Turner Associates

MILESTURNER

AUTOMOTIVE CONSULTANCY

An innovative small consultancy able to draw on experienced managers with extensive Fleet Management experience available for short, medium and interim assignments at competitive daily rates.

Specialists in all aspects of operational volume fleet management including Remarketing, Logistics, Refurbishment, Maintenance and Risk Management.

www.milesturner.co.uk

E-mail us: info@milesturner.co.uk

Telephone: 01252-622521

Mobile: 07766-168168

WORK-RELATED ROAD SAFETY

Caroline Scurr
Programme Manager
Driving for Better Business

Please introduce yourself

I'm the Programme Manager for the 'Driving for Better Business' programme. This is a government backed initiative which aims to catalyse a reduction in deaths and serious injuries caused by driving for work. I have managed the programme for the last two years, since its inception. Prior to working in road safety I worked in advertising, before becoming a local authority Road Safety Officer for West Berkshire Council, specialising in work related road safety. I have contributed to a number of national and international committees and policy groups to advise on Driving for Work and Fleet Safety issues. Over the last five years I have also been involved in the development of resources for the Department for Transport, the Highways Agency and businesses. More recently I was asked to assist in judging the fleet safety category for the Prince Michael International Road Safety Awards and the Motor Transport Awards.

What is Roadsafe?

RoadSafe is a road safety partnership of leading companies in the motor and transport industries in Britain, the government and road safety professionals. It is acknowledged as a leading forum for promoting and devising solutions to road safety problems. It aims to reduce deaths and injuries caused by road accidents and promote safer driving. RoadSafe brings together representatives from government, the vehicle and component manufacturing and road transport industries, road safety professionals and the specialist media, to work together to find new approaches to reducing casualties amongst vulnerable groups.

RoadSafe is unique, as it is currently the only forum which gathers all these representatives to work together. Launched in October 2001, it has grown from the respected Prince Michael International Road Safety Awards which have been recognising outstanding achievement and innovation in road safety since 1987.

RoadSafe manages the 'Driving for Better Business' programme on behalf of the Department for Transport.

RoadSafe's primary objectives are:

* To build partnerships with road safety professionals, the media and government.
* To promote best practice.
* To demonstrate the commitment of sponsors to social responsibility in the field of road safety and traffic management.

RoadSafe is recognised as a 'partner' by the Department for Transport (DfT). We are committed to supporting the government's road safety strategy – Tomorrow's roads: safer for everyone – through developing initiatives in partnership to achieve specific casualty reduction targets.

Our sponsors include SMMT, RHA, the leading car, commercial vehicle and component companies as well as many other companies from the transport sector. RoadSafe is itself represented on a number of professional bodies including AIRSO, IRSO, IAM, and RoSPA.

What is the Driving for Better Business programme? How did it come about?

The Secretary of State for Transport asked the Motorists' Forum how employers could be encouraged to give a higher priority to road safety for those who drive cars or vans for business purposes. Their key recommendations were:

* The need to make employers aware that workplace health and safety legislation applies equally to work-related travel and should be applied in the same way as in the workplace.
* The need for a systematic programme of outreach designed to coordinate a network of employer champions drawn from public, private and voluntary sectors who will work through employer networks and associations to deliver awareness.

How does the programme run?

The Secretary of State for Transport has delegated the development and management of the outreach programme to a Steering Committee which is supported by RoadSafe under contract to the Department for Transport. The Steering Committee consists of experts in work related road safety, business leaders, representatives of the transport industry, and the Department of Transport and its agencies. The Department for Transport wants to avoid imposing further legislation on work related road safety on business. But it wants to improve driving for work standards and believes it can do this by supporting organisations to communicate with business and demonstrate the commercial benefits of effective work related road safety – an innovative approach.

What is the programme trying to achieve?

The aim of the programme is:

> To develop and co-ordinate a network of employers and champions to promote good practice in work related road safety in order to catalyse a reduction in deaths and injuries caused by vans and cars used for business purposes.

Every day of the year more than 150 vehicles driven on company business crash. Every year there are 14,000 road deaths and serious injuries involving people at work. Business pays for this. With the Road Safety Act on the statute book and the advent of the Corporate Manslaughter and Corporate Homicide Act in April 2008, the issue of health and safety in the workplace – the business vehicle – is something business employers are no longer able to ignore.

What progress has been made?

The programme is developing and coordinating a network of employers and their associations in order to deliver awareness. It is engaging partners as well as identifying and supporting Champions. The programme will also implement a communication plan to support other Department for Transport initiatives in work related road safety in a coordinated and sustained way.

The programme has been executed in three phases:

Phase 1: Established a Steering Committee of experts and a Secretariat. This phase is now complete.

Phase 2: Launched a pilot programme focussed on a limited number of organisations. This phase began with the programme launch at the Commercial Vehicle Show on 24 April and ran until December 2007.

Phase 3: Developed and delivered a full scale outreach programme expanding the Phase 2 work into the car fleet management area.

WHERE ARE WE NOW?

We are now well into the third phase of the programme and are still working hard to expand the network and raise awareness about the programme. We have now recruited over 24 organisations as Champions from the private and public sectors, which continue to demonstrate the business case for work related road safety. They have been active in presenting at various events and distributing information through their own communications channels and networks.

WHAT IS THE CURRENT FOCUS OF OUR EFFORT?

We still seek to recruit at least one further champion per month but the main focus is now on the expansion of our wider network, increasing awareness about the programme and working with our existing partners. We are actively targeting leasing firms, trade associations and the FTSE 250 to ensure we are engaging with small businesses as well as large organisations.

CHAMPIONS – WHO ARE THEY AND WHAT DO THEY DO?

Business champions constitute the central element of the Driving for Better Business employer network. They are those firms that are prepared to step forward to champion good practice in work related road safety by taking a business message to business. Business champions, drawn from public, private and voluntary sectors, both company directors and fleet decision-makers, will work through various networks and associations to deliver awareness to their fellow businessmen. The target audience is those businesses operating company car and van fleets, as well as those who rely on staff to use their own vehicles on work-related journeys.

To become a business champion a firm must have:

- A 'top down' commitment to managing work related road safety;
- A positive attitude towards safety, reflected in the behaviour of all its employees (including directors, line managers, contractors and sub-contractors), as part of its 'safety culture';
- Formal policies and practices in line with the HSE / DfT 'Driving for Work' guidance, including internal reporting and measurement mechanisms;
- An honest account of its safety record prior to implementing a risk management system;
- A willingness to present at events and seminars;
- The time and inclination to network with key industry figures;
- A willingness to talk to the media;
- A convincing case study.

RoadSafe supports the Business Champions by:

- Identifying opportunities to deliver their message to their business peers.
- Assisting them to develop their case study and message.
- Providing the administrative support they need to deliver their message.
- Improving their work related road safety ethos by improving their network of contacts and access to expert advice.
- Organising events to allow Champions to network and share best practice.

How bad is road safety in the UK?

Britain has one of the best road safety records in the world but even here there are between 800 and 1200 deaths recorded each year where the driver of the vehicle was at work when the crash occurred. In terms of risk this is high – in comparison all other deaths at work including such obviously high risk occupations such as deep sea fishing total only 250.

Compared with most regions, the European Union is doing well – there is an overall casualty reduction target of fifty per cent to be achieved by 2020. In terms of overall performance Britain vies with Sweden and The Netherlands to be the best; but in the rate of reduction, Britain is lagging behind France (mainly because we drew up our first targets some twenty years ago). The current government-led road safety strategy is on target; last year for the first time since the early 1930s the road death toll in Britain was 2946 – and this was a 7 percent fall on the 2006 total.

Do fleet drivers have a particularly high risk of accidents?

Fleet drivers are the highest risk working group, hence the government's drive to improve this area of management through such campaigns as 'Driving for Better Business'.

Can you give us some examples of organisations that have implemented road safety programmes, and the outcomes of these?

TNT Express:

Time is money to global courier company TNT Express, but ethics and the moral argument are greater, which is why the organisation is focusing on raising road safety standards in every one of the 200+ countries in which it operates.

Just as TNT Express, one of the world's leading business-to-business express delivery service providers, has comprehensive occupational road risk management measures in place in mature markets, such as the UK, it is investing heavily to reduce the number of road crash fatalities and injuries in emerging markets such as Brazil, China, India and eastern European nations.

But summing up the company's view, Birmingham-based health and safety manager Kevin Cook said: "TNT Express does not focus on the financial impact of road traffic accidents. Its primary reason for enhanced road safety performance is the moral benefit to society as a whole and the company feels that to apportion costs is inappropriate compared to the cost of human life and a family's suffering.

"In addition, the company as a whole is already aware of the costs and business implications of accidents within an express delivery service and therefore it is considered unnecessary to further identify costs."

TNT Express, a division of the Netherlands-based TNT business, delivers 4.4 million parcels, documents and pieces of freight each week – and the figure is rising as the business continues to expand, particularly in emerging markets.

The division operates almost 15,000 owned vehicles – HGVs, sub-7.5 tonne vehicles, company cars and motorcycles – and around a further 16,000 vehicles are operated by contractors at a national level depending on seasonal demands, operational benefits and the fact that in some countries such as Italy, India and Germany it is standard practice. In the UK, TNT Express operates 2,002 vehicles above 7.5 tonnes, 370 small trucks and vans below 7.5 tonnes and 988 company cars. TNT Express also operates 47 aircraft and has the single largest door-to-door air and road express delivery infrastructure in Europe.

Mature business units such as the UK, France, Italy and Germany already have well-established road safety policies and procedures for all drivers getting behind the wheel of a vehicle, built around well developed health and safety and employment legislation, and those structures are now being rolled out worldwide.

Initiatives include standards around driver recruitment, on-the-road driving assessments being carried out prior to a post being offered, defensive driver training courses being completed within three months of employment with a refresher after three years, and possible additional training for drivers following a blameworthy crash and when a commercial vehicle driver has been absent for more than three months.

Crucially, contractors are also expected to meet similar high standards – although this presents greater challenges in the developed world than in emerging markets, according to Mr Cook.

"Globally, contractor compliance is the single biggest issue we face," explained Mr Cook, whose role is to help implement and enforce similar standards and approaches to road safety on a country-by-country basis across the world and provide support through auditing global policies and recommending best practice.

"In the emerging markets we tell contractors the safety standards we expect and if they don't comply then they don't get the work. In Europe and the developed world there are legal issues and it is more difficult. However, we explain the TNT Express standard and what we expect of contractors and, where appropriate, provide training and information. We then monitor the contractors and if we are not happy we then go elsewhere."

In 2004 TNT Express saw 19 fatalities involving its vehicles around the world, but it has seen that figure cut to one fatality a month on average in mature markets. However, as the company embarks on a strategy of acquisition in emerging countries it has seen a significant rise in road crashes – last year there were 39 fatalities of which sub contractors accounted for 31 of the incidents with many in the emerging markets.

It is against that background that TNT Express believes that it can make a difference. Mr Cook said: "We will endeavour to work with the national businesses that we acquire to reduce road deaths and crashes and educate drivers. That is why we are giving managers and staff in these countries hands-on support and advice and rolling out best practice from the UK and other mature markets into these countries."

Additionally, an annual global road safety week throughout TNT Express's operations complements its road safety management system, and special programmes and campaigns are designed to keep the issue front of mind amongst all staff – directors, managers and drivers.

Mr Cook outlined how it was perfectly acceptable in India, for example, for a company to ask an employee to undertake a 30-hour journey, but added: "We say that is not acceptable so we have to get policies in place to enable our basic standards to be met. But change must be handled carefully because cultures are very different."

The TNT Express road safety management programme focuses on driver, vehicle and journey management, but said Mr Cook: "TNT Express appreciates that a fourth element of road safety which is not within its road safety management system, but is equally important is road condition, infrastructure and the actions of other road users."

That is why TNT Express has strong links with the Global Road Safety Partnership (GRSP), has signed up to the European Road Safety Charter and has become a 'business champion' under the government's 'Driving for Better Business' programme.

GRSP, which is managed by the International Federation of Red Cross and Red Crescent Societies in Geneva, brings together governments and governmental agencies, the private sector and civil society organisations to address road safety issues in low and middle-income countries.

Meanwhile, the European Road Safety Charter is an appeal and a driving force for all civil society organisations to provide a tangible contribution to increasing road safety in Europe and a forum and platform for the signatories to exchange experiences and new ideas – across national borders – in their efforts towards greater safety on European roads.

By making its policies, procedures and road safety-related materials available to other like-minded organisations, Mr Cook said: "We all share the road; we all share the globe and we all work together. The at-work driving safety measures taken by one organisation may stop a TNT Express vehicle from being involved in a crash and that will help everyone, including our business, which is why we are happy to share best practice."

He added: "By joining organisations and becoming involved in campaigns and initiatives such as 'Driving for Better Business' we can lobby governments for change and promote road safety. We want to reduce road casualties globally and we believe we can make a difference."

Earlier this year, a resolution adopted by the United Nations General Assembly called on private and public sector fleets to develop and implement policies and practices that would reduce crash risks for vehicle occupants and other road users.

"All businesses can learn from each other," said Mr Cook, who explained that all fatal crashes resulted in investigations being launched at managing director level with the aim being to implement measures to stop any repeat incident.

Historically, road safety has been seen as an unfortunate consequence of transport systems and as a problem for the transport sector. However, the direct costs of the growing number of crashes falls mostly on the health sector, businesses and families.

It is with that mind that TNT Express aspires to have the same road safety and health and safety standards not just in the UK, but also in countries as culturally different as Vietnam and Brazil.

"It is not easy," said Mr Cook. "But TNT will focus relentlessly on a zero tolerance policy for the loss of human lives in respect of employees, contractors and third parties."

Greene King

BREWER Greene King cut its road crash costs by more than £150,000 in 2006/7 as its in-house-developed safe driving initiative continued to pay dividends.

In the last four years more than 500 members of staff – HGV, LGV and company car drivers as well as occasional pool car drivers and employees who drive their own car on business – have all completed individual three-hour driving assessments under the eagle eye of the company's driving safety advisor Paul Blackman.

A Greene King Brewing Company dray driver for 11 years until he switched careers four years ago, Mr Blackman is believed to be one of the most decorated driving instructors in the country.

He is Driving Standards Agency registered for car, LGV and fleet, a diploma holder in advanced car instruction a multiple holder of the Royal Society for the Prevention of Accident's gold advanced driving badge and a volunteer chief observer of RoSPA's Bury St Edmunds' Group.

Mr Blackman said: "The company realised that with the growing legislative focus on occupational driving it needed to put a strategy in place. The directors were aware of my interest and advanced driving qualifications so approached me about a change of career."

He readily accepted and used his safe driving expertise to develop the company's own programme, which is focussed around the half-day one-to-one course. That includes a 60-minute presentation and discussion and a 45-mile drive, which is followed by a debrief and a written report that forms part of an employee's employment record.

The company car policy states that all new staff whose work involves driving must have their driving licences checked, report any motoring offences and complete the driving assessment. Further licence checks are made on LGV drivers every three months and car drivers annually.

Any staff who are involved in an accident or commit a motoring offence undergo retraining and specialist training courses are completed by employees who might, for example, have more than six points on their driving licence. Alternatively, a low speed parking manoeuvre resulting in vehicle damage will lead to remedial training taking place 'in the yard'.

As part of the corporate focus on safe driving, all company vehicles are equipped with 'accident packs'. These include information about looking after yourself and others at a crash scene, accident forms to record information and a disposable camera to record all vehicle damage.

In addition, monthly safe driving campaigns, which highlight key issues, such as drink-driving, driver fatigue and tyre maintenance, are run at the company's head office and all depots to ensure road safety remains front of mind for all employees.

As a further step, the company is considering buying its own eyesight testing equipment that could be used by all staff – not just at-work drivers – as research reveals that many people could be driving with their eyesight below the minimum legal standard.

"Not only does Greene King have a duty of care towards its employees, but as a business we want to make sure our staff are safe on the road at all times. We don't want people to lose their job because they lose their driving licence," explained Mr Blackman, whose interest in advanced driving began almost two decades ago when he followed up a local newspaper advanced driving course advert.

The company's success in managing its occupational road risk has been recognised with a second RoSPA gold award this year and it becoming a 'business champion' under the government's 'Driving for Better Business' programme.

Insurance data is independently collated and latest figures reveal that although the fleet has expanded significantly over the past seven years, the number of crashes in 2006/7 was cut by 63 (24%) to 200.

Greene King self insures the first £10,000 of vehicle damage and in 2006/7 costs dropped by more than 54% producing a bottom line saving of £158,000 compared with 2005/6. In addition, the cost of damage to vehicles involved in crashes has been cut by 39% from more than £1,100 per case to £679 as the safe-driving programme means that the severity of incidents has reduced despite inflation contributing to a rise in the cost of repairs in recent years.

Paul Blackman, driving safety advisor, Greene King

"By highlighting the dangers of work-related road risk and recognising the financial costs of accidents, Greene King has been able to improve profitability and contribute to the safety of staff by making them more risk aware," said Mr Blackman.

"I would advise all companies not to bury their head in the sand. Businesses can say that managing occupational road risk is not for them because they have never had anyone killed while driving on business. But that probably means that the likelihood of someone being killed is increasing as the risks faced by drivers is far greater than anywhere else in the workplace."

The company has been a brewer and operated pubs for more than 200 years. It runs a fleet of 271 company cars within an overall fleet of almost 500 vehicles, including 95 drays, with drivers located nationwide.

Company directors and managers have all been through Mr Blackman's assessment and, he said: "Because I work for the company and have been a Greene King dray driver, colleagues know that I understand the issues they are up against.

"Staff have been very receptive to the assessments. Some have gone on to complete their own advanced driving exams and that is very gratifying."

Kaba Door Systems

A multi-faceted action plan to cut the number of road crashes involving employees has resulted in Kaba Door Systems slashing its incident rate by 20% and, as a result, becoming a 'business champion' under the government's 'Driving for Better Business programme'.

Telford-based Kaba Door Systems is a world leader in the supply, installation and service of automatic sliding, swinging, revolving and circular sliding doors together with industrial and commercial shutter and grilles, fire shutters and curtains and moveable partitions.

Employing more than 400 staff, the company operates a 175-strong fleet of which more than half are vans up to 3.5 tonnes and it also includes almost 80 company cars.

The range of safety-focused initiatives introduced across the Kaba Door Systems' fleet has included the company being one of the first in the country to specify that all new vehicles should be equipped with electronic stability control (ESC) as standard.

The anti-skid technology is billed by road safety experts as the most significant life-saving advance since the seat belt, with research on behalf of the Department for Transport suggesting that ESC-equipped vehicles are 25% less likely to be involved in a fatal crash than those without the technology.

The measure was introduced more than 12 months ago and is expected to have significantly contributed to a further reduction in crashes involving company cars and vans when the firm's 2007/8 incident statistics are published.

Crash statistics for 2006/7 revealed a 20% year-on-year reduction in incidents with the company saying that the introduction of an accident financial liability policy played a key role. That sees drivers paying 50% of the cost of their second at-fault crash with a third incident resulting in the driver footing the entire bill.

Fleet manager Ann Dukanovic said: "This measure has been used to encourage drivers to take more care when driving. I have also anonymously visited our nationwide network of depots to inspect vehicle records and these two measures have greatly contributed to the overall reduction in accident rates."

Other safety measures introduced by Kaba Door Systems include:

- Monthly vehicle checks sheets that must be completed by drivers have to and record vehicle condition along with all fluid top ups and last service dates thus ensuring any unreported accident damage can be spotted. Remedial action can then be taken to improve safety.
- Driver logs are also completed to ensure the company knows who was driving a vehicle when and where so any issues can be quickly resolved.
- Reversing sensors fitted as standard on all long wheel base commercials
- All drivers having mobile phones with hands' free car kits.
- All vehicles carrying fire extinguishers and first aid kits

Mrs Dukanovic said: "We are delighted that the safety initiatives we have taken have resulted in a reduction in our accident record. However, we are always looking to further improve the safety of our staff and other road users.

"Being recognised as a 'business champion' by the Driving for Better Business' programme is a tremendous accolade for the company. I hope the initiatives that we have introduced and the success we have had in improving our fleet safety will encourage other businesses to take action."

Commenting on this, I said: "Kaba Door Systems is at the forefront of introducing new initiatives to reduce the number of deaths and injuries on Britain's roads. Our 'business champions' have a crucial role to play in promoting occupational road risk management in their local areas and nationally."

Gateshead Council

It's official! Gateshead Council runs one of Britain's safest fleets and is among the first public sector organisations to become a 'business champion' under the government's 'Driving for Better Business' programmes.

Gateshead Council runs a fleet of more than 350 vehicles including minibuses, light commercial vehicles and HGVs across a range of operations including: construction, refuse collection, highways maintenance and street lighting, gritting, community services and home to school transport.

In recent years Gateshead Council has undertaken a root and branch review of its entire fleet operation and introduced a raft of measures to ensure employees and all other road users are as safe as possible. That has resulted in a crash rate reduction of almost a third in the last three years.

The council policy means that all employees must successfully complete a 'Council Driver Assessment' before operating a council vehicle. Assessments are carried out by one of six trained assessors. Following the initial session, drivers are subject to further annual checks and assessment. The assessment process covers: driver licence checks, eyesight checks, a 45-minute practical driving session and the provision of tips and information on safe driving.

The assessment programme is constantly under review with the aim to continually refresh the information provided and implement improvements. Any driver found to be at fault in a crash or guilty of a road traffic offence must go through the assessment process again. Drivers new to

Gateshead Council must also complete an extended driving induction.

Results of the driver assessment form part of the information used to risk-assess each driver. Accident records are also monitored as well as driving offences and endorsements. If a driver is regarded to be 'high risk', then targeted interventions are implemented including driver training.

The safe-driving initiative, which was introduced in 2006, also includes:

- All drivers carrying out daily checks of vehicles before taking to the road.
- The completion of daily vehicle log records with all journeys accounted for and authorised by line managers.
- Special safe driving briefing sessions for employees under 24 years old.
- An outreach programme to visit users of local authority minibuses to ensure that knowledge of loading, seat restraints and passenger assistance is continually improved.

Alasdair Tose, transport services manager, said: "A number of factors have led to a near 30% decrease in fleet accidents over the past three years. Contributing to this have been our driver assessment/training initiatives, better driver communication and improved vehicle safety features with, for example, all new vehicles fitted with 56 mph speed limiters.

"By reducing our accident record we are saving taxpayers' money and ensuring that service levels within the authority's area continually improve, as valuable time is not spent on dealing with the aftermath of an incident."

"Through the processes we have introduced and, crucially, communication with employees to explain the reasons behind the safe-driving programme, we have changed driving culture within the council."

"We are delighted to be recognised as a 'business champion' and will continue to strive to promote road safety at both a local and national level. I hope the initiatives that we have introduced and the success we have had in improving our fleet safety will encourage other businesses to take action."

Commenting on this, I said: "Gateshead Council is at the forefront of promoting road safety. As 'business champions' local authorities have a crucial role to play in occupational road risk management not only within their own organisations but by using their relationships with businesses in their areas to promote safe driving."

Balfour Beatty

Balfour Beatty Plant & Fleet Services is the most recent organisation to become a 'business champion' under the governments 'Driving for Better Business' safety programme due to its radical approach to road safety and reducing the number of road traffic collisions in its extensive fleet of vehicles.

Balfour Beatty Plant & Fleet Services operates approximately 8,500 vehicles including 4,500 company cars, 3,000 light goods vehicles and 1,000 HGVs. In addition, the Derby-based company manages around 2,000 short-term contract hires every year for Balfour Beatty Group.

The company offers a comprehensive fleet service, incorporating both contract hire and fleet management solutions to Balfour Beatty Group operating companies. This service integrates expert advice, specialised vehicle specification, vehicle procurement, and the coordination of life-long servicing and maintenance requirements to suit the specific needs of their customers. Balfour Beatty Group currently operates in the region of 14,000 vehicles in the UK, ranging from company cars right through to custom-built HGVs.

Key to Balfour Beatty Plant & Fleet Services becoming a 'business champion' has been the introduction of a comprehensive four-stage driver risk management programme that is available to all Balfour Beatty Group employees and includes the introduction of a unique driving simulator.

Balfour Beatty Plant & Fleet Services considers road safety an essential part of its corporate social responsibility. Managing director Steve Farmer reinforces this with the message that 'people are a company asset that cannot be replaced'.

Balfour Beatty Plant and Fleet Services Driver Risk Management programme is aimed at ensuring Balfour Beatty Group employees meet safe driving standards.

The programme is divided into four areas and is overseen by project manager James Burrows and delivered by fleet training manager Martin 'Nobby' Clark, an ex-Cheshire Police traffic officer.

The programme incorporates:

1 Drive Safe, Arrive Safe – a multitude of educational presentations and sessions intended to re-educate drivers in a variety of areas such as defensive driving, drinking and driving, drugs and driving, hazard perception, mobile phone use, and the human cost of road traffic collisions.

2 Company Driver E-Learning modules – drivers are required to complete a web-based e-learning module and assessment, demonstrating that they have reviewed and understood the content of the Company Car or Commercial Vehicle Drivers Handbook. The course targets all employees who drive on business – including own-vehicle and occasional drivers.

3 The Driver Risk Index (DRI) – a web-based technology used to assess driver risk via a psychometric assessment, developed in close association with Cranfield University. The approach assesses the driver's level of risk on the road by taking into account situational, behavioural and attitudinal factors, and provides individualised psychometric profiles instantly via email. The individual driver profiles are then used to develop further tailored driver training.

4 The Driving simulator – a pioneering approach to driver training used by Balfour Beatty Plant and Fleet Services to educate drivers. The Driving Simulator is seen as a dual-edged solution mitigating driver risk alongside enhancing fuel efficiency. The simulator sessions are designed to alleviate the risks identified by the DRI in conjunction with classroom-based driver safety awareness courses.

Steve Farmer added: "It is the ambition of Balfour Beatty Plant & Fleet Services to reduce the number of collisions and consequentially the total collision cost. Increased concentration on driver safety awareness and risk mitigation will significantly contribute to reducing the collision cost incurred. In addition there are many associated costs, which are not considered in this total. Insurance premiums would also reduce in correlation with a reduction in road traffic collisions".

"We are delighted that the safe driving initiatives we have introduced have been recognised by the 'Driving for Better Business' programme. We will continue to strive to improve our fleet safety and hope that the actions we have taken will encourage other businesses to follow our lead."

Commenting on this, I said: "Balfour Beatty Plant and Fleet Services has taken a radical approach to road safety and to reducing its own risk exposure, particularly with the introduction of its own driving simulator.

"The company is fine example of how a range of occupational road risk management initiatives and targeted solutions can be used to put in place a cycle of continuous road safety improvements that will benefit employees, their families and the wider community."

What is your advice to fleet managers on how best to reduce work-related road accidents?

My advice would be to join the Driving for Better Business network via our website to view our case studies and updates on important issues. I would also advise all fleet managers to be prepared to share their experiences with their peers as a way of overcoming common problems.

Our Business Champions are fully aware of the benefits of sharing knowledge and best practice with other businesses, not only from a PR perspective but also from a networking point of view.

Many of the companies and individuals involved in the Driving for Better Business programme have come up against similar obstacles in terms of reducing casualties, reducing costs and managing their fleets and appreciate the support they receive from RoadSafe and each other. The range of experience and enthusiasm demonstrated by our Champions is extensive. Who better to provide guidance and advice on how to overcome fleet safety problems than other fleet managers?

RoadSafe is continuing to develop and support this network of Champions who have tried a range of approaches and interventions and who are willing to share their experiences. We provide opportunities for them to network with each other in order to debate key industry issues and promote their case studies and solutions to problems with the wider business community. Rather than reinventing the wheel, Champions are prepared to put commercial and competitive interests aside in order to tackle work related road safety head on. By sharing information in this way industry is resolving its own issues with minimal legislation or intervention from government, enforcement authorities or the road safety community.

Caroline Scurr,
Programme Manager,
Driving for Better Business,

Driving for Better Business

Between 800-1000 people are killed in the UK each year when driving for work.

Our website features case studies to demonstrate how leading companies manage the risk.

If your organisation takes the safety of employees seriously when they drive for work, join the **Driving for Better Business** network:

www.drivingforbetterbusiness.com

36 RECRUITING FLEET STAFF

Alastair Ames

Alastair Ames Associates

The economy is cooling. How have you seen the job market changing over the last year?

There has been a noticeable change in the automotive sector over the last few months and this has inevitably led to changes in the normal pattern of recruitment activity. There has been an enormous amount of press coverage of the economic effects on the motor trade and this has covered the challenges faced by both retail and fleet businesses. The problems have had a massive effect on the retail sector and in true terms sales of new vehicles and more expensive second hand vehicles have fallen dramatically.

The problem as we know is global and the repercussions are being felt by everybody involved in the business in the UK, Europe and America. The problems really started as soon as money lending stopped and look like they are here to stay for a while. We now have the added problem of currency devaluation, due to interest rate cuts, which will inevitably cause price rises on cars coming into the UK from Europe. This will bring additional gloom to a large proportion of retailers in the market and remove a significant number of jobs.

The fleet sector has been hit hard with both lower residual values and a lower demand for second hand vehicles and this will see them needing to cut costs across the board.

As with every downturn or recession some people will not find employment in the sector again and others will have to reset their expectations and take lesser roles. Car dealerships have grown in size substantially over the last few years and the high availability of credit really meant they really had never had it so good. Cars were bought in unprecedented numbers. There were buyers everywhere for both new and used vehicles and targets and expectations grew and grew. From 2001 until very recently, unemployment had dropped across all sectors. According to the SMMT (Society of Motor Manufacturers and Traders) the automotive sector currently accounts for about 780,000 jobs in the UK with about 190,000 of those in manufacturing. Many of these could now be under threat as demand and sales drop. It had been noticeable that new positions and layers of management kept being created and the population of workers in the car retail sector grew like never before.

The manufacturers and distributors themselves have expanded their work force at a similar rate as dealerships and fleet companies, even if as before, large numbers of people were sub-contracted. Employment in the leasing sector growth has grow but in a slower and more considered way, because advances in technology have gradually cut back office and in-life support teams.

There has been a large growth of leasing brokerages of varying sizes across the country in both the prime and sub prime sectors and business had been plentiful. The lack of available credit over the last few months has meant that several of these brokers have pulled out of the business and probably won't return for some time. The residual value crash has also put a whole series of challenges in place for the larger leasing companies and many are now very cautious about taking on new customers, and will remain so until there is greater clarity in the market place. It has been noticeable that there has been a greater emphasis put into account management, retention and the development of current customers rather than winning new business. There has also been a greater emphasis on remarketing end of contract vehicles and this has led to a wave of recruitment in this area as companies strengthen their internal teams and external companies emerge as specialists.

How do you think the job market will change over the next year or two?

The press have been spreading gloom about the prospects of greater unemployment over the next year or two and unemployment has gone up in several sectors already.

The property, automotive, banking and finance sectors have been hit the hardest first. Redundancy has been very evident across our sector and there is more to come in 2009. The world is changing fast along with people's buying habits and every business in every sector needs to look at how they will be affected. The automotive sector is not exempt from this and has for a long time been producing too many cars and creating a growing but unsustainable market. We have entered into a period of massive uncertainty and this has to be a concern for anybody involved in selling anything, especially to retail customers.

We have been there before and some of us can probably remember the fields of cars that were dotted all over the countryside in the early 1990s. As we know, demand returned and they were all eventually sold. The motor trade has become more glamorous since then and has the overheads to go with it. Costs will have to be cut and jobs will suffer. The commercial property slump has seen the value of the trade's fixed assets fall as fast as the value of their stock and this will, in some cases, put pressure on their ability to borrow money.

Markets can be very fickle and changeable and influenced by all sorts of outside factors. In January 2007 petrol was about 96p a litre and in January 2008 it is under 90p a litre. At one stage in 2007 it hit 117p of course. The oil speculators all got their fingers burnt and the oil companies started finding new oil reserves in all parts of the world. During this period everyone decided that big cars were dead and values were destroyed. The media coverage drove everybody to sell their larger-engined cars at a massive loss and to buy smaller-engined or diesel cars.

It is difficult to predict the future price of oil as it is priced in dollars. Some of the prime car manufacturers have had a disastrous year, notably Land Rover and Aston Martin, as new cars didn't sell and their second hand cars virtually halved in value. The green issue gathered pace and cars came straight into the firing line over global warming. The critics conveniently forgot that cars contribute only 3.5 % of total worldwide carbon emissions. The UK has become very car dependant and there is no doubt that this will continue as there really isn't a wide scale alternative.

Companies will still need to recruit people but are yet to work out what skills they will need over the next 12-24 months. The whole industry will have to quickly adapt itself to survive, move forwards and provide their customers with what they want. There will be noticeable changes in both the fleet and private sectors as customers think about future solutions for the short and medium term.

There are now environmental, economic and governmental issues to be dealt with and customers need a great deal of help and advice. I think it is inevitable that positions will be lost in vehicle manufacturing as the whole industry needs to cut back on volume to protect its long term future and the long term futures of its partners in both the fleet and retail sectors. This will lead to job losses across the industry in OEMs (original equipment manufacturers) and all businesses involved in the distribution and sales cycle.

We know that changes have to be made and that there are bound to be some new positions arising as car technology moves into new areas. Despite some success with battery cars and hybrids, it looks likely that hydrogen power may now be a more viable long term option than the classic internal combustion engine. They have the advantage of being closer in driving characteristics to a fossil powered car and have virtually nil emissions. BBC's Top Gear have recently looked at Honda's new car that is operating successfully in California and certainly think it is part of the future.

There will still be conventional roles in the business in the short term and there will be significant restructures and takeovers taking place during 2009. This will lead to further redundancies, but will also create new opportunities as businesses look to bring in new talent.

We often hear that the role of the traditional fleet manager is dying. Do you think that is true?

Companies have always needed to keep a tight control on their fleets and that situation is not about change. The leasing and fleet management companies have constantly refined the services and products they offer their customers and are very good at what they do. Outsourcing has been through a massive growth in all areas of business and has created what is now the massive service sector in the UK. This has seen the death or dilution of a number of fleet management roles in companies of all sizes. Many companies have simply shifted the various responsibilities to other parts of their organisation.

Over the years the number of vacancies for traditional fleet managers has diminished, but there are always positions around for fleet controllers and administrators.

Fleet managers tend not to leave their jobs unless they have to and this again has been evident over the last 5 years. They tend to be passionate about what they do and make long term career moves. Fleet managers will undoubtedly continue to have a role to play in their organisations but need to look at additional ways to add value in the future.

What sort of experience do employers look for when recruiting a fleet manager?

Recruiters tend to look for experience that relates closely to their own methodology and often take advice from their fleet suppliers as to whom they should consider in the first place. There have been several cases recently where someone has been recruited directly from a supplying leasing company as they understand the requirements of the role either from experience or a tendering process. As with many roles, it is always easier to get a similar position than to move into a completely new field.

What sort of training do employers expect fleet managers to have received?

Employers are always looking for experience and past achievement rather than training and this is common across all positions in all sectors. A CPC is often required when HGVs are involved and we have recently undertaken several such assignments. Normally most applicants tend to have been involved previously in another fleet management role and employers generally have a broad choice of candidates. Candidates tend to have started their careers in an administrative role either within a fleet department or working on fleet matters within another department and they then develop their career from that point.

Have employers begun to recognise the value of Institute of Car Fleet Managers qualifications?

I think that the qualifications could be very useful to someone who is early on in their career and looking for a differentiator that may get them ahead of other candidates in their first or second career move. This is probably true of most functional based training and later on experience and provable expertise count for everything.

Quite a few readers of this book will currently be working within the leasing and fleet management industry. Have you seen any trends emerging over the last few years that have affected employment in those markets?

The leasing and fleet management industry has been through a fair amount of change over the last few years and a great deal of this has been due to changes in technology. This has led to greater efficiency and fewer positions.

There has also been significant consolidation and this looks likely to continue over the next few years. We have seen several mergers and acquisitions and the surviving companies have all worked hard to establish their place in the market and to perfect the services they are offering. We have recently seen the bank owners of two of the largest leasing companies merging and this may well have some repercussions and lead to redundancies.

The overall business has moved further towards providing a total outsourcing solution and can genuinely provide all in-life services to their customers. Individual experts and in some case full teams have been brought in from other parts of the fleet sector as a result.

And how do you see recruitment in this market changing over the next year or two?

The industry is now very mature and most changes are going to be gradual and involve greater system integration with customers. As people are made redundant they seem to be able, in a lot of cases, to find positions through friends in other companies. It probably won't be long before all the slack has been taken up and companies are full.

Recently there has been a noticeable reduction in the number of sales vacancies as companies have looked to recruit fewer but stronger and more strategic new business winners. They are backing up these smaller teams with strong and knowledgeable teams involved in the bid and tendering process. This trend will probably continue as companies look to get greater value from their new business activities.

Do you find that the fleet management function tends to sit within the HR, Finance, Procurement or some other department?

That depends very much on the size of the fleet and the way that the fleet is run. There are still standalone fleet departments in some larger companies, but most companies are now employing fleet administrators to deal with internal matters whilst leaving everything else to their leasing provider. These people seem to be spread pretty evenly across finance, HR and finance depending on how their company is structured. In many cases the person will be responsible for other functions within the business such as facilities and building management.

What are the key objectives that companies are setting for their fleet managers? Cost control? Cost reduction? Risk management? Or simply day to day fleet administration?

This again depends on where the position fits into the organisation. In most cases now it seems that roles are more administrative and involve working closely with one or more outside suppliers. There are specialist organisations that can look at risk management and most other fleet matters can be channelled through a leasing or fleet management supplier.

Who are Alastair Ames Associates and what recruitment services do you provide?

Alastair Ames Associates was established in 1986 and are specialists in search, selection and recruitment in the fleet and automotive sectors.

Over the years we have worked on numerous assignments in both the UK and Europe and have an extensive network of relationships across all areas of the market.

We have undertaken numerous assignments outside the sector, normally through personal recommendations or for groups with multiple business interests.

Alastair Ames
Alastair Ames Associates

37 CAR SHARING

Craig Barrack
Managing Director
Carbon Heroes Limited

What exactly is Car Sharing?

Car sharing is sometimes referred to as lift sharing, car pooling or journey matching. In general, it's when people that would normally take their own car agree to share their journey. It can be for their daily commute, a regular event, the school run or just a one-off journey.

Sometimes passengers make a contribution towards the driver's costs; in other cases the participants alternate driving duties.

In a corporate environment, it's when a company, or group of companies, offers employees the chance to share journeys. The greatest value is normally derived from the regular commute, as this comprises significant mileage for most drivers. Commuting is also ideal for matching, as it is a fairly fixed routine for many employees and the frequency of travel can have a marked effect on fuel expenditure and other running costs. A secondary use for corporate car sharing occurs when colleagues are driving to common events, for example travelling between office locations, to off-site meetings, conferences or to the airport.

This is distinct from car clubs, such as Zipcar, Streetcar and City Car Club, where members typically pay a subscription to have access to rent a communal vehicle by the hour.

How does it work?

Many people car share informally, perhaps without considering that this is what they are doing. Colleagues that are neighbours, students sharing a house, parents whose children are classmates, friends both heading to the supermarket, or even being "designated driver" on a night out, there are many scenarios in which taking one car makes perfect sense.

Carbon heroes makes it easier for people to find convenient matching journeys and to give users a degree of confidence as to with whom they will be sharing.

Companies that are based in business parks can choose to link their car sharing databases, as an increasing the pool of drivers greatly improves the chances of matching them together.

Why would car sharing be of interest to fleet managers?

Personal car use has become something of a pariah in some peoples' eyes. But foregoing personal car use entirely is impractical for most workers – even those that commute by rail often need to drive to their local station.

Many have responded to this by limiting the emissions of the vehicles eligible for selection within their fleets.

The provision of a car sharing scheme is potentially an attractive differentiator; that gives value to the client and reduces their operational costs, whilst improving both company's environmental credentials.

Indeed, when a company operates a car sharing scheme their fleet size remains unchanged, as each employee will still require their own car. If the scheme is effective, the total mileage of the fleet decreases. So the residual values are improved and insurance costs reduced.

If employees wish to share a car, why wouldn't a fleet manager just leave them to do it? Why does the company need to get involved?

We've found that scheme's success depends largely on how actively the company is involved. A company that communicates the availability of the network, how employees can use it, and then offers incentives to participants will have significantly greater uptake than one that is simply made available but then neglected.

Companies that make the effort to publicise the launch of their car sharing scheme, often offering a bounty for signing up, whether in case or gift vouchers, have significant take up and ongoing utilisation of the service.

Typical incentives include:

- Guaranteed parking.
- Free parking where spaces are otherwise charged.
- Lunchtime minibus service to the shops for out of town sites.
- Guaranteed travel home, by another lift, public transport or taxi, if an employee is "stranded" at work.
- Cash incentives and/or credits for company cafeterias.
- Time in lieu for consistent car sharers

Five of the companies in the Department for Transport study paid significant sums (from £100 to £500 a year) to those staff that car share regularly. Exemption from parking charges is a telling incentive, as evidenced by Egg, where a 75p charge encouraged around a quarter of staff to car share, without even having a formal matching service such as carbon heroes in place.

Some companies might question why they want to get involved at all. There are direct cost savings to be made from operating fewer car parking spaces, which can be costly to lease and from reduced mileage from their fleet. Employees that have a significant commute can save considerable sums through regular car sharing, effectively increasing their net income.

Whilst the annual cost of maintaining a car parking space is typically £300-£500 (Source: Department for Transport), leasing a space can cost up to £3,000 per annum in city centres. If a car sharing scheme can reduce the number of vehicles arriving at an office each day, the savings in this regard alone can be substantial.

In May 2008 Nottingham was the first city to pass an order to establish a Workplace Parking Levy. The levy on employer parking spaces affects all employers with more than 10 parking spaces. Due to start at £180 per space in April 2010, it will rise to £350 per space over 4 years, with an annual income target of £10.8million by that time. Other local authorities are considering taking up such schemes, both as a measure to curb congestion and raise capital. Employers will have to choose whether to bear those costs themselves, or to pass them on to those employees that drive to work on a daily basis.

Are many companies actively promoting car sharing at the moment?

Many companies are actively promoting car sharing schemes. Some of the more notable names include Legal and General, Computer Associates, Vodafone, GlaxoSmithKline, Agilent Technologies, Royal and Sun Alliance, Pfizer and BP. It is also popular within the public sector, with some central government bodies and many local authorities endorsing such services.

A Department for Transport survey of companies running car sharing schemes revealed that:

- 34% of Computer Associates' staff signed up to car share 25 days in six months.
- 48% of Marks and Spencer Financial Services' staff registered with their car sharing scheme; 31% share at least one day a week.
- At Egg 26% car share on a daily basis.
- 25% of Legal and General's 2,000 employees at their Kingswood headquarters car share daily.

Whilst high concentrations of drivers make the most active networks, it's important to realise that it doesn't require a vast number of employees to operate an effective scheme. For example, a large office in a city centre, where most use public transport to get to work may have less need for car sharing than an out-of-town site where personal car use is predominant.

Corporate Social Responsibility is one of those expressions we're hearing more of nowadays. What is it and how does lift sharing fit into CSR?

Transport is a major contributor to the carbon footprint of most organisations. Taking an average annual commute of 2,900 miles and average CO_2 emissions of 165 g/km, each employee that drives to work creates almost three quarters of a tonne of CO_2 per annum. If you look at your company car park each day and multiply by ¾; that gives you a reasonable perspective on the emissions that could be reduced.

Companies can promote home working and technologies such as video conferencing, but significant personal car travel is unavoidable, even desirable for efficient business.

An effective car sharing programme reduces the carbon emissions of its members, with minimal inconvenience.

What is key to the carbon heroes proposition is that the system calculates road distances and the detours made accurately and takes the vehicles used into consideration. By that means, realistic carbon emission savings are generated.

Is there any legal requirement for companies to reduce their carbon footprint, or will there be one soon?

The Climate Change Bill, expected to reach the statue books in November 2008, includes a new legally binding climate change and energy saving scheme called the Carbon Reduction Commitment (CRC). It covers large business and public sector organisations and has a significant impact on reducing UK carbon dioxide emissions from such organisations. As things stand, it excludes transport emissions, which is a major oversight in my view.

As the Energy Secretary, Ed Miliband, bowed to pressure to include emissions from shipping and aviation in the UK's overall carbon emission targets within the Bill, I find it difficult to see how transportation can be excluded from the Carbon Reduction Commitment in the future.

In the meantime, progressive companies will take measures to understand their transport carbon footprint and to take measures to reduce it.

The Department for Transport encourages all companies to put in place a Travel Plan. To quote the DfT:

"A travel plan is a package of measures produced by employers to encourage staff to use alternatives to single-occupancy car-use. Such a plan for example, could include: car sharing schemes; a commitment to improve cycling facilities; a dedicated bus service or restricted car parking allocations. It might also promote flexible-working practices such as remote access and video conferencing."

As can be seen, the first reference made is to the establishment of a car sharing scheme.

Car sharing lanes, also known as High Occupancy Vehicle (HOV) lanes have been a feature of cities in the USA, Australia, Norway, Spain and several other countries for years. The Highways Agency has stated High Occupancy Vehicle lanes, are a key component of its strategy. Examples of such lanes are the A47 in Birmingham, the A647 in Leeds, the Avon Ring Road near Bristol and in March 2008 we saw the opening of the first HOV lane on our motorway network, on the M606 from Bradford to the M62 towards Leeds. The then Transport Secretary Ruth Kelly said that similar traffic management measures could be introduced on another 500 miles of motorway.

The economics of car sharing will also be even more apparent for those commuters that pay the London Congestion Charge each day, a scheme that is going to be introduced to cities such as Manchester, Nottingham, Derby and Leicester.

Do you have any statistics to show how much a company's employees could expect to save if they started to lift-share?

The average worker in the UK commutes 2,906 miles and travels 1,622 miles on business by car per annum. If joining a car sharing scheme means that their car is left at home one day per week, the 20% reduction in commuting is around 600 miles. If they can share only 5% of their business travel, then that takes the total to around 700 miles per annum conserved.

Taking a standard cost of 40 pence per mile, that equates to £520 saved per annum.

For fleet car drivers, the commute savings are shared by the employee and the company, for expensed business travel it's the company that saves.

	Petrol savings	Servicing & residual savings
Commuting	Individual	Employer
Business Travel	Employer	Employer
Personal Travel	Individual	Employer

Clearly savings are greatly increased for those able to car share more frequently, those with longer commutes and those with higher business mileage.

What proportion of British workers currently shares a lift to work?

Research from AA insurance in September 2008 quoted that 11% of people currently car share at least once a week.

That figure is significantly exceeded where a well-run car sharing scheme is readily accessible, exceeding one third of employees in some cases.

Research from the AA and Populus in July 2008 showed that over ninety per cent of those surveyed would consider car sharing.

Could lift sharing really provide part of the solution to reducing rush hour congestion?

Yes and no. Eighty-five per cent of commuting journeys only have a single occupant. Clearly that's not an efficient use of vehicles and is a key contributor to rush hour congestion. Individual schemes make a minor difference locally; collectively the uptake of car sharing, particularly during commuting times and at major events, can have a major effect nationally.

This is particularly important within corporate and school schemes, as the focussed times of these journeys make them critical to road congestion. We sometimes see the effect on our roads when fewer vehicles are in use. Every commuter relishes the school holidays, as the removal of those cars from the roads makes travel far easier. The increased price of fuel in the summer of 2008 reduced motorway congestion by 12%. (Source: Environmental Transport Association). Concerted uptake of carbon heroes could make that the norm.

Should the government continue to introduce car sharing lanes on major roads, and introduce congestion charging zones in conurbations, a prominent car sharing service will be required for a significant reduction in congestion.

Can it help employers make their organisations a more attractive place to work?

Most definitely. Research in Sweden has shown that car sharing regularly reduces staff delinquency. If someone is feeling slightly under the weather, they're more likely to surface from under the duvet if a colleague is due to pick them up, or depending on them for a lift to the office.

There's also a social element to car sharing to work. Colleagues get a chance to chat away from the office.

Of course the reduced cost of commuting makes for a more appealing job.

What is Carbon Heroes and how can it help a fleet manager to implement a lift sharing scheme?

Carbon heroes is an online service that allows companies to run private journey sharing networks.

Carbon heroes has the capability to process payments between members, so that passengers can reimburse drivers for some of their incurred costs without cash having to be exchanged. Companies can choose to allow this practice, or disable the capability.

The vehicle registered for each journey is recorded, providing a level of security to passengers if they are unknown to the driver and making meaningful conserved emission statistics possible.

A distinction of carbon heroes is that all members of the database go through a verification process. For members of corporate schemes, this is via their employer; for those that join via the public site, a check against the supplied name, address and payment information is made prior to allowing the first matched journey. An online peer-rating system allows users to leave feedback for one another, again enhancing confidence that members are genuine.

The system also uses route mapping technology to determine journey distances, combining this with vehicle data to give meaningful statistics on saved mileage, and most crucially, reduction in emissions.

Craig Barrack
Managing Director
Carbon Heroes Limited

As motoring costs continue to spiral and concerns over our effect on the environment heighten, it has never been more important to rethink our attitudes towards transport.

Carbon heroes® enables companies to offer employees the chance to save motoring costs whilst reducing their carbon emissions.

Carbon heroes' clients:
- Save money
- Save their employees money
- Reduce their impact upon the environment
- Improve their corporate image

Key features for the company include:
- Reporting – detailed, accurate reports record the uptake and carbon savings of the service.
- Integration with back office HR systems, reducing the cost of ownership.
- Integration with corporate intranets, linking to employee incentive schemes, increasing visibility and uptake.
- Support for multiple locations, with site-specific reporting.
- Advanced matching, rated by convenience and emissions savings, with support for shift patterns.
- Security – all data is protected within a firewalled system, resistant to external hacking.

Key features for the individual include:
- Leisure access – all users are able to extend their usage of carbon heroes® to their private travel.
- User identification – all users' identities are checked, via their employer or payment card validation.
- Vehicle details – these are recorded, so passengers know in which vehicles they will be travelling.
- Peer rating – users can leave feedback, so new members can see which users have reliable track records.
- CRM – users see cost and emissions savings; employers offer incentives to their own "carbon heroes".

ENVIRONMENTAL ISSUES: A MANUFACTURER'S VIEW

Ian Dutfield
Marketing Manager
Mercedes-Benz UK

Please explain a little about how environmental issues are part of your role.

I am responsible for Mercedes-Benz in the UK market, and lead a team that is bringing innovations to UK customers.

Environmental awareness runs through every strand of what we do as a company, both globally and locally. Mercedes-Benz was the first (and is still the only) car manufacturer to be awarded an Environmental Certificate for its products. This certificate looks at how a car's made – the 'green' rating of the factory, the materials used in its construction, how it can be recycled and every other element of its use. Four Mercedes-Benz ranges now have this accolade.

Next year sees the fruition of years of background work in our product marketing team with the roll-out of our clean BlueEFFICIENCY models – more on that later.

We're also bringing in the least-polluting production car in the world in 2009 – the smart fortwo cdi. Just 88g/km of CO_2 and 85.6mpg. Our pioneering smart ed with electric drive is a project about to go global; we've 100 cars on customer trial in the UK – and in coming years this initiative will roll-out across the rest of Europe.

We speak of environmental pollution but there are actually quite a lot of pollutants out there, some that have an impact on climate change and others that don't. Please remind us of the various transport-related pollutants and their impact.

The topic of environmental emissions is a complex and emotive one, and it's nothing new. Back in 1873 a forecast predicted that 'given the constant growth of transport with horse-drawn carriages, the territory of England will be covered by one yard of manure by the year 1961'.

Things have clearly moved on since then, but environmental concerns are ongoing and we all have a part to play. Emissions of carbon dioxide – not poisonous but a contributor to global warming – are an important part of climate change. Since 1997,

CO_2 emissions from new cars have fallen 13% (Daimler, Mercedes-Benz's parent company, has reduced its emissions by 22% over the same period) – and there's plenty more to come as manufacturers increase the pace of change.

Of all the UK's CO_2 emissions, cars make up 11.7% of the total. Heavy industry, aviation and other factors play a much more significant role. Despite this relatively small overall impact, manufacturers such as Mercedes-Benz are making big efforts to act responsibly and in a sustainable way to reduce all our emissions.

For example, Mercedes-Benz and its parent company Daimler is making huge strides here. Our factories are among the very cleanest and most environmentally-friendly in the world. We minimise energy use wherever possible, use low-impact methods and materials and ensure that the environment figures in every aspect of what we do. From designing a new car to recycling in our local offices. We've even installed a wind turbine at our UK headquarters to give 'free' recharging to our – and other – electric cars.

Other pollutants are poisonous and harmful: carbon monoxide (CO), oxides of nitrogen (NOx) and hydrocarbons (largely unburnt fuel). Again, perspective is needed here – because cars are much cleaner now than ever before. It takes up to 60 of our latest executive saloons to emit the same level of pollution as just one family hatchback did in the 1970s.

As engine technology advances, cars become cleaner and pollution levels drop. Cleaner fuels are the next step – and manufacturers are pushing the oil companies to introduce sulphur-free fuel to the UK so the latest – even cleaner – technology can be introduced to UK customers.

Emissions from modern diesel cars are also dramatically lower than you might imagine. Sit next to an idling modern diesel car's exhaust non-stop for an entire year and you'll breathe fewer particulates into your lungs than you would by smoking one cigarette.

How much of an impact does transport have on UK CO_2 emissions and how much of this is due to road transport?

Road transport is a significant contributor to man-made CO_2 emissions, but it is not the only source. In the UK road transport accounts for around 20.1%: cars are responsible for 11.7% and the other 8.4% comes from vans, trucks, buses, coaches and motorcycles. This contrasts with emissions through energy production 35%, domestic use 14% and aviation 6.3%. Aviation is currently the largest growing source of man-made CO_2. None of us can ignore our role.

Source: AEA Engineering and Environment 2005, data includes international aviation (total emissions 503 million tonnes 2005)

What are the various elements that need to be considered if we are to reduce the level of road transport emissions?

Every element of our lives needs to be assessed to minimise our impact on the environment. Insulate your roof at home; fit double glazing; use energy-efficient light bulbs; buy organic food – even LED Christmas lights make a small difference!

For cars, there's plenty we can all do.

- Ensuring tyres are at the correct pressures helps – less energy is then needed to move them (try cycling on a bike with flat tyres and you get the idea).
- Regular servicing ensures the engine is working efficiently – and more economically.
- See the speed limit as a limit and not a target. Aerodynamic drag squares with speed – so driving at 56mph rather than 70 mph causes less drag and increases fuel efficiency.
- Drive using the higher gears – lower revs means less fuel is being used.
- Anticipate the road ahead, braking and accelerating wastes energy, so 'read the road' and act in good time.

We've introduced cars this year which switch their engines off when stationary – so if you're stuck in traffic, consider switching off the engine to save fuel.

Driver behaviour does play a major part in how well or badly a car performs, so it's well worth investing some time, effort and research into what we can do as individuals to 'do our bit'.

Using cars appropriately is important too. Sometimes it's better to take the train, bus or the Tube. It may even be quicker to walk.

Cars do give us an incredible amount of personal freedom, and they run to our personal timetables too. So, in addition to all of the measures mentioned, we should look at our routes. Logistics companies alter their routes depending on traffic conditions and the time of day – it may be quicker (and more efficient) to make a slightly longer route rather than a slow crawl through a congested area.

Modern satellite navigation systems – including our own COMAND system – can 'see' traffic jams ahead, and divert the car around the congestion, saving fuel and time.

How much progress has been made in recent years in reducing the average level of emissions from cars on UK roads, and how have those changes been brought about?

Progress has been dramatic over the past decade, and as emissions regulations get ever-tighter, so manufacturers' efforts increase. For example, Daimler AG – Mercedes-Benz's parent company – spends over one billion pounds a year on reducing CO_2.

Daimler has reduced CO_2 emissions across all its vehicles by 22% since 1995 – substantially more than the UK average over a similar period (13% since 1997).

And despite the misconception that all large cars are 'gas guzzlers', 84% of our product range is below 'Band G', including the S 320 CDI limousine. Next year's new E-Class Saloon range will include a model that emits just 139 g/km of CO_2 – a figure unattainable only a few years ago.

There is a voluntary scheme whereby new cars in showrooms are labelled to show their fuel economy and CO_2 emission levels. Do you think this is making a difference?

It's important to give customers a fair choice and to ensure they know the levels of emissions of any car, before they buy it. Every Mercedes-Benz retailer has signed-up to the CO_2 labelling scheme.

Our customers tend to be well-researched and well-versed when they visit our retailers, so whilst the labels give an indication of exactly how a car performs, they don't tell the whole picture.

What are the various alternative fuels that can be used to power cars, and which are available now?

There's not one magic pill to solve the world's energy issues, and as such research and development needs to explore all avenues. The current focus is on medium and long-term strategies but we shouldn't discount petrol and diesel – there's still plenty of scope in these fuels.

In 2007 Mercedes-Benz introduced its 'Road to the Future' which highlights and focuses on a wealth of different engine technologies, with progressive steps from today's technology to the propulsion technology of tomorrow. Mercedes-Benz has also invented the DIESOTTO engine concept – the petrol engine which thinks it's a diesel. With the power and low emissions of a diesel combined with the torque and efficiency of a petrol, DIESOTTO is a new and exciting future. Fitted to one of our research vehicles, it gives supermini emissions in a car the size – and speed – of a luxury limo.

Diesel is still the real 'alternative fuel'. Diesel engines are getting ever-more efficient and refined. As today's traffic means we use engine torque more than outright power, diesel is coming to the fore. Unfortunately diesel is taxed prohibitively in the UK, so despite its inherent benefits over petrol, its economical use is limited. Sulphur-free diesel taxed at the same rate as petrol would be a compelling combination…

BlueTEC is Mercedes-Benz's diesel innovation – the cleanest diesel technology in the world. BlueTEC uses selective catalytic reduction to clean up emissions. AdBLUE solution is introduced to the exhaust gases to reduce emissions of NOx by up to 90%. The AdBLUE solution splits these oxides of nitrogen into harmless oxygen and nitrogen. BlueTEC is available in the US and mainland Europe. However, a perverse taxation system in the UK – which would effectively penalise BlueTEC drivers – means it's not financially viable for customers to use the technology in Britain. We're lobbying for this to change and as soon as legislation catches up with technology, BlueTEC will be available.

LPG/CNG (liquid petroleum gas/compressed natural gas) are currently taxed at a lower level than regular pump fuels. They offer little benefit technically, and the conversion may invalidate some manufacturers' warranties.

Ethanol – or ethyl alcohol fuel – is used in other parts of the world. It's often grown from food crops – sugar or corn. Controversy surrounds this fuel. Recent research raises questions about the levels of street pollutants it produces. It seems it may produce more pollution – especially ozone - than petrol or diesel. Ethanol has been used in motor racing for years. It gives a lot of power and energy though its invisible flame makes it very difficult to control when 'on fire'.

Bioethanol is a form of bio fuel. Bio-ethanol is often known a 'E85' in the US (and increasingly in the UK). It uses a mix of 85% ethanol with 15% petrol and is therefore taxed at a lower rate than regular fuel. Not every company's cars can run on bioethanol so it's worth checking before filling.

Bio fuels come in two main generations. First-gen bio fuels are largely derived from foodstuffs, which diverts food crops into fuel production. Recent debate has questioned the validity of using food crops for fuel when food is in short supply in parts of the world. Second-generation bio fuels are much better in this regard – the energy is derived from organic waste matter rather than food crops – and as such is more sustainable.

Pure electric cars are a great idea - as long as the energy used to recharge them comes

from a sustainable source. Plugging a car into a regular socket just pushes the pollution elsewhere – maybe a coal-fired power station. With the smart ed project we only included customers who use a green electricity tariff. Wind turbines, solar energy, small scale hydro-electric are all available and can all power cars as simply as a regular supply from the National Grid.

Battery technology is improving too. The latest generation of electric cars uses lithium-ion batteries – similar to those found in mobile phones and laptops – giving more power 'pound for pound'. As technology moves on, electric propulsion is becoming a compelling solution, particularly for urban transport.

Diesel hybrids are 'the quiet man' of future propulsion. The latest generation of diesel engines is remarkable. Piezo injectors deliver precise and incredibly accurately-measured pulses of fuel, hundreds of times a second. Combine these latest engines with hybrid drive and the results could be astounding.

Hybrids can work in a number of ways – as a 'boost' to the combustion engine; as a regenerative braking source; or for 'electric-only' drive at lower speeds. Mercedes-Benz is testing diesel hybrids and is looking to introduce cars to the market within the next two years.

Petrol hybrids are currently popular and are an interesting alternative to a modern efficient diesel engine. Currently incentivised by UK legislation, petrol hybrids can in some cases give electric-only drive, petrol drive or a combination of both. The technology exists in various stages – from start-stop systems, through those that boost and regeneratively charge through braking – to the full hybrid systems.

Mercedes-Benz is soon introducing (into the US and left-hand-drive Europe) the world's first production hybrid with lithium-Ion batteries. This Li-Ion battery technology is more efficient than the first-generation nickel metal hydride batteries – and they're less costly to make. The S 400 BlueHYBRID goes on sale in certain markets later in 2009.

Hydrogen is the most abundant element in the world, so its use as a fuel is something that has been targeted for years. Getting the hydrogen from its ambient state to one that can be used is difficult, so hydrogen technology is in its relative infancy. Hydrogen fuel cell cars are a viable long term goal for manufacturers, and they work in an effective and clean way. Mercedes-Benz has been leading the way with hydrogen technology for over a decade.

The hydrogen is passed through a fuel cell – a thin flexible membrane about the size of a mouse mat – where it mixes with oxygen from the air. This causes a chemical reaction in which the hydrogen and oxygen bond to form water – the only by-product. The clever part is the harnessing of this reaction energy into electrical energy which can then propel the vehicle.

Hydrogen fuel cell vehicles used to be the size of a large van, with a limited range and power band. Today's test vehicles – like the new B-Class F-Cell – have a fuel cell 'stack' of more than 160 fuel cells – all fitting in the space under the vehicle's floor. The mileage range and operating temperatures are also now much better than before (hydrogen freezes easily so it's difficult to use in extreme winter conditions).

Fuel cell vehicles have been on trial around the world for over a decade. Fuel cell buses were used in a trial in London for a number of years – and are in service elsewhere in the world.

Once the efficient production of hydrogen has been introduced, hydrogen fuel cell cars look set to become a strong future mode of transport for the motorist.

What is government doing to encourage the take-up of low-emission cars?

European legislation has recently been announced giving car manufacturers tough new CO_2 targets. 65% of new cars have to average 130 g/km by 2012 – with all new cars averaging this figure by 2015. Tough financial penalties will be imposed for all cars over and above these limits.

Manufacturers are working hard to ensure their cars are as efficient and environmentally-friendly as possible. So, for example, the new E-Class pre-empts forthcoming Euro 5 legislation by being compliant before the new rules come in, for cars on sale from 2011.

Other measures – tyres with reduced rolling resistance, fuel quality, road surfaces and traffic management – all play a part in reducing road transport emissions – as does every driver.

If a fleet manager wants to reduce his or her company's environmental impact, what are the things they should be looking at?

All the measures mentioned throughout this chapter will help every motorist reduce their impact on the environment, and for fleets the results are obviously amplified and multiplied.

As well as selecting cars with efficient engines when ordering new vehicles, myriad options are available. Eco-driver training is a good start – using the cars as efficiently as possible can save fuel costs and reduces wear and tear on other service items. Journey profiling, route planning and service schedules all play a part too. The wealth of information on offer can be overwhelming, so focussing on where the biggest changes can be effected first, is a good start.

It's important to take a balanced view – ensure that the whole life costs (environmental and financial) are considered. A higher initial purchase price may be offset with stronger residuals, lower service costs, and better environmental performance. The Environmental Certificate is a consideration – proof that the car is 'green'. This environmental technology is no longer the preserve of compromised 'hair shirt' cars – you can be green and enjoy dynamic performance and luxurious motoring too.

What is Mercedes doing to help reduce emissions?

Mercedes-Benz is leading the way in research and development – the company invests an average of £10 million every day in this topic. The umbrella term for its environmental work is TrueBlueSolutions – and it works all over the world.

We've already mentioned the world's cleanest diesel technology – BlueTEC – making big changes in the large markets of the USA and left-hand-drive Europe. Closer to home, a wealth of new products is either here or on the way.

We've looked at the best-selling cars in the UK and changed them first. That's why all new A 150, A 170, B 150 and B 170 manual transmission cars have ECO Start/Stop as standard – they're all now BlueEFFICIENCY models. These new cars have an integrated starter-generator (rather than a starter motor and alternator) to give more reliable, regular restarts in traffic. Using ECO Start/Stop can save up to nine per cent of fuel, in urban traffic.

The C 180 KOMPRESSOR is now BlueEFFICIENCY as standard, too. In this model, a number of measures have been taken that combine to deliver fuel and emissions savings of up to 12%. Optimised aerodynamics; low rolling-resistance tyres; energy management (the power-assisted steering doesn't take power when it doesn't need to); and a more efficient drive train all add to the green mix, too. A gear shift indicator advises the driver when to change gear for maximum efficiency; there's an instant fuel consumption monitor. Even the engine has been downsized for efficiency – whilst maintaining the same power and torque output as its predecessor.

And the best part of this standard technology? There's no extra charge for any of it. The forthcoming E-Class range will have BlueEFFICIENCY measures as standard on every car in the range with a four- or six-cylinder engine. And this technology will progressively roll out across the range throughout 2009 and beyond.

All smart fortwos with naturally-aspirated engines (accounting for over 80% of sales) now have micro-hybrid drive as standard. This start-stop technology also dramatically cuts fuel consumption in traffic; and again it's standard and at no extra charge to the customer.

As our Road to the Future continues apace, the innovations and introductions will continue with more models, more technologies and more improvements across the range, across the board.

Vans and trucks from Mercedes-Benz count too. We've been running BlueTEC trucks in the UK for years – and some 3000 of them are on British roads. Our Sprinter vans use Eco-Start to reduce fuel consumption – perfect for urban and regional delivery work. Hybrid trucks are entering their first customer trials too.

It is clear that Mercedes-Benz is well-set to meet these tough challenges, and to meet them head-on with a wealth of innovations, products and services which look set to change the way we choose – and use - our vehicles, for the better.

Ian Dutfield
Marketing Manager
Mercedes-Benz UK

James Langley

Director & Deputy Chairman

Institute of Car Fleet Management

What is your view of the training fleet managers receive?

Sadly, and despite the very positive effect the Institute has had since being formed, we are still focusing on a thinly served population and there is still much to achieve. There are thousands of people who have responsibility for a fleet but for whom the fleet represents only a small part of their complete role. At the other end of the scale are many for whom managing the fleet is a full-time job and one for which they have support staff.

Across this wide spectrum of fleet managers there is a similar wide range of competence levels, with some fleet managers truly pushing the frontiers and others merely dipping a toe in the water.

Managing a fleet is no different from managing any other function and, at the first appointment to a management or specialist administration role, any newcomer has the option of repeating the actions of the predecessor or doing something different. In the case of the former, it seems quite common for the new appointee to have had some connection with the fleet beforehand.

It's perhaps natural that sometimes success is perceived as 'repeating what Harry did', particularly where managing the fleet is just one of several responsibilities.

Certainly, in the smaller operations, where a 'laissez–faire' style is the order of the day and structure, order and control has less attached significance, this 'following Harry' is likely to be the approach. It's little wonder that any 'in-house' training, such as it is, is probably going to be formatted on the basis of what used to be called 'Sitting by Nellie' with the inevitable result that all of Nellie's mistakes and misjudgements are perpetuated and the incoming manager or administrator delivers nothing new whatever to the host business.

In many respects, 'managers' of this type of fleet tend to 'tinker' or 'book-keep' rather than manage. They almost never recommend or deliver initiatives that benefit the host business and rarely get involved with developing and controlling fleet budgets. In the simplest of terms, the business makes only moderate demands and deservedly, gets only compliance (usually, to an ill-defined role specification) in return.

At the other end of the scale, there is usually a real recognition that the costs of running the fleet are likely to be the next highest category of cost after payroll, and an in-depth appreciation of the significance of the fleet to the business. The demands on the person responsible for managing the fleet tend to be greater and, when that person raises a shortfall in either fleet policy or their own competence, the business often tends to be empathetic and will pursue appropriate training programmes in order to access the benefits of improved performance.

In the final analysis, the 'sitting by Nellie' approach perpetuates errors and will never move the overall quality of fleet management forward. Change is only effected when something goes wrong and it is to be hoped that what goes wrong does so only in a moderate sense!

The formal training approach offers many benefits to the employer including real risk awareness, legal compliance, structured application of learning that matches the business requirements and programmes for continuous improvement.

What is the ICFM and why does it exist?

The Institute of Car Fleet Management is the United Kingdom's only independent organisation dedicated to developing the capability and enhancing the standing of fleet professionals. Established in 1992, the Institute exists to connect people who have a genuine interest in car fleet management, in order to provide networking opportunities and the benefits of formal education and training programmes.

What are the aims of the Institute?

The Institute has five aims:

- To provide a structured education and training syllabus and methodology designed to meet the needs of newly appointed as well as established vehicle fleet managers, administrators and fleet industry specialists leading to vocational qualifications recognised and accepted as the requisite for the profession.
- To foster and promote the profession through the development of strategic partnerships and regular contact with members and stakeholders.
- To advance the profession through ongoing research into all aspects of car fleet management and communication of findings to members and interested parties.
- To promote the widespread application of best practices as relevant to vehicle fleet management, particularly those practices appropriate to the environment, duty of care and safety.

- To encourage members to share and communicate knowledge and experience in the application of established and 'leading edge' principles and practices through informal networking and interaction in training programmes and other events.

What are the various levels of membership and how does one achieve these?

The Institute has four levels of membership:

- **Affiliate (Aff.I.C.F.M.)** – For those about to enter the profession or having less then six months experience in any role associated with fleet administration, fleet services support provision or employee mobility management.

- **Associate (A.I.C.F.M.)** – For those with more than six months experience in any role associated with fleet administration, fleet management, fleet service support provision or employee mobility management.

- **Member (M.I.C.F.M.)** – For those who can demonstrate, by reference to their record of successes and other professional qualifications, that they are totally conversant with all aspects of the five units of competence covered in the Certificate in Car Fleet Management syllabus (People Management, Administration, Finance, Acquisition and Law) and who have proven ability in the operational management of a substantial company car fleet.

- **Fellow (F.I.C.F.M.)** – For full Members of the Institute who have successfully completed the advanced course of study leading to the Diploma in Car Fleet Management and have spent an established period in the strategic management of a vehicle fleet (normally for five years), can demonstrate evidence of personal achievement in vehicle fleet management and have made a contribution to the professionalism of the industry.

What are the benefits of membership?

- Access to an invaluable network of contacts and information which will enhance role performance and support the application of best practice.
- Access, via the website, to the Interactive Guide to Fleet Management.
- Eligibility to attend the Members' Conference.
- Access to enrolment on ICFM education and training programmes.
- Access to the Members' Advice Service for specific advice or guidance on policy, operational or strategic matters.
- Recognition through certification, award presentation and, where appropriate, press exposure.
- Opportunities to publish professional articles or exchange ideas and concepts through the website.

What does the Institute do to promote the profession of Car Fleet Management within industry and commerce?

The Institute has wholly altruistic aims. It is a genuine 'not for profit' organisation and its whole effort is focused on advancing professionalism in the industry. We have established standards of performance for fleet managers at all levels and have defined these using competence frameworks which form the basis of our training programmes.

The programmes themselves are aimed at developing fleet policy and changing behaviours – including those of drivers and not just soaking up knowledge but learning how it is best applied.

It cannot be denied that many people currently 'managing' fleets in the UK are not truly fleet managers or administrators but sponsoring organisations can be assured that where an IFCM Member is involved, management of the fleet does indeed assume the level of importance that it deserves.

Has the Institute sponsored research into Car Fleet Management?

The fleet-based projects undertaken in connection with the Diploma programme are pieces of original research and, in most cases, the outcomes are available for reference by other members.

The ICFM tutorial team, along with the Education & Training Manager, undertake constant research on best practice, leading edge technology and forthcoming legislation which is subsequently used to update training material or incorporated as themes or focal points for the annual members' conference.

What work has the Institute done to develop best practice relating to the environment and driver safety?

One of the strong threads which has run through the Institute since its inception has been the Members' Conference. High on our agenda for conference has always been the sharing of best practice – particularly on environmental and safety matters. Council Members are always 'seeking the exceptional' and it's very common for significant papers to be presented at conference by members.

As well as being a key theme of several conferences over the past ten years, environmental and safety issues are given prominent exposure at all levels of education and training programmes – particularly at Certificate and Diploma level.

What is the ICFM's training syllabus? Do you offer courses?

Our education and training framework provides significant opportunities for anyone involved in car fleet management to acquire new, or to develop existing skills, knowledge and competence to standards acknowledged within the fleet industry. It is a three-tier structure, using job-based assignments, examinations or projects as the basis for assessment:

- **Introductory Certificate** – Available through an Online Programme, Key Start (workshop-facilitated programme) and Flexible Learning (CD-ROM or hard copy formats).

- **Certificate** - Fast Track Programme, Flexible Learning (CD-ROM or hard copy formats)

- **Diploma** – Tutor-led Programme only

How much do the courses cost?

The most popular format for the Introductory Certificate is through the Online Programme. The cost of this is currently £99 which includes first year Affiliate Membership (normally £20) and membership administration fee (also normally £20). The flexible learning option costs £55 plus postage.

The Fast Track programme is the most popular format for the Certificate and the cost is just over £2,000, including Institute of Leadership and Management accreditation, plus accommodation costs where appropriate. The flexible learning versions of the five modules cost £96 (excluding ILM accreditation) each.

The costs for the Diploma are £2,700, again including ILM accreditation plus accommodation costs where appropriate.

What is the syllabus?

The syllabus at both Certificate and Diploma level is comprised of comprehensive core modules linked to job-based assignments or projects designed to assess specific competence elements and their application to the participant's car fleet operation (or, in the case of support service providers, the fleet operations of their clients). This provides a flexible learning process leading to tangible results by creating opportunities for individuals to meet their own development needs and adding value to their (or their clients') fleet operation.

The Introductory level programme caters for the training and development needs of new or relatively recent entrants to the car fleet function, in administrative, sales or fleet service support delivery roles.

The Certificate level programme covers the basic principles underpinning effective fleet management at an operational level and is designed to meet the core needs of fleet administrators, managers and service support providers responsible for the effective identification and delivery of either some or all fleet policy elements.

The Diploma level programme covers advanced techniques, skills and knowledge required for the strategic and operational management of the entire fleet function and provides an opportunity for experienced fleet practitioners to develop their existing competence base.

How are results assessed?

Modules at each level have competence-based assessment criteria and, in addition to leading to externally accredited awards, are directly linked to eligibility for upgrading within the Institute membership structure. The methods of assessment are:

- A job-based assignment at Introductory level

- Role/Policy-based assignments and written examinations at Certificate level

- Role/Policy-based projects and a written dissertation at Diploma level.

Programmes at all three levels are externally moderated and endorsed by the Institute of Leadership & Management (ILM) – part of the City & Guilds Group.

If someone wants to progress through the various levels of membership as quickly as possible, do they have to do all the modules? Are any exemptions available?

Exemptions may be awarded (at Introductory and Certificate level only) against the syllabus criteria for individuals who can produce evidence of having attained relevant, recognised qualifications and/or evidence of the applied competence in a past or present car fleet operation.

You personally were the first person to be admitted to Fellowship, the highest level of attainment within the Institute. How did you achieve this and what did it mean to you?

I joined the Institute pretty much at its inception and at the time was working for a major fleet services provider. At the time, I had fifteen years of fleet experience across a wide range of fleets, each with wholly unique business requirements. I felt very confident in my ability to deliver a very comprehensive and competent consulting role but felt it important that my knowledge and ability got a 'Tick of Approval' from an appropriate authority.

I therefore enrolled on the first Diploma programme though I was anxious at returning to an arena of formal education. In the event, the first area of study was my 'pet subject', Advanced Administration and Control and I found myself in a situation in which I felt very comfortable. I excelled in my fleet-based project and this laid a foundation stone of real encouragement for me, particularly through those subject areas in which I didn't feel quite so confident.

In the event, I qualified and achieved my Diploma qualification in 1996, and was elected to Fellowship later that year. For me, the value is that I have clearly demonstrated knowledge and application of the specified competences and have been recognised by a group of eminent peers to have done so. In that sense, I don't have to claim my competence, effectively, others do it for me. It means that I have a good understanding of by far the majority of the situations I encounter and for the situations in which I don't have that comprehension, I know exactly where to go to get the appropriate information.

James Langley
Director & Deputy Chairman
Institute of Car Fleet Management

The Institute of Car Fleet Management is the UK's only independent 'not for profit' organisation dedicated to furthering the education, recognising the achievements and advancing the profession of car fleet management.

Established in 1992, the Institute connects people involved in car fleet management, promotes excellence in car fleet management practices and delivers the industry sector's premier education programmes. Externally accredited vocational qualifications include the Introductory Certificate, the Certificate and the Diploma in Car Fleet Management.

Membership benefits

Membership brings an invaluable network of contacts, opportunities for personal development and access to information which will enhance role performance and support the application of best practice including:

- Professional recognition through certification, designatory letters after your name, award presentation and, where appropriate, press exposure.
- Opportunity to sharpen your professional skills through enrolment on ICFM education and training programmes.
- Access, via the website, to the Interactive Guide to Car Fleet Management.
- Eligibility to attend the annual national members' conference.
- Access to the Member Advice Service for specific advice or guidance on policy, operational or strategic matters.
- Opportunities to publish professional articles or exchange ideas and concepts through the website.
- Network of contacts and access to information.
- Discounts on a range of services.

Contact us

The Institute of Car Fleet Management
Administration Centre
P.O. Box 314
Chichester
PO20 9WZ
Telephone: 01462 744914
Fax: 01243 607591
www.icfm.com

40 SAVING MONEY, SAVING CO₂

Nigel Underdown
Head of Transport Advice
Energy Saving Trust

What is the Energy Saving Trust and why does it exist?

The Energy Saving Trust is a rare commodity in the fleet industry – a not for profit organisation which offers free and independent advice on running a more efficient fleet.

We were set up in 1992 following the Kyoto Agreement on climate change, to help deliver the government's agenda of reducing carbon emissions. Since 1992 our work has included supporting the design and development of new vehicle technologies, grants to encourage the installation of refuelling sites for alternative fuels and in depth advice and support to organisations on reducing emissions from fleet operations.

Government policy is to reduce transport emissions across the board, but in funding the Energy Saving Trust to provide free help to organisations, there is a clear belief in the market transformation that fleets can help achieve; if company fleets are 'clean', the used car market and private purchases will follow.

As Head of Transport Advice my role is to lead a team of regionally based fleet consultants, plus supporting head office staff, and to ensure we are delivering value to the clients we work with, and value to the Department for Transport who provide funding for the work we do. In addition we contribute towards many government consultations on future policy and hopefully bring insight of the practical challenges faced by fleet managers as they juggle the often conflicting priorities of cost, emissions and motivation.

The recent Climate Change Bill has set challenging objectives to reduce carbon emissions in the UK and the Energy Saving Trust looks forward to playing a part in achieving them.

What does the Energy Saving Trust do to help fleet managers?

It's a tough remit for fleet mangers these days. Fleet has always had more than its fair share of daily crises. Accidents, vehicle reliability issues and delayed new car deliveries have always tended to be in the category – 'must solve today'. At the same time, the complexity of new tax regimes, health and safety legislation and being green, mean that while solving today's problems, fleet managers need to have the vision to create new policies that reflect a changing world and be able to sell them to sceptical colleagues.

So the fleet manger needs to be a resourceful fixer, an expert on vehicle technology, thoroughly versed in the complexities of benefit in kind taxation, corporation tax and discounted cash flows, whilst fully understanding the post-tax cost of everything and whether all his staff might leave because a competitor is offering a more attractive company car package. Increasingly this role is given to able managers with no previous background in fleet or formal training and it's almost certain that no-one else in the company will have any more knowledge on which to lean.

So, external support is helpful if not vital to deliver on all these objectives and whilst suppliers are an important source of information, often from real experts in their field, there's nothing like an empty order book to make a nearly good fit for your fleet suddenly become the best that money can buy. The Energy Saving Trust has one simple objective – to help reduce carbon emissions. But we are not evangelists and we know that our recommendations have to be practical, attractive to staff and convince your Finance Director that the numbers add up. It's our business to keep up to date with new legislation, new technologies and what has worked well elsewhere (and not so well). We therefore bring a perspective which is so much wider than can easily be achieved when faced with the myriad of day to day problems every fleet manger knows only too well and with an independence which helps to sell your new strategy internally.

You are well known for offering Green Fleet Reviews. What are these and how much do they cost?

A Green Fleet Review (GFR) is a project which sets out to measure how green your fleet operation is now and to identify how you might reduce emissions in the future and save money.

We approach this from three perspectives;

1   Vehicle choice – are there lower carbon options which also deliver the right answers on cost and desirability? If so, how do you best influence driver choice?

2   Fuel economy – regardless of the vehicle, how do you impact on driver behaviour to achieve the optimum mpg?

3   Mileage – what initiatives would encourage reductions in overall mileage and hence reduce emissions and cost?

In scope are all company cars and vans (up to 3.5 tonnes), plus cash opt out cars as well as private vehicles used by casual users, and our starting point is to map the current fleet; vehicles, CO$_2$ ratings and miles driven. This is rarely straightforward since data will often sit in a number of different systems, but it is fundamental to painting a complete picture of business travel and where the biggest elements of cost and emissions lie. In most cases we will find some data sets are missing and part of the art of a GFR is knowing how to fix this. For example few organisations hold CO_2 figures for cash opt out, but we are able to provide this given registration numbers.

A full appraisal of existing policy documents will complete the understanding of the current fleet makeup and already we will be starting to draw comparisons with the numerous organisations we have previously worked with and our knowledge of what initiatives deliver the best results.

At the end of the project, clients can expect a comprehensive report which proposes recommendations which will save emissions, but which will also quantify the potential savings and how to best engage with staff to ensure success.

We work closely with the fleet manager to sense check findings at each stage and ideally to help sell an agreed action plan to other key stakeholders within the organisation.

All this is free to fleets in England that have a minimum of 50 vehicles (20 in Scotland) and for smaller fleets we provide a telephone based support service for which there is also no charge.

How can a fleet manager determine how much they might save by moving to environmentally friendly vehicles?

If vehicles are sourced on full maintenance contract hire, monthly rentals including unreclaimable VAT are the starting point. Increasingly, the favourable residual performance of low CO_2 cars is showing through in more competitive contract hire rentals compared with less efficient alternatives. If vehicles are purchased outright we would always recommend that lifetime vehicle comparisons should be made by accessing contract hire rates or using databases such as Fleet News' The Costs.

You should then adjust rentals by the 15% leasing rental disallowance for any vehicles over 160 grams (effective April 2009) or congratulate yourself for those lower emission vehicles where all rentals are allowable against corporation tax – assuming of course your organisation pays corporation tax.

Effectively if you have two cars with identical rentals but one is 150 grams/km and the other is 165grams/km, the higher emission car will cost you 15% x 30% = 4.5% more because of the proportion of rental not allowable against tax.

You also need to include employers' Class IA NIC since low emission cars will save you money. Calculate the drivers taxable benefit (P11D value x factor based on CO_2) and take 12.8% (13.5% from April 2010) for annual cost.

Fuel savings are obviously central to choosing more efficient cars so you need to factor these in by agreeing a typical annual mileage for each vehicle on your the fleet (or this part of the fleet), calculating fuel costs at current pump prices (convert to gallons x 4.54) and taking a view as to typical mpg. (Our work suggests the average company car driver achieves the quoted combined mpg less 15%).

$$\text{Annual fuel cost} \quad = \quad \frac{\text{annual mileage x pump price (£ per litre) x 4.54}}{\text{combined mpg x 0.85}}$$

You now have a good measure of the overall cost to the business of individual cars but don't forget to calculate the savings in tax for the driver and the fuel savings for private mileage – you might even be thanked for showing staff how to save money.

You are well known for the Motorvate scheme. What is this and what benefit does it give fleet operators?

Motorvate is an accreditation scheme which sets out to acknowledge on-going carbon reduction. We complete an audit of your fleet operation to set a baseline and subsequent annual audits measure progress in reducing emissions.

This could arise from any, or all of the following;

- Specifying cleaner vehicles
- Changing driver behaviour and improving mpg
- Reducing business mileage

A number of benefits accrue to the Motorvate member but perhaps the most important is being able to provide robust, independent evidence to the Board and your customers that real progress has been made in terms of environmental performance. But in addition, Motorvate provides a forum to share problems and successes with other fleet managers and gain wider experience of different organisations approach to managing change.

The Motorvate bronze award recognises organisations which have achieved a minimum reduction in their carbon footprint of 5%. Silver and gold designate 10% and 15% respectively.

When it comes to reducing emissions, fleet managers have an element of control over their company cars. However they have much less control over employee owned cars used for business purposes – the grey fleet. How does the Energy Saving Trust recommend that fleet managers approach this issue?

Of course it is true that typically fleet managers have less control over grey fleet, but our view is that this shouldn't be the case. The fact is that the grey fleet represents a company purchase – buying transport from your employees. Like any other company purchase, you decide ultimately whether what is on offer is fit for purpose, the right price and the right quality.

That's a big simplification of a quite complex area and we would approach cash opt out rather differently to casual users who travel infrequently.

The important issue is that policy decisions taken on company cars are likely to have a ripple effect on the cash opt out fleet. To give an example; if a decision is taken to put a ceiling on all company cars at 160 grams to support a new environmental agenda, drivers who find this limiting and would otherwise have taken a company car are likely to migrate to cash, secondhand cars and much higher CO_2. The end result could be an overall increase in emissions rather than a reduction. For this reason we would encourage fleet managers to mirror the company car limits for cash takers. The same argument applies to age of vehicle and from both a safety and emissions perspective newer vehicles on average perform better than older vehicles.

For cash opt out staff you can reasonably argue that monthly allowances are there to fund an equivalent to the company car, so that should certainly allow the company a strong say in how the money is spent. Not so a casual user receiving 40 pence per mile for infrequent travel. However, in some organisations grey fleet travel reimbursed at AMAP rates can account for a very significant proportion of total business mileage so any intention to tackle the environmental agenda cannot ignore the grey fleet.

Ultimately you need to decide whether grey fleet transport is critical to delivering the business objectives and to what extent can you reasonably dictate the vehicle which staff provide. Some organisations have decided to strictly limit the age and CO_2 of any grey fleet vehicle but have accepted that some staff will not comply and will need to be provided with a pool car or a daily rental vehicle. The implications may not be as bad as you might think. Journeys in excess of about 90 miles are likely to be cheaper, safer and produce lower emissions in a daily rental car compared with the average grey fleet vehicle (about 7 years old and 185 grams).

The policy you adopt will depend very much on company culture and the mileage patterns of your grey fleet drivers. But regardless of that, your responsibility for health and safety extends to grey fleet just as much as company cars. That alone says you have no choice but to take a very close interest in the cars your staff are using.

What is current best practice if a fleet manager wants to reduce fuel costs?

Every fleet manager would acknowledge the benefit of reducing fuel spend, but frequently the biggest challenge is that there is insufficient data to manage this critical part of fleet operations.

If the fuel spend is represented by a 'pay and reclaim' pence per mile system your challenge is likely to be quite different to a system based on fuel cards. But regardless of compensation method, you need to consider three things;

1   The vehicles on fleet (and their fuel type)

2   The way they are driven

3   How far they are driven

1   THE VEHICLE

It might be stating the obvious that with more economical cars on fleet you should expect lower fuel bills, but there are some dangers in taking too simplistic an approach. We are all used to using the official combined mpg figures (and corresponding CO_2 scores) to compare different vehicles, but the cleanest vehicles will not always deliver the lowest fuel bills. Low emission hybrids will sip fuel in urban driving but struggle to match modern diesels on motorway driving despite official combined figures which might suggest otherwise. Diesels tend to outperform their petrol equivalents by about 20-25%, but don't forget to factor in the premium on diesel pump prices before reaching conclusions.

For most fleets, LPG vehicles are not a mainstream choice not least because only a modest range of new LPG vans is currently available. Price per litre looks attractive and in urban areas LPG offers significant benefits of improved air quality but bear in mind that fuel costs per mile will be no better than diesel.

Electric vehicles offer the lowest fuel costs per mile and if power is generated by renewables the lowest emissions too. As more electric vehicles come to market they will offer obvious potential to reduce fuel costs and help the environment but they are the best illustration that in choosing more fuel efficient vehicles you cannot look at fuel costs in isolation to the capital cost of the vehicle.

2   THE DRIVER

Driver behaviour offers perhaps the biggest potential to reduce fuel bills but also the toughest challenge. Data from a very large sample of fuel card users indicates that the average company car driver achieves 85% of the quoted combined mpg for a given vehicle. The key question of course is 'can you reasonably expect more?' For many drivers the answer is probably yes…but equally you should not expect the same outcome for drivers operating in predominately urban areas compared with those who are undertaking long journeys on motorways. Of course if you reimburse business mileage on a pence per mile basis then you may not necessarily be too concerned about individual drivers' fuel economy, but if reducing costs is your goal, you will need to convince drivers they can achieve better fuel economy regardless of reimbursement method.

For fleets using fuel cards and having many vehicles of the same type, fuel purchase and mileage data provide the opportunity to compare mpg from one driver to another. Consider ranking drivers, publishing the results and providing incentives for the best results. With a more diverse range of vehicles, consider rankings based on a percentage of the published combined mpg figure as a means of identifying good and poor performance. Just the act of measurement has produced results for many fleets and even very modest incentives will increase the focus on improving mpg.

For fleets reimbursing on a pence per mile, a guaranteed method of reducing cost is to reduce reimbursement rates! Many fleets take the easy route of using the HMRC advisory fuel rates, but these are based on a wide range of vehicles and represent the maximum rates you may pay without potentially creating a benefit in kind. But if your vehicles offer better than average fuel consumption there is no reason for you to follow HMRC rates slavishly.

Fully expensed company cars have become much less common as benefit in kind taxation on private fuel has increased. But if they are a feature of your fleet then clearly this is an area where you should be looking for savings. Many drivers still accept this perk without calculating the true value compared with the tax bill that accompanies it, but a typical higher rate tax payer would probably need to drive 12,000 private miles to break even.

3   THE JOURNEY

One research study suggested that almost 40% of business meetings are judged a waste of time. If true, then the potential to reduce mileage and hence fuel bills is enormous. The challenge, of course, is knowing in advance which journeys and which meetings will prove to be of poor value. For the fleet manager this is difficult territory and probably one that can only be managed effectively by line management. However, fleet policy has a part to play; if eligibility for company cars (or an essential user allowance) is based on travelling a minimum number of miles, then inevitably staff have an incentive to travel. Equally if the replacement cycle for a new company car is say four years or 80,000miles, most people enjoy getting a new car and may find reason to travel more rather than less in order to qualify for a new car sooner. Consider revising eligibility based on the nature of the job and the frequency of travel rather than any specific mileage.

Replacement cycles based on time or mileage (whichever comes first) are extremely common, but modern car reliability, even to very high mileages, means that the argument for replacement at a maximum mileage is now considerably weaker. Your drivers will still drive to some meetings ultimately judged to be a waste of time, but at least they will not have a built in incentive to do so.

What is your view of the general level of knowledge about energy saving amongst fleet managers?

There are undoubtedly many knowledgeable and professional fleet managers, but there are also many HR managers, purchasing managers and facilities managers who valiantly juggle the intricacies of fleet along with the day job. For some organisations, size alone dictates that fleet will not be a full time role, but the breadth of challenges involved (funding methods, tax, health and safety, employee motivation, environment and vehicle technology) means there is no comparable function where it will automatically be a natural fit.

The good news is that there is no shortage of information available to fleet managers through trade press, web and events. For mangers who have fleet as just a part of their brief, the value of networking to find independent sources of knowledge and experience cannot be underestimated. Equally the services of organisations like the Energy Saving Trust are there to provide free and unbiased help to mange fleets more effectively.

What energy saving developments have there been in the last few years that have been particularly valuable to fleet managers?

Three significant developments in the last few years have made the fleet managers' task of reducing fuel consumption much easier. Firstly fiscal policy is now firmly aligned with low CO$_2$. Since 2002 benefit in kind taxation has helped to encourage drivers to select lower emission vehicles, but the more recently introduced lower rate band for vehicles of 120 grams or less means vehicles in this category offer big savings for drivers and reductions in employers' NIC. However changes to writing down allowances and expensive car leasing disallowance from April 2009 mean that companies will stand to gain even more by encouraging drivers to choose lower-CO$_2$ vehicles.

Whatever the savings, unappealing vehicles will never encourage drivers to opt for low emissions. So the development of aspirational vehicles which are also low CO$_2$ has been a remarkable achievement in the last couple of years with more than 400 vehicles now on offer in the critical 120 gram or less category. Drivers can now have their cake and eat it; attractive cars with good performance and specification which also deliver low carbon, low benefit in kind tax and low operating costs for the business.

Finally, many organisations have adopted a more environmentally focussed approach to the way they do business, so a lower emission fleet policy is a very visible part of such a strategy and therefore likely to get strong support from the Board.

Is anything happening now or likely to be happening soon that is likely to change the landscape for fleet managers?

Not so much a change of landscape but acceleration of recent developments – the recent Climate Change Bill commits UK Government to an 80% reduction in carbon emissions by 2050. 2050 is hardly soon, but, significantly, Government has also committed to 5 year targets to keep progress on track. These reductions will require a radical change to the way we produce and use energy in the UK and whilst detailed policy is yet to emerge, fleets can expect ever more stringent fiscal policies to change the nature of vehicles we drive and the way we use them.

The King Review, commissioned by Government, concludes that the future of low carbon vehicles is dependent on much greater penetration of electric vehicles and plug-in hybrids, but any review of the current state of this market could only conclude that market shift requires major improvements in the operating range of electric vehicles and increased investment in recharging infrastructure.

Whatever crystal ball you look into, the prospect is for more pressure to reduce the environmental impact of fleet vehicles. This will undoubtedly create fresh problems for fleet managers but also offer exciting challenges for those who are ready to embrace change.

ENERGY SAVINGS TRUST CASE STUDIES

Case Study 1

Company name

Davis Langdon LLP

Fleet profile

445 vehicles, 195 cash for company car opt outs, 1,350 casual users

Business

Leading international project and cost consultancy, providing managed solutions for clients investing in infrastructure, property and construction; 1,800 UK staff; past projects include Tate Modern, London, and the Eden Project, Cornwall

Locations

London and offices throughout the UK

Davis Langdon has embarked on a major programme to reduce emissions for its fleet and is working towards achieving international environmental standard ISO14001. The UK based organisation is a leading international project and cost consultancy, providing managed solutions for clients investing in infrastructure, property and construction – with environmental management a key focus.

With company car drivers and own-car users travelling more than three million miles a year – many in high emission vehicles – the Energy Saving Trust was called in for advice.

As a result Davis Langdon have benchmarked the company car choice list against the existing Vehicle Excise Duty (VED) bands to incentivise drivers to opt for low emission vehicles. It is among the first organisations to take steps to axe use of privately-owned vehicles on business (otherwise know as grey fleet).

Green Fleet Review recommendations implemented so far include:

- Cash incentives to encourage 258 staff company car drivers and 195 cash opt-out employees to drive cars falling in VED bands A–D (165 g/km of CO_2 or below)

- Up to 1,350 grey fleet drivers using public transport or a company paid for hire car instead of their own vehicle

- Financial penalties for company partners (187 in total) if they select a company car above VED band D

- Vehicles driven on company business to have at least a four star European New Car Assessment Programme (NCAP) crash test rating

- Driver licence validation checks

- Video conferencing to reduce vehicle mileage
- 'Root and branch' fleet review

Davis Langdon found out about the Energy Saving Trust's Green Fleet Review when Neil Ashton, the company's Head of Procurement and Supplier Management saw an advertisement in Fleet News. At the time he had already started to undertake a fleet review internally, with input from the organisation's Foresight Group, which was investigating sustainability options for the company.

Neil explained: 'As I began examining the whole lifecycle of our fleet, I thought about the relationship between CO_2 emissions, the cost of fuel and residual values. I feared long-term second-hand values of gas-guzzlers could reduce.

'I contacted the Energy Saving Trust so one of their consultants could carry out a Green Fleet Review. I wanted the review to provide a snapshot of where we were, give some credibility to my thinking, and also come up with some ideas.

'I ended up with a series of recommendations from both the Energy Saving Trust and our own Foresight Group, which were both pulling in the same direction in terms of helping us to reduce our carbon footprint.'

Incentives to choose low emission cars

While average vehicle emissions across the staff company cars were described in the Green Fleet Review as 'moderate', the exhaust output from the largely 'perk' cars driven by partners was described as 'very carbon intensive'. A radically revised car policy based around an emissions cap was therefore recommended.

Instead of using a g/km figure, Davis Langdon has used the actual VED bands.

With an open choice company car policy, staff drivers are incentivised through an allowance system to choose a low emission car – the cleaner the car, the larger the allowance. An identical system is in place for company car opt-out drivers who must now choose a car less than six years old with a minimum four star Euro NCAP rating. Meanwhile, partners who choose a company car in VED bands E–G pay a financial penalty with the cash paid into the company's carbon offsetting programme.

Neil said: 'The scheme is in its infancy so it is too early to have a clear picture of how it's performing. But the initiative has been welcomed by our employees, many of whom are conscientious about their carbon emissions. They also understand that by choosing a low emission car their benefit-in-kind tax liability will be lower.'

In a move to address the health and safety risks of at-work drivers, the organisation has decided to axe the use of private cars for business travel, so staff who need make journeys for work either use public transport or travel by hire car.

'The duty of care risks faced by organisations allowing employees to use their own cars on business are so high that we decided to remove those risks completely,' said Neil. 'We believe we are among the first to take this step.'

Future plans involve setting carbon reduction targets

Talking about the next phase of the Green Fleet Review implementation process, Neil said: 'We have not set any benchmarks at the moment. In 12 months time I think we will have meaningful information that will enable Davis Langdon to set carbon reduction targets across the fleet.'

The introduction of fuel cards to provide useful data on actual fuel usage and mileage is also on the agenda, and Davis Langdon's fleet management company will shortly embark on a car and driver risk analysis that could see a number of strategies put into place, including driver training.

Green Fleet Review promotes credible solutions

'The Green Fleet Review has been extremely useful,' said Neil. 'Being independent it brings credibility to internal debate and promotes new ideas. The actual report and presentation was easily understood by the layman.

'Since receiving the report we have continued to hold extensive dialogue with the Energy Saving Trust as we cement our plans. While we want to reduce our vehicle emissions, we must also offer a car policy that ensures we are competitive in terms of staff recruitment and retention.

'The work undertaken by the Energy Saving Trust has played a significant part in providing Davis Langdon with practical solutions to put the organisation on the road to achieve its objectives.'

Case Study 2

Company name

Commercial Group

Fleet profile

50 company cars, 12 diesel vans; grey fleet travelling 55,000 miles a year

Business

UK's largest independent office services company

Locations

Headquarters in Cheltenham and offices in Plymouth and Cirencester

By transforming their delivery scheduling and having a workforce committed to 'greening' company transport, the UK's largest independent office services company, Commercial Group, reduced fleet carbon emissions by 50 per cent during 2007. This leaves them well placed to achieve a three-year reduction target of 75 per cent.

Success to date has been the result of a company-wide carbon reduction programme, combined with a suite of Green Fleet Review recommendations provided by the Energy Saving Trust. So far the following changes have been made:

- Introducing intelligent delivery journey scheduling using dynamic route mapping and vehicle tracking technology
- Revising vehicle choice lists to encourage company car drivers to choose vehicles emitting less than 160 g/km of CO2
- Introducing pool cars to reduce use of grey fleet (private cars used for business purposes)
- Improving the use of fuel card management reports to proactively manage fuel usage and mileage
- Launching a biodiesel fuel blending bunkering facility at the company's Cheltenham headquarters
- Educating drivers in smarter-driving techniques
- Staff promotions to encourage the introduction of innovative alternatives to car and van use

Passionate about reducing carbon emissions

With a long standing commitment to environmental improvement, the Commercial Group has operated an Environmental Management System that is BS 8555-compliant since 2004, and is expected to achieve ISO 14001 in summer 2008.

Prior to carrying out their Green Fleet Review, Commercial Group discovered that almost 90 per cent of the organisation's CO_2 emissions came from its owned fleet vehicles, other vehicles used for work purposes and staff cars used on home to work journeys. Transport was therefore a priority area to be addressed.

Simon Graham, Environmental Strategist, said: 'As a company we feel very passionate about reducing carbon emissions. We had already introduced many measures to help reduce our carbon footprint, including tackling vehicle use, but we recognised there was still much to be done.'

At the time of the Green Fleet Review Commercial Group was operating 12 vans and 47 cars (diesel and petrol), travelling 1.2 million miles a year and consuming almost 200,000 litres of fuel. Mr Graham recognised that there were many 'hidden inefficiencies' in the company's fleet.

Proactive fuel use and mileage monitoring

The Review identified the need for proactive monitoring of fuel use and mileage. This fitted neatly with the introduction of the company's own biodiesel fuel bunkering facility with in-built monitoring of usage, which will leave only drivers working remotely using fuel cards. The filling station uses locally-produced sustainable biodiesel produced from waste oil in various blends, which will reduce emissions by up to 80 per cent, as well as enabling greater control over fuel usage.

To help reduce mileage, customer delivery journeys were pinpointed as a priority area for change. Intelligent scheduling, dynamic route planning and consolidated deliveries have been introduced and delivery miles have reduced from 435,000 to 276,000 in 2007.

In terms of 'greening' the company car fleet, phase one of the project has involved providing information to encourage drivers to select sub 160 g/km vehicles; phase 2 of the project will encourage vehicles lower than 140 g/km (although average tailpipe emissions have already been reduced by 20 per cent).

Meanwhile all Euro III vans have now been retired and a six year, 300,000 mile replacement policy has been implemented.

Grey fleet and driver education addressed

The issue of employees using their own vehicles for business purposes – otherwise know as grey fleet – was a significant issue for Commercial Group for two reasons. Firstly, concerns over the age of privately-owned vehicles and the difficulty of checking documentation to comply with duty of care rules meant there was a health and safety risk. Secondly, mileage was reaching 55,000 per annum and resulting in large reimbursement claims. To address this, a fleet of more fuel efficient pool cars has been introduced and mileage and fuel reimbursement claims have both reduced.

Training to encourage safer, stress free driving has been piloted and is likely to be rolled out during 2008. Travel awareness days have generated positive results in encouraging staff to reduce vehicle use; staff bus mileage has increased from 940 miles in 2006 to 5,300 in 2007, and one employee even roller skated to work! Cycling to work is also encouraged with bicycle storage, showers and changing rooms provided.

Green Fleet Review drove company forward

Mr Graham said: 'Although we had made significant steps to reduce our carbon emissions, we realised there was a lot more to do and the Energy Saving Trust provided us with the guidance and direction we needed to move forward. 'But we don't want to just focus on our own carbon footprint. We want to spread the message as wide as possible by encouraging customers, staff and suppliers to take action too. We hold an annual CSR day where we not only tell people what we have done but also encourage them to share their experiences of best environmental practices and have made environmental criteria a cornerstone of our supplier assessment programme.

'Overall, the whole process has been incredibly valuable but also challenging and motivational. I hope other companies will follow our lead in running a more efficient fleet and contributing to a better environment.'

Commercial Group's success in reducing carbon emissions was recognised when they were named Runner Up in the Small Fleet (25 –100 vehicles) category at the 2007 Energy Saving Trust Fleet Hero Awards, in association with the Observer and Fleet News.

Case Study 3

Company name

Northern Lincolnshire & Goole

Fleet profile

42 leased scheme cars, 38 pool cars, 60 commercial vehicles and 1,281 grey fleet vehicles

Business

6,000 staff delivering health care at hospitals in Scunthorpe, Grimsby and Goole and across the wider community

Locations

Scunthorpe General Hospital, Diana, Princess of Wales Hospital in Grimsby and Goole District Hospital

Making huge reductions in staff mileage reimbursement claims – with the knock on effect of channelling cash into improving patient care and services – was the key reason behind Northern Lincolnshire & Goole Hospitals NHS Trust undertaking a Green Fleet Review.

In relation to this, a key objective for the Trust is that it aims to cut carbon dioxide emissions by almost 20 per cent over three years. In line with recommendations set by the Review, the following changes have been implemented to help achieve overall objectives:

- Introducing shuttle buses to replace individual car use as staff move between hospital sites
- Replacing existing leased and pool cars and vans with new, lower emission vehicles

Being committed to long term environmental improvement, the Trust has also joined Motorvate, an Energy Saving Trust scheme which recognises and rewards organisations for achieving targeted carbon dioxide reductions from their fleet.

Transport budget focus

An analysis of the Trust's transport operations by the Directorate of Facilities Management revealed annual spending of over £1 million on all aspects of travel and transport services. Following this, Jug Johal was appointed to the newly created post of Transport Services Manager, specifically tasked with improving operating efficiencies and cutting costs.

Addressing grey fleet (staff using private cars for business purposes) was a key challenge for the Trust. More than 1,250 staff including consultants, doctors, midwives, nurses and health workers were using their own cars to travel between three hospital sites in Goole, Grimsby and Scunthorpe as well as other areas. This equated to 1.5 million miles driven annually, costing in excess of £750,000 in mileage claims. A target has been set to reduce that sum by £350,000 over three years.

In terms of the Trust's fleet – a combination of leased and owned cars and vans as well as pool cars – it was identified that more fuel efficient models should be introduced and more employees should be encouraged into the leased car scheme.

Action plan

While Mr Johal has been appointed to address the fleet challenge, external help was required to establish an action plan for moving forward. Grey fleet and mileage reduction were at the core of the Green Fleet Review; however a package of initiatives was recommended to improve overall efficiency and environmental performance.

Changes implemented to date include:

- Introducing a fleet of shuttle buses to transport staff between the three hospitals, which has been highly successful in reducing grey fleet mileage and reimbursement costs
- Installing video conferencing and actively encouraging staff to use public transport when travelling to conferences and events
- Introducing Vauxhall Corsa 1.3 CDTi diesel pool cars and Vauxhall Combo diesel vans onto the owned fleet
- A 'blue light' courtesy car has been purchased which staff can book online. Costs have been recouped in a matter of months due to savings on taxi fares
- Using fuel cards to monitor budgets and miles. A best practice occupational road risk policy has also been developed putting driver health and safety in the spotlight. Driver hand books and safety checks have been introduced and driver training is available.

This was a big task for Mr Johal but having the backing of the Chief Executive and Executive team made it a lot easier. The support of his team in collecting data and staff responsiveness to using the shuttle buses was also very helpful.

The green fleet journey continues

While the Trust has made great progress, particularly in relation to cost savings, it acknowledges there is still much to do.

Determined to achieve existing carbon reduction targets, and move beyond them, Mr Johal has signed up to the Energy Saving Trust's Motorvate programme. By providing expert advice and robust monitoring of carbon reduction strategies, Motorvate ensures specific targets are met. Success is measured by a specialised accreditation process with bronze, silver and gold levels achieved as a result of the annual auditing of vehicle emissions.

The Trust's journey started by establishing a baseline carbon footprint, setting reduction targets and identifying action areas; however the objective is now to ensure initiatives deliver results.

Mr Johal commented: 'The main priority now is to focus on ensuring that recommendations are implemented and integrated into the Trust's business transport strategy. The aim is to ensure new practices work before introducing further initiatives.'

Cost savings to benefit patient care

While cutting transport costs was the prime reason behind the Green Fleet Review, ultimately the main beneficiaries will be hospital patients and the environment.

Mr Johal said: 'We are going to make major financial savings. There is absolutely no doubt about that. And I have every expectation that when we complete our carbon inventory over the next three years, we'll also find out that we have made all the reductions in CO_2 emissions that are expected of us.

'NHS funding is limited so the financial savings that are accruing can be reinvested into services to improve patient care, therefore saving lives and maintaining the health of the community.'

In recognition of their achievements, the Trust was named Winner in the Grey Fleet category at the 2007 Energy Saving Trust Fleet Hero Awards, in association with The Observer and Fleet News. Mr Johal was also named Fleet Manager of the Year in the sub-100 category at the 2008 Fleet News Awards.

Nigel Underdown
Head of Transport Advice
Energy Saving Trust

Add your name to the list of organisations that have saved money and reduced carbon emissions with an Energy Saving Trust Green Fleet Review

Contact us to find out how a **Green Fleet Review** can help you cut costs, improve efficiency and enhance your environmental performance

Call **0845 602 1425**

www.energysavingtrust.org.uk/fleet

Peter Minter
Managing Director
Duncton Group Ltd

Please introduce your company.

Duncton is a vehicle finance and management company with a difference. The company was formed in 1992 to address a gap in the car finance market. We cater specifically for individuals, partnerships and businesses experiencing difficulties in obtaining car finance.

In our experience, the reasons funding applications are declined elsewhere are as numerous and varied as the applicants themselves. Everyone has individual circumstances, so Duncton provides flexible lending solutions tailored to each customer. Our clients include sole traders, those who have experienced credit problems in the past, new start-ups and established businesses with unusual vehicle or finance requirements. We fit the funding to them and the vehicle they require – not the other way around. Being the lender, we're able to consider each applicant, view every case on its merits and tailor competitive funding to fit.

Duncton Group's offices in West Sussex

What sort of deals are available?

We provide contract hire, lease purchase, personal contract hire and personal hire purchase. Inevitably the rates will be higher than normal prime contracts. We will include a service package if required, but this is not a requirement. The client can choose term of 3 or 4 years and mileage between 10k to 30k miles pa. The client may early terminate the contract after two years (if fully up to date on payments) and replace the vehicle with a further contract for a similar vehicle for a further term of 3 or 4 years. There is no upper limit on the value of vehicle. We fund cars and vans, new and used. We are particularly keen on nearly new vehicles as these offer the best mix of economy for the client and security for us.

What finance options are available for the business user?

If your business is making a profit and is VAT registered, contract hire is likely to be the best option for you as long as you intend to change the vehicle within four years. However, if you are looking to acquire a vehicle to keep it for more than four years you may prefer to look at a lease purchase agreement.

CONTRACT HIRE

Contract hire is a method of funding the use of a vehicle rather than its ownership. Duncton hires the vehicle to you for an agreed period, usually 36 or 48 months, for a fixed monthly sum and at the end of the contract you hand the vehicle back to us.

This type of agreement transfers substantially all the risks associated with ownership to Duncton. You are not responsible for selling the vehicle at the end of the contract, subject to the vehicle being kept in good condition and not exceeding the agreed mileage. Service and maintenance plans can be included with contract hire agreements to cater for fixed cost motoring.

You will need to consult your accountant to fully understand all the implications for your business and how to optimise the tax allowances available using this type of agreement.

In order for us to provide the best monthly price the vehicle must be VAT-qualifying. This covers all new vehicles and certain second-hand vehicles depending on the previous keeper's circumstances.

Contrary to popular belief, contract hire is no more expensive than a similar purchase agreement which has a final balloon payment included, and after the tax advantages have been taken into account, it can be considerably cheaper. So all things being equal, you are better off using contract hire as the route to funding your next vehicle.

All contract hire agreements with Duncton provide the facility to upgrade your vehicle and to start a new agreement with us without early termination charges after two years (terms apply).

In summary these are the benefits of contract hire:

- Use of the vehicle for the duration of the agreement without responsibility for disposal at the end.
- Fixed motoring costs – if maintenance package included.
- Tax implications that can make contract hire far more cost-effective than other funding options.
- Change your car every two years without early termination charges (terms apply).
- Ultimately, however, you will need to consult your own advisor to decide what is best for you.

LEASE PURCHASE

The term 'Lease Purchase' was introduced into the finance industry to describe a hire purchase or conditional sale contract with a payment structure similar to a lease. Instead of a deposit, an 'advance payment' may be paid. It is normally a fixed cost, fixed term loan and you become the owner of the goods. However, in law, the title will not pass unless:

- All the regular payments have been made.
- The goods are kept insured.
- The goods are kept in good condition.

On cars over the value of £15,000, Duncton may include a final (balloon) payment on our Lease Purchase agreements to help reduce the monthly payment.

In summary the benefits of Lease Purchase are:

- Lower monthly payments with final (balloon) payment included.
- You own the vehicle – once all payments have been made.

This is intended as background information only. You should consult your financial advisor before making any decisions.

Are there any types of deals you won't do?

It is a basic principle that we will not finance more than the trade value of a vehicle. As a result, the initial payment on a new car tends to be large, making the deal less attractive. On nearly new cars, the size of the initial deposit tends to rely on the ability to source cars of sufficient quality at trade prices, so these cars are easier to finance. We will not finance customers/drivers under the age of 21. Start up companies will probably require a guarantor before we will do a deal

Why would a company fund its cars through a company like yours?

The market for contract hire and lease purchase shrunk dramatically during the second half of 2008 as a direct result of the credit crunch. More companies are struggling to find suppliers of contract hire. There are two reasons for this: there has been a reduction in the number of suppliers willing and able to write business, and those that have stayed in the market have rewritten their credit policies and are now much more stringent about the types of business they will fund.

The market has been in such turmoil that the methods of underwriting that were used in the past in the sub-prime sector are no longer adequate or appropriate. Historically, county court judgements and company voluntary agreements (CCJs and CVAs) would bar a company from receiving regular finance. We have always been happy to supply such organisations. However, the market has now changed to such an extent that such companies now have to be able to demonstrate to us that they will be able to support the agreement for the full term, which in many cases can be hard for them to do.

How does a company like yours manage to operate in a market that other lessors shy away from?

We have developed a very distinctive approach to doing business. These are the key components of the Duncton model:

1   We are very careful to ascertain the precise value of the vehicle. The vehicle is our security and it is essential that we do not over-lend.

2   We are very cautious in setting residual values. Mainstream leasing companies would find our residual values to be highly conservative.

3   We are extremely diligent in ensuring the customer really exists. There have been far too many cases of individuals setting out to defraud the leasing industry.

4   We do all that is necessary to ensure that the car really exists and that we are being given proper legal title.

5   We use directors' guarantees where we need additional security, particularly in start-up situations

This is a more complex contract initiation than most lessors would undertake, and as a result, the cost of the contract will be a little more. However, the larger initial deposit often keeps the monthly payments on a par with prime rates. Also, the use of nearly-new cars reduces the cost further.

What developments have there been in the sub-prime motor finance market in the last few years that have been particularly valuable to fleet managers?

It has virtually ceased to exist. We are one of the very few survivors.

Is anything happening now, or will anything be happening soon, that is likely to change the sub-prime landscape for fleet funding?

The recession started with the so-called toxic sub-prime mortgages in the USA. These have given the whole sub-prime market a bad name, and sub-prime lenders such as us have found it very difficult to obtain funding. You need to consider that even high street banks have been unable to get adequate funding, so for the sub-prime market there has been very little liquidity. All of which is a shame because it is a market that meets a definite need, and meets it efficiently and effectively. There are very few sub-prime funders operating in the market at the moment, and the list is getting shorter. We expect that we will need to wait until the middle of 2009 before anything starts to move again. And when the market does get going we expect it will be on a different business model.

If you were to advise a fleet manager about best practice when it comes to working with a sub-prime finance provider, what would that advice be?

1   The survivors in this market are likely to be the organisations that have been doing this sort of business for a long time. So as a first step fleets should make sure the provider has been in business for some time.

2   If problems do arise during the course of the lease – particularly if the client is running into cash flow difficulties – get in touch with the funder. At that stage they may be able to do things to help; later it may be too late.

3   Make sure you understand the contract you are signing.

4   Resist the temptation to buy cars for the image they project. There will be plenty of time to do that when you have made a success of your new enterprise. If you are in the sub-prime market because of trading problems, your problems will not be helped by hiring top-of-the-line cars.

How can Duncton help fleet managers?

Sub-prime contract hire is a key tool to help business through difficult phases. It is not cheap, so it is essential that you look at other options first. Consider, for example, whether you need the vehicle at all.

Having said that, we can help in situations where your regular finance companies can't get involved, and can be more flexible.

We can tailor the contract to your needs, and provide a useful source of motor industry expertise when making a key investment decision.

Peter Minter
Managing Director
Duncton Group Ltd

Flexible Car Finance.

Founded in 1992 to address a gap in the car finance market, Duncton caters specifically for individuals, partnerships and businesses experiencing difficulties in obtaining car finance.

In our experience, the reasons funding applications are declined elsewhere are as numerous and varied as the applicants themselves. Everyone has individual circumstances, so Duncton provides flexible lending solutions tailored to each customer.

From sole traders to those who have experienced credit problems in the past; from new start-ups to established businesses with unusual vehicle or finance requirements, we fit the funding to you and the vehicle you require – not the other way around.

Being the lender, we're able to consider each applicant, view every case on its merits and tailor competitive funding to fit.

General Enquiries & Broker Sales:
01730 715 300

Sales Enquiries:
01730 818 200

www.duncton.com

Duncton Plc
Wenham Manor Barn
Petersfield Road
Rogate
West Sussex
GU31 5AY

Professor Peter N C Cooke

KPMG Professor of Automotive Management

University of Buckingham

Please tell us a little about your background and your interest in fleet management

I joined Ford Motor Company in 1968, from business school and quickly found myself working in Fleet Sales. As a bright young thing with a Beatles haircut I was asked to see what had been written on 'fleet economics'. Answer after a couple of trips to various libraries and talks with a few journalists – 'nothing' – followed by an over-exuberant – 'should I write something?'

My wife sees that as my downfall. My first book was published in 1974 – '*Financial Analysis of Motor Transport Operations*' – which was in print for some 25 years – and talked about a 'company car costing £1,000'. It has led, over the years to a clutch of books on fleet management in its widest context – focusing on cost control,

managing inflation among others and includes works published in Russian and Polish. There has been a steady stream of reports – including 'Business Car Expectations' series over the last ten years, monographs and articles. I have been published in a dozen languages and have consulted and lectured on fleet and the automotive industry in close to 50 countries.

For the first 20 years of my career I worked in the motor industry, or associated industries with a range of UK, European and wider responsibilities – and I have managed or had overall responsibility for fleets several times on the way through. I seem to have 'attracted fleet management'.

For the past 20 years I have been a business school academic poking my nose into fleet and the automotive industries. I have taught at Henley Management College, Nottingham Business School and, for the past couple of years at The University of Buckingham Business School where I'm currently the KPMG Professor of Automotive Management.

I have developed and launched fleet management programmes at each of those institutions and am currently involved in preparing a university award bearing programme in fleet management.

I'm probably the longest surviving member of the fleet management fraternity still in captivity – whether gainful or not is open to interpretation. I'm probably the only contributor to this tome who does not have a company car so I would claim to be completely objective.

Oh yes, and my qualification to write about fleet management in recession – this is my fourth recession – I hope I have learnt enough in the previous three to be able to offer some useful pointers.

Please give us your view of the current situation

Economic recession is not new; the United Kingdom appears to have one about every ten years. These events are so regular they have a seasonality of their own. Historically, recessions in the UK have been at least part self-inflicted with the rest of the world looking on almost with incredulity. However, the recession we are entering in 2009 would appear to be part of a true global recession triggered, at least in part, by the credit crunch and the associated near collapse of a testosterone-charged 'profit before propriety' global banking system. That banking system, at the time of writing, appears loath to lend on anything with a rating less than AAA investment grade.

A simplistic scenario?

Perhaps – but it sets the scene for the changing shape of business – recession; cash shortage, historically low interest rates – if money will be lent - and a singular lack of business confidence. For once – or at least at this stage of the economic cycle – inflation is not yet prominent on the horizon, although the talk of 'printing money' does set alarm bells ringing.

Given that the current recession is a of a type we have not experienced previously, government may be accused of squandering its interest rate weapon and throwing cash at the economy rather than focusing its limited resources to create immediate demand. Instead it seems to be looking to push through long-term pet projects that will take time to deliver work.

Now, the government is looking to introduce 'quantitative easing' – a sort of financial laxative that will theoretically release cash flow through buying up strings of financial assets – perhaps risking inflation. However, the business person must keep a weather eye on the situation to ensure policy does not collapse further into 'qualitative easing' – buying up rubbish assets.

How will this economic background impact on fleet management?

Well, this diatribe helps set the scene that we are moving into what could be a deep and prolonged recession. Credit availability may be patchy and not totally logical and the company may have higher priorities for those funds than for the fleet. At the same time, a fleet executive working in the real world has to provide a first-class service for his or her organisation, almost certainly with a reduced or restricted budget. Simultaneously the business is perhaps downsizing or almost certainly changing shape more rapidly than at any time in the last 40 years.

I may have exaggerated a little, but let's revisit the scene in three years and see how close I am, historically, to reality.

This chapter seeks to examine a number of questions and suggest steps that might be taken to minimise the negative impact of recession on the fleet and, as the economy emerges from recession, ensure it is in relatively good shape to support the rejuvenation and repositioning of the business.

The chapter initially examines the potential implications of recession on fleets, the changing role of fleet executives during recession and thereafter their role in bringing the fleet out of recession while protecting standards and cash flow.

Fleet management in recession is 'fleet management only more so' but set against a position of a rapidly evolving business. There are few more exciting times to be managing a fleet and the people involved with fleet provision and utilisation.

Do you think the shape of the fleet will need to change during the economic recession – and during the eventual economic recovery?

The contracting economy and the changing of company dynamics to accommodate those changes will ensure the shape of a fleet must change during and after the recession to support the evolved business.

If the organisation fails to respond to changes in its markets and modus operandi it will finish up looking like a camel when the market wants a greyhound. The fleet, led by the fleet executive has to follow and indeed anticipate those changes to be at the front of the curve rather than constantly rushing to keep up.

As the organisation changes, the relationship and self-interest between the different stakeholders changes and that, in turn, will cause changes in the way fleet management is conducted. People will often be one of the more difficult issues the fleet executive has to manage in recession.

There are two interesting paradigms that illustrate the way a business might evolve. The first, shown as Figure 1, are the so-called 'drivers for change on the fleet'. This illustrates the external and business pressures which may directly or indirectly lead to changes in the fleet. Not only does the fleet executive have to manage the internal changes needed to keep the fleet effective but also needs to observe how competition to the business is changing – new players coming into the market, while some others may exit the industry – and judge their implications on fleet provision for employees.

Equally important, the way that the fleet cars will be provided may well change – which may mean different methods of provision and management or indeed the type and numbers of cars provided.

As important, both from the viewpoint of the absolute number of vehicles on the fleet, and their use, are the 'alternatives' shown at the bottom of the paradigm.

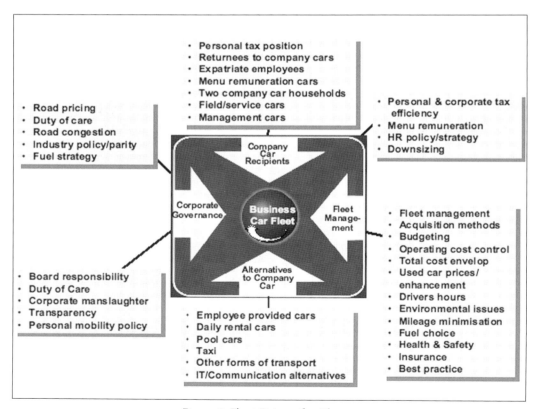

Figure 1: Fleet Drivers for Change
For illustrative purposes only – not comprehensive

Paradoxically, any reduction in the number of field staff or reallocation of tasks may lead to a reduction in miles driven, as field staff replan their activities and utilise alternative forms of client communication as well as reviewing their priorities with regard to the clients which really need to be visited and those it would be 'nice to visit' on a regular basis.

In addition, the 'cash flow as king' methods of vehicle provision may change due to recessional pressures. Will you continue to use the same methods of provision – or sources of units – or seek more cash flow effective methods, short term, either to reduce cost or to improve cash flow?

The wider issues of the marketplace – legislation and best practice – shown on the outside of the paradigm will also move ahead during recession and may well be considered counter-productive with the other tasks the fleet executive has to execute.

Quite simply the Drivers for Change paradigm seeks to put the fleet in context in a recession situation. At least you are not alone! Those same issues will impact on competition as well as on the vehicle suppliers whether OEMs, dealers or leasing companies.

It is a critical part of the role of the fleet executive to watch the market and competition externally during a period of recession, to ensure the fleet is being managed in line with best practice in the sector – standards must not be allowed to slip. Perhaps the best analogy would be to comparing the fleet with a seagull in a storm – you can fight against it or you can ride out the situation.

So much for the macroeconomics of the situation – but one can never stress too highly the importance of watching those external issues and responding, when necessary, even if that is bringing the issues to the attention of management.

The second analysis, which is relevant during a period of recession, is the so-called stakeholder analysis. These players may be internal or external but they can have an impact on both the fleet and the role of the fleet executive – especially during a period of change.

Some pragmatists regard stakeholders as being 'blockers' or those who can stop change moving forward. Thus, we have vehicle providers who may slow down the change of methods of provision or, internally, personnel who may be about to have to surrender their company car – and will fight for it.

You mentioned previously that 'people are one of the most difficult elements to mange in recession'. What do you mean by that?

The company car is, and I think always will be, an enormous ego-trip; a status symbol. Recipients will go to the most devious lengths to justify retaining or even enhancing their company cars if they feel there is any threat to it – even to the detriment of the company.

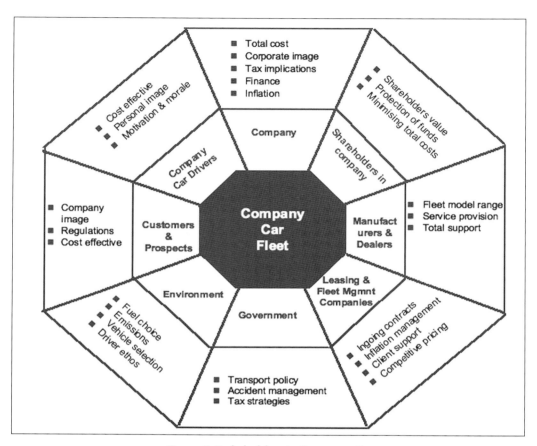

Figure 2: Stakeholders in Company Car
For illustrative purposes only – not comprehensive

Bitter experience has convinced me of this – but we'll not go into that now – it might be libellous!

The stakeholders chart shown in Figure 2 highlights some of the interested parties in the company car – and their interests. The fleet executive needs to be aware of those competing pressures and egos especially in times of recession when potentially disturbing decisions may have to be made – and the fleet executive has to execute them. The company car is an emotional piece of equipment and is subject to a lot of personal involvement. It is amazing what steps employees may take to retain their company car – whatever the cost to the organisation – even its survival.

The fleet executive has a critical role both in watching these external and internal issues and ensuring they do not impact negatively on the business, especially in economic recession.

Managing those HR issues can have a strategic benefit for the fleet executive in that it may well lead to much closer liaison with senior management and their grasping a better understanding of the fleet.

It is an old saying that 'during a recession business moves forward by 10 years'. The fleet, too, needs to move forward by at least that amount and be ready for economic recovery. The business may be totally different at the end of a recession – but can you design and introduce the changes that will be necessary for the fleet?

Do you think the role of the fleet executive will change during recession?

The role of the fleet executive will certainly change during the period of recession, and will change again as the economy starts to emerge from economic downturn.

I think the recession will offer opportunities for the fleet executive who wishes to reposition his or her role within the organisation and to become a genuine advisor to senior management. Specifically, I would highlight the following points;

- Greater involvement in planning personal business mobility – that will mean involvement in planning how executives will travel to obtain best value for money. Equally, it could mean alternative forms of communication within the business and with clients or even territorial redesign.

- Review, as appropriate with other departments, the best methods of providing vehicles using different funding methods. That may include recommending defleeting, if necessary, as well as the substitution of daily rental for cars.

- Watch for fraud; realistically fraud increases during recession – which will mean putting out the word that you are watching like a four-eyed hawk any expenses associated with vehicles – and checking in depth on a random basis. Remember, it is relatively easy to start an ongoing fraud – the challenge is to be able to discontinue it without being discovered.

- It may also include the tacit support of talent management to ensure employees do not leave because of the loss of company cars. That will involve judgement of shades of grey.

- Given the tighter cash position of the company, the fleet executive may have a more hands-on role in terms of juggling the fleet to get the best value and use from the fleet.

Quite simply, the fleet executive may have responsibility for one of the major cost areas of the business and may need to look to the most senior management for support – but that is no bad thing.

You have ranged across many issues so far. Which do you consider the most important ones for the fleet executive to watch during recession and recovery?

The issues of cost control are the usual suspects in recession – but intensified. I think I would identify those shown in Figure 3 as being some of the most important.

> - Residual value management – existing/planned units
> - Funding sources and methods – cash flow and availability
> - Risk management
> - Methods of used vehicle disposal – maybe using more than one
> - Fraud and cost management/monitoring
> - Logical fleet repositioning/downsizing
> - Tax issues – employees and capital
> - Preparation for economic recovery

Figure 3: Financial/Cost Control Issues to Manage during recession
For illustrative purposes only – not comprehensive

These may appear to be obvious issues – they are – but they still need to be managed and it is all too easy to let them slip amid the excitement of change.

My message is 'get out there and grasp the opportunity' – recession can be good news for the fleet executive as it will give you the opportunity to show leadership – both operationally and strategically.

Do you think the role of the fleet executive will change once the economy starts to recover?

While there will be huge challenges for the fleet executive during the recession, these will be even greater for the business as it starts to emerge into a new competitive situation. I think some of the issues will be different – how about these?

- Work with management to decide what has been the change in business requirements for personal mobility – and plan the fleet to fulfil that role.

- Redesign the fleet for the new business model – probably start with a 'make do and mend' strategy to use the resources available and plan the updating of those cars to fulfil the future needs as agreed with senior management.

- Work on cash flow protection – there will be more important places for the cash to be used than the fleet. That may mean all sorts of actions but make sure the issues raised do not increase total costs.

- Look for areas where cash might be released for alternative uses – might mean hire not buy as well as ensuring that used vehicles are disposed of as quickly as possible and that no surplus units are retained.

- Seek to balance the fleet so there is a good age/mileage profile with the whole fleet not needing to be replaced at once.

The most important role of the recovering fleet will be to ensure it is fit for purpose on economic recovery. Part of that planning and thinking can be done while the business is in recession and the new fleet structure and management is pulled together ready for recovery.

The old adage 'when you are up to your a*** in alligators, it can be difficult to remember that the task is to drain the swamp' – the fleet executive has to manage the short-term issues but equally plan for the future. I have been through four economic recessions and think this time, as in the past, we will see some fleet executives emerging with flying colours while others will simply fade away.

You have often said in print that 'the business moves forward twice as fast during a recession as it does in a normal business environment.' Do you think that will be the case this time too?

Absolutely – I think this time the changes could be even more significant and rapid. We will lose a number of companies – how will your competition fare? – and there will be new business opportunities emerging.

The company will want to take advantage of those – and that will mean a greater demand for personal business mobility – or new ways of communicating with the customers. As a fleet executive, if you follow the ideas noted above, demand for company cars will change.

I suppose we are almost calling the fleet executive a juggler, in that the role will demand more ability to keep a growing number of balls in the air without creating a balls-up.

Those business changes will certainly create hot-spots within the business and it will be your task to smooth them over and spot the problems before they actually arise and to defuse potential problems.

While the business may have a strategic plan that offers a vision for five or more years ahead, that could be crushed into 2-3 years – or less – if competition fails or markets change rapidly.

The wider issues will be as much management of the application of business cars as the actual management of individual costs.

Given the depth and speed of recession we appear to be expecting, the fleet executive may well not recognise their role in 3-4 years time –or less.

Given that you are talking about pressure on resources and a more hands-on approach in the short term, what do you think will happen to 'best practice'?

The well-managed organisation is one that retains its standards even during recession. There will be a lot of pressure elsewhere in the organisation to cut corners and the fleet is one area where that simply cannot be allowed to happen – even during deepest recession.

Best practice will mean ensuring the fleet is retained in tip top condition. We do not want to see the roadside littered with shorn and shredded tyres where the remaining vestiges of rubber have sheared off. That is health and safety – think what damage such an incident could do to morale.

Best practice will also mean ensuring the administration does not slip and a proper discipline regarding the fleet is in place and working – that is down to the fleet executive.

Management, too, will be hard pressed, but it is important they are seriously involved in fleet governance. The board needs to know what is happening with the fleet use and incident level – and have the ability to benchmark against previous years – even previous recessions. Management needs to keep a finger on the pulse of the fleet.

The table in Figure 4 shows one of the findings of some research I undertook a couple of years back regarding board attitudes to fleet. I found it concerning and think that management really needs to be involved in fleet.

Not discussed at all	24%
Not considered a board issue	14%
Annually	13%
Every five years	2%
Ad hoc – as required	47%
n = 195	

Figure 4: How often is fleet policy discussed at board meetings?
Source; Corporate Responsibility for Used Car Disposal

I feel the fleet executive needs to place a paper before the board either monthly – or quarterly at the least, showing the incident status of the fleet and any cars used by employees. While the paper need not be discussed every time, it serves to remind the board of their wider responsibilities and, as far as fleet car drivers are concerned, it can be valuable for them to know that any transgressions are likely to show up on a board paper.

Corporate – and fleet – governance are important within the business, especially in recession when staff will have other priorities. Grasp the nettle and make sure the rules and policies are followed – strictly.

Do you think relationships between management and the fleet executive can change during a period of recession?

I mentioned earlier that recession creates new opportunities for those who want to grasp them. The same happened during wartime where new leaders emerged and many able people, who had not had the opportunity to use their potential, rose rapidly in responsibility – far faster than they might have expected in peacetime.

If you think about it, recession is the equivalent of a war. We are all fighting for survival and the most radical, logical people may come through. The fleet executive, because of the very nature of the job, can have that opportunity and the immediate cost opportunities can quickly be recognised by management.

War, whether military or economic, gives talent the opportunity to emerge – and simultaneously compresses the time scales for those actions.

Top management appreciates top professional advice – and that should be the role of the fleet executive.

I know of a number of people who, at the start of previous recessions were in junior management roles managing fleets – but grasped the nettle and used the business turbulence to move their careers forward.

To my knowledge, there are at least three executive directors of top FTSE-100 companies who have served their time with fleet responsibility and used a recession to kick start their careers.

How would you summarise your thoughts about the role and priorities of the fleet executive in the recession?

Technology has offered fleet executives a lot of new management tools their predecessors did not have. Equally, the routine management and costs associated with fleet vehicles have also changed – vehicles that are properly looked after, rarely break down; they are amazingly reliable and robust.

For the fleet executive, that should allow more time for planning and thinking – not just for this week or this month – but also for the recovery.

The role of the fleet executive is increasingly becoming one of 'personal business mobility operations manager' with relatively less to do with the physical mechanics of the fleet and more with its strategic allocation, acquisition, efficiency enhancement and used vehicle disposal.

The role is more one of supervision and management than of checking that the columns of numbers add up!

I see fleet management becoming a stepping stone into operations management – and a recession could give the successful incumbent that first leg up into management.

You make the recession sound almost exciting. Do you think there is sufficient high-quality management training in place to fulfil needs and ambitions? What do you offer at The University of Buckingham?

I think there is a fair amount of training available – and I use the word 'training' advisedly. The role of the fleet executive is surely far more than looking at vehicles but, I am sure, has to become much more involved in the management of the business and the fleet – and the fleet executive needs to understand that – and be involved.

If you think about it, 'fleet management' barely exists as a profession – to most people it is but a stepping stone 'on the way up'. I feel that role has to expand to become 'personal business mobility executive'.

Over the years I have tried to look at the fleet management role in the wider context of the organisation. I think I have reflected this change in my writings.

At The University of Buckingham we are trying to respond positively to the demand for service and support for the industry. Specifically we are planning the following programmes;

- Short – one and two-day reviews of specific programmes looking at issues such as 'managing in recession' where we will be examining short-term management issues. Watch the press for short term programmes which we plan to offer during recession.
- Introduction to Fleet Management; this will be a four module – two day per module programme designed specifically to offer new skills to fleet managers – with special reference to recession management.
- Professional Certificate in Automotive Management – a six, two-and-a-half day module programme that sets management in context – and successful members receive a formal university award at the end of the programme
- International Automotive MBA – will be launched during 2009 – it is going through the validation process as you read this. Again, it's an executive programme – part time – spread over two years – with an opportunity to focus on fleet management.

In addition to these programmes, and details will be posted on the Buckingham website, www.buckingham.ac.uk/business, we are also researching and publishing a range of reports on the industry.

I will not attempt to list the ones we have at present, but again check the website.

There are a string of publications in production that will look at an ever-growing range of issues associated with fleet management.

Any concluding thoughts?

Recession is not nice. But it does offer the business and the individual the opportunity to move the business, and particularly the fleet, forward.

It is the brave who will grasp the nettle and use it as the basis for further personal development – will you?

Professor Peter N C Cooke
KPMG Professor of Automotive Management
University of Buckingham

WWW.BUCKINGHAM.AC.UK

THE ENQUIRIES TEAM
UNIVERSITY OF BUCKINGHAM
HUNTER STREET
BUCKINGHAM
MK18 1EG

TEL: 01280 820313
FAX: 01280 824081
ADMISSIONS@BUCKINGHAM.AC.UK

UNIVERSITY OF BUCKINGHAM

OFFERING A UNIQUE ALTERNATIVE TO THE HIGH COSTS OF GOING TO UNIVERSITY

BUCKINGHAM IS THE UK'S ONLY INDEPENDENT (PRIVATE) UNIVERSITY. AT BUCKINGHAM STUDENTS SAVE TIME AND MONEY BY COMPLETING A TRADITIONAL THREE-YEAR HONOURS DEGREE IN TWO YEARS.

We utilise what would normally be the long summer vacation for an extra term's study, offering a real fast track option with as much teaching content in two years, as other universities offer in three.

We have just over 1,000 students, and one member of academic staff for every 8.4 students - the average in the university sector is 1:17.5. Small group teaching is guaranteed and an open door policy to our lecturers, our students are our customers and we do everything we can to ensure they gain the maximum benefit from their time at Buckingham and progress to successful careers or further study. Graduates have gone on to further study at many of the world's leading universities including Harvard, Oxford, Cambridge and LSE. You will find graduates from the University of Buckingham in law firms, government offices and multinational companies around the world.

Buckingham lies between Oxford and Cambridge and close to Milton Keynes, which has fast and efficient coach services linking all parts of the country. Easyjet fly a regular low-cost service between Jersey and Luton airport just 40 minutes from Buckingham.

We have two libraries and spend more per student on information technology (IT) than most other universities in the UK. Buckingham's annual expenditure on information provision of £281 per student is the 5th highest among all UK universities.

"LITTLE WONDER BUCKINGHAM HAS BEEN VOTED NO1 FOR STUDENT SATISFACTION FOR THE LAST THREE YEARS"

We offer a diverse subject range, including Law (LLB and LLM), Business (including MBA), and a ground-breaking undergraduate degree in Business Enterprise; Accounting, Marketing, Service Management, Psychology, English Language and Communication Studies, English Literature, Journalism, International Studies, Global Affairs, Computing, Business Information Systems and Politics; plus the option to study a modern foreign language alongside all our major programmes.

For further information, please refer to the web site: www.buckingham.ac.uk

43 SPECIALIST INSURANCES

John Chadwick
Group Business Development Director
Lease & Loan Insurance Services Ltd

Please introduce yourself and your company

I am the Group Business Development Director for Lease & Loan Insurance Services Ltd and have been with the company since 1995.

In my career I have always worked within the Sales and Business Development areas. On leaving education, I began my career in Retail management for the Dixons Group. I then moved to providing cleaning equipment and chemicals to the motor trade, ultimately having a franchise for the South Wales area with a particular manufacturer.

The recession of the early 1990s caused me to look elsewhere for a career as the motor trade was hit only second to the construction industry in both severity and speed of decline; and with the resultant career change I found myself in the insurance industry. I started off in life insurance working with Prudential and Lloyds Bank Insurance Services, ending up working for a bank-owned Independent Financial Advisor, where I worked providing products and services to their affinity groups.

In 1995 I was offered the chance to work with a small, American owned insurance agency which had an innovative niche product for the equipment leasing industry and had secured its first two UK clients. This was Lease Insurance Services Ltd.

Lease Insurance Services Ltd was acquired by our current owners in 1998, and with a slight name change the business has since progressed both in the number of products and territories of operation.

Lease & Loan Insurance Services Ltd, as we are now known, specialises in providing insurance products tailored specifically to the needs of the vehicle and equipment leasing and finance markets. As a small and dynamic company we have the flexibility to develop innovative products for our clients in Europe, with the advantage of the stability and backing of Great American Insurance Company, which has been in the business since 1872.

What specialist insurances are available to large and small fleets?

As with most areas of life and business, there are a myriad of insurance products available to both large and small fleets. The most familiar insurance offerings to fleets of all sizes are: Third Party Liability cover, which is a legal requirement for all road licensed vehicles, plus the product with which it is often provided, an all risks protection for the vehicle. The all risks cover protects against the physical loss or damage to the vehicle in the event of a specified peril occurring.

For the purposes of this chapter, I will focus upon some of the other and less well known niche insurance offerings that are available to large and small fleets. I will explain each product, the perils covered and the benefits, who will be the beneficiaries of each product and in what way they will benefit.

Some of these products may be known by different names as insurers tend to brand products their own way to help with differentiation from the rest of the market.

CREDITOR/PAYMENT PROTECTION INSURANCE

Product description

This product is designed to ensure that the finance payments continue on a contract if and when specified events occur, by paying the periodic finance payment on behalf of the lessee. When certain events occur, the total outstanding financial commitment may be paid.

Perils Covered

- Death
- Sickness
- Critical illness
- Temporary or permanent disability
- Accident
- Redundancy
- Marriage break up

Beneficiaries and Benefits

The beneficiaries from the creditor insurance products are potentially the following:

- Lessee
- Fleet manager
- Finance company
- Vehicle dealer

The benefits from the creditor insurance products are typically:

- Additional fee income for funder and/or dealers
- Removes administrative overheads
- Reduces credit risk
- Protects the lessee or fleet manager and helps reduce their financial risk
- Increases satisfaction and ongoing relationships

GAP INSURANCE

Product description

GAP Insurance is a product that, in its simplest form, is designed to ensure no risk of a shortfall between the fair market value covered by the primary insurance and the outstanding financial obligation under the terms of the finance contract when a total loss of the vehicle occurs. This simple form of GAP Insurance is normally called **Finance GAP**.

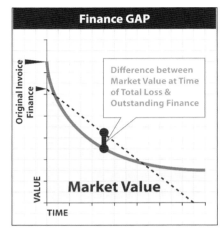

Some variations of the GAP insurance principle have been developed over the years that cover more than just the outstanding financial commitment. A couple of the most common options in the UK market are the following:

- **Return to Invoice GAP**

This is where, at the time of a total loss, the insurance product will pay the difference between the fair market value covered by the primary insurance and the original invoice value of the vehicle.

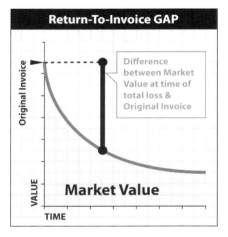

- **Replacement GAP**

This is where, at the time of a total loss, the insurance product will pay the difference between the fair market value covered by the primary insurance and the replacement value of the vehicle.

Perils Covered

Total loss of the vehicle due to

- Fire
- Theft
- Accident damage

Beneficiaries and Benefits

The beneficiaries from the various GAP insurance products are potentially the following:

- Lessee

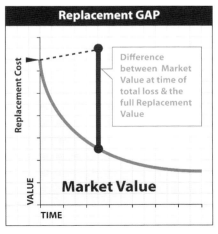

- Fleet manager
- Finance company
- Vehicle dealer

The benefits from the various GAP insurance products are typically the following:

- Additional fee income for funder and/or dealers
- Differentiates a funder's product from the competition
- Removes administrative overheads
- Reduces credit risk
- Protects the lessee or fleet manager and helps reduce their financial risk
- Increases satisfaction and ongoing relationships

Excess wear & tear protection/Return Conditions insurance

Product description

Excess wear and tear protection is a product that provides protection where wear and tear on the returned vehicle is in excess of the agreed return conditions within the contract. The product typically would cover the cost of non-accident damage up to a set limit that has been predetermined.

Perils Covered

The type of damage typically covered would include some or all of the following:

- Stone chips
- Minor dents (<10mm)
- Minor abrasions (<25mm)
- Light scratches (<25mm)
- Bumpers – Limited scuffs
- Screen – No damage in driver's sight-line
- Trim: wear and soiling through normal use
- Wheels – minor scuffs
- Multiple dents on one panel
- Chips through to metal
- Corrosion
- Colour mismatch
- Poorly fitting panels
- Bumpers: cracked, broken or deformed
- Seats: burns, tears, stains
- Wheels: dents or damage

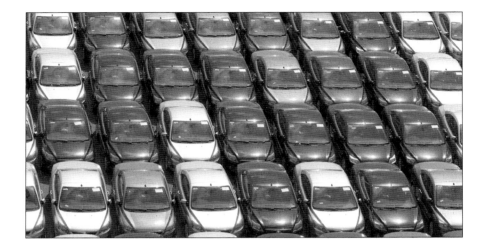

Beneficiaries and Benefits

The beneficiaries from excess wear and tear protection are typically the following:

- Lessee
- Fleet manager
- Finance company

The benefits from excess wear and tear protection are typically the following:

- Protects lessees and fleet managers from excess wear and tear charges
- Removes uncertainty and dissatisfaction at the end of the lease
- Improves customer goodwill and retention
- Protects against losses at lease end
- Key differentiator for funder
- Revenue protection

EARLY TERMINATION INSURANCE

Product description

Early Termination Insurance enables the vehicle to be handed back during the contract if certain events occur to the driver or lessee. The product will pay the difference between the fair market value of the vehicle at the time of its return, and any outstanding financial commitment

Perils Covered

The type of event typically covered would include some or all of the following:

- Bankruptcy
- Unemployment
- Loss of driving license

- Expatriation
- Carer responsibilities (reducing the number of hours worked)
- Resignation
- Death
- Maternity/Paternity leave

Beneficiaries and Benefits

The beneficiaries from early termination insurance are typically the following:

- Lessee or driver
- Fleet manager
- Finance company

The benefits of early termination insurance are typically the following:

For the driver or individual lessee

- Release from financial commitment if circumstances change
- Ability to hand vehicle back, or
- Change vehicle for something more suitable

For the fleet manager

- Flexible solution
- Improved fleet management
- Reduction in fleet management costs
- Peace of mind for employees

For the funder or lessor

- Flexible, tailored solution
- Additional income
- Differentiator in the market
- Improved cost control

DEPOSIT PROTECTION INSURANCE

Product description

Deposit Protection insurance enables the driver or individual lessee to keep their initial deposit, or use the deposit as either a down-payment on a replacement vehicle or a payment towards any outstanding finance due, in the event of a total loss, bankruptcy or redundancy.

Perils Covered

- Total vehicle loss
- Bankruptcy
- Redundancy

Beneficiaries and Benefits

The beneficiaries from deposit protection insurance are typically the following:

- Lessee
- Finance company

The benefits of deposit protection insurance are typically the following:

- Protects lessees against financial loss when key negative events occur
- Removes uncertainty and dissatisfaction
- Improves customer goodwill and retention
- Protects against losses during contract term
- Key differentiator for funder
- Revenue protection

RESIDUAL VALUE INSURANCE

Product description

Residual Value Insurance covers the difference between projected residual value and actual sales proceeds received at lease maturity of the vehicle. The product is quite versatile in that it can be used to protect against risk, is used sometimes to expedite earlier income recognition where a buy back has been offered, or helps change a contract from on to off balance sheet. The main issue at present is that there are few providers of this product and the appetite to take residual value risk in the current economic climate has been severely limited.

Perils Covered

Where the product is used as a risk transfer product: reduced residual values due to:

- Branding issues
- Economic downturn
- Technology advances
- Regulatory or legislative changes

Beneficiaries and Benefits

The beneficiaries from the residual value insurance product are potentially the following:

- Lessee
- Fleet manager
- Finance company
- Vehicle dealer
- Vehicle manufacturer

The benefits of residual value insurance are potentially the following:

- Risk transfer
- Enable off balance sheet transactions
- Expediting revenue recognition
- Providing balance sheet relief

MAINTENANCE OR EXTENDED WARRANTY

Product description

Maintenance or Extended Warranty products provide a way of smoothing and capping the maintenance costs for a vehicle for a period of time by allowing all or defined faults and/or maintenance to be carried out at no additional cost to the driver or fleet manager.

Perils Covered

Maintenance or Extended Warranty products will include all or some of the following:

- Servicing
- Mechanical repair and replacement
- Replacement tyres

Beneficiaries and Benefits

The beneficiaries from the Maintenance or Extended Warranty products are potentially the following:

- Lessee
- Fleet manager
- Finance company
- Vehicle dealer

The benefits of Maintenance or Extended Warranty products are typically the following:

- Provides lessees and fleet managers predictable costs for maintenance and repair to their vehicle/s
- Removes uncertainty and dissatisfaction
- Improves customer goodwill and retention

BREAKDOWN INSURANCE

Product description

Breakdown insurance is a product that provides support and protection to the driver when their vehicle breaks down and needs repair. The insurer normally contracts with a national or international breakdown and recovery company to support the drivers when a claim occurs.

Perils Covered

Breakdown insurance will cover all or some of the following:

- Roadside assistance
- Home start assistance
- Continued journey cover
- Vehicle taken to dealer or home
- Repatriation
- Overnight accommodation
- Hire car costs

Beneficiaries and Benefits

The beneficiaries of the breakdown insurance are the following:

- Driver or lessee
- Fleet manager
- Employer

The benefits of breakdown insurance include:

- Minimised disruption to work and home life
- Predictable costs for breakdown and recovery

There are many other even more niche products available that may offer some benefit to fleet managers. I have listed below a few that are available rather than providing a full description of each product.

MINOR DAMAGE COVER

This protects against the small knocks and scratches that wouldn't be covered by the primary insurance or would fall below the excess level.

TYRE INSURANCE

This is a cost-smoothing product to protect against damage to tyres.

KEY INSURANCE

This is a product to protect against losing the cars keys and the costs of solving the problem.

ETCH

This is a product that will insure against non-recovery of a stolen vehicle after the glass has been etched with the vehicle's unique details.

There has been a flurry of news recently regarding payment protection insurance. Please set out the current position.

Payment Protection Insurance, or Creditor Insurance, has been one of the most commonly sold insurance products in recent years. The product has not only been sold within the motor finance arena but also in most other types of finance markets.

The product (its features and benefits have been described briefly above) offers real benefits to the right person.

This is a product that Lease & Loan Insurance Services Ltd does not and never has offered, but such is its prevalence within the finance world, that it is one we have come across on a regular basis in our discussions with industry professionals.

The product has come under increasing scrutiny in the UK and other countries due to concerns about the potential mis-selling and the levels of commission taken by funders and intermediaries compared to the benefit to the insured.

There have been cases where payment protection cover has been sold on an almost blanket basis, regardless of the need for the product by the individual, offering no indication that there may be alternative providers of the product. In some other cases the fees and commissions charged have been several times of the net cost of the insurance.

The concerns around the selling of the product have reached such a height in the last few years that the Competition Commission has investigated the product and its sale, resulting in a final report recently being published.

A copy of this report setting out the full detail of the findings and recommendations can be found at: www.competition-commission.org.uk

The Finance and Leasing Association recently provided members with an excellent summary of the findings of the report which I have included below:

Competition Commission's main conclusion

The Competition Commission has maintained their familiar argument that firms which offer PPI alongside credit faced little or no competition when selling PPI to their credit customers. They claim that many consumers were unaware that they could buy PPI from other providers, rarely shopped around to compare prices and terms and conditions of PPI policies and rarely switched PPI providers. The Competition Commission argues that the resulting 'point-of-sale' advantage has made it difficult for other PPI providers to reach credit providers' customers and, in the absence of such competitive pressure, consumers were being charged high prices.

Final Package of Measures

Consistent with this analysis, the Competition Commission has published a package of measures very similar to those suggested in their earlier reports.

It says that these will be 'practical and effective' in increasing competition in the market to the benefit of consumers.

The package of remedies comprises:

- A prohibition on the sale of PPI to a customer, within seven days of selling credit to that customer. But a customer can contact the distributor or intermediary on their own initiative from 24 hours after the credit sale.

- A prohibition on the selling of single-premium PPI policies. Premiums can be charged monthly or annually—if an annual premium is charged and the customer decides to terminate the policy, then a pro-rata rebate must be reimbursed. No separate charges can be levied on a customer for administration or other costs arising from the set-up or early termination of a PPI policy.

- Distributors and intermediaries will be required to provide a 'personal PPI quote', which will clearly state the cost of the PPI policy individually and when added to the credit product.

- A requirement on all PPI providers to provide certain information and messages in PPI marketing material (including the price of their PPI, expressed in a common format of monthly cost per £100 of monthly benefit, and that PPI is optional and available from other providers).

- A requirement on all PPI providers to provide certain information on PPI policies to the FSA and a recommendation to the FSA that it uses this information for its PPI price comparison tables. Providers will also be required to supply information to the OFT for the purpose of monitoring the remedies package and to provide information about their claims ratios to any person on request.

- A requirement on all PPI providers to provide an annual statement for PPI customers, including information similar to that provided in the personal quote, to encourage customers to review their policy annually and make it easier for customers to decide whether to switch.

- Where distributors of retail PPI offer an insurance package containing PPI and merchandise cover, they must also offer, as a separate item, PPI cover alone.

The major change to the Competition Commission's remedies has been a reduction in the time period within which PPI cannot be sold following the credit sale, from 14 days to seven days. The FLA lobbied extensively against the 14 day prohibition on the basis that this approach failed to recognise customer buying behaviour and would leave more borrowers without protection.

> ### Timetable for implementation
>
> The Competition Commission expects that the measures will come into force during 2010, with the information remedies in place by April 2010 and other measures by October 2010. This timing coincides with Government's common commencement dates for new legislation and regulation.
>
> ### Next steps
>
> The FLA's General Insurance Group will now be considering the implications of implementing these remedies for the credit industry and we will advise members of The Department for Business, Enterprise & Regulatory Reform implementation programme, following discussions with them.

If you were to advise a fleet manager on the best current practice when it comes to managing their fleet risks, what would that advice be?

An assessment of all the known risks pertaining to the fleet should be conducted and then an analysis as to the potential mitigants for each and every one of those risks made.

Once the assessment has been completed the pluses and minuses (costs and benefits) of each of the different ways of managing that risk should be made. As an example, it may be that a particular risk could be covered by:

- An insurance product
- A provision
- A financial tool like a hedging fund
- A change in processes
- A combination of the above

One of the issues faced by companies when going through this process is that we only know what we know and therefore it may be that you are not aware of all potential mitigants for the risk you are addressing.

If this is the case, bringing in independent outside assistance from consultants or an industry expert will help you to make the best choice or combination of choices to have a comprehensive risk management strategy and policy in place.

Insurance will undoubtedly have a place to some degree in your risk management strategy. Where insurance support in needed, I would advise you to work with specialists who work in the motor finance world rather than a general broker or insurer who may not have the specialised knowledge to provide the best solution for you.

The other thing to mention is that once a reasoned solution is in place with the appropriate internal and external measures taken, ensure that a regular review is taken to ensure that the suite of solutions in force is still the best solution, suited to the current market, regulatory environment etc.

What services does Lease & Loan Insurance Services Ltd provide to managers of large and small fleets?

Our focus in the motor market is primarily to work directly with funders, service providers and intermediaries who then work with fleet managers. We are however, happy to discuss any areas of risk that can potentially be met by insurance products with fleet managers.

What services does Lease & Loan Insurance Services Ltd provide to the vehicle lending and leasing industry?

PRODUCTS AND SERVICES

We offer a range of insurance products and outsourcing solutions which are aimed at the vehicle leasing and finance market:

ETInsurance

Early Termination Insurance - Frees lessees from financial commitment for vehicle lease rentals if their personal circumstances change unexpectedly.

DPInsurance

Deposit Protection Insurance – Enables a lessor to reimburse a lessee's vehicle deposits in the event of total loss of a vehicle or a change in the lessee's personal circumstances.

RCInsurance

Return Conditions Insurance – Protects vehicle finance customers from end-of-lease charges resulting from excess wear and tear.

GAPinsurance

GAP Insurance – Reduces the risk of a financial shortfall when a leased vehicle or asset is written-off as a result of an accident, fire or theft. We provide Finance, Return-to-Invoice and Replacement GAP variants.

In addition, we can customise programmes and we have a progressive approach to developing products and services in response to the needs of the leasing market and the European Insurance Mediation Directive

Please tell us about your company

Lease & Loan Insurance Services Ltd (LLISL) provides niche insurance products and services to the leasing market in Europe. Our strength is in customising insurance programmes to meet the highly specialised needs of finance houses, banks, manufacturers, and vendors. Since 1991 LLISL has provided high quality services and professional support in Europe to help clients:

- Generate additional fee income
- Minimise insurance related administration
- Achieve a competitive edge
- Transfer insurable risk
- Improve return on equity
- Reduce credit risk

Lease & Loan Insurance Services Ltd is a specialist insurance intermediary, registered in the UK and regulated by the FSA. It is licensed to market and administer insurance products and programmes on behalf of insurance companies throughout the EEA. We have representative offices in the UK, France, Germany and the Nordic region.

Together with GAI International Insurance, which was set up in Dublin to write insurance business in Europe and other international territories, which was assigned an "A" financial strength and counterparty credit rating by Standard and Poor's Ratings Services in August 2008, we act as the international arm of Premier Lease & Loan Services®(PLLS). PLLS is part of the Great American Insurance Group, which in turn is a wholly owned subsidiary of the American Financial Group.

The Great American Insurance Group's roots go back to the founding of Great American Insurance Company in 1872 in New York City. The group, now based in Cincinnati, USA, is engaged in property and casualty insurance, focusing on specialty commercial products for businesses, in the sale of annuities, supplemental insurance and life products. In 1973 the American Financial Corporation headed up by Carl H. Lindner acquired majority ownership of Great American and since then, under the Lindner family's leadership, Great American has focused its market presence on being a specialty insurer and is the flagship company of the American Financial Group, Inc. (AFG). AFG's common stock is listed and traded on the New York Stock Exchange ("NYSE") and Nasdaq under the symbol ("AFG").

At the end of 2007, the Great American Insurance Company (GAIC) recorded annual written premiums in excess of US$ 3.9 billion and AFG's total revenue was US$4.4 bn with US$25.8bn in total assets. At the beginning of 2009 GAIC maintained an "A" rating from the ratings agency AM Best.

John Chadwick
Group Business Development Director
Lease & Loan Insurance Services Ltd

INNOVATIVE
INSURANCE

SOLUTIONS FOR VEHICLE LEASING & FINANCE

Significant Benefits

- **Add value** and create product differentiation for lessors
- **Reduce risk** and provide flexibility for fleets and employee car owners

Insurance Products

- Deposit Protection Insurance
- Return Conditions Insurance
- Early Termination Insurance
- GAP Insurance

Find out more about how we can customise an insurance programme for your specific requirements:
+44 117 929 9003   **www.llisl.com**

LEASE & LOAN
INSURANCE SERVICES LTD.

Have you found this book valuable?

Could we have presented the information
in a better way?

Is there something you would have
liked to learn more about?

Did we omit any part of the fleet industry?

If we produce a 2nd edition of this book,
how could we make it even better?

We would like to hear from you!

Please send us feedback via

www.tourick.com

WHAT THIS BOOK DOESN'T COVER

Managing Your Company Cars: Expert Opinion gives you the opportunity to hear what the experts are saying in all corners of the fleet world. It sets out the best practice in contemporary fleet management.

But fleet managers also need a text book.

Somewhere they can look up the differences between the various finance products: contract hire, operating lease, contract purchase, finance lease, hire purchase, lease purchase, conditional sale, credit sale, loans and bank overdrafts.

Where they can learn what to look for in a lease agreement.

Where they can find out about the mathematics of leasing and lease accounting.

If you need a fleet management textbook, you need **Managing Your Company Cars.**

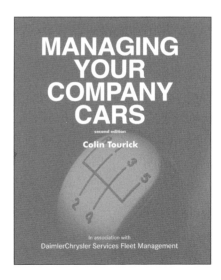

Managing Your Company Cars

ISBN 978 1902528212

Eyelevel Books, 2005

A comprehensive guide for the beginner and expert.

520 pages, 172,000 words.

The textbook for fleet managers – 'a tour de force of vehicle finance'

LeasingLife magazine

Every profession should have a reference book; if you're in fleet management, this is it!

James Langley, Chairman, Training & Education Committee,
Institute of Car Fleet Management

This book is essential reading for fleet decision-makers. It is the single most authoritative information source for all fleet funding and operational issues.

Ashley Martin, Industry analyst/consultant,
Former editor of Fleet News.

Managing Your Company Cars is the 'number one' reference book for the fleet industry.

Paul Ashton, Managing Director, Equalease

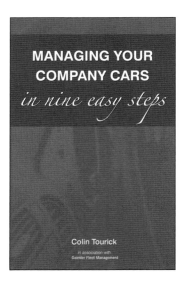

Managing Your Company Cars in Nine Easy Steps

ISBN 978 1902528243, Eyelevel Books, 2008. List price £15

Available in hard copy from good bookshops, amazon.co.uk and www.tourick.com

Also available as pdf download fromwww.tourick.com

In many areas of business – human resources, property management, manufacturing, IT and so on – there are thousands of books to help company managers make the right decisions, reduce costs and manage risks.

However, even though most new cars are bought by businesses, and the cost of the car fleet can be a very significant business expense, there were almost no textbooks on this important subject. Colin Tourick wrote Managing Your Company Cars to fill this gap. Now in its second edition, it continues to sell around the world.

In this new book, Managing Your Company Cars in Nine Easy Steps, he takes the most essential material from Managing Your Company Cars and condenses it into a much slimmer volume, making it an excellent introduction to this specialist topic.

This is the definitive text for anyone devising and implementing an effective company car strategy. It's essential reading for all procurement and finance professionals operating a fleet.

Martyn Moore, editor, Fleet News

A no nonsense guide to fleet management – by an authority who has successfully managed a large contract hire fleet.

Professor Peter Cooke, KPMG Professor of Automotive Management,
University of Buckingham

Clear and unbiased. Professor Tourick explains the jargon and gives the fleet manager all the tools necessary to make the right choices in this highly complex area.

Jo Tacon, Editor, Motor Finance

An essential handbook for all those thinking of running a fleet of company cars.

Brian Rogerson, Consultant Editor, Leasing Life

I have yet to find a better source for understanding the complexities of fleet management.

Ralph Morton, editor, BusinessCarManager.co.uk

CT&A

Building Profit, Developing People

Colin Tourick and Associates Limited is a management consultancy specialising in the leasing and fleet management market.

We help leasing and finance companies boost revenues, reduce costs, increase profits, develop new products and develop their people.

We help fleet managers cut costs, manage their fleets more effectively and save tax.

We help leasing and finance companies outside the UK apply UK know-how to develop their businesses.

We help all manner of businesses restructure their balance sheets.

The business was formed by Colin Tourick in 1992. Colin has 29 years' experience in vehicle management and asset finance.

Hilary Davis is a management coach with 12 years' professional experience working with senior management teams in Top 100 companies.

CT&A
Management Consultants
Colin Tourick and Associates Limited
London
postmaster@tourick.com
www.tourick.com